THE AGE

OF ENERGY

OTHER BOOKS BY
HOWARD MUMFORD JONES

The Double Corliss Engine at the Philadelphia Centennial Exposition.

HOWARD MUMFORD JONES

THE AGE
OF ENERGY

Varieties of
American Experience
1865–1915

NEW YORK : THE VIKING PRESS

FOR BESSIE

ACKNOWLEDGMENTS

Charles Scribner's Sons:
From *The Hermit of Carmel and Other Poems*
by George Santayana

The disparity of epochs is due to the fact that the clash of the two antagonistic principles of freedom and necessity gives rise to new ages and new conditions.

—VON RANKE

Preface

THIS BOOK is written to a thesis or at least on a theme. I have read innumerable books and articles ranging from general surveys to special monographs, all having to do with American development from 1865 to 1915—that is to say, from our emergence out of the mingled stupidity and glory of the Civil War to our somewhat reluctant entrance into what used to be called the Great War. For us the sinking of the *Lusitania* in 1915 made participation in it inevitable. We came out of the Civil War a great military and economic power, strong, unpredictable, and parochial. Then on the whole we turned our gaze inward under a succession of presidents who at the best were high-class mediocrities and at the worst U. S. Grant. Eventually William McKinley, a mediocrity also but (save for Benjamin Harrison) the only chief magistrate in the period distinguished for excessive piety, proved to be both religious and indecisive. Under him we stumbled overtly into imperialism, and under Theodore Roosevelt we discovered we were a great world nation, a potent member of the concert (unfortunate term) of the Great Powers. The difficulty with most of the literature dealing with these fifty years, so far as I have read it, is that it does not for the most part address itself to any governing philosophic concept.

We became industrialized. We undertook, and almost wrecked ourselves on, a series of fatuous policies for the post-bellum South. We passed in literature from the standard classical American authors, mainly romantic, to another set of writers who afterward became standard—such as Henry James, William Dean Howells, and Mark Twain—men who as often "Europeanized" as not, who essentially abandoned the older doctrine that American writing should be unique and accepted the doctrine that American writing should study European theories.* We produced a large number of painters who also "Europeanized," as did most of our leading architects, and we patronized American composers mainly educated in Europe who wrote contemporary cosmopolitan music as, we fondly imagined, Stephen Foster, that naïve follower of Schubert, had not done. After the importance of Agassiz and the Darwinism of Asa Gray, our scientists, toward the close of the nineteenth century and after, achieved a modest equality with Europe: witness the cases of Willard Gibbs and Thomas Hunt Morgan. Our philosophers—William James, George Santayana, Josiah Royce, George Mead are representative—debated on equal terms with thinkers such as Bergson and F. C. S. Schiller and Lotze, and with system-builders of the rank of Alexander von Humboldt and Herbert Spencer. And we walked through the valley of humiliation under Grant, again after the panic of 1873, and once again during most of the 1890s.

Theoretically we welcomed the poor of the world to our democratic shores, the symbol being a statue donated by France, with an inscription on its base written by a Sephardic Jewess named Emma Lazarus. Practically, however, we kept the Negro in his place; the Indian on his reservations (which we steadily shrank); the Mexican in his alley; the Jew, except for a minority, in the ghetto; and the Slav, so far as we could, under the tyranny of the czar by trying to keep him away through literacy tests and, eventually, national quota systems. Our politics were furious, confused, and sectional. Was not the tariff a local issue? Was not the free coinage of silver necessary to the West? Was not government to aid Eastern industry and, through court decisions, curb the labor force and the radicals? Our municipal governments were then the worst in the world, our state and national police clashed and clawed at each other when there were strikes and riots, and in the Spanish-American War the doctrine of states' rights and the control of the militia confused such military policy as we hastily evolved. We came to conservation, public health, hours of labor, and the like social commonplaces long after Bismarck's Germany had shown what the social responsibilities of the modern state

* It is astonishing how much time Mark Twain spent abroad, and interesting how much of his later work dealt with European themes. Witness among other titles *A Connecticut Yankee in King Arthur's Court*, *Tom Sawyer Abroad*, and *The Mysterious Stranger*.

truly are. In the 1880s our navy had sunk to a level about that of Chile's and our army, at the outbreak of the Cuban War, was about thirty thousand. We were probably worse prepared for the Cuban, Puerto Rican, and Philippine campaigns than, given the opportunity for military education, we had been at First Bull Run.

Yet during these decades, at once depressing and brilliant, we produced the most amazing gallery of powerful and picturesque personalities we have fostered in any age, not excepting the great days of Webster, Clay, and Calhoun. If we gutted the land, staged some of the bloodiest conflicts in our industrial history, and suffered from a continual neurosis of sectionalism that led us to snarl and sniffle without becoming really belligerent, we also gave birth to a race of dreamers and reformers—Henry George, Edward Bellamy, Laurence Gronlund, Ignatius Donnelly, and the leaders of populism—the like of which we had not seen before, not even during the time of Albert Brisbane and Brook Farm. In this half-century every reformer carried a utopia in his head, every protest was against the whole establishment, every dismal prophecy predicted the coming transformation of the country by violence into a tyranny or, contrariwise, saw beyond immediate collapse a communal heaven ultimately to be reached by evolution and reform.

We did not, as did Mexico, experience either a dictatorship or a genuine class war. We did not, as did China, break up into shards and fragments of power, each under a war lord who, if he began as a traditionalist or as a radical, ended by heading private armies of his own. We were not, as was the Austro-Hungarian empire, held together by habit because nobody could think of any better way of getting along.

Such is the picture as I see it. My difficulty with the vast and brilliant library that has been collected around these amazing years is that I can find in it no center. Political historians have their special excellence, but their able books seldom or never recognize much connection with the cultural or scientific history of the period, though they dwell on invention; or, if they do find such connections, deal feebly with art and thought. The social historians are wonderful on topics like urbanization, the peopling of the West, conflicts between labor and capital, the Americanization of immigrants, and populist discontent. The literary scholars make a bow in the direction of the Gilded Age, which they commonly excoriate, but one would not guess from their pages that there were Americans then alive named Thomas Eakins, Augustus Saint-Gaudens, Daniel Burnham, Jacques Loeb, or Charles W. Eliot. That driest of historical branches, the history of science (peace to its practitioners!), could not be worse written if one wants to find out something about the rise of the laboratory, the philosophy of medical teaching, or the difference between able mediocrity and creative genius in these years. Books on painting or architecture with few exceptions exist in a vacuum; and when they get around to so important an event as the World's Columbian Exposition of 1893 seem to regard it as a belated expression of something Victorian, artificial, French, and genteel.

In all this library I do not find any leading principle that might serve to make sense out of American development as a whole from the age of Andrew Johnson to the presidency of Woodrow Wilson. In hunting for some clue in this rich confusion, in seeking for some standpoint from which to survey the tumult, I have hit upon the idea of energy as being central. By this I mean the discovery, use, exploitation, and expression of energy, whether it be that of personality or of prime movers or of words. By the idea of energy in words I mean that, except for islands of linguistic calm in some magazines and some colleges, the verbal style of the period has the same sort of fury that characterizes the public language of today. Abuse in politics is no new thing—Washington, John Adams, and Jefferson all complained of it. With the possible variant of the Log Cabin Campaign ("Tippecanoe and Tyler Too"), public discussion seems to have been relatively less violent before 1865 than it was thereafter, always excepting, of course, the controversy over slavery and secession. But after Appomattox it was as if the enormous energy concentrated by the Civil War, not satisfied with killing or wounding a million men or more, could not check itself at the peace but went on to gigantic verbal clashes over reconstruction, industry, politics, and theology. Never was oratory more orotund, propaganda more reckless, denunciation more bitter, reform more strident—until now. A people thus verbally unrestrained must have been filled with exuberance and wrath. Hence I call this book *The Age of Energy*.

Although I think of the book as a study of culture I have not tried to define culture, and I have sometimes glossed it as the intellectual side of civilization and sometimes as the desires and values of the apparently dominant class. I have on occasion discussed emotional drives. But I have not confined myself to culture in any anthropological sense; and if anybody wishes to accuse me of imprecision, I shall have to admit the impeachment. My only defense must be that nobody really knows what is meant by the culture of a nation, espe cially of a nation in a state of violent change; and, next, that it is sometimes more important to be curious than it is to be consistent.

All great periods have their characteristic motions of tension and release. What is the conflict at the heart of these fifty years? I think it is hinted at in the concluding chapters of *The Education of Henry Adams:* we have to deal with a tension between unity and multiplicity. Yet to set this forth as a bare central doctrine does not really shed light. Adams confined himself to the effects of science, invention, and industry upon the creation and control of physical (mechanical) energy. My guess is that the conflict was more complicated.

In truth the tension between unity and multiplicity could not be reduced to the simplicity of a battle between the Virgin and the Dynamo. On the one hand, after Appomattox the drive for general order, for restoration, for a national policy, an American philosophy, an American idiom in the arts, in literature, in theology, in other forms of thought. On the other hand, the inexpugnable desire of major regions in a continental empire to remain themselves, the belief that American culture was not created for uniformity but for variety (hence the local-color schools), the concept that if the federal government now overarched the states, regionalism and the richness of imported alien cultures might be simultaneously fused into a useful outlook and yet retain their autonomy, their quality, and their color. After the Civil War the nation for the most part threw off its fear of Europe. It felt that Japanese, Chinese, Hindu, Turkish, Egyptian, and even Amerindian patterns of art and thought had some thing to contribute to a representative republic. After 1865 the wounds of war healed so slowly that even in 1970 they are still raw; yet a united nation pushed out to take in Alaska, Hawaii, Cuba, Puerto Rico, Guam, the Philippines, and various other parcels of real estate, including the Panama Canal Zone. The opposition to these measures, at best weak, was seldom sectional. The same decades that developed toward a restatement of one-hundred-per-cent Americanism saw opera, the museum, the university, the magazine, architecture, and the book trade bringing to Columbia, the gem of the ocean, treasures and traditions from the total globe. At the same time, American specialists studied the archaeology of Yucatán or ancient Egypt, American historians wrote about Italy and the Inquisition, American scholars staffed the classical school in Rome, American businessmen furnished oil for the lamps of China.

The traffic was not all one way. If American missionaries clothed naked South-Sea islanders in Mother Hubbard gowns, French chefs took over the kitchens of smart restaurants and modish "cottages" at Newport. Germany became the country where you went for proper research training. American architects studied in Paris. Baudelaire and Huysmans, Ibsen and Gorki, Schopenhauer and Bergson were read in the United States. Toward the end of our period the Armory Show seemed to indict American parochialism.

Yet the Armory Show was the creation of a group of American artists and lovers of art. There arose a demand for the Great American Novel, but critics of the caliber of James Gibbons Huneker insisted that the way to become a cultivated American was to become a good European. Henry James, though he became a British subject, remains in all the histories of American literature. John Philip Sousa wrote national marches, but his contemporary, Theodore Thomas, played the music of Europe to attentive American ears. If James McNeill Whistler went abroad to live, Oscar Wilde came to America to lecture. To be patriotic it was no longer necessary to be merely provincial.

But how catch up with the years lost through isolation, how absorb a world-wide pattern of culture and yet remain a republic? Were we to be an agricultural nation as William Jennings Bryan apparently thought, or an industrial nation as Andrew Carnegie desired, or a nation dominated under God by white Anglo-Saxon Protestants as the Reverend Josiah Strong and Senator Albert J. Beveridge believed? Were we to be a melting-pot democracy, an example to the world? Or a nation worried by popular tumults, sectional divisions, racial antagonisms, religious hostilities, and the contentiousness of regions that distrusted each other and, above all, distrusted those two symbols of national unity, New York and Washington? These tensions are something different from a mere conflict between industrialism and tradition.

It is true that movements of reform during the age took over the doctrine, and something of the language, of the religion of humanity common in Europe during its more revolutionary years. Perhaps as a consequence historians have not always been able to escape the influence of certain powerful terms. Thus the battle cry of the progressive was that "the people" should control. But "the people" is a term then and now never closely defined, so that it was often asserted, in contradiction to the axioms of the Founding Fathers, that the cure for the evils of democracy was more democracy. The progressives had a good case, they fought for it gallantly, and in the end they not only forced into being some social control of big business, but also taught the soulless corporations that a concern for the commonwealth was part of their economic responsibility.

Such considerations both accent and diminish the features of a picture in which a democratic St. George conquers the dragon of Big Business. Once again, however, the situation is not that of an either/or simplicity. The robber barons were not less American for being rich Americans. If they regarded themselves as the economic disciples of the man who wrote "The Way to Wealth," they also acted as followers of the Franklin who retired from business to work for the public good. They came to accept some doctrine of cultural responsibility. They turned into creators, patrons, or supporters of art, medicine, education, research, social reform, and other institutions and causes usually thought of as forward-looking; and this in an important degree links them with the great merchant princes of the Renaissance. I venture to suggest that this aspect of American life has been obscured by the tendency of biographers to look at each tycoon separately, and of liberal historians to look at them in the context of "reform" and nothing else. Of course there were spendthrifts and selfish men among them, but we would not have the Chicago Art Institute, Vanderbilt University, the Boston Symphony Orchestra, the Carnegie Foundation for the Advancement of Teaching, the Rockefeller Institute, or the Morgan Library if the robber barons had not had larger minds than legend credits them with. It will not do to say that the use of wealth for social and cultural ends came late in their lives so that it was a confession of "guilt" that led them into philanthropy. The important truth is that, to a degree beyond that of any other society in the period under survey, wealth in the United States came to accept an increasing degree of social responsibility. One has only to think of the Krupp family in Germany to sense the unique American achievement.

The base line on which these chapters rest is of necessity the Civil

War. But a history of that conflict and its complex antecedents is too
vast for my book. I therefore go on to a survey of the United
States in terms of the general tension between regions and nation. Then I analyze particular forces at work, and conclude with the
struggle of the 1890s, the emotional unity brought about by the
Spanish-American War, however indefensible that conflict may be
judged to have been, and—I am sorry to use so trite a phrase—the
"new nationalism" of Theodore Roosevelt and William Howard
Taft.

Part of this book formed the substance of the Jacob C. Saponeskow
Memorial Lectures I was honored to deliver at the City College of
New York in 1966. Other portions I presented as the Trask Lectures
at Princeton University in 1968. The discussion of the Genteel Tradition I gave as a paper at the ceremonies honoring Merle Curti at the
University of Wisconsin when he retired. This paper has been
printed in the *Harvard Library Bulletin*, January 1970. Another portion was condensed and read before the Massachusetts Historical Society and appeared in their *Proceedings* in 1968. I am grateful to
these institutions and periodicals for the honor they did me and for
permission to reprint the material here, though in each case further
study has modified my earlier statements. I am grateful for a grant in
aid from the American Council of Learned Societies and to the Guggenheim Foundation for a fellowship. I also express my indebtedness
for the help I have had from Sigmund Diamond, Benjamin Rowland, Linda Rideout, Ralph H. Wetmore, Sue Walcutt, Bessie Z.
Jones, Ernst Mayr, Malcolm Cowley, Marshall A. Best, and the late
Edith Gray in ordering these pages.

Thanks are due to Glendon T. Odell for his patience and care in
helping to prepare the index.

—HOWARD MUMFORD JONES

Cambridge, Massachusetts, April 11, 1970

CONTENTS

THE AGE

OF ENERGY

I

American Panorama

A nation may be said to consist of its territory, its
people, and its laws. The territory is the only part
which is of certain durability.

—ABRAHAM LINCOLN

1

WHEN LEE SURRENDERED at Appomattox on April 9, 1865, the
Union was still ripped asunder. Parts of it were without any
government, other parts were under military government, and still
others, though they were theoretically civil in structure, had governments that of necessity were strongly colored by martial law or military necessity. There were prison camps in the North and fear of starvation and riots in the South. The regions beyond the Mississippi,
mostly Northern in sentiment but with islands of Southern sympa-
thizers (abortive attempts to bring California and the Southwest into
the Confederacy included the brief capture of Santa Fe by a Southern
military command) were, with the exception of a fringe of states
along the west bank of the Mississippi and of Texas, virtually unor-
ganized territory. The few trans-Mississippi states included Missouri,
torn by partisan bitterness; California, almost an autonomous republic; distant Oregon; and Nevada, a product of the war and virtually a
satrapy of the Republican party. For the first time in history a president of the United States had been assassinated, and it soon appeared
that his successor, Andrew Johnson, was to involve himself in the
worst conflict between Congress and the executive branch the country had ever experienced, the president escaping impeachment by a
single vote. To say that the South lay in ruins is an exaggeration, but

unwise handling (in part owing to inexperience with a state of affairs hitherto unknown, in part created by a Northern thirst for vengeance, in part a result of continuing Southern intransigence) meant that normal government was not to be restored to all the former Confederacy until the withdrawal in 1877 of the last Federal forces of occupation, after the 1876 election of Hayes, which many had felt to be fraudulent. But the restoration of constitutional rule in the South had been gained mainly by fraud or by violence or the threat of violence in most of the seceding states, where, as elsewhere, the freedmen were denied elementary rights guaranteed them in theory by the Fourteenth and Fifteenth Amendments.

When the Germans sank the *Lusitania* on May 7, 1915, half a century later, the United States was a closely knit nation. Violent political disagreements and bloody conflicts between capital and labor or between radicals and the police had at no time threatened to overthrow constitutional government by force of arms. The only march on the national capital had been that of Coxey's army, ludicrous rather than threatening. In 1863–1864 Napoleon III had assumed that he could ignore the North American republic when he sent Maximilian and a French army to create an empire in Mexico. (Among Maximilian's mistakes was the appointment of ex-Confederates to important Mexican posts.) But by the end of the century the imperial republic had not only forced the downfall of that rickety kingdom; it had also declared to the world that the United States was dominant in North and South America because its infinite resources, combined with its isolated position rendered it practically invulnerable as against any or all other powers.[1]* It had bought Alaska. It had wrecked the remnants of the Spanish Empire in the West Indies and the Pacific Ocean. It had annexed Hawaii. It had sent a fleet around the world. It was getting ready to pour two million men into Europe to preserve France from German conquest and Britain from defeat. A Southern president by the name of Woodrow Wilson was in the White House, the first since the Civil War, and nobody held it against him that he was the son of a chaplain in the Confederate Army. Changes as remarkable as these are as striking as the contrast between France of the Revolution of 1789 and France of the Second Empire of 1852.

---

* Numbered reference notes, which include additional material by the author, begin on p. 437.

The American population increased from about thirty-one and a half million in 1860 to almost one hundred and six million in 1920. In 1860 there had been thirty-three states; in 1915, there were forty-eight of them. In 1860 the population per square mile of the land area of the continental United States was 10.6; in 1920 it was 35.6. In 1860 the center of population was somewhat to the south of Columbus, Ohio; in 1920 it was southwest of Indianapolis, and thirty years later it was to cross the Illinois line, Between 1860 and 1890 about twice as many immigrants entered the United States as had entered it between 1815 and 1860, and between 1890 and 1930 the ten million of the previous epoch had doubled in number. One million or more came in 1906, 1907, 1910, 1913, and 1914, the peak year being 1913, which welcomed 1,285,349. Some immigrants of course returned; and the labor troubles of the 1870s and later, fear of radicals, smoldering anti-Catholicism and anti-Semitism, and superficial doctrines of racial superiority led to a succession of restrictive laws, among them a literacy test put into effect in 1917 over Wilson's veto. In 1921 a quota system based on doctrines of race was made national policy, and the epoch of the melting pot came to an end, or at least simmered down. Enormous numbers of immigrants settled in the industrial cities— but not for that reason alone did Americans become more and more urbanized. By 1920 more than half the population lived in cities. Perhaps because of urbanization an important element in American writing, American humor, and American painting during these years was a nostalgia for the farm: Whittier's *Snow-Bound* was published in 1866, his "Maud Muller" in 1867, Will Carleton's *Farm Ballads* in 1873, and Riley's *"The Old Swimmin'-Hole" and 'Leven More Poems* in 1883. Denman Thompson's *The Old Homestead,* first produced in Boston in 1886, held the stage for about twenty-five years, and the great popular success in painting at the World's Columbian Exposition of 1893 was Thomas Hovenden's "Breaking Home Ties." Even after the local-color tale of rural or village life had seemed to run its course elsewhere, Zona Gale could bring out between 1908 and 1919 four volumes of saccharine stories about "Friendship Village," a place which knew nothing of industrialism, war, crime, corruption, or realism.

Farming, however, declined in many areas, notably in the Northeast and parts of the South, and the proportionate number of farmers also steadily decreased. Yet by 1920 the value of livestock production was more than ten times what it had been in 1860, and the value of crops rose from about $769,000,000 in 1860 to more than $7,-500,000,000 in 1920. The Department of Agriculture had been created in 1862, partly as a war measure; the Secretary of Agriculture was given cabinet status in 1889. These developments in agriculture are the more noteworthy in view of the collapse of the cattle industry in the 1880s and the agricultural distress through about half the period, which found expression in the Granger movement of 1867, the Greenback party of 1874–1875, and the Populist movement of the 1890s. The United States by the time of World War I had become the leading industrial nation of the globe; yet the little more than two million farms in 1860 had increased to almost six and a half million by 1920, and agricultural acreage had more than doubled, rising to over nine hundred and fifty-five million acres in 1920. Oddly enough, though modern mechanization made big farming profitable, the average farm, which had included almost two hundred acres in 1860, dropped to a little under one hundred and fifty acres in 1920. Undoubtedly tenant farming had something to do with this shrinkage. But though it became a minority element in a manufacturing republic, the farm bloc exercised throughout the half-century a political influence beyond its numerical strength—an influence the more lasting because of the peculiarities of state boundaries and of congressional districts, and political reluctance to redistrict any state for election purposes.

The year 1860 was crucial in the development of parties in the United States. The old political order had broken up. The Whig party lay in fragments; what was left of it reappeared rather hopelessly as the Constitutional Union party that nominated John Bell and Edward Everett for president and vice-president. The Democrats were divided; they were not to enter the White House until the election of Cleveland a quarter of a century later. The young Republican party could not quite make up its collective mind whether its primary object was to further the cause of industry and transportation or to restrict slavery; and Abraham Lincoln, receiving only 1,865,594 votes out of 4,689,569, though he was elected by 180 electoral votes out of 293, was a minority president. Once in office, Lincoln was to grow into greatness; yet it must not be forgotten that the Republican party, though it opposed the extension of slavery, demanded high tariffs and national support of a transportation system that would aid industry to distribute its products and collect its materials from all parts of the nation. Industrial markets were increased by the Homestead Acts, and the railroads were given hundreds of thousands of acres of national land. Nor is it without significance that as a lawyer Lincoln had once represented the Illinois Central Railroad, and at another time the McCormick Reaper Company in a suit charging infringement of patents.

The Civil War and the Republican party accentuated, though they did not create, the enormous expansion of industry and of technology in a nation that had now abandoned the agrarian democracy of Thomas Jefferson for the "liberal" political economy of the British classical school. There were of course industrial corporations in the first half of the nineteenth century, organizations that, it has been said, mainly arose from selling stock to friends. By 1900 there were about one hundred and eighty "trusts" in the United States, and in 1901 what was then the largest trust ever created came into being with the organization of the United States Steel Company, combining the interests of Andrew Carnegie, J. Pierpont Morgan, and other leading bankers and industrialists and controlling about seventy per cent of the national output in iron and steel. At the end of our fifty years corporations employed about eighty per cent of the wage earners of the country. For all but eight of the years from 1861 to 1912, the Republicans held the presidency and usually controlled Congress, and, under the benevolent disinterestedness of a Supreme Court that seemed always to have a conservative majority, Big Business managed most of the nation most of the time.

In 1860 there were fewer than a million and a half factory workers in the country; by 1920 this number had grown to eight and a half million. Discoveries of gold and silver in the West, of copper in Montana, Michigan, Utah, and Arizona, of vast deposits of iron and coal (the latter often turned into coke for industrial purposes), and of course of petroleum after 1859 fed this enormous industry. Thus millions of immigrants, not all of whom were unskilled and many of whom, or their descendants, as technology grew more necessary, became plant managers, engineers, inventors, and experts in business and finance. In 1860 there were about thirty-one thousand miles of railroad in the United States; by 1915 there were something under two hundred and forty thousand miles. In 1910 fewer than half a million automobiles were manufactured. This vehicle was just beginning to lose status as a luxury item; by 1920 the annual output was about eight million. Drivers demanded better roads and got them. Ships of iron and steel traversed the Great Lakes (the locks and canals at Sault Ste. Marie were the greatest ship highway in the world, the Panama Canal not being fully opened to traffic until 1915). They brought ores from the mines to the industrial ports on the lakes or grain for the elevators of the Middle West. After long neglect the inland waterways were being improved, notably the Ohio-Mississippi system; between 1905 and 1918 the former Erie Canal was modernized as the New York State Barge Canal. If the picturesque Mississippi River steamboat had almost vanished from the Father of Waters, a steady increase in barge traffic marks the opening decades of the twentieth century. There were those who lamented the decline of the United States international mercantile marine fleet, but industry found no difficulty in selling its products abroad and importing its raw materials from afar.

The first stages of industrial development were raw and brutal, and organized labor fought against exploitation as the farmers did, but the muckrakers and the progressives had their day in court under the presidency of Theodore Roosevelt. Though the half-century saw pitched battles between strikers and troops in Pennsylvania or Illinois, the traditional American dream of a perfected republic produced in the period such writers as Edward Bellamy and Upton Sinclair and a whole library of novels in which a young political idealist battles successfully against the dark forces of corruption. Examples include Winston Churchill's *Mr. Crewe's Career,* Paul Leicester Ford's *The Honorable Peter Stirling,* Booth Tarkington's *The Gentleman from Indiana,* and Brand Whitlock's *The 13th District.* Indeed, the line of reform stretches unbroken from Roger Williams through Brook Farm and the Oneida Community, the Bellamy Clubs and the Nationalist Movement to the New Freedom of Woodrow Wilson, who announced he would not accept the Democratic nomination if success in his election depended upon Tammany Hall. Despite the somber truth in Bryce's observation that municipal government [2] was the greatest failure of American political life, despite the two great financial panics of 1873 and 1893, despite the discontent, despair, and fury that created numerous but ephemeral parties of protest and pressure groups, often illegal (the Ku Klux Klan and the American Protective Association), the renovated two-party system was not really shaken during these fifty years. Foreign observers, used to a higher degree of consistent political philosophies, might be bewildered by the American system, but its very illogic was the secret of its durability.

The early portions of these years have been decorated by such pejorative phrases as the Gilded Age, the Great Barbecue, and the Age of the Robber Barons. From the point of view of what modern critics are pleased to think of as their own sophistication, its later years have been dubbed the Age of Innocence. Life in Eden, it is held, steadily diminished and finally disappeared some time after the First World War or after the Second, critics being a little vague in their chronology. The Reconstruction years have occasioned a flood of studies, most of them until recent times, accusatory. The title of one widely read volume, James S. Pike's *The Prostrate State* (1874), which was even translated into Dutch, indicates the moral passion of a good many treatments. Modern scholarship is more objective and inclines to more temperate views.

It would, however, be a nice exercise in comparative judgment to measure the amount and deleterious effect of corruption in France under Louis Philippe or under Napoleon III as against the corruption in the United States under Ulysses Simpson Grant, and the relative burden of military government in the South from 1865 to 1877 as against the British performance in India from the Mutiny of 1857–1858 to the proclamation of Victoria as Empress of India in 1876.

The difficulty in many treatments of American history of the period is that scholarship tends to be moralistic. Who can applaud the Gilded Age? Who nowadays dares support our war with Spain? Who does not know that Thaddeus Stevens was a Bad Man, William McKinley a Weak Man, Henry Ward Beecher a Vain Man? Morality is desirable, and wickedness is detestable, and should be especially so to those who remember the Hitler years, but one suspects that the distribution of virtue and vice in the United States from 1865 to 1915 was about what it has been in any other fifty years. The signs of evil —the brazen corruption under Grant, the Tweed ring, the tough-gutted financiers such as Daniel Drew, unlovely bandits like Jesse James, the vulgar revivalists, the walking delegates of the labor unions, the hypocritical ministers of wealthy congregations—are evident. But let us not underestimate the forces of honesty—the earnest churches, the political and social reformers, the idealistic critics of the arts; the proponents of civil-service reform, of the rights of women, primary elections, and the popular election of senators; the founders of universities, hospitals, museums, libraries, and research institutions; the creators of green belts and public parks; the pioneers in modern scholarship, modern science, and modern health programs; the battlers for freedom of thought; and the educators who tried to invent a public school system that would be flexible enough and practical enough for a nation that was forever enlarging and forever changing.

In this half-century it was possible for that arrant snob, Ward McAllister, to proclaim that Society consisted of four hundred names, but in the dark tunnels of the copper mines under Butte it was questionable whether society even existed. Yet it was possible for settlement work to advance, for a movement for the arbitration of labor disputes to gather force from 1888 to 1920,[3] and for an increase in laws intended to restrict the length of the working day, protect the health and safety of factory employees, and lessen the hours of employment of women and children.[4] Doubtless an age that sent Maxim Gorki into Coventry because he came here with a mistress was ridiculous, yet the same age digested the moral upset of Darwin's *The Descent of Man,* and the 1890s took on von Hartmann, Schopenhauer, the *Rubáiyát* and such "problem novels" as E. L. Voynich's *The Gadfly* and Harold Frederic's *The Damnation of Theron Ware.* A culture that could not think of Mark Twain seriously as an artist guffawed over *Peck's Bad Boy* and *A Slow Train Through Arkansas,* it is true; but the same culture shaped Yosemite and Yellowstone National Parks, supported the Chicago Art Institute, and created that dream of beauty, the World's Columbian Exposition. Doubtless the period erected the incredible Philadelphia City Hall, but it also gloried in the soaring lines of the Brooklyn Bridge. If it turned its eyes away from the lynching bees in the South, it supported the American Society for the Prevention of Cruelty to Animals. If it produced those two strange enchantresses, Victoria and Tennessee Claflin, one of whom ran for president of the United States while the other married a man who later became the Viscount de Monserrat,[5] it likewise produced Jane Addams. "The Man That Corrupted Hadleyburg" is one sign of the times; Josiah Royce's *The Philosophy of Loyalty* is another.

II

Are there lines to be followed through this rich confusion, other than that implicit between the naïve confrontation of the Age of Scandal with the Age of Reform? I think there are. The economic historians of course have their patterns, the social and political historians have developed theirs, and the literary specialists and historians of the fine arts have constructed their own frameworks. One should not quarrel with the specialists, each of whom, if one grants his premise, is sound enough, and many of whom are still quietly seeking something better than chronology as explanation. Yet I venture the opinion that there may be three or four general clues to be found in this riotous and contradictory epoch, even though one must deal with such opposites as William James and Elbert Hubbard, Percy MacKaye and the Ringling Brothers, A. A. Michelson and Lydia Pinkham, Frank Lloyd Wright and whoever planned and executed that most extraordinary of wooden houses, the Carson mansion in Eureka, California. Everything was flexible, everything was possible—the New South, the Great West, university reform, physical education (for example, the movement for calisthenics in the public schools), aesthetics, greater "sophistication," higher morality, the strenuous life, art for the people, more millionaires, a juster distribution of the national wealth. One is tempted to quote the opening of *A Tale of Two Cities:* "It was the best of times, it was the worst of times, it was the age of wisdom, it was the age of foolishness, it was the season of Light, it was the season of Darkness, it was the spring of hope, it was the winter of despair."

The first governing idea that seems useful is that these decades were years in search of a style. For a long time no agreement appeared. In ante-bellum America there had been a relatively orderly society, North or South, and the settled parts of the Union were content to accept simultaneously a system of status and a system of democracy. It is true that there must always be some conflict between these polar ideas, but for a variety of reasons the United States before the war, despite the so-called Jacksonian revolution, was able to reconcile quality and equality, position and populism. The Civil War shook the caste system in the South and flooded the status pattern of the North with wave after wave of the newly rich, inundations caustically recorded by Edith Wharton, George Ade, Arlo Bates, and others. Meanwhile the West tried to create, as it were overnight in areas like San Francisco, a pattern of Old Families with a general hospitality to individualism. Before the war it had been comparatively easy to assimilate immigrants into the American system. Afterward it was increasingly a puzzle how to make good citizens out of the newcomers, who brought with them from Russia or the Far East cultures that radically differed from the American way. A powerful republic was no longer timid about Europeans, to be sure. A nation that had conquered itself in the years from 1861 through 1865 was no longer afraid of being overwhelmed by monarchy, even though it had a haunting fear of European radicals. Increase of travel abroad was partially a result of the modernization of ocean-going ships that, decade after decade, were swifter and more commodious, so that what had been a venturesome thing when Emerson went abroad in the 1840s had become standard performance, at least among the wealthy, in the 1900s. Moreover, the intellectuals were persuaded that the secret of research could be learned only in European universities. Artists, aesthetes, and the American equivalent of *les flâneurs* now went to Paris, which eclipsed Rome and Düsseldorf for gaiety, worldliness, and art. The tone of magazine comment on things foreign veered after 1865 from toploftiness and suspicion to acceptance and admiration, even though the French remained morally questionable—a heroine reading a yellow-back French novel automatically classified herself in the period as either "advanced" or dissolute. The United States was, then, far more open to a multitude of influences after 1865 than it had been in 1815. What the historians have lumped together as the execrable taste of the late Victorian-American world is better interpreted as eclecticism, the weighing of various styles, the search for something both national and modern.

By any standard, bad taste in the period is evident enough. The three-color lithographs of saccharine domestic scenes and Sunday-school cards, the incredible patent medicine advertising, gimcrackery on mantelpieces draped with velvet or velours, the bamboo furniture, the beaded curtains that hung in doorways, the cabinet photographs in sepia, the overelaborate sets for overelaborate melodramas like *Under the Gaslight* and *The Heart of Maryland,* the Brussels carpets with roses bigger than cabbages, the gilt on "subscription" books, the miniature birchbark canoes labeled "Niagara Falls" (pyrography, by the way, came in among the genteel), the peacock feathers, the china vases shaped into lilies or young girls wearing nightgowns, the gilded bulrushes, the shaving mugs bearing their owners' names in Gothic letters, the overstuffed sofas, the ornate music cabinets with leather music-rolls on top, the Moorish alcoves, and the English dens—who does not know these products of the decades? I say nothing about costume, since every age looks ridiculous to its successors—though many years later the despised garments may become quaint and even be revived. Yet the bustle, the shirtwaist, the trailing skirt, the ostrich plume, and the buttoned shoes, the high collar, the watch chain, the swallow-tailed coat, the full bathing suit, and the stovepipe hat do not, one guesses, offer much for aesthetic approbation.

Every age presumably gets the ugliness it deserves, but ugliness is both chronologically and topographically a relative term. One can imagine the comments of Thorwaldsen on modern sculptural "constructs" or the bewilderment of Erwin von Steinbach if he were called upon to pass judgment on the Carpenter Center at Harvard University. Now that art dealers are salvaging nineteenth-century paintings from basements and storage bins and even the tidy has come back on chairs, the relativity of taste is once more exemplified. The old-fashioned kitchen range with its mass of decorative design in black, its bow legs, and its incised nickel trim is now fashionable in country houses maintained as vacation spots by city people, and though the hall tree has not reappeared, the commode and the marble-topped table or washbasin are again fashionable. If we tear layers of Victorian paper off the sham walls that conceal a brick fireplace and envy Victorian Americans their high-ceilinged rooms, it is more important to ask why the stove was decorated, why was the flowered paper pasted on the walls of drawing rooms so crowded with things as to make navigating them a perilous voyage. (Dresden shepherdesses and Japanese fans were likely to be swept off shelf or table unless the strictest rules of decorum in movement were observed!) The answer to the riddle seems to lie in the wide-ranging, eager curiosity of the Americans after each new thing. The importation of Canton china and the exhibition of scrimshaw work were simple matters in the age before Sumter, but the avid curiosity of these later years was not thus easily satisfied. Exemplifying the Spanish proverb that he who would bring back the wealth of the Indies must carry the wealth of the Indies with him, the Americans wished to know, to experience, to experiment, to taste, to try. Having been repeatedly told that American life was thin and raw but that the United States was the heir of all the ages in the foremost files of time, they demanded whatever the world could offer. There was not a perdurable native style; there was only a conglomerate of styles, out of which they hoped in the end to fashion something that would do—as, indeed, they did in the work of Dankmar Adler and Sullivan, Winslow Homer and Stieglitz, Mark Twain and Robert Frost.

They tried almost everything. Fashion went in for the baroque of the Second Empire, for Tudor houses, for Queen Anne dwellings, for Romanesque libraries and railway stations, for Gothic churches and Oriental synagogues, for the curlicue of *l'art nouveau,* for Renaissance architecture in stone, for German romanticism in stone, brick, stucco, and shingle, for bulbous domes and Spanish theaters. The mining camps were raw, the dusty villages bare, the small towns too often merely hideous; yet Main Street was likely to have a two-, three-, or four-story business block with plate-glass windows on the ground floor, lettered in gold. Who invented the amazing courthouses that dot America I do not know, just as I do not know who carved the little stone soldier that stands with his innocent musket keeping watch over Confederate cemeteries or, with a slight change in uniform, over the Union dead. It is, however, instructive in this search for satisfaction to walk through the Mount Auburn Cemetery in Cambridge, or one in Milwaukee, or the grounds at Gettysburg and observe the constant experiments with monumental forms borrowed from the classical past or from Egypt, France, the Gothic North, or the distant East. A city like Rochester, New York, is an architectural museum, a jumble of structures, sometimes appalling, sometimes curious, sometimes beautiful. But the restless curiosity, the insatiable energy that built or adapted or invented these edifices is unparalleled in the previous history of the United States.

Inevitably the search led to contradictions. Naturalists might write about determinism and chemisms as Theodore Dreiser did, and farm life might be as dreary as Hamlin Garland said it was, but in America everything was possible. How else could you explain Jacob Riis and George Washington Carver? The decades that froze the Boston Brahmins into their stately brownstone fronts on Beacon Street saw John Philip Sousa, son of a Portuguese immigrant, rise to fame as the greatest composer of military marches in the world. Nourishing the tradition of Canova, Lorado Taft carved the "Solitude of the Soul," now in the Chicago Art Institute; the same period found Albert Pinkham Ryder painting his fantastic visions: "I am trying," said he, "to find something out here beyond the place on which I have a footing." The era that produced *The Portrait of a Lady* and *Daisy Miller*, two adroit studies which seemed to show that the independent American female was doomed to destruction, also nourished Horatio Alger, whose one hundred and thirty-five books celebrated the virtue of honesty and industry in a society that welcomed energy and the Benjamin Franklin way to wealth. Fashionable despondency took over parts of American art and thought in the 1890s, but the people were still reading those sentimental triumphs of the age, Helen Hunt Jackson's *Ramona*, Lew Wallace's *Ben Hur; A Tale of the Christ*, and Charles M. Sheldon's *In His Steps*. The last sold by hundreds of thousands of copies and was supposed to prove that the application of the simpler principles of Christianity would build the New Jerusalem. The Western state that nourished William Jennings Bryan and his flamboyant rhetoric also nourished the classical simplicity of Willa Cather. Samuel Gompers, a Dutch Jew born in London, organizing labor, counterpoints Andrew Carnegie, a poor Scots boy, organizing steel, and delightedly serving later on as host to Matthew Arnold when the apostle of culture came to the United States. The businessman was constantly satirized from Emerson to Sinclair Lewis, yet the businessman built the University of Chicago and the Monadnock Building and made way for such non-Anglo-Saxons as Daniel Guggenheim, Michael Pupin, Carl Laemmle, and Ole Hanson, a realtor who became mayor of Seattle, broke a strike, developed Los Angeles and Santa Barbara, and wrote a book called *Americanism vs. Bolshevism*.[6] In the Napoleonic armies every private carried a marshal's baton in his knapsack; in the age of eclecticism the doctrine of rags to riches made a good deal of sense. If the reader is tempted to murmur something about social Darwinism at this juncture, he is right to do so; eclecticism in taste and social Darwinism were supplementary or complementary terms.

The mention of social Darwinism is not so extraneous as at first it seems. The evolutionary doctrine rested on the general supposition of the survival of the fittest in the struggle for existence, and what applied to economic life or politics applied also to such social manifes-

tations as painting, music, art, architecture, and books. But a problem arises. Historians of the fine arts, when they come to the
nineteenth century, particularly its latter half, take an odd turn. In
discussing some earlier age—for example, the painting and architecture of the Renaissance—they look for what seems most richly to embody or express the values of that age; they do not demand that Renaissance art shall be "modern." When, however, they come into the
nineteenth century, a period that may still lie too close for proper
perspective, they do not ask what best expresses the values of the
nineteenth century. They hunt out artists who anticipate the years of
the modern, the forerunners of cubism, or abstractionism, or some
other movement favored by the twentieth century. It seems probable,
however, that the nineteenth century, as did the Renaissance, knew
what it wanted and tried to find it; and that if it liked Twachtman
and Elihu Vedder, William Merritt Chase and Edwin A. Abbey, John
La Farge and Abbott Thayer, and failed to applaud the later water
colors of Winslow Homer or the visions of Arthur B. Davies or the
paintings of Middleton Manigault or Louis Eilshemius, it may be because this second group did not say what the nineteenth century
wanted said. In sum, the period did not exist as an imperfect prophecy of twentieth-century America; it lived in its own right.

Emerson's dictum that every scripture has a right to be read in the
light of the circumstances that brought it forth is true of any period,
but it needs most strongly to be asserted of these fifty years. The
moderns insist that until the Armory Show of 1913, the Americans
were wandering in the wilderness. Yet if anybody were to assert that
eighteenth-century drawing and engraving were all wrong until the
happy arrival of William Blake, the absurdity would be apparent. It
is important not to make this sort of mistake about the years from
1865 to 1915. I have said, I think rightly, that the age was seeking a
style; I have said, I hope correctly, that the age was filled with contradictions, so that the first effect upon the observer is that he is
watching a kaleidoscope. But the characteristic style was not proto-
modernism. The technique of John Singer Sargent is quite as remarkable as that of Jackson Pollock, just as the brushwork of William Morris Hunt is quite as mature as the brushwork of Andrew
Wyeth. The important thing is not to label the age weak-minded because it hung Bouguereau on its walls and failed to buy Toulouse-
Lautrec. As there is usually a lag between technical and thematic in-

novations and the acceptance of change by the general public, I suggest that these years were hesitant to accept "radicalism" prophetic of our own style (or styles), less because they were backward in taste (a charge that hardly equates with their capacity to import all sorts of novelties from abroad) than because the innovators seemed to deny some fundamental tenet held by the critics and the public. The style to which, amidst all the contradictions I have sketched, they finally came, the style that makes their work as unmistakable as the work of the Italian primitives, is a style that richly, flexibly, and strongly expresses their profound conviction that the visible world exists. Probably it owes something to the vogue of photography.

In one way this style was simply a continuation of the hold upon thoughtful Americans of the Scottish common-sense philosophy. In another sense, however, it expresses a determined turning away from the illusions of romanticism or, more accurately, of the romantic philosophy—the outlook of the transcendentalists, of Poe, of Thomas Cole's insistent attempts to paint the goodness of God in nature rather than the American landscape. For persons like Emerson, or Jones Very, or Amos Bronson Alcott, "reality" lacked real existence. It was only a shimmering and rather annoying veil let down between their eyes and eternity. Emerson's *Nature* perfectly states this point of view, as, in another context, does *Moby Dick*, virtually a philosophical allegory, or Poe's "Al Aaraaf," a poem in which "the murmur that springs/ From the growing of grass" and various other enumerated phenomena is transformed into "the music of things," whatever that may mean. Hawthorne, too, wanted to transcend the instant and the material: Maule's curse, mysteriously descending without regard to biology through several generations of Pyncheons, at last catches up and ruins that family in 1851.

By 1865, however, hundreds of thousands of American feet had tramped the earth from Atlanta to the sea and from Maine to California. That generation and their successors learned that the world exists, that rain falls, that snow freezes, that wealth can be torn from the soil and out of the hills, that rivers run to bear traffic, space exists for railroads, oil to be burned, forests for making two-by-fours, electricity to be transmitted over cables and wires. Skyscrapers rose above the level land. Wealth in the period, not surprisingly, expressed itself in the acquisition of things (it is significant that most financial tycoons wanted a gold currency); and when you look at the

paintings, the sculpture, the architecture, the books, you are overwhelmed by the conviction of their creators that the world is as we
see it and that the business of style is to be a mode of representing
things as they are, sometimes a little heightened, sometimes a little
imagined, but always as physical fidelity. We, who mainly project our
queer images of life rather than register actuality, we who live in con-
torted and private universes of our own devising, cannot understand
this emergence out of the chaos of war and the clouds of romanticism
into the daylight of physics and chemistry, industry and invention, of
a way to picture things as they exist. Formerly a problem of the soul;
now flesh and blood, stone and steel, meat and drink, landscape and
building. This was the great transformation in style these fruitful
years accomplished.

The style is everywhere evident. In characteristic canvases of the
time individual objects are lovingly portrayed as they are, not as they
might be imagined if you saw them in four dimensions. The portraits are bold and "real"; the subjects live in normal bodies, character looks out from their faces, and the painter does not satirically dis-
tort arm and leg, neck and chest, eye and coloring into a private
alphabet of his personality. A landscape is something you can walk
on, not something imagined. An undeniable glory of the time was
the Ashcan School; if you cut into the flesh of people portrayed by
Luks or Bellows or Sloan or Marsh, they will bleed, precisely as the
patients in canvases by Eakins bleed when the surgeon opens their
flesh. The architecture is visible and earthy: Richardson's Romanesque buildings are arrangements of actual stone and tile, not something out of transcendental geometry; Ware and Van Brunt's Memorial Hall at Harvard is as solid and ugly and imposing as the Civil
War and does not merely pretend to be a building like Yamasaki's
blown-up sham Japanese temple across the street. It is obvious that
realism and naturalism in the literature of these years express the
same conviction about actuality. The recording of speech in *The
Story of a Country Town* or *The Octopus* or *Jennie Gerhardt* is a
couple of light years away from what purports to be conversation in
The Scarlet Letter or *The Last of the Mohicans*. To say this is not to
denigrate Cooper or Hawthorne but to define what the style attempted. So likewise in statuary. Sculptors such as John Quincy
Adams Ward or Bela Pratt or Daniel Chester French may have pretti-
fied or idealized man, but they had studied anatomy, they knew that

man is a plantigrade animal that walks the streets; they did not dream of erecting anything like the Picasso sculpture that is supposed to beautify modern Chicago. Only in music does the general principle seem to weaken; [7] yet even in our musical development from 1865 onward music retained its humanistic intent. If it could in no sense be "realistic," it could at least carry on a grave tradition, noble and sympathetic. Contrast, whatever the merits of the two styles, MacDowell's *Sonata Tragica,* intended to express grief for the death of his teacher, Joseph Joachim Raff, with the *musique concrète* of our time, which, whatever it expresses, does not express general emotion and scarcely mathematical relationship. If we insist (and we do) that art in some sense mirrors its own epoch, the five decades to be surveyed must surely be allowed to express themselves and not some later time—allowed also to create a style satisfactory to those who used it without anticipating a style that was not to be dominant until half a century after the Battle of the Marne.

III

Style, however, is but the outward and visible sign of an inward and basic belief. If one looks more closely into this fascinating age, another general formula appears amid the eclecticism and the contradictions: the search for some sort of unifying law or principle in every important field of endeavor. At first sight this does not seem to differentiate this age from any other. Intellectuals of the eighteenth century thought they had found unifying explanation in the universality of reason. In ante-bellum America the universe was sometimes mechanical and sometimes dynamic and sometimes both. But it was always divinely ordered. The shattering effect of the Civil War, of the evolutionary hypothesis of Darwin and the evolutionary philosophy of Herbert Spencer, of German biblical scholarship, and of a flood of new ideas from Europe (for example, the philosophy of Hegel), tended to antiquate the older cosmogonies and to demand newer explanations.

But one must distinguish. For the man on the street unitary explanation of the universe was what it had always been; for most Americans, Christian theology; for others, a naïve fatalism or a naïve belief in progress. One must therefore look to the intellectual minority for the stir of curiosity about modern explications. Most of the intellec tuals, one supposes, were graduates of colleges or universities or at least of the better secondary schools, public or private, since the proportion of self-educated intellectuals seems to diminish during these decades. One must sort out and put aside disciples, however intelligent, of Spiritualism and Christian Science, faiths that had their private doorways to truth that was never affected by the cosmic weather. One must also subtract small groups still more distant from the intellectual center, followers of this or that leader or sage or mystic to whom a vision had been vouchsafed, simple in substance and esoteric in vocabulary, which, taught to disciples, was to clarify living, morality, and love. Madam Blavatsky, for example, who lived in New York during the 1870s, promulgated theosophy, and the assumptions of New Thought can be studied in such books as E. W. Hopkin's *The Science of New Thought* (Bristol, Connecticut, 1904) and B. MacLelland's *Prosperity through Thought Force* (Holyoke, Massachusetts, 1907), or in a periodical founded at Los Angeles in 1911 with the engaging title of *Eternal Progress Magazine*. One notes that Elizabeth Stuart Phelps's *The Gates Ajar*, a novel in which the living communicate with the dead, sold steadily for thirty years after its publication in 1868.

At the end of the Civil War it is probable that the majority of American Christians were in a general sense fundamentalists.[8] Despite the vogue of Emerson, transcendentalism seems to have had little general appeal. Most Americans accepted the story of creation narrated in Genesis, God as a loving father and an almighty judge, the fall of man in Adam, an atonement made possible through the incarnation of the Son, and salvation through grace if one truly repented and tried to live a better life. Repentance assured the soul present peace and everlasting bliss hereafter in a heaven where family relationships were to endure eternally. Around each of these basic concepts theological controversies had eddied and were to eddy, but most Christians thought they believed these tenets, together with the idea that God had made the world, ran it, and would destroy it on a day called the Last Judgment. Fundamentalist theologians were, it is true, likely to be bellicose, but it is easy to mistake the lions for the lambs—easy also to dismiss all fundamentalists as bigoted or ignorant men. There were believers of high caliber among them, as witness the quality of arguments in the famous Andover trials.

Many fundamentalists believed that Satan was still abroad, enticing souls into his kingdom with the blandishments of playing cards, wicked shows, godless books, agnosticism, atheism, sensual women, gambling, whisky, and "worldliness." [9] Heaven was to recompense the faithful for a life beset by temptations, even though the celestial landscape grew fainter with the passing years and the angelic hosts were principally evident at the Christmas season. But the earth was, nevertheless, the Lord's and the fullness thereof; and if human life was imperfect, the universe was good because it was run on principles evident in Addison's famous hymn, sung in a thousand churches, "The hand that made us is divine." Even if the seven days of creation in Genesis were not literal days, traditional Protestantism could accept mild modifications of meaning since God often spoke in symbols rather than literally, for example, in the rainbow and the burning bush. Sound education, sound theology, and sound natural philosophy agreed that the cosmos displays the extraordinary skill, prescience, and goodness of Deity.

So ran general belief when *The Origin of Species* appeared in 1859, reviewed in this country by Asa Gray and Francis Bowen. For the time being, however, evolution was muted by the noise of war. Most Christians were content with the reassurance of the most influential scientific personality of the age, Louis Agassiz, who told them that not geology, comparative zoology, or paleontology could disturb their faith:

> As soon as we recognize in nature a harmonious plan pervading all its parts,—as soon as it is understood that this plan has been carried out, in the course of time, successively towards one definite end, developing always the same train of thoughts,—we are justified in concluding, that as it is now it has been from the beginning, at every following period, the result of a free determination of the Creator, unlimited, unrestrained in his works, save by his own decision.[10]

But the war ended. American thought was more and more Europeanized, and the intellectual minority had to choose, or so it seemed, between opposed explanations of the universe, both in a sense traditional. One, relatively easy to grasp, was the theory of the Newtonian universe. The other, more emotionally satisfying to many and also more difficult to comprehend, was the dynamic universe of Schleiermacher and Humboldt, Goethe and Carlyle. In the Newtonian universe, though there might be cyclical movements in history (but is not a circle a mathematical concept?), and though God was needed to give the first push to the vast machine (but is not push a mechanical concept?), mathematical analysis explained everything except the soul, and the atomistic theory of matter was happily paralleled by the atomistic psychology of Locke. Planets swept along in their majestic orbits; animals were what they had always been, copies of each other ceaselessly produced (it is true, some animals had dropped out); and man, though he could rise to the excellence of Plutarch or sink to the barbarism of ignoble savages, could neither improve nor decay sufficiently to alter essential human nature. The invention of the calculus had made it possible to measure with great accuracy quantities that altered by imperceptible degrees, so that the system could take care of most sorts of change. Such a world was compatible with theism and even with Christian theology.

In the minds of many of the Founding Fathers, it is true, this interpretation induced an attitude of stoic resignation, since, on the cyclical theory of history, even the best government could only postpone decay. History was the record of the crimes and follies of mankind. Thus, writing to John Adams January 12, 1812, Jefferson could declare that he had taken final leave of politics and given up the newspapers for Tacitus and Thucydides, Newton and Euclid, finding himself happier for concentrating on the eternal verities, and a good many ante-bellum Southerners were inclined to agree that human nature never changed. If a minority thought the cosmic machine also produced progress (and surely a Jefferson was superior to a Hottentot), as late as 1888 the Reverend James McCosh, who retired from the presidency of Princeton in that year, though he accepted evolution (his version), was still teaching that things are as they are under a divine dispensation and that the mind of a Princeton student did not differ from the mind of Adam. Each needed to be educated.

The dynamic, organic, or organistic point of view had been shaped by romantic philosophy and early nineteenth-century science, unless one prefers to think that the romantic world-view was the product of a dynamic interpretation of the cosmos. The shift was from mechanism to vitality, from the mathematical way of reasoning to the idea that the universe was a sort of enormous animal, from the particularistic psychology of Locke to an all-embracing subjectivism in which the universe did not create mind but the mind created the universe. The American heritage from transcendentalism was not, as I have hinted, widely important, though the vogue of Emerson in this period as America's most representative writer was great. But the inheritors, such as they were, took the romantic point of view. So did the Hegelians in St. Louis.[11] Others were led into pantheism, or into a doctrine of immanence, or, like John Fiske and Francis Ellingwood Abbot, into some form of theism.[12] Long before Sir Charles Lyell's *The Antiquity of Man* (1863) and Darwin's *The Descent of Man* (1871–1872), among the American romantics the universe was not so much inert matter whirling on invisible circular belts as it was some mysterious entity filled with life.[13] The drift of the romantic interpretation was in the direction of Vitalism, Basic Law, Force, Spirit, or Mind, all surrogates for Deity. The century tended to believe that you proved the existence of an abstract truth if you capitalized the noun.

For a good many Americans simplifying seemed to lie with evolution. Among the ignorant or the half-educated, of course, Darwinism was materialism or atheism or both, and the philosophy of Spencer was equally bad. But in biology, once that area was out from under the shadow of the influential Agassiz, most scientists had by 1880 come to accept the hypothesis, or some variant of it, expounded in that marvel of patience and modesty, *The Origin of Species*. Geologists and astronomers had long since given up special creationism and had taken over some form of uniformitarianism as explanation for change. By the 1870s the controversy mostly eddied around *The Descent of Man* (Sir Charles Lyell's *The Antiquity of Man*, had got lost in an America preoccupied with Gettysburg and Vicksburg) and around the astonishing generalization of Herbert Spencer,[14] who, if he left room for God in a mysterious region called The Unknowable, took a dim view of deity, even though Spencer had been subsidized by American money and should therefore have been kinder to Christianity. Did one mean by evolution the ponderous syllables of the famous theorem in the Synthetic Philosophy or the succinct statement of Joseph Le Conte, who said evolution involves continuous progressive change according to certain laws and by reason of resident forces? Le Conte's language comforted many, especially among the theologians, but even if Spencer's universe was geared to run down, you could be at least as optimistic about it as the Founding Fathers had been in the universe of Newton. Of course if you felt that the struggle of the fittest to survive was the law at the heart of things, so-

cial Darwinism was justified, but if you held with the Synthetic Philosopher that "evolution is an integration of matter and concomitant
dissipation of motion, during which the matter passes from an indefinite, incoherent homogeneity to a definite, coherent heterogeneity"
while the "retained motion undergoes a parallel transformation,"
once it had been explained that this meant everything was supposed
to move from the simple to the complex, that "development" was improvement, and that industrial society, which is complex, is superior
to savage society, which is simple, you could argue that the state, that
outward form of social man, develops by force of inward law and
that the best thing for you to do was not to interfere and not to let
anybody else interfere.

If, however, you were inclined to advanced views—for example, to
socialism—you might still infer that progress ("development") was so
inevitable that all you had to do was to give it a helpful push.[15] In
either case the heart of the matter was Law. If scientists thought
Spencer was too philosophical and philosophers thought he was not
philosophical enough, the Spencerian theorem which hitched all the
dynamic universe to the enginery of development, did not encourage
defeatism. When the great man came to New York after journeys
into Canada and from Boston to Chicago and back, he was given a
dinner at Delmonico's, where, however, he begged William Evarts,
who presided over a gathering of notables, to talk to him as little as
possible, said he became "tolerably callous" to eulogies, and delivered
a speech disappointingly critical of American determination to develop by working too hard.[16]

Not every interpretation of evolution was sweetness and light. At
Yale the tough-minded William Graham Sumner, who detested sentimentalists, wrote an essay, "Sociology," in 1881, almost the year of
the dinner to Spencer, in which he denounced novelists, utopians, socialists, "dilettanti," the half-educated, and reformers who assume
"that we men need only to make up our minds what kind of a society
we want to have, and then that we can devise means for calling that
society into existence." Human life, he said, is maintained by a struggle against nature and by competition with other forms of life, since
"the prime condition of this society will lie in the ratio of its numbers to the supply of materials within its reach. For the supply at any
moment attainable is an exact quantity, and the number of persons
who can be supplied is arithmetically limited." Therefore "con-

straint, anxiety, possibly tyranny and repression, mark social relations," because "the law of population . . . combined with the law of the diminishing returns, constitutes the great underlying condition of society." If socialists and sentimentalists did not like this state of things, their complaints, if they were to be made at all, should be directed "against the author of the universe for the hardships which man has to endure in his struggle with nature." Sumner combined the harsher aspects of Malthus, Ricardo, and the Darwinians with a deep respect for the laws of thermodynamics.[17]

If Sumner was no optimist, the Adams brothers, Brooks and Henry, were even grimmer in their final analyses of the course of history under scientific law. The very titles of two of their books, *Law of Civilization and Decay: An Essay on History* (1895–1896) and *The Degradation of the Democratic Dogma* (1919), breathe what Dr. Johnson called inspissated gloom. It is an intricate problem in the history of ideas to determine accurately the sources and development of Henry Adams' thought as well as the relation between his final outlook and that which his brother arrived at on quasi-independent lines. Both accepted evolution, and each was profoundly shaken by the inferences they drew, necessarily before the discovery of atomic energy, from their understanding of the first and second laws of thermodynamics as enunciated by Lord Kelvin. Henry Adams added to this what he called "the rule of phase applied to history," an idea he got from Willard Gibbs, who "stood on the same plane with the three or four greatest minds of the century." The universe was running down, and the human race was consuming greater and greater quantities of solar energy, for which no replacement was possible. Man was clearly of animal origin; thought consumed energy quite as much as did muscular exertion; and thought, by creating machines, accelerating commerce, and multiplying wants, was leading man into a dizzy dance toward ultimate destruction. The assumption by American historians that progress was guaranteed by evolution was, thought Henry Adams, quite unfounded, because the restoration of energy was impossible, and it seemed to him misleading to teach "progress" when destruction was in the long run sure. Brooks and Henry took over the "phase rule" from Gibbs. As under change of temperature or pressure a homogeneous mixture passes through solid, liquid, and gaseous phases (for example, ice, water, and vapor), so thought undergoes a series of changes, each successive phase decreasing in length by a law of inverse squares somewhat fantastically applied to history. The religious phase of mankind lasted about ninety thousand years, ending in 1600 with Copernicus and Galileo; the mechanical phase went on for three hundred years (the square root of ninety thousand); the electrical phase (hence the worship of the dynamo), on the same principle, would last from 1900 to 1917; and a final phase of, apparently, pure thought would last about four years and reach its end in 1921, perilously close to the final dissipation of cosmic energy.

Toward the end of *The Education of Henry Adams* and of course in *Mont-Saint-Michel and Chartres* the Virgin appears to counterpoint the dynamo, but she is a Protestant virgin. Since for Henry Adams woman was both a source and a consumer of energy, it is somewhat difficult to see how the worship of the Queen of Heaven really alters what the brothers assumed to be cosmic law. The *Law of Civilization and Decay* works out with more specific application to the Western world this proposition: "The theory proposed is based upon the accepted scientific principle that the law of force and energy is of universal application in nature, and that animal life is one of the outlets through which solar energy is dissipated. . . . Human societies are forms of animal life. . . ." One may or may not prefer Henry Adams' statement:

> In short, the social Organism, in the recent views of history, is the cause, creator, and end of the Man, who exists only as a passing representative of it, without rights or functions except what it imposes. As an Organism society has always been peculiarly subject to degradation [that is, dissipation] of Energy, and alike the historians and the physicists invariably stretch Kelvin's law over all organized matter whatever.[18]

As might be expected and as Charles A. Beard points out, Theodore Roosevelt, though he read Brooks Adams with care, found the book not altogether to his liking.

A hard-line interpretation of evolution as unity might have been expected to appeal to the dark strain of Calvinism in America, but though the dogma of man's inherited wickedness flourished among fundamentalists, discourse of the Sumner-Adams kind was beyond the comprehension of many, or, if it touched them at all, confirmed their opinion that evolution and atheism were interchangeable terms.[19] A principal citadel of Calvinism in the North had been the Andover Theological Seminary, founded in 1807–1808 by a combination of

Old Calvinists and Hopkinsians, who, if they did not wholly agree, set up a creed (or rather two variants of a creed) supposed to be forever changeless. On their appointment members of the faculty were expected to subscribe to this. There had been a few earlier deviants, but in 1885 Professor Egbert C. Smyth and four others published a collection of essays called *Progressive Orthodoxy*,[20] the general purport of which was, like Cardinal Newman's doctrine of "development," to subject static and eternal theological truths to changes of interpretation that harmonized them with evolution. This book, together with Smyth's editorial conduct of *The Andover Review*, incensed conservative alumni, who brought charges before the Board of Visitors saying that the offenders were unfaithful to their original pledges to the creed. The case was argued for three days in December 1886, legal counsel appearing on both sides. It was agreed to simplify proceedings by taking the conduct of Professor Smyth as representative. The Board found him guilty but dropped the case against his four colleagues. After some maneuvering the matter was eventually referred to the Massachusetts Supreme Court, which vacated the decision of the Visitors to discharge Smyth and sent the case back on the ground that though the Visitors had jurisdiction, the Trustees had not been properly represented or heard. In effect, the Visitors eventually allowed the matter to drop. But the Andover trials [21] attracted national attention; they were regarded as a test of strength between the old theology and the new liberalism.

The Andover controversy highlighted but did not originate the struggle of theological liberals to unite evolution (or "development") with Christian theology and simultaneously to prevent modern biblical scholarship from eroding the basic tenets of Christian faith. Unity between science and religion, harmony among Christian theologies, accommodation to be somehow achieved among dogmatic absolutism, the historical point of view, and a universe in constant flux — such were the goals of liberals in the ministry and the divinity schools. What they unconsciously did was to transfer vitalism as a principle from science to theology.

There were various awkward points to be got around or got over. If Jesus Christ was God Incarnate, how could you reconcile his human qualities (which must be, if evolution was correct, the products of evolution), with his divine qualities, which were presumably absolute? If God loved mankind, why had He waited so long to offer them redemption, and what about the luckless billions who had never had a chance to believe? Did not other religions have their redeemers and their miracles and their ethical systems, and why was Christianity superior or unique? If the Bible was the product of an evolution of texts, what part of it was nevertheless inspired, how did you identify the inspired portions, and who was to judge? Even if you granted that evolution was merely God's way of creating things, what evidence was there that He had in these latter days infused souls into men? At what stage of the evolutionary process did man cease to be an animal and take on eternity? And why—if these few years on an inferior planet attached to an inferior star in the corner of the universe were a period of moral probation—should one assume that spiritual evolution, if it exists, stops with this brief earthly life? Why not a probationary period indefinitely beyond the grave? If striving upward was characteristic of man, why should he suddenly stop? Given the assumption that the great familiar Christian creeds were eternal truth, these riddles were insoluble; yet, fearful of disruption and desirous of shaping some unifying formula that would hold together the church and civilization, religion and science, a great library of earnest Protestant books strove to forge some theory of religion that would be progressive and flexible, eternal and true, and, discarding what was false in tradition, would find some sort of pragmatic unity in this theological and philosophical diversity of views.

It is impossible to give an account of this large library of liberal theology, often acute, sometimes emotional, frequently shallow, and more rarely profound. In a general sense its immediate ancestor so far as Protestantism is concerned was probably Horace Bushnell, whose influential volume, *Christian Nurture* (1861) and one of its successors, *The Vicarious Atonement* (1866), appealed to many. In effect Bushnell denied the doctrine that children come into the world hopeless little sinners, thought they could be educated into religious truth and, what is more important, shifted the ground of belief from dogma to intuition and experience.[22] Through the breach that he had made in orthodoxy others followed—not merely the Andover five but such men as Newman Smyth, William Newton Clarke, Charles A. Briggs, Levi Leonard Paine, Henry Churchill King, and the tough-minded George A. Gordon. There were liberal preachers and popularizers like Henry Ward Beecher, Phillips Brooks, Lyman Abbott, and Washington Gladden. There were scientists like Joseph

Le Conte who, insisting there is no necessary connection between evolution and materialism, thought that

> the spirit of *man* developed out of the *anima* or conscious principle of animals, and that this, again, was developed out of the lower forms of life-force, and this in turn out of the chemical and physical forces of Nature; and that at a certain stage in this gradual development, viz., with man, it *acquired* the property of immortality precisely as it now, in the individual history of each man at a certain stage, acquires the capacity of abstract thought.[23]

A popularizer of evolutionary philosophy, John Fiske, as early as his *Outlines of Cosmic Philosophy* (1874), concluded that Force cannot be identified with Deity, that, theologically speaking, "the question is whether the creature is to be taken as a measure of the Creator," and asked whether "the highest form of Being as yet suggested to one petty race of creatures by its ephemeral experience of what is going on in one tiny corner of the universe is necessarily to be taken as the equivalent of that absolutely highest form of Being in which all the possibilities of existence are alike comprehended," and in a later book, *The Destiny of Man* (1884), averred that "whereas in its rude beginnings the psychical life was but an appendage of the body, in fully developed Humanity the body is but the vehicle for the soul." [24] Lecture series were set up, at least in the North, anthologies put together, and histories of American religion published to demonstrate that evolution did not mean the death of God.[25]

When in 1885 Henry Ward Beecher defined religion as "that state of mind in which a man is related by his emotions, and through his emotions by his will and conduct, to God and to the proper performance of duty in this world"; when Lyman Abbott in 1887 proclaimed that "every spring is a creative spring. God is always creating"; when Henry Churchill King in 1901 declared that evolution points to just such "a larger dominant spiritual order, in that man is its goal, with whom the physical evolution is arrested and the spiritual unending evolution begins," [26] they thought they had found a unitary principle, and in some sense they had. More radical groups like the Free Religious Association, the proceedings of which were published from 1867 to at least 1907, and the Ethical Culture Society of 1876 went beyond them in a reduction of theology to humanism, aspiration, and rather cloudy notions about God,[27] so that Washington Gladden might well ask, in the title of a book published in Boston in 1898, *How Much Is Left of the Old Doctrines?* But among liberal Protestants, at least, evolution and Christianity were at unity with themselves.

Moderns find this unity misleading. The age of Tillich and Reinhold Niebuhr does not accept the reduction of theology and a philosophy of science to spirituality, personalism, and a vague identification of God with immaterial force. Even in the period itself basic difficulties appear. "Traditional" theology, whether one likes it or not, had an intellectual cutting edge to it; "liberal" theology is vague in its definitions, permissive as dogma, and reaches unity only by fusing into one a blurred notion of science, a blurred notion of history, and a blurred notion of religious faith. As a result, the Protestant sermon soon ceased to have much intellectual content and fell back on vague emotional appeal and moral uplift, as George A. Gordon confessed in 1903 when he lamented the separation of religion into theology controlled by professionals and preachers without mental stamina, the result of the fact that "the teaching that controlled our fathers has lost its authority." [28] One has only to read an eighteenth-century American sermon and one by Phillips Brooks to see the decline in intellectual rigor. Finally, the social gospel,[29] that admirable resolve to forget casuistry and build the kingdom of God on earth rather than wait for it in heaven, presently discovered the inadequacy of churches and Christian settlement workers to deal adequately with the modern city and the urban proletariat. The job was taken away from them, so to speak, by the rising demand for trained social workers, social psychologists, and, eventually, psychiatrists. All this, however, should not conceal the truth that "liberals" in the period solved the unification of science and religion to their own satisfaction.[30]

IV

I have now sketched the development of a search for a common style amid the clash of tastes and preferences in the period; and I have hinted at the belief to be found in many fields of thought that some unifying principle could be educed from the conflict of theories and the welter of discoveries and inventions during the age. I have illustrated this last argument principally from the adoption or adaptation of the evolutionary principle and the attempt of theology to ingest, as it were, this new enemy of traditional Christian faith. Other fields could be examined—for example, the physical sciences (as Henry Adams did), sociology, and psychology, even though the search for general principle is less evident in some of these areas than it is in the biological sciences. I turn now to a third commanding idea, the new, or at least the revised, concept of nationhood.

The ideas of nation, nationalism, nationality, and nationhood are of course ancient and have often shifted their meanings. Students at medieval universities, for example, quarreled with each other, sometimes to the death, because they belonged to different "nations," but nation in this context does not in the least imply our nation-state. One great element of the romantic movement was the conviction that particular races, or nations, or traditions, or states had each its unique quality which, even when it had been obscured by time and conquest, could, if necessary, be resuscitated and form the basis not merely of the nation's collective identity, but also of a revived and modern national art and national thought. This sort of thing was powerful even before the French Revolution, as is evident in the vogue of the "Gothick" north, the Celtic revival, the interest of the generation of Lessing in throwing off neoclassicism and reviving a true Germanic culture. The French Revolution began by trying to restore the ancient customs of the French kingdom, but soon developed into an ambiguous force that theoretically ignored political boundaries drawn by "tyrants" and simultaneously created, by sympathy or opposition, an emotional support for that fusion of race, rights, traditions, and history which is the basis of the modern nation-state. Even the American Revolution faced both ways. It appealed to the traditional rights of Englishmen expressed in powerful seventeenth- and eighteenth-century theorists, and also to the general traits of human nature.[31]

But though the young republic could not avoid such complexities, it is on the whole true that the United States prided itself on being a nation built on the general philosophical principles about men and government expressed in the Declaration of Independence and the Constitution of the United States, and that, by virtue of being "radical," the new nation was thought to be a danger in a world of monarchies. This attitude the country paid back in kind, as in Washington's Farewell Address with its warning against entangling alliances and in the Monroe Doctrine, which declared not only that the United States wanted to be let alone but also that it proposed to protect other New World republics against molestation. Among citizens emotional attachment to the new republic was by no means lacking; Yankee brag, much complained of by European travelers and sometimes satirized by American writers, is one evidence of this attachment, and the truth that such patriotic songs as "Columbia, the Gem of the Ocean," "The Star-Spangled Banner," and "America" are all products of the ante-bellum years is another. Obviously the shrill crusades for an American literature, an American art, and an "American system" are as often emotional as they are philosophic and sometimes have behind them economic or social forces. Yet it seems to be true in general that the unique quality of American existence before 1861 was felt to lie in its political system, whatever poets might sing about Columbia and whatever satirists might say about a character like Birdofredum Sawin in Lowell's *The Biglow Papers*. Of course the political system did not exist in a social vacuum. The novels of Cooper are often examples of the attempt of a gentlemanly conservative to equate the political pattern of the American government as he understood it with the social pattern of American life as he thought it ought to be. But the central public questions of the first half of the nineteenth century, including slavery, whatever modern economic history has to say about them, turned on questions of political theory.

What was a republic? What was sovereignty? Could it be divided? What was the proper relation between the general government and that of the several states? What was the function of the federal judiciary? How were the powers of the presidency to be defined and, if necessary, circumscribed? If, as Gladstone said, the American Constitution was the most remarkable political document produced by the human intellect in modern times, the intellectual history of the country from 1789 to 1861 includes one of the most remarkable political debates in modern history. One has only to think of the decisions of John Marshall of the United States Supreme Court, or of the great Webster-Hayne debate, or the controversy over nullification aroused by the tariff of 1828 and its sequel, or the struggle over the legality of internal improvements, a national bank, and the power of the central government to lay down terms for the creation and admission of new states, or of the great climax in 1850 when Webster, Calhoun, and Clay reached heights and depths of tragedy in an effort simultaneously to impose particular theories upon the nation and avoid that conflict between North and South which, eight years later, William H. Seward was to call irrepressible. Foreign observers like Tocqueville and Grund might talk about democracy or aristocracy in the American republic and analyze the demography, the economics, and the sociology of life in the United States; but to most Americans the national issues were political and moral. The Constitution was a great legal charter; it was not yet sacrosanct.

But the war came, the Union was preserved, and thereafter language regarding nationhood becomes increasingly mystical. Doubtless the peroration of Webster's "Reply to Hayne" has its rhetorical grandeur, but Webster's appeal was something a Macaulay could understand because it was a practical warning against anarchy. It did not lie under the penumbra of Edmund Burke's theory that government was virtually a religious institution. The war not only re-established the union, it transformed it into a Burkeian entity. The process is evident in Lincoln's speeches. In 1854 at Bloomington, Illinois, he could refer to "our federal compact"; in 1858 he could write that the "Republicans have never contended that congress should *dictate* a constitution to any state or territory; but they have contended that the people should be *perfectly* free to form their constitutions in their own way," all as if the Constitution were only a superior sort of charter or contract. But by the time of the First Inaugural Address we have this vision of the country:

> The mystic chords of memory, stretching from every battle-field and patriot grave to every living heart and hearthstone all over this broad land, will yet swell the chorus of the Union when again touched, as surely they will be, by the better angels of our nature.[32]

The religious note is sounded again in the Gettysburg Address—"this nation, under God, shall have a new birth of freedom"—and in the Second Inaugural one hears not only that the judgments of the Lord are true and righteous altogether, but also the spiritual injunction:

> With malice toward none, with charity for all; with firmness in the right, as God gives us to see the right, let us strive on to finish the work we are in; to bind up the nation's wounds; to care for him who shall have borne the battle, and for his widow, and his orphan—to do all which may achieve and cherish a just and lasting peace among ourselves, and with all other nations.

These passages can of course be dismissed as the elevated discourse common in wartime. Moreover, the Declaration of Independence has its emotional appeal, as do the essays of Thomas Paine. But one cannot quite imagine President Thomas Jefferson referring to mystic chords of memory or employing in public discourse the biblical phraseology of Lincoln's speeches, terms that translate the idea of a federal republic out of the category of something set up by a political charter into the category of something so sacred that secession became treason and the military records of the Civil War were published under the title *The War of the Rebellion*.

It is difficult to differentiate among emotions, images, and times. It is quite possible that Timothy Dwight's poem of 1777,

> Columbia, Columbia, to glory arise,
> The queen of the world, and the child of the skies! [33]

—a poem by a minister—aroused as much emotional allegiance in its day as Katharine Lee Bates's "America the Beautiful" aroused in 1898 and after. Even before the Civil War Walt Whitman was merging into a single whole the United States, the New World, the religion of humanity, and an expansive ego. Despite Roger Asselineau's well-argued theory that during the Gilded Age Whitman lost an absolute faith in his country and in *Passage to India* (1871) substituted for patriotism faith in cosmic design,[34] I feel that the *Drum-Taps* of 1865, "When Lilacs Last in the Dooryard Bloom'd," and *The Wound-Dresser*, posthumously published the year of the Spanish-American War, contain and enrich a greater mystique about the American republic than is found, to use this critic's term, in Whitman's earlier pan-Americanism, which was not a little tainted with chauvinism. If *Passage to India* was occasioned by news of the opening of the Suez Canal, it was also a celebration of completing a railroad to the Pacific coast. An important poem published the next year begins:

> Thou Mother with thy equal brood,
> Thou varied chain of different States, yet one identity only,
> A special song before I go I'd sing o'er all the rest,
> For thee, the future.
>
> I'd sow a seed for thee of endless Nationality,
> I'd fashion thy ensemble including body and soul,
> I'd show away ahead thy real Union, and how it may be accomplish'd.

The poem continues a little later:

> As a strong bird on pinions free,
> Joyous, the amplest spaces heavenward cleaving,
> Such be the thought I'd bring of thee America,
> Such be the recitative I'd bring for thee.
>
> .   .   .   .
>
> And for thy subtler sense subtler refrains dread Mother,
> Preludes of intellect tallying these and thee, mind-formulas fitted for
>   thee, real and sane and large as these and thee,
> Thou! mounting higher, diving deeper than we knew, thou tran-
>   scendental Union!
> By thee fact to be justified, blended with thought,
> Thought of man justified, blended with God,
> Through thy idea, lo, the immortal reality!
> Through thy reality, lo, the immortal idea!

In this poem Longfellow's "Ship of State," which, in "The Building of the Ship," was instructed to sail on, becomes the "ship of Democracy," and we are told:

> With thee Time voyages in trust, the antecedent nations sink or
>   swim with thee,

The United States is turned into a

> Land tolerating all, accepting all, not for the good alone, all good
>   for thee,
> Land in the realms of God to be a realm unto thyself,
> Under the rule of God to be a rule unto thyself.
> (Lo, where arise three peerless stars,
> To be thy natal stars my country, Ensemble, Evolution, Freedom,
> Set in the sky of Law.)

I do not see how any other form of words could more succinctly turn patriotism into virtually a religious belief in the nature and destiny of the United States. If it be argued that Whitman was mainly read by the highbrows and the radicals, one finds other poets giving similar emotional interpretations of the nation as possessing a sacrosanct character and a divinely appointed mission: for example, in Arlo Bates's "America," where the country is "the last hope of man and truth"; in Woodberry's "My Country," where it is a "destined land with Throned Freedom," set apart on the North American continent, who "bids her future for the past atone"; in Frank L. Stanton's "One Country" with its injunction: "We must be / The makers of her immortality"; in Richard Hovey's "Unmanifest Destiny," which says the poet cannot prophesy under what skies or on what seas the ships of state will voyage, but that "I only know it shall be high, / I only know it shall be great." [35] Perhaps the culmination of this new mystique is in two odes by William Vaughn Moody, "An Ode in Time of Hesitation" and "On a Soldier Fallen in the Philippines," grave descants both on the moral duty of America to renounce imperialism and serve humanity:

> Was it for this our fathers kept the law?
> This crown shall crown their struggle and their ruth?
> Are we the eagle nation Milton saw
> Mewing its mighty youth,
> Soon to possess the mountain winds of truth,
> And be a swift familiar of the sun
> Where aye before God's face his trumpets run?

Here a fusion of language from the great Christian epic poet and from the Bible combines to delineate an America divinely appointed for a special end.[36]

Again, it can be argued that these expressions do not radically differ from the language of the New England theocracy, that of a providential view of American history, or the concept of manifest destiny clearly expressed in the "Young America" movement of ante-bellum days. But there is, I suggest, a difference in tone. It is as if the principle of vitalism, more and more obsolescent in the sciences, had been transferred to still another emotional center. The concepts of the inevitable superiority of the Anglo-Saxon race and the triumph of Protestant Christianity on earth are also involved in this mystique. In transforming the theory of the United States as that of a rational political society under a charter into the notion of the United States as a divinely appointed nation, the country was taking its place alongside of Holy Russia, the Hegelian or pseudo-Hegelian picture of the future of Prussia (and Germany) as the triumph of Reason, an emerging doctrine in Latin-American states about a "cosmic race," and other glorifications of nationhood in other states and races elsewhere on the globe. The United States was expressing the nationalism of the nineteenth century, but what is significant is that the utopias of Henry George, Bellamy, Gronlund, and William Dean Howells do not recognize the existence of the separate states and say nothing about states' rights.

The process by which the Constitution ceased to be a mere charter
and turned into a sacred scripture was noticed by Hermann Eduard
von Holst, whose *Constitutional and Political History of the United
States* appeared at intervals from 1873 to 1892. In the second chapter
of the first volume one reads:

> At first it [the Constitution] was looked upon as the best possible consti-
> tution for the United States. By degrees it came to be universally consid-
> ered as a masterpiece, applicable to every country. This was preached
> with so much unanimity and honest conviction, although internal quar-
> rels were raging all the time, that the propagandism of the new faith
> reached even to Europe. In the United States this conviction grows stead-
> ily stronger. . . . From the close of the century, that is, from the time
> when the opposing principles assumed a fixed form, the constitution has
> been the political Bible of the people. The child sucked in with his
> mother's milk the conviction that this was the light in which he should
> regard it. The paternal *sic credo, stat fides pro ratione*, was a guaranty
> for the rightfulness of this conviction.[37]

Possibly the central event in this transformation of a charter into a
scripture was a huge celebration held at Philadelphia, September 15,
16, and 17, 1887 (not to be confused with the Centennial Exposition
of 1876), on the one-hundredth anniversary of the framing of the
Constitution. There were enormous parades both civic and military.
On one day, for example, the industries and labor parade began at
ten in the morning and lasted until half-past six in the evening. One
spectator wrote concerning it: "A hundred years of history had just
passed in review before our eyes." Of course there were speeches and
banquets, President Grover Cleveland delivering the principal address. His speech (and the celebration) culminated in this paragraph:

> When we look down upon one hundred years and see the origin of our
> Constitution, when we contemplate all its trials and triumphs, when we
> realize how completely the principles upon which it is based have met
> every national need and every national peril, how devoutly should we
> say with Franklin, "God governs in the affairs of men," and how solemn
> should be the thought that to us is delivered this ark of the people's cov-
> enant, and to us is given the duty to shield it from impious hands. It
> comes to us sealed with the test of a century. It has been found sufficient
> in the past, and will be found sufficient in all the years to come, if the
> American people are true to their sacred trust. Another centennial day
> will come, and millions yet unborn will inquire concerning our steward-

ship and the safety of their Constitution. God grant they may find it un-
impaired; and as we rejoice to-day in the patriotism and devotion of
those who lived one hundred years ago, so may those who follow us rejoice in our fidelity and love for constitutional liberty.[38]

Cleveland's peroration, it is true, re-echoes the conclusion of Joseph
Story's influential *A Familiar Exposition of the Constitution of the
United States* (New York, 1840), which commended that document to
American youth as something "reared for immortality" unless public
negligence subvert it. What is new in 1887 lies in Cleveland's tincture of a religious vocabulary: "solemn thought," "ark of the covenant," "stewardship," "impious hands," "sacred trust." Indeed, the
stream of a religious interpretation of the Constitution mounted
higher than the Philadelphia celebration. In 1883–1884 Oscar S.
Straus delivered two lectures before the Long Island Historical Society of Brooklyn, in which he derived the republic from ancient Ju-
daism and equated the Founding Fathers (who were mostly deists)
with the prophets of ancient Israel:

> No one but He who rules the destiny of nations in all ages could have
> ordained that the bright sun of Canaan should rise again in after ages
> with refulgent splendor over the vast continent of America, and that the
> pure and unselfish spirit of Moses, Joshua, and Samuel should live again
> in a Franklin, a Washington, and an Adams. May we, the people of
> America, who have learned so much by the example of this ancient com-
> monwealth in its rise to glory and freedom, also profit by the lessons of
> its decline.[39]

A whole library of books concerning the Constitution and constitutional law appeared in the 1880s, some of them merely analytic, some
of them expressive of this new emotional nationalism. Against this
new theory John Randolph Tucker's *The Constitution of the United
States* (1899) is a neo-Confederate protest. Yet even Tucker, professor
of constitutional and international law and equity at Washington
and Lee University, spoke the language of godliness: the "Body-poli-
tic is the means Divinely ordained to secure the inalienable rights of
men," and liberty is the prize "which God holds out as reward of
moral elevation." A set of lectures on constitutional law delivered in
1888 or 1889 at the University of Michigan is interesting. One lecturer cited Francis Marion Crawford's "New National Hymn":

Thy sun has risen and shall not set
Upon thy day divine;
Ages of ages unborn yet,
America are thine!

A student of what was taught about the Constitution in schools and colleges during the period finds that the teaching of "civics" was relatively weak until about 1880 and that not until the 1880s did political science gain its place in the academic curriculum. As early as 1863, however, the National Teachers Association, a forerunner of the National Education Association, unanimously voted that history, "polity," and the Constitution should be taught in all schools where the children were mature enough to understand it. The instruction was presumably more formal than pragmatic, but one can be sure it was reverential. "We must plant and perpetuate in the hearts of our youth reverential love for the Constitution," declared a speaker before the American Institute of Education in 1881. In 1891 in his *Easy Lessons on the Constitution* Alfred Bayliss wrote of that document as "the cornerstone and rock of defense of the greatest nation God's sun ever shone upon"; and in 1899 John Bascom, once president of the University of Wisconsin, felt that the only organization to compare in comprehensiveness with the nation was the church.[40] A movement away from civics toward "social studies" occurred during the twentieth century, as the impact of the teachings of Lester F. Ward, Albion W. Small, and Edward A. Ross, and the educational doctrine of John Dewey began to reach the public schools. Throughout most of our fifty years, however, the Constitution was untouched by cynicism. Indeed, looking back on the age from 1957, the late Robert G. McCloskey, introducing a volume of *Essays in Constitutional Law* usually pragmatic and sometimes cynical in tone, could nevertheless say with truth that

the 19th. century did achieve a comparatively well-accepted consensus about the Constitution and the Supreme Court. Disaffection with the standard myths was not unknown, and skeptics could be found even in the contemporary legal fraternity. But . . . there was . . . a kind of synthesis in American constitutionalism.[41]

The Constitution as a secular Bible was still operative.

If the Constitution came to be regarded as sacrosanct and only to be amended after long debate, and neither rewritten nor overthrown,

the Supreme Court in these same years turned into a Sanhedrin possessing miraculous powers of interpretation. Addressing students at
the University of Michigan Law School in 1889, Mr. Justice Miller
(Samuel Freeman Miller) acknowledged the special quality of the
court: "It has no army, it has no navy, and it has no purse. It has no
patronage, it has no officers, except its clerks and marshals, and the
latter are appointed by the President and confirmed by the Senate."
Yet, as Professor Henry Wade Rogers remarked, "Feeble as it may
thus appear to be, yet in reality the Supreme Court of the United
States is more powerful in its influence on the character of the government than is the President or the Congress." [42] This fact is apparent when one realizes that attorneys representing some of the former
Confederate states appeared before the Court "not to defend their
clients on trial, but to arraign and deny the authority of the law-
making power, and to plead anew the issues of the cause already decided by the sword. After accepting the terms of surrender, they propose in the Supreme Court to test the very right admitted by their
surrender," says a contemporary account. It is difficult to think of
any other nation in which this kind of action would have been possible.

Despite bitter attacks during the Reconstruction Era, notably after
the decision in the famous Milligan case of 1866 (which denied the
president the right to institute trial by military tribunes in localities
where civil courts were open); despite the continuing disaffection of
economic and political radicalism during these decades,[43] and despite
the fact that every appointment was a political act, it is probable that
the Supreme Court was regarded as the sacred guardian of the ark of
the covenant in these five decades more seriously than in any other
half-century. The epigraph of the official history of the centennial of
its founding runs:

> What, sir, is the Supreme Court of the United States? It is the august
> representative of the wisdom and conscience and justice of the whole
> people, in the exposition of their Constitution and their laws. It is the
> peaceful and venerable arbitrator between the citizens in all questions
> touching the extent and sway of Constitutional power. It is the great
> moral substitute for force in controversies between the People, the States,
> and the Union.[44]

As every church must have its central edifice, so mystic nationalism,
before the erection of the Lincoln Memorial in Washington, re-

garded the chamber of the United States Supreme Court. In the galleries of the House of Representatives or of the Senate you came to observe and perhaps be amused, but you entered the Supreme Court room as if you were entering a shrine.

The official celebration of the centennial of the court was held at the Metropolitan Opera House in New York February 4, 1890. There was the inevitable parade. There were the inevitable decorations. There were also speeches, the New York Bar Association acting as host, since the first sitting of the court had been held in that city. The official history of the court published for the occasion concludes with a eulogy on modern nationalism and a neat reference to religious symbolism from the classical past:

> The steady expansion of principles, and the vigorous as well as irrepressible growth of the doctrine of Nationality are conspicuous phenomena [in the history of the court]. Constitutional principles have been vitalized; Acts of Congress have been made to breathe; situations, conditions and circumstances, unprovided for by either, have been nurtured into living forces, presenting, when drawn up in array, a noble and imposing body of jurisprudential facts which, when studied and understood, will prove the best title to renown of the distinguished jurists to whose care and protection they were committed, the ceaseless source of the gratitude and veneration of posterity, and the best and most enduring bulwark of National greatness. As the safety of Troy depended upon the preservation of the heaven-descended statue of Pallas, holding a spear in her right hand, and in her left a distaff and spindle, so the Supreme Court of the United States enthroned in majesty and invested with power, wielding the imperial sceptre of National Sovereignty, while jealously guarding the rights of the States, will prove, as long as our institutions endure, the Palladium of the Republic.[45]

Even Charles Warren, by no means uncritical as a legal historian, in concluding his great history of the court, said it had fully and worthily fulfilled the purposes for which it was designed and quoted Tocqueville, who placed the court at the head of all known tribunals.[46] It is, I think, significant that the mode of electing senators has been altered and the possible terms of a president limited to two, but the only change in this mysterious body has been an enlargement of its members to take care of the increase of business brought before them. The solemnity of the court, in a sense its secrecy, its time-honored rules, and the epochal results of some of its decisions persuade

Americans even today that here is the true and secret heart of the American nation.

If the Constitution became the inerrable scripture of the new nationalism, and the Supreme Court turned into a secular priesthood in a secular temple, the translation of the American flag into a religious symbol was also symptomatic of the new attitude toward nationhood. Up to about 1824 nobody quite knew what the shape or pattern of the national banner might be. The origin of this symbol, like the origins of other powerful symbols, is shrouded in mystery and obscured by conflicting stories. Even as late as the Civil War there were acceptable variations in the pattern of the national flag. By 1892, however, a pledge to the flag as a sacred symbol of the republic was printed in *The Youth's Companion,* and with one mild variation this was adopted by the National Flag Conference in 1923 and soon became obligatory in the public schools. Eventually the Supreme Court had to rule on the constitutionality of requiring the salute, or the pledge, or both, from children whose families did not regard a piece of bunting as a religious symbol. In 1905 national legislation forbade the use of the flag, the great seal of the United States, or any similar emblem as part of any commercial trademark. By 1917 desecration of the flag became a criminal offense; the next year Congress voted that any official or employee of the United States government found guilty of disrespect to the flag should be dismissed from the service. Meantime an elaborate ritual governing the display of the flag on buildings, over streets, as drapery, or on platforms was worked out, as was the proper posture for civilians when the flag went by in a parade. This ritual was formally confirmed in 1942. In 1931 "The Star-Spangled Banner" officially became the national anthem—note the religious noun—and in 1914 the President of the United States urged, though he did not order, that the flag be displayed on that peculiarly American (if commercial) invention, Mother's Day. I suppose the final triumph of secular religiosity came about when the national emblem was carried in some churches in procession alongside the cross and the two emblems were displayed during services, one on each side of the altar.[47]

V

A new or renewed sense of nationhood was not of course confined only to, or caused merely by, the three components I have sketched—

the concept of the Constitution as a sacred writing, one of the Supreme Court as a secular priesthood, and the interpretation of the national flag as a religious emblem. I shall later show with what distrust the several sections of the republic continued to look at each other after the Civil War. Of course the massive and rapid growth of industry, transportation, and communication, swelling like genii released from magic bottles, made any return to mere state control or to a constitutional doctrine, like that of Calhoun, so impossible that the states, still retaining the power to regulate intrastate business and banking, railroads and telephones (but not always all of these), followed the lines laid down by national legislation or the regulations of such bodies as the Interstate Commerce Commission. Although the Constitution does not mention education, that activity became increasingly uniform and nationalized when the states found it easier to imitate each other, sloughed off the Scottish or English origins of their universities, and accepted European concepts of state-directed education for all and the characteristics of German universities, those wonders of the world, as institutions supported by the state. Originally the states had regulated immigration; now this problem became a federal responsibility. Formerly there had been state banks and state bank-notes, but beginning with the National Banking Act of 1863 and continuing through the creation of the Federal Reserve System in 1913, the control of currency and credit more and more became a national responsibility. Other examples in agriculture, public health, conservation, the regulation of hours of labor, the control of foods and drugs, and so on will occur to the historian. The point is not to deny this development, nor to seem to confute the sound theory that the new nationalism was economically and politically inevitable, whether one has in mind the shaping of tariff laws in favor of infant industries or an appeal from the populace for the national government to act because the individual states will not or can not. There is a distinction between an interpretation that verges on economic determinism and an interpretation that inquires why a nation tragically sundered by the Civil War, less than forty years later should emotionally unite on a moral crusade to liberate Cuba and destroy the tyranny of Spain. Frank Freidel puts the case succinctly:

> It was not the business community that was howling for war. Nor was it instigated solely by the sensationalism of the jingo press. . . . Perhaps it can be attributed in part to the American restlessness in the 1890s, and

in part to a desire to see the United States function like a great nation, complete with powerful navy and strong overseas bases. More than these factors, it was a crusading morality. Above all, the reform element in the population—those who had been Populists and those who became Progressives—clamored for the United States to rescue the Cuban people from the Spanish malefactors.[48]

It is significant that the first land battle of the war found the American army under the command of "Fighting Joe" Wheeler, who had been in charge of the Confederate cavalry in the West during most of the Civil War, and that though the Rough Riders were principally recruited from the Southwest, Roosevelt was besieged by potential recruits from every state in the union, particularly from the South.[49]

I have discussed what seem to me three basic components in the search for unity in American culture between 1865 and 1915. Other formulas can be cited. The social historian, for example, once he has dealt with the wars between capital and labor and the problems of urbanism against village folkways and the countryside, might point with justice to the doctrine that a leading—indeed, a decisive—characteristic of American life was the growing acceptance at all social levels of the norms of middle-class life. It is true that in the upper group (Veblen's conspicuous expenditure is here relevant) millionaires and their kind frolicked in ways that shocked the bourgeoisie and that were frequently both childlike and appalling. But the old aristocracies in Boston, New York, Philadelphia, Charleston, St. Louis, Natchez, New Orleans, and other centers steadily declined into islands of genteel obsolescence in these years; and at the other end of the social spectrum labor, on the whole not greatly moved by social revolutionaries, wanted middle-class homes, middle-class comforts, and middle-class status. The middle-class norm came to be accepted in the public schools, the churches, social usage, and value judgments. It is remarkable in this context that all the presidents from Grant to Theodore Roosevelt were middle-class in upbringing and standards and that Roosevelt, born into a prestigious New York family, emphasized the obvious bourgeois virtues of health, frugality, manliness, patriotism, and Protestant morality. Many artists complained that the middle-class family dominated their markets. Undoubtedly the increase of department stores, of mail-order houses, of courses in domestic science in school and college, and of groups such as Chautauqua and clubs like the Sorosis group tended to standardize taste. So in the book trade the concept of the best seller as a publishing norm, a term that came into use early in the present century, radically altered judgments of acceptance and rejection in publishing houses, just as it altered book advertising and book distribution. Magazines were, in the main, family journals, a fact that created hostility among the avant-garde and derision among some sorts of literary historians. Any examination of the manuals of conduct (or for that matter of letter writing) in these decades reveals that the patterns set in these handbooks were eminently middle-class. Indeed, the "momism" thought by some social critics to be a peculiar American trait flourished in these days. Mother's Day began its conquest of the country in 1907.

Or one can argue that the drive for unity was eminently a striving for equality and social justice, and so it was. The Civil War ended slavery, and the rise of the Negro population from dependence and illiteracy, a struggle upward too often thwarted by hatred, prejudice, violence, and greed, is one of the wonders of the time; and if living proponents of black self-consciousness are at this writing too embattled to judge objectively the work of Booker T. Washington, or of the founders of Atlanta University, or the spread of literacy and schooling among ex-slaves and their children, or the increasing revulsion even in the deep South against lynching, we shall simply have to wait for a fairer estimate. Programs in Americanization are also relevant, as is the work of settlement houses, adult education courses, newspaper and magazine, both secular and sectarian, in educating immigrants and their children, as well as the poor, the ignorant, and the unlucky, into some comprehension of their rights and duties as electors and citizens. The extension of the franchise to women in certain elections, notably in the Western states, and the agitation for women's suffrage culminating in the adoption (1920) of the Nineteenth Amendment are further evidence of this drive toward equality. So in some measure was the adoption of the Seventeenth Amendment in 1913, which, it was thought, would end the United States Senate as a house of privilege and return it to the plain people.

Oddly enough, two opposed drives were each intended to insure equality among the Americans. On the one hand, the anti-Oriental agitation, the anti-Catholic ferment, anti-Semitism, and other unlovely manifestations of xenophobia were in theory intended to prevent some alien or privileged group from becoming financial or political or religious overlords of the American people. On the other hand, liberal condemnation of this sort of thing assumed that all men are brothers and that to be an American was to assert and accept fraternity for all mankind. Ungenerous critics say that this crusade for an American egalitarianism prevents or retards the recognition of excellence. Other interpreters, heirs whether they know it or not of the Jeffersonian doctrine of an aristocracy of talent, prefer to believe that democracy, a term that came more and more into use, opens every field to ability, and stoutly argue that cultural pluralism in the United States insures a fair field and no favor. A favorite slogan among the progressives after the turn of the century was that the cure for the evils of democracy was more democracy. Cities might thicken and decay, natural resources be wasted, farms be abandoned in the Northeast or the upper South, the incidence of disease, crime, insanity, and malnutrition increase,[50] but the current of American life, so runs the argument, had set in the direction of equality, opportunity, and progress for the country and for mankind.

All this is true enough, and the reader may prefer these explanations or some other to the three I have analyzed in this chapter. My own feeling is that the general acceptance of middle-class values and the general, if uneven, drift to egalitarianism are symptoms rather than causes—the outward and visible forms of that inward and spiritual grace (if it be one) I have called a mystique of nationhood developing after the Civil War. In the following chapters I shall discuss what seem to me some of the interesting aspects of American culture in these tumultuary years. There will be times when the reader may think I have forgotten my own doctrine of a thirst for unitary explanation. Yet I shall try, even in chapters devoted more to dissidence and confusion than to union and harmony, to show that the social glitter, the sectional animosities, the struggles over race and ideal, cosmopolitanism and nature do not in the long run deflect the slow, deep current of desire for some unity of belief, some basic perdurable value underlying the clash and restlessness, the gaudiness and varied accomplishments, of the Americans in these fifty years.

II

———— ◆ ————

But Yet a Union

—But yet a union in partition.
—*A Midsummer Night's Dream*

I

AT THE CONCLUSION of any great war the belligerents commonly look for a miraculous dawn of unity and peace. The Civil War was no exception.[1] After the cessation of hostilities such phrases as "let us have peace," "bind up the nation's wounds," Lowell's "O Beautiful! My country! Ours once more," and Robert E. Lee's "united in the restoration of the country and the reëstablishment of peace and harmony" expressed this feeling. Great forces seemed to move or were about to move in the desired direction, and to some of these I shall come. Here it is sufficient to say that energies created in the war or growing out of it, whether these took shape as the exploitation of natural resources, mechanical inventions, powerful personalities, corporations operating on a national or international scale, the multiplication of national associations of scientists, economists, scholars, technologists, and businessmen, or the steady expansion of the central government emphasized the general trend. The postal system was a force for union, and so were the railroads, the telegraph networks, the telephone companies, and the distribution of electric power as these developed or came into being.[2] The necessity the federal government was under to feed and reorganize the South, a necessity partly humanitarian, partly political, and partly exploitative, preluded the growing dominance of federal activities in all the states. Magazines sought a continental circulation. Book publishers created regional depositories, national advertising, and ever-widening sales systems, developments that moved the country more and more in the direction of a common ideology. The proliferation of cities in the half-century is astonishing, as is the growth of individual urban communities, to use a contemporary term; and though places like New Orleans, Butte, Charleston, and San Francisco retained strong local characteristics, urban culture is almost by definition national and cosmopolitan, not regional and parochial. The interlocking of stockbrokers, bankers, directors, and trustees is a phase of this nationalism, so that, partly under their guidance, what the elder Arthur M. Schlesinger labeled "urban imperialism" eroded the folkways of the countryside and replaced neighborliness with impersonal social responsibility.[3] A curious mark of change was the tendency of humor to polarize around two opposite typologies—that of the hayseed and that of the city slicker, an old contrast set in a new context. Another interesting result of urban nationalism was the tendency of regional theorists and local colorists to fall back upon the mountain people of Appalachia, or Western cowboys, or Maine fishermen, or Southern Negroes as untainted representatives of true local color. Viewed positively, these trends and others like them increased unity in the nation, a unity that reached an emotional climax in the fervor of support both North and South for the Cuban war; viewed negatively, it reaffirmed what many observers had called the flatness and monotony of American life.

But though the forces of change were powerful, the era never really attained either political or cultural unity. The United States remained essentially what it had been—a tumultuous republic, a nation under perpetual stress and strain. Despite the vast central area of prairies and plains, its terrain was, and is, extraordinarily diverse;[4] a continental country that varies from alluvial deltas to the peaks of the Rockies and from sea-level swamps to the elevated deserts of Utah and New Mexico. Florida, or much of it, is subtropical; North Dakota shares the winters of central Canada. The lower Mississippi is one sort of river, the Colorado another, the Humboldt still a third. Lives in Alabama, in upper New York State, in Montana, and on the Eastern Shore of Maryland differed as greatly as life in the Mediterranean basin differed from life in Finland. The Old South had one feeling for history, Utah a second, Plymouth a third, and Santa Fe a fourth. If today the supermarket and the throughway, the motel and the filling station emphasize monotony, American feeling for time and distance is still tribal, local, and subjective: in the matter of patience compare a New York journalist, a wool-hat from Georgia, a New England lobsterman, a Negro in Savannah, and a Colorado forest ranger. This rich heterogeneity has latterly been increased by the admission of the forty-ninth and fiftieth states, since Alaska and Hawaii could scarcely differ more in location, climate, population, history, and economic outlook. But do they differ more in 1970 than Delaware differed from Minnesota in 1870?

Although the half-century moved toward nationalism and uniformity, that movement was continually slowed or checked by tensions among various regions and bickering segments of the American people. The obvious instance is the continuing hostility of the South toward the North and the lingering suspicion of the North about the South, scotched but not killed by Appomattox and revived after Andrew Johnson's proclamation of May 29, 1865, which extended amnesty to North Carolina. Throughout our history the East, however defined, has been simultaneously superior to and suspicious of the West, however changing. The Thirteenth Amendment ended slavery; yet in the face of the amazing progress of the Negro race toward literacy and economic stability in these fifty years, the South kept Negroes subdued and the North had little use for them. The Indian and the white man were in continuing, if intermittent, conflict. Old Americans at once feared and desired the New Immigration; and if Americanization proceeded more smoothly than anybody had a right to expect,[5] Scandinavians were viewed with alarm in the Middle West; distrust of Italians provoked the Mafia riots in New Orleans (1891); and the political success of Catholic Americans, notably the Irish, helped create that unlamented organization, the American Protective Association. If Jews were not persecuted, they were often shunned. Nor should one forget the antagonism aroused by the Chinese and the Japanese.

Moreover, tensions between Christians and Jews, Protestants and Catholics, fundamentalists and "advanced" thinkers not only continued but were sometimes augmented by sectional and regional differences and conflicts between an urban culture and an agrarian or small-town culture. Industrial warfare was necessarily regional because of the concentration of heavy industry and its financial control in certain areas, and its absence (or the presence of a debtor class) in others. This economic tension was coupled with the existence (or lack) of an organizable labor force. Cotton mills moved South, attracted by "cheap labor," but steel manufacturers, railroads, and mining companies could not move and had to face combat situations in particular areas and cities. Political life was also determined by sectional or regional interests more often than most persons realize: the Republicans tried to keep in power by waving the bloody shirt, a banner that drove the South back upon a one-party stance; most of the Granger movement can be plotted on a map of the Middle West and the prairie states; and Populism was a complex product of impoverished Southern agriculture, an embittered farm belt, small businessmen in the West and South, angry housewives, and puzzled small-town intellectuals. It may therefore be useful to analyze, however superficially, some leading components of regionalisms characteristic of the American story after the Civil War.

II

From the Confederate point of view anybody who fought against the South, whether he came from Maine or California, was a Yankee. This is a comprehensible bit of wartime emotion, but what was meant by the North from 1865 to 1915? Upon the most cursory examination the North appears to have consisted of something called the East and something called the Middle West (the Old Northwest), albeit citizens of Ohio, Indiana, or Illinois, for example, were known as "Western men" even after 1876. The East, as soon as one looks at the map, splits in two. One of the parts is definite, the other indefinite. The definite part is New England, to which I shall come; the indefinite part is what is left when one has taken New England out of the "East." What does one have left? The East seems to include New York, Pennsylvania, New Jersey, and, rather doubtfully, Delaware and Maryland, both commonly labeled border states. New Jersey offers no problem. But does "the East" include all of New York and Pennsylvania? The West used to begin at Harrisburg and the State of Pennsylvania has in Erie an important port on the Great Lakes. Describing Buffalo, New York, a Baedeker of 1900 calls it "an important emporium for much of the traffic of the great North-West" and notes that nine thousand vessels with an aggregate burden of more than fourteen million tons annually entered or left the harbor. Buffalo was long an autonomous cultural center, nor is it insignificant today. It was the home of two presidents, Millard Fillmore and Grover Cleveland, and the city where another president, William McKinley, was assassinated while he was addressing a large audience at the Pan-American Exposition of 1901, which drew more than eight million visitors. When Mark Twain's father-in-law, upon the humorist's marriage, presented the bride and groom with a house in Buffalo, the gift implied social status. Mabel Dodge Luhan's *Intimate Memories: Background* (1933) gives a charming account of upper-middle-class culture along Delaware Avenue. The place of Buffalo in the Catholic world has been important, and its museums, historical society, libraries, and institutions of higher learning were noteworthy. Does all this make Buffalo a western outpost of the East or an eastern outpost of the West?

The municipal personalities of Boston, New York, Philadelphia, and Baltimore, Atlantic seaports all, are distinct, if not as distinctive as those of San Francisco and New Orleans. But what makes them Eastern? There were those who would read New York City out of the nation on the ground that it did not really represent America.[6] Yet, with the possible exception of Baltimore, these cities are all in the North. One is sometimes tempted to think that aside from sea-borne commerce and big finance, the common characteristics of these metropolises were large immigrant populations, municipal corruption, and slums, but even in these bad qualities New York seemed to stand apart, perhaps because of the literary skill of such a writer as Jacob Riis.[7] Cities like Chicago and St. Louis had these elements too. One can of course fall back upon topography and define the East as the Atlantic coastal shelf north of the Potomac and extending westward to the Appalachians, and probably this is right, but it is not altogether accurate with respect to New England, the Champlain Valley, the Catskills, and the Adirondacks. Geography is only a partial aid.

I therefore abandon the topographical puzzle to try a different approach. Perhaps the East was not so much an area as a set of beliefs or fictions about an area, or what modern critical jargon calls a myth. The East was what people thought it was, and the people who thought about it were Southerners, Westerners, and Easterners. To the South the North (and I shall have to use the East and the North as virtually interchangeable terms in this analysis) was the haughty victor, strangely cruel and stupid in the sequel. The North was New England abolitionists coming south to exult, and New England schoolteachers coming there to reform. It was the officers and soldiers of an army of occupation enforcing an unacceptable government or rather a series of unacceptable governments. The North was the home of cotton thieves and carpetbaggers, mudsills (or at any rate ignorant men) and immigrants, shifty financiers and crafty politicians, Radical Republicans like Thad Stevens of Pennsylvania and unconscionable rogues like "Beast" Butler of Massachusetts. The North held the gallant South of the Lost Cause in military subjugation, political bondage, and financial leading strings. Who but wealthy Northerners (Easterners) had enough risk capital to re-establish Southern plantations, Southern mills, Southern factories, Southern railroads, and Southern banks? If the tired Confederate soldiers reconciled themselves to things as they were, not so, by all accounts, the outraged Southern gentlewomen, who continued to nurse their wrath, insisting among other things that Southern schools should teach Confederate victories and not the triumphs of Sherman and Grant. The North, in this view, was something you had to put up with or dodge around.

But the situation was complex. The North was also that part of the country, mortgages aside, with money rather freely put to work to get the South back on its feet, the home of skills to restore Southern agriculture, and the source of generous, if occasionally mistaken, charities—educational, religious, and medical. It was also, astonishingly, a region not averse to encouraging Southern writing, and eager, especially after 1876, to publish Southern memoirs, biographies, histories, poetry, novels, and short tales. Northern political realists did not, it was discovered, really like the Negro en masse; Northern realists reconciled themselves to a new variant of white supremacy that aided industrialism; and by 1886 Northern realists were gratefully accepting Henry W. Grady's description of a New South as he pictured it to the New England Society of New York City. Grady, however, spoke only for the elite, and not for all of that.

The West, however bounded, has traditionally feared, distrusted, or envied the East. In colonial and revolutionary times, as population spread westward, new settlements, towns, counties, and states tried to throw off or combat the indifference, greed, or superiority of the East. Like the postwar South, the ante-bellum West had learned to fear exploitative risk capital and self-seeking political influence from that older part of the United States. A separatist Western psychology can be traced, exemplified in successive eras by the existence of Vermont as an independent republic, the abortive state of Franklin, the attempt at an autonomous German commonwealth in Ohio, various communal settlements in the Middle West, demands for a quicker transition out of territorial dependence into statehood, and the long resistance of the quasi-independent State of Deseret and its successor, the Territory of Utah, to Eastern control. Exploitation of natural resources and development of land beyond the Mississippi required risk capital available mainly in the East, and the East therefore became the legendary home of predatory wealth. Distrust developed into distrust of Eastern banks, Eastern inventors (for example, barbed wire was supposed to be imposed upon the range by Easterners coming west), Eastern politicians, Eastern tariff policies, Eastern women, and Eastern clergymen—a set of prejudices astonishingly like those of the South. After the panic year of 1873, notably after the land boom collapsed, agricultural prices fell, and a drought ruined the crops, angry ranchers and farmers, small-town merchants and bankers, housewives and workingmen, looking for somebody to blame, created Wall Street as a symbol of evil, a symbol gratefully accepted by the same classes of persons in the South.

One gets a glimpse into this distrust of the East by reading the pronouncements of the Populist party in the 1890s. Here are some samples:

> On one side are the allied hosts of monopolies, the money power, great trusts and railroad corporations, who seek the enactment of laws to benefit them and impoverish the people. On the other are the farmers, laborers, merchants, and other people who produce wealth and bear the burdens of taxation.

> The newspapers are largely subsidized or muzzled; public opinion silenced; business prostrated; our homes covered with mortgages; labor impoverished; and the land concentrated in the hands of the capitalists.

> . . . The fruits of the toil of millions are boldly stolen to build up colossal fortunes for a few, unprecedented in the history of the world, while their possessors despise the republic and endanger liberty.

The Boy Orator of the River Platte, William Jennings Bryan, in the famous "Cross of Gold" speech, said that cities did not matter but that farms did: "The great cities rest upon our broad and fertile prairies. Burn down your cities and leave our farms, and your cities will spring up again as if by magic; but destroy our farms and the grass will grow in the streets of every city in the country." Mary Ellen Lease was more explicit: "Wall Street owns the country. It is no longer a government of the people, by the people, and for the people, but a government of Wall Street by Wall Street and for Wall Street. The great common people of this country are slaves, and monopoly is the master. The West and South are bound and prostrated before the manufacturing East." [8] That there were Western millionaires and Southern robber barons, or that the Chicago Stock Exchange and the Kansas City Stockyards, not to speak of Western railroads, followed the policy of Eastern magnates, did not matter. Wall Street and Tammany Hall were emblems of all political wickedness.

It was charged that Western and Southern wealth, but particularly Western wealth, was perpetually draining eastward—out of the copper mines near Lake Superior or from Montana, out of the gold and silver deposits of the mountain states, out of struggling towns and lonely farms along Western railroads over which farmers, ranchers, and cattlemen were compelled to ship their products at rates fixed in the East. Large sections of the South came also to believe this. Nothing the East could do altered the myth, even though Boston continued to be a center of radical thought (consider B. O. Flower and *The Arena*), even though Grover Cleveland was an honest man from New York State, and Teddy Roosevelt, educated at Harvard, wrote *Hunting Trips of a Ranchman,* took over a regiment known as the Rough Riders, and denounced malefactors of great wealth.

The East, furthermore, was inhabited by mongrel races denounced by sociologists like E. A. Ross—new immigrants by whom the Old American stock was being swamped, demoralized, and deprived of all the manly virtues. The scandals of the Grant administrations, though they involved Westerners,[9] were attributed to the low state of political and financial morality in Northern cities, a view that James Bryce's *American Commonwealth* (1888) did nothing to alter. When in 1906 David Graham Phillips published his articles, "The Treason of the Senate," though he did not neglect senators from other states, he tended to focus on Eastern senators. Nelson W. Aldrich of Rhode Island is an example, a senator who was by no means weak or wicked but who did not believe in lowering the tariff and regulating the corporations.[10] What else could you expect from a state where millionaires and their families and friends disported themselves on exclusive Bailey's Beach and from their gigantic Newport "cottages" looked down on the toiling masses of mankind? The rich, if they could not make it at Newport, went to Tuxedo Park or Long Island or some other fashionable Eastern area. New Jersey and Delaware, thought to be lax in laws governing corporations, were satrapies of the wealthy. The East was known to view with alarm such democratic ideas as votes for women, the initiative, the referendum, and the recall. Did not "Czar" Reed, Speaker of the House after 1889, come originally from Maine, the home of James G. Blaine, despised of the Mugwumps? Did not "Uncle Joe" Cannon, though born in North Carolina and a quondam lawyer in Illinois, imitate Reed? Was not the Eastern political power structure based on the votes of ignorant immigrants, shepherded to the polls by ward bosses whose money came ultimately from the corporations? Chicago, St. Louis, and San Francisco, it is true, had lost their pioneer virtues and their primitive wickedness, but were they not now professionally corrupt, so to speak, after the example of New York and Philadelphia?

Nor was this all. To right-thinking Americans in other parts of the republic it was evident that the East not only nourished millionaires, city bosses, ward heelers, and masses of immigrants, but also produced undesirable types of upper-class males: soft, effete, snobbish, decadent, aesthetic, incapable of physical exertion, disdaining work, unable to ride a horse in the proper fashion, fearful of bears, unskilled in hunting, tracking, or canoeing except under the watchful eye of guides in the puny wilderness of Maine. The clubman, the stage-door Johnny, the tenderfoot, the effeminate clergyman, the long-haired poet (or musician, actor, painter, or dancer), the artistic poseur, the absent-minded professor—these were Eastern products, undemocratic and essentially un-American. Nor were their women more admirable: the vacuous debutante, the snobbish mother, the Eastern clubwoman, the Boston girl and the Boston matron loaded with culture, the wife of the millionaire who ruled the servants with a heavy hand but could not cook, nurse, wash clothes, or rear children. It is of course ironical that these stereotypes were supported by cartoonists, partly under European influence, and it would not have softened dislike to know (what few realized) that the severest attacks came from caricaturists of Eastern birth and breeding,[11] or that Edith Wharton, born to the purple in New York City, scored and scorned snobbery.

A legend is a legend, and this legend was re-enforced by other literature. As early as *A Chance Acquaintance* (1873) William Dean

Howells, who became editor of the *Atlantic Monthly,* to be sure, contrasted a healthy-minded Western girl from Eriecreek and Milwaukee with the condescension of Miles Arbuton of Boston. In *Harvard Episodes* (1897) Charles Macomb Flandrau exposed "rounders, poseurs, and butterflies" in that Ivy League college. But the cowboy and the clubman simply could not get together, the Boston girl and the Charleston belle were culturally apart. A thousand books and plays from *Roughing It* (1871) and *The Virginian* (1902) through William Vaughn Moody's *The Great Divide* (1909) to Harry Leon Wilson's *Ruggles of Red Gap* (1913) and *Ma Pettingill* (1919) dramatized a conflict of cultures. It is an old conflict, which goes back at least to Leatherstocking and which was re-enforced by dime-novel Westerns, and, in the case of the South, by such plays as *The Heart of Maryland* (1895). A diminished ghost, it still haunts television. Europe, Emerson pithily wrote, extends to the Alleghenies, a remark by an Easterner that removes the East altogether from the United States.

This was not the whole story. The West also looked back upon the East with longing and envied its long tradition. Southerners, when they could, fled to New York City, and other Southerners wished that their section had as much wealth, as many libraries, as much education, and a Southern version of Northern modernism. Easterners were naturally a touch complacent. The oldest part of the republic except for Virginia and a few scattering settlements like St. Augustine and Santa Fe, the East took pride (as why should it not?) in its long history of statesmanship, business, science, education, society, culture, and religion. It was the great publishing area of the nation and therefore the principal diffuser of ideas. Most of the national magazines had their principal offices in Boston, New York, and Philadelphia, and in New York City especially the literary agents lived, the great advertising firms developed, and leading critics wrote, such as James Gibbons Huneker, Henry E. Krehbiel, and Royal Cortissoz. More and more it became the center of the nation's theater. It had most of the famous art museums, and its library resources surpassed those of any other area. Easterners could look upon their achievements with a certain pride in no way diminished by the outcome of the Civil War.

The East tended to be the focus of American intellectual life. If it did not have all the oldest colleges, it had the most prestigious universities, colleges, and private schools. Eastern cities and Eastern institutions were accepted on the whole more easily by visiting European worthies than were cities in the South and West, which seemed somehow odd. The great intellectual and professional organizations had their headquarters in Boston, New York, Philadelphia, or Washington (on the border of the North). The great academies of learning —the American Philosophical Society in Philadelphia, the American Academy of Arts and Sciences in Boston, the American Antiquarian Society in Worcester—were in the East. The Massachusetts Historical Society, oldest of such organizations, served as a model for similar state societies elsewhere. Save for the Hegelians in St. Louis and random professors at Michigan or Chicago, the East nourished the influential persons in philosophy during these decades.

The East maintained its special and mysterious control of fashions for men, women, and children, and in a more limited sense of polite conduct. It knew how to manage dinners, cotillions, and fancy-dress balls, even though the South had its tradition and the West was catching up. It created the Junior League. Its men's clubs were in the main the leading clubs—organizations such as The Century Association of New York. It furnished diplomats to important foreign capitals because its elite had the proper savoir-faire. It possessed West Point, Annapolis, and in a sense, the national capital. And all these things were the manifestations of wealth and tradition—the very wealth and tradition the Populists attacked. If, then, it is difficult to define the East, even as part of "the North," the East nevertheless existed as a state of mind, the occasion of an *odi et amo* valuation: indefinable, vigorous, splendid, despised, and envied, one of the most dynamic elements in the cultural history of the times.

III

New England is a definite geographical entity. The area divides into sub-areas, but here it is sufficient to talk about upper New England and lower, or southern, New England. The fertile Connecticut River Valley bottom lands in southern New England raised profitable crops including tobacco, and Aroostook County potatoes ("Maine potatoes") entered the national market, but in this half-century New England agriculture steadily declined; [12] towns and villages in upper New England stagnated or dwindled, and promising New England harbors turned into secondary or tertiary seaports. Dairy farming, however, slowly developed with the rise of cities, though the lumber industry, until the demand for pulp paper increased, could not rival mills in Michigan, Wisconsin, and other Western areas.[13] French Canadians competed with Yankees on the subsistence farmlands, in the mill towns, and in the industrial centers.[14] Skiing had not yet become a popular winter sport, and if the summer hotel business became lucrative after about 1870, not until the general use of the automobile and the creation of good roads did "summer people" contribute importantly to the New England economy.[15] Sarah Orne Jewett, Mary Wilkins Freeman, Alice Brown, and others reflect in poem and story both the poignancy and the crank humor of isolated lives in villages and on intervale farms, writing with such success that notions of regional decline became an obsession with later commentators. Thus Van Wyck Brooks said of the 1880s in New England:

> The heats and the rigours of the past were long forgotten, the passions of the war, the old crusades, and a mood of reminiscence possessed the people, for whom the present offered few excitements. Society had lost its vital interest, and the Boston mind was indolent and flaccid, as if the struggle for existence had passed it by. Its ambition seemed to be atrophied, except on the practical plane, and this was equally true in the rural regions. Many a clock had gone dead in hamlets that had hummed with life, where the men . . . were torpid and listless; and farmers sat in the village stores, wagging their beards all day, chewing and whittling. . . . The old strain was wearing out.[16]

Some of this is mildly and some of it is wildly inaccurate. New England manufacturing could not compete on equal terms with the industrial cities strung from Schenectady to Minneapolis, railroad transportation in the region was never satisfactory,[17] and in the mid-1890s New England textile mills began a perceptible movement South.[18] Yet in the region the cotton industry continued to expand until 1914. Boston had long since yielded its pride of place to New York as an import-export harbor.[19] But New England industry was by no means a lost cause—on the contrary, cities like Bridgeport, Worcester, Providence, and Boston maintained themselves as industrial centers.[20] More important, New England finance, mainly concentrated in Boston,[21] Providence, and Hartford, made sound investments in insurance, Western railroads, mines,[22] and the service industries, and was to do even better in electronics. Wholesale fishing flourished. If New Americans manned the factories and the fishing fleets and dominated politics in lower New England, Old Americans controlled most of the professions, the world of finance, real estate, education (except in the Roman Catholic schools and colleges), the public school systems, and the arts.

Van Wyck Brooks apologizes for concentrating on Boston and Harvard, and he is right to do so; it is unwise to ignore Providence, Hartford, New Haven, the New England colleges from Middlebury and Bowdoin in upper New England to Trinity and Wellesley in the south.[23] There were lively intellectual movements in theology,[24] science, politics, sociology, architecture, and the representative arts. If ante-bellum Boston could boast of Bulfinch, post-bellum New England is where H. H. Richardson made his home and where he built Sever Hall in the Harvard Yard, Trinity Church in Copley Square, Boston, and various public libraries, homes, warehouses, and railway stations. Russell Sturgis helped remake the Yale campus, McKim, Meade and White planned the Boston Public Library and Symphony Hall for the Boston Symphony Orchestra, founded in 1881 by Major Henry Lee Higginson. Burgess made a master plan for Trinity College, Edward H. Sears constructed (or reconstructed) the Isabella Stewart Gardner Museum on the Fenway in Boston (1902), and Shepley, Rutan & Coolidge planned various buildings, public and private, scattered over New England. For good or ill, Newport sprouted the Renaissance opulence of its millionaires' houses with Richard Morris Hunt among the architects; their construction, whether we nowadays like them or not, marked a notable period in American architecture. Toward the end of this age Horace Trumbauer planned the Widener Library (1913–1914) at Harvard, supposed to be at the time the finest library building in the country. One should not forget the New England Conservatory of Music (1867), eventually housed on Huntington Avenue in Boston, nor Eben D. Jordan's support of the Boston Opera Company (1909), also housed in a building [25] remarkable for its decade.

As an artist Winslow Homer is superior to Washington Allston, and he is but one of a remarkable group of New England artists—among painters, William Morris Hunt and among sculptors, Bela Pratt. In decorating Trinity Church and the Boston Public Library Boston inaugurated mural painting in the United States, employing artists of the rank of John La Farge, Edwin A. Abbey, and John Singer Sargent. The Boston Museum of Fine Arts was founded by private citizens in 1870, was housed in a Ruskinian brick building on Copley Square, and moved to its present Roman imperial structure on Huntington Avenue in 1909. In Providence the prestigious Rhode Island School of Design was founded in 1876. In 1894 Yale established its School of Music (it had early acquired the Jarves gallery of Italian art). In *America's Music* Gilbert Chase devotes a whole chapter to the "Boston classicists"—Daniel Gregory Mason, Arthur W. Foote, George W. Chadwick, Charles Martin Loeffler, Horatio Parker, Edward Burlingame Hill, and Mrs. H. H. A. Beach—who as a group, he says, "gave to the American composer a professional dignity, a social and artistic prestige, and a degree of recognition both at home and abroad, such as he had not previously enjoyed." [26] Meanwhile a quondam Yale student named Charles Ives (1874–1954) was quietly revolutionizing American music; he began his *Second Symphony* in 1889, and the *Concord Sonata*,[27] written in the midst of a business career, occupied him from 1909 to 1915. It is difficult to see that either the Boston mind or New England was indolent and flaccid between 1865 and 1915.

Such a judgment is further denied by the contributions of New England to science, medicine, psychology, general philology, history, education, publishing, and other fields. A few examples will illustrate the activity in these areas. In the 1870s and early 1880s Willard Gibbs at Yale was enunciating principles that led one scientific commentator to call him the greatest synthetic philosopher since Newton; at Harvard Benjamin Osgood Peirce and William E. Byerly were creating a new era in mathematical physics; and in Boston William Barton Rogers laid the foundation of the Massachusetts Institute of Technology, now perhaps the greatest institution of its kind in the world. At Cambridge from 1891 to 1928 Theodore William Richards carried on research in chemistry that was to bring him the Nobel prize in 1914.[28] Charles William Eliot reorganized the Harvard Medical School in this half-century, but this was only a part of his transformation of Harvard College into Harvard University, a radical innovation in the Law School being equally important. Though other institutions, for instance Cornell and Johns Hopkins, exemplified both the university idea and the elective system, Eliot became the great philosopher of American higher education and an important force in the development of secondary education in the United States.[29] Psychology was furthered by G. Stanley Hall at

Clark University in Worcester and William James and his colleagues at Cambridge. At Yale William Dwight Whitney, after trying geology, botany, ornithology, and medicine, turned into one of the great comparative philologists of the world, editing from 1889 to 1891 the *Century Dictionary* in six volumes. At the Paris Exposition of 1889 G. and C. Merriam of Springfield were awarded a gold medal for their latest edition of Webster. In history: Francis Parkman between 1865 and 1892 completed his triumphal work on France and England in North America; Albert Bushnell Hart edited in twenty-six volumes *The American Nation: A History,* the first great multivolume work on the subject by specialists; John Fiske applied Darwinism and the ideas of Herbert Spencer to the development of America down to the adoption of the federal constitution; and Charles Francis Adams, Henry Adams, and Brooks Adams wrote history in a new key.[30] At Harvard in 1873 Charles Eliot Norton began "the first continuous university instruction in the history of the fine arts as related to social progress, general culture, and literature." [31] If the publishing center had moved to New York, Horace E. Scudder of Houghton Mifflin Company performed one of the most amazing feats in the history of American books: through the founding of the Riverside Literature Series for the schools and the creation of both the Cambridge Poet series and scrupulously edited texts of the great New Englanders, he persuaded the country to accept Emerson, Thoreau, Whittier, Hawthorne, Lowell, Longfellow, and Holmes as the core of classical American literature.[32] In Portland Thomas B. Mosher was producing the "Mosher books" after the manner of William Morris, and in Cambridge two youngsters named Herbert Stuart Stone and Ingalls Kimball were doing fine printing of a superior sort.[33]

Although the importance of New England lessened in economics, banking, transportation, and industry, the area was more important in the intellectual and cultural realms in these fifty years than it had been before the war. Major writers and reformers who outlived the war did not mysteriously end their labors when the ideas of the abolitionists triumphed with the Thirteenth Amendment in 1866.[34] Bryant, now in New York of course, Mrs. Stowe (her famous *Lady Byron Vindicated* in 1870, first printed in the *Atlantic,* was a document about the wrongs women suffered), Julia Ward Howe, Amos Bronson Alcott with the Concord School of Philosophy in his backyard, Emerson, Longfellow, Lowell, Whittier, Holmes, Wendell Phil-

lips, Garrison, Sumner, and others were unaware that they had de-
cayed. As late as 1890 Whittier was capable of so Greek and lapidary
an inscription as this for a bas relief portraying the last Indian and
the last bison:

> The eagle, stooping from yon snow-blown peaks,
> For the wild hunter and the bison seeks,
> In the changed world below; and finds alone
> Their graven semblance in the eternal stone.[35]

Longfellow wrote his admirable *Tales of a Wayside Inn* from 1863 to
1873, his fine translation of Dante was done between 1865 and 1869,
and his better lyrics and sonnets came to him in these later years
when he no longer felt required to live up to his image as the children's poet.[36] Lowell's well-known "On a Certain Condescension in
Foreigners" dates from 1869, his more influential address, "Democracy," was delivered at Birmingham in 1884, and at home he denounced graft and corruption in politics. Holmes's "medicated" novels run from *Elsie Venner* (1861) to *A Mortal Antipathy* (1885),[37] his
Mechanism in Thought and Morals from 1871, and his *Medical Essays* from 1883. Scholars, at least, know that in *Oldtown Folks* (1869),
Sam Lawson's Fireside Stories (1872), and *Poganuc People* (1878),
whatever trash she may have written, Mrs. Stowe created in Sam
Lawson a folk hero, and cultural historians are aware that in the
minds of elite readers Lowell turned into a culture hero comparable
to Goethe and Arnold. It is sometimes held that Emerson fell into
vain repetition after *The Conduct of Life* (1860), but he became
from 1865 to 1915 America's philosopher as John Locke had been before him. Dedicating the Soldiers' Monument at Concord in 1867, he
said bluntly that "the theory and practice of liberty" at the North
"had got sadly out of gear," denounced political corruption in a Phi
Beta Kappa address that same year, and in "The Fortune of the Republic" in 1878 had this to say about the rich and the idle:

> We have seen the great party of property and education in the country
> drivelling and huckstering away, for views of party fear or advantage,
> every principle of humanity and the dearest hopes of mankind; the trus-
> tees of power only energetic when mischief could be done, imbecile as
> corpses when evil was to be prevented.
>
> The class of which I speak make themselves merry without duties. They
> sit in decorated club-houses in the cities, and burn tobacco and play

whist; in the country they sit idle in stores and bar-rooms, and burn tobacco, and gossip and sleep. They complain of the flatness of American
life; "America has no illusions, no romance." They have no perception of
its destiny. . . . The felon is the logical extreme of the epicure and cox-
comb. Selfish luxury is the end of both, though in one it is decorated
with refinements, and in the other brutal.[38]

Nor did other reformers fall silent. Senator Sumner nowadays suf-
fers from a bad press, though at the end of the war he was with
Abraham Lincoln the most powerful political personality in the
United States. By and by he broke with the radical Republicans,[39]
(some said out of vanity), fought the Grant administration, opposed
the cynical move to annex Santo Domingo, worked for international
peace, denounced political favoritism, supported movements for civil
rights, and opposed "Caste" in an address of 1869 he often repeated.
Wendell Phillips, once more unpopular with the moneymakers,
thundered against drink, favored woman suffrage (Sumner wouldn't
have it), spoke out vehemently on the wrongs of Ireland, fought for
the Negro, battled contract labor, opposed fundamentalism, wanted
public education, advocated the right of labor to organize, and demanded an eight-hour day. When he died in 1884 there was a public
funeral, though not until 1894 did the Boston City Council put up a
tablet in his honor.[40]

In the next generation men like Edward A. Atkinson, Mayor
Henry L. Pierce (Phillips's "Diogenes' honest man in the mayor's
chair"), Charles Francis Donnelly, B. O. Flower, Robert Treat Paine,
William Jewett Tucker, Robert A. Woods, and Andrew Preston Peabody worked for social and political reform.[41] Edward Bellamy published *Looking Backward* at Boston in 1888 and founded a national
party. In that city the Radical Club met from 1867 to 1880; and
there the philosophic anarchist, Benjamin Ricketson Tucker, wrote
editorials by day for the Boston *Globe,* and in his free hours translated Proudhon's *What is Property?* and Bakunin's *God and the
State,* printed Tolstoi's *The Kreutzer Sonata* in spite of the censor,
edited *Radical Reform* and *Liberty,* a sort of anarchist broadside,
and was called in 1899 to address the Conference on Trusts held by
the Chicago Civic Federation.

I can but briefly mention here the Free Religious Association, heir
of the transcendentalist movement, but a force in the so-called liberal
movement in New England theology, which became sufficiently na-

tional to color the important World Congress of Religions at the Columbian Exposition of 1893. Francis Ellingwood Abbot called it no more than a debating society, but the debaters included Octavius B. Frothingham, John Weiss, David A. Wasson, Felix Adler, Frank Lester Ward, Cyrus A. Bartol, and Abbot himself, men quite as intelligent as the transcendentalists and more effective. A final representative incident illustrating the alertness of New England to intellectual issues is represented by the presidency of Elisha Benjamin Andrews at Brown University in Providence from 1889 to 1898. During the agitation over the free coinage of silver, the trustees said his views on this question and on free trade were costing the university the millions it needed from gifts and legacies and pressed him to keep still or alter his views. Instead, Andrews resigned. Thereupon twenty-four Brown professors, six hundred alumni, and about one hundred distinguished Americans declared that if the resignation were accepted free speech would everywhere be endangered, and Andrews was reinstated—a crucial episode in the development of academic liberty for the whole country.[42]

The fact seems to be that, far from being decadent, from 1865 to 1915 New England was a major dynamic force in the life of the nation, an *officina philosophorum* which poured forth incessantly educators, college presidents, critics, artists and architects, liberal theologians, political radicals and political conservatives—intellectual missionaries sometimes gratefully received and sometimes hotly resented but never to be ignored. New Englanders crossed the Vermont line into central New York, entered the Old Northwest, passed on into Iowa, Kansas, Nebraska, and Colorado, went forward into Utah, Washington, Oregon, and California carrying New England with them.[43] They also penetrated Hawaii.[44] New England was charged with parochialism and snobbery, but whatever losses it may have sustained in politics and finance, it remained an area possessing intellectual vitality to a degree probably beyond that evident in any other large section of the United States.

IV

More definite in boundary than the "North" or the "East," the Middle West is not as topographically explicit as New England. The heart of the region is the Old Northwest, which became Ohio, Indi-

ana, Illinois, Michigan, and Wisconsin under the terms of the Northwest Ordinance of 1787. But the "West," even the "Great West," once
began at Pittsburgh and the Alleghenies, and, moreover, settlers
came to push across the Mississippi into southern Minnesota and
Iowa, even into northeast Missouri, sending northward-running
streams into southern Michigan and Wisconsin and up the Mississippi to the Twin Cities in Minnesota. Kentucky, sometimes called
the mother of Western states, lies south of the Ohio River and cannot
be included in the Middle West. A special problem is represented by
St. Louis, a great river port, the entrepôt of the fur trade, and the
starting place for exploring expeditions, military forays, and bands of
settlers moving into the Great Plains and beyond. St. Louis was also
the seat of the Catholic Vicar-General, to whom the Chicago area was
for a time subordinate.[45] Yet, despite these connections with the westward movement, St. Louis is seldom considered a part of the Middle
West and occupies, as it were, a cultural principality all its own. The
"lake states," Michigan and Wisconsin, stand a little apart from their
sisters by virtue of difference in terrain, climate, and natural resources.

Despite these complexities it is proper to talk about the Middle
West as an entity sometimes thought of as the heartland of America.
Into this area the original swarms of settlers came down the Ohio
River; or, dividing into two principal branches north of the Ohio,
moved west along the National Road and beyond it or went through
central New York to the southern shore of Lake Erie or across its waters into northern Ohio, Indiana, or southern Michigan. As a consequence of this bifurcation the southern counties of Ohio, Indiana,
and Illinois were tinctured with Southern values, and during the
Civil War the Confederacy had some hope of aid from them. Cincinnati was fearful of attack, and anti-abolitionist sentiment, pro-South-
ern secret societies, and the smuggling of supplies across the Ohio or
down the Mississippi into the Confederacy perplexed political and
military policy in the North. But southern Illinois furnished more
than its quota of volunteers to the Federal forces, Morgan's raiders
were not gratefully received above the north bank of the Ohio, and
Cairo rose briefly into prominence as a military center for Union
forces. The rest of the area, though it did not care for abolitionists or
for Negroes, was on the whole pro-Union.

To geologists the Old Northwest has a particular interest. If one forgets Michigan and Wisconsin, what must have struck travelers moving westward from the mountain passes or pushing up from the Ohio was the accessibility of the terrain and its lack of real obstacles to migration and settlement. Allowing for local elevations and river beds, hills and swamps, an immigrant going from Zanesville, Ohio, to Quincy, Illinois, found the land growing steadily flatter and more uniform—the average elevation of Ohio above sea level is eight hundred and fifty feet, that of Illinois six hundred feet. By all accounts this great expanse of prairie and plain was originally a region of striking, if monotonous, beauty, well timbered and well watered, though the winters could be dangerous and the mud in spring or fall was as tenacious as Southern gumbo. Accessibility, ease of clearing, plentiful waterways, the fertility of the soil, and the discovery of such natural resources as coal and lead in Illinois made the area attractive. It developed a special sense of expansiveness, a challenge to energy under these endless skies.

During the nineteenth century no part of the republic moved with more amazing rapidity from a state of nature to a state of industry. The population of Ohio in 1800 was estimated at about 45,000; just before the Civil War it was 2,339,511. In 1825 there were only an Indian agency and about fourteen houses at Chicago. By the mid-1850s Chicago had become one of the great grain ports; at the time of the Great Fire of 1871 the population of the city was over 300,000, and just before the World's Columbian Exposition it held well over 1,000,000 inhabitants.

We are so accustomed to think of the Middle West in terms of Bryce's charge that it was dominated by materialism and the middle class, or as it is pictured in Ed Howe's *The Story of a Country Town* (1883), Dreiser's *Sister Carrie* (1900), Sherwood Anderson's *Winesburg, Ohio* (1919), and Sinclair Lewis's *Main Street* (1920),[46] it is difficult to grasp the truth that in its earlier history the Middle West anticipated and telescoped the phases of the Far West—the struggle with Indians and animals, the appeal of wild beauty, the sense of immemorial antiquity, melancholy, and vastness, the allure of a new beginning for humanity, though humanity was half rascals and half heroes, and infinite challenges to greed and altruism. It will dramatize the rapid transition from the wilderness to industrial exploitation, as well as help us to understand better why the Middle West had a good conceit of itself if we glance briefly at some descriptions of the region between 1800 and 1860. The style of many of these passages is of the spurious grandiose or the spurious sentimental order; by looking past the rhetoric to the intention one can understand the mixture of wonder, hope, and greed the writers were struggling to express.

Here, for example, is Jacob Burnet, talking to the Cincinnati Astronomical Society in 1844, trying to put into language a general vision of vanishing enchantment. He declares that:

> . . . the country was one of the most delightful on the face of the earth; exhibiting a fertility of soil—a grandeur of forest, and a beauty and richness of prairie, never excelled; and that as far as original, creating power was concerned, everything had been done, which the imagination of man could anticipate, or desire. When the early adventurer penetrated the forest, his feet sunk in the loose rich soil, on which he trod, and as he traversed the extensive prairie, which nature, in the imaginary person of *Flora,* had beautified with her richest gifts, painted with every variety and mixture of colors of the rainbow, his feelings could not be adequately expressed. The further he advanced into the interior of the great Valley, and the more he saw of the rivers, which intersected it in all directions; and of the endless variety of its luxurious vegetable, and rich mineral productions, the more readily did he yield to that frailty of human nature, which prompts us to covet and invade the rights of our neighbors. This beautiful region, however, was in the state, in which nature had made it. The hand of civilized man, had not then been employed, to change its appearance, or mar its native beauty.[47]

Of the first view of the Ohio River from Wheeling Charles Fenno Hoffman declared that it was:

> . . . worth a journey of a thousand miles. The clear majestic tide, the fertile islands on its bosom, the bold and towering heights opposite, with the green esplanade of alluvion in front, and the forest-crowned head lands, above and below, round which the river sweeps away, to bless and gladden the fruitful regions that drink its limpid waters,—these, with the recollections of deeds done upon its banks—the wild incidents and savage encounters of border story, so immediately contrasted with all the luxuries of civilization that now float securely upon that peaceful current,—these make up a moral picture whose colours are laid in the heart, never to be effaced:—no man will ever forget his first view of the Ohio.[48]

The English traveler, Charles A. Murray, saw the upper Mississippi in autumn:

> The deep and solemn foliage of the nobler trees was relieved by the brilliant colours of the scarlet creeping-vines which were twined around their mighty limbs, and hung in festoons forming natural bowers, wherein poets might dream, or dryads repose. Over all this enchanting scene, and over the wide expanse of water, the setting sun had cast his rosy mantle, and bathed it in a flood of crimson light.[49]

To Bryant the prairies had the encircling vastness of an ocean:

> The clouds
> Sweep over with their shadows, and beneath,
> The surface rolls and fluctuates to the eye;
> Dark hollows seem to glide along and chase
> The sunny ridges. Breezes of the South!
> Who toss the golden and the flame-like flowers,
> And pass the prairie-hawk that, poised on high,
> Flaps his broad wings, yet moves not.[50]

Accepting the then current theory of the Mound Builders, Bryant thought solemnly of vanished races and nations long ago.

Caroline Kirkland faced innumerable difficulties in pioneer Michigan, yet she indignantly repudiated the notion that there was anything mean about the landscape with its meadowland, swelling hills, rich variety of foliage, innumerable streams and lakes, and multitudes of wild fowl.

> No spot on earth possesses a more transparent atmosphere. . . . The heavenly bodies seem to smile upon us without an intervening medium. The lustre of the stars and the white glittering moonlight seem more pure and perfect here than elsewhere.

> The waters are more like molten diamonds, and the herbage like living emeralds, because the lustrous sky brings out their hues in undimmed intensity, adding depth to shadows, and keeping back nothing of brilliancy.

Every one of the three thousand lakes in Michigan was, she thought, "a mirror set in verdant velvet and bordered with the richest fringe." [51] And Mrs. John H. Kinzie in *Wau-Bun,* printed in 1856, remembered the hundred or more Indian canoes converging on Mackinac (Michimillimackinac), the central trading post of the Old Northwest, and "those pure, living waters, in whose depths the fish might be seen gliding and darting to and fro, whose clearness is such that an object dropped to the bottom may be discerned at the depth of fifty or sixty feet." A companion exclaimed: "Oh! I could wish to be drowned in these pure, beautiful waters!" [52] There were even those who, though they reported on travelers frozen to death on the prairie, thought Midwestern winters superior to those in the East. A lasting sense of difference developed by a thousand descriptions of this kind, made the Mid-Westerner feel he was a being a little apart, a truer American than people living elsewhere.

But this alluring land, fit for only poets and heroes to occupy, was swiftly filled with as motley a set of human beings as were ever found in familiar legends of the Far West: sullen Indians, New Englanders both of the pious and the slippery sort, Mexican caballeros, shouting evangelists and poverty-stricken ministers, quiet nuns, colonies of Germans, Irish, Italians, Slavs, Frenchmen, Jews, Cornish miners, Finns, freed Negroes and decrepit ex-slaves, keelboatmen and river rats, border ruffians and gentility, gamblers, fancy women, starry-eyed teachers and academicians, reformers, naturalists, scientists, newspaper editors, Southerners of every sort, wandering limners, daguerreotypists and photographers, demagogues, Nantucket whalers,[53] founders of Utopias such as Nauvoo, New Harmony, and Icaria,[54] and speculators—always speculators—in canals, railways, patent medicines, towns, banks, and above everything else, land.[55] A Western speech developed with idioms of its own, a Western egalitarianism that collided with social and professional hierarchies, a Western type of male exemplified in Abraham Lincoln, even though Stephen Douglas, the Little Giant, also came from Illinois. There were cultivated families and gangs of ruffians, elegance and filth, claims for an eternity of health and lamentations about ague, fever, and the "milk sick," attempts at the amenities and contempt for them, abolitionists and racists, Old Americans and New Americans, believers in people and believers in profit—all in the Middle West.

It was no small source of satisfaction that Grant, a Western general, had captured Vicksburg and compelled Lee's surrender, just as it was right and proper that Mark Twain's celebrated speech of 1879, picturing Grant as a baby trying to put his big toe into his mouth, was delivered at the Palmer House in Chicago at a reception by that famous Western force, the Army of the Tennessee; a Western humorist making a Western joke about a Western hero. Nor is it without significance that of the nine presidents of the United States holding office by election after the administration of Andrew Johnson through the first administration of Woodrow Wilson, six were Western men, and that one of the Easterners, Theodore Roosevelt, presented himself as a Rough Rider, a Westerner who got things done.[56]

The striking and in a sense quintessentially "American" fact about the Middle West was the unparalleled rapidity with which in three generations it passed from being a wilderness into a predominantly agrarian culture (at first, subsistence farming) and then into becoming the industrial heartland of the United States. The factory did not destroy the farm but came to overshadow it. The great inventions of a gigantic industrial order (not that they were unique here)—the endless freight trains, the cyclopean steam engines, and after them the dynamos, the steel mills, the packing houses, the breweries, the distilleries, the oil refineries, the automobile companies, the power plants, and the power lines—grew more and more formidable, occupied more and more space, scarified more and more of the landscape, and polluted more and more air, water, and soil as the years marched on. Like evil genii, they drew their thousands from the country, from the East and the South, and from Europe, hordes of laborers, skilled and unskilled, who lived in planless wildernesses of ugly houses or in slums that steadily worsened, homes that the new millionaires of meat, petroleum, steel, transportation, wheat, corn, flour, electricity, or banking never saw or, seeing, regarded as regrettable side-products of progress to be somehow spirited away by the magic of progress.

In the Middle West a new order of politicians arose between the opposing forces of capital and labor, using one element of this seething and dissatisfied society against the other. The ward heelers, the city bosses, and the venal legislators make one think of the parasites of ancient Rome, hangers-on of wealthy and cynical families. From time to time a spell of reform would seize this or that area, when a Tom L. Johnson or a "Golden Rule" Jones would arise to counterbalance such personalities as Hinky-Dink and Bath-House John, the most picturesque Chicago aldermen of the period. The rapidity of change from farming to heavy industry, from the yeomanry to the proletariat, varied from state to state. Michigan and Wisconsin belonged to the lumber kings until the timber was exhausted, leaving the upper counties dreary, cut-over wasteland with islands here and there of hopeless farms and isolated hamlets, and leaving also complex problems of reconstituting state governments and modernizing state responsibility for the population. Urbanites, middle-class and upward, would discover in the northland cheap real estate, secluded lakes, and streams full of trout. But otherwise population tended more and more to concentrate in the southern tiers of counties as the industrial order rolled relentlessly westward from Pittsburgh and Youngstown, Cleveland and Toledo, to swallow up Detroit, Grand Rapids, Gary, Chicago, Milwaukee, Madison, and Peoria. Lake Erie was turned into the largest area of liquid pollution in the New World as William Blake's dark, satanic mills spewed forth their waste and bewildered cities considered how to dispose of garbage and human excrement.

Despite the excellence of agricultural colleges in the Middle West and the scientific modernization of farming, political and financial power slipped from the farm belt to the industrial cities, where cloud and sky were replaced by smoke, steam, and soot, a change that increased after the election of 1876. A William McKinley in a rocking chair on his front porch in Canton, Ohio, affably receiving delegations of the faithful, a smooth puppet manipulated by Mark Hanna, king maker from Cleveland, is a dramatic opposite to Abraham Lincoln, the Rail-Splitter, though an interval of only thirty-one years separates the death of the one from the election of the other. Lincoln is now an American saint; nevertheless he was until his election a small-town lawyer, a local politico not above the cunning of the "smart" young attorney, a man who shared the country amusements of the boys, liked their ribaldry, wrestled well, distrusted elegance, and possessed both the mysterious melancholy and the physical skills of a whole generation of youth growing up this side of the wilderness. Contrast William Howard Taft, elected less than a half-century after Lincoln's assassination, scion of a cultivated Cincinnati family (Cincinnati was once the intellectual capital of the Middle West), moving easily from Ohio to the East and, for that matter, around the world. Taft was born the year of the Dred Scott decision, a year before Lincoln delivered his famous "house divided against itself" speech, three years before the election of 1860.

If it be true that America came of age by the time of Woodrow Wilson, it is equally true that the Middle West became industrially mature in the same epoch. There were great universities, great hospitals, great art museums, great libraries, great symphony orchestras,

great architects and builders, sculptors and painters in the Middle
West, and they produced the World's Columbian Exposition and the
Chicago "Renaissance," which, it was thought, would make that city
the literary center of the United States. The Middle West invented
the skyscraper, the Great Lakes ore boats, the best state universities in
the country, and much else; but the characteristic quality of the area
became energy and conflict rather than aestheticism and calm. Carl
Sandburg's *Chicago Poems* (1919) and Sinclair Lewis's *Babbitt* (1922)
summed up one side of the Middle West; Robert Herrick's *Clark's
Field* (1914) and Booth Tarkington's *The Magnificent Ambersons*
(1918) and *Alice Adams* (1921) summed up another; Vachel Lindsay's
brassy *General William Booth Enters into Heaven and Other Poems*
(1913) sums up a third; perhaps Eugene Field and the celebrated Mr.
Dooley of Archey Road express a fourth, a humorous, indulgent, and
skeptical commentary upon the other three.

V

The South is the most controversial region in American history, an
enigma to itself and a riddle to the nation. By the geographical
South one usually means the states that made up the Confederacy,
but of these Florida was in a class by itself, Texas and Arkansas, save
for their eastern counties, are usually classed as belonging to the
Southwest (sometimes the West), and Tennessee, which was theoretically in the Confederacy, like Kentucky, which did not secede, was
split down the middle, the eastern half being pro-Union. The South
spills over into Maryland and Delaware and over the Ohio River
into southern Ohio, Indiana, and Illinois. Virginia seceded, but the
western counties broke off and were admitted to the Union as West
Virginia in 1863. If one identifies the South with the Confederate
States of America, one finds that short-lived republic occupying in
theory about 766,665 square miles, or one-fourth of the area of the
continental United States in 1915. In this vast territory there was an
extraordinary range of climate. If all of Texas be counted in, this
range runs from the sudden winter cold of "northers" sweeping into
Texas from Canada, to the semitropical temperatures of the Gulf
Coast. The South, however defined, fronts on the sweep of the Atlantic from Delaware Bay to the tip of Florida and along the Gulf Coast
westward to the Rio Grande, a seacoast that offers relatively few good

harbors. It has its mountain ranges in the southern Appalachians and the broken masses of the Ozarks; it shares the Mississippi River Valley with the Middle West, and in western Texas it rises by way of the Edwards Plateau and the Guadalupe-Davis-Santiago mountains to an altitude like that of New Mexico, El Capitan, a little east of El Paso, reaching over 8000 feet. West Texas is, however, scarcely Southern.

If one confines the South to the territory vaguely thought of as Dixie, it still exhibits a diversity of terrain and development from the Florida Everglades to the Cumberland Plateau and from the iron and steel complex around Birmingham to that vastest of Federal projects, the TVA, which affects the economy of seven, eight, or nine commonwealths. Apples are grown in the Shenandoah Valley, tobacco in North Carolina, cotton in Mississippi, tung-oil nuts in Louisiana, and oranges in Florida. Southern life ranges from persistent poverty in Appalachia and parts of the Deep South to the swank residential sections of modern Atlanta.

In the years here under survey components of the contemporary South grow increasingly evident. They couple, however, with lingering bitterness and self-pity created by the Civil War and Reconstruction, a race problem that was to diffuse itself over the whole country, and a series of virtual political revolutions accompanied by occasional bloodshed and more frequent corruption or disregard of the democratic process. I refer to the various Reconstruction governments, the restoration of white supremacy by fraud, violence, and intimidation, and populist revolts against the "mummies"—that is, political Bourbons who, often in conjunction with Northern money, made political capital of their military or civil prominence in the Confederacy. If the South is not yet wholly reconciled to an indissoluble union with the rest of the United States, enthusiasm for the Spanish-American War and widespread Southern support for World War I at least diminished sectional antagonism. In 1897 the British traveler G. W. Steevens wrote: "I had, before I went South, the belief that the war feeling was dead and buried years ago; I was astonished at the bitterness that survives." [57] Nowadays the Confederate flag is defiantly flown in Alabama.

Unfortunately for historical simplicity, this enormous region, uncolored in the main by the new immigration, exhibited a wide variety of indigenous types. Among the blacks the spread was from the "old-timey darkey" and the unskilled Negro laborer in the city or humble farmer in the country to the rising Negro middle class that was to make Durham, North Carolina, a financial center for their race, and the earnest teachers and idealists who created Atlanta University. The white population was equally diverse—representatives of the Southern gentry conscious of family, history, defeat, and Protestantism; ignorant tenant farmers; poor whites drawn into the dreary mill towns; industrial, railroad, financial, mill-owning, or ecclesiastical magnates, who, if they had emigrated from the North, soon took on a Southern veneer; rabble-rousers like "Pitchfork" Ben Tillman and Cole Blease; Jews, some of them of historical lineage in South Carolina or Louisiana, others newly come to the cities and towns, usually as peddlers and small shopkeepers, many of them rising to later eminence; a Christian ministry more often fundamentalist than not; editors, politicians, and public men of the type of "Marse" Henry Watterson or Josephus Daniels; and reformers such as Charles B. Aycock or Leonidas L. Polk. Their wives and daughters were equally diverse in culture and outlook. It is difficult to generalize about a population so complex. Moreover, all generalizations are contradicted by those who want to generalize otherwise.[58]

Some argue that frontier values lingered longer in the South, even among the planters, than they did elsewhere this side the Mississippi;[59] others stress a traditional social order undervalued or misinterpreted by Northern historians. Indeed, the contrast between the elegance of ante-bellum Natchez and the sordor of Natchez-under-the-hill[60] is as striking as that between ante-bellum parochialism and Senator Jefferson Davis, then a senator from Mississippi, fighting to establish the Smithsonian Institution. The University of North Carolina before the Civil War had a larger enrollment than Harvard College, evidence perhaps of a high culture supposed by abolitionists to be lacking in the ante-bellum South.

Outside the mountain areas and a few others, heat and humidity conditioned Southern architecture, ways of life, family customs, and general outlook. Life in Georgia or Mississippi was lived outside the house as it could not be lived in a New Hampshire winter. If the plantation palaces were fewer and more sparsely scattered than legend allows, the characteristic lower-middle-class Southern house in town or country, set a few feet above the ground on cedar posts or brick columns, with no cellar hole, an iron kettle in the yard over the ashes of a fire, domestic animals beneath the floor or invading the porch, a breezeway separating the two halves of the structure—such a dwelling would have been uncomfortable in Maine or Montana. If the South has many climates, what W. J. Cash calls a "cosmic conspiracy against reality in favor of romance" tended to blend the South into a single, legendary setting for courtesy and violence. Cash is penetrating and eloquent:

> The country is one of extravagant colors, of proliferating foliage and bloom, of flooding yellow sunlight, and, above all perhaps, of haze. Pale blue fogs hang above the valleys in the morning, the atmosphere smokes faintly at midday, and through the long slow afternoon cloudstacks tower from the horizon and the earth-heat quivers upward through the iridescent air, blurring every outline and rendering every object vague and problematical. I know that winter comes to the land. . . . I know there are days when the color and the haze are stripped away . . . but . . . the dominant mood, the mood that lingers in the memory, is one of well-nigh drunken reverie—of a hush that seems all the deeper for the far-away mourning of the hounds and the far-away crying of the doves—of such sweet and inexorable opiates as the rich odors of hot earth and pinewood and the perfume of the magnolia in bloom.[61]

An important generalization about the South is that its white population has been on the whole more nearly homogeneous than that of any other great portion of the United States. Like any other on this topic, the generalization is open to exceptions; for instance, the Acadians in Louisiana are a separate group. But it is a good working generalization, especially in view of the attempts of several Southern states—South Carolina and Georgia are examples—to induce European immigration to turn southward, attempts that commonly failed. Homogeneity did not destroy traditional castes in the region but made it easier to support the doctrine of white supremacy and a uniform value system not merely about race but also about religion, the economic order, the politics of status (at least until the rise of Populism, which, however, did not destroy status), the position of women (happiest at home), and an ambiguous attitude toward education. "Book-larnin'" was for the happy few, although step by step agricultural courses took hold, technological education spread, and Southern universities slowly approached the level of those in the North. Through these fifty years the Southern home was the center of Southern culture, two lamentable side-results being the mediocrity of

Southern hotels, except in a few cities and resort areas, and the mediocrity of Southern restaurants. The South, save for one or two cities, never learned to delight in the variety of menus—Greek, Italian, Chinese, French, German, Russian, Austrian, Swedish, and so on—that gave color to eating out in San Francisco or New York. Indeed, a disinclination to experiment with food and the monotony of diet among the poor, in part a function of poverty, in part a function of the hookworm, reduced personal energy among many Negroes and poor whites. Nor was "soul food" necessarily the best possible diet for health among the blacks. An unhappy result was a high rate of infant mortality.

Slavery and the Civil War are two fundamental and familiar data in Southern history. The South was the only part of the United States to experience the widespread destruction of four years of a modern war, the results of which turned the existing social pattern inside out, temporarily putting political control of the former master class in the power of the former slave and the former enemy. The war crippled or killed thousands of human beings, damaged a rising generation, ruined scores of cities, towns, villages, plantations, and farms, destroyed a transportation system that, if it was never good, had had some chance of getting better, bankrupted the wealthy, offered wide opportunity for the unscrupulous to grow rich, left large portions of the South for months without any sure system of government, and created the soil out of which demagoguery and lawlessness developed. One cannot summarize this agony, albeit vivid accounts of travels in the South just after the war permit us to participate in some of it. A sense of the consequences of warfare and ruin in a single Southern state can be realized by reading two volumes published by the Mississippi Department of Archives and History in 1961, *Mississippi in the Confederacy as They Saw It* and *Mississippi in the Confederacy as Seen in Retrospect*.[62] These accounts need only to be multiplied for other seceding states.

According to legend, all the Confederates were gallant and all the Union men were brave. As a matter of cold fact desertions from the Union armies numbered more than two hundred and seventy-five thousand and from the Confederate forces over one hundred thousand, and these deserters came to control large sections of the United States south of the Federal lines. They were joined by bushwhackers, thieves, and other lawless men, and set up kangaroo governments of their own. If the Federal armies and the Reconstruction governments restored order more rapidly than might have been predicted, violence, especially under and just after "Black" Reconstruction, remained a force, nor did it disappear with the restoration of white supremacy.[63] By the 1890s segregationist lines had been established more firmly than they were in 1877 when President Hayes withdrew the last Federal regiments from the former Confederacy. Little in this crowded and tumultuous history altered the character of a Southern legend that went back to colonial times; much in it enriched the legend, the existence of which became the chief emotional support for the "otherness" of Southern life. Soil erosion, too long unchecked, kept the poorer farmers in a permanent state of poverty and hopelessness; and when they, or their wives, or their daughters, or the entire family moved into the mill villages to occupy unlovely company houses, they infected each other with racial and religious attitudes. Legend, meanwhile, insisted upon seeing them as quaint Anglo-Saxon folk who dipped snuff, sang old English and Scottish ballads in the mountains, and spoke a picturesque Elizabethan or Jacobean English. Another Southern legend saw the Negro either as Uncle Remus, Aunt Jemima, and cute little pickaninnies, or, what was more, as a bestial threat to white Southern womanhood. The history of lynching in the South at the end of the nineteenth century and into the twentieth is shameful; the organized protests of white Southern womanhood (which the lynchers thought they were protecting from rape) was one of the most potent forces in reducing it.

The political history of the post-bellum South is not here our main concern, nor, except in summary, is the emergence of the New South. The New South implied the acceptance of industrialization as a major way of life alongside of agriculture; the permanent subordination of the Negro to the white man; the modernization of farming for both races; the rationalization of large wholesale crops like cotton and tobacco; the exploitation by modern technology of such natural resources as sulphur, oil, and coal; the improvement of transportation by railroad, canal, river, and road; the updating of Southern education; better programs for public health; and the creation of trained civil servants for the state, this last being the least successful item in the program. In these fifty years modernization did not affect the one-party system, traditional Southern attitudes about the tariff, public lands, foreign policy (for example, "imperialism"), resentment of "interference," nor the firm belief that the South understood both the South and the Negro better than any Northerner could understand either. Nor did it alter Southern hostility to "radicals," godless evolutionists, Northern education, Northern journalism, and Northern critics.[64] It is paradoxical that as the South was modernized, the Southern legend was enriched.

In 1898 Thomas Nelson Page, born and dying in Virginia, published a novel about the Civil War and Reconstruction called *Red Rock*. The preface declares the story is laid "somewhere in that vague region partly in one of the old Southern States" and partly in memory.

> It was a goodly land in those old times—a rolling country, lying at the foot of the blue mountain-spurs, with forests and fields; rich meadows filled with fat cattle; watered by streams, sparkling and bubbling over rocks, or winding under willows and sycamores, to where the hills melted away in the low, alluvial lands, where the sea once washed and still left its memory and its name. The people of that section were the product of a system of which it is the fashion nowadays to have only words of condemnation. Every ass that passes by kicks at the dead lion. It was an Oligarchy . . . but has one ever known the members of a Democracy to rule so justly? If they shone in prosperity, much more they shone in adversity; if they bore themselves haughtily in their day of triumph, they have borne defeat with splendid fortitude. Their old family seats, with everything else in the world, were lost to them—their dignity became grandeur. Their entire system crumbled and fell about them in ruins—they remained unmoved. They were subjected to the greatest humiliation of modern times: their slaves were put over them—they reconquered their section and preserved the civilization of the Anglo-Saxon.[65]

This landscape is like something by Howard Pyle. The only possible comment on his picture is to read Ellen Glasgow's *The Deliverance* (1904) and to meditate on the symbolical significance of old Mrs. Blake in that dated but important novel.

All legends look backward; no American legend looks backward longer or more consistently than the Southern legend, the origins of which are difficult to ascertain. Unless one is willing to interpret William Byrd's conviction that he really belonged to fashionable London as the basis of Southern nostalgia for aristocracy, one does not know where to start. In Byrd's *History of the Dividing Line* the Southern aristocrat is so secure that he can deal with the lower orders on terms of easy affability. The generation of Jefferson seems to have felt little desire to turn the clock back to the Cavaliers; and if anything like the Southern legend existed before the War of 1812, its fragments do not form a living unit. The legend gathers force in the time of Andrew Jackson. Its components include soil exhaustion (the old plantation is always on the point of bankruptcy), cotton culture, slavery (but only of the domestic sort), the vogue of oratory,[66] the search for a usable Southern past as intersectional tension grew, the special vogue of British romanticism among the Southern gentry,[67] and after the Civil War a determined effort to romanticize a vanished culture. Elements of the plantation legend are early evident in such novels as George Tucker's *The Valley of Shenandoah* (1824) and John Pendleton Kennedy's *Swallow Barn* (1832; revised, 1851). Inflated rhetoric is already rampant in William Wirt's *Sketches of the Life of Patrick Henry* (1817), which gives us the "Demosthenes of America" delivering the famous "Liberty or death" speech, in some degree the invention of Wirt and more nearly like Cicero than it is like the Greek.[68]

Southern rhetoric expressed an important part of the Southern tradition, in character not different from flamboyance anywhere, but in its universality within the region it was a troubling barrier to intellectual life. Orators insisted upon the iterative theme and the expectation of stock responses. Here is William Lowndes Yancey denouncing the North in 1860 and picturing the horrors that must follow the election of Lincoln:

> Suppose this is the case—that the frontiers of the country will be lighted up by the flames of midnight arson, as it is in Texas; that towns are burned; that the peace of our families is disturbed; that poison is found secreted throughout the whole country in immense quantities; that men are found prowling about our land distributing that poison in order that it may be placed in our springs and our wells; with arms and ammunitions placed in the hands of this semi-barbarous people [the slaves], what will be our fate? . . . Can you expect any people of spirit or courage, true to themselves, true to their firesides, true to their own families . . . to give up all regard for the Constitution, permit it to be trampled under foot, to acknowledge this "higher law" government, to give it their assent? [69]

This outburst is no worse than the rant of the Northern abolitionists; the Southern difficulty was the lack of any efficient intellectual counter-criticism. The following passage shows the extreme to which Southern rhetoric could go:

> Woman is earth's angel. She is the morning star of man's infancy, the day star of his manhood, and the evening star of his old age. This is her golden opportunity to play an angel's part in her country's salvation. Let but the daughters of the North and the daughters of the South meet with their floral offerings annually on some great national memorial day on the fields where our heroes fought their last battle and sleep their last sleep, and let their flowers mingle their fragrance as they fall together with their hearts upon the lowly pillows of the loved and lost. Let them kneel together there, and let their prayers for the welfare of their common country rise, as it were, on the wings of one breath and soar to heaven; angels will be waiting at the portals of the skies to bear them to the footstool of the great white throne. God will hear and answer them, and fraternal feelings will revisit this riven land, man will recognize again in man his brother, sectional prejudice will pass gradually away, radicalism will be rebuked, and peace and prosperity, harmony and happiness will crown a national glory and grandeur without a parallel in the annals of ages.[70]

The sentiment is admirable, and possibly such a passage does not differ from elegant oratory in the North; the point is that defeat increased Southern satisfaction with this emotional fustian. From the beginning the South had relished a highly ornamental style.[71] The region had not failed to produce some tough-minded thinkers, but these latter tended to be smothered in the sea of rhetoric that swept over them.[72]

I have hinted at concepts of chivalry and the Cavaliers. Perhaps, as Hubbell suggests, these go back to Burk's *History of Virginia* (1804–1816). The ring tournament and the Mardi Gras carnival in New Orleans with its excessive amount of fake royalty and aristocracy clearly continue the tradition. In the ring tournament "knights" bearing such titles as Knight of the Red Cross, Knight of Bowling Green, Knight of the Golden Fleece, Knight of Darkness, and so on "jousted" in a "tourney"; that is, armed with a lance, on a galloping horse, each tried to transfix a ring suspended in air. The winning knight crowned some Southern belle the queen of love and beauty, and maids of honor were selected to accompany and support the queen.[73] The New Orleans Mardi Gras and other municipal festivities like it are too familiar to require description: "Comus" seems to

date from 1857, the "Carnival Rex" from 1872.[74] As for the doctrine
that this sort of thing did not affect actual life, let us remember that
Philip Pendleton Cooke once galloped twenty miles across country to
throw a bouquet into the window of a female cousin (said to be the
original of the girl in his poem, "Florence Vane"), George Tucker
argued that dueling maintained the better features of our national
manners, Francis Orray Ticknor wrote during the Civil War:

> But aye the Golden Horseshoe Knights
> Their old Dominion keep,
> Whose foes have found enchanted ground,
> But not a knight asleep, . . .

and John Esten Cooke, though he confided to his private notebooks
that war is only fit for brutes and brutish men, publishing *Mohun* in
1869, was capable of passages like this: "They will remember the
martial form of Stuart at the head of his *sabreurs,* how the columns
of horsemen thundered by the great flag; how the multitudes
cheered, brightest eyes shone, the merry bands clashed, the gay bugles rang; how the horse artillery roared as it was charged in mimic
battle." At Gettysburg, he wrote, "every man's veins seemed to run
with quicksilver instead of blood. Every cheek was glowing. Every
eye flashed with superb joy and defiance" as "if under the effect of
champagne or laughing gas." [75] Sidney Lanier's *Tiger-Lilies* (1867),
though part of the dialogue pretends to be common speech, is likewise afflicted with this romantic rhetoric.

If the war for Southern independence had been a total disaster, insistence upon a Southern literature continued. This campaign came,
so to speak, in three successive phases. The first, illustrated by
Mohun and *Tiger-Lilies,* not to mention that earlier masterpiece of
sentimentality, Augusta J. Evans Wilson's *Macaria; or, Altars of Sacrifice* (1864), continued the Scott-Bulwer-Byron strain. In the 1870s
there began an enormous library of *pièces justicatives*—histories, personal memoirs, biographies, documents, disillusioned fiction about
the process of Reconstruction such as Albion W. Tourgée's *A Fool's
Errand* (1879); and the first fine runnings of Southern local color, for
examples: Joel Chandler Harris's *Uncle Remus; His Songs and Say-
ings* (1880), collected from various newspapers; Irwin Russell's Negro
dialect poems, G. W. Cable's *Old Creole Days* (1879); and the stories
of "Charles Egbert Craddock" (Mary Noailles Murfree), which began

appearing in *Lippincott's Magazine* in 1874. In 1869 the Southern Historical Society was founded. It was reorganized in 1873, and for a time after 1896 there was a rival organization, the Southern History Association. In 1889 the first general organization of Confederate veterans was formed, and in 1894 the United Daughters of the Confederacy was founded. The creation of these associations tended to solidify a reading public in the South and coincided with the spread of local-color literature and the popularity of historical romance in Britain and the United States.[76] What better theme for historical romance than Southern colonial life, or the Lost Cause, the latter an idea now being bruited about?

The result was the weaving of a shimmery literary veil not only between the South and the rest of the country but also between the South and reality itself. Charming tales of humor and sentiment such as F. Hopkinson Smith's *Colonel Carter of Cartersville* (1891) must, a fortiori, be true pictures; gallant stories of love and honor in the colonies like Mary Johnston's *To Have and to Hold* (1900) must reflect history. And on a lower literary level collections like E. R. Brooks's *Stories of the Confederacy* (1912) must be correct—the compiler enriched Southern prose with this valuable paragraph:

> The matrons of Rome, who poured their jewels into the treasury for the public defence; the wives of Prussia, who with delicate fingers clothed the defenders against French invasion; the mothers of our Revolution, who sent forth their sons, covered with prayers and blessings, to combat for human rights, did nothing of self-sacrifice truer than did these women of our fallen Confederacy, which was wiped from the map of the world April 9, 1865 (p. 15).

The vogue of Booker T. Washington, who addressed the Cotton States and International Exposition in Atlanta in 1895, showed how much the South loved the Negro, whereas W. E. B. Du Bois, whose *The Souls of Black Folk* came out eight years later, was a "radical." All this the prescient Tourgée saw coming in 1868: "Within thirty years after the close of the war of rebellion popular sympathy will be with those who upheld the Confederate cause rather than with those by whom it was overthrown; our popular heroes will be Confederate leaders; our fiction will be Southern in its prevailing types and distinctively Southern in its character."

C. Alphonso Smith at Louisiana State University said ten years

later that the great advantage of the South over the North with respect to literature was having lost the Civil War, for "literature loves
a lost cause, provided honor be not lost." [77] Before one dismisses
these statements as excessive, let him reflect upon the popularity of
The Birth of a Nation, the film made from Thomas Dixon's *The
Clansman* (1905), the enormous reading public for Margaret Mitch
ell's *Gone with the Wind* (1936), and the general consensus that William Faulkner is one of the major novelists of the English-speaking
world. Moreover, accompanying the flowering of all this post-bellum
writing, there developed one of the most extraordinary literary discussions in the history of the United States—that concerning the nature and nurture of Southern letters and their relation to the cultural
health and economic and social welfare of this vast section of the republic. [78] One may grant that the dollar crosses all lines and that a
national depression affects all parts of the Union. If I have seemed to
lay undue stress upon Southern literature as an expression of "South-
ernness," it is because the insistent note in that literature continues
to persuade the South that Southerners even in the industrial age are
and propose to remain a special and peculiar people.

VI

The West was once all America. By the end of the Revolution its
eastern boundary had retreated to the Appalachians; by 1815 it
meant Kentucky, Tennessee, the "Old Northwest," and areas along
the lower Mississippi. Beyond that river lay the vague unknown of
the Louisiana Purchase. By 1861, though citizens of Wisconsin or
Ohio were still "Western men," the West, slowly metamorphosing
into the Great West, meant the trans-Mississippi world. Some, however, would put Washington, Oregon, and California in a separate
category partly because the last two of these states were admitted to
the Union in the 1850s, partly because of climatological peculiarities
affecting the coast to the line of the Cascades and the Sierras, and, in
the matter of rainfall, the area from San Francisco Bay to Puget
Sound. Settlements along the right bank of the Mississippi were,
moreover, often extensions of the Middle West, and the eastern
boundary of the Great West is a confusing problem of climate and
culture. As the prairies melt insensibly into the Great Plains, they
rise inexorably to a mile above sea level at Denver, and the climate,

particularly the rainfall, changes also. A line wandering between the 98th and the 100th meridians separates an arid region westward from an eastward area having an annual rainfall of from twenty to thirty inches, sufficient for standard agriculture. The area thus bounded makes an irregular belt from, on the one side, Brownsville, Texas, to Pembina, North Dakota, and on the other, Corpus Christi to Duluth, Minnesota. Here, at least for most of this fourteen-hundred-mile strip, the Middle West dissolves into the Great West. In its largest sense the Great West comprises two-thirds of the continental United States exclusive of Alaska, and falls into three divisions: the Great Plains, the mountain states, and the three states on the Pacific. Yet within these sub-areas there is an extraordinary topographical diversity: the eastern half of Montana, for example, belongs to the Great Plains, and eastern Washington, eastern Oregon, and much of southern California are arid. One must also allow for the basin of the Great Salt Lake.

During our half-century the West was an area at once beautiful and brutal, alluring and destructive, fertile and desolate, full of unparalleled wonders and incredible hardships with which nothing had prepared immigrants to cope. Size was greater, distance longer, mountains higher, canyons deeper, unshaded plains more terrifying or beautiful, deserts more hazardous than anyone had dreamed. Nature was a perpetual surprise, a continuing revelation, an endless peril, and a furtive trap. Extremes characterize the country. In California Mount Whitney rises to 14,495 feet; Death Valley, mainly in the same state, is 280 feet below sea level. The first reports on the wonders of Yellowstone Park were labeled lies. The Llano Estacado in western Texas runs to about 400 miles. Colorado has more than fifty mountains over 14,000 feet high. The Great West includes Iceberg Lake on Trail Ridge road in the Rockies, about 11,500 feet above sea level, and in 1913 the West recorded a temperature of 134 degrees Fahrenheit in Death Valley. The depth of the Grand Canyon of the Colorado and that of the Snake River exceed in measurement and terror anything else on the continent, but Leadville, once the highest mining town in the United States, makes the tourist gasp for breath. Nothing is more magnificent than the Grand Tetons, nothing more weird the Dakota Bad Lands, nothing more awe-inspiring than a sunset that paints the Sangre de Cristo Mountains in New Mexico with all the colors of the palette. The beautiful forty miles of

South Park in Colorado balance the cactus trees in the Saguaro National Monument near Tucson, and the timeless relics of the cliff dwellers, an indigenous part of the landscape, counterpoint crumbling ghost towns, intrusions into the landscape, in Idaho or Colorado.[79] An impression of age broods over these landscapes, many of them younger in geological time than their humbler equivalents east of the Mississippi, and this sense of eternity is mixed with delight, with awe, and with melancholy.

Let us add the alternations of plenitude and desolation once characteristic of the Great West—the hundreds of thousands of buffalo, the endless herds of deer, antelope, and mountain sheep, the innumerable prairie dogs, the snakes and lizards, the sea gulls of the Great Salt Lake, the bears, the rivers filled with fish, and always the Indians, elusive and eternal, keeping to an ageless sedentary culture in the Southwest, a nomadic culture in the North, unpredictable, cruel, burning with a justifiable sense of outrage as the government failed to protect lands ceded or defined for Indian use, waging an intermittent warfare against the whites, a people who like the Celts always went forth to battle and always fell.

Driving in comfort over deserts where once prospectors perished or across mountain passes that formerly took their toll of human life, the modern tourist has difficulty in picturing what the West was like between 1865 and 1900, nor do commercialized rodeos, dude ranches, "Old Western" saloons, and the glitter of Las Vegas or Reno tell him much he can believe. I therefore select at random some representative descriptions from an immense narrative literature.

A prairie fire was one of the terrors of the plains, a theme of romantic paintings by Catlin, Bierstadt, and others. Here is Catlin's vivid description of such a catastrophe:

> The prairies burning form some of the most beautiful scenes that are to be witnessed in this country, and also some of the most sublime. Every acre of these vast prairies (being covered for hundreds and hundreds of miles, with a crop of grass, which dies and dries in the fall) burns over during the fall or early in the spring, leaving the ground of a black and doleful colour. . . . These scenes at night become indescribably beautiful, when their flames are seen at many miles distance, creeping over the sides and tops of the bluffs, appearing to be sparkling and brilliant chains of liquid fire . . . hanging suspended in graceful festoons from the skies.

But there is yet another character of burning prairies, that requires . . . a different pen to describe—the war, or hell of fires! where the grass is seven or eight feet high, as is often the case for many miles together . . . and the flames are driven forward by the hurricanes, which often sweep over the vast prairies of this denuded country. . . . The fire . . . before such a wind, travels at an immense and frightful rate, and often destroys, on their fleetest horses, parties of Indians, who are so unlucky as to be overtaken by it . . . the dense column of smoke that is swept before the fire . . . alarming the horse, which stops and stands terrified and immutable, till the burning grass which is wafted in the wind, falls about him, kindling up in a moment a thousand new fires, which are instantly wrapped in the swelling flood of smoke that is moving on like a black thunder-cloud, rolling on the earth with its lightning's glare, and its thunder rumbling as it goes.[80]

Here is Albert D. Richardson, a professional writer, who, after narrating the hardships of a climb up Pike's Peak, expatiates on the view:

Eastward for a hundred miles, our eyes wandered over dim, dreamy prairies, spotted by dark shadows of the clouds, and the deeper green of the pineries; intersected by faint, gray lines of road, and emerald threads of timber along the streams; and banded on the far horizon with a girdle of gold. . . . Eight or ten miles away, two little gems of lakes were set among the rugged mountains, holding shadows of the rocks and pines in their transparent waters. Far beyond, a group of tiny lakelets, "eyes of the landscape," glittered and sparkled in their dark surroundings like a cluster of stars. . . . To the west, the South Park, and other amphitheaters of rich floral beauty—gardens amid the utter desolation of the mountains—were spread thousands of feet below us; and beyond, peak upon peak, until the pure white wall of the Snowy Range rose to the infinite blue of the sky. . . . Upon the north side of the Peak, a colossal plowshare seems to have been driven fiercely down from the summit to the base, its gaping furrow visible seventy miles away, and deep enough in itself to bury a mountain of considerable pretension. Such enormous chasms must the armies of the Almighty have left in heaven when, to overwhelm Lucifer and his companions, "From their foundations loosening to and fro,/ They plucked the seated hills with all their load,/ Rocks, waters, woods, and by the shaggy tops/ Uplifting, bore them in their hands." [81]

In 1869 Samuel Bowles wrote of a thunderstorm in Breckenridge Pass, about twelve thousand feet high:

A cold storm gathered upon the snow-fields above us, wheeled from peak to peak in densely black clouds, and soon broke in gusts of wind, in vivid lightning, in startling close and loud claps of thunder, in driving snow, in pelting hail, in drizzling rain. We were below the storm's fountain, but near enough to see all its grand movements, to feel its awful presence, to be shaken with fear, to gather inspiration. The rapidity of its passage from side to side, from peak to peak, was wonderful; the crashing loudness of its thunderous discharges awful; one moment we felt like fleeing before the Lord, the next charmed and awed into rest in His presence.

But it was dreary enough, when the thundering and the flashing ceased, and the clouds stopped their majestic movement, and hung in deep mists over all the mountains and the valleys, and the rain poured ceaselessly down. . . . It seemed a long ride down mountain side and through valley to Hamilton,—woods that made us feel even more pitiful; open valleys that made the rain more pitiless; streams twisted out of place and shape by ruthless miners; desolated cabins, doorless, windowless,—even the storm was more inviting.[82]

In 1870 John C. Van Tramp describes a ride of eighty miles from one water hole to the next, a ride known as the *Jornada del Muerto,* or journey of death, and expatiates on its emotional effects:

Sometimes the trail led us over large basins of deep sand, where the trampling of the mules' feet gave forth no sound; this added to the almost terrible silence, which ever reigns in the solitudes of the desert, rendered our transit more like the passage of some airy spectacle, where the actors were shadows instead of men. Nor is this comparison a constrained one, for our way-worn voyagers, with their tangled locks and unshorn beards (rendered white as snow by the fine sand with which the air in these regions is often filled), had a weird and ghostlike look, which the gloomy scene around, with its frowning rocks and moonlit sands, tended to enhance and heighten. There were other matters, too, to render the view impressive: scattered along our route we found numerous skeletons of horses, who at some former period had dropped down and died by the wayside.[83]

In contrast, here is C. H. Crawford publishing in 1898 his memories of a cloudburst near the Humboldt Mountains in the Owyhee River country (Nevada-Oregon):

It commenced to pour. How can I describe it truthfully, for it seemed like we were all going to be drowned as we traveled on, and even after we had taken shelter behind an adobe building, which was fast melting away, it seemed no better. The only idea that I can give of that storm is to say that the little cloud which came floating over us was like a cistern, a fourth of a mile in diameter and the same in height, filled with water to the brim when all at once the bottom fell out and that immense body of water all came down at once. In a few moments our once dry gulch was a raging torrent, at least thirty feet wide, but we had taken refuge behind an adobe saloon which was located on the ground above the torrent that went rushing past us. The saloon keeper saw his saloon building melting away like wax before a blazing fire and he stood and cursed his maker for sending a storm that had ruined his business and broken his bottles of rum. Below the house, perhaps a hundred and fifty yards, the hills closed in forming a wall on each side of the creek while the only road through that mountain gorge was down this stream which had so lately been nothing but a dry gulch. . . . the water rose fifteen or twenty feet in height leaving its mark on the rocky walls. The flood rolled large rocks out on to the Humboldt flat that must have weighed several tons.[84]

Possibly the grasshopper ("locust") plague in the Dakota country belongs with my paragraph on the plenitude of "animated nature" in the Great West, but its primitive and elemental quality classes it with the experiences I have illustrated. Grasshoppers came at irregular intervals (the seven-year cycle seems to be a misnomer) to plague the land throughout the nineteenth century. Here is a representative description:

It came in disguise, masquerading as a welcome rain cloud that blotted out the sun and cast its great shadow over the land. But as the cloud drifted nearer, [the settler] heard a low, humming sound like the beating of distant wings; the great gray mass resolved itself into millions of locusts which swooped down on the green crops and covered the whole prairie with a crawling, hopping, shimmering blanket. The incessant sound of myriad crunching mandibles on the tender stalks roused the family to futile action.

They beat at the loathsome invaders with clubs, pounded with sticks on kettles . . . set fires that were smothered . . . by the very juice of the frying creatures. And still they came, in a stream seemingly endless, blighting the grass and the green crops, stripping the bark from the trees. . . . trains had been halted by crushed millions of grasshoppers that made the rails slippery . . . other millions had perished in the Missouri River and washed up on the banks in foot-deep windrows whose stench could be smelled for miles. . . . There was no defense against such a foe. . . .

When General Sibley marched toward the Bad Lands in 1864, "the country of the Little Missouri was covered with myriads of grasshoppers, which had entirely destroyed the grass":

> The only thing spoken about here is the grasshopper. They are awful. They actually have eaten holes in my wagon covers and in the tarpaulins that cover my stores. A soldier on his way here lay down to sleep on the prairie in the middle of the day—the troops had been marching all night. His comrades noticed him covered with grasshoppers and awakened him. His throat and wrists were bleeding from the bites of the insects.

In 1868 at Devils Lake in North Dakota the bodies of the grasshoppers formed rows from four to six feet long and two to three feet wide.[85]

What could puny man achieve amid this combination of space and savagery? The environment dwarfed the individual, a moving speck on the Great Plains or an insect slowly crawling up the gigantic mountains or slowly moving through the difficult passes. It was a land at once beautiful and terrible, varied and monotonous, a region alternately alluring and repellent. Yet somehow it had to be explored and defined, somehow it had to be peopled and exploited.

If we except the Mormons, early settlements in western Oregon, and the gold rush to California, the striking migration into the Great West began in the 1850s, slowed during the Civil War, and resumed after Appomattox.[86] The peopling of the area was a movement that extended from 1850 to 1890, although this does not mean that Americans did not drift westward before 1850 or that they have not continued to do so since that time: witness the extraordinary increases in population of California and Arizona. But in the 1890s came the famous announcement of the "closing" of the frontier, an announcement mildly premature. In that decade or its successor industrial or wholesale exploitation replaced individual enterprise, so that by World War I Owen Wister's cowboy in *The Virginian* (1902) and Alfred Henry Lewis's "Old Cattleman" in the Wolfville books (1897–1908) had become as legendary figures as Captain John Smith and Daniel Boone. In a general sense the Great West was something that existed between 1865 and 1900, after which it turned into the "Old West," a land as mythical as the ante-bellum South.

For, to a greater degree than even the South, the West has been seen through a veil of illusion of its own creating. The newest part of the country is nevertheless known as the Old West. Nostalgia colors most of the books about it, each author being certain that he, and only he, remembers or discovers what has been and cannot come again. In that legendary area the farmer and his family live or die heroically or happily in their little old sod cabin on the plain; the cowboy and his buddies, forever young, gallop into town firing six-shooters from horses borrowed from Frederic Remington; the saloon and the dance hall are open day and night, faro and poker being occasionally interrupted by gunfire, which, once the corpses are removed, is followed by drinks all around; the miners take their cues from Bret Harte or *The Girl of the Golden West;* the United States cavalry either fights to the last man, as in pictures of Custer's last stand, or arrives at the penultimate moment to save the fort, the ranch house, the wagon train, or a white woman from a fate worse than death; the badman dies with his boots on, still retaining in his heart, however, an image of his dear old mother; the stagecoach dashes madly down the mountain passes; women are either worshipped, pitied, or paid for, according to their status as maid, wife, mother, or prostitute; the Indian perpetually grunts "How," makes a sly attempt at massacre, and slips into the sunset; men are judged by what they are or can do, not by race, religion, or origin; and the handshake is still a little stronger out where the West begins.

All legends have their basis in fact, and so does this. One example must serve for a thousand—that of the Western desperado. As early as 1836 Washington Irving sketched the type that was to become classical, the villainous Trampas of Wister's immortal *The Virginian,* in presenting Edward Rose in *Astoria:*

> The plot of Rose to rob and abandon his countrymen when in the heart of the wilderness, and to throw himself in the hands of a horde of savages, may appear strange and improbable to those unacquainted with the singular and anomalous characters that are to be found about the borders. This fellow, it appears, was one of those desperadoes of the frontiers, outlawed by their crimes, who combine the vices of civilized and savage life, and are ten times more barbarous than the Indians with whom they consort. Rose had formerly belonged to one of the gangs of pirates who infested the islands of the Mississippi . . . often perpetrating the most atrocious murders.

He plotted with other members of his gang to desert to the savages, carrying off with them the horses of the outfit and packages of goods and committing murder if necessary to their success. They collogued with the Crow Indians, but were outwitted by the noble-hearted leader of the party, Wilson P. Hunt, who "felt a sensation of relief as he saw the whole crew, the renegade Rose and all, disappear among the windings of the mountain, and heard the last yelp of the savages die away in the distance." [87] A thousand "Westerns" have revolved around Rose and his evil progeny.

Discussing the development of the upper Missouri Valley, Harold E. Briggs organized his study into six sections: the frontier of the miner, that of the buffalo (i.e., its hunters), that of the cattle-rancher, that of the sheep-rancher, that of the settlement, and that of agriculture. [88] Prelude this with the trapper and add that of the lumberman; remember that the trader accompanied these phases, sometimes as an itinerant with a packtrain and sometimes, turned sedentary, as the owner of a general store, and one has in the large the stages of Western development—albeit not all phases, nor necessarily in this order. For prudential reasons cattlemen took some care of the range, fighting off shepherds on the theory that sheep spoiled the grass, and making life unpleasant for "nesters" (settlers) fencing off farm lands in the open range. Other waves of development unfortunately ravaged more than they conserved and created islands of ugliness and waste in the solitude and majesty of nature. The huntsman slaughtered the buffalo and much else, leaving behind him rotting meat, stinking hides, and quantities of bones. The miner violated the beauty of stream and forest and constructed for his temporary abode and as cover for his machinery some of the ugliest towns ever built on the continent. [89] As early as 1863 John William Draper grimly observed that "agriculture has never been practised in the United States. We are miners, not farmers." [90] He was summarizing the lesson of Edmund Ruffin in his pioneer volume on soil renewal, *An Essay on Calcareous Manure* (1832), [91] and reflecting the indifference of "practical" farmers to scientific agriculture. The abandoned farms of New England, New York, and Pennsylvania and the exhausted soils of the South held no warnings for settlers swarming behind the plow that broke the plains, who thought that rain follows the plow, and discovered too late that traditional Eastern agriculture would not do in the West. They helped to induce a series of agricultural disasters unparalleled in American history. So good a Westerner as Wallace Stegner is eloquent on the consequences of their blindness to the warning of John Wesley Powell's *Report on the Lands of the Arid Region of the United States:*

> Much western history is a series of lessons in consequences. That is what the busted homesteaders straggling back from western Kansas in the early 1890s were getting; or the cattlemen counting carcasses and salvaging hides in the corners of the barbed-wire fences after the Big Die-up of 1886–87; or the politicians who looked up one day in Washington, D. C. in 1934 and saw the sky over the Potomac darkened with Plains dust; or the residents of Willard, Utah, who on an afternoon in the summer of 1924 scrambled onto the railroad embankment during a shower and watched a flash flood from the cut-over mountain-side fill their fields and houses with twelve feet of mud and gravel; or the Dustbowl farmer who remarked that the best place to locate a farm in Colorado was over in eastern Kansas; or the lawyers endlessly debating the rights of the several states to the waters of western rivers. What works in a wet country does not necessarily, or even likely, work in a dry one, and when a mistake has been made—when a watershed has been logged off or the range overgrazed or a sloping field gullied by carelessly handled irrigation water— the wounds do not heal naturally as they would in a country of ample rain, but grow worse unless they are actively stopped by such rescue operations as total rest of the land, watershed planting, range re-seeding, and the brushing and damning of gullies.[92]

In a general sense, though the conservation movement made a good beginning in 1890 with John Muir's campaign to save the Yosemite from the devastation of sheep-grazing and made important advances under the presidency of Theodore Roosevelt, the half-century never really awoke to the damage "pioneering" had done. Heroic individualism was supposed to compensate for anything. When, as often happened, the subsistence farmer gave up the struggle and was replaced or preceded by bonanza ranches, the result was too often what Sidney Lanier shrewdly noted in 1880—the destruction of human values evident in large-scale industry during these decades. His analysis concerned the Grandin farm near Fargo, which had about five thousand acres in wheat, and

> where five hands do all the work during the six winter months, while as many as two hundred and fifty must be employed in midsummer; where

the day's work is nearly thirteen hours; where, out of the numerous structures for farm purposes, but two have any direct relation to man . . .
where the economies are . . . wholly out of the power of the small
wheat-raisers . . . where the steam machine, the telephone, and the telegraph are brought to the last degree of skillful service. . . . It appears
plainly enough . . . from . . . all those associations which cluster about
the idea of the farm, large farming is not farming at all. It is mining for
wheat.[93]

Finally it should be observed in this context that a characteristic
"note" of Western life in these decades was restlessness and transience
—the prospector and the miner perpetually trudging from disappointment to a gleam of wealth and back to disappointment; the
cowboy always in the saddle; the lumberjack moving from one destroyed forest to another he will destroy; the migrant laborer going
from ranch to railroad and from railroad to ranch; the land speculator slipping from boom town to boom town; the Indian roving until
the Ghost Dance War of 1890 and the slow failure of the well-meant
Dawes Act settled him on a reservation, at least for a time.[94]

But it is easy to be wise after the event. The West was settled and
adaptations were made. In those vast spaces—Yavapai County in Arizona once included sixty-five thousand square miles, an area as big as
the six New England states together—men marched beyond the bor-
ders of law and had to invent codes and systems of their own.

The trapper and the mountain man had to take over Indian foods
and clothing, methods of trailing, hunting, and concealment, sexual
habits, and some portion of their code of ethics. The art of managing
range cattle was, like its vocabulary, borrowed in large measure from
the Mexican vaquero, and neither stock nor technique improved
greatly until these more primitive patterns were abandoned after the
hard winter of 1886–1887 had ruined the existing herds, railroads
had pushed farther into the open range, and ranch-owners learned
that longhorn steers were not necessarily the best sort of beef for the
world market. Placer mining and other primitive methods of extract-
ing gold were ancient techniques revived and modified in the West;
only when the surface ore became rare, and underground or stope
mining began to grow did scientific engineering become standard. If
most settlers mistakenly applied to dry-land farming methods traditional back home, a minority learned better; for example, irrigation
was successfully practiced by the Mormons. Though there was noth-

ing new about Western stagecoach lines with their stations and relays of horses, the nature of the terrain developed special skills in the drivers, just as river transportations, ranging from canoes to steamboats, given the uncertainty of Western waters, called for special aptitudes in those who drove or piloted the boats.

Such adaptations were to be expected. More significant was the emergence of certain social patterns and their long-run political results. If man was to survive in the Great West, he had to adopt two opposing patterns of behavior: a capacity to operate within a fusion of democracy and dictatorship, and an ability to live an individual, often an isolated, life. Social order was necessary to survival in areas beyond the reach of conventional law, and groups in the West developed almost instinctually little democracies under leaders who might exercise unusual dictatorial powers, virtually military in character, during an emergency. Life in the West was therefore both communal and individualistic.

The greatest of all American communal enterprises was of course the Church of Jesus Christ of Latter-day Saints, patterned on the economy of the ancient Jews to a degree beyond the dreams of seventeenth-century Massachusetts. It was organized around a sacred and peculiar book. It had a high priest in the person of the president of the church, who alone could receive revelations like a later Moses and whose mandates could be final; elders corresponding to the ancient judges; a people divided and governed after the manner of the tribes of Israel; a distrust of "Gentiles" that sometimes deepened into war and massacre; [95] a holy of holies; tithing; polygamy; and in its beginning the assumption that social happiness rests upon a pastoral and agrarian culture.[96] All this of course was later modified. But the immigrant train toiling over the plains and through the mountains adopted, like the Pilgrims in Plymouth harbor, a self-created code of regulations, electing a leader, setting up simple rules, and agreeing to obey the commands of the chief. The cattle outfit operated under an admirable, though unwritten, code that placed care for the moving herd, cooperation in any emergency, Homeric hospitality, the repulse of enemies, and the punishment of those who broke the code, far above any such city concept as an eight-hour day or a jealous division of labor. The boss of the moving outfit had the responsibility of the captain on an ocean liner, and so long as the cowhand accepted wages from his employer, his loyalty was to the community whether on the trail or on the range. Only after he was paid off was he on his own.

So, too, when there was a rush to some new mining discovery, anarchy would have resulted if a form of government somewhat after the fashion of Rousseau's primitive state had not been quickly set up.[97] From these mining camps developed a complex code of claims, dips, shares, lodes, and other matters, not to speak of the use of running water, that strongly influenced Western law. There grew up professional or vocational associations parallel with and sometimes anterior to county or territorial government [98] and in intention on the side of law; and lawlessness itself was organized—even groups of cattle rustlers had their code. Moreover, in a region often beyond the reach of formal legal processes and sometimes contemptuous of them, or in communities like San Francisco in one stage of its development, when law seemed to have broken down and organized crime threatened to take over, vigilantes operated in the name of justice, usually simulating the ancient Anglo-Saxon pattern of jury trial before the offender was hanged.[99] Religion seems not to have produced many of these quasi-spontaneous societies. A variety of deism satisfied this masculine world, and the minister was apparently looked upon as a fifth wheel except at burials, weddings, and christenings. As settlements developed, churches developed also, but the incompatibility of middle-class value judgments in the settled East with the ethos of Western life was not easily erased. To this generalization there is an important exception over and beyond the Mormons: when companies of Germans, Norwegians, Bohemians, Poles, Russians, and others from the Old World came to take up land in the Great West, they not infrequently came as congregations bringing their church organizations with them, and in such communities the Lutheran minister, the Roman Catholic priest, and his Orthodox equivalent enjoyed a prestige and exerted an authority not yielded to a bourgeois American clergyman.

In the earlier decades Western society was in fact heavily masculine, and much is made of the resulting egalitarianism. Egalitarianism, however, had its limits. Except in individual cases, it did not include Indians, Mexicans, the Chinese, or the Negro. Hatred of the Indians is understandable not only because of Indian cruelty but also because it is natural to hate whomever one has deeply wronged, and white intrusion into Western lands specifically reserved for Indian use is one of the less honorable facets of Western history. In the Southwest the "Anglos" and the Mexicans got along well enough by the device of living in separate cultures; yet, despite all that Americans owed to the Mexican tradition, that unfortunate people were usually kept below the salt. Negroes suffered less discrimination, in the main because they were a rarity, but they were confined to meaner walks of life. Western discrimination against the Chinese, however, is somewhat more mystifying. Members of this great branch of the human family were imported to build railroads and perform a variety of menial tasks, but they were not permitted to take up mining claims and were subjected to brutal treatment in San Francisco and elsewhere.[100] Wyoming was admitted to the Union in 1890 as the "Equality State"; but in living memory restaurant doors in Wyoming towns have borne signs to the effect that Mexicans, Negroes, and Indians were excluded.

Until the rise of wealthy families in San Francisco and a few other places (and with the exception of the status retained by one or two of the great Spanish families in California and the Southwest), within the confines of the white race Western society did tend to accept men and women at their proved values. Hence it is not inconsistent to find this masculine universe, or at least much of it, ready to adopt woman suffrage, willing to accept colonies of foreigners as entitled to their special ways of life, and prepared to allow the individual considerable latitude in getting wealth, spending it, fulfilling personal and sometimes eccentric desires, playing practical jokes, and exercising justice outside the law, provided always the male subscribed by his conduct to an unwritten but powerful code.

Individual violence is supposed to be a colorful element in Western history, a tradition supported by dime novels, "Westerns" in the movies or on television, the fame, often artificial, of this or that bandit, cattle rustler, card sharp, or professional killer, not to overlook epic-minded sheriffs who shot it out and won. Life in the West was sometimes violent and bloody; Indian wars, outlaws, feuding, and vendettas, and occasional crimes of passion can be authenticated.[101] But it would be difficult to prove statistically or otherwise that the West was more given to violence in these decades than was the East with its murderers, bank robbers, and other criminals quite as vicious as anything beyond the Mississippi. It must be remembered that the cowboy was under a strict, quasi-military discipline, and that the miner who did not attend to business was not likely to make it. Undoubtedly the great open spaces gave opportunity for roaming banditti of one sort or another, but Eastern slums also offered excellent opportunity for concealment and disguise. It does not seem, on reflection, that the Johnson County War of 1892 was half as bloody as the Homestead strike in Pennsylvania that same year, and if Federal troops had to intervene during the strike at the silver mines in the Coeur d'Alene country, Federal troops intervened almost simultaneously in the Pullman strike of 1894.

Possibly because land seemed to be illimitable, the ownership of real property, except in the mining world, did not produce the violence that might have been predicted from disputed claims. And claims were disputable. Some titles went back to vague grants by the Spanish kings; some were cloudy because of Mexican law; some were doubtful as a result of the dispute over the Oregon boundary, the same acreage having been granted in good faith by the British and by the American governments. Some claims were so vast (like the King Ranch or the JA Ranch that Goodnight created in the Palo Duro arroyo in the Texas Panhandle) that nobody knew where the boundaries were. Thousands of acres had been granted to railroads, but it was not always clear what acres were involved. And what were the elusive boundaries of Indian reservations, which no white man was bound to respect anyway? The national government sold land, and so did the state or territorial government, and sometimes it was the same acreage, precise surveying being difficult. Squatters had a habit of moving in or moving on, and the doctrine of squatter sovereignty, though modified, had not died with the passing of Stephen A. Douglas. Only in mining were the disputes really bitter.

It is important to note a curious reversal of land development in the Great West. East of the Mississippi, railroads had sought out towns; west of the Mississippi, they often created them, whereupon the railroad or the speculator or both campaigned to persuade somebody to inhabit a town, and afterward launched a propaganda campaign to get farm and ranch land taken up in order to support the trading center.[102] If this was not everywhere true, it was common enough to cast doubt on the theory that land-hungry Americans flocked into the agricultural Eden of the Great West. The doctrine can of course be supported by the epic rush to take up Oklahoma land in 1891,[103] but the picture of a spontaneous, individualistic rush of settlers westward requires modification. In the earlier years wagon-trains had to be organized, and not every land-seeker had the capital to participate. Historical emphasis has necessarily been on those who went and stayed, but it forgets those who turned back and spread disturbing reports about the cost, the danger, the isolation, and the hardships of the enterprise. The speculator, furthermore, was as unconscionable a plague as the grasshopper, and fraudulent "deals" were unfortunately as common then as they were in later real-estate booms, with the added difficulty that courts and attorneys were usually far away.

But the most important reason for questioning the so-called safety-valve theory of the peopling of the West appears in the necessity railroads, territories, and states were under to organize great land-selling campaigns in the East or in Europe. These campaigns were skillful, enormous, and expensive; they involved pamphlets, posters, special agents, lecturers here and abroad, low rates on steamship and railroad, assurance that schools, churches, banks, and towns would be financed, and arrangements about taxes.[104] Immigration thus induced seems to have been as common as what may be called spontaneous and individualistic migration. In his admirable study, *North Dakota: A Human and Economic Geography* (Fargo, 1956), Melvin E. Kazeck discusses the remarkable campaigns of the land commissioners of the Northern Pacific and Great Northern Railroads to lure settlers into North Dakota, the population of which rose from 3000 in 1870 to 646,872 in 1920. Large fractions of this increase, he says, came from abroad, usually in groups and colonies—from Norway, Canada, Russia, Denmark, Sweden, Poland, Czechoslovakia, and so on, and he notes how many counties in the state bear the marks of this international migration. Doubtless North Dakota may be a special case; doubtless the problem of the size of the individual farm made some difference; doubtless no similar ethnographical change appears in Utah. Nevertheless considerations of this order throw some doubt on the simplistic notion that the unemployed from the cities flocked westward during a depression.[105]

But within less than half a century after the Civil War twelve Western states were admitted to the Union, seven of them in the two decades from 1880 to 1900. In the nation as a whole, and notably in the Senate, if one adds Oregon, Kansas, and Nevada, admitted earlier, the Great West was a major political force. Between 1865 and 1915 it ceased to be the frontier; it developed its special grievances, and until the defeat of Bryan in 1896 it threatened to control the monetary policy of the United States. But in the 1890s the individual enterpriser gradually yielded to corporate control; heavy industry, scientific mining, huge lumbering companies, scientific stock-raising and, though not sufficiently, scientific agriculture remade the West. The space and the scenery remained much as they had been, but the area increasingly oriented itself toward problems created and dominated by the big cities from Kansas City to San Francisco, from Seattle to Salt Lake, from Denver to Los Angeles. In this sense the concept of the Old West as nostalgia is justified, and it is perhaps significant to the historian that such books as Walter Prescott Webb's *The Great Plains* (1931) and Henry Nash Smith's *Virgin Land* (1950) would probably not have been possible during the decades of the buffalo, the miner, the nester, and the open range.

III

The Age of Energy

Power when wielded by abnormal energy is the most
serious of facts.

—HENRY ADAMS

I

THE AMERICAN CIVIL WAR was the first great modern war. Napoleon had exploited speed and the massing of force as instruments of victory, but the rapidity of his armies was still that of the foot soldier, and his concentration of artillery to make a gap in the opposing line did not differ essentially from the impact upon the enemy of the Macedonian phalanx. As late as the Crimean War troops were principally transported by sailing vessels. Even in the Civil War essential military elements were lacking, many had to be improvised, and there was a feeling of amateur effort during the early months of the conflict. One thinks of the incredible camp sanitation, the even more incredible food, the irregular enlistment periods, the conflict between the authority of the state and the authority of the general government, the ghastly, if well-intentioned, medical service, the long and tortuous road to centralized command. Generals did not understand that in modern war cavalry was no longer a weapon of assault upon infantry supported by heavy guns, nor realize that its essential function was to act as the eyes of the staff. One thinks of the uselessness of the Confederate cavalry at Gettysburg, off on a raid and unable to supply Lee with necessary information.

The armies fought with any firearms they could procure. The War Department in Washington failed for years to recognize merit in many a modern weapon; the standard, though not the universal, equipment of the Union infantry was a muzzle-loading percussion-cap .58 rifle, though breech-loading rifles (and carbines) were known. Besides the muzzle-loader some fifty other types of small arms were distributed to Federal regiments, each chambered for its own ammunition, some of them manufactured here and some abroad. The Confederates fought with a miscellany of small arms, attempts to run any considerable quantity of guns through the blockade having failed. The seceding states had of course a considerable supply of Colt's revolvers thoughtfully stored in Southern arsenals during 1860–1861 by John B. Floyd, Buchanan's Secretary of War.[1] They captured much material from the enemy,[2] and attempted to manufacture small arms themselves, but owing to the lack of proper machines and tools, the irregular supply of metals, and the want of an efficient force of skilled mechanics, the attempt was relatively unsuccessful.

In the beginning neither side had a competent navy, a competent medical service,[3] a competent service of supply, nor a competent provost-marshal general's staff. In 1861 the national army had numbered only about some seventeen thousand officers and men, and these were scattered over the West and Southwest and along the coasts. Enlistment was on a volunteer basis. When the war broke out, the state was still considered by both sides to be the principal furnisher of soldiers. Therefore, when a state-raised regiment was called into service there was confusion about primary allegiance. Some "militia" regiments in the South would not pass beyond state boundaries, and at First Bull Run a Wisconsin regimental surgeon refused to care for any wounded man unless he came from Wisconsin. Governors North or South authorized somebody to raise a regiment, usually commissioned him a colonel, often commissioned subordinate officers (who were sometimes elected by the troops themselves), and in the beginning appointed the regimental surgeon. In these and other respects the war was at first a war waged by amateurs. But it changed its character.

By the end of the struggle more than two and one-half million American males had at one time or another enlisted or been conscripted. On the Union side, once Grant became general-in-chief, there was unified strategy, something the Confederacy never achieved, partly because of states' rights, partly because Jefferson Davis fancied himself as a military strategist. Both sides were forced to institute a draft. Riots resulted; the measure was so bitterly resented on the Union side that in 1863, the month of Gettysburg, New York City, for example, was ruled for a week by a mob that hanged Negroes to lampposts, murdered army officers, and destroyed property. In the Confederacy some state governors—for instance, "Joe" Brown of Georgia—opposed conscription, blocked the appointment of officers by anybody but themselves, and sometimes refused both men and supplies to the principal Confederate forces because to send them would "weaken the state." Badly though it was administered, conscription was inevitable in a conflict, the total casualties in which (of all kinds) were about a million and the total desertions about four hundred thousand. This was an epic struggle, and the rapidity with which the combatants created modern, if imperfect, military organizations is among the wonders of American history.

Obviously in this respect the North was in a better position than was the South. One military historian remarks with asperity that Northern industry and Northern technicians, not Northern generals and untrained Northern troops, won the war. The enormous Federal armies and navies had to have guns, food, training camps, tents, ships, ambulances, hospitals, medical supplies, Bibles, calomel, clothing, shoes, scalpels, flags, frying pans, and much else. The demand for arms enabled Samuel Colt to double his factory at Hartford and led the Sharps Rifle Manufacturing Company to recover a bankrupt factory at Windsor, Vermont, and open a second one at Hartford. And of course the national arsenals were very busy—by 1863 the Springfield Armory was turning out twenty-five thousand stands of small arms a month, and textile factories, short of cotton, sometimes went in for the manufacture of weapons. The army had to be shod; and Gordon McKay, who had a monopoly of shoe-making machinery, became a millionaire. The army had to be clothed, and the ready-made clothing industry mushroomed; sewing-machine factories in the North made more than one hundred thousand machines a year in 1860. The army had to be fed; and Cyrus McCormick, who before the 1850s had dared to locate his principal plant at Chicago instead of Cincinnati, sold his reapers on the installment plan. Persons dealing in food found new ways of packaging or shipping it, and whole herds of beef cattle were sent by rail or went on the hoof to be slaughtered at central points, among them Washington, D.C. A navy had to be created, and somebody had to build, buy, or rent ships, usually at a profit. The symbiosis of modern war and modern industry is perfectly illustrated by the American Civil War.[4]

But if the war had its effect in quantity production, mass movements, wholesale purchases, the urge toward labor-saving devices, and the emphasis upon the validity of interchangeable parts in the manufacturing process, it had another effect. Novelty after novelty was introduced into the struggle: military orders sent by telegraph, the use of railways on a gigantic scale as an element in strategy, armored fighting ships, river gunboats,[5] the repeating rifle, however sparsely issued, the Gatling gun (1862), the observation balloon (not new), the camera (one remembers Brady's great Civil War photographs), the booby trap (those left by the Confederates when they evacuated Yorktown in the Peninsular Campaign seem to have been deeply resented), ether masks (a Southern invention), an organized sanitary service [6]—these and like innovations are part of the war. Another important creation was the national banking system, put into shape by 1864, the operation of which led James Bryce to marvel at the rapidity with which the huge war debt of the North was paid.

In the 1850s and 1860s other innovations were preparing. Thus the St. Mary's Canal connecting Lake Superior and Lake Huron was opened in 1855, ready to channel huge shipments of ore after the struggle to the expanding industrial cities of Ohio, Illinois, Indiana, and Pennsylvania. By 1857 California was producing $50,000,000 in gold. In 1859 F. L. Drake at Oil Creek, Pennsylvania, drilled the first oil well; and that year the Comstock Lode was opened in Nevada (Henry Comstock died a pauper), and Nevada, which applied for statehood in 1863 and got it in 1864, displayed an enthusiasm for the Union evident in Mark Twain's *Roughing It,* notably the chapter on the sale of the sack of flour for the United States Sanitary Commission. Naturally its three electoral votes went for Lincoln. In 1861 the first telegraph wire stretched to San Francisco, messages being interrupted from time to time by the Indians, who cut off pieces for purposes other than communication. In 1862 Congress passed the first of several bills to create a railroad to the Pacific coast. In 1863 John D. Rockefeller softly entered the oil industry. In 1865 Samuel Van Syckle built his first oil pipeline. In 1866 the Atlantic cable was at last really working. In 1869 Leland Stanford drove the last spike, a gold one, into a tie at Promontory Point, Utah, to complete a line of rails across the continent. Chicago was already the greatest lumber center in the world. Various patents and processes by Kelly and Bessemer were prophetically consolidated into the Bessemer Steel Company in Pennsylvania in 1866, the precursor of United States Steel. The Civil War did not directly "cause" inventions like these; but it dramatized ingenuity, it accustomed people to mass and size and uniformity and national action, it got them used to ruthlessness, it made clear the dominant place of energy in the modern state.

Indeed, the intellectual center changed as the old philosophical assumptions weakened or vanished. On the vast continent, most of it owned by this majestic empire, from which political philosophy seemed for a long time to disappear, any man of push and energy could make his fortune or go emphatically broke. There had been a doctrine of individuality before the Gilded Age, the product of Protestant ethic and Lockean psychology. Now individual activity, not philosophizing; the application of science to the material world, not civic virtue; entrepreneurship on a national or international scale,[7] not industry and frugality in the corner drygoods store—these were the changes in value that were to characterize a new epoch.

II

We have no good name for the period from the end of the Civil War to the opening of World War I, but I call this half-century the Age of Energy. I shall not use the term "energy" with scientific exactness. The word has many meanings. It may refer to force or vigor in style, particularly literary style, as when one says that Emerson's style is marked by energy. One may refer by energy to the exercise of power, to the actual operation, working or activity of man or thing, or to the product or the effect of such energy. One may mean by it personal vigor of action or utterance, as when one says that Theodore Roosevelt was characterized by energy. One may have in mind the individual power or capacity to produce such and such an effect, as in the phrase: "At least he had enough energy to run away." One may mean what the physicist tends to mean: the power of doing work possessed at some moment by a body or system of bodies, and speak of static or potential energy or energy of position. Common to all these meanings is the idea of energy as the power by which anything or anybody acts effectively to move or change other things or persons. In this rough general sense it may be said that the Age of Energy was distinguished by producing in two generations (perhaps one should include those born in an elder generation who came to maturity after the Civil War) some of the most extraordinarily energetic persons in American history, and that in the physical sense the period from 1865 to 1915 created or multiplied the number of prime movers [8] available to American industry in quantities undreamed of before that time by either engineer or physicist.

I suggest that as an idea energy is both amoral and ambiguous. It takes on a quality of utility or of morality, of evil or good intent, only in context. When, for example, an engineering project is found to waste energy, we regard waste as a mark of inefficiency, not of evil. Inefficiency is here an intellectual demerit. When energy is used or abused in a social or political context and when in such a context it harms the individual or society in some physiological, intellectual, ethical, or, for that matter, political or economic sense, one may fairly say that power is exerted for evil or in the contrary case for good. In many instances judgments will be mixed or variable. Thus in the Age of Energy Frederick W. Taylor's studies of the productive capacity of men working at machines as measured by the economy of their motions were sometimes twisted into glaring examples of the exploitation of labor by capital, and this judgment was turned into a charge of real or potential social evil. Many persons thought the devices used by the Standard Oil Company and other "trusts" to kill off competitors were wicked but, in the long run, the enormous cumulative capacity of such companies, constantly availing themselves of more efficient instruments for the production, management, and distribution of energy, was an economic good. One can say without being paradoxical that the vision of John D. Rockefeller, Sr., paralleled the vision of Walt Whitman—a picture of a happy, wasteless, and plentiful society. Evaluation of energy is always a little baffling, even in the world of engineering. Moral judgments of immediacy must be weighed against long-run social gains, and engineering judgments of utility must not be confused with ethical judgments of value. I postpone, therefore, the consideration of energy as industrialism, corporate management, the creation of prime movers, the transmission of power and other devices for the quick creation of wealth, and confine myself here to what I may call energy of personality as this expressed itself in the lives and the tastes of the successful during the Gilded Age and after.

Activism has long been thought to be a characteristic American quality. "Pioneers, O pioneers," sang Whitman, and contemporary social commentators sang the same chorus. "It is strange to see with what feverish ardour the Americans pursue their own welfare," wrote Tocqueville in 1840; and in 1861 Bayard Taylor in a lecture on "The American People" said the Americans were essentially a nervous people, excitable and ceaselessly active. In *The American Commonwealth* James Bryce remarked that in the United States "it is usually hard for any one to withdraw his mind from the endless variety of external impressions and interests which daily life presents, and which impinge upon the mind." "The type of mind which American conditions have evolved," he went on to say, "is quick, vigorous, practical, versatile," and he charged that it wants patience to bring ideals to perfection. Possibly Bryce's verdict was influenced by George Miller Beard's study, *American Nervousness: Its Causes and Consequences*, published in 1881. American nervousness, Beard thought, was on the increase because American civilization was the victim of technological advances and of urbanization. In 1901 Dr. John H. Girdner sought to apply the soothing hand of Christianity to the fevered brow of business energy. Let the victim learn altruism:

> Culture will cure a patient of this money mania, by reminding him that, at most, he has only a few years to stay on this planet, and can take nothing away with him. . . . It will bring him to a realizing sense of the fact that . . . the amount of his earthly possessions can have no sort of effect on his standing in a future state.

Christian culture can lure the New York stockbroker out of the treadmill of his calling, reduce his egotism, and make him a "citizen of the universe." [9]

Many elements of the Age of Energy are as old as human nature, but these motives coalesced with other components in the special social pattern that dominated the first phase of the Age of Energy, the Gilded Age. A spending economy replaced the Benjamin Franklin virtues. A philosophy of self-aggrandizement tended to overthrow or overshadow both republican virtue and Christian altruism, despite the growth in church membership and the increase of philanthropic giving and of charitable associations. The egalitarianism of an agrarian culture was swallowed up in what has come to be called social Darwinism, the latter regarded by sound thinkers of the age as the proper management of the universe. Viewed morally, the result was the Great Barbecue; viewed merely as the discharge of enormous energies, the Gilded Age is as fascinating as the Regency in England, the post-Napoleonic period on the Continent, and the Second Empire in France. The first of these spendthrift times was chronicled by Byron, the post-Napoleonic world was pictured by Balzac,[10] and the age of Louis Napoleon had its imaginative historian in Zola. Unfortunately, there is no American equivalent, since the novel by Twain and Warner which gave its name to the Gilded Age is curious rather than masterly, possibly the worst constructed novel ever put together by two intelligent men. It may be that Whitman's *Democratic Vistas* is the central literary document for the American era; Whitman had a vision of American democracy threatened with a sort of *Götterdämmerung,* though he saw light at the end of the story.

With all its waste, vulgarity, corruption, and silliness the Gilded Age accomplished more toward transforming the United States in a short time than did any earlier epoch. Equally, however, no previous age except the Civil War displayed such a passion for destruction. Energy fascinated the period. Energy was fiercely sought after by the North during the war years and as frenetically desired by the South; and when peace came, the accumulated energy of the North now balked of military expression, avidly sought other outlets. Inevitably this avidity was colored by the experience of war. There was a continent to ravage. The discovery that energy could be channeled into vast and profitable projects of destruction created in the era a kind of fierce, adolescent joy in smashing things—in stripping mountains to get at the ore, laying forests waste for their better timber, plowing up the plains whether normal crops could grow on them or not, slaughtering millions of bison, five animals being killed for every useful buffalo robe, scarifying whole counties with the poisonous fumes of smelters, polluting rivers with sludge from oil wells, slaughterhouses, and city sewage, driving business rivals to suicide in a stock-market crash, killing, maiming, or otherwise incapacitating factory workers for lack of elementary safety devices, seizing public lands by fraud and so preventing or postponing the possibility of conservation, erecting buildings so rickety they soon fell in; and, as a final ironic touch, crippling the business leaders with high blood pressure, too much food, too much drink, too much activity in a period when only women went to the seaside in the summer and vacations were thought a waste of time. The strikes of the period have all the aspects of war, being vast, bloody, and destructive—from the great railroad strike of 1877 with its pitched battles between the militia and the mob, to the anthracite coal strike of 1902, when the president of the Reading Railroad uttered his celebrated sentence: "The rights and interests of the laboring man will be protected and cared for, not by labor agitators, but by the Christian men to whom God in His infinite wisdom has given control of the property interests of the country." Small wonder that as late as 1891 Ignatius Donnelly, author of that anti-Utopia, *Caesar's Column,* pictured American development as ending in a general massacre.

It is difficult to assess verbal expression in comparative terms, but since the Age of Energy saw the flowering of what used to be called yellow journalism, it is fair to examine the language of the time. It must sometimes seem to the reader that writers—not the greater writers, but advertisers, journalists, propagandists, and the merely literate —sought to gain their effects by screaming. Thus in 1882 a production of *Uncle Tom's Cabin* in Chicago was advertised: "NEW AND BEAUTIFUL SCENERY, THE MAGNOLIA JUBILEE SINGERS, THE TRICK DONKEY 'JERRY,' AND THE FAMOUS TRAINED SIBERIAN BLOOD-HOUNDS, the most savage of their species, which will engage in the Realistic Picture of the terrible SLAVE HUNT." One suspects that the cowed canines who crossed the stage were actually nothing of the sort. The Baker Library of the Harvard Business School contains an incredible collection of patent-medicine advertisements from the period. One "before and after" card begins: "MISERABLE! MISERABLE! Yes, he looks miserable! He is BILIOUS; and biliousness with its killing complaints—bad unnatural taste, loss of appetite, imperfect sleep, headache, chills, fever, etc.—do not tend to make anyone feel happy or cheerful." Another nostrum will "Positively Cure SLEEP-LESSNESS, PARALYSIS, OPIUM HABIT, DRUNKENNESS, HYSTERIA, NEURALGIA, SICK HEADACHE, SCIATICA, NERVOUS DYSPEPSIA, LOCOMOTOR ATAXIA, HEADACHE, OVARIAN NEURALGIA, NERVOUS EXHAUSTION, EPILEPSY, ST. VITUS' DANCE, NEURAESTHENIA, &c." A third proclaims in capital letters it will "POSITIVELY CURE" the backache in two hours and deafness in two days.[11] The placard that called together the open-air meeting in Haymarket Square, Chicago, read: "REVENGE! WORKING-MEN, TO ARMS! Your masters sent out their bloodhounds—the police; they killed six of your brothers at McCormicks this afternoon . . . If you are men, if you are the sons of your grandsires, who have shed their blood to free you, then you will rise in your might, Hercules, and destroy the hideous monster that seeks to destroy you. To arms, we call you, to arms!" One has to wait for the racial riots of the 1960s to equal this verbal recklessness.

Lest it be thought I quote only material addressed to the mob, I turn to the peerless Robert J. Ingersoll, whom Mark Twain thought the greatest orator he ever heard. Ingersoll said:

> I want you to know that every man that thinks the State is greater than the Union, is a Democrat. Every man that lowered our flag from the skies was a Democrat. Every preacher that bred bloodhounds was a Democrat. Every preacher that said slavery was a divine institution was a Democrat. . . . Every man who shot the emaciated maniac who happened to totter across the deadline,[12] with a hellish grin on his face, was a Democrat. . . . The keepers of Andersonville and Libby, those two wings that will bear the Confederacy to eternal infamy, were all Democrats. The men who proposed to give our Northern cities to the flames were all Democrats. . . . The men who wanted to assassinate Northern Governors were Democrats.[13]

The above example is from politics. Excess of language in religion may come out either as mawkishness or as invective. The great evangelist team of the period was Moody and Sankey. Here is a solo, once sung by Ira D. Sankey:

> When the dewy light was falling,
>   And the sky in beauty smiled,
> Came a whisper, like an echo,
>   From a pale and dying child;
>
> "Mother, in the golden region,
>   With its pearly gates so fair,
> Up among the happy angels,
>   Is there room for Mary there?
>
> "When my baby-sister calls me,
>   And you hear my voice no more,
> When she plays among the roses
>   By our little cottage door,

> Never chide her when you're angry—
>   Do it kindly and in love,
> That you both may dwell with Mary
>   In that sunny land above."

The force of bathos cannot further go; in fact Sankey had to give up the song.

The sermons of the Reverend Dwight Lyman Moody could on occasion also be tearful, but he could reach an equal excess in the other direction, as in a famous sermon on blood, and another comparing salvation to a city of refuge:

> Don't you know that death is on your track now, and is ready to have you a victim? Don't you know that he may be only a few years, a few weeks, a few days, or even a few moments only, from you? . . . Haste then to a place of refuge. If you are outside the city you perish; if you come within the walls of salvation you are secure.

Edwards has the same note of desperation, Pascal's famous wager has the same tone of urgency, but the Reverend Mr. Moody's pastoral style is somewhat below that of either.

What of imaginative expression generally? Here is a single sentence from that greatest of evangelical novels, *Ben Hur* (1880), part of the immortal chariot race. I italicize the action words:

> Out *flowed* the *many-folded lash* in his hand; over the backs of the *startled* steeds it *writhed* and *hissed*, and *hissed* and *writhed again and again*; and though it *fell* not, there was (*sic*) both *sting and menace* in its *quick report*; and, as the man *passed* thus from quiet to *resistless action*, his face *suffused*, his eyes *gleaming*, along the reins he seemed to *flash his will*; and *instantly* not one, but the *four as one*, *answered with a leap* that *landed* them alongside the Roman's car.

This, to put it mildly, is not the style of Henry James's *The Golden Bowl*. And for verse, here are some stanzas from Ella Wheeler Wilcox, the self-styled poetess of passion:

> On the white throat of the useless passion
>   That scorched my soul with its burning breath
> I clutched my fingers in murderous fashion
>   And gathered them close in a grip of death;
> For why should I fan, or feed with fuel,
>   A love that showed me but blank despair?

So my hold was firm, and my grasp was cruel—
    I meant to strangle it then and there!

I thought it was dead. But with no warning,
    It rose from its grave last night, and came
And stood by my bed till the early morning,
    And over and over it spoke your name.

.   .   .   .

A lighter sin or a lesser error
    Might change through hope or fear divine;
But there is no fear, and hell has no terror
    To change or alter a love like mine.[14]

If this is a touch excessive, excess was a characteristic of the writer. Mrs. Wilcox once wrote a poem that begins:

God and I in space alone
And nobody else in view,

which she submitted to Richard Watson Gilder, then editor of *The Century Magazine*. Gilder returned it on the ground that readers might just misunderstand Mrs. Wilcox's conception of herself and the Deity.

It is not here pretended, however, that hyperbole is an invention of the Age of Energy but only that hyperbole and violence were acceptable to its taste for strong flavors. To compare *Little Women,* which has no melodrama,[15] with *The Adventures of Tom Sawyer* and *The Adventures of Huckleberry Finn* is not merely to move from charming domesticity to a world of juvenile rebelliousness, but also into a universe of discourse in which melodrama and violence (consider the Indian Joe plot in the one book and the Shepherdson-Graingerford feud in the other) are considered necessary to make books about juveniles "go." But to discuss the complications of belles-lettres and stylistic development among the greater writers would take us far afield.[16]

Style is not something confined to writing, and the Age of Energy also nourished a wild variety of styles in architecture, furniture, clothing, the intercourse of Society, theatrical entertainments, and much else, commonly denigrated as American Victorianism. Styles exist for people and are created by them; and it may be wiser at this point to glance at some of the notable personalities of the Gilded

Age. Possibly the houses, the decorations, the values, and the parties of the Age of Energy were not any more grotesque than our own.

III

I have elsewhere noted the curious revival of the metaphor of piracy to characterize the lawlessness of financiers and industrial magnates in the Gilded Age, and also the curious parallelism of their values and their actions to those of the Italian mercantile princes of Renaissance.[17] Leading personalities of the age were as excessive in their egotism as was Ingersoll's oratorical style. The men suggest the buccaneers of the Spanish Main, the condottieri of the Italian Renaissance, the morality of Benvenuto Cellini, Machiavelli, and Cesare Borgia; and the women were often like the men. On the other hand, if the robber barons accumulate wealth, like the Medici they seek to patronize culture, and like the medieval feudal lords they turned to philanthropy for the salvation of their souls. They seek also in many cases to perpetuate a personal dynasty, which may or may not come off: the Rockefellers continue as great public leaders, but other families tend to validate the folk wisdom of shirt-sleeves to shirt-sleeves in three generations. In that earlier work I noted the incredible fusion of cruelty and culture, of coarseness and Christian philanthropy that characterizes the first generation of American millionaires. Their skill in economic exploitation, in creating combinations and trusts, or in such things as the Heinze-Daly copper war in Montana, the fight for a railroad empire in the Northwest, the buying up of courts and legislatures, senatorial elections and appointments to the federal bench, the manipulation of stock markets, the use of rebate, drawback, and simulated panic, prices artificially lowered and taxation artificially increased to crush a competitor—in sum, the epic of the Gilded Age and its aftermath—must be balanced against their founding of libraries and art museums, hospitals and institutes, the support of opera and orchestra, the creation of schools, colleges, and universities, the patronage half scornfully, half enviously extended to writers, musicians, painters, sculptors, decorators, fashion designers, and cooks, the beginnings of vast foundations for scholarship, scientific research, medicine, charity, and education.

I have said also that the parallel between the Fuggers of Augsburg

and the Rockefellers of New York or that between the Florentine
merchant princes and the Huntingtons of California or the Guggen-
heims of Colorado is close and instructive. It is also instructive to
remember that the palaces of Italian cities were in fact the models of
some of the palaces that once lined Fifth Avenue, and that the difference between the Farnese family building the first modern theater in
Parma and Samuel Insull and his friends building a lush Civic
Opera House in Chicago is minimal. Indeed, if Florence owes its
great art galleries to mercantile munificence, Chicago owes its great
Art Institute to the munificence of the Hutchinsons, the Spragues,
the Ryersons, the McCormicks, the Bartletts, the Fields, the Palmers,
and others. Gertrude Stein is supposed to have said to Mrs. Charles
B. Goodspeed of Chicago: "Never make the mistake of fraternizing
with artists—*command* them!" The saying is worthy of Cosimo de'
Medici.[18] The egotism of Venetian merchants, who thought the
world existed for their profit, precedes but does not surpass an attitude expressed, for instance, by Sam Wilkerson, an associate of Horace Greeley, who wrote back from Puget Sound: "There is nothing
on the American continent equal to it. Such timber—such soil—such
orchards—such fish—such climate—such coal—such rivers— . . .
And the whole of it is but the Western terminus of our Railroad . . .
Jay [Gould], we have got the biggest thing on earth. Our enterprise
is an inexhaustible gold mine." Not only is the language as excited as
that of Robert Ingersoll, but the image is that of wealth to be plun-
dered: there is no indication of anything like republican virtue or of
a redeemed society.

The difficulty in dealing with these men is to know what is fact
and what is fiction. The Age of Energy produced its own legends as
readily as it produced its own lives. How shall one find out where
truth begins? It seems doubtful that the parlor houses of Leadville
and Denver or the madams of San Francisco were as glamorous as
legend and nostalgia picture them.[19] It is virtually impossible to
trace any Robin Hood qualities in Jesse James (1847–1882), trained
in murder by the infamous Quantrill organization, who, if he was capable of spurts of egotistical generosity, was capable also of cold-
blooded assassination, including the killing of one of his own men on
the mere suspicion of treachery. Nevertheless, the fifteen years of his
lawless career passed into folklore and produced a ballad, a play,

numerous impostors who insisted that Jesse James had not been shot by Robert Howard, and a whole subliterature of romanticized biography and misleading fiction.[20]

On a higher plane the faults and virtues of George Armstrong Custer (1839–1875) of the curly locks still excite debate, some calling him the most brilliant cavalry leader America ever produced and the last of the cavaliers, and others denouncing him as a rash, vain, reckless, and irresponsible officer.[21] Or consider "Ned Buntline" (Edward Zane Carroll Judson, 1823–1886), cabin boy, midshipman, scout, editor, liar, duelist, hymn-writer, rioter, a man who survived being lynched, four marriages, innumerable wounds, several unextracted bullets, sciatica, and heart trouble, but who gave a name to the once popular Know-Nothing party, wrote a play for Buffalo Bill, and produced, or is said to have produced, more than four hundred dime novels. How much is truth, how much deception in a career like this? [22] Take a much better known personality, that of Mrs. Eddy. Her life is passionately defended by the faithful as the story of a pure spirit moving through clouds and darkness into sunlight and spiritual truth, but her career, to less fideistic biographers, is a jumble of hysteria, illness, marriages, law suits, Quimbyism, malicious animal magnetism, mesmeric poisoning, and the like. Her genius for business organization is indisputable, and when she "passed on," she left behind her a religious organization of about one hundred thousand (since increased), a book, *Science and Health with a Key to the Scriptures,* that during its manifold revisions has sold by thousands of copies, and a personal estate worth about two and a half million dollars.[23]

The startling fact is that many seemingly incredible careers are well authenticated. An example is the life of Annie Oakley (1860–1926), who began marksmanship at the age of nine, paid off a mortgage on the old farm, teamed up with Frank E. Butler, whom she later married (happily), and was for seventeen years part of the great Buffalo Bill Show. She could slice a playing card held with its thin edge toward her, hit dimes tossed into the air, and shoot six holes into another playing card before it fell to the ground. She once shattered 4772 out of 5000 glass balls thrown upward, and the Crown Prince of Germany, the future Emperor William II, insisted that she shoot a cigarette held between his lips.[24] The career of Mrs. Frank Leslie (Miriam Florence Folline Leslie c. 1836–1914) is both authenticated and unbelievable. She got through four marriages, one of them to the brother of Oscar Wilde, and crossed the continent with her first husband, Frank Leslie, in a sumptuous parlor car (she wrote a chronicle of the trip in *California: A Pleasure Trip from Gotham to the Golden Gate,* 1877). On Frank Leslie's death she took over his publishing business, then burdened with a deficit of three hundred thousand dollars, and made a go of it for fifteen years. She was apparently a woman of great magnetism and executive ruthlessness, and she once claimed on heaven knows what evidence to be a baroness.

Before one turns to the better-known world of business and politics, consider Wild Bill Hickock (1837–1876), credited with killing more than a hundred men, though a careful biographer can find only fourteen. An expert marksman, he was also a fop, wearing on high-toned occasions a boiled shirt with detachable collar and cuffs, a sleeveless Zouave jacket of scarlet, slashed with black velvet and ornamented with silver buttons (at least I think they were silver), and trousers of black velvet or of buckskin! This costume he sometimes varied by donning a Prince Albert coat, an embroidered silk sash, and custom-made boots with high heels. Killed while he was playing poker in Deadwood, he was buried in a "handsome coffin" "with silver ornaments," in which he lay, "a picture of perfect repose" (one thinks of Bret Harte's Oakhurst):

> His long chestnut hair, evenly parted over his marble brow, hung in waving ringlets over the broad shoulders; his face was cleanly shaved excepting the drooping moustache, which shaded a mouth in death [that] almost seemed to smile, but which in life was unusually grave; the arms were folded over the still breast. . . . The corpse was clad in complete dress-suit of black broadcloth, new underclothing [*sic*], and white linen shirt,[25]

and his "trusty rifle" was buried with him. Buck Fanshawe's funeral? Not at all. A sober newspaper account of Hickock's.

But let us add to our gallery some figures more nearly central to the American economy. There was Daniel Drew (1797–1879), originally a cattle driver, illiterate, sharp-witted, by all accounts unscrupulous, greedy, and grasping, yet a devout Methodist ("I got to be a millionaire afore I knowed it, hardly"), and founder of Drew Theological Seminary (now Drew University), once dedicated to fundamentalist Protestant theology. Consider Jay Gould (1836–1892), to whom Sam Wilkerson wrote his letter—undersized, keen-minded, unscrupulous, melancholy, friendless, driving his first partner to suicide, at fifty the owner of millions, his principal recreational outlet being a mild passion for gardening. There was Cornelius Vanderbilt (1794–1877), ruthless, bumptious, tobacco-chewing, hard-headed, hard-swearing, the father of thirteen children, a man who, according to one biographer, committed his wife to a sanitarium because she wouldn't move to Manhattan and break into society, a father who did not recognize ability in his eldest son until the younger man cheated him over some loads of manure. He was also a shipowner, a railroad king, and a modernizer of transportation. Under the influence of his second wife he became the founder of Vanderbilt University, and in his later years turned to the consolations of religion and had hymns sung every evening. John Jacob Astor (1822–1890) rewrote telegrams to save a word, commended the Tweed Ring comptroller of New York City for honesty, bought up real estate but often failed to insure buildings because it was cheaper to let them burn; he was also the creator of the Astor Library. John D. Rockefeller, Sr. (1839–1937) gave away dimes, installed an accounting system accurate to the third decimal, dominated the growing petroleum industry at thirty-eight, went to his office on the New York Elevated because it saved money, and became to zealous reformers the archetype of all that was evil in American finance; yet he gave a great many million dollars to the University of Chicago. One catches glimpses of his personal power in this comment by a lesser oil refiner: "You never saw such eyes. He took me all in, saw just how much fight he could expect from me, and then up went his hands and back and forth went his [rocking-] chair."

These are examples from the East. Move West and consider the lives of John W. Mackay (1831–1902), James Graham Fair (1831–1894), James Clair Flood (1826–1888), and William S. O'Brien (1826–1878), once kings of the Comstock Lode in Nevada. Mackay broke Jay Gould's monopoly of the American telegraph system; Fair became a senator of the United States and was sued for divorce on the grounds of "habitual adultery"; Flood died alone in a hotel bedroom in Heidelberg, Germany; and the expensive mausoleum that O'Brien built for himself was broken into in 1930 and used as a home by a group of tramps who thrust a stovepipe through one of the stained-glass windows.

Who has ever solved the complex personality of George Hearst

(1820–1891)? He made a fortune in Nevada in 1859, held vast possessions in the Ophir, Homestake, and Anaconda mines, not to speak of real estate scattered from Alaska to Mexico, bought the San Francisco *Examiner* in 1880, and became a United States senator in 1886 by appointment and in 1888 by legislative election. In 1887 he gave his son this same paper. William Randolph Hearst (1863–1951), at thirty-two so diffident that Ambrose Bierce compared his voice to the fragrance of violets made audible, revolutionized the *Examiner* and made it the foundation of the most famous newspaper chain in American history, comprising at its peak papers in seventeen cities. At one time Hearst also controlled the International News Service, three radio stations, and four or five magazines, went to Congress, was enthusiastic for Franklin D. Roosevelt and then bitterly opposed him. There were those who said he started the Spanish-American War. The Hearsts created at San Simeon, California, an estate of two hundred forty thousand acres, including an ocean frontage of fifty miles; the son spent about a million dollars a year for fifty years on anything he thought was art. This he shipped to San Simeon. He once purchased a monastery in Spain, erecting a new church there to replace the monastery, and building a mountain road and a railroad spur to carry away the original structure piece by piece. One of the unpredictable autocrats of journalism, essentially without taste, he nevertheless hired Bierce, an interesting if artificial stylist, to write for the *Examiner,* gave him entire freedom of expression even at the risk of libel suits, and protected him throughout their stormy connection, just as he hired Arthur Brisbane in 1897, a writer who, in the view of many high-minded critics of the newspaper world, did much to corrupt journalism. Though he also gave Brisbane entire freedom, Hearst was quite capable of firing anybody at a moment's notice on any paper he controlled.

Then there were the Montana copper kings—F. A. Heinze (1869–1914), Marcus Daly (1841–1900), William Andrews Clark (1839–1925)—and their curious connections both with Boston capitalists and with the Standard Oil Company. Heinze and Daly were true condottieri, their employees fighting savagely underground for the possession of ore while the leaders fought bitterly and cunningly in the courts, state and federal, above ground.[26] Clark began his Montana career by buying tobacco for the miners, then opened a general store, and afterward contracted to carry the mail between

Missoula, Montana, and Walla Walla, Washington, Indians or no Indians. He made millions in Butte and in 1899 was elected United
States senator, but that body threw him out on charges of bribery.
He was, however, again returned by the legislature and, *mirabile
dictu,* became an ardent advocate of national conservation. He built
a mansion in New York City known as "Clark's Folly," where he collected a magnificent gallery of great paintings from the Renaissance
through the Barbizon school, as well as tapestries, rare rugs, old lace,
and so on; these are now in the Corcoran Gallery of Art in Washington. Once again the parallel of the Renaissance merchant-prince is
validated.

Nor should one forget the California "Big Four." One of them was
Collis P. Huntington (1821–1900), active, profane, cynical, six feet
tall, two hundred pounds in weight, who had been a watch peddler
and became master of the Southern Pacific, not to mention other enterprises on sea and land. A second, Leland Stanford (1824–1893),
mediocre as a lawyer, strongly Unionist in sentiment, came to California, some said, poor as a church mouse. He outweighed Huntington by sixty-eight pounds. He turned into a mediocre governor and a
mediocre senator, and a biographer wrote of him that reading in economics seems to have confused rather than clarified his mind. Yet the
fortune of the one was the basis of the great Huntington Library and
Art Gallery in San Marino; and the other founded the most
distinguished private university on the Pacific Coast. The third was
Charles Crocker (1822–1888), who weighed even more than Huntington, whose life alternated between fits of furious activity and fits of
unaccountable quiescence (he died in a diabetic coma), and who
lived in a San Francisco house delicately described as a "delirium of
the wood carver" (it contained Meissonier's "The Smoker" on an
easel in the drawing room).

The fourth was Mark Hopkins (1813–1878), a thin, stubborn man,
who, when he found the price of vegetables in Sacramento outrageous, put in a vegetable garden of his own and sold the surplus to
the neighbors at full market prices. Famous in the annals of San
Francisco is the Mark Hopkins mansion, built to suit Mrs. Hopkins,
who read Bulwer-Lytton, Ouida, and Mrs. E. D. E. N. Southworth.
The incredible castle that incarnated the results of this reading had
no particular style except that it was "romantic." The drawing room
was modeled on a room in the palace of the doges in Venice, the din-

ing room was large enough to seat sixty, there was a master bedroom finished in ebony and inlaid with ivory dotted with semiprecious stones, and a library so beautiful that "only poetry should be read there." [27]

Only the San Francisco of this period could nourish "Norton I, *Dei Gratia*, Emperor of the United States and Protector of Mexico," who on August 12, 1869, formally dissolved both the Republican and Democratic parties as he had previously banished all spiritualists from his wide domain; his gravestone stands in Woodlawn Memorial Park.[28] Where else but in the Great West among the robber barons?

Other figures in the public eye were quite as remarkable. Roscoe Conkling (1829–1888), the great spread-eagle orator and boss of New York State, was described by James G. Blaine as a majestic, supereminent overpowering turkey gobbler. He was nevertheless once a nominee for the presidency of the United States. Blaine (1830–1893) was called both the "plumed knight" and "the continental liar from the State of Maine." Of him the sober *Dictionary of American Biography* confesses that he became wealthy without any visible means of income, and his reputation for political intrigue was such that when, in the election of 1884, it was discovered that Grover Cleveland had fathered an illegitimate child, a Democrat advised: "We should elect Mr. Cleveland to the public office he is so admirably qualified to fill, and remand Mr. Blaine to the private life which he is so eminently fitted to adorn." Nevertheless, Blaine made one of the ablest secretaries of state of the century. Then there was Henry Ward Beecher (1813–1887), lusty, exuberant, unstable, enthusiastic, a reformer, a moralist, a preacher who weekly addressed a congregation of two thousand five hundred and who, charged with committing adultery with Mrs. Theodore Tilton, wife of the editor of *The Independent*, a Congregational weekly, braved it out during a trial that lasted six months and ended with a hung jury. Plymouth Church, where Beecher preached, smothered the courtroom with flowers when the case came on. Beecher served the Union well by his speeches in Great Britain during the Civil War and persuaded many Protestants that Charles Darwin was not Satan in disguise.

The women were often as extraordinary. Consider Mammy Pleasant of San Francisco, who lived in an opulent house of thirty rooms with carved mantelpieces, elaborate doorways, mirrors with gold-leaf frames, rock-crystal chandeliers, and a spiral staircase that went up three stories. This former Georgia slave managed the "House of Mystery" and flits in and out of the marital and judicial antagonisms of William Sharon, quondam senator from Nevada; Thomas Bell, a San Francisco businessman; Judge David Smith Terry, once of the California supreme court, shot by a bodyguard of Stephen J. Field, a future justice of the United States Supreme Court; and, finally, Field himself.[29] Then there is Adah Isaacs Menken (1835?–1868) of the numerous marriages, including one to John C. Heenan, the "Benecia Boy" of prize-fighting fame. The seemingly unclad star of *Mazeppa*, bound naked on a wild horse, she was the toast of the mining towns, the idol of Paris, the woman who, according to legend, bet she could seduce Swinburne. Poetess and adventuress, she was posthumously described by the Boston *Globe* on Thursday, December 11, 1869, as a "large-waisted, full-bosomed, Oriental-looking creature, with short, boyish curls, elaborately hung about and piled upon by false hair. A very Messalina of a woman, condemned to a life of sensuality, even before she was born," "the opulence of mature flesh upon her." She brought out a volume of verse in 1868, which she audaciously dedicated to Charles Dickens. It is entitled *Infelicia* and has among its gems a poem entitled "Myself." This includes such passages as

Still I trim my white bosom with crimson roses; for none shall see the
  thorns.
I bind my aching brow with a jeweled crown, that none shall see the iron
  one beneath.
My silver-sandaled feet keep impatient time to the music, because I cannot
  be calm.
.   .   .   .
After all, living is but to play a part!
The poorest worm would be a jewel-headed snake if she could!
.   .   .   .
When the purple-and-gold of our inner natures shall be lighted up in the
  Eternity of Truth, then will love be mine!

Love was certainly hers. Even the gray pages of the *Dictionary of American Biography* grow feverish when they chronicle her career.[30]
One must not forget Victoria Woodhull (1838–1927), known as the terrible siren, who once worked in a patent-medicine show, later fascinated Cornelius Vanderbilt (he thought she was psychic), ran for President of the United States, and published an advertisement in a

THE AGE OF ENERGY

newspaper to explain why her husband and a former husband were living with her simultaneously. Then there was Lillian Russell (1861–1922), known as "airy, fairy Lillian," apparently because she was neither, the friend of Diamond Jim Brady, four times married, making five contracts for a single theatrical season and breaking all but one of them, and getting out a permanent injunction to prevent any theater manager from requiring her to wear pink tights.

Diamond Jim Brady (James Buchanan Brady, 1856–1917), interested in all sorts of people, all sorts of "art," all sorts of manufactured articles, collected chorus girls, Oriental rugs, prize fighters, automobiles, bicycles, pictures—anything and everything. He once bought a gold-and-white piano for four thousand dollars. He bought an electric brougham, waited two years to get it, and had it shipped to him on a special flatcar. He had a Turkish room in The Rutland, an apartment house, stuffed with hand-painted coal scuttles, pyrographic work, burnt-leather cushions, gilded rolling pins, and inlaid tabourets. The rumor was that he gave parties where naked girls waited on the guests. He owned a farm where gold-plated milk pails were used. He gave Lillian Russell a gold-plated bicycle with tiny chip diamonds on its frame, handle bars of mother-of-pearl, and diamonds, sapphires, rubies, and emeralds set in the hubs and spokes, which she kept in a blue plush-lined case and took with her on her tours. He once said of it to Lillian: "God, Nell, ain't it grand!" The exuberance, the vitality, the sheer, passionate paganism of the epoch are in that remark.

I come finally to the incredible Jim Fisk (1834–1872), who despoiled the Erie Railroad and whose attempt to corner all the gold in the nation reached its climax on Black Friday, 1869, when hundreds were ruined. He was shot by Edward Stokes, man-about-town, in a quarrel over the favors of Josie Mansfield, Fisk's current mistress. Fat, jovial, impudent, vulgar, Fisk put on French light opera, was the "admiral" of the Fall River steamboat line and colonel of the Ninth New York Militia Regiment. Visiting Boston with his regiment on Bunker Hill Day in 1871, he asked permission to celebrate divine services on the Common. He lodged the officers of the Erie Railroad in Pike's Opera House in New York, had his room thickly carpeted, his chair studded with gold nails, and his corner washstand surrounded by a frieze of naked nymphs dancing against a background of rose and gold on the wall. Somewhere there was a wife, the obscu-

rest person in the Fisk ménage. His funeral has seldom been surpassed. It was taken charge of by Tammany Hall, the Ninth Regiment escorted its late colonel to the train, there was a band of two
hundred pieces, Brattleboro, Vermont, stayed up till midnight to receive the body, and a Vermont minister informed the nation: "We
have every reason to believe that he gave testimony to his faith in
Jesus." As for Josie Mansfield, she once appeared on the witness
stand during a libel suit, and was thus described in a contemporary
newspaper:

> The lady merits some brief description, as she is well known from Maine
> to Oregon, for her connection with Mark Antony Fisk and Octavius Cae-
> sar Stokes . . . [She is] above the medium height . . . with a pearly
> white skin, dark and very lustrous eyes, which, when directed at a judge,
> a jury, or a witness, have a terrible effect. Her delicate white hands were
> encased in faultless lavender kid gloves, and over her magnificent tour-
> nue [sic] of dark hair was perched a jaunty little Alpine hat, with a
> dainty green feather pinned thereon. Her robe was of the heaviest black
> lace over Milanese bands of white satin. A gold pin glistened and height-
> ened the effect. Her hair was worn à la Clèopatre, and a superb black
> mantle covered her shoulders.

Sex is no recent discovery.[31]

IV

This magnificent breed of men and women lived as exuberantly as
they loved, fought, and flimflammed the public. When in 1877 an
outcry was raised about certain aldermen who at a dinner called for
public business ate, each one, seventeen dollars worth of food, not to
speak of the drinks they consumed, the *Atlantic Monthly* rose to
their defense, congratulating the United States on possessing men
who had a capacity for eating and drinking comparable to that of
the heroes of Homer and remarking that "their stomachs were as heroic as their hearts, their bowels as magnanimous." [32] A generation of
free spenders built enormous kitchens, enormous wine cellars, and
enormous dining rooms. Their hotels were on the same magnificent
scale. They patronized vast mahogany bars, behind which the bar-
tender, virtually an invention of the age, stood with his sweeping
mustache, his diamond pin, his rings, his spotless white coat, his
regal manner, creating on occasion drinks like the Blue Blazer and

raising the cocktail to a level of social esteem.[33] Behind him was an extensive mirror, frequently bearing designs or scrolls or the names of drinks, and reflecting the glitter of bottles. Centered over it was a lush saloon nude, and at either end of a few of the finer bars might be two nude female statues of ample proportion and vaguely classical stance. The drink of the era was champagne. It was served in the high-class brothels. It ran from one of the three faucets in the butler's pantry at the elegant Perry H. Smith mansion at Pine (now part of Michigan Avenue) and Huron streets in Chicago, finished in 1878. It filled the water tank of a mine superintendent in Nevada on the occasion of a wedding.[34] It furnished the punch line to popular songs intended to celebrate the stage-door Johnny who waited in the alley for the girls to emerge from the chorus of *The Black Crook* or (later) *Florodora;* and lobsters and champagne turned into a tag phrase for metropolitan pleasures. Champagne of course suggested the Gallic tradition; and a rage for hiring a French chef developed among the wealthy, who competed with the high-toned restaurant and the fashionable hotel for his valuable services.

In wealthy circles voluptuous eating and drinking became the hallmark of success. In that silliest, yet most illuminating, of social commentaries, Ward McAllister's *Society As I Have Found It* (1890), a whole chapter is given to Madeira, "the king of wines," and another to champagne, claret, and sherry. Since "a New Yorker does not live in his New York residence, at most, more than four or five months in the year," during the other months the servants are likely to drink up the wines, but a good wine merchant will get you around this regrettable behavior. Before giving a dinner, you must first have "an interview with your *chef,* if you have one, or *cordon bleu,* whom you must arouse to fever heat by working on his ambition and vanity." Grave problems immediately present themselves. Do not let two white or brown sauces follow each other, nor have truffles twice on the same menu. The first battle, however, is over the soup. Shall there be one or two? That being determined, remember that if, early on, you serve *mousse de jambon,* your guests will relax, knowing that they are in able hands. Let us therefore pass to the problem of fish. Salmon? Only in spring or early summer. Terrapin? Terrapin, with us, is "as national a dish as canvasback," and at choice dinners may be substituted for fish. Then we discuss the *relevé,* for which there are half a dozen possibilities; after that, the entrées, which for a simple dinner seating twelve or fourteen need not be more than three—two hot and one cold, and for the latter a "sorbet" is recommended since "it is digestive and is intended as such." The penultimate problem is the salad; then perhaps a hot pudding (though not for a ladies' dinner) with some ices—perhaps "a *pouding Nesselrod*," provided of course your cream is good.

But this is only a modest dinner for the ladies; our main concern is for the male animal. After two pages of valuable advice on choosing poultry, meat, grapes, coffee, and *paté de foie gras* in the markets, our specialist offers for the man of *ton* this simple:

Menu of an Old-Fashioned Southern Dinner

Terrapin Soup and Oyster Soup, or Mock Turtle Soup.
Soft shell or Cylindrical nose Turtle.
Boiled freshwater Trout (known with us at the North as Chub)
Shad stuffed and baked (we broil it).
Boiled Turkey, Oyster Sauce, A Roast Peahen.
Boiled Southern Ham.
Escalloped oysters, Maccaroni [*sic*] with cheese. Prawn Pie.
Crabs stuffed in shell.
Roast Ducks. A haunch of Venison.

Dessert
Plum Pudding. Mince Pies. Trifle. Floating Island.
Blanc Mange. Jelly.
Ice Cream.

The wine list was separate. A more elaborate affair, served at Delmonico's in 1873, the menu printed in gold, ran as shown on the facing page.

Men rose to fame by their ability to manipulate this sort of life, Ward McAllister being one example, "King" Lehr a second. A third, was "Sam" Ward, a notable Washington lobbyist who marketed for terrapin and tea, used his chef and his dinners as instruments for getting votes, and, says Allan Nevins, "really did something for American civilization; at his quarters on E Street Plaza dining was an art." [35]

But mere eating and drinking eventually ceased to suffice; what one commentator called culinary vaudeville also set in. At one dinner

Menu

Potages
Consommé Impérial Bisque aux Crevettes

Hors d'œuvre
Timbales à la Condé

Poisson
Redsnapper à la Vénitienne
Paupiettes d'éperlan sauce des Gourmets

Relevé
Filet de bœuf à l'Égyptienne

Entrées
Ailes de Canvas-back sauce bigarade
Côtelette de volaille Sevigne

Aspergas froides en branche

Sorbet à l'Ermitage

Rôts
Chapons truffes   Selle de mouton

Entremets
Choux fleurs sauce crème Cardons à la moëlle
Petits pois au beurre
Poires à la Richelieu
Gelée aux ananas Gaufres Chantilly Julienne
Gateaux à la Reine Coupole à l'anglaise
Pain de pêches maréchale gelée aux fruits

Desserts
Délicieux aux noisettes, Biscuits forêts
Fruits glacés
Petits fours
Bonbons
Pièces montées

Mr. Lukemeyer

the soup alone cost ten dollars a plate. At another there were hand-painted menus, complete sets of gold plate for a ten-course meal, and a liveried and powdered footman behind each pair of guests. A dinner at the Waldorf in New York for eighty-six was estimated to cost about one hundred and twenty dollars a setting. One at the St. Regis in the same metropolis for a hundred and fifty guests compelled the florist's men to wear white felt shoes to slide along the immense table in arranging trails of roses and carnations. The Grand Pacific Hotel in Chicago annually served a "game banquet" to invited guests, the dining room being turned into a miniature forest with stuffed animals and birds' nests, the menu including every meat and fowl from bear to reed birds. At another Waldorf dinner at the close of the century nightingales sang in groves of transplanted rose trees and artificial arbors were hung with hothouse grapes. At still another, a monkey was jocosely presented as the guest of honor. A dog dinner was staged at Newport for about one hundred pet animals; one of the dogs collapsed from overeating. There was a horsemen's dinner, all the guests sitting on horseback. At a birthday party for twelve in Diamond Jim's honor, arranged, it is said, by Stanford White in his Hall of Mirrors at the top of the Old Madison Square Garden, waiters brought in a huge Jack Horner Pie; the guests were given ribbons and told to pull, the pie opened to reveal a nude girl, who climbed off the table, sat on Brady's lap, and fed him his dessert. The guests were shortly favored by the presence of eleven other naked girls. What is one to believe? At another party naked girls in swings hung from the ceiling were supposed, in swinging, to allow the guests to snatch food from the platters they carried in their laps, but the guests snatched at the girls instead.[36]

There were always gambling, horse racing, and sports when eating and drinking failed to stimulate. People in the Age of Energy began the lavish support of the National Horse Show, they imported the four-in-hand tallyho coaching fashion, and some of them rode to hounds. Their stables were imperial; some had forty or fifty horses. They created the National Baseball League in 1876 and got intercollegiate football put under Walter Camp's rules, two American interests that have led to the building of stadiums larger than the Coliseum and to the American equivalent of the Roman doctrine of bread and circuses. They liked prize fights. They loved to gamble either on the stock market, in gambling clubs, or at private poker tables. In the 1870s there were two thousand gambling establishments in New York City alone, and other gambling centers were strung over the continent—Washington, New Orleans, Chicago, Denver, and San Francisco. Las Vegas is our characteristic inheritance from the era. In New York John Morrissey rose from the sidewalks to become a noted pugilist, a politician, a gambler who lost one hundred and twenty-four thousand dollars in a single night, a state senator and a United States congressman. When he died in 1876 he owned, it is said, three-eighths of the gambling casino at Saratoga Springs and a one-third interest in the race track; state senators were pall bearers at his funeral, and fifteen thousand mourners followed his body to the grave through the rain. Morrissey's losses were impressive, but "Bet-you-a-million" Gates, who made his money in barbed wire and became a Wall Street speculator, lost, it is said, a quarter of a million dollars at poker in a single sitting.

These pleasures had to be tasted in appropriate environments, and the age, to the intense disgust of all right-minded historians of art and architecture, created the most colorful period of feverish eclecticism the country has ever known. Some glimpses of their taste we have already had. When they wished to be transported by other means than a coach-and-four or a private yacht, they insisted on splendor. George Makepeace Towle, in *American Society* (1870), devotes a whole chapter to the glories of American steamboats:

> A handsomely-gilded and carved door leads to the ladies' cabin, which is richly carpeted, and plentifully supplied with sofas, armchairs, marble-top tables, mirrors, pictures, and books. . . . Below deck is the gentlemen's cabin, which is more spacious, and, if less luxuriously decorated than the ladies' cabin, is quite as comfortable. . . . On the upper deck, closed in on all sides, is a long and really magnificent general saloon, or drawing room. You ascend to it by a winding staircase, the steps of which are mounted with brass plates; you enter an apartment replete with every luxury which money can procure, and where you might imagine yourself in the drawing room of some Fifth Avenue mansion. It is richly carpeted, often with velvet carpet, or the most expensive Brussels; there are the softest and most yielding sofas and fauteuils, ottomans, circular cushioned seats around the pillars, ornate mirrors, marble tables supplied with fanciful clocks and elegant vases full of flowers, painted panellings, heavy chandeliers supplied with gas, a variety of illustrated books dispersed on the tables, and often a bookcase with a library . . . or a piano, on which any one may play.

And the bridal suite on board is composed of "sumptuous apartments."

He found "first-class" American railway travel equally wonderful. For example:

> Carriages are converted into restaurants, with circular or square marble-topped tables placed here and there. You enter and sit down; are handed an elaborate bill of fare, with the price affixed to the name of each dish; are served with neat appliances, and well-cooked meats and vegetables, much as you would be in a city restaurant.

As for the parlor car,

> [it] is supplied with all that can serve to pass away pleasantly the hours of travel. Here may the young ladies rival each other on the piano; they have at their side choice collections of music. A library of the most popular books stands against one side of the saloon; the newspapers of the day cover an elegant centre table; and sofas and armchairs, bulging with soft and velvet-bound cushions, invite the post-prandian [sic] siesta and lazy reverie. Smaller compartments, equally luxurious, are fitted up for the reception of families. . . . To the family saloons are added little state rooms for the night; every possible modern convenience; so that you may live as comfortably as if you were at home.[37]

But this is for the nearly or the merely rich; let us look at true elegance—for example, the private car used by Adelina Patti when she made her numerous farewell tours. Its cost was thirty thousand dollars. Its walls were covered with embossed leather. It was decorated by Parisian artists, and the sides and ceiling were adorned with painted morning glories.

> The parlor . . . was lighted by plate glass windows and a gold lamp which hung from above. The windows were ornamented with designs representing the four seasons. The hand-carved piano of natural wood corresponded with the rest of the woodwork in the room. There was a couch, with satin pillows ornamented with bows and lace tidies. . . . A square table, covered with plush, stood in the center, and all around were easy chairs of luxurious depth. . . . The bed-chamber was largely pink. The paneling was of satin-wood, inlaid with ebony, gold, and amaranth. Bevelled mirrors were abundant. The couch had a silk plush cover of gold, embroidered with trailing pink rosebuds and with the monogram "A.P." in the same delicate shade. Over the velvet carpet, beside the bed, was a leopard skin.

There was also a concealed bathtub and a toilet. The table service was of solid silver, china, and glass, all bearing the singer's monogram.[38]

Nor was this luxury confined to Europeans. The same writers who describe Adelina's private car tell us about the reception in San Francisco of Emma Wixen, an opera star who changed her name to Emma Nevada, who was graduated from Mills College, and who billed herself as the California Patti. In March 1885 she sang in *La Sonnambula* at the Grand Opera House amid immense excitement. Bouquets fell on the stage like hail. There were handed over the footlights a floral chair from her sister, a yacht made of pink roses on a sea of forget-me-nots from Mills College classmates, a satin cushion with "Nevada" in silver letters across its surface, a branch of a lemon tree laden with fruit, a laurel wreath from Mills with an attached red streamer on which was printed:

> With fragrant bloom,
> And living green
> We crown thee song's
> Victorious queen.

In addition, there were an orange satin basket filled with roses and marigolds resting on a tall copper standard, on the surface of which appeared a horseshoe entangled in a spider's web, a floral basket containing a note of congratulation in a satin case, the lid of which was decorated with a painting of the Golden Gate, and a purse of two thousand dollars in five-dollar gold pieces.[39] Miss Nevada stayed at the Palace Hotel.

Hotel furnishings and the furnishings of parlor houses participated alike in this eclectic magnificence. The great Palace Hotel in San Francisco was principally the creation of William Chapman Ralston, whose house on Pine Street was valued at one hundred forty thousand dollars and whose estate at Belmont, twenty miles south of San Francisco, was reached by guests on a special fast train. The Palace was a quarter of a mile in circumference, and its seven stories contained eight hundred rooms. The walls were two feet thick, set on masonry twelve feet in depth and reinforced every four feet by double strips of iron bolted together, the outside heads of which were gilded and shone against the vast external walls, painted white. The central court, 84 feet by 114, contained a circular driveway for the carriages of arriving guests. There were 5 miles of pipe and 125 miles of electric wiring. The marble used in the interior came from 15 separate firms and was used to make 804 mantels, 900 washstands, and 40,000 square feet of pavement. The woods with which the interior was finished were mahogany, East India teak, primavera from Mexico, rosewood, and ebony. The woods were often hand-carved. The public rooms were originally painted pink, there were specially woven French rugs, a special manufacture of Haviland china, Belfast linen, 9000 cuspidors, Eastlake furniture, and—a great novelty— Negro waiters, porters, and chambermaids instead of Chinese. Everybody stopped there; the hotel stood until the fire and earthquake of 1906, when Scotti and Caruso were guests, as Patti had been. They escaped with their lives.[40]

The Baldwin Hotel, also erected in the 1870s, countered by having what was probably the longest bar in San Francisco, a billiard room for women, and four-in-hand coaches that conveyed departing guests to the ferries and the trains.[41] As for the Waldorf in New York, opened in 1893, where the plush rope across a doorway was invented as a device to make people want to get in because they thought they were being kept out, it contained, according to contemporary reporters, every costly and artistic "accoutrement" that could be found in an Old World palace. There were tapestries, paintings, carvings, marble and onyx mosaic work, rich and expensive furniture, costly tableware, chandeliers, ferns, flowers, a canopied bed upon a dais, enormous dining rooms and great ballrooms. There the famous Bradley Martin ball was held. There at another dinner the Bradley Martins entertained eighty-six guests, only six of whom were not multimillionaires, all in a delirium of diamonds and useless magnificence.[42] The floor of the barbershop in the Palmer House in Chicago was inlaid with silver dollars; as for that hotel in general, let Kipling describe it:

> They told me to go to the Palmer House, which is overmuch gilded and mirrored, and there I found a huge hall of tessellated marble crammed with people talking about money, and spitting about everywhere. Other barbarians charged in and out of this inferno with letters and telegrams in their hands, and yet others shouted at each other. A man who had drunk quite as much as was good for him told me that this was "the finest hotel in the finest city on God Almighty's earth." By the way, when

an American wishes to indicate the next country or state, he says, "God
A'mighty's earth." This prevents discussion and flatters his vanity.[43]

Swank brothels (parlor houses) patronized by the rich were equally
luxuriant. In Chicago the famous Everleigh Club (originally the
House of Mirrors) was run on lavish lines by two girls from Kentucky. It had Moorish, Egyptian, Japanese, and Chinese parlors, the
dinners were sumptuous and accompanied by music furnished by a
violin, a cello, a piano, and a harp. The furnishings were also sumptuous and so, it was alleged, were the girls. Josie Arlington's house in
"Storyville," New Orleans, four stories high, with bay windows and a
cupola, was a riot of gilt, plush, velvet hangings, Oriental carpets,
damask chairs, sofas, lace curtains, beveled mirrors, cut-glass chandeliers, and Turkish "corners"; the Blue Book of the red light district
called it "absolutely and unquestionably the most decorative and
costly fitted out sporting palace ever placed before the American
public . . . Within the walls . . . will be found the work of great artists from Europe and America," not to speak of "curios" galore and a
collection of steins that had to be padlocked against theft. Of New
York parlor houses a contemporary remarked that "no hotel is more
elegantly furnished. Quiet, order, and taste abound," the "lady board-
ers" are selected "for their beauty, grace, and accomplishments," and
"all that grace and attraction can do to secure visits is employed." [44]
One is reminded of Zola's Rougon-Macquart novels.

In their struggles toward taste the moguls of the Age of Energy
and their ambitious wives erected some of the most striking specimens of domestic architecture. The Potter Palmer House in Chicago
(1885) had no exterior doorknobs or outside locks, and contained an
octagonal hall three stories high, the floor being a marble mosaic.
There were a French drawing room, a Spanish music room, an English drawing room, a Moorish corridor, a Turkish parlor, a Greek
parlor, a Japanese parlor, and a private elevator; and Mrs. Palmer's
bed, a Louis XVI affair, was ten feet high. Yet this monstrosity also
contained an incomparable collection of jade and one of the earliest
collections of the French impressionists to be found in America. In
Milwaukee the Dake house had a "tent" ballroom, the ceiling covered with a two-toned beige fabric draped in swathes, behind which
musicians could be concealed; and there were tapestries picturing the

romance of Antony and Cleopatra, an "Oriental" chandelier in orange, green, and red, and windows on three sides running from floor to ceiling and giving a view of Lake Michigan. After touring Europe for two years, Ellery Orrum, the wife of Sandy Bowers, a teamster who struck it rich, sent back to Reno marble mantels, French furniture, and heaven knows what else to furnish an "elegant mansion of stone" with two wings, mansard roofs of pale blue and white checkerboard slate, round dormers, and a stone-paved court.[45] Strolling through Eureka, California, Hildegarde Hawthorne came upon that most extravagant of wooden mansions, the Carson House, built in the 1880s by a redwood millionaire:

> It has all the intricate elaboration of the late Victorian era as it found expression in wood here in America. Nothing is missing. The scalloped verandah, its roof supported on fantastic posts, the innumerable decorated gables, the tower with its sharp-pointed top, its balconies and tiers of small windows. The roof has a square portion surrounded by a railing, the windows of the various floors almost disappear behind columns and porches, there is a turret, and there are many pinnacles. All is meticulously emphasized and picked out with darker and lighter shades of brown and tan and white. Lawn and flower-beds, a palm or two, shrubs and a wide curved driveway are contained within the wrought-iron fence.

A biographical sketch of Carson announces that "this palatial dwelling, not excelled by any other home in the state, was one of his most important contributions to the beautifying of his chosen city." [46]

The same heady exuberance, the same avid thirst for experience, the same desire to taste other cultures and sample other centuries created or filled the palaces on Fifth Avenue in New York, on Michigan Boulevard and adjoining streets in Chicago, at Newport or Tuxedo Park, or elsewhere. Among the Chicago millionaires statues of bronze or alabaster, scimitars, antlers, Oriental lamps, and sculptured busts vied for attention with canvases by Bouguereau, Meissonier, and artists of more perdurable fame. So did Eastlake furniture, French rococo *objets d'art,* Dresden china, elaborate silver, brass bedsteads, and upholstered sofas. In the Cyrus McCormick mansion in Chicago the main hall was patterned after a castle of Henri IV of France, and tapestries from the period hung on the dining-room walls. The ceiling of the room touchingly combined the cross of the French Legion of Honor, a reaper, sheaves of grain, and the names of Pomona, Flora, Ceres, and Diana. "Armsmere," Samuel Colt's home in Hartford, was basically "Italian," but it had an Oriental dome or two, various attached greenhouses, and, in front, an equestrian statue. Frederick E. Church's "Olana" above Hudson, New York, built by Calvert Vaux and now an official historic site, was called by a contemporary art journal "Persian in inspiration," with "shallow arches, over doors and windows . . . bordered with mosaic tiles, its minarets [and] spindle-like columns painted originally in bright colors," all supposed to suggest something on the Bosphorus or in the Near East.

For the W. K. Vanderbilts, Richard Morris Hunt built the "Marble House" in Newport at a total cost of eleven million dollars. Of this house Henry James heartily disapproved. Mrs. Vanderbilt, who later divorced her husband and married O. H. P. Belmont, had a Chinese teahouse erected on the grounds but apparently forgot a kitchen. She therefore had a miniature railway constructed from the main house to the red-and-gold lacquer temple, and, if Cleveland Armory is to be believed, footmen in full livery, squatting in the little cars, could be seen holding up silver tea trays as they rode majestically from the vast main kitchen to the Oriental pavilion. But the "Marble House" had its rival in "The Breakers," built for Mr. and Mrs. Cornelius Vanderbilt II (by the same architect) out of marble and Caen stone. It was two years in construction, and the central element is a covered courtyard, the ceiling of which is painted to look like the sky. The circular staircase has a fountain under it, the music room and the morning room were designed in France and shipped to Newport, the billiard room is marble and alabaster, and the WPA guidebook to Rhode Island displays more than classical restraint in calling it "the most striking and magnificently appointed of Newport 'cottages.' " The imagination flags before this procession of structures built to demonstrate conspicuous expenditure and exhibit conspicuous waste.

I have imperceptibly drifted out of the Gilded Age in the usual sense of that term into the last twenty years of the nineteenth century and the first decade of this. It would be tedious to record the continuing tensions between the old families in New York, Boston, Philadelphia, and other centers and the new millionaires;[47] tedious also to chronicle the Great Social War between the tyrannical Mrs. Astor and the clever Mrs. Vanderbilt. Nor need one enumerate the steam yachts, the expensive carriages, the automobiles (when they came in), the diamonds, pearls, rubies, and emeralds, the furs, the lap dogs, the companies of servants, or the international marriages celebrated with incredible pomp and circumstance and too often leading to disaster. Nor is it necessary to describe more Lucullan banquets. Yet one other activity of the American millionaire and his wife needs to be cited because of its implications. This is the fancy-dress ball, that curious rebirth of the *trionfi* of the time of Lorenzo de' Medici. These balls were numerous, a sign that one had "arrived." They employed the services of scores of costume-designers, interior decorators, florists, and even research workers who sometimes toiled endlessly to see that a historical costume was an accurate reproduction of the real thing, and they were expensive.

Two will do as well as twenty. For the famous fancy-dress ball of 1883, which marked the capitulation of Mrs. William Astor to the rising power of Mrs. W. K. Vanderbilt, held as a housewarming of the new Vanderbilt palace on Fifth Avenue, the halls and drawing rooms were lined with roses and the upstairs gymnasium was turned into a supper room set in the tropics. Mrs. Vanderbilt was dressed in what she and her research workers thought was the costume of a Venetian princess, a figure somewhat rare in the history of that republic.[48] Her brother-in-law Cornelius Vanderbilt II was dressed as Louis XVI of ill-fated memory, and his wife was smartly modern as "Electric Light," a costume that involved some sort of concealed battery. (At another affair a woman appeared with a headdress lighted by gas.) There were among the guests all sorts of historical characters, and one real one—General U. S. Grant, who came as himself. There was a Hobby-Horse Quadrille, which had been two months preparing because the dancers all had to appear to be four-legged. There were also a Mother Goose Quadrille, a Star Quadrille, a Dresden Quadrille, and others beside. Henry Clews, the British-born Wall Street broker, who rather admired the Vanderbilts (William H. Vanderbilt's "investments had always a healthy effect upon the market") thought well of it:

> So far as cost, richness of costume and newspaper celebrity were concerned, that ball had, perhaps, no equal in history. It may not have been quite so expensive as the feast of Alexander the Great at Babylon, some of the entertainments of Cleopatra to Augustus [*sic*] and Mark Antony, or a few of the magnificent banquets of Louis XIV, but when viewed from every essential standpoint, and taking into account our advanced

civilization, I have no hesitation in saying that the Vanderbilt ball was superior to any of those grand historic displays of festivity. . . .

Mr. Clews thought well of riches also:

As a matter of fact, the assistance which Americans of great wealth have given the nation in the founding and preservation of institutions for the public benefit, and in other ways, has never been sufficiently appreciated or acknowledged.

This he said before the annual banquet of the Economic Club of Boston in 1906.[49]

Following the Clewsian doctrine that the country necessarily benefited from wealth, in the winter of 1897 the Bradley Martins determined to give a ball in order to decrease national unemployment during that panic year. It was held at the Waldorf-Astoria, and the total expenditure was said to be three hundred and sixty-nine thousand dollars. The guests came dressed as Renaissance, Elizabethan, Dutch, or French historical characters; and Mrs. Martin, who had appeared as Mary Queen of Scots at the Vanderbilt festival, resumed that ominous role fourteen years later. Her husband, defying augury, appeared as Louis XV. Mr. R. W. G. Willing, under the direction, it is said, of a Harvard ethnologist, was costumed as an Indian chief, and Anne Morgan appeared as Pocahontas. There was a cotillion in which gentlemen in Colonial costumes got rather entangled with their swords. There were of course quadrilles, and a general atmosphere of Neronian splendor. But it was the last festival of its kind. The Bradley Martins were so severely attacked by press and pulpit, anarchists and agitators, the representatives of labor and social workers that they withdrew from the United States altogether.

Two years later Thorstein Veblen published *The Theory of the Leisure Class,* in which the American millionaires found themselves classified with Polynesian chiefs and would have learned, had they read the book, that the beauty of an object "is best served by neat and unambiguous suggestion of its office and its efficiency for the material ends of life." In 1906 William Balfour Ker drew his celebrated picture of men and women of Society recoiling in terror from the menacing fist of a laboring man thrust through the parquet floor of a fashionable restaurant where a dinner dance is going on.[50] The floor of the banquet hall, it will be recalled, is unwillingly supported on the bowed heads and shoulders of the proletariat. In this decade Teddy Roosevelt was declaring that if J. Pierpont Morgan came to call, he would be received, but only like anybody else. By 1911 Frederick Townsend could publish *The Passing of the Idle Rich*. Income taxes, death duties, and other "socialistic" measures began to reduce the fortunes gathered in the Age of Energy.

Undoubtedly much of this luxury was senseless. Undoubtedly much of it was vulgar. Undoubtedly reformers were right in checking it by legislation. The preachers were less likely to denounce the wealthy, but when they did, it was probably for cause—at least the muckraking novels seem to say so. There is no contesting the truth that managed capitalism is superior to predatory wealth and invidious comparison. And yet what the modern student may well feel is not so much a sense of economic outrage as a sense of personal pathos. Wealthy men in the Age of Energy toiled terribly for what they got. Most of them had had no childhood, nor were their wives characteristically the carefree, handsome young women into whom Charles Dana Gibson was to transform their daughters. When, therefore, they had a chance to play, they played in a kind of delayed childhood. They resemble the Gargantuan boys and girls H. G. Wells imagined when he wrote *The Food of the Gods* and pictured some of the human young as quite normal but blown up to giant size. As these giant capitalists had no history, they faked one. They had not been born in castles or palaces, so they pretended they were knights and ladies, feudal lords and chatelaines issuing orders to retainers in uniform. If they had no rich heirlooms, they bought them. If they sprang up in a country without a hereditary nobility, they pretended to be that nobility, as in Balzac, Lucien de Rubempré campaigns to overcome the aristocratic world by sheer determination. If the Southern gentry or the aristocracy of Little Old New York looked down upon them as *nouveaux riches,* they spent their riches defiantly enough to compel the traditional families to come to heel.

But all this came late in their feverish and superhuman efforts to get on. Consequently there is a touch of pathos in their play. Like children dressing up, they turned their play hours (or let their wives so turn them) into a make-believe world with disastrous imitation toys. Except in the area of business, they invented nothing at all— not a book, not a philosophy, not a religion, not a scientific discovery, not a single new mode of art or culture, but only an occasional machine like the reaper and harvester. They never gave a single mechanical invention freely to the world. And as everything came to them too late, so everything had in it a touch of transience, a feverish compression in time, an unacknowledged but desperate feeling that the night was coming on, that they must therefore eat, drink, make love, dance, build houses, ride fast horses or fast trains before it was too late. It is surprising how many millionaires prophetically planned their own mausoleums. I think it significant that the great vogue of the *Rubáiyát of Omar Kháyyàm* in America came precisely during the decade of the very rich. They had to get away from the immense tedium of being rich. They relived, as I have said, the lives of the wealthy merchants of the Italian Renaissance; and could they have sung Italian, they might have trilled with Lorenzo de' Medici:

> Ciascun apra ben gli orecchi.
> Di doman nessun si paschi;
> Oggi siam, giovani e vecchi,
> Lieti ognun, femmine e maschi
> Ogni triste pensier caschi;
> Facciam festa tuttavia.
> Chi vuol esser lieto, sia:
> Di doman non c'è certezza.
>
> . . . .
>
> Quant' è bella giovinezza
> Che si fugge tuttavia! [51]

IV

Energy, Expertise, and Control

> It is my impression that there is more open-minded-
> ness and willingness to examine carefully the prem-
> ises underlying a new or unfamiliar thing, before
> condemning it, in the world of business than in the
> world of music.
>
> —CHARLES IVES

I

I HAVE DISCUSSED the energy of personality.[1] I turn now to another phase of this extraordinary time. If one puts aside persons and meditates on the Age of Energy as a whole, two clusters of images tend to form, the one mobile, the other motor; that is, either images of movement, or images of machines that incite motion in other things or persons. As examples of the first, one thinks of the dispersal of armies after the Civil War, hundreds of thousands of men roaming like ants over the enormous countryside; the long trains of settlers rolling westward, or, in certain years, returning east like fragments of a defeated army; immigrants pouring into New York, Boston, Detroit, Port Huron, and thence fanning out, usually into the swarming ant-hill slums of the cities; the long range-cattle drives; the reapers moving across the vast bonanza farms; Coxey's army of the unemployed gathering numbers and then oozing away; the seasonal migration of thousands of tramps like the mysterious movements of destructive grasshoppers; pipelines creeping sinuously through the earth or over it; railways stretching always onward, their feeder lines growing out of the trunk systems; street railways, subways, interurban lines, cable cars, elevated railroads; pleasure steamers restlessly moving on lake, river, or ocean; ferries crossing innumerable straits and rivers; and eventually blots and trickles of automobiles, first clustering in the cities, then tentatively flowing into the countryside in little rills that by and by swell into rivulets and rivers penetrating more and more of the landscape.

The other image is motor. By this I mean the contained energy of steam, the energy of the internal combustion engine, the energy of the dynamo, translated into a thousand other forms. Paradoxically, the second of these was to have a more disturbing influence than the first or the third, but no giant embodiment of it appeared to compare with the Corliss engine or the dynamo. Queerly associated with these sources of power are the early motion pictures, a prophetical burlesque intermediary between the mobile and the mechanical, reducing men to puppets jerked across sight like frogs twitched by a galvanic battery. The step from the Kinetoscope of the early 1890s, in which topical views were gradually replaced by naïve narrative films like the *Life of an American Fireman*, to the first multireel movies was more than an increase in length; it also represented an extension of puppetry across space. The dolls no longer jumped about in a box as they did in "What the Bootblack Saw" or the film of Little Egypt doing a belly dance on a property stage. They moved across, through, or against space—in real landscape or imitation towns and cities. In an upside-down sort of way they expressed a technological distaste (like William James's distaste) for a block universe; they also prophesied twentieth-century restlessness. But let us return to the motor image.

The hundredth anniversary of the Declaration of Independence, coming eleven years after the close of the Civil War and preceding by a few months the Hayes–Tilden election, required recognition; and as early as 1866 Professor John L. Campbell of Wabash College called attention to the propriety of holding a great international exposition in the United States, testimony to the renewal of American unity. Three years later the idea was picked up by the Franklin Institute. What more appropriate place than Philadelphia, the home of Independence Hall? After the usual congressional pulling and hauling (why Philadelphia? why not Washington, New York, or some other site?), Congress passed in 1873 a bill creating a Centennial Commission, and on July 3 President Grant declared Philadelphia would be the city and the time from mid-April to mid-October—that is, from the month of Lexington and Concord to the month when Columbus landed. (The Exposition actually opened May 10 and closed on November 10, 1876.) There was the usual haggling over who was to pay for what. Congress proved niggardly, an understandable attitude in view of the depression of 1873, but the Centennial Commission pushed forward. Americans studied the Crystal Palace Exposition of 1851,[2] the New York exposition of 1853, and more recent expositions at Paris and Vienna, and, with notable skill, created on 236 acres and in 194 buildings in Fairmont Park the first international exposition on a grand scale ever held in the United States. On the opening day Theodore Thomas's orchestra played thirteen different national anthems, as well as Richard Wagner's "Inauguration March," commissioned for the occasion, which, like most commissioned compositions, has long since faded. Bishop Simpson prayed an endless prayer, Whittier's "Our fathers' God from out Whose hand" was sung to John Knowles Paine's music, Sidney Lanier's cantata was also sung, and North and South being thus neatly balanced against each other, General Hawley "presented" the Exposition to General Grant, and the first of eight million visitors entered the fair, most of them at fifty cents a head.

Patriotism, union, and peace were the notes of the show. The official *Illustrated Catalogue of the Centennial Exhibition, Philadelphia, 1876* (printed in New York) has a frontispiece showing Columbia in a liberty cap giving wreaths to three other female figures representing Europe, Asia, and Africa, while with her other hand she holds an American banner, furled, the American eagle standing peacefully at her side. Frank Leslie's *Historical Register of the United States Centennial Exposition, 1876* (New York, 1877) in ten parts sold by subscription, opens with a chromolithograph of America clad in the stars and stripes, an elaborate helmet on her head, her costume much bejeweled, her one visible leg sheathed in a Roman military shoe held by appropriate bindings around her calf. She stands atop a high cliff and with a wave of her shapely hand and arm calls the attention of three women, Europe, Asia, and Africa (who kneels), to the wonders of modern life. On her other side a sort of cigar-store Indian also kneels and looks at her rather than at the national capitol, Philadelphia, the sailboat, the steamer, or, most conspicuous of all, a locomotive belching steam, its tender labeled "Pacific," drawing a train of passenger cars. The national note was further sounded by Joaquin

Miller's elaborate "Song of the Centennial," a cantata without music in which a "minstrel" addresses the people. Among the speakers in Miller's poem are an Oregonian, a hunter, a muleteer, a chorus of miners, and a ranger who proves to be an ex-Confederate. More prosaically, Thomas Bentley in *The Illustrated History of the Centennial Exhibition, Philadelphia, 1876* (New York, 1876) argued that the "generous rivalry of nations" has "extinguished the old mistakes of seclusion," and that the Centennial Exposition is proof that the United States is taking her place in the comity of nations by her remarkable progress "in all those attainments of art, science, literature, and the industrial arts which refine and civilize mankind, and promote the peace, the happiness, and the wealth of nations" (p. 4). One visitor described the fair as a "series of incredibly brilliant pictures"; "words cannot paint it; song cannot describe it," [3] and so far as the future is concerned, "if America has not attained her highest eminence, she will attain it."

As Zeus subsumed all lesser deities into himself, so the steam engine now absorbed all its primitive originals; and the focus of the Philadelphia Centennial was inevitably the gigantic Corliss engine. It was created by a New Englander who later sold it to the Pullman Palace Car Company, thus uniting, so to speak, the motor and the mobile images.[4] This vast idol, one of "the largest and most powerful stationary engines in the world," a "beneficent Titan which is one of the greatest wonders of the Exhibition," stood in the center of Machinery Hall, itself an enormous building. The monster was a double-acting, duplex vertical engine installed on a platform fifty-six feet in diameter, three and one-half feet above the floor of the hall. The cylinders were forty-four inches in diameter with a ten-foot stroke, and between the two engines revolved a flywheel weighing fifty-six tons, thirty feet in diameter, with a twenty-four-inch face. This made thirty-six stately revolutions every minute to govern 1400 horsepower of energy furnished from twenty tubular boilers outside the building. By an ingenious arrangement of cogs and underground shafting, the Corliss engine transmitted power to all the other machines in the hall, of which there were about eight thousand in position when the Exposition opened. (A lesser engine supplied power in the Agricultural Building.) [5] On the opening day President and Mrs. Grant were accompanied by the Emperor and Empress of Brazil.

All being in readiness, President Grant and the Emperor Dom Pedro grasped the handles of the acting valves, and at a concerted moment turned them. There was a slight hissing of steam audible, and then the huge walking-beam was seen to move, and, gathering momentum, was soon in full play. At the first visible movement a great shout arose, and at the same time the multitude of machines in the vast building began its din and clatter, as if they understood and responded to the acclamation.[6]

The engine ceased its service only when on the last day of the Exposition President Grant sent the last of thirteen successive signals, one for each of the original states, telling it that the work was over.

What effect did such an idol have upon visitors? We do not have to wait for a Henry Adams to tell us. In 1877 Edward C. Bruce published an account of the Exposition. What he says of Machinery Hall and the Corliss engine shows that like Mark Twain in *What Is Man?*, he was hard put to it to know where man ended and machine began. His description is headed "The House of the Iron Hand," and it is revelatory:

The label of Machinery Hall is hardly distinctive. It might be clapped on all the lookers-on and on everything looked at, artificial or natural, since all are machinery, built up on a system and working to fixed ends by fixed laws. The human machine, impelled by an internal motor that rests not day or night, looks around at those of iron without recognizing brotherhood. Nay, it calls them its creatures and makes them its slaves. Its action has brought theirs into play—checks, stops, renews, and accelerates it at pleasure. The machine conscious of this power and action of creation—and creation for a purpose—claims the possession of a will, and is by the latest philosophical advices credited with the same. It separates itself, accordingly, from those which do not boast that attribute, and declines to don the common badge and number. Acolytes and chattels, from the Corliss engine down to the candy-mixer, they are, in its view—as truly as those others, less easily classified as clearly having a will, which trot about in harness or wriggle in aquaria.

Spectators complained of the heat generated by the great engine but, says Bruce, "a world of automata insists on breathing an atmosphere of its own." [7] His prose might be improved; what he says is haunted by the modern fear that he who creates robots may turn mankind into machines.

Less than twenty years later a better known and more prestigious fair opened in Chicago, the World's Columbian Exposition, originally scheduled for 1892, four hundred years after the landing of Columbus. I shall return to certain aspects of this great show in another connection. Here it is sufficient to note that although two other enormous Corliss steam engines, each 2000 horsepower, surpassed the Philadelphia monster, they had to yield pride of place to a new breed of creatures, the industrial dynamo, which they set in motion and kept running. There were twelve of these in the Westinghouse exhibit, each larger than any previous dynamo. The fair was lighted and "run" by electricity, a fact that, together with its architectural harmony and wonderful arrangement of space, made it one of the great American achievements.[8] Henry Adams twice visited the Chicago World's Fair, but though he wrote John Hay that he "looked like an owl at the dynamos and steam-engines," Adams was too greatly harassed by fears generated from the financial panic and perhaps by provincialism to take in the significance of the dynamo.[9] His comments were principally on the architecture. But as all the world knows, he haunted the Paris Exposition of 1900, where Samuel Pierpont Langley, if Adams is to be believed, though Langley "said nothing new," explained everything and threw out "every exhibit that did not reveal a new application of force." The effect on Adams was something he could have got at Chicago, but the lesson had been postponed seven years. For Adams the dynamo became a symbol of infinity. The chapter in the *Education* on "The Dynamo and the Virgin" is of course one of the classical passages in the history of American ideas:

> The planet itself seemed less impressive, in its old-fashioned, deliberate annual or daily revolution, than this huge wheel, revolving within arm's-length at some vertiginous speed, and barely murmuring—scarcely humming an audible warning to stand a hair's-breadth further for respect of power—while it would not wake the baby lying close against its frame. Before the end, one began to pray to it; inherited instinct taught the natural expression of men before silent and infinite force. Among the thousand symbols of ultimate energy, the dynamo was not so human as some, but it was the most expressive.

The foci of force, he thought, were situated at either end of a catenary curve of history running from the Virgin to the dynamo. But Adams' Virgin has not proved satisfactory to Catholic thinkers. An instinct for elaborate mystification apparently led him to overlook Boyesen's "iron madonna," the vast murals at the Chicago Exposition, Daniel Chester French's statue of "The Republic"—to these I shall come in another connection—the Gibson girl, and the presentation of American womanhood by Howard Chandler Christy.[10] Simply as embodiments of energy, American women now emerged from the pale white flower phase of femininity beloved of Poe and his contemporaries, and represented energy even if they misrepresented sexuality.[11]

II

Let us consider the mobile image before we go on to discuss the control of motor energy. In ante-bellum America, still committed to the ideal of agrarian equality except in the slavery South, the simple Jacksonian doctrine of a career open to the talents was the hallmark of republican virtue. In politics this shaped itself into the theory that any adult male could fill any public office; and if you pushed Jeffersonianism, or Jacksonianism, or, for that matter, the communal ideals of Albert Brisbane or Robert Owen or John Humphrey Noyes to their logical conclusion, you arrived at social harmony. The doctrine remained acceptable to the business world, it was acceptable to the Federal armies and even to the Confederate forces though in lesser degree, and it remained basic in that great American Biblia Pauperum in many volumes, the success stories of Horatio Alger. After 1865 it was still fundamental to most Americans, but a new value, or rather the intensification of an old value, enriched the gospel of getting on. Mobility, which had been a mark of a westering society from the beginning, became an absolute virtue in an industrial democracy wherein mechanism put a special premium on speed and movement and a special disadvantage on standing still. You might stay where you had been or where your ancestors had been, but there was for the most part no advantage in doing so.

To this general precept there were exceptions, many of them more apparent than real. The old New England family, poor but proud, or, if not poor, certainly proud, in town or village; the Southern aristocrats still clinging to their ancestral halls or clustering in smaller Southern towns or cities like drowsy bees not yet incited into activity; old families in Little Old New York quietly disintegrating in all but caste values as the millionaires pushed in; older groups in central New York or Pennsylvania, Old Washingtonians, and their like— these incarnations of tradition remained, just as father and mother, grandfather and grandmother stayed on the old farm or in the old manor house. The old farm, indeed, was a base camp to which the exploratory younger generation could return for fresh supplies in case of disaster, and visits were paid to the old home in the village or its equivalent in the plantation South for which a certain fondness remained, as portrayed in nostalgic novels of the South and dutiful autobiographies praising the simple integrity of farm and village. But as industrialism covered more and more of the United States, it be-came less and less necessary to return except for funerals, family reunions, or family settlements, just as it was commonly felt that these islands of an older America lay outside the main channel of modernity. The elder generation was pitied or envied for its pride and poverty, and simultaneously ridiculed and admired for its in-ability to accept progress. The ambiguity of attitudes is evident in much of the fiction of these years, in which, though descriptions are given of an older way of living thought to be simpler, more pastoral, less "nervous," or more chivalric, the climax of the tale commonly centers upon progressive youth. The restless generation of veterans undoubtedly contributed to the Great Uneasiness, but nobody has troubled to find out what really happened to the lost generation of the Civil War.

For the majority of Americans mobility was progress. Except as conservatism was upheld by family distinction, not to be able and willing to migrate implied stagnation. During this period terms like "whistle stop" and "one-horse town" came into common parlance. Not to move meant not reflectiveness but defeatism. Stagnation cre-ated or implied apathy, parochialism, or bitterness. The isolated farm or ranch, cut off from neighbors or from store or village because the roads were bad or impassable in the mud season or during floods or when they were blocked with ice and snow; crude cabins in the piny woods of the South or along some uncivilized riverbank; shacks lived in by frowsy families, white or black, on a back road, their own-ers usually suspicious, illiterate, and lawless; moonshiners up a moun-tain cove; gaggles of defeated gold-seekers still haunting ghost towns in Nevada, California, or Colorado; defeated pioneers, wrinkled and prematurely old, in sod huts or sun-blistered frame houses on the

Great Plains—these people were obviously failures, to be interpreted as pitiful or quaint, living museum pieces preserving fragments of seventeenth-century English, local versions of old ballads, or mysterious African rites—spells, charms, voodoo ceremonials, and superstitions. Such things were to be collected by folklorists or transcribed by the sentimental. To these shreds and patches of an immobile America one must add, when the aborigines were finally conquered, Indian reservations and towns, to which reformers, tourists, and anthropologists made reverential or condescending expeditions. Art lovers bought Navaho rugs and Indian basketwork, simultaneously supporting primitivism and dodging responsibility for an answer to the question: what is the future of the primitive in an industrial world? To most Americans such persons or communities were inexplicable relics that could not be equated with the doctrine of general motion.

Other types, scarcely more respectable in status, at least embraced mobility as their way of life, even if the embrace did not imply the virtues of going upward and on. The squatter, the speculator, the patent medicine man, the quack doctor, the traveling salesman, the hired man, the migrant worker who toiled on the railroads in summer or at seasonal harvestings and retreated to the West Side of Chicago during the winter, the traveling "tent" evangelist, the itinerant prostitute, the flimflam artists who moved from county fair to county fair or from north to south as the weather dictated—these, too, participated in the Great Restlessness. Books like Josiah Flynt's *Tramping with Tramps* (1899) and *Notes of an Itinerant Policeman* (1900) were written about some battalions of this aimless army,[12] and so were studies like *The Workers: The East* (1897) and *The Workers: The West* (1898) by Walter A. Wyckoff, a Princeton theologian who later became a professor of political economy. Most of these submarginal lives were parodies of the great central theme of mobility. The hobo as a comic figure ("Wearie Willie") and the tramp as a sinister apparition at the back doors of middle-class homes did more to engender an atmosphere of fright than did novels like John Hay's *The Bread-Winners* (1884) and Jack London's *The People of the Abyss* (1903).

These types were, however, only skirmishers or outriders in the general army of mobility. The town or village on Saturdays attracted the farmer, who, the chores being done, hitched up his team to the wagon, put his wife and children on boards for seats, and drove into town, where he bought supplies, gossiped with his cronies in the courthouse square or on the front porch of the general store, and drank lager beer in the saloons. His wife did her shopping and glanced enviously at city notions in the cases or on the counters, and the children stared at the "townies" and sucked licorice sticks or hard candies. Toward nightfall the wagon rumbled back to an unlovely house, the horses were unharnessed by lantern light, the children were put to bed, and the chores were belatedly done up by the weary farmer if the hired man was still off on his weekend drunk. Glimpses into the colorful world of town did much to make the younger generation want to leave the farm, especially when young adolescent males could slip off to listen to drummers on the hotel veranda tell stories of their exploits in the bright lights of the metropolis, and they whetted the desire of farm daughters for pretty things and lessened toil. The invention of the mail-order catalogue, if in one sense it brought the city to the farm, in another sense increased the hunger of the farm family for a life less drab and more colorful. The telephone and radio were to brighten things and various labor-saving devices for barn and household and for planting and harvesting were to appear among farmers who were better off. By 1910 the farm wagon was likely to be replaced by the Model T Ford, the Tin Lizzie of happy memory.[13]

But if the town thus attracted the farm, the city attracted the town. The clerk in the village store gaped at the costumes and witticisms of the traveling salesman from the metropolis; the owner of the store, when he visited wholesale houses at some larger distributing point, learned something about the lure and glitter of the city. Ambitious young women, finding no challenge in schoolteaching or clerking in the village store, longed to go to a metropolitan "business college" and become "typewriters" in some city firm, or if not that, clerks in a store like Marshall Field's in Chicago. The village banker and his wife were less likely to move; nevertheless, when they went to the big city to put up at some smart hotel during the state bankers' convention, they felt a little awed, a touch entranced, and brought back anecdotes about leading bankers, politicians, businessmen, and big legal lights they had met or listened to, not to mention the latest word in men's overcoats, suitings, and necktie pins, or women's hats, chinaware, house furnishings, and decoration.

The city was wicked; it was also fascinating. Ranchers and farmers could, and did, rebel against the domination of the "money trust," but the rural virtues and the mores of the village began to seem old-fashioned as this half-century swept on. Novels such as Hamlin Garland's *Rose of Dutcher's Coolly* (1895) and Dreiser's *Sister Carrie* (1900) represent the lure of the bright lights for the female sex; Robert Herrick's *Memoirs of an American Citizen* (1903) and Ellen Glasgow's *The Voice of the People* (1900) do the same thing for the male. The classic forerunner of these and others is presumably Howells' *The Rise of Silas Lapham* (1884), in which a Vermont farm boy goes to the city, makes his pile, is tempted, falls in the moral scale, fails in business, and rises in the scale of traditional morality. Fictionists might be cynical or sentimental about the pull of the city on the hinterland, but their theme was more often the lure of the city for the country than it was the attraction of the countryside for the jaded metropolitan.[14]

The farm seemed drab, the village dull, the town stagnant. Every force in America, it sometimes seemed, was in the direction of speed, scatter, and mobility. To be modern was to be mobile and to be mobile was to be modern. If speed-up cut down labor, it sometimes increased an empty leisure. Beginning about 1850 and reaching relative perfection about 1880, the mechanical reaper harvested grains with a sweep and precision that ended the life of Whittier's Barefoot Boy and Riley's Raggedy Man. In 1880 it took a unit of about 20 manpower to harvest an acre of wheat; by the opening of World War I this had been cut to 12.7.[15] The automatic binder came into its own about 1880. Milk production was rationalized. The town (and indeed the city)[16] had formerly depended for their meats upon the local butcher, who in turn got them from the local slaughterhouse, but as early as the 1830s Cincinnati was developing teamwork processes in killing and dressing hogs, the presence of which in the city Mrs. Trollope detested. After Swift, Armour, and Morris had developed their vast designs for killing, dressing, and shipping meats to all parts of the nation and the world, what Giedion has called the mechanism of death triumphed. Meat was no longer a product of the farm at hog-killing time, but the business of wholesalers—a titanic complex which assumed, as he says, that vast areas agree to draw their provisions of meat from four or five central places. Moreover, when the old-line farmer failed and the mortgage fell in at the bank, hard-boiled business managers were sent out to take over, a procedure this same writer compares to the enclosure of common lands in the eighteenth century. By 1910 agriculture was no longer Jeffersonian but Brobdingnagian; Sidney Lanier in the essay I have cited about "wheat mining" on bonanza farms in the Great West and Frank Norris in *The Octopus* with its unforgettable picture of a regiment of harvesting machines sweeping over a vast field anticipate or parallel historical development. Even the hen was metamorphosed into an egg-laying machine lodged in one cell among tier on tier of cells.

Science, efficiency, speed, movement—these were the ideals. Persons displaced from farm or village had to go somewhere. Sometimes they went farther west only to face again the problem of machine displacement or bad weather or both; sometimes they drifted into the planless cities of the century. As Spengler hints in *The Decline of the West,* the picture of Socrates wearing a wristwatch is virtually indecent. But as mobility grew into either a necessity or a virtue, time became a prominent element in culture. By the date of the World's Columbian Exposition, the Waterbury watch was being manufactured at a rate of five hundred thousand a year. By 1919 seventy million Ingersoll watches had been sold, and in the period clock making, once the occupation of artists and artisans, under the direction of engineers had become a matter of interchangeable parts. A clock or watch is of course no more than an instrument to measure the flight of time in a culture conscious of both time and movement. In the period geniuses like Marey, Muybridge, and Gilbreth were measuring the speed of movement in birds, horses, swordsmen, and men walking or running in space. Science and invention no longer found much interest in stillness; only that which moved, and preferably that which moved swiftly, really fascinated inquiry. In 1887 the Michelson-Morley experiment seemed to settle the problem of the speed of light as an absolute; in 1893 an engineer on locomotive # 999 of the New York Central drove his train at a rate of 112.5 miles an hour; in 1894 Edison's Kinetoscope, which speeded up pictures, was publicly revealed; and in 1896 the Vitascope first threw moving pictures—note the adjective—on a screen in a New York music hall. By 1903 the Wright brothers were flying their first airplane, an invention that, except for the atom bomb, has done more to destroy a static culture than even the automobile. As an illuminating footnote to this thirst for movement, it is well to remember that in *Tom Sawyer* (1876) the boys stay in or near the village, but in the incomparably greater *Huck Finn* (1885) we have one of the great journey books of American literature.

I have hitherto written as though only the movement from the farm or village to the city was paramount. Obviously cities mushroomed. But this is to simplify. As I have already said, hundreds of thousand of immigrants, lured to the New World by rumor, glittering promises in poster or delusive pamphlets about new Edens in the West, talks by publicity agents of American railroads, steamship lines, or, in some cases, states, attracted by letters from relatives in America, or driven from their homeland by poverty or pogrom, streamed like lemmings into the United States. Discovering that being packed into ghettos or slums was, aside from "freedom," an unsatisfactory life, they squirmed out of the slums into better metropolitan neighborhoods or into areas of greater space.

But the flow of passengers was not all one way. In the period the steamship companies strove for more comfortable, safer and speedier service from American ports to Europe (sometimes to Asia), the travel agent made his debut, books like Stoddard's *Lectures* were sold in sets, and the commercialization of itinerancy to the Old World, Asia, the Pacific, and Africa became another element of mobility. Moreover, millionaires moved east from Texas, Montana, Colorado, or Alaska; consumptives went south or west to Florida or Colorado; Southern Negroes drifted north to get jobs as waiters, Pullman porters, attendants at barbershops, gambling dens, and baser places; Northern debutantes went south to learn charm, college boys made a point of going to school somewhere else, college girls got summer jobs in seaside hotels or inns in the national parks; and American tourism, a rising industry, took in not only the rest of the world, but the White Mountains, Quebec, the Adirondacks, Saratoga Springs, Yellowstone, the Yosemite, and much more.

It was the age of the summer-resort hotel, the carryall, the sunshade, and the guided tour, just as it was the age of yachting,[17] bicycling, and of course horse racing, an ancient sport of kings that threatened to become the sport of crooks. In track, records began to be kept and broken as runners trained by careful coaching dashed around ovals at speeds that would have astonished Leatherstocking. But this period was to turn into the age of the automobile with its emphasis on speed. We began motorcar racing (as the phrase went) in 1895, and by 1911 we opened the Indianapolis Speedway. In all this speed-up two attitudes predominate: if in Europe the United States was accused of materialism, the charge increased rather than retarded the desire of immigrants to come here and prosper; and, despite tourism, nobody really wanted to return to Europe permanently. Such expatriates as existed were regarded as un-American snobs, probably trying to dodge taxation.

But the giant central agency in American mobility was the railroad, which in these fifty years entered upon its golden age. The development of railroad transportation from 1850 to World War I is an epic chapter in an epic time. In 1850 there were a little more than nine thousand miles of railway in the country, all of them east of the Mississippi, all of them short-line roads, the rolling stock being dangerous and primitive.[18] Already, however, agitation had begun for the extension of a railway to the Pacific coast,[19] and in 1853–1854 surveys were made by the government to "ascertain the most practicable and economical route for a railroad from the Mississippi River to the Pacific Ocean." These surveys are recorded in one of the most magnificent sets of documents ever issued by the United States.[20] Trains then ran at from eighteen to thirty miles an hour, accidents were frequent, there was no uniform signal system, and since railroad corporations were usually the result of local enthusiasm, the concept of a through route on a uniform gauge from one important city to another was slow in forming. Yet by 1853 it was possible to travel from the Atlantic to Chicago by rail, though one had to change roads frequently, by 1854 there was a railhead on the Mississippi River, and by 1870 a train left Chicago every fifteen minutes. Not even the panics of 1857 and 1873, not even stock-market speculation, overcapitalization, strikes, bad management, and physical disasters could stop the proliferation of the railway. By 1900 there were about one hundred and seventy-five thousand miles of track in the country or approximately two-fifths of all the railroad mileage of the world.

One curious element in this development is the extent to which New Englanders pioneered, whether as engineers and builders or as directors or managers. A typical instance is the upright John Murray Forbes of Massachusetts, the principal creator of the Chicago, Burlington & Quincy, one of the soundest railroad systems of the age; another is Charles Francis Adams, who, having exposed the criminal actions of speculators in his *Chapters of Erie* (1871), became the first chairman of the Massachusetts Board of Railroad Commissioners in

1872, chairman of the government directors of the Union Pacific in 1878, and president of that company in 1884. Granville M. Dodge, a great construction engineer and the chief engineer of the Union Pacific, came from Danvers, Massachusetts, and John A. Poor of Maine devoted his considerable talent to creating a viable connection by rail between eastern Canada and New England. These are but four among many.

In the East short lines were rapidly consolidated into railway systems, the control over which occasioned gigantic battles among millionaires. West of the Mississippi the construction of roads into unsettled or sparsely settled areas, through the mountain ranges and the inland desert into California and the Pacific Northwest, is a colorful chapter in the history of the continent, one that includes armed conflicts between Indians and railroad construction crews and soldiers, battles between gangs working on rival projects,[21] the importation of labor from abroad (in one famous case Chinese coolies), and the eternal struggle to pierce mountains or ward off heavy snows or sudden floods. In the majority of cases Western trunk lines could not have been built without substantial aid from the federal government, the extent of which, like charges of graft and corruption, has been exaggerated.[22]

It is obvious that the enormous industrial centers and the national distribution of goods and services, not to speak of the export-import trade, modern postal service, the railway express service, and much else, would have been impossible without the railroads, but our present concern is their encouragement to human movement. After novelty wore off and public apprehension grew because of the mounting number of lurid railroad accidents, companies began to discover there was revenue in safety, comfort, speed, and luxury, qualities that became more and more apparent in passenger service after 1870. As somebody has said, the aim of the roads was to create moving hotels encompassing speed, laziness, safety, and luxury. The Pullman car, the diner, the smoking car with its bar, the chair car, the observation car, and eventually the vista-dome car made for luxury; the air brake, the vestibule train, steel coaches, heavier rails, improved roadbeds, safer trestles and bridges, electric signal systems, and careful scheduling made for safety. Speed was insured by all these inventions and by more powerful locomotives, by the distinction between the limited and the local train, and by creating a professional, even a technological, pride in punctuality. One railway advertised itself as the "On Time Road," and Arnold Bennett in *Your United States* (1912) takes a mild, malicious delight in recording the discomfiture of the conductor, brakemen, and other officials of the crack Twentieth Century Limited when, because of accidents, it rolled into Chicago some two hours late.[23] Railroads advertised the glory of riding from here to there. Their agents solicited travel, their publicity representatives got out illustrated booklets full of allure, the companies advertised excursions to the seashore, the mountains, the lakes, the large cities, or to meetings and conventions; they created personally conducted tours, built or helped others to build resort hotels, and had their trains pause for a moment for a glimpse of Niagara Falls or some other scenic wonder. Even the local train encouraged mobility. It offered father and mother and the children cheap transportation to a town fifty miles away to see grandma and grandpa.

The railroads were also, as I have indicated, an important agency in peopling great blank spaces on the American map. A classic instance is the campaign of the Illinois Central to induce immigrants and settlers to take up farms on the hundreds of thousands of acres in government grants along its right of way. One advertisement in 1860 reads: "Homes for the Industrious in the Garden State of the West. The Illinois Central Railroad Company have for Sale 1,200,000 Acres of Rich Farming Lands in Tracts of Forty Acres and upward on Long Credit and at Low Prices." The road distributed this and similar come-on advertisements everywhere. It issued attractive brochures, it sent agents to talk to farm groups in this country and to foreigners abroad. If not all the purchases were bona fide, if the farms were not uniformly rich and the prairie sod was somewhat tougher to break with the plow than publicity said it was, if the company had to fight off squatters and timber thieves, this road was nevertheless a primary agent in increasing the population of Illinois, adding, says the historian, over one hundred thousand people to the state between 1854 and 1870.[24] What the Illinois Central had done other roads could imitate; later this railroad and the state were disturbed to see Illinois farmers moving west to Nebraska and beyond. The transcontinental lines also needed traffic and population. At one time James J. Hill was transporting farmers prepared to take up land along the Northern Pacific, from the Atlantic seacoast to, say, Montana, for about ten dollars. It is too crass to remark that this encouragement of mobility was merely for profit, since some roads took care that towns along the right of way had sites for churches and schools, a courthouse, and a jail. But they had no control over speculative purchasing, and nobody heeded the warnings of John Wesley Powell [25] about the danger of deep plowing in the semiarid Great Plains—so that when disaster struck, bitterness flavored politics, and aimless mobility, the result of disappointment, led people to migrate eastward. One recalls the earlier legend on settlers' wagons: "Pike's Peak or Bust," which became "Pike's Peak: Busted" when they crawled away from misadventure.

III

But how were the energies of these human armies, these vast machines—locomotives, steam engines, dynamos, industrial presses, gigantic cranes, endless belts, buckets of molten steel, and all the rest —to be controlled? Who was to direct the exploitation of the earth, the air, and the sea and bring together into any meaningful design the coal and iron and copper, the wheat and beef and poultry, the cotton and wool and timber, the leather and clay and oil, and all the other primary elements and forces industry demanded for its existence? Who was to build, supervise, repair, and tear down these furnaces, these incredible mills and slaughterhouses, these grain elevators, flour mills, textile factories, ore boats on the lake, and mile-long trains of freight cars? Who was to oversee the penetration of the cities and the countryside with endless lines of telegraph or telephone wires, and cables for the distribution of electric power? How direct, how manage the speed, ruthlessness, energy, and movement, each essential to wholesale production and to retail trade? On the one hand, the constant encouragement to mobility; on the other, the continuing expansion of a raw industrial order. How rationalize a seething life of exploitation, manufacture, distribution, and consumption beyond anything the world had ever known?

At this point the student confronts a curious dilemma. Those who felt that the growth of the giant Industry and the ogre Monopoly were the results of devilish cunning believed, naturally enough, that there must be at the center of this expanding evil some inhuman genius whom it was the business of all honest citizens to identify, expose, and either cripple or destroy. Hence there arose a kind of brassy rhetoric of reform among the Grangers, the Populists, the Socialists, the Anarchists, the Communists, the Silver Democrats, the Bellamy Nationalists, and the Henry George Single-Taxers, and to this rhetoric social historians have, quite properly, paid a great deal of attention, analyzing the grievances that created it and estimating the success or failure of the reforms it proposed. There has come into being a remarkable library of specialized history about social and economic legislation and legal decisions, the working of state or federal commissions, the influence of national leaders on fiscal policy, the tariff, taxation, railroad rates, labor laws, the imposition of competition by statute, and the retention in the last quarter of the nineteenth century of the simpler ethos of business a century earlier. Nor is it here denied that legislation was needed and that control was often effective.

On the other hand, as soon as one picks up a history of invention and technology [26] for the same period, politics and social history drop out of sight, and the eddies of social and political history are replaced by the clear, untroubled forward-running stream of science, invention, and technology. One moves into a universe of discourse so totally different from that of the social historian that one begins to wonder whether the same nation is under survey. From this second point of view the years from 1865 to 1915 are a brilliant epoch, during which the creation and utilization of new sources and forms of energy and the distribution of that energy or its products go steadily forward, driven on by a mysterious compulsion known as progress. Progress, it is true, is sometimes marred or blocked by financial depressions, quarrels among inventors and those who exploited them, lawsuits over patent rights, attacks by "agitators," and ignorant struggles of individualists, liberals, and labor unions to reverse an inevitable trend. These are, however, temporary blots on a fair record. The machine by definition lightens toil, increases comfort, creates more wealth and more science, and is a primary power for the general welfare. The warnings of Guglielmo Ferrero that modern America might be following the path of ancient Rome in its accumulation of easy riches and its creation of a vast proletariat fell on ears that were deaf in a period when Teddy Roosevelt was preaching against race suicide. Considerations of this sort did not disturb the euphoria of those who chronicled the development of industrial science in the United States, and not until the rise of critics like Lewis Mumford and Siegfried Giedion did any one seriously question the ultimate effect upon human life of man's increasing separation from natural processes.

And, in truth, the historians of industry and invention have a case. Here, for example, is a partial list of important innovations:

1863 the first "Mogul" locomotive
1864 the first Bessemer steel plant (Wyandotte, Michigan)
     the first practicable Pullman car
1865 the first oil pipeline
1866 the Atlantic cable in operation
1867 the first practicable refrigerator railway cars
1868 the Westinghouse air brakes for railway cars
1869 the first transcontinental railway track completed
1870 the first silos
1871 Hoe's web perfecting press used for the New York *Tribune*
     the Ingersoll compressed air drill
1873 Janney's automatic car coupler
     the first cable cars in San Francisco
1874 the third rail for subway and elevated traction
1875 the first cash carrier for stores
1876 the Bell telephone
     the hydraulic dredge
     machines for making cigarettes
     barbed wire manufactured on a large scale
1877 the phonograph
     Selden's automobile
1878 the first public telephone switchboard (New Haven, Connecticut)
     Wanamaker's store in Philadelphia lighted by electric lamps (carbon)
     the Sholes typewriter
1879 the first hydroelectric plant at Niagara Falls
     the streets of Cleveland, Ohio, lighted by carbon lamps (arc lights)
     the first automatic railway signal system
1880 the first successful incandescent electric lamp
1882 the first public electric lighting system (New York)
1883 the first elevated electric railroad (Chicago)

1886 the linotype
      the alternating electric current commercially viable
1887 the vestibule passenger train
1888 Dunlop's pneumatic tire
      the first municipal trolley car system (Richmond, Virginia)
1889 the De Laval turbine
1892 the first electric passenger elevator
      the Ford car
1896 the first commercial movies (New York City)
1900 American tinplate processing perfected
1903 the apparent failure of Langley and the success of the Wright
        brothers in flying

Almost every date is in dispute; almost every invention is claimed by various persons both here and abroad. The list does not include the creation of new tools and machines for flour milling, mining, lumbering, the loading and discharge of bulk cargo, vast changes in industrial chemistry that only an expert can chronicle, various advances in ice-making, textiles, woodworking, metalworking, the operation of hospitals, new tools and instruments in dentistry and surgery, the creation of patent foods, new modes of sinking caissons and building bridges, progress in printing, computing machines, paper-making, and much else.

The historian's problem is still that posed by Henry Adams in the *Education*. Why, if technological skill could thus drive irresistibly forward, was there such social chaos? How reconcile the regular pulsing of the Corliss engine and the smooth purring of the dynamo with constant jars and breakdowns in the political and social order? On the one hand, the proliferation of labor-saving devices; on the other, a tumultuous life that recalls the pages of Gibbon when he is describing the disorders of the later empire. Why, when causes and crusades were thus passionately advocated, was distress so deeply felt? why was the gap between the exploiters and the exploited so obviously widening, and why did the multitude not turn on their masters, the monopolists and the inventors of machines? The march of industry was not checked; the magnates continued to expand and to exploit the channels and instruments of energy. No left-wing group or party triumphed in a republic whose legal system was supposed to be sensitive to the will of an outraged people. How reconcile order and anarchy? Stability and confusion? Technology and chaos?

It is a platitude that the years from 1865 to 1915 saw the development of the modern corporation in the United States. Where their ante-bellum predecessors had been not much more than enlarged partnerships confining their relatively simple operations to a state, a region, or a single business, these new creations, expanding both horizontally and vertically, took the nation, the continent, or the world for their empires, swelling rapidly into institutions that rivaled government, the church, the courts, and the schools as instruments of social energy. Usually the creation and sometimes the victim of the robber-baron generation, the industrial corporation was a fictive, yet immortal entity, legally the creature of a single state, though its business might be done in any or all states or abroad. It might dissolve but it could not die as a human being dies, even though the courts declared it was legally a person. It might and sometimes did melt its curious immortality into the immortality of a larger "trust," and this larger monster was more terrifying to simple citizens than the jinni of the Arabian Nights. Theoretically the possession of its stockholders, the corporation was in fact really the creature of its directors or a competent moiety thereof, who might drive it to shipwreck in some financial storm or, contrariwise, steer it over the sinking hulk of an enemy vessel. The corporation existed as a screen for the dark doings of speculators, as a shield to hide the actual operations of competitive ruthlessness, and as a vast new device for the exploitation of power, the diffusion of energy, and selling the products of energy. To the rural mind and the liberal thinker the corporations, at least when they were damned as "trusts," were uncontrollable evil giants that were turning an agrarian republic into an empire of greed. To the capitalist, the engineer, the investor, and the business genius the corporation was the last fine flowering of the Protestant ethic, the philosophy of individualism; it was the inevitable product of, and (simultaneously) the modern answer to, what came to be known as social Darwinism. The reformer said the corporations were soulless. The cartoonist pictured them as Goliaths with bloated bellies. The politician denounced them in general and collogued with them in particular. The labor unions fought them. The legislature tried to restrain them. The corporation lawyer found new ways of getting out from under the bounds of legal restraint.

The corporation, it is clear, could be denounced as a modern revival of ancient practices of monopoly, regrating, engrossing, covin, and other violations of the theory of a just price, against which church and parliament had thundered in past centuries; or it could be praised as the great "creative response" to new technologies, expanding markets, full employment (the full dinner pail is a phrase of the 1890s), the fulfillment of the promise of American life. If the "trusts" were the children of malefactors of great wealth,[27] proponents and defenders felt that only through the large corporation could American technology bring happiness to the country and the world. Happiness lay with technology. Thus the engineer, Henry G. Prout, told some Cornell alumni in 1905:

> the engineer more than all other men will guide humanity forward until we come to some other period of a different kind. On the engineer and on those who are making engineers rests a responsibility such as men have never before been called upon to face, for it is a peculiarity of the new epoch that we are conscious of it, that we know what we are doing, which was not true in . . . preceding epochs, and we have upon us the responsibility of conscious knowledge.[28]

This duality of valuation underlies so keen an analysis as Herbert Croly's *The Promise of American Life* (1909), for in one and the same chapter Croly describes business competition as "a fierce and merciless affair" and admires the "justifiable and ameliorating purpose" of John D. Rockefeller in endeavoring to "escape from the savage warfare." What Rockefeller really sought was the conservation of economic energy.

If patterns making for economy of motion and the reduction of friction were essential to the triumph of the Corliss engine, the dynamo, and the internal combustion engine, were not more efficient patterns of social organization also possible? A fascinating aspect of the period is the search for societal and economic forms that would reduce or eliminate social friction. The outcome of the Civil War had basically altered acceptable notions of the relation between the states and the federal government, so much so that the kind of hostility represented by nullification and the kind of antagonism represented by secession were no longer possible. If in theory the individual commonwealths still retained their political autonomy, the years since 1865 have seen the slow erosion of states' rights and a steady increase in the power of the central government, a movement toward centralization that, though it creates vast problems of its own, has diminished the points of controversy between these two great components of the federal system. This slow shift, principally under the general welfare clause and under a concept of interstate commerce that would have bewildered the Founding Fathers, was, however, so imperceptible from administration to administration as not to be one of the recognized dominant organizational patterns of the age. The dominant organizational patterns from 1865 to 1915 were, I think, the corporation, conspiracy, and the national association. I have already touched on the corporation and all too briefly hinted that it came to be regarded as a fine instrument for the conservation of energy. It is now necessary to turn to the idea of conspiracy and then to the concept of the national association.

Charges of conspiracy are likely to be made in any period of extreme tension or of social unrest. Conspiracy is a pejorative term. To most Americans it is an idea thoroughly against the American grain. Yet conspiracies or charges of conspiracy are common enough in the national history. The Boston Tea Party was a conspiracy; so was the treason of Benedict Arnold; and conspiratorial actions have been charged against Revolutionary generals like Lee and Gates. No one has ever succeeded in freeing Aaron Burr from the suspicion of conspiracy; and as for General James Wilkinson, governor of the Territory of Louisiana, he seems secretly to have run with the hare and hunted with the hounds. Conspiracy was hotly alleged in the presidential election of 1824—rank bargain and corruption, it was said, sent John Quincy Adams to the White House. Charges of conspiracy flew back and forth between North and South during the years that preceded the Civil War. One faction supposed there was a conspiracy on the part of a slaveholding oligarchy to dominate the government and the other side charged that John Brown's raid on Harpers Ferry was only the latest of Northern or abolitionist plots against the peaceful South. The assassination of Lincoln and the attempted assassination of Seward were officially announced to be the results of a conspiracy, for which four persons were executed and four imprisoned after the death of John Wilkes Booth. During Reconstruction the Ku Klux Klan, the Knights of the White Camellia, and other white supremacy groups were declared conspiratorial by legislation. In the Far West, Henry Plummer, to all appearances a gentleman, elected marshal, elected sheriff, elected a legislator, headed a gang of bandits who were said to have robbed or murdered more than a hundred persons in southern Montana and adjacent parts of Idaho. For this Plummer was hanged in 1864, as were twenty-four of his associates. Since a countervailing force was necessary, a secret society of vigilantes was organized to rid the area of thieves and murderers.[29] Similar groups of vigilantes appeared elsewhere—for example, in Nevada and in San Francisco. There were other gangs of bandits, too: Sam Bass and his thieves in the cow country, the Dalton gang in Oklahoma.

The technical legal definition of a conspiracy implies that two or more persons unite to do an unlawful or criminal act or an act innocent in itself that, being done by the concerted action of the conspirators, becomes criminal or uses unlawful means for the commission of an act not unlawful in itself. The courts and the legislature also distinguish between a criminal conspiracy and a civil conspiracy, the latter being a concerted effort to defraud or cause injury to persons or property that results in damage to the person or the property of the plaintiff. The distinction is an important one. In popular terms, however, a conspiracy may be entered into either to make evil prevail or to hasten the triumph of good over evil. To put down evil and make the good triumph was the aim of the original members of the Ku Klux Klan. Since trade unions were long illegal under common law and declared to be conspiracies by statute, it will surprise nobody to learn that the original idea (1869) of the Knights of Labor was that of a secret society, the secrecy being partly for glamor, partly to prevent infiltration by spies, *agents provocateurs,* and private detectives in the pay of employers. Indeed, the notion of the labor union as a dark conspiracy of radicals or of lawless men seemed justified when in 1876 the Molly Maguires were exposed, a terrorist organization of miners, ten of whom were hanged for murder. The attempt of Jim Fisk and Jay Gould to hoodwink President Grant into allowing them to corner gold, the failure of which resulted in "Black Friday" of 1869, the exposure of the Tweed ring in 1871, the Crédit Mobilier scandal of 1872, and the revelation of the Whisky Ring affair in 1873 all pointed to conspiracy as a potent force in America. Anarchists, Communists, Socialists, and radicals generally were thought to be conspirators, so that by the 1870s and 1880s the concept of conspiracy as a form of organization was familiar to most Americans. How else account for the price of food, or of shipping grain, or the cost of clothing, or real estate, or fuel, or a wide variety of other necessities?

The novelists, those abstracts and brief chronicles of the time, often make conspiracy some part of their plots. The activities of Senator Dilworthy in *The Gilded Age*, of Van Harrington, the hero-villain of Herrick's *The Memoirs of an American Citizen*, of Servosse in Tourgée's *A Fool's Errand*, of Magnus Derrick in Norris's *The Octopus*, of Dreiser's Frank Cowperwood in the so-called trilogy of desire, involve or disclose conspiracy in the business or political world. In John Hay's *The Bread-Winners* the labor movement is infiltrated by conspirators, and the same imputation colors F. Hopkinson Smith's lesser but illuminating *Tom Grogan*. Thomas Nelson Page's *Red Rock*, Thomas Dixon's *The Clansman*, and Booth Tarkington's *The Gentleman from Indiana* feature the Ku Klux Klan as a conspiracy justified or unjustified according to the predilection of the novelist. In Donnelly's *Caesar's Column* and Jack London's *The Iron Heel* the government of the United States is taken over by conspirators who, when they are strong enough, use force and violence to complete the job. A good many reform novels—Winston Churchill's *Coniston* is representative—reveal, sometimes as melodrama, sometimes as ironic comedy, the central place and secret ways of conspiracy in political and legislative life or reach a climax when the young lawyer reveals in a stunning courtroom scene the facts of a business conspiracy against the city, the county, or the nation.[30]

The concept of civil conspiracy is less lurid than that of criminal conspiracy. If we interpret the former as a quiet agreement among the big captains of industry to accomplish this or that end, it becomes evident that, shorn of its darker moral coloring, conspiracy was a standard form of business action in the Age of Energy. The granting of rebates and drawbacks, the unostentatious acquiring of public lands or franchises, the management of a price war against a competitor, the buying or selling of stocks and bonds through third parties for the purpose of acquiring a rival firm or wrecking a competitor, abrupt demands for injunctions before some complacent judge, the creation of trusts, pools, and interlocking directorates—all these aims or devices were more efficiently managed by methods that bordered upon or fell within the definition of civil conspiracy. In

furthering these aims the corporation lawyer, virtually a creation of
the period, a specialist whom Croly singles out as one of the four
great shapers of the new industrial society, became an expert in conspiracy. The popular mind, unable or unwilling to distinguish between criminal conspiracy and civil conspiracy, naturally gave the
worst possible interpretation to these practices, arguing that if the
leaders of Tammany Hall meeting in a smoke-filled room were justly
called conspiratorial, the directors of some large corporation meeting
in a more elegant chamber were likewise bent on plundering the
pocketbooks of the plain citizen. Unfortunately, many of them were.
If you didn't believe that the masters of money were conspirators,
you had but to read the denunciations of populist-minded muckrakers, for example, *Monopolies and the People,* "Dedicated to the Patrons of Husbandry," by D.C.Cloud, where you would learn:

> It is a fact to be admitted by every candid thinker, that of late years, cor-
> porations, rings and single speculators have, by united and persistent
> efforts, obtained control of the government; that their interests are
> guarded, and protected by the legislative, executive, and judicial depart-
> ments of the government, both state and national. The men who are
> thus combined in opposition to the people do not belong to any one po-
> litical division; they are found in all parties; they are firmly united for
> the purpose of grasping power, of controlling the government in their
> own interest, of fastening upon the people oppressive monopolies, and of
> enriching themselves at the expense of the public.[31]

If this were too much of an *ad captandum* and vulgar argument,
then you could read in the *Atlantic Monthly* for March 1881 the
"Story of a Great Monopoly" by Henry Demarest Lloyd (the issue
had to be reprinted seven times), the basis of his influential *Wealth
against Commonwealth* (1894), or, if not that, Ida Tarbell's *History of
the Standard Oil Company* (1904).[32]

In common law monopoly and civil conspiracy were often thought
to be synonymous; and state legislation in various commonwealths
had attempted to check or destroy the piratical purposes of the captains of industry. In 1887 the Interstate Commerce Act was aimed
against rebates and toward the power of the federal government to
regulate railway rates, and in 1890 the Sherman Anti-Trust Act became law, the intent being to put down both monopoly and conspiracy, the latter word being directly used in the legislation. It cannot
be said that the Anti-Trust Act was effective, even though its lan-

guage declares that "every contract, combination in the form of trust, or otherwise, or conspiracy in restraint of trade and commerce among the several States" makes persons guilty of a misdemeanor "who shall monopolize or shall attempt to monopolize or combine or conspire with other persons to monopolize trade and commerce among the several States." But what constituted monopoly? What constituted conspiracy? Was bigness in itself a crime? Was the efficient management of the fruits of energy, merely because it was on a large scale, evidence of conspiracy? Decisions by the Supreme Court for twenty or thirty years seemed to waver in their definitions of conspiracy, and despite the agitated prose of the later muckrakers, as recently as the administrations of Theodore Roosevelt the metaphysical distinction between a "bad" trust and a "good" trust was not established. Meanwhile the efficiency of what might be deemed conspiratorial practices was more and more evident.[33]

Political and social historians are naturally bemused by the drama of the plain people rising in their wrath to put down industrial conspiracies, and have not sufficiently dramatized the defense of business, interesting at this point because it tends to combine four major arguments: that of evolution (big business is inevitable), a stout plea for laissez faire, a protest against "radicalism," and, most interesting of all, an argument of efficiency. In 1899 a "Conference on Trusts" was held under the auspices of the Civic Federation of Chicago. Attended by economists, politicians, officers of business corporations, and others, the gathering solemnly voted that "this conference is without authority, and it would be inexpedient for it to adopt resolutions purporting to declare the sense of the conference upon any aspect of the subject of discussion," even though William Jennings Bryan had been in attendance.[34] In 1900 Jeremiah W. Jenks, though he admitted that trusts should be regulated by sound legislation, opposed Bryanism and held that "the Trusts afford greater scope for individual power and independent management than has been ordinarily suggested." A book of essays edited by James H. Bridge in 1902 (the contributors included James J. Hill) argued that "America is now in the front in the race for industrial supremacy. The main factor that has placed her there is the system of consolidation. Surely, such results do not argue for a restriction, but rather for the continuance and enlightened development of the system." In 1905 John Moody held that Standard Oil and the Morgan interests "constitute the heart of the business and commercial life of the nation" and that "the modern Trust is the natural outcome or evolution of societary conditions and ethical standards which are recognized and established among men to-day as being necessary elements in the development of civilization." In 1907 the redoubtable Chancellor James Roscoe Day of Syracuse University denounced the "demagogic and socialistic agitation" in the land, "an insult to our intelligent working people and mechanics," and found that "evils in corporations and individual enterprise" could be "corrected by strong thinking brains as we move forward." [35]

Emotion obviously colors statements like these, but the modern business historian merely rephrases the argument. The naïve stage of exploitation, unless regulated by considerations internal to the industry, soon burns itself out. Once past that stage, and putting aside naïve stereotypes of the capitalist and the entrepreneur, any large business will find that for survival it must turn from exploitation to expertise. Industrial corporations are driven to efficiency. They do their own buying and selling. They weaken or abolish the middleman and the jobber. They create large marketing and purchasing organizations of their own. They locate their manufacturing activities in advantageous locations, they systematize and standardize all sorts of processes from bookkeeping to transportation, they lower costs, and they seek to create better public relations.[36] The first pressure was apparently from bankers; [37] the second move was the employment of experts by industry and the giving of increased attention to the opinions of experts outside the corporation, even if these opinions were unsympathetic. The expert could control energy efficiently; the mere investor was likely to waste it. But where were the experts to come from? [38]

IV

In ante-bellum America societies existing for a particular cultural, scientific, religious, historical, or other professional or specialized purpose were regional in scope, or, if not regional, then bounded by state, county, or municipal lines. Even when the title of the society implied national membership, the organization rarely took in the whole country. A historical society was usually confined to a single commonwealth; a society for agricultural improvement rarely went beyond the boundaries of the state and, if it did, seldom extended beyond a limited region. Movements for the improvement of manufacturing, or commerce, or education, or such great branches of science as geology were similarly limited. Examples abound. Thus the Massachusetts Historical Society, said to be the oldest of its kind in the country, is defined by its title; the American Antiquarian Society, though national in scope, was in fact long limited to New England. In the South, when the ante-bellum industrial pioneer, William Gregg of Graniteville, wanted to propagandize for Southern cotton mills in 1849, he addressed the South Carolina Institute for the Promotion of Art, Mechanical Ingenuity, and Industry rather than a nonexistent National Association of Manufacturers or an equally nonexistent New York Cotton Exchange, created only in the 1870s. There were no great national associations of law schools or of medical schools, and the National Association for the Advancement of Science was not yet truly national. Despite the ecumenical pretensions of many religious bodies, the state association of Baptists or some local or regional conference of churches or ministers was the characteristic form of most Protestant sects, which, with the exception of the Episcopalians, were further split in the 1860s by the creation of the Confederate States of America.[39] Scientific laboratories were long the possession of individual natural philosophers, the study of law generally meant "reading law" in somebody's office, and American economists like Francis Wayland, or Henry C. Carey, or George Tucker were, when they taught, likely to be professors of moral philosophy. If they had no school connections, they were publicists, publishers, or businessmen who took on economic theorizing as part of a political program. As late as the time of Herbert Baxter Adams' appointment at The Johns Hopkins University (1876) there were so few national professional journals in history or political science that Adams had to write to his friends to send him copies of publications which would later have reached any university library as a matter of course. The situation was explicable: the causes include the lack of good systems of national communication, the superior attraction of the state or the locality over that of a distant nation, and the sort of *ad hoc* or amateur spirit that colors the writing of many public men during these decades. Membership in the American Philosophical Society, the most nearly national of learned bodies, was, to be sure, more widely distributed than in its younger rival, the American Academy of Arts and Sciences, but the APS was a society of gifted amateurs rather than an organization of specialists in a single discipline.

Not until after the Civil War was the national association discovered to offer an effective pattern for the control of both energy and the products of energy. In fact it was not until after 1876, with the nationalization of business, of transportation, and for that matter of education, sports, religion, and so on—indeed, not until after the nationalization of the country itself. This transformation of local and disparate societies and individuals into unions of representative specialists is one of the profoundest changes in American intellectual history. It has had equally profound effects upon all phases of national life.

The *World Almanac* for 1963 lists about 1034 American associations and societies.[40] Of these only 60 were founded before 1860. The creation of national bodies, sometimes with international overtones, goes steadily forward from that date: in the 1860s, 18; in the 1870s, 76; in the 1880s, 61; in the 1890s, 102; in the first decade of this century, 119; in the second decade, 169. These associations are of all kinds, from the Associated Wheelmen of America to a society for commemorating the War of 1812, but what is most striking is the steady increase of professional organizations on a national scale during the half-century under consideration. Thus, the seventh edition of the index of American scientific and technical societies, published by the National Research Council in 1961, lists 1836 organizations, of which about half are state or local. A sampling of 100 societies clearly national in scope listed in this index shows that only 4 were organized before 1860, 0 in the 1860s, 4 in the 1870s, 10 in the 1880s, 6 in the 1890s, 14 in the first decade of this century, 11 in the second decade, and 49 between 1920 and 1960. (Two seem indeterminate.) Of the 34 professional societies now (1969) constituting the American Council of Learned Societies (founded 1919), only 3 were born before 1815, only 2 between 1815 and 1860, but 16 were created between 1861 and 1915, and the rest since that time. Of the 7 major societies constituting the Social Science Research Council in 1923 only 1 was founded before the Civil War, 2 in the 1880s, 2 in the 1890s, and 2 in the first years of this century. Various attempts at a national association for the advancement of science were made before 1848, all more or less abortive. Not until the Association of American Geologists and

Naturalists turned itself into the American Association for the Advancement of Science in September 1848 was an enduring national organization born. The AAAS had a struggle. From 1851 to 1860 attendance at annual meetings fluctuated between 1004 and 605; the society did not meet during the Civil War, and in 1867 only 73 members attended. As late as 1870 the membership was only 536, nor did it pass the thousand mark until 1879. The Association was incorporated in 1874.[41] By 1960, however, the AAAS was one of the most powerful organizations in the country, meeting in 18 sections, each with its specialty. In that year it was affiliated with 245 national or regional scientific societies and about 46 state or regional academies.

Two notable categories of national societies have relevance to the proper control of energy. The first includes those in the social sciences; for example, the American Economic Association (1885), the American Academy of Political Science (1899), the American Sociological Society (1905), and the American Historical Association (1884). Associated with these in the sense that they contributed to the formation of national opinion are such groups as the American Forestry Association (1884), the American Psychological Association (1902), the Advertising Federation of America (1905), and the Association of National Advertisers (1910). With these I class the American Association of University Professors, created at the very end of our half-century (1915), a powerful force in protecting the university professor from unfavorable outside social pressure. Of these societies and others like them it can be said that they helped produce climates of opinion tending to check the exploitative phase of big business and to induce the more modern concept of "service."

The second category is made up of associations of experts in technology and applied science (and of course some in "pure" science as well). Here the development of specialized associations in the single field of engineering will illustrate the trend. The American Society of Civil Engineers goes back to 1852, but the steady drive toward expertise is evident in the creation of the American Institute of Mining, Metallurgical and Petroleum Engineering in 1871, the American Society of Mechanical Engineers in 1880, the American Institute of Electrical Engineers in 1884, and the American Institute of Chemical Engineers in 1908. Of considerable moment also is the creation of the Society for the Promotion of Engineering Education, at the World's

Columbian Exposition in 1893, the annual proceedings of which permit us to watch the growth of professional and sociological responsibility in a key situation. To these I shall come.

Obviously the growth of such associations rested in part upon the increase of institutions of higher learning in the United States, the proliferation of specialized faculties, the creation of professional and vocational curricula increasingly directed toward the needs of an industrialized society, and the granting of more specialized degrees to more students. Aside from the universities, notably the state universities that profited from the Morrill Acts to found schools of engineering and agriculture, an important element was the increase in technological institutions. In the first quarter of the last century American engineering education was confined to West Point and the Rensselaer Polytechnic Institute of Troy. In the year after the Civil War there were only 6 engineering schools of repute in the country. But by 1915 the Society for the Promotion of Engineering Education, which had begun with 75 members, had increased to 1405 individual members and 49 "institutional members" from 194 institutions teaching engineering in some form.

Political and social historians have naturally made much of the melodrama of political action, devoting most of their attention to the rise and legislative influence, direct or indirect, of pressure groups such as the Granger movement and the Populist party. They are right to do so. The long history of the regulation of railroad rates is a familiar example of the way exploiters were brought under some degree of political control for public service. But to concentrate upon this aspect of public opinion is to overlook the slow but powerful development of the organization of expertise and its influence in remolding corporate behavior, and the control of energy.

The behavior of American business leaders falls into several successive phases. In the first or predatory stage, that of the unscrupulous entrepreneur, the expert is merely a human tool. The predatory capitalist captures or creates a corporation for immediate gain and does not look beyond tomorrow. The policy is the famous public-be-damned doctrine. In the extractive industries such men want to get all the riches they can as quickly as they can, without regard to the welfare of the industry, the region, the workers, or the nation, and they will hire an engineer or a foreman and throw him aside when they are through with him. The expert simply takes and carries out orders, uttering only such warnings about, say, the safety of a mine as a minimal sense of human responsibility demands.[42] In the lumbering world the drive was to get the timber cut and get it out fast. As for transportation, the careers of Fisk, Gould, the elder Vanderbilt, and their kind were notorious for exploitation. They ran their railroads chiefly for plunder, sanctioned or passed over careless engineering, the faulty construction of bridges, passing tracks, signal systems, and the like, and cared less about the reputation of their lines for endangering human lives than they did for the stock market. The amusing burlesque of the Salt Lick Branch of the Pacific Railroad and its manipulation of the "engineers" narrated in *The Gilded Age* magnifies but does not essentially falsify this fusion of political corruption, financial jugglery, indifference to either public or professional responsibility, and the subordinate place of the expert in the corporate scheme.

But in the midst of this same generation more thoughtful capitalists arise, men who, without abandoning the doctrine that profit is the legitimate aim of capitalism, ask whether profits cannot be stabilized. They take the longer view, they return to the Benjamin Franklin virtues. The race-track psychology of the fast buck yields to the philosophy of prudence. Reckless aggression against man and nature is modified by a horror of that cardinal economic sin, unnecessary waste, and it is discovered that intelligent organizational control is more profitable in the end than unscrupulous daring. Managerial geniuses like John D. Rockefeller and Andrew Carnegie enter the field. The virtues of a Rockefeller are prudence, planning, and complete calm. He learns not merely how by manipulating railroad rates he can bring his competitors to heel or destroy them. He learns the need for supreme and careful organization, he learns that you do not need quite so many inches of metal around your oil barrels, that there are circumstances wherein pipelines are more economical than tank cars, that a uniform tally sheet will not only save money but give you a quicker scanning of profit and loss, that running even charities on a business basis pays better than yielding to humanitarian impulse. Such a man has a genius for ferreting out importance in apparently trivial detail. Ida Tarbell, in what is perhaps the least biased book in the library of muckraking, devotes an admiring chapter of her *History of the Standard Oil Company* to the greatness of its achievement, which lies in economy and organization. Organization, of course, will be for the sake of the owners, but it is at any rate socially superior to mere exploitation. So, too, an Andrew Carnegie, virtually unschooled, can suggest for his epitaph, "Here lies the man who was able to surround himself with men far cleverer than himself," but in truth he has an instinct for reliable expertise and is prepared instantly to scrap even a new installation for a better one. He knows that his brother Thomas has a feeling for business, and that his famous employee and friend, "Bill" Jones, although without an engineering education, possesses a genius for tools, machines, devices, inventions, plants. In this second stage of the capitalist-expertise symbiosis the capitalist still hires the expert, but the expert advises and sometimes controls him on major issues even though the relation is that of master and servant. They agree that the great sin is waste. Efficiency replaces exploitation, but we are still in the kingdom of laissez faire.

It is illuminating to read the annual *Proceedings of the Society for the Promotion of Engineering Education,* which begin in 1894 (for 1893). In 1896 it is possible to look back at a quarter-century of progress in engineering education, but the papers delivered before the Association for the next ten years revolve around four problems: the relation of the engineer's education to the liberal arts, the relation of the engineer to industry, the relation of theoretical training in the schools to practical training in the field, and the philosophic aim of technical education. In 1896 a speaker is still complaining of the low esteem in which the profession is held; two years later "engineering education is gradually winning its title to intellectual respect." The president of the Association in 1900, looking back, saw a virtual reversal in the attitude of the employer to the engineering school graduate:

> Twenty-five years ago practitioners doubted the value of a technical training for young engineers, and distrusted the engineering graduate, but now general managers and chief engineers prefer technical graduates, since they have been trained in scientific methods of working, and have a knowledge of the fundamental principles underlying all engineering practice, and look out upon the world of truth from the view point of a man of science.

That same year another speaker noted that "the relation between the engineer and the business world is very close, in fact, so close that engineering is more properly called a business pursuit than a profession," and still a third paper rejoiced that manufacturers were now on the watch for technically trained men of commercial interests. If in 1909 the Association was listening to addresses entitled "Why Manufacturers Dislike College Students," by 1913 it was listening to papers on "How Can the Colleges and the Industries Cooperate?" and, what is even more striking, the last years of this half-century see the exaltation of efficiency as the god of engineering idolatry. Efficiency and the elimination of waste are virtually the theme song of meetings in 1912 and later years.[43]

Our modern eagerness to get children into college makes it impossible for us to comprehend the basic revolution of attitude toward higher education then evidenced in the industrial world. It is necessary to go back to Mr. Dooley's "The Education of the Young" and his "Colleges and Degrees," to R. T. Crane's *The Utility of All Kinds of Higher Schooling* (in his opinion it had none), to George Horace Lorimer's *Letters from a Self-Made Merchant to His Son* (dedicated to Cyrus Curtis, "a self-made man") to realize the profound suspicion in which college education, whether technological or not, had been held by the masters of American business. Writes Lorimer in his assumed character of John Graham, a Chicago pork packer: "There are two parts of a college education—the part that you get in the schoolroom from the professors, and the part that you get outside of it from the boys. That's the really important part. For the first can only make you a scholar, while the second can make you a man." This ambiguity was echoed by Theodore Roosevelt, O. Henry, and George Ade in his tale, "The Fable of the Corporation Director and the Mislaid Ambition." [44] But being merely a man no longer sufficed for the world of the distribution of energy; you also had to become an expert and avoid waste.[45]

It was impossible to discuss waste as merely a mechanical error, as too much friction in the distribution of power from a prime mover, or as something else mechanical. Waste had uncomfortable social implications. A book like George Perkins Marsh's classic, if effusive, *Man and Nature,* which sold out its first edition in 1864 and was reprinted under varying titles throughout the period, developed at alarming length the damage the ruthlessness of man had done to man and nature.[46] In 1898 the Society for the Promotion of Engi-

neering Education printed a presidential address expressing a like
warning:

> We have exhausted a large portion of our lands by spendthrift and im-
> provident agricultural methods, and have moved on to the next new
> country to repeat the process until we have reached our uttermost
> bounds and have been turned back by the inhospitable mountains and
> desert plains; we have squandered our forest resources and are even now
> seeking timber supplies from our northern neighbors; we have wasted
> our natural gas supplies in a most foolish and prodigal manner . . . we
> have foolishly trifled with our finances and with our civil and consular
> services, in a way to bring upon us the contempt and loss of confidence
> of all honest and intelligent nations,

and much more, including overburdening the people with taxation
that brings profits only to the "coffers of our multi-millionaires." [47]
Precisely ten years later President Charles S. Howe of Case Institute
addressed the same association on "The Function of the Engineer in
the Conservation of the Natural Resources of the Country." He had
returned from the White House conference where both James J. Hill
and Andrew Carnegie had read papers, and he insisted: "In the future, waste of raw material should be abhorrent to the engineer and
his aim should be to conserve the materials which nature has provided for his use." He passed in review man's recklessness in the forests, in the diminishing supply of fuel, in iron and steel, in the creation of waste lands, and much else.

> In the past the engineer has been concerned with getting results. If the
> results were obtained, the waste and destruction of the natural product
> has scarcely been considered but in the future, economy of the natural
> product as well as economy in the final result must receive careful atten-
> tion. [48]

In a kind of Wagnerian counterpoint, while a doctrine of social responsibility was timidly invading technological education, the Adams
brothers were developing the wastefulness of technology, or rather
their understanding of entropy, into total catastrophe. I have quoted
Henry Adams, but his opinion is so important, I quote him again:

> The social Organism, in the recent views of history, is the cause, creator,
> and end of the Man, who exists only as a passing representative of it,
> without rights or functions except what it imposes. As an Organism so-

ciety has always been peculiarly subject to degradation of Energy, and alike the historians and the physicists invariably stretch Kelvin's law over all organized matter whatever.[49]

But Henry Adams' views scarcely affected the merchants of energy. What did affect them was a far more complex influence. At the opening of the twentieth century and increasingly after World War I, great industrial corporations, having profited from the use of expertise in the worlds of engineering, chemistry, geology, and other fields of applied science, came to believe that social scientists (for example, economists) and the graduates of colleges of commerce might make a like contribution toward efficiency in the marketing of energy and its products. In the same period they also came to believe that applied psychology in the form of personnel management and social psychology in the area of practical public relations would do them no harm. The most dramatic example of change of heart is perhaps the Standard Oil Company, which was formerly wedded to taciturnity. A pioneer in the field of public relations, Ivy L. Lee (1877–1934), newspaperman, student of political science, and aide to various politicians and political groups, opened an office in New York City, reshaped the public image of the Pennsylvania railroad, was made publicity counsel to John D. Rockefeller in 1915, and, though inevitably nicknamed "Poison Ivy" Lee, became the leading public relations man in the United States.[50] Side by side with this development eventually came the rise of employee counseling and the acceptance of the idea that the managerial function was itself a profession.[51] Expertise in the social sciences and in psychology affected corporate management since specialists in economics, business practices, social psychology, and public relations were not so much telling management what it could do as telling management what it could not do. In this third phase of the entrepreneur-expertise relationship, though experts were still hired by management, expertise had grown to a virtual equality with management in many areas of the exploitation and marketing of energy and its products, for example, in questions like the location of new plants, the sales potential of a new product, the new packaging of a familiar product, and so on.

But this is not the whole story. The development of professional societies in turn meant the development of informed professional opinion increasingly inaccessible to political and economic pressures and at the same time increasingly interested in national problems, national welfare, and predictive judgments. The rise of the national association tends to equalize expertise over the nation and in some sense, even if indirectly, to equalize the problem of energy. An example is found in electric power, which no corporation can now monopolize—it was once charged that United States Steel and Standard Oil had virtually monopolized production in their fields. Moreover, the national association, as it develops, steadily diminishes the area in which the exploiter can control or rid himself of the lonely expert. Even in the 1890s it was impossible either for politicians, corporations, or colleges to prevent economists or any other specialized group from joining a professional association, attending its meetings, reading its publications, and discussing professional questions with colleagues. A consensus of professional opinion thus developed, beyond the control of either exploiter or manager.[52] If corporation magnates during the half-century often flouted the courts, the legislatures, and the law, they overlooked the insidious influence of national organizations dealing with expertise. Popular attention was fixed on conspicuous wickedness in the "trusts," and political campaigns concentrated on the drama of stock manipulation, pools, combinations, the ways by which corporation lawyers evaded federal laws, taxes, or what not. Meanwhile as the need for expertise steadily increased, so did membership in national associations of specialists, and so did the demand for specialized education. In demanding "practical" education business leaders of the baser sort did not realize that the faculty members of institutions offering professional training were living in a climate of opinion created by these national associations, not by the business world, which was rather an object of study and analysis than a despot benevolent on many occasions, tyrannical on others. It is possible that the influence of professional societies was greater in taming industrial excess than were the denunciations of plutocracy by populist and progressive.

At this point one may wax ironical with W. H. White in *The Organization Man* and C. Wright Mills in *The Power Elite* by contrasting the traditional Protestant ethic with the developing social ethic and comparing the original doctrine of competitive individualism with the later ideal of social cooperation. But one can be overly bemused by the drama of social Darwinism. When one remembers that in ending *A Connecticut Yankee in King Arthur's Court* Mark Twain could see only general massacre as the climax of technological processes, and when one imagines what American life might have been had the savage strife among entrepreneurs and between labor and capital continued unchecked, one may reasonably conclude that if legislation did something to reduce both greed and the waste of energy, the marshaling of expert opinion on a national scale may have quietly done quite as much.

Industrial corporations are now in many instances bigger than they were in the days of Teddy Roosevelt, and the amount of energy of all sorts in the country is incalculably greater. When one asks why popular opinion about these gigantic businesses has changed, one faces a nice question of historical interpretation. Legislative control had something to do with it. So did the admitting into managerial positions of the specialist. But in the concluding years of the Age of Energy and increasingly in our own time one marks the emergence of a new word, or rather an old word in a new context. That word is "service." One cannot imagine Commodore Vanderbilt or Henry Clay Frick or H. H. Rogers being greatly interested in "service." Today, however, "service" is a corporation goal much touted by public relations counsels who practice an expertise unknown in the days of U. S. Grant. We are perhaps too close to the doctrine of "service" to realize how idiosyncratic and national it is. When, however, one reads advertising by a chain of undertaking establishments (morticians!) which runs: "Serving the bereaved for over forty years with compassion and understanding," or finds a great chain-store system proclaiming: "We care. Caring about you is just plain good business. . . . We better care how we serve you, about what we serve you, about being fair, honest, and dependable," one realizes the enormous distance the corporation has come from the public-be-damned policy of earlier decades.

Doubtless "service" is a hypocritical word. Doubtless hypocrisy lurks in the glossy color-printed annual reports published by any large company to soothe its stockholders. Doubtless there was something epic and engaging in the fierce infighting among great plungers and enterprisers of the exploitative era. But this shift from the raw power-thrust of a predatory plutocracy to the smoother image of public servants, all questions of profit being discreetly subdued, if it be in part a function of legislation, in part a function of the managerial revolution, and in part a change of goal among industrialists, is also a function of the influence of expertise on energy.

I am unable to trace the steps of this important, if silent, revolution, but as early as 1868 Andrew Carnegie wrote this memorandum to himself: "To continue much longer overwhelmed by business cares and with most of my thoughts wholly upon the way to make more money in the shortest time, must degrade me beyond hope of permanent recovery." [53] In 1886 he published *Triumphant Democracy* and in 1900 he accumulated a series of essays in *The Gospel of Wealth.* Carnegie's "philosophy" was in one sense entirely within the Protestant ethic of the obligation to prosper in order to do good, and he was the sole determiner of his own generosity. Nevertheless, he was already dimly sketching out the theory of corporate conscience, a concept of sociological responsibility among the unduly rich in control of energy, and not merely paving the way for a "Bill" Jones and an Ivy Lee. He was also looking into the future when expertise would have a major role to play in the equable distribution of energy and its products over the United States. In these various ways, then, the expertise necessary to running an industrial culture moved from exploitation to unity, sometimes in harmony with political trends but more characteristically running silently toward the goal that Godkin and James Russell Lowell had hoped to reach as a result of civil war.

V

Culture and Race

A colossal machine for the manufacture of Philistines?
—MATTHEW ARNOLD

I

THE AGE OF ENERGY heard without astonishment that Chicago intended to make culture hum. That city, rising from the ashes of the great fire of October 1871, sustained between 1876 and 1914 a more striking cultural life than it had experienced before or has known since. These decades saw the founding of the American Conservatory of Music (1883), John W. Root's building for the Art Institute (1887) and its new structure (1893), the beginning of Hull House (1889), the opening of the John Crerar Library (1889), the great Chicago Auditorium of Adler and Sullivan (1889), at the dedication of which Adelina Patti sang "Home, Sweet Home" with variations, the founding of the Chicago Symphony Orchestra (1891),[1] the great World's Columbian Exposition (1893), the opening of the new University of Chicago (1893), the creation of the Field Museum (1894), and the organization of the Chicago Civic Opera Company (1910). A center of cultural energy was the Cliff Dwellers Club, of which Hamlin Garland seemed to be perpetual president. In these years the city supported *The Dial* from 1880 to 1916, *The Chap-Book* from 1894 to 1898, *The Drama Magazine* after 1911, and *Poetry: A Magazine of Verse,* founded in 1912 by that formidable entrepreneuse, Harriet Monroe. In that year also Maurice Brown created his Little Theater, two years after the Drama League of America had made Chicago its headquarters. Publishing firms included: the Open Court, distinguished for books in philosophy, science, and religion;

179

Fleming H. Revell, a notable publisher of religious volumes; and the firm of Stone & Kimball (1893), begun in the Harvard Yard by two young men devoted to *l'art nouveau,* William Morris, aestheticism, realism, and the gentle art of shocking.[2] Henry Adams' astonishment at finding culture on the prairies was naïve but natural. The Chicago system of parks and boulevards promised to be the wonder of the world. The parks were adorned by statues—French's "The Republic," reduced in size from the giantess at the Exposition, and by Saint-Gaudens' two statues of Lincoln; and after 1913, next to the Art Institute stood Lorado Taft's "Fountain of the Great Lakes." Intellectual and literary life included such persons as George Ade, Finley Peter Dunne, Hamlin Garland, Robert Herrick, William Vaughn Moody, Henry Blake Fuller, Thorstein Veblen, Robert Morss Lovett, A. A. Michelson, Rollin D. Salisbury, and their fellows; at a lower level cartoonists such as John T. McCutcheon, H. T. Webster, L. D. Bradley, and John T. Lederer, and the columnists, "B. L. T." (Burt Leston Taylor) and Eugene Field. A row of one-story frame buildings on East Fifty-fifth Street, left over from the World's Fair, served to house a Bohemian quarter, which later drew Sherwood Anderson, Floyd Dell, and Carl Sandburg to mild Bohemian evenings, and young musical and dramatic talent was irresistibly attracted from the farms and villages of the Middle West (for that matter, from the towns) to a metropolis that was expected to become the literary center of the United States.[3] As for the development of architecture in Chicago—from the White City and Sullivan's Transportation Building, the Home Insurance Building, and the Tacoma Building through Frank Lloyd Wright's Robie House on the South Side—is it not writ large for all men to see?

But what was culture? What *is* culture? No question is more difficult. Culture has a complex of meanings when it is used by social scientists [4] and another when used by disciples of Matthew Arnold, who are never quite certain whether they are talking about self-development ("the study of perfection") or some social ideal ("to make reason and the will of God prevail"). Among the entries under "culture" in the New English Dictionary the only illuminative phrase in this context is that culture can be thought of as "the intellectual side of civilization."

Bewildered as one may be about culture, the Age of Energy in one sense simplified and in another sense was fearful of the word. Avoiding all metaphysical and professional definitions, one can say that American culture in the period tended to live on one of three planes. The first was popular culture.[5] The pursuit of folk art, folk singing, and folk customs being then only a minor branch of scholarship, popular culture in these decades meant the appeal of the popular media, their ancestors, or their equivalents—the dime novel, the magazine or newspaper intended for easy reading and quick emotional response, comic journalism, the comic strip, "popular" sheet music, band concerts, sentimental pictures (spring landscapes or Christmas snow, sentimentalized children, family episodes, lovers in romantic attitudes, anecdotal paintings, chromolithographs, religious subjects, and so on), the subscription book business, verse by Will Carleton or James Whitcomb Riley, and "comic" books ranging from *Peck's Bad Boy* and *Samanthy Allen at the Fair* to *A Slow Train Through Arkansas*. I suppose one should also include such matters as the three-color-process cards picturing ball players and actresses that boys used to collect when they or their big brothers bought cigarettes. My examples are illustrative, not exhaustive, but the power of conventional condescension toward popular culture is illustrated in the long, long time it took Mark Twain to climb out of the category of being a funny man into being recognized as a major literary genius. Popular culture was of course exploited by profit makers and sometimes invaded by writers potentially, at least, of the "better" class. Examples are found in children's literature of the period, like "Martha Farquharson" (Martha J. Finley), who wrote the Elsie Dinsmore books, twenty-eight in all, and "Burt L. Standish," creator of the Frank Merriwell series, which are said to have sold about twenty-five million copies.[6]

At the other end of the spectrum was high culture, generally denominated the genteel tradition. High culture was the expression of values cherished or aimed at among several disparate elements: minority groups of traditional family status; new wealth yearning to be recognized by the establishment; liberal arts colleges; private secondary schools (whose interests colored the curricula in public high schools); the "better" churches; and public men who professed to be statesmen operating within a traditional pattern of responsibility. One thinks of figures as different as George William Curtis, Chauncey Depew, "Marse" Henry Watterson, and Henry Cabot Lodge. The fact that persons of culture launched the Mugwump movement did not, however, mean that all cultured persons were either progressive or untainted by the easy political morality of the Gilded Age.

Between these polarities there were two broad cultural bands more difficult to define. With some trepidation I shall call one of these the culture of the middle class, and with greater assurance refer to the other as the culture, or rather the cultures, of the new Americans. The second of these offers less difficulty of definition. Immigrant groups for a span of years kept to their own language, their own reading matter, their own churches, their own social organizations, and their own amusements. We tend to picture these groups as racial enclaves within the cities. Probably we are influenced to think so by the dramatic life of the ghetto Jews in the Lower East Side in New York. But a lingering affection for the homeland and familiar ways was not a product of the ghetto only; racial minorities might break through that sociological barrier, rise in the economic scale, and still maintain a culture differing from "normal" American life. An example is the culture of Germans in Wisconsin, who long clung to their churches, theaters, and newspapers, their Saengervereinen, Turnerhalle, beer gardens, and breweries. Indeed, such a group need not be confined to a city. The residents of the village of Coon Valley, Wisconsin, at the opening of the present century spoke Norse oftener than they did English, were guided or dominated by the Lutheran pastor, suffered an English-speaking school, but sent their children after school hours to get religious instruction in Norse. Such groups also kept up a good many Old World eating and drinking habits. Willa Cather's *My Ántonia* is eloquent on the felt difference between "old American" habits and the mores of the Shimerda family, who are Bohemians. The continued existence of a foreign-language press in the United States, a matter of anxiety to some ardent patriots before and during World War I, is a measure of the relatively long life of these transplanted cultures, which by some Americans were supposed to interfere with the operation of the melting pot. Today, of course, interpretation moves in the opposite direction and lauds the contributions of foreign-language cultures to the totality of American life.[7]

I turn with greater diffidence to a statement about middle-class culture. My difficulty lies in the haziness of the term "middle class." Does one mean the *haute bourgeoisie*, the *petite bourgeoisie*, or something in between that one calls in desperation the middle

middle-class? [8] The middle class, however stratified or defined, set up
no goals opposed to the genteel tradition, on the whole supported its
general aim, and tended to disparage a good many expressions of
popular culture while covertly enjoying them. Their patronage sustained the best sellers (but the best sellers were not all mediocre or
sentimental). Middle-class patrons furnished the bulk of the theater
audiences and the bulk of the newspaper readers, and *were* the public for magazines of wide circulation, domestic amenities, the serialization of "good" fiction, and intelligent but cautious discussions of
the issues of the day—the *Ladies' Home Journal* and *The Saturday
Evening Post* are representative, not Flower's *The Arena* or Godkin's
The Nation. But such persons also read the *Atlantic Monthly* and
Scribner's Magazine. The beauty of the World's Columbian Exposition was as much a revelation to them as it was to Henry Adams, but
they had no part in planning it, a matter they left to "leaders."

The middle class liked a cheerful religion, conventional office
buildings, upright pianos, Sousa's band, historical romance, Stoddard's *Lectures,* the tent chautauqua, pyrography, cut-glass bowls for
the table (or a reasonable facsimile thereof), Maxfield Parrish, the
Copley prints, Teddy Roosevelt's heartiness, and the classic profile of
Richard Harding Davis. They wanted a better America for their children and sent them to high school and, when they could, to college.
If they held a mild allegiance to the idea of a cosmopolitan world,
they were suspicious of British condescension, German materialism,
and the loose-living French. The villains in their fiction were often
dark-skinned Spaniards or Latin Americans, the Negro was the
source of comedy and the object of intermittent charity, and only a
few of them could see anything "worth while" (a favorite phrase) in
the arts of the American Indians. They were honestly provincial, yet
they had some vague feeling that the Old World was no longer the
eternal enemy of the New.

It would once have been possible to call their values the value of
respectability without being misunderstood, for they were respectable
in the nineteenth-century, if not the eighteenth-century, meaning of
the word, and they would never have understood a literary culture
that turned "respectability" into derision. They helped maintain, and
indirectly shaped, the genteel tradition. And if one says such a magazine as *The Arena* was not characteristic of their interests, this judgment does not mean that it lacked middle-class readers, that the mid-

dle class was never "progressive" or never moved by books like Jacob Riis's *How the Other Half Lives,* Sinclair's *The Jungle,* or Jane Addams's *Twenty Years at Hull House.* Middle-class culture was conservative but not therefore reactionary; if it made a success of Lew Wallace's *Ben Hur,* it did not turn away from the fiction of William Dean Howells; and if it liked Hovenden's "Breaking Home Ties," modern art criticism is beginning to find merit in this domestic piece. This class admired Saint-Gaudens' "General Sherman" which has been called the greatest equestrian statue in modern American art.[9] After all, the middle class helped to send Grover Cleveland twice to the White House, though he was the father of an illegitimate child. How far the uproar that expelled Maxim Gorki and his mistress from a number of American hotels was factitious and how far genuine is anybody's guess, even though Mark Twain opined that "laws can be evaded and punishment escaped, but an openly transgressed custom brings sure punishment." [10]

II

The genteel tradition, as we shall see in the next chapter, was an operative fusion of philosophic idealism and a renewed instinct for craftsmanship that dominated high culture throughout the period. Its leading ideas were shaped by artists, critics, philosophers, and educators, and were supported by an elite [11] minority. But the elite minority was divided into two segments often socially and economically hostile to each other, however much they might agree on the general principles of the tradition. Conflict between these segments was the theme of innumerable novels, short stories, plays, humorous verse, prose satire, cartoons, and solemn social commentaries both before and during the age.

The intellectual and aesthetic core of the genteel tradition and, in some measure, its social status were guarded by upper-class "Old American" families—the Boston Brahmins, the traditional mercantile and banking aristocracy of New York, Main Line families of Philadelphia, and their counterparts in Baltimore, Washington, Richmond, Charleston, and other centers on the Eastern seaboard, in Western cities like St. Louis, and newer metropolitan places like Chicago and the Twin Cities, which lagged not far behind. In the Far West the situation was more complex. In the Far West time moved to a different drummer and such cities as San Francisco developed a dominant group (old San Francisco families), the members of which, though by the calendar parvenus in comparison with Boston or Philadelphia, regarded themselves as both a cultural and a social elite. This group arose within a few years of the Gold Rush and soon learned to look down on later comers. In centers such as Los Angeles, Santa Fe, or San Antonio "old" Spanish families of birth and breeding had thrust upon them, or reacquired, an unofficial aristocracy of status never won by ordinary Mexicans or middle-class Americans from back East. Yet the Western situation was complicated by the fact that scions of upper-class Eastern families moving westward sometimes carried status in their baggage, and that army officers of superior rank, provided they were "gentlemen," were assimilated by dominant groups, as is evident in the novels of Charles King, various biographies, and stage plays in which a cavalry colonel saves the day or the heroine or both.

All these superior groups developed "leadership" [12] from their own ranks, or associated to themselves talent from the arts, education, philosophy, and so on, when it was not boorish. The "Old American" elite was of course accused of being among other things dull, conventional, prim, and tyrannical. Nevertheless, without its support no opera company or symphony orchestra, art museum or artist, public library or civic enterprise, and with few exceptions no great publishing house, upper-class magazine, leading church, privately endowed school or college, philanthropic enterprise, hospital, first-class hotel, summer resort, and men's or women's club pretending to distinction, could flourish.

"Elite" (the modern term is The Establishment) is a word that engenders democratic distrust, but the distrust is only partially justified. In any modern society the few who either by nature or by nurture consciously assume that a high degree of civic and cultural responsibility rests upon them, that they can discharge it, that they are by tradition or training capable of admitting to the "in" group eligible members of any "out" groups or of rejecting them when outsiders seem incapable of an instinct for the discipline of the secret on which the "in" group tacitly agrees—these are elementary observations. The elite usually has a higher, or at least a keener, sense of history than do other social classes, so that even during international tensions it can retain an instinctual understanding of the elite among the enemy. In times of peace a Boston Brahmin could communicate with a member of the British upper classes or with French intellectuals in a manner denied to a wandering Nevada mining entrepreneur and his shrewd, uncultivated wife. A graduate of Yale in the period was more apt to be at ease in Athens or Florence than the most earnest YMCA secretary from the Dakotas. Members of the elite, moreover, might belong to opposing political parties, be modern or traditional in their aesthetic tastes, conventional or progressive in their ideals of education, join almost any church above the fundamentalist level, and take up economic radicalism or reaction, provided they retained the indefinable sense of solidarity that overrides all coarse political, economic, or religious enmity. They were less tolerant in racial issues. Whatever the Brahmins thought of Wendell Phillips's outrageous views, he was still "one of us," to be snubbed if necessary, but not to be permanently excommunicated, whereas, however conscientiously Mark Twain might become an apologist for wealth, imperialism, or the genteel tradition, he remained until late in life persistently an *arriviste*. Edith Wharton was "in," Theodore Dreiser was not; John Singer Sargent was respectable, Whistler was not; a German-born symphony orchestra conductor of the rank of Theodore Thomas was, by and large, of the establishment; a band conductor, for example, the Irish-born Patrick Gilmore, was of more dubious vintage.

Although the elite was to furnish both support and leadership for the genteel tradition, in exact contradiction to this celebration of activism, one fraction of the elite was capable of turning idleness into a virtue—something on which Thorstein Veblen was to seize in his *The Theory of the Leisure Class*. Doubtless the ancestry of idleness as status goes far back in European history. If an honest pride in civic responsibility or the support of the arts was a "note" of the American elite during the nineteenth century, a curious countervailing virtue (which owes something to European, notably English, aristocracy and something to the romantic movement) was a denigration of activism as an end in itself—not merely of business but virtually of any vocation or occupation that interfered with the cultivation of the self. Typical of this point of view during the first third of the century are both the title and the general attitude expressed in *The Idle Man* (1821–1822) by the elder Richard Henry Dana. For example:

Have we lived so many years in the world and been familiar with its affairs, only to part off men into professions and trades, and to tell the due proportions required to stock each? Must we for ever travel the straightforward turnpike road of business, and not be left to take the way that winds round the meadows, and leads us sociably by the doors of retired farms? . . . Must all we do and all we think about have reference to the useful, while that alone is considered useful which is tangible, present gain? [13]

The theme is developed by Washington Irving, his brother, and James K. Paulding in the *Salmagundi Papers;* it appears in Cooper and Poe; [14] in altered form it turns up in Emerson and Whitman, each of whom thinks the richness of life will follow when one has a chance to loaf and invite one's soul. The idle-man tradition continued to influence the young throughout the century. A series of passages from the biography of Thomas Wentworth Higginson in the 1840s is illuminating:

My great intellectual difficulty has been having too many irons in the fire (1841). . . . [But I] made the day an era in my life by fixing the resolution of not studying a profession. . . . The resolve is perfectly settled and perfectly tranquil with me, that I will come as near starving as [Jean Paul] Richter did—that I will labor as intensely and suffer as much—sooner than violate my duty toward my Spiritual life (1842). . . . [Although] various old gentlemen . . . ask me every time they see me what my profession is to be, I do not expect my plans to be understood or approved; I shall expect to be frowned at by many and laughed at by some (1843). [15]

This was of course during the period of the "Newness."

Higginson's disinclination to be bound by any vulgar occupation had its basis in a philosophy, however adolescent. But there was a less spiritualized explanation for refusing to earn money, namely, the desire to imitate the European who lived on his income, devoting his time to pleasure, society, and culture. Even in the Jacksonian period this was remarked by competent observers. Says Tocqueville: "When an opulent American arrives in Europe, his first care is to surround himself with all the luxuries of wealth: he is so afraid of being taken for the plain citizen of a democracy, that he adopts a hundred distorted ways of bringing some new instances of his wealth before you every day." At the end of the 1830s Francis J. Grund, who had lived ten years in the United States, wrote a sardonic analysis of the "bloods" of New York, society in Boston and Philadelphia, and life in Washington. This was *Aristocracy in America*. He said:

> "An American exclusive," resumed my friend [really Grund], "is not yet a finished 'aristocrat'. There are yet a thousand things about him which betray his low origin, or, as the English have it, 'smell of the shop'. Though extravagant and wasteful he has not yet learned to spend his money with ease and gracefulness. The women do not know how to speak French or Italian, and the boys, brought up sometimes at a public school, (for there are few families in the Northern States incurring the expense of a private tutor,) would necessarily imbibe some of the *vulgarising* spirit of democracy. As a finish . . . to the education of father, mother, and children, and perhaps, also, to drown in oblivion the tedious particulars of their rise and progress, our highest and best families emigrate for a short time to Europe, in order, in the society of noblemen, to attain that peculiar high polish and suavity of manners which it is impossible to acquire amidst the bustle of business and the vulgar turmoil of elections." [16]

The doctrine that the gentleman does not soil his hands with retail trade is old, just as the parvenu is a social type inciting ridicule as far back as Horace and Aristophanes. But America was a philosophic republic, a democracy in which everybody was supposed to imitate the village blacksmith, beginning some task each morning and bringing it to a close each evening; hence the special significance of the doctrine of virtuous idleness, made to stick more fiery off.

Since an industrial society had less and less room for idlers, however admirable it might be to purchase white hyacinths for the soul, a kind of distribution of parts between the ideals of activism and idleness came about, notably after the Civil War. Heads of families, men in the prime of life, energetic younger sons, some mature women, and many younger ones delighted in some sort of occupation; and a smaller fraction of those who inherited wealth or status or who had married wealth and acquired status, wives among the elite, society girls of a certain type, and some young men in cities (commonly known as clubmen) went as far as they dared in the direction of the idle man; that is, they strove to retain an intelligent amateur standing in a society that demanded more and more specialization. On the weaker side the young American male at this social level apparently took his cue from the European *flâneur* and was frequently caricatured as if he were a weak-minded young British aristocrat, but the stronger element in this same group kept to an ideal of the virtuoso and collected books, art, pottery, and *objets d'art,* sometimes went in for teaching in elite schools, and were useful not merely in organizing cotillions but also in setting up art shows, charity drives, and so on. Caught between the traditional Protestant ethic of industry for its own sake and the British tradition of the elder son of a landed proprietor (consider the novels of Trollope), they enjoyed both the scorn and the envy of their parents and some part of the populace.

All elites have to fend off the intrusion of *novi homines* and their families, the chief difference between the Age of Energy and earlier epochs in this respect being the sudden appearance of scores of new millionaires. Among the formidable weapons, whether of offense or defense, were the social sponsor, the social secretary, the society reporter, and the creation of an American equivalent of Beau Nash in the persons of a Ward McAllister and a "King" Lehr.[17] The *nouveaux riches* had two principal alternatives. They might, often through the ambition of a wife to shine or her desire as a mother to acquire status for her children, climb or intrude or creep into the fold of the "Old Americans" by various ingenious devices. Or they might bludgeon their way to recognition by using wealth for impressive cultural projects such as collecting manuscripts, books, paintings, subsidizing orchestra or opera companies, creating or contributing to universities, colleges, and schools, and aiding hospitals. In most such cases it became impossible to deny the millionaire donor a place on the board of directors; and though business acceptance did not immediately guarantee social assimilation, it was a promising first step. Since some of the newly rich were without much formal education and as the majority came from the middle class or from immigrant groups with only a modest education, the head of such a family, though he might in rare cases have an instinct for taste, commonly secured the services of experts for his purchases and his philanthropies. He also tacitly assented to two rather contradictory doctrines: one, that woman being the purer vessel, he ought to turn culture over to her; and two, that females being a restless breed, his wife and his daughters, after breaking into society, ought to satisfy their thirst for meaningful life by patronizing artists and other odd types who aroused in the business magnate a mixture of contempt and bewilderment. The success of the Wharton School of Commerce and Finance (1881) at the University of Pennsylvania and the growing influence of the American Economic Association after 1888 persuaded some business magnates that academic economists, though they never met a payroll, might be useful in controlling governmental enterprises and the tariff and in keeping down "socialism." The same approbation was not extended to professors of the humanities, long-haired pianists and poets, and irresponsible fellows like painters, even though a liberal education was vaguely a good thing.

The complex web of familial status and idleness, excellence in taste and dilettantism, energy and lethargy, social security and social aspiration, good manners and the naïveté of honest rusticity, the etiolation of the family through causes ranging from loss of money to thinness in the blood, the rude vigor of *arrivistes* who cloaked uncertainty by bluster, the qualities of the "American girl" and the Ivy League college graduate—these themes appear repeatedly in literature. The novels of Henry James, Howells, Edith Wharton, Francis Marion Crawford, Arlo Bates, David Graham Phillips, Booth Tarkington, and others, appealing to various levels of the public—consider the distance between the Corey family in *The Rise of Silas Lapham* and the caricature of the adolescent idler in cartoons—often turn on such topics as the social comedy in this pattern, sometimes pushing into farce, and its pathos sometimes darkening into tragedy. Bronson Howard's amusing comedy, *The Henrietta* (1887), is projected against this complex, and so, in another sense, is Langdon Mitchell's *The New York Idea* (1908). Mr. Dooley is eloquent on these topics, so was George Ade, and Eugene Field's satirical *Culture's Garland* (1887) anticipates Don Marquis's *Hermione and Her Little Group of Serious Thinkers* (1918) as an ironical comment on culture and pseudo-culture. Among a hundred such volumes Edgar Fawcett's unjustly forgotten *Social Silhouettes* (1885), a series of sketches and impressions by "Mr. Mark Manhattan," lies somewhere between the venom in the *Salmagundi Papers* and the subtler satire of Mrs. Wharton's *The Age of Innocence* and Robert Grant's *The Chippendales*. Fawcett's volume contains what the seventeenth century knew as "characters," that is, sketches running from grave to gay, from lively to severe, of types like "The Lady Who Can Be Vulgar with Safety," "The Young Man Who Pushes His Way," and "The

Young Lady Who Tries Too Hard." He is capable of such *sententiae* as:

> She looked upon her mother as a great lady, a thorough-paced patrician. This was by no means a case where the American daughter had shot ahead of and overtowered the American mother (p. 91).

> I might have been a *châtelaine*, with Gladstone, and Browning, and Ruskin, and Froude, and Huxley, and Daudet, and François Coppée, and even Victor Hugo, for my guests and friends . . . the immense mistake was that I came to New York from the West, and caught the absurd fever of wanting to be a *grande dame* here (pp. 152–153).

Fawcett's world is a world of form, where money is taken for granted as in the novels of Henry James. One lives in it by an unwritten breviary of elitism. His chapter, "A Millionaire Martyr," is a small masterpiece in its ironical yet poignant dramatization of the tired father, the pushing wife, and the young girl obediently trying on culture as she would a new dress.

III

One can distinguish with some particularity the centers where the elite controlled and supported "culture," and also some of the social modes of that support. On the Eastern seaboard three cities were paramount—Boston, New York, and Philadelphia (Baltimore and Washington following meekly after); Charleston and other Southern centers were still wrapped in their memories of "The War."[18] Boston and Philadelphia were regarded on the whole as Anglophile; whereas New York was "cosmopolitan," so much so that leaders of opinion there were fearful that the "Old American" tradition would be submerged by immigrants and newcomers from the West. Thus George William Curtis, a New Englander who long occupied the Easy Chair of *Harper's Magazine,* lamented on occasion that there were no statues in Central Park commemorating New Yorkers and gave a good deal of space in his essays to "Old American" values.[19]

To distinguish among cities would be invidious. Nobody challenged the greatness of New York. Philadelphia had its collection of historic shrines, its libraries and museums, its American Philosophical Society, writers like S. Weir Mitchell and Agnes Repplier, and painters like Eakins, and it sheltered the younger years of the Ashcan school. Cincinnati boasted of Duveneck, St. Louis nourished the American Hegelians and for a while Kate Chopin. San Francisco had the *Overland Monthly* and the circle around Ina Coolbrith. Yet there was a general feeling that if Washington was the political capital of the United States, if New York was its financial capital, then Boston was its cultural capital, or at least that culture was at once more solid and more rarified in Boston than anywhere else. Foreign travelers and some Bostonians said so.

Postwar Boston exhibited a superior cultural vitality. The Boston family, the Boston matriarch, the Boston *jeune fille,* the Boston man of family were felt to be *sui generis.* Boston culture was obviously that of the "Old Americans," Boston supported a Browning Society, the *Atlantic Monthly,* and what became Houghton Mifflin Company. Like Philadelphia, Boston had its Revolutionary past; like New York it was a financial center. It was, people thought, a curious and baffling place, so that between Lydia Maria Childs' *Hobomuk* in 1824 and L. P. Osborne's *Through Purple Glass* in 1946 more than two hundred novels examined this metropolis. If one puts aside the historical romances and such triumphs of sentimentality as Maria Cummins' *The Lamplighter,* there remains a solid core of substantial interpretations running from Howells to Marquand. It is worthwhile pausing on two or three of these books because, though their tone is commonly ironical or satiric and their themes the universal ones of social pretentiousness, snobbery, and prudishness, they make one feel not so much that Boston alone exhibited these qualities, as that Boston culture, with Harvard College on one side of the Charles River and the Boston Museum of Fine Arts on the other, was really formidable. The common topic in Arlo Bates's trilogy (*The Pagans,* 1884, *The Philistines,* 1889, and *The Puritans,* 1899)—and Bates, according to one commentator, was supposed to have touched more facets of Bostonianism than any other fictionist—is the conflict between joy and art on the one side and an overpowering sense of duty and inheritance on the other. His books are filled with epigrammatic dialogue and brilliant observation; their weakness is Bates's inability to generate plot out of character. For him the Pagans represent the protest of the artistic soul against shams, whereas the Philistines substitute "convention for conviction," no new topic; yet as one watches the degeneration of Fenton from an honest and fearless artist to

merely a fashionable painter, one has a sense of both the strength
and the weakness of this elite group and of the ambiguity of the relation between it and "culture." In *The Philistines* we read:

> Mrs. Frostwinch belonged, beyond the possibility of any cavilling doubt,
> to the most exclusive circle of fashionable Boston society. Boston society
> is a complex and enigmatical thing, full of anomalies, bounded by waver-
> ing and uncertain lines, governed by no fixed standards, whether of
> wealth, birth, or culture, but at times apparently leaning a little toward
> each of these three great factors of American social standing. It is seldom
> wise to be sure that at any given Boston house whatever, one will not
> find a more or less strong dash of democratic flavor in general company,
> and there are those who discover in this fact evidences of an agreeable
> and lofty republicanism.

Through the eyes of a visitor, a Miss Merrivale, domiciled at the
house of Mrs. Staggchase, who is "arty," we get a glimpse of female
Boston:

> [Miss Merrivale] had been at a luncheon at Ethel Mott's, given in com-
> pliment to herself, where she had sat nearly speechless for an hour and a
> half while half a dozen young ladies had discussed the origin of evil
> with great volubility, and what seemed to her, however it might have
> impressed metaphysicians, astounding erudition and profundity. She had
> assisted at that sacred rite of musical devotees, the Saturday night Sym-
> phony concert, where a handful of people gathered to hear the music,
> and all the rest of the world crowded for the sake of having been there.
> She had been taken . . . to a select sewing-circle—that peculiar institu-
> tion by means of which exclusive Boston society keeps tally of the stand-
> ing of all its young women. She was somewhat bewildered, but enjoyed
> what might be called a hallowed consciousness that she was doing exactly
> the right thing.

Mrs. Ranger observes: "Doesn't it seem to you that the modern fashion of admitting artists into society is mixing up things terribly?
Nowadays one is always meeting queer people everywhere, and being
told that they are writers or painters," on which an old lady remarks:
"It is worse than that. . . . You even meet actors in quite respectable
houses." [20]

In *Her Boston Experiences* (1900) by Margaret Allston, illustrated
with photographs of Boston in the 1890s, the heroine comes to that
city, experiences the "intellectual" tone of Boston society, and is put
off by what she thinks is the cavalier treatment of a Boston young

man, though she eventually marries him. She discovers a rather genteel Bohemianism. These two passages are revelatory:

> During my first week in Boston I received the impression that I had
> found my way into a mammoth woman's club where the principal idea was
> to doubt and weigh every proposition, then disprove it if possible. I was
> oppressed with the feeling that I alone was always found wanting, until I
> discovered how general is the individual failure, how deficient every new-
> comer appears in the local eye.

> Before the evening was over I became so mixed in my mind, what with
> expressions of polite anarchy, the imminence of the socialistic idea, the
> importance of college settlements, and other theories hinged on to those
> . . . that I wondered how the world could be large enough to hold them
> all where each man and woman overflowed with explosive ideas directed
> oppositely.[21]

Truth Dexter (1901) by "Sidney McCall" (Mrs. Mary McNeil Fe-
nellosa) turns on the worn theme of reconciliation between North
and South (a quixotic young Boston lawyer marries a Southern girl
and saves her estate), but it also chronicles a rite of passage into Boston. Faith comes there for the first time:

> Scanning the faces of pedestrians on the Boylston Street Mall, the little
> bride remarked, with some relief, that they did not look altogether inhu-
> man. But the shop-fronts, with their enormous plate-glass windows, mosa-
> iced [sic] in gorgeous costumes, deep-toned Oriental rugs, or glittering
> Japanese screens, seemed visions of impossible splendor. The squareness
> of the streets, the absence of trees, the vista of colossal stone palaces
> along Arlington, the carved animals over the windows of the Natural
> History Building, the terraced steps of the Institute, the air-hung pyra-
> mids of Trinity's towers, and, more than all, the stupendous white for-
> tress of the Public Library dominating Copley Square, oppressed her
> with a sense of magnificence, of civilization, of the power of the North,
> of the presence of man, which belied every generalization of her rustic,
> untutored youth. It was her first revelation of a real city.[22]

If I have avoided citing better books by James or Howells, it is because these more average fictions seem to me characteristic samples of
average responses to Boston, a city that, if it denied space to Mac-
Monnies' "Dancing Bacchante," got Puvis de Chavannes to paint murals in its Public Library.[23]

It will be understood that Boston, even Greater Boston, was not
the sole support of the genteel tradition in New England. On the

contrary, Providence, Hartford,[24] and New Haven are examples of other cultural centers; and colleges from Williams and Amherst to Smith and Wellesley, not to speak of private preparatory schools of the caliber of Exeter and Groton, readied the rising generation to maintain the tradition. What has been said in detail of Boston could in some degree be said of New York, Philadelphia, Baltimore, New Orleans, and so on, and of lesser metropolises like Buffalo, Cleveland, Cincinnati, and Louisville. Modern commentators find the genteel tradition barren; one gets a glimpse, however, into its excitement if one reads Homer Saint-Gaudens' *The American Artist and His Times* (New York, 1941) on his youth in New York:

. . . there has vanished with the "Diamond Horseshoe" much of the plu-tocratic romance that rustled down on its red plush seats bought for the ample wives of the railroad kings who strutted it wide and handsome . . . I was duly impressed when I was sent as part of my education to hear Emma Eames and the de Reszke brothers sing in "Faust." "Cousin Louise" Homer appeared in that opera as Siebel, and what discussion there was in the family as to the length of her blouse and the tightness of her tights!

In those days my father, wise beyond the times as to the bringing up of his son, insisted that on Wednesday matinees I watch Ada Rehan, the toast of Broadway, give "The Taming of the Shrew" with John Drew at Daly's Theater, or sit in the front row of the balcony at Abbey's Theater on the east side of Broadway at Thirty-eighth Street. To my father a proper background for a boy included the best that the theater had to offer along with the best of literature and sculpture and architecture and music and painting. Such an interrelation of the arts was taken for granted. So "willy-nilly," I did see Mounet-Sully go blindly to his death in "Oedipus Rex," and Jane Harding mount the steps of her tumbril as she parted from the elder Coquelin in "Thermidor," and Henry Irving as Charles I, his wife's miniature in hand, look back at his family as he vanished through the door on the way to the scaffold. This was the era in which my father brought home stories from the Players, the private house on Gramercy Park which Edwin Booth had given as a club to con-genial men of all the arts. Nothing like that has happened since or can happen now in actor land.

Then I was brought to listen to chamber music in the Rembrandt Room of the Henry O. Havemeyers' house on Fifth Avenue. There artists and plutocrats assembled before one of the finest groups of pictures of our land. . . . It was not a dealer's collection either, for the Havemeyers, by way of their own taste and that of their friend, Mary Cassatt, had toured through Europe to buy what they liked when they liked it. Sunday afternoons the Kneisel Quartet played in my father's studio, with an accompaniment of beer and pretzels, to men of art and men of affairs. Art in those days did not seek out the millionaire. The millionaire sought art.[25]

One important form of support for the genteel tradition was the club, particularly the men's clubs [26] organized by artists and businessmen. Some of these were founded before the Civil War. The names of many of them betray their purpose; for example, in New York The Tile Club, The Authors, and The Players. The Century Association in that city goes back to 1847; the constitution of 1857 declares it is devoted to the advancement of the arts and literature. The Penn Club in Philadelphia, founded just before the Centennial Exposition of 1876, described itself as an association of authors, artists, men of science and the learned professions, and amateurs of music, letters, and the fine arts. In Boston The St. Botolph Club, begun in 1880, exists for the promotion of social intercourse among authors and artists and other gentlemen connected with or interested in literature and art, and The Tavern Club in that city, dating from 1883, began as a lunch club among young painters. In St. Louis The Wednesday Club, in San Francisco The Bohemians, in Chicago The Cliff Dwellers, in Washington The Cosmos Club exist wholly or in part for similar purposes.

The importance of these organizations lies in the fact that publishers and editors, painters (if they were successful), musicians (if they were the right sort), authors (if they were not radical), and architects (if they had no nonsensical ideas) could lunch and drink and dine with those who represented family, finance, and tradition. Clubhouses, moreover, were maintained in some cities by alumni of the various Ivy League colleges, and university clubs, open to any reputable alumnus of a reputable school, also developed. Women's clubs were organized to pursue culture—in "Xingu" Mrs. Wharton tells us that "Mrs. Ballinger is one of the ladies who pursue Culture in bands, as though it were dangerous to meet alone"—and only gradually went over to politics, social service, and talks on international politics.[27] A common sense of values developed between artist and patron, poet and publisher; and though by the nature of club organization, records are fragmentary, one can be reasonably sure that a climate of opinion about art and education, culture and the support of culture was engendered by casual conversation, talks at club dinners, annual club revels, and club nights when music was played, readings given, or pictures exhibited. It is symbolic of the relation between clubs and culture that Richard Watson Gilder is supposed to have named *The Century Magazine* after The Century Association; and it is true that Matthew Arnold, on his famous lecture tour, was passed from club to club and from wealthy host to wealthy host as he made his way from New York to Chicago, St. Louis, and Richmond.[28] (The contrast with Emerson, whom Arnold in some sense patronized, making his way from hotel to hotel on the lyceum circuits is interesting.)

Members of the "Old American" elite tended to dominate boards of trustees for private schools and colleges, boards of regents for most state universities, boards of trustees for museums and art galleries, and lay boards associated with the leading Protestant denominations. School, college, church, museum, and art gallery therefore tended to support or echo the values of the genteel tradition. One special area of general education and value judgment, somewhat removed from "The Establishment" and yet supporting the genteel tradition, needs special discussion. This was that unique invention, the Chautauqua movement, its rivals and imitators.

The remote ancestor of Chautauqua was the camp-meeting, the nearest progenitor the lyceum, and its grandfather was perhaps the church assembly. If the genteel tradition was a gallant attempt to apply idealism to living, the Chautauqua movement was its shrewdest commercial performance (in an ideal way) toward making these ideas a sort of ecumenical force in American middle-class culture.[29] The original concept was the invention of John H. Vincent, who rose to be a bishop in the Methodist Episcopal Church, and of his colleague, Lewis Miller. These two turned a potential camp-meeting site at Fair Point (later Chautauqua), New York, into the Chautauqua Assembly, which in turn gave birth to the Chautauqua Literary and Scientific Circle, the Chautauqua School of Theology, and a variety of other improving enterprises that would be assembled into a lay university. One of their most potent inventions, *The Chautauquan: A Monthly Magazine Devoted to the Promotion of True Culture,* edited in the first instance by Theodore L. Flood, offered reading lists, instruction, and uplift to the country at large. It ran (in various formats and under various titles) from 1880 to 1914, and it spawned various imitations,[30] just as the Chautauqua movement proper developed rivals like the Bay View Reading Circle and the Home-Culture Clubs, the latter at one time under the direction of George Washington Cable. As for the concept of summer assemblies, by 1885, when Vincent published his expository history, *The Chautauqua Movement*, they had come to dot the map from Puget Sound to Florida.

The original Chautauqua Assembly began as a combination of school and summer camp for Sunday-school teachers, lasting about two weeks. By the opening of the 1880s the sessions were lengthening toward a ten-week period, the original concept of training Sunday-school teachers had been lost in the creation of an unofficial four-years college program, and in 1882 the first "class" was graduated. Theoretically open to any respectable person, Chautauqua classes tended to draw more women than men, since the American business male could scarcely afford to take so long a vacation. The first "graduates" called themselves "The Pioneers," and chose as their motto "From Height to Height" and as their emblem the hatchet.[31] This class included a grandmother of eighty-one and her granddaughter as well as "women who grace the highest circles and personify the ripest culture of the land." By and by there developed the Chautauqua salute, apparently first used to greet General Grant when he was presented with a Bible, which he received in silence. This salute was the enthusiastic waving of white handkerchiefs, transmogrified into lilies in a poem by May Bisbee:

> Have you heard of a wonderful lily,
>   That blooms in the fields of air?
> With never a stem or a pale green leaf,
>   Spotless, and white, and fair?
>
> Unnamed in the books of wise men,
>   Nor akin to the queenly rose;
> But the white Chautauqua lily
>   Is the fairest flower that grows.

With a keen eye to sentimental values the founders devised an elaborate ceremony for the graduating class, which was "admitted to this sacred grove," passed under "arches" dedicated to Faith, Science, Literature, and Art, was formally admitted to the "Society of the Hall in the Grove," and sang an "Anniversary Ode," the first stanza of which runs:

Bright beams again Chautauqua's wave,
And green her forest arches,
As with glad heart and purpose brave,
The student homeward marches.

If we are to believe one "witty" commentator, the homeward-marching student came to have a surprising influence:

Now, all over the land are groups of ladies who meet with their sewing to discuss, not their neighbors' virtues, but the conduct of the Greeks and Romans, or listen to a selection from some great author, or to a translation from Homer or Vergil. Travellers, both old and young men, on the railway car and steamer, one sees conning their Chautauqua textbooks, and there are home circles, where the kings of Old England are reviewed at the breakfast table, and social gatherings with criticism and cream mingled in pleasant proportions.

One may be a little skeptical about the number of breakfast tables where the kings of England passed in review and wonder whether the cloudy Christian idealism of the Chautauqua enthusiasts ever came down to earth,[32] but one cannot altogether laugh off a movement enrolling thousands upon thousands of earnest seekers either in reading courses or as students physically present in the summer Chautauqua meetings.

The original Chautauqua Assembly drew teachers and lecturers of the caliber of Phillips Brooks, Washington Gladden, Herbert B. Adams, M. L. D'Ooge (the classical scholar), Richard T. Ely, G. Stanley Hall, Henry Drummond, Bliss Perry, Jacob A. Riis, Ram Chandra Bose, J. P. Mahaffy (the Irish classicist), and William James. James, indeed, had mixed feelings after "meeting minds so earnest and helpless that it takes them half an hour to get from one idea to its immediately adjacent next neighbor," he was sorry the students "seem to have little or no humor in their composition," and escaped to Buffalo after a week, "glad to get into something less blameless but more admiration-worthy," but all this did not prevent him from giving lectures that later turned into his *Talks to Teachers,* and, as his latest biographer observes, he tried to enter into the spirit of the place.[33] And though *The Chautauquan* carried advertisements for corsets, patent medicines, and garden seeds and had violent objections to Chinese immigration, in its earlier volumes it made few concessions to mere popularity. By 1891, however, serialized fiction appears, and the periodical advertises itself as a "high-class literary magazine adapted to the needs of practical people who think and want to think," and by 1900 under a new editor it goes in for popular articles on minor subjects, though still theoretically clinging to altruism and self-culture.

But there are human enterprises in which nothing is more fatal than success. Chautauqua proved to be one of these. James Redpath, abolitionist and entrepreneur, capitalizing on the old lyceum circuit, founded in 1868 the Boston Lyceum Bureau; Major James Burton Pond bought into the business in 1875, and four years later opened his own lecture bureau in New York. By 1906 the revived lyceum-cum-entertainment world had so developed that A. August Wright produced *Who's Who in the Lyceum*, the preface of which solemnly states that "whatever belongs indubitably to spiritual aesthetics—the realm of life's most significant and most intimate drama—belongs to the Lyceum." Redpath and Pond between them "managed" most of the popular speakers of the country, shrewdly combining instruction and entertainment in a fashion more appealing, if less intellectual, than Chautauqua proper; and though the original assembly carried on, the commercial combination of William Jennings Bryan and the Swiss Bell Ringers was more attractive than ritual. It proved easy to fuse the chautauqua (with a small letter) and the lyceum circuit into a single whole, the tent chautauqua, which was run for profit rather than for uplift, playing a week-long stand in one city and then like a circus pulling up stakes and moving on. Like Artemus Ward's, the tent chautauqua was a moral show. It required no reading. It united laughter and "inspiration." The altruism that had made the original Chautauqua a unique product of American earnestness faded out of its commercialized offspring, and the traveling chautauqua ended as genteel vaudeville.[34]

IV

Elite supporters of the genteel tradition found themselves struggling with an insoluble problem—the clash of two value systems, a clash that involved both religion and race. The general doctrine ran that Western tradition is a seamless whole, a unity that overrides time and nationality, church and race. One began with the Greeks, one swept majestically along the shores of Egypt into the Roman em-

pire, thence through the Middle Ages, the Renaissance, and the Enlightenment into the progressive nineteenth century, wherein, wrote
the Reverend Josiah Strong, there is a tremendous rush of events
which is startling.[35] In this great sweep particulars melted into the
oneness of "Art," which was universal, "Beauty," which was ennobling, and "Wisdom" (sometimes "Faith"), which was expressed by
Great Thinkers. The Old Testament was the work of the Jews; Plato
and Socrates were Greeks; Christianity eventually suffused the
Roman world; Gothic cathedrals and *The Divine Comedy* embodied
the medieval vision; the great Renaissance painters were Catholics;
Milton was a Protestant; Montesquieu, though skeptical, was progressive; Goethe, perhaps a pagan, believed in self-culture as did Tennyson, James Russell Lowell, and the Reverend James Freeman
Clarke.[36] And there was always Shakespeare, who was not for an age
but for all time. They all represented mankind yearning for the
Ideal. Therefore the true believer,

> in his ears
> The murmur of a thousand years,

strove like Arnold's poet in "Resignation" to see life unroll before
him as one placid and continuous whole. If the panorama was spotted by wars and racial hatreds, religious strife and political dissen-
sion, these were accidents, not substance. The believer strove for insight:

> Deeper the Poet feels; but he
> Breathes, when he will, immortal air,
> Where Orpheus and where Homer are.

The unity of the development of mankind was certified by philosophy, by Christianity, and by evolution.

Nevertheless one was forced to select. Among the Greeks and Romans a thousand years of schoolteaching had singled out figures like
Homer and Sophocles and thrust aside the scurrility of lewd fellows
like Lucian and Petronius. In the Christian era, before the invention
of Protestantism, another pragmatic sanction was possible: one took
the medieval writer, architect, or artist as a naïve Catholic, unconscious prophet of sound Protestant religion, and the bawdiness of,
say, the goliards could be set aside for study by specialists. With the
Renaissance of course difficulties increased. One could not deny the

splendor of Renaissance painting, yet how was one to distinguish between the Ideal and the flesh? Between an alluring Magdalen and an
alluring Venus? Petrarch and Castiglione were all right, but what
about Boccaccio and Aretino? Anglo-Saxon sensibility collided with
Mediterranean sensibility. Undoubtedly the Latin races had their geniuses, but were they not susceptible to unpredictable lapses from purity? There was the divine Raphael with his "Sistine Madonna," but
there were also Titian's nudes. Was all this because they were Catholic or because they were Latin?

Overwhelmingly of the white, Anglo-Saxon, Protestant tradition,
the elite wanted to be amiable to agreeable Jews and cultured Catholics. But they had an uneasy sense that their birthright was being
threatened by pagan or decadent art, by theories about art imported
from Europe, and by hordes of non-Anglo-Saxon, non-Protestant immigrants from all sorts of places, including Asia. A belief in univer-
sals like Truth, Wisdom, Art, and Faith meant, it was discovered, a
belief in Truth, Wisdom, Art, and Faith satisfactory to the Protestant
mind, so that the reconciliation of aesthetic, philosophic, and religious values in the Ideal was somehow never quite fused with the
practical facts of religion and race.

The doctrine of the inherent superiority of the Anglo-Saxon was,
of course, not a nineteenth-century invention. The Germanic tribes,
if Tacitus was to be believed, had had a loftier ethical standard than
the decadent Romans; and in the seventeenth and eighteenth centuries it was discovered that the "Gothick" north was both the mother
of parliaments and the womb of virile virtue.[37] The doctrine picked
up auxiliary aid from the conviction of New Englanders that they
were under Providence a lamp unto mankind, replacing the Jews as
the Chosen People, and moved into the nineteenth century as an
amazing compound of the will of God, virtue, the adaptation of a
race to environment, evolution, progress, and manifest destiny. True,
the American Constitution forbade the establishment of religion, but
everybody knew that the United States was a Protestant country.
Protestantism was a characteristic invention of the Germanic peoples.
John Higham points out that Sharon Turner's *History of the Anglo-
Saxons*, first published in England from 1799 to 1805, was reissued in
Philadelphia in 1841.

But it did not require an English historian to establish the doctrine of Anglo-Saxon greatness. In 1843 that amazing genius, George

Perkins Marsh, addressed Middlebury College on *The Goths in New-England*. His lecture shows some influence from Lyell's *Principles of Geology* and fully exemplifies the theory of Anglo-Saxondom. The principles of American government, he said, precede the Revolution; they arise from "the intellectual character of our Puritan forefathers," which "derived by inheritance from our remote Gothic ancestry," free of the shackles and burdens which "the spiritual and intellectual tyranny of Rome had for centuries imposed" and deriving its moral character from "a superinduction of the temper and spirituality of Christianity upon the soul of the Goth." During the Reformation, "the English mind . . . was striving to recover its Gothic tendencies, by the elimination of the Roman element." New England was clearly descended from the Reformation. His audience, Marsh thought, was

> too well instructed to be the slaves of that antiquated and vulgar prejudice, which makes Gothicism and barbarism synonymous. The Goths, the common ancestors of the inhabitants of North Western Europe, are the noblest branch of the Caucasian race. We are their children. It was the spirit of the Goth, that guided the May-Flower across the trackless ocean; the blood of the Goth, that flowed at Bunker's Hill.

In Marsh's view the eighteenth-century respect for classical Rome was an error, for "Rome was essentially a nation of robbers." Roman art "attracts by the . . . voluptuous beauty of the external form," whereas "the Goth pursues the development of a principle, the expression of a thought, the realization of an ideal." For this reason:

> The Roman, holding the essence and efficacy of Christianity to consist in its ceremonies and its symbols, sinks the preacher in the priest, makes the minister a juggler, and conceives of Christianity as a middle term, a *punctum indifferens* between Judaism and idolatry . . . ; the Goth feels it to be a living, spiritual influence, involving the abnegation of both, and believes that all its outward rites are symbolical of that internal work, by which the mind is elevated, and the heart purified.

The founders of New England "belonged to the class most deeply tinctured with the moral and intellectual traits of their Northern ancestry," and for that reason fled the Romish Stuarts and fought against the tyranny of the House of Hanover. The Anglo-Saxons will prevail. "The mighty West will look back with filial reverence to the birth-place of the fathers of her people, and the schools of New-England will still be nursing mothers to the posterity of her widely scattered children." [38]

The doctrine was re-enforced by the magazines. Thus an article in *The American Whig Review* for January 1848 argued that places and times have been divinely appointed for the several races, and that the infiltration of the Anglo-Saxons into the tropics, Asia, and the isles of the sea is divinely guided because,

> the Anglo-Saxon race has ever been distinguished from all others, by moral elevation, by religious fervor . . . we cannot resist the conclusion that Providence has raised up, and sustained, and qualified the Anglo-Saxon race, to perform a great work in reclaiming the world; has guided and protected them from temptation, or brought them from it *purified*, and ennobled by every scene of trial; and has given them—to *us*—the destinies of the world.

> The efficient feature, then, in modern civilization is *enterprise*—social, moral, intellectual, and political enterprise; and in this race for distinction, England and America have been first and foremost.[39]

In 1851 an article entitled "The Anglo-Saxon Race" in the *North American Review,* ostensibly a notice of two books by Klipstein on Anglo-Saxon language and literature, left philology behind to rejoice in "the old Anglo-Saxon love of liberty and equal rights." "The American, however democratic he may be . . . is yet proud to assert that he too is the free-born child of the same stock; for, a thousand years of progressive civilization, transportation to a new continent, revolution, change of governmental form, have not sufficed to change the nature of the Anglo-Saxon." "The destiny of the Anglo-Saxons," wrote the happy author, "is to conquer the whole earth." The Spaniards failed in the New World "because they are incapable of holding any rational idea of liberty." Though most of the article is a popular history of the Anglo-Saxons and the Danes through the reign of Alfred, the heart of the doctrine is this:

> We are progressive and yet conservative, wandering and yet inhabitive, ready to win from the forest or the savage all the earth we can ever hope to use, and then equally ready to bring it under the dominion of civilization, law, and religion. We are intensely attached to our own customs and institutions, and yet ever ready to adopt improvements from whatever source they may come. Our love of freedom, if not always wise, is always indomitable; but just as strong is our conviction that freedom can be insured only by the dominion of laws; a conviction which is often as-

sailed, and sometimes apparently suppressed, yet always has conquered, and we trust always will conquer, in the battle with lawlessness. We are the most mixed race that ever existed; and yet the admixture of other races has never been such as to weaken or impoverish the original Saxon stock;—on the contrary, it has infused into it new life and energy. We believe that the Teutonic race excels all others in the possession of these traits of character; and that the Saxons are pre-eminent or typical for possessing them in a higher degree than any other members of that race.[40]

The sense of the irreconcilability of the Protestant and Catholic worlds, of the Germanic and the Latin races, together with the conviction that God had chosen the Anglo-Saxons as His special people, began to influence historical writing. The opening of Parkman's *The Conspiracy of Pontiac* (1851) announced that the Indian was doomed before the onrush of Anglo-Saxon civilization. The second chapter is a rapid sketch of the French and British in North America from 1608 to 1763; it is evident that the French are ordained to lose:

> Feudalism stood arrayed against Democracy; Popery against Protestantism; the sword against the ploughshare. The priest, the soldier, and the noble, ruled in Canada. The ignorant, light-hearted Canadian peasant knew nothing and cared nothing about popular rights and civil liberties. Born to obey, he lived in contented submission, without the wish of the capacity for self-rule. Power, centred in the heart of the system, left the masses inert. . . .

> If we search the world for the sharpest contrast to the spiritual and temporal vassalage of Canada, we shall find it among her immediate neighbors, the Puritans of New England, where the spirit of non-conformity was sublimed by a fiery essence, and where the love of liberty and the hatred of power burned with sevenfold heat. The English colonist, with thoughtful brow and limbs hardened with toil; calling no man master, yet bowing reverently to the law which he himself had made; patient and laborious, and seeking for the solid comforts rather than the ornaments of life; no lover of war, yet, if need were, fighting with a stubborn, indomitable courage, and then bending once more with a steadfast energy to his farm, or his merchandise,—such a man might well be deemed the very pith and marrow of a commonwealth.[41]

Moses Coit Tyler, the great historian of colonial and revolutionary American literature, noted with pride that from the primal community of twenty one thousand persons in New England, three and one half millions have descended, "who compose the present population of New England; while of the entire population now spread over the United States, probably every third person can read in the history of the first settlement of New England the history of his own progenitors," a statement he based on John Gorham Palfrey's *History of New England*. Tyler described the literature of the American Revolution as mirroring a period of "upheaval, perturbation, tumult, in which the English race in America appears to be in desperate struggle for self-preservation against fatal assault from without and from within." The Scotch-Irish, the Dutch, the Germans, the Huguenots, the Swedes, and the Welsh (and the Irish?) were all apparently absorbed into the master race.[42]

Herbert Spencer, Charles Darwin, and a doctrine of evolutionary progress were called on to substantiate the theory. The popular philospher-historian, John Fiske, keyed his histories of the American colonies, the Revolution and the so-called "Critical Period" to the same dominant theme. The first chapter of *The Beginnings of New England,* an amplification of a passage in *The Destiny of Man,* which in turn echoes his *Outlines of Cosmic Philosophy,* develops a long comparison between the "Roman idea" and the "English idea." The English idea possessed the incomparable merit of being Aryan and including political liberty:

. . . the merest glance at the history of Europe shows us Germanic peoples wresting the supremacy from Rome . . . we shall discover a grand and far-reaching Teutonic Idea of political life overthrowing and supplanting the Roman Idea.

From the days of Arminius and Civilis in the wilds of lower Germany to the days of Franklin and Jefferson in Independence Hall, we have been engaged in this struggle, not without some toughening of our political fibre, not without some refining of our moral sense.

. . . we find all the tremendous force of this newly awakened religious enthusiasm coöperating with the English love of self-government and carrying it under Cromwell to victory. From this fortunate alliance of religious and political forces has come all the noble and fruitful work of the last two centuries, in which men of English speech have been laboring for the political regeneration of mankind.[43]

Fiske also felt that the atheism of the French *philosophes* had had no great effect in America, and in his influential *Civil Government in the United States with Some Reference to its Origins* (1890), after a few philological flourishes, derived representative government from the Anglo-Saxon clan system and the Old English *tungemot.* If American municipal government was a failure, "the great mass of ignorant voters, chiefly foreigners without experience in self-government" was to blame.[44]

And Senator Henry Cabot Lodge's *Early Memories* opens with a chapter on heredity that approves of Darwin, Galton, and Mendel. In an essay of 1891 he thought the New England town a reversion to "forms which our remote ancestors brought out of the German forests." So did Henry Adams. Out of 14,243 persons of superior ability in American history Lodge found 10,376 to be of English origin, though he never clearly defined "English."

Even heavier artillery was brought to bear upon the problem. In *The Descent of Man* Darwin had said that "the wonderful progress of the United States, as well as the character of the people, are the results of natural selection," and quoted the Reverend M. Zincke to the effect that "All other series of events—as that which resulted in the culture of mind in Greece, and that which resulted in the empire of Rome—only appear to have purpose and value when viewed in connection with, or rather as subsidiary to . . . the great stream of Anglo-Saxon emigration to the west."[45]

Lecturing in America, Matthew Arnold insisted (out of a population of about 55,000,000, about 24,500,000 were immigrants or the children of immigrants) that:

> You are fifty millions mainly sprung, as we in England are mainly sprung, from that German stock which has faults indeed. . . . Yet of the German stock it is, I think, true, as my father said more than fifty years ago, that it has been a stock "of the most moral races of men that the world has yet seen, with the soundest laws, the least violent passions, the fairest domestic and civil virtues."

In shaping this stock "the discipline of Puritanism has been invaluable, and the more I read history, the more I see of mankind, the more I recognise its value." Mediterranean culture would not do: the French worship the goddess Lubricity.

The influential British historian, Edward A. Freeman, author of *Comparative Politics,* toured the American academic circuit from Cambridge to St. Louis. One of his lecture series was called "The

English People in its Three Homes," the three being Germany, Great Britain, and the United States. In a later travel book he declared that in America "the English kernel is so strong as to draw to itself every foreign element" and that if "men of various nationalities" are "easily changed into good Americans," the good American must be, "in every case that is not strictly geographical, a good Englishman." He thought that Rhode Island and Delaware were strikingly like the German-speaking Swiss canton of Uri; and in an "Introduction" to *American Institutional History* written for Herbert Baxter Adams' monograph series, he said the institutions of Massachusetts and Maryland

> are part of the general institutions of the English people, as those are again part of the general institutions of the Teutonic race, and those are again part of the general institutions of the whole Aryan family.

> To me the past history and present condition of the United States is, before all things, a part of the general history of the Teutonic race, and especially of its English branch.[46]

It was but a step toward books of general racial and religious theorizing, of which one may select two for comment. The first, already mentioned, is Josiah Strong's *Our Country,* said to have sold about 175,000 copies by 1916. Backed by the Home Missionary Society, Strong had a profound faith in the American system, thought the world was going to be Christianized and civilized by the Protestants, distrusted the Roman Catholics and the Mormons, took a reserved view of unrestricted immigration, denounced socialism, revived the doctrine of wealth as trusteeship for Christianity, and, though he detested the gambling spirit, held that "the West is being filled with a *selected* population, and the principle of selection is the desire to better their worldly condition." This social datum is somehow the basis for Anglo-Saxon domination, Protestantism, and the improvement of mankind. "Race" is with him virtually a portmanteau word. One reads that "most of the spiritual Christianity in the world is found among Anglo-Saxons and their converts; for this is the great missionary race"; yet Anglo-Saxondom is something that is going to "include all English-speaking peoples," so that apparently the ability to speak English will assimilate a Chinaman to the Anglo-Saxons. The inherent contradiction in his argument is clear in the following passages:

Does it not look as if God were not only preparing in our Anglo Saxon civilization the die with which to stamp the peoples of the earth, but as if he were also massing behind that die the mighty power with which to press it? My confidence that this race is eventually to give its civilization to mankind is not based on mere numbers—China forbid! I look forward to what the world has never yet seen united in the same race; viz., the greatest numbers and the highest civilization.

There is here [that is, in the United States] a new commingling of races; and, while the largest injections of foreign blood are substantially the same elements that constituted the original Anglo-Saxon admixture, so that we may infer the general type will be preserved, there are strains of other bloods being added, which, if Mr. Emerson's remark is true, that "the best nations are those most widely related," may be expected to improve the stock, and aid it to a higher destiny. If the dangers of immigration, which have been pointed out, can be successfully met for the next few years, until it has passed its climax, it may be expected to add value to the amalgam which will constitute the new Anglo-Saxon race of the New World.

Among the striking attributes of the Anglo-Saxon (that is, the original Anglo-Saxon) are his money-making power, his genius for colonization, and his energy, which "becomes peculiarly American." This confused logic comes out as: "It seems to me that God, with infinite wisdom and skill, is training the Anglo-Saxon race for an hour sure to come in the world's future," at which time the Anglo-Saxons, however defined, are to "move down upon Mexico, down upon Central and South America, out upon the islands of the sea, over upon Africa and beyond." Strong could not make up his mind whether the Anglo-Saxons were to be a dominant race or whether the triumph of the melting-pot theory was to remake the Anglo-Saxons.

Others were concerned lest the American Anglo-Saxons be swamped by lesser breeds. Assuming as a matter of course that "the Anglo-Saxon branch of the Nordic race is again showing itself to be that upon which the nation must chiefly depend for leadership, for courage, for self-sacrifice and devotion to an ideal," in *The Passing of the Great Race,* Madison Grant sorrowed in 1916 over the fact that "one of the greatest difficulties in classifying man is his perverse predisposition to mismate." He argued against amalgamation, that "widespread and fatuous belief in the power of environment" born of the "loose thinkers of the French Revolution and their American mimics," and denounced both the Church of Rome and unrestricted immigration. He thought it "highly unjust that a minute minority should be called upon to supply brains for the unthinking mass of the community," including "an ever increasing number of moral perverts, mental defectives and hereditary cripples," said that genius was not a matter of family but is produced by race and only by race, described the Nordic race as "domineering, individualistic, self-reliant and jealous of their personal freedom both in political and religious systems and as a result they [sic] are usually Protestants," and toward the end of his volume presents this remarkable discovery in art:

> In depicting the crucifixion no artist hesitates to make the two thieves brunet in contrast to the blond Saviour. This is something more than a convention, as such quasi-authentic traditions as we have of our Lord strongly suggest his Nordic, possibly Greek, physical and moral attributes.[47]

Perhaps the best comment on this curious confusion between the inevitable dominance of the Anglo-Saxon and the theory that the Anglo-Saxon would dominate only by assimilating almost anybody not an Anglo-Saxon is that of Dunne's Mr. Dooley:

> I can tell ye, whin th' Clan an' th' Sons iv Sweden an' th' Banana Club an' th' Circle Francaize an' th' Pollacky Benivolent society an' th' Rooshian Sons of Dinnymite an' th' Benny Brith an' the Coffee Clutch that Schwartzmeister r-runs an' th' Turned'ye-mind an' th' Holland Society an' th' Afro-Americans an' th' other Anglo-Saxons begin f'r to raise their Anglo-Saxon battle-cry, it'll be all day with th' eight or nine people in th' wurruld that has th' misfortune iv not bein' brought up Anglo-Saxons.[48]

One catches glimpses of the impact of this doctrine of racial superiority in the writings of Theodore Roosevelt. In 1896 he wrote Henry White: ". . . though I greatly admire the Boers, I feel it is to the interest of civilization that the English-speaking race should be dominant in South Africa, exactly as it is for the interest of civilization that the United States themselves, the greatest branch of the English-speaking race, should be dominant in the Western Hemisphere." The next year he told his British friend, Cecil Arthur Spring Rice: ". . . there are still great waste spaces which the English-speaking peoples undoubtedly have the vigor to fill. America north of the Rio

Grande, and Australia, and perhaps Africa south of the Zambesi, all possess a comparatively dense civilized population, English in law, tongue, government and culture, and with English the dominant strain in the blood," and he contrasted this vigor with the decadence of the French. That same year he wrote Augustus Lowell apropos of giving some Lowell lectures that he would like to do six that would end by showing Western ranch life as a kind of condensed paradigm of expansionism:

> I could sketch briefly in outline the whole western movement; that mighty westward thrust of our people which established the dominance of the English blood, tongue, and law from the seacoast of the Atlantic to the Pacific; showing how this has really been a part of the great move-ment which within three centuries has made the expansion of the Eng-lish-speaking peoples infinitely the greatest feature in the world's history. And then I would come down finally to the ranch life . . . to show that it was really repeating, in extremely abbreviated form, for our people a stage of civilization which in other peoples—among the Russians for instance—has lasted for many centuries of their development.[49]

Apparently speed-up in empire building was also an Anglo-Saxon virtue. In *The Winning of the West* (1889–1896) Roosevelt followed Parkman in assuming the inevitable triumph of the virile Teutonic stock over the French, the Spanish, and the Indians, and in collec-tions of autobiographical sketches, essays, and addresses ranging from *Hunting Trips of a Ranchman* (1885) to *The Strenuous Life* (1900) he tirelessly proclaimed the superior morality of physical vigor proper to Anglo-Saxons (or in a larger sense the Germanic stock). He likewise denounced the decadence of other races (who were commit-ting race suicide) and of much recent art and thought.

Even Roosevelt could not express the ultimate glory of the expan-sionist philosophy. This remained for Albert J. Beveridge of Indiana, who announced in the Senate on January 9, 1900, that: "Of all our race, God has marked the American people as His chosen nation to finally lead in the regeneration of the world. This is the divine Mis-sion of America, and it holds for us all the profit, all the glory, all the happiness possible to man. We are trustees of the world's prog-ress, guardians of its righteous peace." [50]

It is not here pretended that the American elite, as I have tried to define them, were all for Anglo-Saxondom and the Big Stick. On the contrary, one of the most characteristic expressions of moral idealism proper to the genteel tradition was the anti-imperialism of 1898–1900. Men, it was vehemently argued, should not be governed without their consent if the Declaration of Independence had universal meaning. In acquiring colonies the United States was being false to the principles of Washington's Farewell Address. In Brahmin Boston worthies like Gamaliel Bradford and Moorfield Story organized on the model of the American Revolution committees of correspondence to arouse protest against the policies of McKinley and Roosevelt, and founded in the autumn of 1898 an Anti-Imperialist League, which, while retaining George S. Boutwell of Boston as president, shortly had forty-one vice-presidencies scattered over the country. The cynical Senator Lodge found the movement comical, but a year later the League had so increased that it held an anti-imperialist convention with delegates from thirty states, and in 1900 it called a "Liberty Congress" in Indianapolis. Such distinguished representatives of the elite as President Charles W. Eliot of Harvard, President David Starr Jordan of Stanford, William James, John Burgess, Henry Van Dyke, and other academics, ex-President Harrison, Speaker Reed of the House, Senator George F. Hoar of Maine, Godkin of *The Nation,* John Sherman, Leonard W. Bacon, Jane Addams, Thomas Wentworth Higginson, William Dean Howells, W. G. Sumner, Mark Twain, and "Mr. Dooley" were of the movement. A scholarly analysis of the membership shows that it was composed of former mugwumps, present political reformers, older Republicans, Democrats like Grover Cleveland and William Jennings Bryan, and churchmen; representatives of business and industry were naturally less numerous and those of labor were few.

Anti-imperialism had its literary expression, running from Mr. Dooley's satire to William Graham Sumner. Henry Blake Fuller broke into vituperative verse in which he called McKinley a "sweating chattel slave" and Roosevelt the "Megaphone of Mars." Mark Twain, thoroughly aroused, published one of his most savage essays, "To the Person Sitting in Darkness," in the *North American Review* for February 1901, and earlier, in the New York *Herald* for December 30, 1900, printed "A Greeting from the Nineteenth to the Twentieth Century," which begins: "I bring you the stately nation named Christendom, returning, bedraggled, besmirched, and dishonored, from pirate raids in Kiao-Chou, Manchuria, South Africa, and the

Philippines, with her soul full of meanness, her pocket full of boodle, and her mouth full of hypocrisies. Give her soap and towel, but hide the looking glass."

William Graham Sumner devoted *The Conquest of the United States by Spain* (Boston, 1899) to the thesis that expansion and imperialism are at war with the best traditions, principles, and interests of the American people. Probably the most enduring of these literary expressions of outrage are three poems by William Vaughn Moody, "An Ode in Time of Hesitation," "The Quarry" (on the attempt of the Great Powers to carve up China), and the "Ode on a Soldier Fallen in the Philippines." "An Ode in Time of Hesitation" is set on the Boston Common, where on a spring day the poet has paused to look on Saint-Gaudens' memorial to Robert Gould Shaw and his Negro regiment and to meditate on the meaning of liberty. Part of the poem runs:

> Alas! what sounds are these that come
> Sullenly over the Pacific seas,—
> Sounds of ignoble battle, striking dumb
> The season's half-awakened ecstasies?
> .   .   .   .
> Lies! lies! It cannot be! The wars we wage
> Are noble, and our battles still are won
> By justice for us, ere we lift the gage.
> We have not sold our loftiest heritage.
> The proud republic hath not stooped to cheat
> And scramble in the market-place of war.

Whether the heritage was sold or not, the anti-imperialist movement lacked coherence, was put together from too many disparate components, and could not exert practical political pressure. Nevertheless, better than any other single political episode, the expansionist doctrine and its counterpart show how difficult is it to generalize about the elite and the genteel tradition.[51]

V

My discussion of the genteel tradition as an expression of the values of an elite, of the nature of the elite, and of the inevitable inferences to be drawn from some aspects of elite values has up to now been prejudiced, or seems to be so, toward a tradition that is in fact one of the major aspects of mature American culture. To ignore the social setting of nineteenth-century idealism seems to me, however, to leave the genteel tradition hanging in mid-air, where, to be sure, many historians and many critics would like to keep it. On the other hand, to indicate some of the practical difficulties faced by its adherents is to seem to join those who have no patience with what they think of as futile and unreal.

Members of the elite who supported its value system can be found on both sides of many public questions. Not all the supporters of the tradition were ardent Protestants *ipso facto* hostile alike to Catholicism and to all other forms of religion. Some of them held that the country was a melting pot; some deplored the mixture of races this implied. Some advocated fulfilling the role manifest destiny had assigned to the American republic; others vehemently argued that there is no manifest destiny but only goals appropriate to national ideals. Human beliefs are seldom consistent; the important thing is not hastily to charge that hypocrisy or blindness was built into the very nature of idealism.

Yet the practical weakness of the general theory is clear. This weakness arose out of a failure to see a necessary connection between past and present time. Intellectuals could look upon history as a whole and then fail to show how or why this wholeness had somehow broken just before the contemporary world began. Thus members of the Dante Society in Cambridge could honestly believe that Dante was a great and universal poet, but fail to see any connection between the pulsing life of Florence in the last quarter of the thirteenth century and the pulsing life of the North End in Boston in the last quarter of the nineteenth century. Admirers of Ibsen proclaimed that his dramas were great universal poems; they somehow failed to translate this admiration into much concern for Norwegian immigrants in Wisconsin. One read the Bible as literature and one avoided contact with Russian Jews on the East Side in New York. One could be fascinated by the Parthenon and the theater at Epidauros and repelled by the Greek candy-store merchant and his family six blocks down the street. Dvořák's *New World Symphony* was charming, one could even be "intense" about Oscar Wilde's charge that Dvořák wrote "passionate, curiously colored things" (in "The Critic as Artist"), but few among the elite paused to inquire why Dvořák elaborated his famous composition in Spillville, Iowa, a village of Bohemian immigrants.

Paderewski of the leonine mane was a huge success; Polish-American immigrants in Buffalo or Hamtramck were more dubious. When the universal and the beautiful were defined principally as great efforts in past time, it proved difficult or impossible to bring the implication of universality into the present tense and the living generations. It was not the incoming of "realism" that killed the genteel tradition so much as it was that the universal lived and moved and had its being only in the storied centuries. And yet, as we shall see, the genteel tradition performed a radically necessary service to American art and thought.

VI

The Genteel Tradition

Beauty will not come at the call of a legislature.

—EMERSON

I

THE GENTEEL TRADITION, which has been more often traduced than analyzed, was a necessary major phase in the development of American culture. The term itself was brought into vogue by the irony of George Santayana, and there have been various attempts to refine his interpretation.[1] By the genteel tradition I shall mean an operative fusion of idealism and the instinct for craftsmanship, which dominated high culture from 1865 to 1915 and which infiltrated the culture of the middle class. During this half-century the genteel tradition was our cultural norm; that is, it was a central principle for aesthetic values, philosophy, upper-class religion, and higher education, which influenced secondary education importantly in these decades. The genteel tradition was also consonant with a renewed admiration for important aspects of European culture, particularly British literature, "classical" music, and the approved great masters of sculpture, painting, and architecture. The decorative arts were also involved. Its idealism was at once moral, aesthetic, and philosophical, and its criticism tended to set up kinds of judgment that W. C. Brownell, its most representative critic, called standards. Like all important expressions of cultural value the tradition is difficult to bound in time and define in content. One may, however, begin by looking at certain phases of American art and literature before the Civil War.

Many literary historians label the years between the Battle of New Orleans and Appomattox the period of American romanticism, though no one has succeeded in defining either romanticism in general or romanticism in America [2] to the satisfaction of scholarship. After the waning of Federalist culture and the weakening of judicial criticism,[3] a variety of forces—ranging from a renewed drive toward cultural nationalism and novel doctrines in religious belief to a sympathetic admiration for exciting ideas out of European art and philosophy or concerning the nature of genius—radically altered older concepts of the way of genius and the theory of art. The glories of the Golden Day and the American Renaissance have been too often extolled to require recounting here. It is, however, essential to discuss certain weaknesses of American romanticism even at the risk of seeming to cavil at a great creative epoch.

Whatever one means by romanticism, loftiness of purpose rather than perfection of workmanship tends to be one of its literary hallmarks.[4] Its performances were at the worst ejaculatory and at the best unpredictable, since in theory art sprang from a divine afflatus that was by its very nature intermittent. As in Europe, so in the United States: literary genius was tantamount to inspiration, and inspiration came and went. The results were rarely architectonic. Among the greater men Emerson, though wise, is aphoristic; he often writes by sentences rather than by paragraphs. Irving is diffuse, only occasionally condensing into memorability. Cooper sprawls. Lowell is subject to learned whim. In *The Scarlet Letter* Hawthorne for one wonderful moment wrote something as firmly shaped as *Madame Bovary* (though one may question the propriety of the "Custom House" essay), but except for a handful of tales and sketches he never again reached this pitch of perfection. Thoreau has unity of tone, rarely unity of structure. *Moby Dick* is stuffed with chapters the ordinary reader wishes away and critical casuistry struggles to justify. Whittier seldom knew when he had finished a poem. Whitman goes on and on; and though verbal affluence is part of his greatness, his constant tinkering with *Leaves of Grass,* the uncertain diction of his prose, and the equal uncertainty of his aesthetic judgments are part of the same general weakness. The only three firm technicians among the great writers are Bryant, Poe, and Longfellow, and when one passes to lesser figures—Margaret Fuller, William Gilmore Simms, Jones Very, and Harriet Beecher Stowe—uncertainty of control over material is only too evident. It was painfully evident to Poe, much of whose book reviewing was devoted to elementary lessons in diction and syntax and most of whose criticism concerns problems of structure, as in the essay on *Barnaby Rudge,* his critique of Hawthorne's *Twice-Told Tales,* and his own account of the writing of "The Raven." The key sentence in the critique is: "A skilful literary artist has constructed a tale." Its antithesis is in Emerson's essay, "The Poet," where one reads: "With what joy I begin to read a poem which I confide in as an inspiration." The two approaches to the art of writing can be reconciled, but they are opposed polarities.

American music in the period did not exist on any such scale as American literature, but in other major arts (architecture, sculpture, and painting) the situation was similar, though more complex. There were plenty of honest craftsmen in the building trades, but the exaltation of soul over technique often appears in "higher" architecture, where the two significant trends were the Greek revival and the vogue of Gothic. Though such geniuses as Bulfinch, Upjohn, and Renwick did excellent work; though many Greek revival structures are admirable—for example, the Bank of the United States in Philadelphia—and though Gothic included among its triumphs American pine Gothic, simple and sincere, the difficulty with too many Greek-revival structures and too many Gothic buildings was that aspiration outran capacity. (The ultimate absurdity of aspiration was probably Bronson Alcott's summer house in Concord, though that was scarcely a problem in architecture.) In sculpture Greenough's "Washington" was grandiose rather than great. Greenough theorized that form follows function, but he was inclined to regard *colossal* as a meritorious adjective.[5] Hiram Powers' "Greek Slave" was gracile rather than Greek. The "Greek Slave" is, as Adeline Adams somewhere rightly says, an anecdote. The implied anecdote saved it for "purity," but neither anecdotage nor purity improves it as a statue.

The situation in painting was more complicated still. Once past the wandering limner phase of its development, American painting, or at least the American painters that art history and art criticism still find worth discussing, developed technical proficiency with astonishing speed. Thomas Cole, for example, was virtually self-taught; and though modern taste may find the smooth finish, the melodramatic coloring, and the attention to minute detail distasteful, American achievement is, given the circumstances, amazing. Confronting their canvases nowadays, especially their landscapes, one feels that the artist was not satisfied to render the subject in itself but something beyond the subject, like infinity, or nature, or the American dream, or wildness, or the goodness of God. Cole is perhaps the extreme example of this confusion between paint and theology. Beginning as a transcriber of the beauties of the American landscape, he went on to pomposities as in "The Course of Empire" series, and what Bryant characterized as his "ardent imagination" turned many of his later canvases into settings for a Meyerbeer opera. His biographer, Louis Legrand Noble, thought that as a landscapist Cole saw unity arising out of infinity (one thinks of Emerson); and in proposing to his best patron, Luman Reed, the "Course of Empire" Cole suggested, "a series of pictures . . . that should illustrate the history of a natural scene, as well as be an epitome of Man,—showing the natural changes of landscape, and those effected by man in his progress from barbarism to civilization   to luxury—to the vicious state, or state of destruction—and to the state of ruin and desolation." [6] However interesting as a philosophy of history, this is scarcely painterly.

The most prominent writer on painting in the half-century was probably Henry T. Tuckerman, by no means deficient in technical knowledge, but the epigraph to his *Artist-Life; or, Sketches of American Painters* (1847), taken from the poet Charles Sprague, could scarcely be more "ideal":

> When, from the sacred garden driven
> Man fled before his Maker's wrath,
> An angel left his place in heaven,
> And cross'd the wanderer's sunless path.
> 'Twas Art! sweet Art! new radiance broke
> Where her light feet flew o'er the ground,
> And thus with seraph voice she spoke:
> "The curse a blessing shall be found."

Passages in the text are equally seraphic. Henry Inman is thus described:

> His air and smile, the lines of mental activity in his face, the very fall of his long hair would stamp him in a crowd as a weaver of "such stuff as dreams are made of." His countenance has that interest which lies in expression, an interest far transcending mere regularity of outline or beauty of individual feature. . . . It seems less the offspring of accident, has a more intimate relation with the soul, and is a characteristic over which time has no power.

Tuckerman thought that

> Catholicism is the religion of Art. With all her errors, she has ever met
> the native sympathies of the heart, and obeyed the great law by which
> the True is sought through the Beautiful. Puritanism represents Christi-
> anity as an opinion, Catholicism as a sentiment; the former addresses the
> intellect, the latter the feelings and imagination.[7]

The point is not shrewdness in evaluating Catholic art; the point is
that the intellect is minimized, feelings and the imagination maxim-
ized. The true and the beautiful require capital letters. But feeling
and imagination do not *ipso facto* produce technique.

It is difficult to insulate the beginnings of a renewed drive for
craftsmanship; it is, as I have said, a major interest in Poe, and of
consequence in the books of Andrew Jackson Downing, as in *Theory
and Practice of Landscape Gardening* (1841) and *Cottage Residences*
(1842). The thesis can also be defended that in a sense, craftsmanship
was one of the chief hobbles on American painting up to the mid-
century.[8] But the development of literary and historical scholarship,
by insisting on differences among styles, inevitably swung attention
from genius to technique, and in literature particularly the power of
craftsmanship became a paramount consideration after the Civil
War. E.P.Whipple is a transition figure in this criticism. Edmund
Clarence Stedman in *Victorian Poets* (1878), *Poets of America* (1885),
and *The Nature and Elements of Poetry* (1892) argued for the Horatian labor of the file, admired Tennyson for his perfect workmanship,
and declared that poetry was the easiest art in which to dabble and
the hardest to master.[9]

About the middle of the century the French were becoming the
great teachers of technique. Paris was supplanting Rome and Düsseldorf as a center for painting and had become a musical center as
well, and French criticism and French literary theory were therefore
the subjects of innumerable articles in serious American magazines.
Not unnaturally Henry James launched in *French Poets and Novelists* (1878) that long series of explorations of the relation of craftsmanship to creativity that culminates in the famous prefaces to the
New York edition of his fiction. But James was a little remote from
America, and the greatest teacher of the theory of craftsmanship was
probably Brander Matthews of Columbia University, who began
with *Theatres of Paris* (1880) an enormous productivity.

What is the mechanism of success in writing? Matthews assumed with Dr. Johnson that they who live to please must please to live, and in books running from *Aspects of Fiction* (1896) to *The Principles of Playmaking* (1919) and in innumerable magazine essays he explored virtually every literary form except the epic. He noted that fiction begins with the improbable (*The Arabian Nights*), moves on to the impossible (medieval romance), passes next to the probable (Balzac, Thackeray), and comes down to the inevitable (*The Scarlet Letter, Anna Karenina*). This progress represents an increasing sophistication of technique. The noble qualities in any literary work are insufficient, he thought, unless they are sustained by technical competence. The true artist hungers after technique for its own sake, well knowing the nourishment it affords, and even goes outside his art in search of unforeseen but fascinating difficulties. If the business of art is to delight, the business of criticism is to understand the technical problems in any work, and by illuminating the technique to increase the reader's pleasure. Matthews even laid down twelve rules for book reviewers,[10] and though he was often superficial, he was immensely influential in stressing form, technique, style, and clarity as goals.[11] Partly because of Matthews' influence, partly because of the magazine editors, the American short story became increasingly deft, and, from our point of view, "slick." Moreover, the period is the era of the "well-made play."

Propaganda for technique might produce a merely mechanical approach, as in "How-To" books like those fabricated by Sherwin E. Cody (*How to Write Fiction*, 1895) [12] and magazines directed at the creation and selling of manuscripts such as *The Writer* (1887—). It created courses of both the collegiate and the commercial sorts on the "you, too, can write" doctrine. Or it might offer general advice to readers like that expressed by Lewis E. Gates of Harvard in *Talks to Booklovers* (1901).[13] But at a higher level it brought into being not merely James's essays but also Howells' confused yet perennially interesting *Criticism and Fiction* (1891), in which, amidst much about morality and Americanism, there is an attempt to identify and associate formlessness with sentimentalism and to differentiate honest romance from the falsities of romanticism. From the point of view of an analysis of writing novels Howells' neglected *Heroines of Fiction* (1901) is better because it is more like conversations in a literary workshop.

On a still loftier plane the discussion of technique, form, and style was beautifully articulated by William Crary Brownell, along with Matthews one of the chief channels through which a sense of European, especially of French, concern for craftsmanship was brought to American readers.[14] Long the chief editorial adviser to Charles Scribner's Sons and one of the great American editors of his time, Brownell found the key to French art in the influence of the intellectual as distinguished from the sensous instinct, remarking that as one strayed through a French art gallery, one was "impressed by the splendid competence everywhere displayed." French sculpture resembled Greek sculpture in being "the production of culture, which in restraining wilfulness, however happily inspired, and imposing measure and poise, nevertheless acutely stimulates and develops the faculties themselves." [15] Style, he thought, results from the preservation in every part of some sense of the form of the whole, a sense of relations as well as of statement—in other words, results from superb craftsmanship; and he denounced injunctions to American artists to "be themselves" and throw away craftsmanship for a purely abstract originality. He insisted that, barring the miracle of genius, arts and letters have been produced mainly by special and arduous training.[16] In *Victorian Prose Masters* and *American Prose Masters* he applied the doctrine to the writing of prose. His theory cannot be further from the injunction to write on the lintels of the doorpost, Whim.

This stress on craftsmanship parallels the stress on industrial expertise. Before glancing at the celebration of technique in other major arts we may pause to note the intimate relation between professionalization in publishing and the critical doctrines I have sketched. The period from 1870 to 1915 is a kind of golden age in the American novel as it was in the history of American magazines. Before the Civil War we had no real publishing center, only a series of little centers —Boston, New York, Philadelphia, Cincinnati, Charleston, and so on. Until the rise of James T. Fields (1817–1881) the publisher was still a printer and bookseller, a small businessman with virtually no professional standing. Book production was local and casual, book distribution was inefficient (before the proliferation of railroads, books were mainly distributed by water, a method usually impossible during winter months in the North), and even a novelist as notable as Cooper had to make individual bargains with local printers, often assuming half the production costs. Book advertising was naïve, book illustration amateurish. There was virtually no magazine serialization of novels, and most American periodicals were short-lived, edited by amateurs, and uncertain in paying authors. Before the acceptance by the United States of the international copyright law, every foreign edition of an American work had to be separately negotiated (if at all), usually by the author.

In the post-bellum era, especially after 1870, writing ceased to be an avocation for gentlemen and became more and more professionalized concomitantly with the emergence of New York as the publishing center. Contracts and royalties were standardized as publishers assumed the total risk of manufacturing, distributing, advertising, and wholesaling books. The literary agent appeared: in the first volume of *The (American) Bookman* (1895) an article avers that the literary agent has been a potent figure in the world of letters for a decade and has revolutionized the relation of writer and publisher. Books were now uniformly and quickly distributed by rail. Improved techniques in composition, presswork, and binding were everywhere in use by 1885, and the linotype came in during that decade, the monotype in the 1890s. If paper declined in durability, it increased in cheapness.

More important is the notion that publishing is an honorable profession rather than a trade.[17] The profession was adorned by such men as Charles Scribner, Henry Holt, the two George Putnams, Frank Scott of Century, and George Brett of Macmillan. With them developed a great generation of editors exemplified not alone by Brownell but also by Horace E. Scudder of Houghton, Mifflin and Edward Burlingame of the house of Scribner. All these men were sensitive to workmanship. Printing and format steadily improved, whether in the book or the magazine world. By such designers as Daniel Berkeley Updike, founder of the Merrymount Press in Boston in 1895, typography was raised to a fine art.[18] In the same years Bertram Goodhue did book decorations for publishers such as Copeland & Day and Small, Maynard, and for *The Chap Book*.[19] Magazine covers were designed by artists of the rank of Elihu Vedder. Book and magazine were enriched by the most dazzling generation of illustrators the country has ever known, including Winslow Homer, E. A. Abbey, Frederic Remington, Howard Pyle, Maxfield Parrish, N. C. Wyeth, E. C. Kemble, A. B. Frost, and their rivals. The superb wood engravings of old masters which *The Century Magazine* commissioned Timothy Cole to make in and after 1883, in an age less crowded with technical brilliance would have given this periodical a repute equal to that of *The Savoy* or *The Yellow Book* for incomparable pictorial work. The *Autobiography of Joseph Jefferson* (1892) was the first important book to be illustrated by the new halftone process of reproducing pictures. The book jacket and the book poster were improved by advances in design and color printing, the poster in particular was raised, here as in Europe, to the dignity of an important minor art.[20]

It would take too long to analyze a parallel movement toward a celebration of technique in the other arts. After 1880 musical criticism matured in the hands of Gustav Kobbé, Henry De Koven, Edward J. Stevenson, Henry Krehbiel, Henry T. Finck, Louis Elson, James Gibbons Huneker, and others; and Hugo Leichtentritt observed twenty years ago that "the Boston of 1895 was considerably superior in its love of fine music and in its support of artists to the Boston of 1945." [21] Ralph Adams Cram counted the years between 1880 and 1900 the most remarkable in American architectural history [22] as, in his opinion, American architects outdistanced their predecessors in technical proficiency. Perhaps Montgomery Schuyler's essays, *American Architecture* (1891) [23] are as good a record to consult as any other. The opening lecture on "Modern Architecture" in this collection concludes:

> What may we not hope from the union of modern engineering with modern architecture, when the two callings, so harshly divorced, are again united, and when the artistic constructor employs his cultivated sensibility and his artistic training, not to copying, but to producing, no longer to the compilation of the old forms, but to the solution of the new problems that press upon him; when he shall have learned the use of the studies that teach not their own use.

This plea for originality differs basically from that of the romantics in its demand for a fusion of technical competence and artistic invention.

The situation in painting was complicated. It is not irrelevant to point to the vogue of Louis C. Tiffany in the minor arts of stained glass, textiles, jewelry, and decoration as exemplifying a general attitude toward craftsmanship that, if it owes something to Ruskin and William Morris, has no predecessor in the history of the arts in America.[24] The same concern appears in the biographies, autobiographies, and studio talks of the age—examples are William Morris

Hunt's two series of *Talks on Art* (1875, 1883) and the long essays on
the technique of Greek art in William Wetmore Story's *Excursions in
Art and Letters* (1891). Just as engineering schools multiplied, so did
schools of art and so did a demand for instruction in art, or at least
in drawing, in the public schools. The Englishman, Walter Smith,
who came to Boston in 1870, became the principal of the Massachusetts Normal Art School in 1873. The founding of Pratt Institute in
Brooklyn followed in a few years. Of course the arts and crafts movement is not a synonym for craftsmanship; yet American concern for
technique in all the arts owes much to the vogue here of the Pre-Raphaelites, just as instruction in manual training (sloyd) owes something to the Scandinavians. How complicated the situation was is evident in an article by Albert Bush-Brown, which demonstrates that
the Ruskinian members of the newly founded American Institute of
Architects were defeated by the Huxleyite champions of functional-
ism.[25] Which side emphasized technique? The scientists and the engineers seem to have branded Ruskinian theory as politically undemocratic and ornately Catholic, whereas the technicians wanted mechanistic "naturalism" and believed that adaptation to use produces
beauty and is "democratic."

II

The injunction laid on artists to master technique had its parallel
in the injunction laid on critics to master scholarship as a discipli-
nary formula. Evident in W. C. Brownell, this doctrine is strongly expressed by John Jay Chapman, that strange compound of Byron and
the Shorter Catechist, Voltaire and Ralph Waldo Emerson. Chapman
had read everything, had soaked himself in Europe, had taken up
mysticism and self-torture, liberalism and doubt, culture and cynicism, the history of art and the reform of politics, and came in his
maturity to believe that tradition only will, in Robert Frost's phrase,
steady us down. Two books by him are revelatory. In *Learning and
Other Essays* (1910) Chapman argued that though we may almost believe our feeling for art is original with us, "the great reason of the
power of art is the historic reason." In such and such a manner these
things have been expressed; in a similar manner mankind will continue to express them. Fine craftsmanship, he says, was forgotten in
the business of settling a continent, and the Americans ever since

have in consequence been buffeted by pragmatic experimentalism. Therefore the duty of scholarship is to bring about familiarity with greatness, "an early and first-hand acquaintance with the thinkers of the world, whether their mode of thought was music or marble or canvas or language." He did not recommend subserviency to Europe but subserviency to intellect, which has a long history in the Old World.[26] Though in *The Greek Genius and Other Essays* (1915), he complained that the universities are filled with pedants, expressed his detestation for Gilbert Murray's translations, longed for an American school of "classic cultivation, half as interesting as this Neo-Hellenism of Oxford, quaint and non-intellectual as it is," he nevertheless compared universities to "great furnaces of culture, largely social in their influence, which warm and nourish the general temperament of a nation." [27] This queer metaphor at least shows where he thought heat and energy might originate. Brander Matthews was a university professor, as was Barrett Wendell. Other critics, such as William Dean Howells and W. C. Brownell, were thought of for university posts.

But how bring about familiarity with greatness? Museums were useful, but they were perhaps static. I have remarked on the development of the force of expertise based on professional organizations as a mode of control in business and industry. Development in history and the humanities followed a parallel course. A curious illustration, extending even to a figure of speech, is Woodrow Wilson's tribute to Herbert Baxter Adams, student of the great German historian Bluntschli, follower of E. A. Freeman, and pioneer in the new historical method. At Johns Hopkins Adams was midwife to a series of specialized monographs, presided over distinguished seminars, and aided in creating the American Historical Association. Wilson wrote:

> If I were to sum up my impression of Dr. Adams, I should call him a great Captain of Industry, a captain in the field of systematic and organized scholarship. I think all his pupils would accord him mastery in the formulation of historical inquiry, in the suggestive stimulation of research, in the communication of methods and ideals. His head was a veritable clearing house of ideas in the field of historical study, and no one ever seriously studied under him who did not get, in its most serviceable form the modern ideals of work upon the sources; and not the ideals merely, but also a very definite principle of concrete application in daily study. The thesis work done under him may fairly be said to have set the pace for university work in history throughout the United States.[28]

But Adams was representative, not unique: a whole generation of historians in post-bellum America, trained in German methodology or students of German-trained scholars, overthrew rhetorical and romantic histories. Though fault has been found with Germanic notions of scholarship, the injunction to get at sources, to present text and artifact as they truly are (contrast Jared Sparks's edition of the *Writings* of Washington with that by Fitzpatrick), to comprehend art and thought developmentally, and to accept development as a postulate in philosophy and the arts no less than in the sciences—all this matured the higher learning in the United States. The emphasis upon the craft of scholarship is clear.

The symbolic date is 1876, when The Johns Hopkins University, essentially a modern graduate institution, opened its doors. Gilman at Hopkins, Charles W. Eliot at Harvard, Andrew D. White at Cornell, James B. Angell at Michigan, G. Stanley Hall at Clark, and William Rainey Harper at Chicago are representatives of a presidential generation that founded or reshaped modern universities in the United States. Some institutions held back for a time, regarding themselves as guardians of an ancient tradition and remembering that previous attempts to modernize the American college had failed. The famous "Yale Report on the Classics" of 1827 had tended to freeze both the curriculum and modes of instruction for a half century; and since that curriculum, resting on an honorable mixture of medieval and Renaissance traditions, had interpreted the classical tradition as virtually a timeless absolute, the forces of change had much to overcome. But again one has a symbolic date—1883, when the Modern Language Association of America was founded, a creation that signalized the passing of Greek and Latin from their academic pride of place. The MLA was but one among many.[20] And of course with the multiplication of societies and the augmentation in the number of scholars there came an increasing flood of professional journals in the humanities, history, and the social sciences.

Learning ceased to be the work of gifted gentlemen amateurs and turned into the professional "disciplines" of modern academic jargon. In the literatures and the languages teachers (among them William Dwight Whitney, Francis James Childs, Albert Stanburrough Cook, Morgan Callaway, Jr., James Wilson Bright, Hiram Corson, and Arthur Beatty, names I choose at random) applied Germanic methodology to their subjects, and the same thing was done in the other humanities. A new standard of writing was established, a new attitude toward criticism, literary history, and literary theory and research was taken. Younger scholars, appointed to teaching positions in the undergraduate colleges, necessarily taught their subjects in a fashion quite different from the rote-memory system of the ancient regime. There were of course mavericks at all levels—one thinks of Harry Thurston Peck, George Edward Woodberry, and in some sense William James—but in the main the new methodology conquered. People who didn't like it referred to it as the "Ph.D. octopus."

Octopus or not, the system exposed the student to greatness in a regular temporal order. Genesis and chronology became elementary conditioning terms. The weight of interest in the new dispensation was mainly on older periods this side of the classical past—the late Roman empire and the earlier middle ages, to which one could trace the origins of modern European languages, many literary conventions, and some painterly and architectural forms; the Renaissance, by definition more splendid than any portion of the industrial world; the Augustan ages; even the romantic movement and, more cautiously, the nineteenth century. Daring persons like Corson came down as far as Browning, and the equally daring Moses Coit Tyler taught the earlier portions of American literature. On the whole, however, right-minded scholars tended to look upon American writing as an inferior province within the imperium of British literature, its better authors being, so to speak, imitation Victorians. As we shall see, "idealism" was by no means sacrificed to developmentalism and the genetic point of view; a countermovement essentially non-national in character dwelt upon the glories of the arts without much reference to evolution. But art ceased to be a sudden glory; it was, on the contrary, a knowledgeable fusion of an inheritance of acquired characteristics with whatever novelty the talent or genius of the living artist could contribute. The doctrine was so far sound that, as has been remarked, paintings are born out of paintings and poems out of poems. Light was really shed on at least one aspect of writing by carefully studying the sources of the artist's material, and the same was in a general sense true of the other major arts.

The contributions of American scholarship became increasingly important and influential not only in the study of great poets (Chaucer, Shakespeare, Milton, Wordsworth, and so on) but, by and by, in the case of the American literary classics—New Yorkers, including

Irving and Cooper, the great New England line, and Poe and Simms from the South. Cultivated English became the norm; that is, the English which looked to British practice for the ultimate standard of speech as well as to the speech proper among upper groups in the United States. Since English of this sort was to be learned mainly by being born into the right families or, failing that, associating with the right persons, reading the right books, and attending the right courses, composition classes burgeoned everywhere. The models were commonly Macaulay and Robert Louis Stevenson. Some teachers took over the "sedulous ape" theory of the author of *Kidnapped*. Dictionaries like the great *Century Dictionary* (1889–1891) were expected to substantiate nice discriminations in usage, something that a recent edition of Webster has failed to do and was reproached for not doing. It is of course not argued that there were no standards of style and no scholarship before the Civil War, but only that the last third of the nineteenth century was a kind of golden age in scholarship also, when graduate work and humanistic research were new and exciting, and disciplined minds demanded disciplined writing. A minor proof of the hold of this theory is William Dean Howells' gallant attempt to please the cultivated by announcing that Mark Twain was a well of good English. Cultivated readers, however, read *Innocents Abroad* or *Roughing It* with a mild sense of literary slumming. Indeed, Mark Twain's insistence in the brief preface to *Huckleberry Finn* that he has been careful to distinguish among dialects and to use each one consistently is in its way a tribute to the general doctrine. A like tendency to study historical masterpieces is evident in the world of art. Sepia prints of Guido Reni's "Dawn" hung in many a schoolroom and over many a fireplace in a domestic library. The difficulty with much American music of a serious sort was that it was overwhelmed by musical tradition. Yet a sculptor like Lorado Taft in a work as poignant as "Solitude of the Soul" succeeds in suggesting the technical proficiency of both Michelangelo and Rodin.

This vast campaign was directed to creating discrimination in taste no less than the historical view in criticism, and in certain magazines —*The Nation*, *The Dial* (originally published in Chicago), the *North American Review*, and in some degree the *Atlantic Monthly*, *Harper's*, *The Century*, and *Scribner's*—the contributions of the scholar-critic were welcomed. In the same period dignified publishing houses brought out the *American Men of Letters* series, edited by

Charles Dudley Warner, and the Cambridge edition of the leading American poets; and excellent sets of the collected writings, at least of the New Englanders and sometimes of others, brought dignity to the notion that there were American classics.

Graduate education directly affected only a small fraction of the population, but historicism as a mode of artistic interpretation was increasingly diffused until a reaction against it appeared in the twentieth century. The more general impact was probably through the undergraduate college. The concept of a liberal education uneasily combined an inheritance from ante-bellum America with elements arising from this new, genetic, or evolutionary approach. In its earliest stage the college had been mainly directed to the education of the Christian ministry; before the Civil War it had changed to the education of character through a Christianized view of the arts, philosophy, and science; after about 1870 this concept was transmogrified into the education of a gentleman (and in coeducational institutions and women's colleges his female equivalent). Charles Franklin Thwing, president of Western Reserve, averred that the college could be "content with nothing less than training men for complete living." Guy Potter Benton, president of Miami University, said its mission "is not to prepare directly for business or profession. It does prepare for life." Henry Parks Wright, dean at Yale from 1884 to 1909, declared the college offers the undergraduate "a higher ideal of manhood, a broader culture, a better social standing, a love of books, and a capacity to appreciate the best things." A popular manual for freshman classes edited by three Wisconsin professors was an anthology on the meaning of a liberal education; characteristic is this passage from Dean Birge of that institution. He is speaking of why he went to college:

We did not suppose that Livy and Demosthenes, calculus and natural theology, or any combination of these studies, would be of "practical value" to us in later life. We knew that the life of the college was dissociated from the life to follow it; that it led directly to no calling, to no profession. This was one reason for our going to college. We took four years of our youth and devoted them, quite unconsciously, to the intellectual life and to the ethical spirit . . . we sought and we gained, both from work and from play, each according to his desires and his capacity an entrance to the intellectual life. We acquired, most of us without becoming conscious of the fact, the rudiments of a liberal education—the education of a free man in a free state; the education which, preparing him for no particular calling, fits him for a life of freedom.[30]

In these representative passages the reader will detect a fascinating amalgam of medieval theory about the seven arts, Renaissance doctrine concerning a gentleman's education, the "idle man" of Federalist culture, and the assumption, partly Miltonic, partly Jeffersonian, that the aim of a liberal education is to create responsible citizens in a democratic culture.

This doctrine could not be contaminated by any of the elements of a "servile" education. Liberal education was directed at young gentlemen or at young Americans who by instruction and association could become gentlemen, an assumption basic to the teaching of Charles Eliot Norton and to books by his colleague at Harvard, Barrett Wendell, in which genteel culture, laissez-faire economics, and the advantages of a liberal education were fused into a philosophy that his president charged with snobbery.[31] Since the Greeks had believed in healthy bodies, college athletics were all right, but not professional sports. "Pure" science was within the canon because it revealed intelligence, "applied" science was servile. Foreign languages could be pursued as a part of culture; studying them with a commercial purpose in mind was wrong. Literature and the arts were broadening, and formal deference was still paid to Greek and Latin though fewer and fewer undergraduates could read them. Philosophy was a good thing still in the period before pragmatism, logical positivism, and the technology rather than the substance of epistemology overwhelmed the schools of idealism regnant after the passing of the Scottish philosophy. Typical in this respect is Howison's translation of the City of God into an Eternal Republic which somehow subsumes evolutionary doctrine under eternal process.[32] Enriched by ancient tradition and intellectual inquisitiveness, the male graduate was theoretically ready to study for one of the professions (certainly few of them took up farming), but in fact, despite this able disclaimer of utility, most of them went into white-collar jobs in business as the antagonism to college education diminished among stockbrokers, bankers, industrialists, and their kind. From the point of view of the liberal college thus conceived, poverty was either ephemeral or a mark of inferiority, and sex and brutality were sublimated into love and manly strength.

III

Although the development of scientific research on a plane of positive philosophy and as a mensurative approach to truth was eventually to overcome the tendency to think of cosmology first and experiment afterward; although emphasis upon technique in art and scholarship seemed to avoid or contradict the need for philosophical goals; and although Germanic scholarship inevitably tended to fragment learning into disparate units,[33] the genteel tradition sought to correct mere expertise by fusing into a single whole the technique of art, the discipline of scholarship, and a vague but powerful belief in the ideal. The romantics had celebrated the ideal either on a Platonic or a transcendental plane or as some variant of mysticism or hylozoism. In one sense the theorists of the genteel tradition did no more than keep alive a valuable inheritance, which they wed to craftsmanship. In another sense they made a fresh start, one the more necessary in that evolution, realism, and naturalism (not to overlook the force of empiricism, Comtean theory, greed, and "scientism") threatened both the dignity of man in general and the nobility particularly necessary to the health of a representative republic. To trace the history of American philosophical thought in the period would take us far afield. But one can say that in decades when philosophy moved out of the pulpit into the lecture hall, the dispute between idealists of whatever sort and empiricists of whatever kind is neatly epitomized in the difference of outlook between Josiah Royce and William James. Everyone knows the amusing photograph of these two friends sitting on a rock wall somewhere in New England; James points a comic finger at the philosopher of loyalty and exclaims: "Royce, you're being photographed! Look out! I say *Damn the Absolute!*" In the event, the absolute was damned; but the fact that it would be preposterous to deny idealism to the author of *Talks to Teachers on Psychology and to Students on Some of Life's Ideals* (1909) and of "The Moral Equivalent of War" (1910) shows both how elastic the meaning of idealism is and how it continued to pervade the Age of Energy.

Fortunately it is not necessary to the present inquiry to ask why a philosopher who denied absolute idealism was nevertheless an idealist, if of a different strain. Writers, artists, and critics were less concerned for epistemological niceties than they were for the operational validity of a force they wanted to oppose to crass materialism; and in so doing they were the heirs of Emerson and Thoreau. Their struggle to validate idealism as the capital mode of art was at once their noblest effort and, from the point of view of the contemporary cynic, their greatest failure. The ideal might mean the highest morality, or it might mean that art is to mirror perfection, or it might mean a system of aesthetics that owed its origins to Plato, Aristotle, Schiller, or Hegel. If idealism was the tenor, culture was usually the vehicle of their crusade. When one considers the human tendency to belittle any set of ideas because its proponents are not geniuses, the reluctance of our contemporaries to think of idealism as anything other than self-deception, and the truth that the idealists themselves fell into the sentimentalism they were trying to avoid, one can see why the image of the genteel tradition is dim. All this, however, does not affect its importance in American intellectual history, nor alter the truth that any consideration of the Gilded Age which ignores the idealistic strain in art, morals, philosophy, and religion, is one-sided.

I suppose Edwin Percy Whipple is again a convenient link between romanticism and the post-bellum period, but there are, I think, more forceful exemplars of the ideal than this faded figure. One such critic was Edmund Clarence Stedman, who was, along with Brownell, the maturest theorist of the age. In 1891 he was called upon to deliver the Percy Trumbull Memorial Lectures on Poetry at The Johns Hopkins University, the only chair then established in any American university having poetry for its sole province; and after paying due compliments to Sidney Lanier, who had lectured at that university in 1879, Stedman launched upon a full-scale discussion both of the theory of poetry and of poetry in a world view. He defined poetry as "rhythmical, imaginative language, expressing the invention, taste, thought, passion, and insight of the human soul." His doctrine is an interesting compound of Plato and Aristotle. Poetry depends upon insight (inward vision, second sight, the prophetic gift of certain personages); and to support this theory Stedman refers to Plato's "Ion" and to von Hartmann's *Philosophy of the Unconscious*,[34] wherein he had read of "the activity and efflux of the Intellect freed from the domination of the Conscious Will." Modern poetry seemed to him to originate from the depths of some divine despair. He tried to steer an intelligent middle course between "transcendentalists who invoke the astral presence and underrate the fair embodiment" of art and "technical artisans who pay regard to its material guise alone." If Schiller had distinguished between naïve and sentimental poetry, Stedman differentiated between the Me and the Not Me in verse. Poetry that seems to spring from the Not Me "appears the more creative as being a statement of things discerned by free and absolute vision" (objective poetry), whereas poetry springing from the Me (poetry of the subjective order) is poetry sprung from a "relative and conditioned imagination."

In either case poetry is the ideal expression through words," and Stedman tries to strengthen his theory by saying that sculpture expresses ideas of form arrested in movement and time, painting gives similitude to an ideal moment, and music to the highest kind of supernal beauty. An earlier, somewhat puzzling passage about "Vibrations" becomes clearer when one reads that "in truth, if the intercourse of a higher existence is to be effected through sound vibrations rather than through the swifter light-waves or by means of aught save the absolute celestial insight, one may fondly conceive music to be the language of the earth-freed." This is an inheritance from romanticism. Romanticism and "Platonism" combine in a statement to the effect that poetry "enables common mortals to think as the poet thinks, to use his wings, more through space and time, and out of space and time, untrammelled as the soul itself. . . . Through poetry soul addresses soul without hindrance, by the direct medium of speech. . . . [Its] idealized language . . . as it ever has been the earliest form of emotional expression, appears almost a gift captured in man's infancy from some 'imperial palace whence he came.' "

Poetry is not the antithesis of prose, but the antithesis of science. The scientist gives us the facts, the artist the semblances, as these are known to eye, ear, and touch. If this epitome makes Stedman sound like an echo of Poe or Emerson or both because poetry is referred to the ideal, the reference is carefully guarded. The original concept of a work of art may be spontaneous and imaginative, but its working out brings into play the conscious intellect of the craftsman.[35] An idealist who disliked the formlessness of the sentimental and the romantic, Stedman was also averse to minor bardlings who became so fascinated by the ballade, the rondeau, the sonnet, and other technical displays that they left out the poetry altogether.

In literary criticism Stedman was, as I have said, along with Brownell, the most intelligent of this group. One has to forgive the idealists a good deal. Thus, a book like Hamilton Wright Mabie's *My Study Fire* (1890) with its stereotyped sweetness (in October "I catch in this transient splendor a vision of the deepest meaning which life and art have for me") is a sitting duck for any critical marksman.[36] But the firelight shines on Homer, Dante, Shakespeare, Milton, Goethe, and Cervantes; and Mabie notes that

> they are the great, vital works which belong to all races and times; the books which form the richest inheritance of each new generation, and which the whole world has come to hold as its best possession. . . . The conviction deepens in me year by year that the best possible education which any man can acquire is a genuine and intimate acquaintance with these few great minds who have escaped the wrecks of time and have become, with the lapse of years, a kind of impersonal wisdom, summing up the common experience of the race and distilling it drop by drop into the perfect forms of art (pp. 43–45).[37]

How does this differ from Mortimer Adler's Great Books theory? Mabie's was a second-class, even a third-class mind, but it was an honest mind; and if one wants to understand the components of the genteel tradition, one can do worse than read the nine volumes he published between 1890 and 1900, of which *Books and Culture* (1896) is typical. He was doing in a more popular vein what Stedman and Lowell, Norton and George Edward Woodberry were doing on higher levels.

Possibly Woodberry was the only consistent Platonist of his generation (or should one say Neo-Platonist?), a writer whose intellectual vagueness and fuzzy verse make it difficult today to understand his enormous power as a teacher. (A Woodberry Society was created to propagandize his views.) Though he claimed that Henry Adams helped to form his mind,[38] he seems to have been ignorant both of science and of the theory of science; and if his criticism was founded on ideal principles, it was colored by anthropology and doctrines of race.[39] He was also full of self-pity [40] and could not stand the young University of Nebraska.[41] But he wrote excellent studies of Poe, Emerson, Hawthorne, and in a way of Swinburne, and published volumes of poems, critical essays, and literary appreciation, even a treatise on wood engraving. For him there were two worlds of being: the world of the actual—of science, of ugliness, for which he had very little use; and the realm of the ideal—of perfected human nature, of an eternal spiritual order, the basis of virtue and wisdom to be reached not through science but by art. Man, he thought, is the only object of interest to man; and in a curious, rather formless philosophic drama, *Agathon,* the *dramatis personae* of which include Agathon, Diotima, Eros, Urania, and a Phantasm, he tried to indicate that the principle of the universe is love. He struggled to spiritualize evolution:

> In fair things
> There is another vigor, flowing forth
> From heavenly fountains, the glad energy
> That broke on chaos, and the outward rush
> Of the eternal mind; and as they share
> In this they to the soul are beautiful.

Manfully he tried to reinstitute the idealism of Plato, Spenser, and Shelley.[42] His Platonism got mixed up with racial theory and with Christianity, and the Anglo-Saxons, so far as I can make out, became the chief purveyors to the modern world of the "master-ideas" of history, the greatest of which is self-sacrifice.[43] His studies of literature tried to substitute the vatic inspiration of the bard for the scientific analysis of truth. He wrote:

> Immortal love, too high for my possessing,—
> Yet, lower than thee, where shall I find repose?
> Long in my youth I sang the morning rose,
> By earthly things the heavenly pattern guessing.

The contemporary world is not altogether persuaded by this spiritual gallantry.[44]

To the idealists access to the changeless world of immortal love and heavenly perfection, even if one were not a Platonist, was through the medium of the intuitive imagination, a "faculty" of the soul they constantly praised. Again Mabie, being simple, is invaluable:

The more closely we study human knowledge and thought, the more clearly do we perceive that this word "imagination" has more compass and depth of meaning than any other word which we apply to our faculties. It includes all that we possess of constructive power,—the power of holding masses of facts so firmly and continuously in the field of vision as to enable us to discover their unity and the laws which govern them; in other words, science,—the power of seeing the permanent in the transitory, the universal in the particular; in other words, of things visible, and of the real construction of the ideal; philosophy,—the power of perceiving and realizing the soul; in other words, art,—the power of discerning the spiritual behind the material, the creator behind the creation; in other words, religion.[45]

Imagination was like the Socratic daimon: it seized upon the fortunate specialist, possessed him utterly, and raised him above all mundane concerns. The Platonic dialogues between Belton and Mullett which constitute that neglected minor masterpiece by William Wetmore Story, *Conversations in a Studio,* are eloquent on this point. The moment art becomes a business it is degraded; the fact that millionaires buy pictures does nothing for art, and the qualities of a painting or a piece of sculpture arise from the "unconscious effluence" of the artist's soul.

> My notion is that our best work is done when we are possessed by an idea, and not when we are striving after one. Inspiration is the in-breathing of an influence from without and above, that can only really live in us and become an essential part of us when the interior nature is in a condition to be fecundated. The individual mind is, as it were, the matrix which is impregnated by the universal mind, and then alone can it conceive.

Religion and art go hand in hand throughout history.[46] An artist (this is Goethean) must learn the virtue of renunciation.[47]

There was, then, a necessary identity between the spiritual power as the secret of universal life, and poetic ("creative") madness. But the madness had to be controlled. Not for the idealists the doctrine that intelligence plays but a minor role in the shaping of life or art. Hence, the endless concern of these men not merely for the ideal, but for the ideal form, for the doctrine that the highest morality requires the most perfect expression. To this end there were principles compared to the "laws" of science, as Gilder, Brownell, Stedman, Mabie, and the rest endlessly reiterated; and when Brownell defined style as something that "results from the preservation in every part of some sense of the form of the whole" and not "the mere expression of the moment"; when at the Whitman birthday dinner of 1889 Gilder burst out: "I am a stickler for form in literature and one thing I admire in Walt Whitman is his magnificent form"; when Lloyd Mifflin begins a sonnet on a sonnet:

>Still let a due reserve the Muse attend
>Who threads the Sonnet's labyrinth;

when Story, denying that art is a special faculty, proclaimed that "to conceive a great statue and embody a noble idea,—not simply by imitation of the model, but by a grand treatment of form and a noble character of design and expression," [48] these theorists were not merely combatting realism (though Story called *Nana* "the literature of the brothel"), they were simultaneously arguing that the solution of the problem of art by realism is unphilosophical, and also setting up a universe of discourse of cosmic grandeur. The theory may be mistaken but it is not unintelligible.

Possibly the most influential figure among the idealists was Charles Eliot Norton, Harvard professor of the history of art, who began teaching in 1874 and kept at it for a quarter of a century. If in book and classroom he insisted on the close study of Greek, medieval, and Renaissance craftsmanship, he likewise insisted that technique was a vehicle for the ideal. He was a complex personality. Many thought him a snob. Apropos of Lowell's famous address, "Democracy," he wrote that democracy was likely to work "ignobly, ignorantly, brutally." The progress of democracy in Europe saddened him by its "destruction of old shrines, the disregard of beauty, the decline in personal distinction, the falling off in manners." There is a legend that when he confronted his class at Harvard, he used sadly to observe that few among them knew what is meant by a gentleman. He thought the face of Wendell Phillips had lost nobility and taken on a "bitter and malign look"; he argued that if "men are not worse than they were," democracy exposed them "in larger numbers to temptations which they were not prepared to resist, and which are threatening the public welfare"; and he was of course depressed by American political corruption, materialism, and the imperialistic stridency of 1898. He lost faith in Christianity, writing Goldwin Smith that he, Norton, was "the more complete agnostic" and had given up faith in the invisible with "no sentimental regret at its vanishing." Yet from the opening of the Civil War to his death in 1906, the republic had no more faithful citizen. As did Godkin, George William Curtis, Olmsted, and other Mugwumps, he opposed Blaine. His famous annual dinners at Ashfield, held from 1879 to 1905, were foci of all sorts of liberal causes ranging from civil-service reform to the education of the Negro, and were addressed by notables from America and from abroad. He was not afraid of modernity. He paid tribute to Daniel Burnham, the chief planner of the World's Columbian Exposition, which seemed to Norton, despite its "border vulgarities," "a great promise, even a great pledge." He approved of Whistler. He liked writers as different as Henry Blake Fuller, Santayana, John Davidson, Kipling, and William Dean Howells. He was one of the founders of *The Nation,* was influential in preserving Niagara Falls for posterity, helped create the Archaeological Institute of America and the Dante Club, and could write of an International Council of Liberal Thinkers held in Boston in September 1907 that it was "the strongest assemblage of this kind which has ever met."

Friend of Carlyle and Ruskin, Norton clung to the doctrine that the purpose of art was to enrich culture through idealism. For him the Parthenon was "almost a code of aesthetics," and he wondered "why the Athenians alone should have invented such subtile laws of harmony in building" or be endowed with a sense of form as characteristic as the Venetian sense for color. If only the "sane thought" of the Greeks could be brought to bear upon modern youth! But there were difficulties in raw America: "an Italian sunset," he wrote Woodberry, "is better than a Californian" because it is infused with history, and for some queer reason a daisy was "of more worth than a sunflower." Yet it is easy to exaggerate Norton's *préciosité.* The world, he averred, had never been a pleasant place for a rational man to live in, and if "the old America, the America of our hopes and our dreams has come to an end," he stoutly maintained that because most Americans descend "from the oppressed, the servile, the peasantry, without intellectual traditions," "seeking material comfort in a brutal way," the wonder is they are not worse.[49] He wrote Henry Blake Fuller: "I hold with the poets and the idealists; not the idealizers, but those who have ideals, and, knowing that they are never to be realized, still strive to reach them and to persuade others to take up the same quest." He was no mere aesthete, but a tough and resilient man.

Norton's pedagogical purpose was simple: he wanted to reform a culture by insisting on idealism, and though it is a nice question whether his idealism was Plotinian, Platonic, Coleridgean, or Ruskinian, the question is in a sense irrelevant, for he was not a meta-

physical man. An article by him in the *Educational Review* for April
1895, "The Educational Value of the History of the Fine Arts," is a
kind of *summa* and is so recognized by the editors of his correspondence:

> It is through the study and knowledge of the works of the fine arts, quite
> apart from the empirical practice of any of them, that the imagination,
> the supreme faculty of human nature, is mainly to be cultivated. . . .
> And nowhere are such study and knowledge more needed than in Amer-
> ica, for nowhere in the civilized world are the practical concerns of life
> more engrossing; nowhere are the conditions of life more prosaic; no-
> where is the poetic spirit less evident, and the love of beauty less dif-
> fused. The concern for beauty, as the highest end of work, and as the no-
> blest expression of life, hardly exists among us, and forms no part of our
> character as a nation. The fact is lamentable, for it is in the expression
> of its ideals by means of the arts which render those ideals in the forms
> of beauty, that the position of a people in the advance of civilization is
> ultimately determined.[50]

The indictment is over-severe, but it cannot be called effete.

Absorbing the historical idealism of Norton, or Woodberry, or
other high-minded members of the faculty in fifty other liberal arts
colleges, the graduate was supposed to attain to a lofty and melancholy purposefulness, yet turn this into the civic idealism of a young
Madison or Alexander Hamilton, a *civis Americanus* who could lead
the multitude into right ways of responding, thinking, and voting.
The political responsibility of educated men became a favorite com-
mencement address and a favorite lecture topic. Civism and culture
were two faces of the same coin. Great examplars were cited—
Goethe, but a Goethe moralized, his love affairs and the *Roman Ele-
gies* left out, and keeping the striving upward of *Faust;* James Russell
Lowell, diplomat and public man, who knew so many languages and
had read so many books; and, above all, Matthew Arnold. It is true
that on his visit here beginning in October 1883 Arnold had aroused
considerable antagonism. His treatment of the Bible, his interpretation
of Emerson, his lecture on civilization in the United States, and his
wretched public speaking were all elements in his unpopularity.[51]
Nevertheless, Arnold, perhaps because he was a more controversial
figure than Goethe or Lowell, powerfully helped to shape the concepts of idealism, of culture, of the relation of both to public life, as
some characteristic American comments show:

Many of the thoughts, inferences, and impressions, so clearly and emphatically stated in this genial volume [*Essays in Criticism*] are familiar to the conversation of intelligent Americans.

Mr. Arnold's writings have been widely read here. They have a natural relationship to this country. He is an admirer of democracy, and has thought a great deal about the future of human character and society.

Mr. Arnold will doubtless find in America much that will offend his taste, much worship of the Philistine gods, material prosperity, progress and success, and the ends that men call "practical". Of "light" we may have something, though in "sweetness" it is to be feared we are sadly wanting. But Mr. Arnold will also find in America many warm admirers who will acknowledge with enthusiasm their debt of gratitude for his influence and teaching.

Mr. Arnold has shown Americans that art, literature, religion, and education are not ends in themselves, but factors in the intellectual development of the nation.

Arnold is a gifted man who can be of use. No other English writer has represented "the European world of fine literature".

It will perhaps be long indeed before Mr. Arnold's true greatness is understood and the profoundness of his ideas and their connection with present needs are properly weighed and felt.[52]

Even though all this was addressed to the upper class of readers, Arnold's emphasis upon self-development chimed with American individualism. James Freeman Clarke's *Self-Culture* is a somewhat watery American parallel. "Perhaps the future of culture in this country, the growth of a true criticism of life," wrote Edward Fuller in 1895, "is not quite hopeless, although one might almost be excused for believing that it is." Teddy Roosevelt was optimistic—that is, if you interpreted culture as vigor and not mollycoddle-ism; and Stedman affirmed that even in Chicago rich men appear "enthusiastic with respect to art and literature." [53] Thus the tradition was supposed to create leaders for democracy.

IV

The power of the genteel tradition vigorously sustained most of the major arts in the period with a resiliency and freedom unfortunately concealed from those who see the history of the arts from 1865 to 1915 principally as a battle between an emergent and admirable modernity and a senescent and deplorable romanticism. The period was, as I have said, virtually a golden age in the development of the American novel, which was principally written on what I have elsewhere [54] called the classical mode in fiction: that is, a structured narrative that moves to denouement, climax, and resolution in a pattern of plot involving characters whose motives are rational and whose ethical choices are clear. From its beginning, if one excepts a few types like picaresque romance, Western fiction has commonly narrated a conflict between good and evil, between what is noble and what is not, that is, between the forces of light and the forces of night. In America the pattern was virtually uniform. It is found in the novels of writers of talent such as the class represented by Albion W. Tourgée, George Washington Cable, Francis Marion Crawford, S. Weir Mitchell, Ellen Glasgow, and others. It is a *donnée* for local color (witness Westcott's *David Harum*), it is basic to the reform novel like Paul Leicester Ford's *The Honorable Peter Sterling,* to the adventure story, and to historical romance of the type of Mary Johnston's *To Have and to Hold.* Nor do the greater men escape from it. James's *The Portrait of a Lady,* however subtle, still distributes its characters between villainy and idealism, which in the long run is preferable; Howells' *The Rise of Silas Lapham* by its very title betrays its commitment; and *Tom Sawyer* and *Huckleberry Finn* differentiate between what is ideally desirable and what is morally wrong. Nascent realism and nascent naturalism, furthermore, kept within the purlieus of the ideal: witness Garland's *Rose of Dutcher's Coolly,* mentioned before, and Crane's *The Red Badge of Courage,* in which, modernity to the contrary notwithstanding, Henry Fleming, inspired by the regimental flag ("a carved treasure of mythology"), recovers his courage, and, coming closely in touch with death, "found that, after all, it was but the great death," and so became a man. Thus also the grandiose spread of Norris's *The Octopus* is sustained not only by mystical apprehensions of immortality and beauty, but also by an epic nature in the ranchers led by Magnus Derrick, who resemble Homer's Trojans. This is not to say that every book was sustained by the genteel tradition—one thinks of *The Damnation of Theron Ware,* the short tales of Ambrose Bierce, or *The Man That Corrupted Hadleyburg*—but dominant assumptions are in the tradition. The distrust with which European naturalism was viewed sprang from and enforced the tradition. Naturalism was a product of Old World decadence.[55]

Most poetry in the period was written in the same context. The works of Stedman, Bayard Taylor, Gilder, E. R. Sill, Thomas Bailey Aldrich, Louise Imogen Guiney, Santayana, Moody, Bliss Carman indeed, of most of the poets of the age appearing in Stedman's influential *An American Anthology*—represent a striving to fuse exquisite workmanship, reality, and "ideal passion" into a seamless whole. The publication of the anthology was virtually a national event. I have noted the dinner in Stedman's honor at Carnegie Hall in New York, where poems, letters, messages, and speeches from eminences such as John Hay, William Dean Howells, Henry Van Dyke, James Whitcomb Riley, and others deluged the banker-poet. The general doctrine was also underwritten, so to speak, that same year by George Santayana, whose *Interpretations of Poetry and Religion* was dedicated to the thesis that:

> religion and poetry are identical in essence, and differ merely in the way in which they are attached to practical affairs. Poetry is called religion` when it intervenes in life, and religion, when it merely supervenes upon life, is seen to be nothing but poetry.

> [Human life] is not merely animal and passionate. The best and keenest part of it consists in that very gift of creation and government which, together with all the transcendental functions of his own mind, man has significantly attributed to God as to his highest ideal.[56]

Here are representative poetical utterances on the theme:

> Hark at the lips of this pink whorl of shell
> And you shall hear the ocean's surge and roar:
> So in the quatrain's measure, written well,
> A thousand lines shall all be sung in four.

> ———

> Keep back the one word more,
> Nor give your whole store;
> For, it may be, in Art's sole hour of need,
> Lacking that word, you shall be poor indeed.

> ———

> Passion is a wayward child,
> Art his brother firm and mild.
> Lonely each

Doth fail to reach
Hight [*sic*] of music, song, or speech.

If hand in hand they sally forth,
East or west, or south or north,
Naught can stay them
Nor delay them.
Slaves not they of space or time
In their journeyings sublime.

———

Still let a due reserve the Muse attend
Who threads the Sonnet's labyrinth. As some bell
That tolls for vespers in a twilight dell,
So in the octave, let her voice suspend
Her pomp of phrase. The sestet may ascend
Slowly triumphant, like an organ-swell
In opulent grandeur rising—pause, and dwell
With gathering glories to its dolphin end:

So, oft at eve around the sunset doors,
From up-piled splendors of some crimsoned cloud
Storm-based with dark—unrolling like a scroll—
Forth the accumulated thunder pours
Across the listening valley long and loud
With low reverberations, roll on roll! [57]

What is wrong with the doctrine is patent; and the generation of Pound, Sandburg, and Vachel Lindsay reacted with extreme violence against poetry stifled in "literature." Nothing, however, is more "literary" than Eliot's *The Waste Land,* or Pound's erudite performances, so that, though poetic elegance seemed lifeless, Eliot had afterward to react against the reaction by urging individual talents to return upon tradition. It is a mistake to think that post-bellum poets carved intaglios only and were incapable of passion. The poems of Louise Chandler Moulton include some amazing anticipations of Edna St. Vincent Millay's amatory candor; Sidney Lanier cannot be shrugged off; Moody's poetic dramas, of which *The Masque of Judgment* is representative, have their large discourse, and Santayana could produce his solemn poetry.[58]

The period saw an increased and lively literary interest in painting and music; that in painting is manifested not merely in familiar works by Henry James, such as *The Tragic Muse,* but also in poems and novels by such lesser figures as F. Hopkinson Smith (for example, *The Fortunes of Oliver Horn*), who was himself a painter, and in music by Francis Marion Crawford (as in *A Roman Singer* and *The Primadonna*). Books by such budding realists as Hamlin Garland, Stephen Crane, and Theodore Dreiser offer a convenient transition to other major arts. In the other arts the doctrines of craftsmanship and culture inevitably Europeanized American practice to a greater degree than in the art of words. If they were to broaden themselves, American libraries had to import bibliographical treasures from abroad and buy richly in European books, and with the publishers and booksellers they did much to familiarize the American novelist and literary critic with current European practice.

American architecture became more and more enthralled with Beaux Arts training, more and more resolved to translate to American soil contemporary European practices in Gothic, Romanesque, Empire, or "classical" buildings. The Americans had always imported music, but the tendency increased after the Civil War. American schools of music, beginning perhaps with the New England Conservatory in 1867, hired Europeans or persons trained in Europe, for their faculty and were proud to do so. The leading American symphony orchestras, not yet numerous, were mostly made up of European-trained players, led by European-trained conductors, and accompanied European-trained soloists in compositions from abroad. When the Metropolitan Opera House opened in 1883, the first production was that glittering Parisian success, Gounod's *Faust*, sung by a cast without a native American in it; [59] and when on the second night Alwina Valleria starred in *Lucia* few remarked that she was a soprano from Baltimore, who had changed her name to something more prestigious, studied in Europe, and sung in Russia, Germany, Italy, and Great Britain in order to gain status in the United States.[60]

Composers Europeanized. They had to, if they were to receive first-rate professional education. All, or nearly all, the so-called Boston classicists studied abroad and returned to write music colored by Mendelssohn, Liszt, Wagner, Brahms, or somebody else. It is significant that what seem to be their three leading successes were Horatio Parker's *Hora Novissima* (1893), a choral setting of a medieval Latin poem, John Knowles Paine's incidental music for *Oedipus Tyrannus* (1881), and Charles Martin Loeffler's *A Pagan Poem* (1901), suggested by the eighth eclogue of Vergil. Edward MacDowell, then the great hope of American music, went abroad, attracted the attention of Franz Liszt and Joseph Joachim Raff, returned, as somebody said, bringing Germany with him, and, though he could call music a "soul language," took a reserved view of musical nationalism. The two leading composers of light opera were Reginald De Koven of *Robin Hood* fame and Victor Herbert, who wrote *Naughty Marietta* and *Babes in Toyland*. Each went to Europe, each wrote a serious opera on an American theme (*Rip Van Winkle* and *Natoma*), and each failed to bring it off, apparently because the musical idiom was neither American nor European. The point is not to complain—how else was craftsmanship, how else was the great tradition of idealism to be mastered?—the point is that the genteel tradition, by emphasizing technique and universality, necessarily undercut the demand for a unique American art.

Perhaps the best area in which to estimate the virtues and defects of the genteel tradition is that of the graphic arts. As did musicians, American painters and sculptors went abroad, as, indeed, they had been doing before the Civil War. But now they tended to concentrate in Düsseldorf or Munich, and especially in Paris or in the farms and villages that attracted the Barbizon school. Sculptors lingered in Italy. In the romantic period American artists in Italy had talked much about soul, ideality, and the infinite; the new generation went to assimilate, sometimes to repudiate, the technical training of a Couture or a Courbet. Their talk was about pigment, light, brush stroke, compositional rhythms, impression, and of course about the ideal. American critics and historians of art encouraged them to be both expert and idealistic. It would be tedious to quote discussions of technique. Let us take these for granted and note how the historians of art insisted on the moral or spiritual idealism of painting. Wrote John C. Van Dyke in the introduction to *The Art Tradition in America:* "Three generations at least are supposed to be necessary to the making of a thorough gentleman. Is it possible to make a thorough artist in one?" His statement denies instant romantic inspiration. He lamented that the men who had created the Society of American Artists lacked any "patrimony of style." He said of Wyant that he had brooded over nature so long that "the disturbing prose of facts was no longer there. The poetry of light, air, and color alone remained," and he admired the "strong influence" of the "refined gentlemanly personality" of Alexander.

Discussing George de Forest Brush, Charles H. Caffin wrote:

There are periods of sorrow when the world seems very empty and desolate to-day; there still are yearnings after higher things, the flutterings of
doubt and hope that precede the beginning of growth of something better; and still a grandeur in the solitude of nature and maybe in that of a
man's own communings with himself . . . if a picture can recall the past
and show it as part of the eternal relation of spirit and matter, we are
justified in honouring its author.

Samuel Isham, who gives both the best specific account of the
training of younger Americans in European ateliers and a vivid picture of the difficulty American artists experienced in selling their pictures in the United States in competition with imported European
canvases, was nevertheless happy about the wholesome sanity of
American painting, which exhibited no taste for pain and misery,
blood and terror. "Our annual exhibitions," he wrote, "tell of the joy
and beauty of life with hardly a discordant note." "Art is still so new
an interest with us that we have not yet had time to weary of the
simple, natural things of life, and so be forced to go in search of the
abnormal and eccentric in order to stir a jaded taste." [61]

With the exception of such painters as Eakins, Homer, the Ashcan
school, Albert P. Ryder, and Frank Duveneck, present taste has
turned away from the canvases of the period; yet such men as Inness,
Wyant, Blashfield, Tryon, and Homer Martin show a distinct advance in "painterliness" over the genre pictures and studio landscapes
satisfactory to ante-bellum America. If William M. Chase and John
Singer Sargent were charged with having so much technique that
they concealed the "soul," if John La Farge and William Morris
Hunt were occasionally reproached with too much idealism and insufficient technical achievement, the norm lay between these extremi-
ties, as biographies of the artists reveal. [62] I think the most characteristic expression of actual practice is probably Robert Henri's *The Art
Spirit,* published in 1923, but compounded out of utterances by
Henri during the preceding years. Henri was capable of writing:
"Through art mysterious bonds of understanding and of knowledge
are established among men. They are the bonds of a great Brotherhood. Those who are of the Brotherhood know each other, and time
and space cannot separate them."

But he was also full of technical advice:

I think the true Yellow is rather more green than the yellow generally accepted as "true." I am speaking of paint and I am thinking of the functioning power of the pigment.

The grip of a line. Note how a line takes hold. It hooks the vital parts together. It binds the composition. Look well at the model and look well at the drawings of masters and you will see why I speak of the *hook* of a line, which grips. See the drawings of Rembrandt, the Chinese and the Japanese masters.

The direction of the nose may decide the way the hair shall go. The painting of a nose is the painting of an expression.

A background is good in color and form when it is so certainly there that you do not think of it.[63]

An interesting element in the Henri book is that while the painter continues to hammer away at technical problems, the underlying philosophy of what he says slowly shifts in the direction of the psychology of the painter. But the important thing, even with the Ashcan school is the dedication of all these artists to bringing the great tradition and whatever is great about it up-to-date. (I paraphrase a statement made by the living Boston artist, Jack Levine, in the Boston *Sunday Globe,* February 1968.)

Anecdotal, sentimental genre studies, slick easel-paintings, and conversation pieces still abounded—the popularity of John G. Brown's smiling newsboys continued apparently unchecked—but they are not the true measure of the genteel tradition. Landscape raised no questions of morality, nor did most portraiture, but when in the high art of the period one gets around to the problem of the nude, complexities of idealism, morality, propriety, and technique begin to multiply, and the strength and the weakness of the tradition are revealed. The nude has had a troubled history in the United States. Powers' "Greek Slave" had passed inspection, Erastus D. Palmer's "White Captive" had got by, even Vanderlyn's lush "Ariadne" had, after some debate, passed muster and Page's "Venus" (derisively known as "Venus on the Half Shell") had been exhibited in Philadelphia; yet a shipment of plaster casts from the antique that had been sent to the Pennsylvania Academy of Fine Arts could be viewed by men and women on alternate days only. Greenough's "Chanting Cherubs," commissioned by James Fenimore Cooper, had been attacked before it was acceptable. Hawthorne was embarrassed by the nudes he looked at in Europe.

Oliver Larkin tells us that a Mr. Fazzi was hired to make fig leaves for imported statues at the Ladies' Academy of Art in Cincinnati.[64] The biographer of Healy reports the visit of an American "lady" to Powers' studio in Rome, where she could find nothing to admire because, said she, "I am not accustomed to see ladies and gentlemen naked, so I can't tell whether they are good likenesses or not." Various religious bodies denounced "representations" of the voluptuous in art, and the ancient legend that a female who poses in the nude thereby loses her modesty was still so powerful that when young William Merritt Chase went to New York in 1869, "life" models usually meant the janitor or somebody like him and to secure the services of an undraped female was almost impossible. Eakins was forced out of the Pennyslvania Academy of Fine Arts because he preferred living models to plaster casts and once posed male and female models together to demonstrate the differences in human anatomy. He told one girl: "Respectability in art is appalling!" Popular debate over the morals of du Maurier's Trilby, who posed in the "all-together" (that prodigy of hypnotism and song appeared in the novel named for her in 1894), was almost as heated as the debate over Hardy's Tess of the d'Urbervilles, that "pure woman faithfully presented," who fluttered the dovecotes in 1891–1892.[65]

Now the problem was up again. On the one hand, a long tradition associated ideality in the nude with gods and goddesses, heroes and heroines, Renaissance paintings by revered great masters, and symbolical figures by eighteenth-century or romantic artists. On the other hand, though we returned upon Europe, we were, as I have indicated, suspicious of European naturalism and European decadence. The realism of Courbet presented not nudity but nakedness. Could it be denied that Moreau's "Salome" was erotic? or a good many pictures and drawings from Fuseli to Edvard Munch, Toulouse-Lautrec, and Aubrey Beardsley? What should one do about Courbet and Renoir? What about Ingres' odalisques? or Manet's "Olympe"? or that even more doubtful canvas showing a naked woman stretched shamelessly on the grass in a park together with two Frenchmen fully clad? This was all very well for the French who were somehow responsible for all the lush saloon nudes in the country, but this was not purity, this was not republican virtue, this was not the ideal in art. The problem of sensuality versus symbolism concentrated on the representation of the human form, particularly the female form. The working solution came to be a formula I may call "nude to the waist."

One must pass over much: William Wetmore Story's queer sentence that "women should be made of swan's down and velvet and nothing else"; [66] the fascination of unripe girls for painters like Benjamin R. Fritz and R. Siddons Mowbray; Childe Hassam's "Lorelei,", who carefully turns her back on the spectator; Daniel Chester French's "Memory," her knees and drapery concealing everything below her waist; Rudolph Evans' "Golden Hour," a statue of a young girl with drapery covering her right hip and revealing only her left leg; Abbott Thayer's "Caritas," a painting in which, as Larkin puts it, Thayer's wife and children are transformed into cheesecloth classicism. Nor shall I pause on the innumerable "Fine Arts," "Graces," "Muses," and other Parnassian females who float in gilt plaster over the proscenium arches or the side boxes of aging theaters and "opera houses," their maiden forms revealed only to the navel. I turn rather to mural painting.

In the midst of a business depression Chicago energy turned a virtual swamp and wasteland into a vision of classical splendor such as the country had never known. This great enterprise seems to be the climax of the order and idealism the genteel tradition advocated. Here it is sufficient to note that the buildings of the Exposition revealed on a grand scale the latest American acquisition from European practice, and simultaneously faced the problem of design, symbolism, and nudity since, by convention, nonreligious mural painting required any quantity of nude or seminude figures.

Mural painting had had its beginnings in Boston, where in 1876 a group of artists including La Farge decorated the interior of Richardson's Trinity Church. Here no problem of nudity had to be solved. About the same time William Morris Hunt painted two murals for the State Capitol at Albany, but he was so ill-advised as to paint in oils directly on damp walls; the pictures have not survived, and all we have of them now are preliminary cartoons, in which the symbolical characters tend to be nude to the waist. Other murals were randomly done between 1876 and 1893 for a few private houses and a few public buildings. But covering the walls of the Exposition buildings was the first extensive use of murals in American art.

The magnitude of the task was appalling. The roofs and wall spaces to be covered were many times larger than similar spaces in St.

Peter's in Rome. The project was put in charge of Francis D. Millet, who, with a company of painters and their wives, virtually lived on the grounds for months. It was a prolonged artistic picnic. There had to be agreement about themes and style, and the agreement was on the whole for neoclassical idealism. Thus, "The Glorification of the Arts and Sciences" that decorated the Manufacturers Building showed Apollo, crowned with laurel, seated on a marble throne, and surrounded by groups and figures emblematic of the divisions of human knowledge.[67]

Of the treatment of the nude, particularly in mural painting, Charles H. Caffin wrote somewhat unsympathetically:

> [The ideal picture] involves the use of the nudes or figures wrapped in draperies, for the most part, supposed to be "classical". This class of motive is based upon the assumption that the painter's duty and privilege is to improve upon the imperfections of the human form and to give the figure an ideal perfection. Therefore the world of real men and women will not do; the painter must invent some fancy of his own. As a rule, he does not so much invent as follow along well-worn ruts that have led for centuries to the same goal. Here some nymph of antiquity for the thousandth time disposes of her maiden beauty to invite the approach of her divine or human lover; or steps into her bath or emerges therefrom; or beautiful youths and maidens pose themselves in self-admiring groups, or wave their bare limbs and nicely calculated draperies into a rhythmic mass.[68]

An extraordinary number of sexless females, draped in white or the national colors or some other appropriate tinted garments and variously labeled "Justice," "America," "The Law," "Alma Mater," "The Future," "The Triumph of Manhattan," or "The Ballet," adorned various theaters, courthouses, university libraries, and other public edifices from 1890 onward. Perhaps the epitome of the saccharine treatment of nudity was Will Low's "Homage to Woman," painted on the ceiling of the ladies' reception room at the old Waldorf. In this enormous candy-box-cover composition a cupid, a flock of doves harnessed by blue, pink, and mauve ribbons ("feathered captives," says Miss King), two youths and a maiden coyly seated on banks of cloud, four girls in mauve, violet, blue, and green draperies, and a couple of lyre players called attention to Woman, a female figure in a delicate shell, her mass of golden hair floating modestly around her. There was no hint of carnality in the painting. Woman was very like the American Girl as portrayed by James Montgomery Flagg, a healthy, vigorous, provocative, and sexless creation. Still extant and quite as characteristic are the nudes by Howard Chandler Christy that adorn the walls of the Hôtel des Artistes in New York City.

To many moderns the image of woman represented in the nude-to-the-waist formula or the Gibson girl, who was always fully clad, validates H. H. Boyesen's famous essay about "The Iron Madonna," [69] who was supposed to strangle the novelist in her fond embrace and so stultify American realism. It may also be hilariously argued that since the ideal nude might expose her breasts, the genteel tradition likewise validates the mom complex charged against Americans. In this context, however, it is curious to see how closely the Viking heroines dear to Frank Norris and Jack London resemble or anticipate the treatment of the female nude. In fact, if proponents of the ideal hit upon the glorification of womanhood as an expression of goodness, beauty, and truth, they were both accepting and modifying an ancient tradition. Venus and Helen, the *alma mater genetrix* of Lucretius, the *Ewigweibliche* of *Faust* are variant symbols of a desire and an ideal deep in the history of Western man. The sculptors and painters who turned the female into French's statue of "The Republic" were not necessarily evasive. In a sense they were approximating, even if they did not forcefully state, what Whitman meant:

> Thou Mother with thy equal brood,
> Thou varied change of different States, yet one identity only
> .   .   .
> Brain of the New World, what a task is thine,
> To formulate the Modern—out of the peerless grandeur of the
>   modern,
> Out of thyself, comprising science, to recast poems, churches, art,
> (Recast, may-be, discard them, end them—maybe their work is
>   done, who knows?)
> By vision, hand, conception, on the background of the mighty
>   past, the dead,
> To limn with absolute faith the mighty living present.

The American Virgin, secular and chaste, rose superbly over the dynamos beneath her feet. Let us be just to painterly idealism, remembering its work was done in a period succinctly described by Homer Saint-Gaudens:

Naturally the American millionaire, backed by no tradition whatsoever, wanted a bit of spectacular and grandiose plastic elaboration to blind strangers' eyes to crude beginnings, and so splashed his wealth about his Fifth Avenue mansion. Naturally ruthless men, in the pride of new-found wealth and power, gave diamonds, trotting horses, and champagne to their lady friends. . . . Those were the days when Mrs. Levi Leiter ran Chicago society from her lavish mansion on Rush Street, and was preparing to join her daughter in matrimony to Lord Curzon by taking the young miss to Europe to be "painted by the Old Masters." [70]

The astonishing thing is not that from the point of view of the moderns the genteel tradition seemed ineffective; the astonishing thing is the high courage of its proponents in trying to correct the point of view of Mrs. Leiter.

V

Although the genteel tradition remained important until the 1920s, when it was attacked under the specious charge of "puritanism," the Exposition of 1893 at Chicago was its climax. Like the genteel tradition, the Chicago Fair has been sniffed at by modern critics who assert that this enterprise set American architecture back by whatever term of years the critic is inclined to stipulate. The charges are commonly three: that the adoption of the Beaux-Arts ideal was a major error; that the genius of Adler and Sullivan was slighted at the Fair; and that the planners ignored such promising inventions as the skyscraper and the new domestic architecture of Frank Lloyd Wright. I find it difficult to think of a world's fair made out of skyscrapers, and in 1893 Frank Lloyd Wright had not got beyond rather simple domestic architecture. These matters aside, one still finds it difficult to follow the logic of the detractors. It is true that all the buildings facing the Court of Honor were by agreement kept within the bounds of "classicism" loosely defined. To retain symmetry, it was agreed that no cornice should be more than sixty feet from the ground and no bay (the vertical division in a wall) should exceed twenty-five feet in width, and that the general decorative scheme, supervised by Saint-Gaudens, should be harmonious—harmony being defined by a Beaux-Arts education, the only tradition the architects had in common. These do not seem horrendous stipulations and, moreover, outside the Court of Honor considerable latitude was al lowed. Thus the Palace of Fine Arts, now the Museum of Science and Industry, was formally Greek, the Fisheries Building had roofs of glazed Spanish tile and a variety of cupolas and towers, and the buildings of the foreign nations and the American states were constructed in styles thought to be appropriate to the country or commonwealth which put them up. As it is sometimes argued that the Beaux-Arts "conservatives," because they were horrified at Sullivan's "originality," pushed aside his Transportation Building, it should be observed that a structure housing locomotives and railroad cars had to be where the railway tracks ran, that Sullivan's masterpiece occupied one side of the Lagoon, one of the three principal divisions of the grounds (the Fine Arts Building was much farther away), and that its famous Golden Door, undoubtedly beautiful, betrayed the strong influence of Mogul architectural motifs and decoration.[71] As for isolating Sullivan, the firm of Adler & Sullivan was one of the five architectural firms that met, agreed to work together, and resolved also to seek the counsel and cooperation of leading architects, designers, painters, and sculptors from all over the United States. At no time in American history has a brilliant group worked more harmoniously toward a common artistic goal than those enlisted in creating the Exposition—a truth attested to by Saint-Gaudens' famous assertion on looking around a plenary session of the artists and planners: "Gentlemen, do you realize that not since the Renaissance has a comparable group been brought together for an enterprise like this?" [72]

Beyond any other art in the United States, architecture had been suffering from an overdose of eclecticism. Eclecticism had of course its good side in flexibility and openness to experiment. It gave scope to the genius of H. H. Richardson and created the dignity of the Back Bay in Boston. It built the Brooklyn Bridge with its great stone piers, now much admired.[73] It put up the Monadnock Building in Chicago, the last really tall building in which a thick, solid foundation supported a wall. It created Sullivan's Auditorium and the Auditorium Hotel. It permitted William Le Baron Jenney to experiment with the first real skyscraper, and Richard Morris Hunt to dream up a French chateau for George Washington Vanderbilt, "Biltmore," at Asheville, North Carolina.

But it was also capable of such curious structures as Eidlitz's (and Richardson's) State Capitol at Albany, of Hunt's odd Scroll and Key Building at Yale, of Firehouse No. 15 in San Francisco (the pinnacles

shaped like fireplugs and the gargoyles caricatures of firemen), of
Mullett's unmanageable State, War, and Navy Building in Washington, of Peter Wright's National Academy of Design in New York (a
Venetian palace strayed on to dry land), and of such lush and indeterminate creations as "Olana," built for Frederick Church. These
buildings are fantastic rather than fine. Eclecticism (or carelessness)
also built the faceless "business blocks" that lined a thousand Main
Streets, the airless tenements in the slums, frame houses alternating
between carpenter's frenzy and gaunt clapboarding over a balloon
frame, pine-wood medievalism sometimes topped with a mansard or
an Oriental roof or tower, ugly "store-front" boxes in ugly hamlets,
and grim brick schoolhouses set in grimmer playgrounds among the
crowded wards of cities east and west. There was no national style in
a nation concerning which Van Brunt could write in 1866 that it totally lacked any standard of architectural criticism.[74] Nor in the time
at their command could the creators of the Fair possibly have invented one. Yet in view of the truth that every building designed by
the collaborators had a specific purpose to fulfill, it can be argued
that seldom before has form followed function so excellently on so
vast a scale as at Chicago in 1893.[75]

The holding of an exposition to commemorate the four-hundredth
anniversary of the discovery of America by Columbus had been
under discussion since the mid-1880s. Chicago had organized a five-
million-dollar company in 1890 (which later doubled that amount)
to bring the Fair to Illinois, and after the usual bickering among
other leading metropolises, Chicago was approved by Congress and
the President as the site of the celebration. Meanwhile, governing
boards had been set up, more money had been appropriated by the
Illinois legislature, and the opening date was established by President Benjamin Harrison as May 1, 1893, the buildings to be dedicated on October 12, 1892. The site was not determined until February, 1891—five hundred acres of sandy and swampy water and land
on the edge of Lake Michigan near Jackson Park. The site was chosen largely by the advice of Frederick L. Olmsted, who turned this
wasteland into a perfectly designed landscape setting for the Exposition, taking advantage of the very defects of the place—the feature-
less flora, the fact that no sand dune was more than six feet above
lake level, and the distance from the heart of Chicago, a distance that
permitted a modern solution of the traffic problem in getting to and

from the Fair and in circulating within the grounds. Olmsted was the chief landscape designer; Daniel H. Burnham and John W. Root were the consulting architects; but in fact, after Root's untimely death and after the resignation of Abram Gottlieb, the chief engineer, the principal executive burden fell on Burnham, who met all sorts of emergencies with extraordinary ability.

Tempting as it is to chronicle the swift and efficient solution of a series of technological problems, one must agree that the national signficance of the World's Columbian Exposition lay in three great achievements: the working together of painters, architects, decorators, landscape designers, engineers, and day laborers [76] in realizing an ideal that kindled their enthusiasm and redoubled their energies; the beauty of the Exposition as a whole; and the range and variety of intellectual congresses held at the Fair or called by it in 1893. The congresses were under the direction of a board called the World's Congress Auxiliary and they ranged from banking and finance through charities and corrections to labor [77] and education; the climactic one was in all probability the World Parliament of Religions held in September, which included over forty denominational bodies. In most cases the proceedings were recorded and published. Thousands who never participated in any congress nevertheless felt that Europe and Asia were no longer foreign powers to be shunned but differing civilizations to be studied.

The evanescent beauty, the wonder of the Exposition, notably the Court of Honor, was what thousands remembered as long as they lived. The formal central basin was dominated by Daniel Chester French's standing statue, "The Republic," a smaller replica of which still exists in Jackson Park. It was supposed to be balanced by Mac-Monnies' fountain at the end of the basin, and in a sense it was, but the fountain seems to have been, at least in its main element, clumsy and ill-conceived. Its principal component was an absurd ship having a pedestal with a seated figure in place of a mast and at the prow a winged figure holding out a laurel wreath to nobody in particular. (There were also four female rowers on each side of the pedestal, an effect that gave the vessel an air of either laboring forward or tipping backward; and the figure of Time was using his scythe as a rudder!) Any dissatisfaction that one might feel, however, concerning a particular statue was lost in the total impression of majesty, of harmony, of hope and futurity conceived by Burnham, Olmsted, Saint-Gaudens, and all the glorious band of associated architects, sculptors, and painters, who managed to instill into the great basin and its adjoining architecture their own passionate ideality. Calling the style classical, or Beaux-Arts, or Renaissance, or anything one likes, one could not forget this vision of an imperial country, the great offspring of republican Rome, taking shape as a White City adorned with columns and statues, colonnades and triumphal arches, made fair with stately buildings and illuminated at night by that new wonder, the electric light. Here was a mingling of the Old World and the New, an embodied idealism, a sense not of what the United States was but of what the United States might become. The possibilities of civic planning were made evident also, but the deeper impression of wonder is what lingered in the mind.

Among a hundred descriptions of the World's Columbian Exposition two in particular seem to me to convey the intoxication of delight that the visitor experienced. The first is by James Fullerton Muirhead, long associated with the Baedeker *Handbooks* and later with guidebooks of his own, who wrote:

> We expected that America would produce the largest, most costly, and most gorgeous of all international exhibitions; but who expected that she would produce anything so inexpressibly poetic, chaste, and restrained, such an absolutely refined and soul-satisfying picture, as the Court of Honour, with its lagoon and gondolas, its white marble steps and balustrades, its varied yet harmonious buildings, its colonnaded vista of the great lake, its impressive fountain, its fairy-like outlining after dark by the gems of electricity, its spacious and well-modulated proportions which made the largest crowd in it but an unobtrusive detail, its air of spontaneity and inevitableness which suggested nature itself, rather than art? No other scene of man's creation seemed to me so perfect . . . the aesthetic sense of the beholder was as fully and unreservedly satisfied as in looking at a masterpiece of painting or sculpture, and at the same time was soothed and elevated by a sense of amplitude and grandeur such as no single work of art could produce. . . . The glamour of old association that illumines Athens or Venice was in a way compensated by our deep impression of the pathetic transitoriness of the dream of beauty before us, and by the revelation it afforded of the soul of a great nation.

The sense of evanescence of ideal beauty moved William T. Stead, present on the closing night, to unusual eloquence:

Beneath the stars the lake lay dark and sombre, but on its shores gleamed and glowed in golden radiance the ivory city, beautiful as a poet's dream, silent as a city of the dead. It was more wonderful to have seen that city in the silence and solitude, with no one near except the lonely sightseers fleeting like wandering ghosts across the electric lighted square into the dark shadows of the projecting buildings, than to have seen it even on Chicago Day, when three-quarters of a million visitors crowded into Jackson Park. . . .[78]

VII

Cosmopolitanism

the best Cosmopolite
Who loves his native country best.

—TENNYSON

I

THE GENTEEL TRADITION sought to know and acclimatize the best that had been thought and said in the world, but for most Americans during this half-century the best that had been thought and said in the world, despite books and lectures, concerts and colleges, was still remote. Life was too often dull. Observers of the national scene had traditionally associated drabness with American life. The classic statement is presumably found in Hawthorne's preface to *The Marble Faun* (1860):

> No author, without a trial, can conceive of the difficulty of writing a romance about a country where there is no shadow, no antiquity, no mystery, no picturesque and gloomy wrong, nor anything but a commonplace prosperity, in broad and simple daylight, as is happily the case with my dear native land. . . . Romance and poetry, ivy, lichens, and wall-flowers need ruin to make them grow.

This is dated from Leamington, England, and Hawthorne had been seven years abroad. For him as for Cooper, "romance" had a technical meaning, and it is possible he wrote this famous passage with his tongue in his cheek. Nevertheless, analogous statements were made by other observers. Tocqueville had written some years earlier that if the emergence of the United States stimulated and fed curiosity, "in the end, the spectacle of this excited community becomes monotonous, and, after having watched the moving pageant for a time, the

259

spectator is tired of it." ¹ Hawthorne's view was, moreover, endorsed by his most famous biographer. Discussing Hawthorne's notebooks, Henry James wrote in 1879:

> . . . as I turn the pages of his journals, I seem to see the image of the crude and simple society in which he lived . . . it takes such an accumulation of history and custom, such complexity of manners and types, to form a fund of suggestion for a novelist. . . . one might enumerate the items of high civilization, as it exists in other countries, which are absent from the texture of American life, until it should become a wonder to know what was left. No State, in the European sense of the word, and indeed barely a specific national name. No sovereign, no court, no personal loyalty, no aristocracy, no church, no clergy, no army, no diplomatic service, no country gentlemen, no palaces, no castles . . . cottages, nor ivied ruins; no cathedrals, nor abbeys, nor little Norman churches; no great Universities nor public schools—no Oxford, nor Eton, nor Harrow; no literature, no novels, no museums, no pictures, no political society, no sporting class—no Epsom nor Ascot!

The effect of such an environment, James thought, upon an English or French imagination would have been "appalling." ² Hawthorne and James were of course literary men, and James was an Anglophile, but because of the special historical relations between Great Britain and the United States, cultural comparisons by others than novelists between England and this country were easy and sometimes painful. Mediocrity was a common charge by British travelers. The cases of Captain Basil Hall and Mrs. Trollope in the ante-bellum period had been notorious; just before the Civil War and long after it much the same fault was alleged by other Britons.

Thus Thomas Colley Grattan, once British consul in Boston, in his *Civilized America* (1859) let drop these remarks:

> In observing the great mass of good, and its natural result of general well-being among the people at large, throughout the United States, I must admit that it is produced by a sacrifice of individual eminence, and consequently of personal enjoyment.

> The intense pursuit of gain, the little cultivation of the higher order of intellect, the shifting way of life, the fluctuations of fortune, all tend to reduce the standard. . . . It is quite painful to observe at present the striking change for the worse in most of the sons of the men from sixty to eighty years of age who are now fast dropping off from the scene. But painful as this degeneracy is, in an individual point of view, it would be

far better for the country at large were these weak scions of good old stems aware of their inferiority, and content to become merged in the general mediocrity (I am forced to reiterate the word) to which everything in the United States is tending.

The frontier, which he called "the rude ways of physical existence," seemed to him to explain this mediocrity, together with the fact that everything of merit had been accomplished in the Old World, so that all America could do was to import thought and art:

> . . . all the higher duties of human improvement are done for her. The exercises of lofty thought, and the elegancies of art, all come from Europe. She has no such indigenous standard of taste and knowledge as that in which they have their source. She obtains the little that she wants of these ready made. Yet a servile and jealous admiration of the Old World leads to attempted imitations, uncouth and clumsy.[3]

Since the 1850s have been regarded as a kind of golden decade in American cultural development, Grattan can be charged with obtuseness. But the indictment continued. Thus, in 1883 Edward A. Freeman, a powerful force in popularizing racial doctrines, published *Some Impressions of the United States;* and though this country was, with England and Germany, one of the "three Germanies" (i.e., countries happily dominated by Germanic stock), "there is something very strange in going through a vast land in which there is not one ancient building, where no historical association can be anything like three hundred years old, where the chief historical associations are only one hundred years old." [4]

In 1888 Matthew Arnold's *Civilization in the United States* was published. This critic announced that a true civilization—for example, that of Greece—was "interesting," but that American civilization was not interesting because American cities offered nothing to a trained sense of beauty, American newspapers supported American self-glorification and self-deception, and in what concerns the higher culture, Americans lived in a fool's paradise.[5]

The fullest statement of the theme is probably found in Bryce's *The American Commonwealth* (1888). In a chapter entitled "The Uniformity of American Life," Bryce mildly disagreed with Arnold, saying that American cities might be pleasanter and cleaner than European towns but, he declared, "their monotony haunts one like a nightmare." Again we read of our lack of historical antiquity. Bryce adds that although the Americans come from varied racial stocks, the nation remains a land of monotony, even if it be a happy monotony. Will variety eventually introduce itself? Bryce excepted certain cities and areas, but he was pessimistic about the future as a whole:

> Many of the small towns of to-day will grow into large towns, a few of the large towns into great cities, but as they grow, they will not become less like one another. There will be larger theatres and hotels, more churches . . . and handsomer ones; but what is to make the theatres and churches of one city differ from those of another? Fashion and the immense facilities of intercourse tend to wear down even such diversities in the style of building or furnishing, or in the modes of locomotion, or in amusements and forms of social intercourse, as now exist.

He ventured a cautious hope that time might take away "the monotony which comes from the absence of historical associations" and looked for a decline in the dominance of the business mind.[6] Books like *Main Street* and anthologies like Harold Stearns' *Civilization in the United States: An Inquiry by Thirty Americans* (1922) were to continue where the British observers left off. It is superfluous to point out that the problem remains today.[7]

In an old-fashioned analysis of that master, Elizabeth Luther Cary points to a scene in James's *Roderick Hudson* (1876) that is virtually symbolic of the yearning for color and variety felt by many Americans of the period. Rowland, who has financed Roderick Hudson's trip to Italy, visits him in his studio:

> "Tell me this," said Rowland, "do you mean anything by your young Water-drinker? Does he represent an idea? Is he a symbol?" Hudson raised his eyebrows and gently scratched his head. "Why, he's youth, you know; he's innocence, he's health, he's strength, he's curiosity. Yes, he's a good many things." "And is the cup also a symbol?" "The cup is knowledge, pleasure, experience. Anything of that kind!" "Well, he's guzzling in earnest," said Rowland. Hudson gave a vigorous nod. "Aye, poor fellow, he's thirsty." [8]

The sculptor is vague, the patron confused, but the thirst and the curiosity were real. How infuse into this drab culture, this uniformity of existence, which every day threatened to become more unendurable, the color, the tang, the variety it lacked? The genteel critics were admirable, but there remained something abstract and theoretical

about aesthetic idealism. To satisfy this thirst for the picturesque and
the exotic a variety of forces was developed by American activism.

II

At no time in their history have the Americans imitated the
Chinese and shut themselves off from foreign lands. From the creation
of the republic (even before) residents of the United States have traveled abroad not merely on diplomatic or commercial missions but as
general observers of mankind. The results enriched the ante-bellum
nation. When one thinks of the exotic treasures brought home from
China, Japan, or the South Seas, or perhaps even Africa, the importation of French wallpaper, bottled water from the River Jordan, Italian "Old Masters" (even though the canvases might be fakes or copies), or meditates on the pirating of European literature or on the
effect of European fashions, European philosophy, European theology, and European science upon America before the Civil War,[9] one
becomes cautious about generalizing. It is a commonplace that as
population and wealth increased and as ocean travel became easier,
safer, and less expensive, more and more Americans found it both desirable and possible to visit other parts of the world.

Changes in the make-up of travel books as between ante-bellum
and post-bellum America are of course difficult to define, but I venture on three generalizations concerning such literature prior to 1861.
The first is that many early travelers took to heart Jefferson's famous
injunction to visit courts and monarchies as one would visit a zoo,
the consequence being an anti-monarchical or pro-republican bias, a
tendency to attribute the faults of a foreign land to its monarchical,
aristocratic, or "feudal" system, and to contrast the decaying Old
World with the bright social promise of the New. The second is that
a good many American travelers were militantly Protestant, had no
sympathy with any other sort of religion (the association between
Protestantism and a republican form of government was for them
fundamental), and were often violently hostile to Roman Catholicism. Protestant clergymen sent abroad for a vacation by admiring
congregations often found it necessary to denounce the Scarlet
Woman of Babylon, as did the Reverend Orville Dewey in 1836. I
have noted that even so distinguished a person as Charles Eliot Nor-

ton, when he published his *Notes of Travel and Study in Italy* serially in *The Crayon* in 1856, salted his discussion of art in Rome with
a good many anti-Catholic objurgations.[10] My third observation is
that the travel book of the earlier period is likely to be naïvely pedagogical or didactic, a tendency that explains the tedious repetition of
descriptions of the Tower of London, or the Apollo Belvedere, or the
Colosseum, or the romantic scenery of the Rhine. Later, one could
take these things for granted. Indeed, Mark Twain's *Innocents
Abroad* (1869) finds the basis of its burlesque partly in the teachy-
preachy quality of these earlier works.

After the Civil War travel books by Americans no longer tended to
be addressed solely to political, or religious, or democratic man. Except for "funny" books or obviously didactic accounts, these volumes
ignored the farmer, the laborer, or the immigrant to concentrate
upon genteel readers who liked "good books." Travel to foreign
lands was broadening; and if you could not go yourself, the next best
thing was to read a sensitive account by someone who had been
there. Cosmopolitanism even at second hand enriched a liberal education, and the picturesque, whether in words or photographs or pen-
cil sketches, ink, or water color was almost as good as seeing the real
thing. The style in these volumes is that of cultivated conversation
touching upon seaports, landscapes, famous buildings, custom and
costume and amusing anecdote, personal reminiscence, and sympathetic portrayals of peasants or porters, priests or peddlers, more
rarely of the nobility and gentry. Famous public figures were of
course included, as were thoughtful, if not final, estimates of religion,
government, and politics, the place of women, the value and mode of
education, politeness or the lack of it, sanitation, and food—usually
with some comparison to like things in the United States, not always
to the benefit of American pride. Such books were produced by authors of the standing of Howells, Henry James, F. Hopkinson Smith,
Bayard Taylor, Edith Wharton, and Richard Harding Davis. There
were also throwbacks to the earlier polemical travel account; and
there were wonderful studies like Howells' *Venetian Life* (1866),
which preserves the whole subculture of Venice under Austrian rule,
John Hay's *Castilian Days* (1871–1899), Edward S. Morse's magisterial *Japan Day by Day, 1877, 1877–1878, 1882–1883* (1917), Percival Lowell's *Chosen: The Land of the Morning Calm* (1885), thought
to be the first full-length account in English of Korean life, Lafcadio

Hearn's *Two Years in the French West Indies* (1890), and Price Collier's *England and the English from an American Point of View* (1909), probably the best American account of English life in succession to Emerson's *English Traits*. An important new element, though a negative one, is the relative absence of condescension toward foreign lands.

After the war, and particularly after 1870, the chip-on-the-shoulder attitude formerly characteristic of the Yankee abroad was outmoded. Nothing is more interesting than the new American attitude toward England.[11] The monarchy now becomes a wise institution, the aristocracy a proper mode of maintaining social distinctions; Great Britain is the home of poetry and history. English political institutions, English literature, and the "Anglo-Saxon" inheritance are assumed to be joint possessions of the two countries. Representative books are William Winter's *The Trip to England* (1879) and *Gray Days and Gold* (1892), Anna Bowman Dodd's *Cathedral Days: A Tour in Southern England* (1899), Josephine Tozier's *Among English Inns* (1904), Marcus B. Huish's *The American Pilgrim's Way in England to Homes and Memorials of the Founders of Virginia, the New England States, Pennsylvania, etc.* (1907), Henry C. Shelley's *Literary By-Paths in Old England* (1906), and Katharine Lee Bates's *From Gretna Green to Land's End: A Literary Journey in England* (1907). Winter would not have recognized an English slum if he saw one. "My sketches of travel," he writes, "are the spontaneous creations of genial impulse." At Windsor he comprehends at a glance "the old feudal system . . . the imaginative mind wanders over vast tracts of the past, and beholds, as in a mirror, the pageants of chivalry, the coronations of kings," and much else; a "luminous twilight" envelops both Stoke Poges and the *Elegy Written in a Country Churchyard;* at Kenilworth he experiences "peace, haunted by romance"; and in the region around Windsor he "saw many a sweet nook where tired life might well be content to lay down its burden and enter into its rest."[12]

Anna Bowman Dodd drove a horse named Ballad to the cathedral towns. Henry C. Shelley's book is full of literary and cultural reverence. Katharine Lee Bates, though she has a section on a "group of industrial Counties," seemed mainly distressed by the fact that "smut" disfigures buildings in Manchester. She noted only that families in Liverpool herded together by threes and fours in a single dirty cellar, merely wondered where they find the money they spend in the pubs, and then hurried through Cheshire, quoting local balladry, to get on to Knutsford with its memories of Mrs. Gaskell. She made this excursion with two women "faring-mates," visited all the literary shrines she could, and was more concerned about her balky automobile than she was about industrial grime.[13] (I remark parenthetically that a book by Clifton Johnson, entitled *Among English Hedgerows,* is unusual in devoting many pages to the British yokelry, who, however, are mainly portrayed as quaint historical relics.[14]) King George III was now, so to speak, dead and had been succeeded by Queen Victoria and then by Edward VII, that jolly patron of beautiful women and fast horses. In the reign of the queen, American thirst for color and culture could be gratified; in the reign of her son, American thirst for social recognition. Meanwhile, watercolorists, etchers, and photographers increased the American reader's feeling for the English picturesque.[15]

Three or four authors in this extensive library deserve special notice. One illuminating volume is Andrew Carnegie's *An American Four-in-Hand in Britain,* first published in 1883, then several times reprinted. The steel magnate rejoices in a British coaching trip, the guests for which included Mr. and Mrs. Matthew Arnold, John Morley, Edwin A. Abbey, Sir Edwin Arnold, William Black, two Gladstones, and the James G. Blaines. There is something enchanting about Carnegie's naïve acceptance of Scotch feudalism ("modern castles in England built to order are only playthings, toys; but in Scotland they are real and stir the chords"). But the future Laird of Skibo Castle also expertly played the role of Mr. Facing-Both-Ways: on one hand, he was boyishly delighted to be accepted by the English nobility and admired English genius in the arts; on the other, he prophesied the coming of an English republic, which, "when it comes, will excel all other republics as much as the English monarchy excelled all other monarchies." Calling the British "a great race," he urged them to "go to work and get rid of their antiquated prejudices." The Black Country horrified him:

> rows of little dingy houses . . . tall smoky chimneys vomiting smoke, mills and factories at every turn, coal pits and rolling mills and blast furnaces, the very bottomless pit itself; and such dirty, careworn children, hard-driven men, and squalid women. To think of the green lanes, the larks, the Arcadia we have just left. How can people be got to live such

terrible lives as they seem condemned to here? Why do they not all run
away to the green fields just beyond?

Perhaps he meant to answer this question in two ways: "the English
exalt politics unduly and waste the lives of their best men disputing
over problems which the more advanced Republicans have settled
long ago"; and "the working classes in England do not work so hard
or so unceasingly as do their fellows in America." [16]
Since moderns find it difficult to penetrate the smooth text of the
prose of William Dean Howells to the acid social commentary beneath, one may reasonably infer that volumes such as his *London
Films* (1905)—photography, not cinema—*Certain Delightful English
Towns with Glimpses of the Pleasant Country Between* (1906), and
Seven English Cities (1909) were felt to cater to picturesqueness,
antiquity, mellow charm, and tradition. Henry James's *English
Hours* [17] and the leading essay in *Essays in London and Elsewhere*
(1893), which is devoted to London, that "dreadful, delightful city,"
are more complicated. James is by no means blind to the sordid elements in English life,[18] but "he reflects with elation that the British
capital is the particular spot in the world which communicates the
greatest sense of life"; and however superficial or intermittent his acquaintance with the English gentry may have been, he continued to
picture in his novels, save for the unfortunate attempt at "radicalism"
in *The Princess Casamassima* (1886), the gracious life of the country
houses, the London "season," and the servant class immediately dependent upon the hierarchy. Certain chapters in *The Portrait of a
Lady* (1881) were a paradigm of the way the American millionaire
would like to live; a short story like "Brooksmith," that portrait of
the perfect gentleman's gentleman, represented a tradition Newport
vainly strove to develop. To compare the shrill denunciation of England in Tom Paine ("a French bastard landing with an armed banditti and establishing himself king of England against the consent of
the natives") with the mellow acceptance by Henry James of traditional English upper-class life is to see how the cosmopolitan spirit
has triumphed over propaganda and parochialism.
How far a sympathetic interpretation of English life had gone can
be judged by reading Price Collier's *England and the English from
the American Point of View* (1909). Collier is in no way disturbed by
the hierarchy of English society (which includes the servants), for he

calls England a country of personal freedom and personal responsibility, where justice "is swift, unprejudiced, impartial and sure. The lord, the millionaire, the drunkard and the snatch thief are treated the same." He admits there is a dark side to English prosperity—drunkenness, prostitution, under-nourishment, lack of public education, slums—but from the original Saxon stock there "has percolated down a million men who rule the world" (that is, the British empire), a ruling class constantly recruited from below on the "Saxon system." The king is no more than a prominent gentleman, England is not an aristocracy and never has been, outdoor life and sports demonstrate the English feeling for democracy, radicalism loses its force in this moist island and its feverishness among these hard-playing islanders. The kingdom has a good many elements he doesn't like—the drabness of English cooking, the worship of money, the dominance of the male, the inability of government to come to grips with Ireland; nevertheless, he thinks England is the most hopeful of nations, as these excerpts will reveal:

> Though the problems here are faced as courageously and discussed as frankly as elsewhere, there is no throwing up of hands in despair, no dyspeptic politics to put it briefly.

> If we have learnt anything from this admirable people, and this wonderful Empire, it has been how much may be done by liberty loving men, with the wealth and leisure to ensure courage, patience, and loyalty.

> Radicalism in England, whether social, political, or literary, was for a long time only a costume and a way of wearing the hair; it is now a philosophy with considerable political and some social power. It is not, however, of the integral tone and temper of the English people.[19]

Collier was no lover of socialism and not prophetic enough to foresee the Lloyd-George cabinet and the Labor Party, but how far he is from the denunciation of George III in the Declaration of Independence as a bloody despot whose every act is one of tyranny!

The chief Catholic countries of the Continent offered another sort of problem. If it was no longer right to blame their backwardness on wrong traditions, wrong governments, and a wrong religion, what did the traveler do? There was a language barrier to be overcome. He often insisted that the French were greedy or immoral, the Italians and the Spaniards backward or bigoted or dirty. But the concept of Paris as sensuous delight ("when good Americans die, they go to

Paris"), the legend of sunny Italy and romantic Spain persisted, even among the high-and-dry Protestants, and it is fascinating to watch travelers struggling among these points of view and with the embarrassment occasioned them by political events—the rise and fall of the Second Empire, the Dreyfus case, the Carlist wars in Spain, anarchy, change of monarch, and the growing dislike of Spanish administration in Cuba, and of course the problem of the unification of Italy and the virtual imprisonment of the pope.

Here are some sample judgments from what I may call average travel books. Writing of her experiences in France from 1867 to 1873, Mrs. Henry M. Field said of the Bois de Boulogne:

> It is one of the strangest spectacles in the world. Here all sorts of people, —high and low, rich and poor, good and bad; kings and princes, and needy adventurers; the high-born duchess, and the woman of pleasure flaunting in her gay attire; brazen-faced vice jostling against innocence and purity; rank and wealth and empty pretension,—all in one common throng, meeting, mingling, and rolling on together to that boundary of life where they shall all be separated by the eternal Judge.

She listened to the famous Père Hyacinthe at Notre Dame, was shown an old hag who had once been the Goddess of Reason of the French Revolution, thought the Catholic church in a state of paralysis, and complained of the lack of popular education in France. In 1875 Albert Rhodes, after a "lengthy foreign residence in the consular and diplomatic service," though he called the French "the Chinese of the West" and said they killed liberty as soon as it was in their power, found "the wide dissemination of art-feeling" to be a "refining tendency on the manners of all classes," and said that "even in the women given over to vice, pagan cultivation redeems it of its most revolting features," the prostitutes being "generally polite, orderly, and well dressed—in striking contrast to the Anglo-Saxons of the same class." He printed sympathetic accounts of French restaurants, French diners, and French gourmets, spent a chapter on the picturesque ragpickers of Paris, and described the professional attitude of everybody concerned with modeling in the nude. To Nathan Sheppard, who had a subacid contempt for the Paris mob, Paris was "everything delightful and everything abominable," "a volcano on which flowers may be plucked and children may gambol"; and Stuart Henry in 1896 (he had seen Verlaine drinking absinthe and writing verses in the Café du Soleil), published a book full of amusing vignettes but without moral judgment. He sketched literary and social figures, the theater, the salons, the Latin Quarter, Parisians at the beach, and included a sardonic account of a meeting of the French Academy. French newspapers were notoriously corrupt, the Boulevard des Italiens was on the decline, the French café was doomed, and he noted the enormous popularity of Rossini (*William Tell*), Ambroise Thomas, and Auber as instances of shallow taste. But his sardonicism does not conceal his admiration: "Of course French art and fashions will reign supreme, and the French will always teach nations taste, delicacy, lucidity. It would be a heavy world, indeed, were the French taken out of it."

One can put aside Henry James as *sui generis* [20] and take Richard Harding Davis's *About Paris* (1903) as representative of American interpretation. Americans go to Paris to enjoy themselves. If there are dangerous classes there, the Parisian criminal has no special environment, the Halles are lively, the tourists mildly stupid, and the dynamic life of France is the life of art:

> The American artist who has taken Paris properly has only kind words to speak of her. He is grateful for what she gave him, but he is not unmindful of his mother-country at home. He may complain when he returns of the mud in our streets, and the height of our seventeen-story buildings, and the ugliness of our elevated roads—and who does not? But if his own art is lasting and there is in his heart much constancy, his work will grow. . . . New York and every great city owns a number of these men who have studied in the French capital, and speak of it as fondly as a man speaks of his college. . . . These are the men who made the Columbian Fair what it was, who taught their teacher and the whole world a lesson in what was possible in architecture and in statuary, in decoration and design. . . . They are the best examples we have of the Americans who made use of Paris, instead of permitting Paris to make use of them."

If this is a little highbrow, one can turn to Berkeley Smith's *How Paris Amuses Itself* for the Paris of du Maurier's *Trilby* or of Toulouse-Lautrec. But books about France are legion.[21]

It is impossible to examine everything, but one can note half a dozen characteristic books about Italy and Spain. The emphasis of William Wetmore Story's *Roba di Roma,* for instance, is on the historical and the picturesque: "it was dirty, but it was Rome; and to

any one who has long lived in Rome even its very dirt has a charm
which the neatness of no other place ever had." The common people, peasants in the fields or laborers in the city, forever sing:

> Whether this constant habit of song among the Southern people, while
> at their work, indicates happiness and content, I will not undertake to
> say; but it is pleasanter in effect than the sad silence in which we Anglo-
> Saxons perform our tasks,—and it seems to show a less harassed and anx-
> ious spirit. . . . The demon of dissatisfaction never harries them. When
> you speak to them, they answer with a smile which is nowhere else to be
> found.

As for the past,

> this is one great charm of Rome,—that it animates the dead figures of
> history. On the spot where they lived and acted, the Caesars change from
> the manikins of books to living men; and Virgil, Horace, and Cicero
> grow to be realities, when we walk down the Sacred Way and over the
> very pavement they may once have trod. . . . The air seems to keep a
> sort of spiritual scent or trail of these old deeds, and to make them more
> real here than elsewhere. The ghosts of history haunt their ancient habi-
> tations. Invisible companions walk with us through the silent deserted
> streets of Pompeii. Vague voices call to us from the shattered tombs
> along the Via Appia; and looking out over the blue sea, through the col-
> umns of that noble villa, lately unearthed at Ostia, one almost seems to
> hear the robes of ancient senators sweeping along its rich mosaic floors.

It is tempting to quote some of the passages of sensuous description
by Story of spring in Rome and its environs.[22]

F. Hopkinson Smith saw Italy, particularly Venice, through the
eyes of a painter:

> That first morning in Venice! It is the summer, of course—never the
> winter. This beautiful bride of the sea is loveliest when bright skies bend
> tenderly over her, when white mists fall softly around her, and the la-
> goons about her feet are sheets of burnished silver: when the red olean-
> ders thrust their blossoms exultingly above the low, crumbling walls:
> When the black hoods of winter *felsi* are laid by at the *traghetti,* and
> gondolas flaunt their white awnings: when the melon-boats, with lifeless
> sails, drift lazily by, and the shrill cry of the fruit vendor floats over the
> water.

It was a joy to live in Venice "in this selfish, materialistic, money-get-
ting age,"

where a song is more prized than a soldo; where the poorest pauper laughingly shares his scanty crust; where to be kind to a child is a habit, to be neglectful of old age a shame; a city the relics of whose past are the lessons of our future; whose every canvas, stone, and bronze bear witness to a grandeur, luxury, and taste that took a thousand years of energy to perfect, and will take a thousand years of neglect to destroy . . . to know her thoroughly is to know all the beauty and romance of five centuries.[23]

I have already mentioned Howells' admirable *Venetian Life;* in later books about Italy he combined an eye for the picturesque with an eye for political and sociological meanings, as in his *Italian Journeys* (1872) and *Roman Holidays and Others* (1908). He made honest appraisals of pictures, statues, and architectural monuments (he thought the Roman forum was a jumble of bad architecture, crowding, and ruins), and a paragraph in the second book is especially pertinent to the Age of Energy:

Genoa, Venice, Pisa, Florence, what state their business men housed themselves in and environed themselves with! Their palaces by the hundreds were such as only the public edifices of our less simple State capitols could equal in size and not surpass in cost. Their *folie des grandeurs* realized illusions in architecture, in sculpture, and in painting which the assembled and concentrated feats of those arts all the way up and down Fifth Avenue, and in the millionaire blocks eastward could not produce the likeness of. We have the same madness in our brains; we have even a Roman megalomania, but the effect of it in Chicago or Pittsburgh or Philadelphia or New York has not yet got beyond a ducal or a princely son-in-law. The splendors of such alliances have still to take substantial form in a single instance worthy to compare with a thousand instances in the commercial republics of Italy.[24]

As for Henry James's *Italian Hours* (1919), a collection of essays written from 1882 forward, the reader will find it an astonishing blend of sensibility and sociology. The sociology takes form as commentary on the misery of Venice, the people having little more to call their own than the "bare privilege of leading their lives in the most beautiful of towns," and on the social pressures of Genoa, where

a traveller is often moved to ask himself whether it has been worth while to leave his home . . . only to encounter new forms of human suffering, only to be reminded that toil and privation, hunger and sorrow and sordid effort, are the portion of the mass of mankind.

James wonders why people who three hundred years ago had the best taste in the world now have the worst. Nevertheless one can be happy in Venice "without reading at all—without criticising or analysing or thinking a strenuous thought," for there "life was so pictorial that art couldn't help becoming so," and he struggled to maintain his sense of the past of Italy while brooding over the tawdry present "modern crudity" runs riot "over the relics of the great period." [25] Whatever the perplexity of life in modern Italy, the picturesqueness, the pleasantness, and the sense of the past in that country were praised or pictured by scores of Americans writing books about it. Representative volumes can still be found in virtually any large college or public library.

Consensus about Spain was harder to come by. In a thoroughly Protestant, yet intelligent, book, John Hay was dubious about Roman Catholicism, the prevalence of superstition, the questionable morals of the clergy, the ignorance of the women, and the out-of-date quality of Spanish education, but he dutifully reported on art, architecture, cities, and country life, was happy that a Protestant could now (1871) live in Spain and be buried there, and indirectly flattered American complacency in this passage, suggested by a passion play:

> Spectacles like that which we have just seen were one of the elements which in a barbarous and unenlightened age contributed strongly to the consolidation of that unthinking and ardent faith which has fused the nation into one torpid and homogeneous mass of superstition. . . . By dwelling almost exclusively upon the story of his [Christ's] sufferings, they excited the emotional nature of the ignorant, and left their intellects untouched and dormant. . . . Is there not food for earnest thought in the fact that faith in Christ, which led the Puritans across the sea to found the purest social and political system which the wit of man has yet evolved from the tangled problems of time, has dragged this great Spanish people down to a depth of hopeless apathy, from which it may take long years of civil tumult to raise them? [26]

This is obviously a long distance from Washington Irving.

Kate Field's small *Ten Days in Spain* is a chronicle of incompetence, cheating, dirt, and insolence; she could not find that Spain had improved since Irving's time. The picturesque colors James Albert Harrison's *Spain in Profile* (1879), though he complains of begging, ignorance, and superstition.

All over the peninsula the same jumble is found, the same *canaille,* the same eating, singing, and carousing manhood and womanhood, trying to get the best of everything for the least possible price; trying to outwit you and everybody else in a bargain; trying to drive you farther than you engaged for to make more money; trying to show you castles and abbeys and churches and palaces, whether you will or not . . . begging in every imaginable crevice and corner; throwing coins out of their poverty-stricken pockets over the silver railings as an offering at the shrine of some sumptuous Virgin; eating and dancing in the street with delightful naïveté; going to bed to wrestle with *pulgas* and *chinches.*

But though any posada is more than likely to be filthy, romantic Spain has not vanished; at Valencia

the tinkling guitar and clashing castanets are heard everywhere, from the poor blind men leaning pathetically over the fence which separates the railway from the road, where they stand and play in the hope of beguiling a copper out of the traveler when the train stops, to the wanderers that make the music in the streets under the balconies and hotel windows, even before one is up in the morning.

Moreover, "the Moors seemed to build by moonlight and to breathe through their architecture the plaintiveness, tenderness, and purity of the perennial star," and, observing a square in Seville of an evening, he writes: "Life is not an even flow with these people; it is a tumult, a sort of passion. . . . Where the air never sparkles with frost, all the sparkle has gone into the people."

William Howe Downes in 1883 took a somewhat toplofty view of everything, commonly found the lodgings dirty or full of smells, disliked the Escorial, disliked Andalusia, and disliked Spanish trains; nevertheless he saw Spain through the eyes, as it were, of both Gautier and Bizet. Like virtually every other American, Charles Augustus Stoddard hated bullfighting, dwelt on religious bigotry, and was somewhat put out that the women in the tobacco factories of Seville did not resemble Carmen; but he wrote of Cordova: "The stillness and solemnity of the place are good for tired nerves and weary brains, which have been excited and worn in the atmosphere and action of American life; but there is also a reaction from the enforced slowness and moderation which characterize everything here."

The Workmans took a bicycle trip in Spain, found the roads awful, frightened horses and mules, were threatened by mule drivers and riders, and discovered that most of the inns were bad, and they were not impressed by the Spanish postal service or the manners of the children. Nevertheless, Cordova in the moonlight was enchanting, and so was a Corpus Christi service at Toledo.[27] These excerpts are, I think, representative of a large library; and however the accounts may differ in prejudice or impartiality, Spain remained a country of romance, revolution, and ragamuffins, antithetical to American energy and in that sense attractive.

The "new" kind of travel book was written about European countries from Iceland and Russia to Greece,[28] but one does not have space for every country. Two final observations should, however, be made. One concerns the rise of the professional traveler, of whom Bayard Taylor is a literary, and John Lawson Stoddard, of *Stoddard's Lectures*[29] fame, a commercial type. Of travel books concerning more exotic lands I shall speak in another connection. But one should not overlook the spate of volumes of all kinds concerning the Latin-American countries. The Brazilian empire of Dom Pedro drew a good deal of favorable attention, the West Indies came under greater scrutiny as tension with Spain increased, and books about Mexico, often sociological, sometimes anti-Catholic, frequently tended to stress the picturesque; for example, F. Hopkinson Smith's *A White Umbrella in Mexico* (1889), in which one finds such passages as: "I thank my lucky stars that I still know a few out-of-the-way corners where the castanet and high-heeled shoe, the long, flowing, and many-colored tunic, the white sabot and the snowy cap, and the sandal and sombrero, are still left to delight me with their picturesqueness, their harmony of color and grace."[30]

A good many accounts of the South American republics are commercial in intention, but one must except from this categorization books like Professor and Mrs. Louis Agassiz' *A Journey to Brazil,* overflowing with the picturesque, the Reverend Titus Coan's *Adventures in Patagonia: A Missionary's Exploring Trip,* an almost incredible narrative, Charles Augustus Stoddard's *Cruising among the Caribees: Summer Days in Winter Months,* full of lush descriptions, and Richard Harding Davis's amusing *Three Gringos in Venezuela and Central America.* As early as 1851 a forgotten author named John Esaias Warren was capable of this: "In addition to the crew and the Indians, we observed several beautiful Rio Negro girls, whose dreamy eyes and dark tresses, hanging in dishevelled masses over

their handsomely rounded shoulders and well-developed bosoms, left
an impression upon our *susceptible hearts* that was not soon erased."
Half a century later Davis could describe scenery in Honduras in this
fashion:

> We left La Pietà early the next morning, in the bright sunlight, but in-
> stead of climbing laboriously into the sombre mountains of the day be-
> fore, we trotted briskly along a level path between sunny fields and deli-
> cate plants, and trees with a pale-green foliage, and covered with the
> most beautiful white-and-purple flowers. There were hundreds of doves
> in the air, and in the bushes many birds of brilliant blue-and-black or or-
> ange-and-scarlet plumage, and one of more sombre colors with two long
> white tail-feathers and a white crest, like a macaw that had turned
> Quaker . . . we plunged into a forest of manacca-palms, through which
> we rode the rest of the morning. This was the most beautiful and won-
> derful experience of our journey. . . . The branches of these palms were
> sixty feet high, and occasionally six feet broad, and bent and swayed and
> interlaced in the most graceful and exquisite confusion. Every blade
> trembled in the air, and for hours we heard no other sound save their
> perpetual murmur and rustle. Not even the hoofs of our mules gave a
> sound, for they trod on the dead leaves of centuries.[31]

Whatever else might be true of this variegated library, it did not
describe winter on the Illinois prairie or drought on the Great
Plains, and it encouraged not merely the wealthy but also the well-
to-do to go abroad. Immigrants who made money in the United
States were also to return to Greece or Ireland, Germany or Norway
on visits that refreshed and sometimes saddened their memories of
their old homelands. These visits were made possible by the steady
decrease in the cost of international travel.

It is impossible, as I have said, to generalize except tentatively
about American reports on foreign lands, but if one contrasts passages by Andrew Preston Peabody, who published *Reminiscences of
European Travel* in 1868, and others by Harry Thurston Peck, who
brought out *The New Baedeker* in 1910, the change in tone is obvious and the increase in American "sophistication" is evident. Peabody expresses no horror of the nude and but a tempered anti-Catholicism; his book is the report of a solid and substantial citizen.
England "manifests everywhere the accumulated opulence of an age
of many centuries." London is an admirably governed city, Paris is
the cleanest city he ever saw, even though it is essentially atheistic,

and he rejoiced in the Protestant bookstores he found in Rome, where, however, he discovered no medium between the splendid and the squalid. An old-fashioned genteel idealism informs this description of the Capitoline Venus: "The Venus of the Capitol is peerless in beauty, combining with consummate symmetry, grace, and loveliness, the freedom and energy which belonged to the ideal of woman not yet limited and enfeebled by the restraints of artificial life," an interesting judgment from a man who rejoiced "to recognize, not so much human genius, taste and culture, as the Divine inspiration in art." This is solid and substantial writing.

When, however, one drops down some forty years to *The New Baedeker,* he finds himself reading prose covered with a veneer of, in the modern sense, sophistication. "Whether you cross the Atlantic with a millionaire's menagerie or whether you are satisfied with a real ship," writes Peck, "if, after a week of ocean, you wish something to emerge before your sight slowly and serenely and with a mellow beauty of its own—a beauty that grows on you and resolves itself into minor beauties and delicate tones of foreign strangeness," Liverpool won't do, Southampton won't do, Hamburg and Dover are dull, Rotterdam "is a horror," and Cherbourg is "a little tea-boardy . . . suggestive of a chromo [chromolithograph]." Le Havre is, then, where you must land.

> Nothing can be more delightful than to approach the wide-spread mouth of the river Seine a little before daybreak and while darkness still broods upon the scene. You rise joyfully and go for the last time into the *salle-à-manger* (why *will* the French employ upon their ships the same words and names which they employ on shore?) and your own particular *garçon* brings you a cup of coffee and bowl of savory *soupe à l'oignon;* and then, fortified by the excellent meal, you light a cigarette and proceed on deck.

There follows a paragraph on Maupassant, and after that:

> presently comes a flush of rose into the sky, and from the deck you see the smooth white shores on which the water dimples in the dawn. The steamer moves majestically along until finally you behold the lighthouse, snowy white, and the huge semaphore, and then the ship turns inward. The tricolour is run up at the mast-head; a small brass cannon bangs vociferously on the upper deck, and soon you pass along the front of the Grand Quai.

Precisely how this differs from landing at any other port may be questioned, and the style is a throwback to the affectation of Nathaniel Parker Willis, but the point is the psychological distance that separates Peck in 1910 from the Reverend Orville Dewey in 1836.[32]

III

There were a thousand other ways by which the Americans were made aware of both the validity and the "otherness" of foreign cultures. Museums desirous to increase their stock of masterpieces bought heavily abroad, and so did millionaire collectors and commercial art galleries. Books were pirated, and then properly imported after the acceptance in 1891 of international copyright by the United States; the pirated books were often luridly got up in cheap paperback form.[33] "Foreign" restaurants—Chinese, German, French, Italian, Greek, and so on—multiplied in the Eastern cities. Immigrant groups enriched American life with customs ranging from processions on some Italian saint's day to the German or Scandinavian kaffeeklatsch. Learned men got their doctorates in Germany, learned Europeans lectured in America. The sentimental valentine, the comic valentine, the caricature, and the cartoon exhibit foreign influences.[34] Costumes and manners were borrowed from abroad—from Paris and the Court of St. James, to name two important sources. Music and drama were enriched. The ancient republican horror of "luxury" increasingly gave way to the importation of perfumes and French wines, lingerie and foreign jewelry, limited editions of books, porcelain figures, china, silverware, Scotch tweeds, Irish linen, and much else.

Moreover, Americans, or at least Americans of the middle and upper classes, were made aware of the importance of philosophical, theological, and aesthetic systems from afar; examples in philosophy include the vogue of Hegelianism in the United States, of various systems of European evolutionary philosophy, and the "foreign" elements fused into the pragmatism of William James.[35] One might also recall American interest in pessimism and the "philosophy" of the decadence, evident in the vogue of Schopenhauer and the *Rubáiyát* in this country, and the fame, however transient, of Max Nordau's *Degeneration*,[36] the self-conscious little magazines which exploited the aesthetic movement, and literary theory and criticism of the kind rep-

resented in Percival Pollard's *Their Day in Court* (1909), which, however, is but faintly decadent in tone. An incidental but important
phase of the belief that the end of the nineteenth century marked a
total decline in civilization was the re-enforcement of the stereotype
that the French were a sensual, pleasure-loving, and decadent nation,
the proof being the Dreyfus case, and the belief that "French dancing
girls" in side show or burlesque were products of the lascivious amo-
rality of Paris.

Of considerable importance to the cultural life of the nation were
the international contacts at the three great world fairs of the period
—the Centennial Exposition at Philadelphia in 1876, the World's
Columbian Exposition of 1893, and the St. Louis Louisiana Purchase
Exposition of 1904. At the Philadelphia Exposition Continental
painters were poorly represented, but England sent her best, Howells
found the vigor of Spain surprising, and an anonymous running account in the *Atlantic Monthly* (July–December 1876) emphasizes the
unexpected mingling of racial representatives and the merits of the
Japanese exhibit, the latter making everything else look "commonplace, almost vulgar." Some part, at least, of this glowing tribute deserves quotation:

> The gorgeousness of the specimens is equaled only by their exquisite del-
> icacy. . . . Here is the handicraft of those extremest Orientals, five, eight,
> eleven hundred years old, if we can believe it, with a grace and elegancy
> of design and fabulous perfection of workmanship which rival or excel
> the marvels of Italian ornamental art at its zenith; and as one of discern-
> ment standing by said, there is no decline nor degeneracy, no period of
> corruptness and coarseness, such as the Renaissance shows in its decay.
> . . . The Japanese seem to possess the secret which the modern pre-Ra-
> phaelites have striven for without success, the union of detail and effect.
> . . . The commonest object of pottery or cotton-stuff for daily use has a
> merit of design or color which it does not owe to oddity alone. . . .[37]

So far as one can distinguish among three rather incommensurable
events, the Philadephia Exposition was less notable for an intellectual program than for machinery and objects. By 1890, however, an
International Congress of Americanists had been held in Paris, where
a presidential address was delivered by Armand de Quatrefages,
"The Advent of Man in America," and this congress was sufficiently
prominent to justify reprinting the speech in the *Annual Report of
the Smithsonian Institution for 1892*.[38] That this congress (and oth-

ers like it) led the managers of the World's Columbian Exposition to speculate on the desirability of holding international meetings in Chicago cannot be asserted, but the Fair was notable, as I have earlier said, for the variety and maturity of the congresses that were held.[39]

The intellectual fare at Chicago was probably surpassed by that offered at St.Louis in 1904. Nothing less than universal knowledge was to be there embraced by the Congress of Arts and Science held under the auspices of a distinguished board of scholars—Nicholas Murray Bulter, William R. Harper, R.H.Jesse, Hugo Münsterberg, Simon Newcomb, Henry S.Pritchett, Herbert Putnam, and Albion W.Small, the director being Howard J.Rogers. The proceedings were published in eight volumes, which included addresses long and short and relevant bibliographies; and the congress considered philosophy, mathematics, politics, history, economics, law, religion, the languages, literature, art, all the sciences, sociology, technology, medicine, and education. If the attendance of foreign scholars was smaller than had been anticipated, nevertheless many of them came; and if, inevitably, Münsterberg's over-all scheme was attacked as too ambitious, there is plausibility in the assertion that the St. Louis Congress might be called the most notable assembly of scholars the modern world had seen. At any rate, American intellectual parochialism, if it ever existed, was now certainly dead; American scholars were prepared to associate on equal terms with scholars and scientists from the rest of the world.[40]

There was never a time when American magazines neglected foreign thought, but it is generally true of the ante-bellum period that much of the commentary on men, measures, and opinion overseas was bellicose, defensive, or propagandistic as embattled American writers sought to fend off influences deleterious to the republic, to democracy, and to Protestant Christianity. Much of it was, but of course not all; writers like Nathaniel Parker Willis strove to be cosmopolitan, and even when American periodical criticism battled against British arrogance or French immorality, it did not totally condemn European art, literature, and thought. After 1870, however, bellicosity weakens, the Arnoldian doctrine of knowing the best that has been said and thought in the world increases, and the range of materials dealing with the rest of the earth is widened. The *Atlantic Monthly* is commonly thought to have been, if not a parochial, at least a regional magazine, but any thoughtful examination of its issues from 1857 to 1914 will reveal the most amazing variety of travel articles, critical accounts of foreign masterpieces or current foreign writers, discussions of art, philosophy, religion, statesmanship, education, and politics in foreign lands. I select the *Atlantic* at random, but the same policy generally governed other "class" magazines such as *Scribner's* and *The Century*. When *The (American) Bookman* was founded in 1895 it gave almost as much space to foreign literature as it did to native writing, and to go through the files of *The Publishers' Weekly* (1872–1873—) is to be instructed in the immense hunger of readers and publishers for books from abroad. Scholarship has devoted laborious attention to the vogue in the United States of various foreign writers in this period—Turgenev, Zola, Ibsen, Verlaine, Baudelaire, Balzac, D'Annunzio, Verga, Björnson, Palacio Valdés, Tolstoi, Oscar Wilde, and many more, but the process of investigation has only begun and, moreover, academics tend to confine their researches to elite literature. Yet from 1865 to 1914, if one accepts as a gauge of popular taste, the tables of best sellers in Frank Luther Mott's *Golden Multitudes,* out of one hundred and seventy-three titles, seventy-one are by foreign authors; and if some of these rise no higher than Jules Verne, Ouida, and Hall Caine, other books widely read are by Dickens, George Eliot, Thomas Hardy, Karl Marx, R. L. Stevenson, and Rudyard Kipling. Magazine publication undoubtedly helped to popularize some of these names, since even *Munsey's Magazine* and *McClure's* found it profitable to serialize authors of the rank of Kipling, Hardy, Israel Zangwill, Stevenson, and Conan Doyle.[41] American taste was made more cosmopolitan by this general reading.

Moreover, this was the age of "sets": Balzac, Molière, Sue, Hugo, Paul de Kock, Dumas, Ibsen, Auerbach, Dickens, Thackeray, George Eliot, Scott, Wilkie Collins, and Stevenson were thus sold. Translation became a minor industry in the hands of craftsmen like Nathan Haskell Dole and Katharine Prescott Wormeley.[42] Other sets were got up for "libraries": *The Library of the World's Best Literature* in thirty volumes edited by Charles Dudley Warner (1896–1897), *The World's Great Classics* (1899–1900), *The World's Best Poetry,* ten volumes (1904), *The World's Wit and Humor* (1906), the *Harvard Classics* of somewhat ambiguous fame (1909–1910), *The Library of Literary Criticism* in eight volumes (1910), and the *German Classics* in twenty (1913–1914). These books, often attractively printed and bound, filled shelves in mansions erected by the newly rich, but they were also bought, often on the installment plan, by the middle class and others. They flooded public and school libraries and were purchased by, or given to, college and university libraries. To this day many of them are consulted by pupils, students, club members getting up papers on some foreign theme or author, and sometimes (tell it not in Gath, publish it not in the streets of Askelon) even by professors and specialists.

In an era when the reading of fiction and going to plays supplied the kind of entertainment now partitioned among books, the stage, movies, radio, and television, a good many Americans got their impressions of other peoples from the theater, short stories, and novels. These appealed to various segments of the public. The international novel as written by Francis Marion Crawford, Henry James, Edith Wharton, more occasionally by William Dean Howells (*The Lady of the Aroostook* demonstrates how the moral purity of Lydia Blood triumphs over European and American worldliness), and others has been frequently studied by scholarship and interpreted by criticism. Whatever else may be true of its varied examples, a general formula seems to be that the American hero or heroine, though he or she may be naïve, is more virtuous than the cynical foreign society into which the plot precipitates the central character. Even the subtleties of Henry James tend to rest on this elementary distinction. At lower levels than that represented by *The Portrait of a Lady* (1881), the black-white, goodie-baddie, American-foreigner distinction is cruder; for example, in the forgotten melodrama by Lem B. Parker, *Thorns and Orange Blossoms,* a dramatization of the Bertha M. Clay novel of that title, the haughty Duchess of Ryverswell with the aid of the villainous Carstone vainly tries to break the spirit and asperse the virtue of the suffering heroine, who, in the adaptation that made the round of the stock companies in the 1880s was, as I remember, an American.[43] It has been remarked that in the American theater and in much American fiction the villain tends to be dark-haired, dark-skinned, and, if possible, dark-eyed—characteristics attributed by popular lore to the Latin or Latin-American races—albeit Orientals, the cruel Russian with a knout and, after 1914, the brutal Prussians were also plausible.

Foreigners were, of course, not all wicked, and it would be an engaging task to number and examine virtuous Europeans in fiction

and on the stage. If male, they were sometimes younger sons of aristocratic families, but knighthood might flower anywhere, and the
invention or re-invention of historical romance in the late 1880s fostered the mythical European state—Graustark or Ruritania. A char
acteristic example is Richard Harding Davis's *The King's Jackal*
(1896), in which the worthless king of Messina, a monarchy not
found on any map, is surrounded by a set of precious rascals who,
under pretext of collecting money for the monarch to reconquer his
kingdom, are really feathering their own nests. But a quixotic American journalist and a queenly American girl get involved; in the best
light opera manner they persuade the lesser conspirators to install
the little prince rather than the villainous father in the kingdom;
some of the corrupt court still cherishes idealism; and a typical passage has to do with the appearance in the king's entourage of Gordon, the American reporter. The king instructs Kaloney, a leading
courtier, to pay Gordon whatever blackmail is necessary to get rid of
him. Says Kaloney: "Your Majesty is thinking of the Hungarian Jews
at Vienna, who live on *chantage* and the Monte Carlo progaganda
fund. This man is not in their class; he is not to be bought. I said he
was an American." [44]

"Actual" historical romance was not always more veracious; the villain in Mary Johnston's *To Have and to Hold* (1899–1900), a story
of Jamestown, is somewhat improbably named Lord Carnal; and the
purveyors of this sort of fictional confection continued the costume
novel of Scott, Cooper, and Dumas without being able to equal these
masters in creating unforgettable characters. From this sweeping
judgment I would of course exclude certain triumphs; for example,
the Saracinesca series of Francis Marion Crawford and his remarkable evocation of Philip II in *In the Palace of the King*.[45] But if the
international novel and historical romance too often took the easy
way out of one of the difficult problems in novels of manners, they
nonetheless placed vivid images of foreign lands and characters under
the eyes not only of an elite group but also of the common reader
who got his books out of the public libraries or from reading clubs.[46]

IV

But American energy cannot exhaust itself in travel to Europe, in
museums, in the importation of jewels and antiques, bibelots and cas-

tles, translations and sets of books, nor can it be always attending lectures, discussion clubs, and extension courses to learn what the Old World is like. The cosmopolitan spirit becomes paradoxical, at once tireless and in need of repose. It discovers the charm of the exotic, a word that can be defined only in terms of the sensibility which experiences it. Dictionary definitions confine themselves to variants of "foreign," "extrinsic," "barbarous," "imported," and the like, but, as Fowler says, "exotic" is a vague word, and in our national usage it implies that strangeness which, in a phrase borrowed from Bacon, Edgar Allan Poe described as a necessary component of exquisite beauty. Sometimes the strangeness is more sought after than the beauty. "Exotic" implies rarity: "exotic" foods imply a special curiosity of the palate, "exotic" clothes, or ornamentation, or, for that matter, personality, connotes languor, sensuousness, sensuality, sexuality, a revolt against the commonplace that may be either active or passive or both. The sensibility that seeks out the exotic usually associates the quality with remote, tropic, primitive, or "different" lands. Examples may clarify. Thus, in the dictionary sense the English sparrow is, or was, an exotic brought from abroad, but nobody now applies the adjective to this little pest, whereas the myna bird, at least in the first flush of fashion, was thought to have an exotic quality. French restaurants are not exotic; Polynesian restaurants declare they are. The waltz, originating in Europe, was never so dubbed, but the burlesque shows advertise a specially sensual striptease artist as an exotic dancer. The isles of Greece are not exotic, but the islands of Oceania seem so, at least to many Americans. I shall therefore mean by "exotic" a special variety of experience, commonly sensuous, often sensual, associated with the South, the semitropical, the tropical, the ancient, the primitive, the intensely colorful, the strange; and to this I add a special interpretation of the Orient by some Americans. The exotic is pagan, not Christian; amoral not ethical; lazy rather than laboring; languid and never strenuous.

What I may call the exoticism of the soul entered American writing before the Civil War, or may be seem by reading the poems of Freneau (for example, "The Beauties of Santa Cruz"), or the poetry and prose of Poe, as in "Romance":

> Romance, who loves to nod and sing
> With drowsy head and folded wing,

Among the green leaves as they shake
Far down within some shadowy lake,
To me a painted paroquet
Hath been,

and in the prose poem, "The Domain of Arnheim," with its "dream-
like intermingling to the eye of tall slender Eastern trees—bosky
shrubberies—flocks of golden and crimson birds—lily-fringed lakes"
and much else. This invention of imaginary exoticism is continued by variations as different as those in Edgar Saltus, H.P.Lovecraft
in *The Shadow Out of Time,* and Poictesme, the dream country
of James Branch Cabell, in which Dom Manuel and Jurgen had
their curious experiences. I suppose the first full-length evocation
of the actual exotic must be Melville's *Typee* (1846), with its
lush scenery, its bevies of naked girls, its pagan freedom, and its
picture of Fayaway, perhaps the most perfect representation of sensuous female loveliness in the American nineteenth century:

Her free, pliant figure was the very perfection of female grace and
beauty. Her complexion was a rich and mantling olive, and when watching the glow upon her cheeks I could almost swear that beneath the
transparent medium there lurked the blushes of a faint vermilion. The
face of this girl was a rounded oval, and each feature as perfectly formed
as the heart or imagination of man could desire. Her full lips, when
parted with a smile, disclosed teeth of a dazzling whiteness; and when
her rosy mouth opened with a burst of merriment, they looked like the
milk white seeds of the "arta," a fruit of the valley, which, when cleft in
twain, shows them reposing in rows on either side, imbedded in the red
and juicy pulp. Her hair of the deepest brown, parted irregularly in the
middle, flowed in natural ringlets over her shoulders, and whenever she
chanced to stoop, fell over and hid from view her lovely bosom. Gazing
into the depths of her strange blue eyes, when she was in a contemplative mood, they seemed most placid yet unfathomable; but when illuminated by some lively emotion, they beamed upon the beholder like stars.
The hands of Fayaway were as soft and delicate as those of any countess.
. . . Her feet, though wholly exposed, were as diminutive and fairly
shaped as those which peep from beneath the skirts of a Lima lady's
dress. The skin of this young creature, from continual ablutions and the
use of mollifying ointments, was inconceivably smooth and soft. . . . The
easy unstudied graces of a child of nature like this, breathing from infancy an atmosphere of perpetual summer, and nurtured by the simple
fruits of the earth, enjoying a perfect freedom from care and anxiety, and

removed effectually from all injurious tendencies, strike the eye in a manner which cannot be portrayed.[47]

One did not have to go to the Pacific for sensuous experience. During the Civil War Thomas Wentworth Higginson became colonel of the first Negro regiment in the Union army, a regiment that operated chiefly along the coast of South Carolina and in Florida. Higginson recorded his experiences in *Army Life in a Black Regiment* (1870), commonly classed as a document in race relationships, which it is, but it is also a fascinating account of the way a Unitarian clergyman transformed himself into a sea-island pagan. He lets himself go, he yawns, he expands, he accepts and delights in all that is warm, colorful, lazy, and exotic. Once or twice remembering the "pure, clean, innocent odors" of a Massachusetts spring, he nevertheless devotes a whole chapter (VI) to the sensuous (and dangerous) pleasure of swimming during a warm Southern night. He accepts this strange world of profuse and tangled vegetation, of bare gray sand that turns yellow when you dig into it, of magnolias and oysters, death and luxuriance, flowery lanes and green alleys through whose miles of arching roses he endlessly rode. The sea, in which the sun sets like a great illuminated bubble, is as romantic as the land. When he is sent to Jacksonville, he hears the mockingbirds sing all night long, their notes trickling down through the sweet air of the blossoming bough. Can this be America? In South Carolina

> I look out from the broken windows of this forlorn plantation house, through avenues of great live-oaks, with their hard, shining leaves, and their branches hung with a universal drapery of soft, long moss, like fringe-trees struck with grayness. Below, the sandy soil, scantly covered with coarse grass, bristles with sharp palmettoes and aloes; all the vegetation is stiff, shining, semi-tropical, with nothing soft or delicate in its texture.

As for the troops at night:

> All over the camp the lights glimmer in the tents, and as I sit at my desk in the open doorway, there come mingled sounds of stir and glee. Boys laugh and shout; a feeble flute stirs somewhere in some tent, not an officer's; a drum throbs far away in another; wild kildeer-plover flit and wail above us, like the haunting souls of dead slave-masters . . . from a neighboring cook-fire comes the monotonous sound of that strange festival, half pow-wow, half prayer-meeting, which they know only as a "shout."

He writes of "the brilliant fire lighting up their red trousers and gleaming from their shining black faces . . . the mighty limbs of a great live-oak with the weird moss swaying in the smoke, and the high moon gleaming faintly through." This mingling of sensuality and death could not be further from Walden Pond.[48]

Another masterpiece is Lafcadio Hearn's *Two Years in the French West Indies* (1890), which differs from other travel accounts of the Caribbean by its intermingled sorrow, intense color, sense of otherness, and the perpetual presence of death or decay:

> How gray seem the words of poets in the presence of this Nature! . . . The enormous silent poem of color and light—(you who know only the North do not know color, do not know light!)—of sea and sky, of the woods and peaks, so far surpasses imagination . . . defying all power of expression. . . . Nature realizes your most hopeless ideals of beauty, even as one gives toys to a child. And the sight of this supreme terrestrial expression of creative magic numbs thought. In the great centres of civilization we admire and study only the results of mind . . . here one views only the work of Nature,—but Nature in all her primeval power. . . . Man here seems to bear scarcely more relation to the green life about him than the insect; and the results of human effort seem impotent by comparison with the operation of those vast blind forces which clothe the peaks and crown the dead craters [of Martinique] with impenetrable forest. The air itself seems inimical to thought.

Even the artist, he said, would feel his helplessness, since the "luminosities of tropic foliage could only be imitated in fire." While the Americans were celebrating the doctrine of progress and Teddy Roosevelt was writing about *The Winning of the West* by sturdy members of the Germanic races, Hearn was meditating on disintegration:

> There is something in tropical ruin peculiarly and terribly impressive: this luxuriant, evergreen, ever-splendid Nature consumes the results of human endeavor so swiftly, buries memories so profoundly, distorts the labors of generations so grotesquely, that one feels here, as nowhere else, how ephemeral man is, how intense and how tireless the effort necessary to preserve his frail creations even a little while from the vast unconscious forces antagonistic to all stability, to all factitious equilibrium.

How the odor of death and fecundity hung over St. George in Grenada!

. . . here the powers of disintegration are extraordinary, and the very air would seem to have the devouring force of an acid. All surfaces and angles are yielding to the attacks of time, weather, and microscopic organisms; paint peels, stucco falls, tiles tumble, stones slip out of place, and in every chink tiny green things nestle, propagating themselves through the jointures and dislocating the masonry. There is an appalling mouldiness, an exaggerated mossiness—the mystery and the melancholy of a city deserted. Old warehouses without signs, huge and void, are opened regularly every day for so many hours; yet the business of the aged merchants within seems to be a problem;—you might fancy those gray men were always waiting for ships that sailed away a generation ago, and will never return.

This forsaken city, "patched with the viridescence of ruin," is a far cry even from Hawthorne's customhouse in Salem served by half a dozen Rip Van Winkles, two or three of whom, gouty and rheumatic or perhaps bedridden, never appeared during the winter months but crept out into the warm sunshine of May or June and betook themselves to bed again. Salem prolonged life; Martinique seemed intent upon destroying it.[49]

Melville was of course not the first or the last to find sensuous beauty in Oceania—the number of British books on the theme, many of them read by Americans, is legion.[50] I must confine myself to two or three prerogative instances. In 1873 Charles Warren Stoddard published his extraordinary *South-Sea Idyls;* a new edition brought from Howells a paragraph in which he remembered his joy in accepting "A Prodigal in Tahiti" for the *Atlantic* and in recollecting how Stoddard's stories "rise up like old memories of delight—graceful shapes, careless, beautiful, with a kind of undying youth in them." For once this minor literary figure struck a major note. His book is still remarkable. He tried to convert a native, Kána-aná, to Christianity, but the native returned home and died, and the conscience-stricken Stoddard wrote:

I can see you, my beloved, sleeping, naked, in the twilight of the west. The winds kiss you with pure and fragrant lips. The sensuous waves invite you to their embrace. Earth again offers you her varied store. Partake of her offering, and be satisfied. Return, O troubled soul! to your first and natural joys; they were given you by the Divine hand that can do no ill. In the smoke of the sacrifice ascends the prayer of your race. . . . Alas, Kána-aná! As the foam of the sea you love, as the fragrance of the flower you worship, shall your precious body be wasted, and your untrammelled soul pass to the realms of your fathers!

This is pure Gauguin. And here is Stoddard describing a dance on Tahiti when the "palms rustled their silver plumes aloft in the moonlight; the sea panted upon its sandy bed in heavy sleep; the nightblooming cereus opened its waxen chambers and gave forth its treasured sweets."

> . . . the dancers posed for a moment with their light drapery gathered about them and held carelessly in one hand. Anon the music chimed forth—a reiteration of chords caught from the birds' treble and the wind's bass; full and resounding syllables, richly poetical, telling of orgies and of mysteries of the forbidden revels in the charmed valleys of the gods, hearing which it were impossible not to be wrought to madness; and the dancers thereat went mad, dancing with infinite gesticulation, dancing to whirlwinds of applause till the undulation of their bodies was serpentine, and at last in a frenzy they shrieked with joy, threw off their garments, and were naked as the moon.[51]

But I suppose the most distinguished purveyors of Oceanic exoticism among the Americans were John La Farge and Henry Adams, both too fastidious to do more than hold island life at arm's length. Adams, who wrote Elizabeth Cameron that "one's imagination is the best map for travellers," was as often repelled as allured by Oceania —his account of visiting Stevenson on Samoa is notable for its emphasis upon slovenliness—though his account of a "siva" dance on Samoa (in the aftermath, "general nudeness most strangely mixed with a sense of propriety") is sympathetic. Yet when he got to Tahiti, he could write: "I never saw a people that seemed so hopelessly bored as the Tahitians" and he complained of "this eternal charm of middle-aged melancholy." But "the sensation of seeing extremely fine women, with superb forms, perfectly unconscious of undress, and yet evidently aware of their beauty and dignity, is worth a week's seasickness to experience," and he sympathized with La Farge's aesthetic excitement. It is characteristic that, except for letters home, Adams' chief memorial to life in the South Seas is a historical work and that, although he learned something about color and tried to paint under La Farge's tutelage, he seems to have left these Edens without a sigh.[52]

Perhaps because he was a painter, La Farge managed to be less morally intransigent. Life on Samoa seemed to him "Homeric" in its "splendid nakedness." "From out of the darkness, as if from out of the shade of antiquity" on one occasion, a half-naked girl, "something as beautiful and more heroic than the Bacchanals that are enrolled on the Greek vases," stepped forward to dance. The colors intoxicated him (as, indeed, they stirred Adams):

> . . . the blue and green that belongs to the classics; that is painted in lines of Homer; that Titian guessed at, once, under a darker sky; and far off the long sway and cadence of the surf like the movement of ancient verse—the music of the Odyssey. . . . If . . . you can gather my impression, can you see something of an old beauty, always known, in these new pictures, you will understand why the Greek Homer is in my mind; all Greece, the poetry of form and colour that comes from her, as well as her habits; just as the Samoan youngster who rose shining from the sea to meet us, all brown and red, with a red hibiscus fastened in his hair by a grass knot as beautiful as any carved ornament, was the Bacchus of Tintoretto's picture, making offering to Ariadne.[53]

But La Farge's water colors, mildly charming, lack the depth of Gauguin's oils.[54]

Even under the vague definition I have set up, the American response to the Far East becomes difficult to analyze. American taste for chinoiserie descends from the eighteenth century, and aside from vulgar notions about Chinese sexuality, joss houses, and opium dens, it is problematical whether things Chinese served greatly to quench any thirst for the exotic.[55] Books like Arthur Henderson Smith's admirable *Chinese Characteristics* (1890) offer no conceivable basis for exoticism. On the other hand, in *Java Head,* a novel slightly beyond my chronological limits, Joseph Hergesheimer wishes to create an ironical context for the suicide of Taou Yuen, the exotic Chinese wife. "A connoisseur of the particular period," as an editor calls him, Hergesheimer heaps up a long list of Oriental objects in a Salem house of Hawthorne's time:

> . . . she stopped to examine the East India money on the lowest shelf of a locked corner cupboard. There was a tiresome string of cash with a rattan twisted through their square holes; silver customs taels, and mace and candareen; Chinese gold leaf and Fukien dollars; coins from Cochin China in the shape of India ink, with raised edges and characters; old Carolus hooked dollars; Sycee silver ingots, smooth and flat above, but roughly oval on the lower surface, not unlike shoes; Japanese obangs,

their gold stamped and beaten out almost as broad as a hand's palm; mohurs and pieces from Singapore; Dutch guilders from Java; and the small silver and gold drops of Siam called tical.

Laurel Ammidon is bored by all these as "with dragging feet" she makes a "reluctant progress to the piano." So, I suspect, is the reader.[56] I doubt that the collection makes any appeal to the senses, or to languor, or to anything except a mild distaste for the falsely erudite.

Since we are in an atmosphere and an area where exact scholarship cannot much help us,[57] let us content ourselves for the moment with the American response to Japan. That country was, as all the world knows, "opened" by an American naval officer (Matthew Perry's *Narrative of the Expedition of an American Squadron to the China Seas and Japan* appeared in 1859), and the arrival of the first Japanese mission to Washington excited much interest, as did the Japanese exhibits at the Philadelphia Centennial of 1876 and the World's Columbian Exposition of 1893. One must again distinguish, however hazily, between curiosity value and the allure of the unknown. The impact of Japanese art upon American sensibilities was increased (or prepared for) by its vogue in Europe, and there are those who point to the high-piled female hair-do and female clothing styles as representing an exotic Japanese influence. Gilbert and Sullivan's *The Mikado* (1885) had an enormous run, paving the way for such later theatrical successes as *The Geisha, The Mayor of Tokyo, Cherry Blossom River, A Flower of Yeddo,* and *The Lady of the Weeping Willow Tree.* Sir Edwin Arnold, who had considerable following in the United States, produced a melodrama, *Adzuma; or, the Japanese Wife* in 1893, but the love-'em-and-leave-'em theme had its greatest success in fiction, stage, and music, with *Madame Butterfly*.[58] The vogue of the poster, an art form that owed much to Japanese influence, was in turn transmuted by magazine illustrators into a fusion of exoticism and Pre-Raphaelitism.[59] Articles by painters fascinated with Japanese life and art began appearing in upper-class periodicals; for example, Theodore Wores, "An American Artist in Japan" in *The Century* for September 1889, and a series by Robert Blum, "An Artist in Japan," which began in *Scribner's* in April 1893. Then there were books, for example, John La Farge's *An Artist's Letters from Japan* (1897). I do not know when the Japanese lantern first invaded the American garden and the Japanese kimono first came into the dressing-room, but by the 1880s they were giving an additional foreign touch to the world of Grover Cleveland. In this connection John Singer Sargent's pleasant painting in the Boston Museum of Fine Arts of some little girls with Japanese lanterns should not be forgotten. But it would be naïve to assume that because an artist or an art collector writes about Japan he is per se contributing to exoticism; *Japan Day by Day* and *Japanese Homes and Their Surroundings,* both by Edward Sylvester Morse, scientist, traveler, and expert on Japanese art and culture, are equally substantial as public monuments.[60]

Although in the 1890s the influence of Japanese art, combined with a "decadent" enthusiasm for Aubrey Beardsley, influenced American pictorialism in the direction of strangeness and sensuousness, and remembering also that Ernest F. Fenollosa was an influential art collector and the author of *Epochs of Chinese and Japanese Art* (1922),[61] one can still assert that the principal architect in developing the image of Japan as a land of delicate exoticism was Lafcadio Hearn. Hearn operated from two principal philosophical assumptions. One, evident in his previously mentioned book on the French West Indies, is explicitly stated in a letter to Henry Krehbiel, written from New Orleans in the 1880s: "I eat and drink and converse with members of the races you detest like the son of Odin that you are. I see beauty here all around me,—a strange, tropical, intoxicating beauty. I consider it my artistic duty to let myself be absorbed into this new life, and study its form and colour and passion." The other is laid down in a letter to his brother from Japan in 1892: "The heathenism of Japan is infinitely better religion than the Christianity of Christendom, and shows better results."[62]

Whatever his individual peculiarities and however disappointing he found it to become a Japanese citizen, Hearn, a perfectionist in art (he once worked eight months on seventy-three lines) repudiated "Puritanism," the genteel tradition, and the United States. Hearn's books on Japan fall into two general categories. The first (which frequently includes Chinese themes) was devoted to the occult, to mystery, to ghosts, to strange religious rituals. The second, solid, informational, and penetrating, was an excellent interpretation of Japanese society and history. The first has titles like *Some Chinese Ghosts* (1887), *Gleanings in Buddha Fields* (1897), *Exotics and Retrospectives* (1898), *Japanese Fairy Tales* (1893–1903), *In Ghostly*

Japan (1899), *Kwaidan* (1904), and *Shadowings* (1900–1907). The masterwork of the second category is presumably *Japan: An Attempt at an Interpretation* (1904). Nothing in Hearn's interpretation prepared Americans for Pearl Harbor, but the style in which books of the first class are presented attaches sensibility to exoticism, as in this passage from *Shadowings:*

> The moon had not yet risen; but the vast of the night was all seething with stars, and bridged by a Milky Way of extraordinary brightness. There was no wind; but the sea, far as sight could reach, was running in ripples of fire,—a vision of infernal beauty. Only the ripplings were radiant (between them was blackness absolute);—and the luminosity was amazing. Most of the undulations were yellow like candle-flame; but there were crimson lampings also,—and azure, and orange, and emerald. And the sinuous flickering of all seemed, not a pulsing of many waters, but a laboring of many wills,—a fleeting conscious and monstrous,—a writhing and a swarming incalculable, as of dragon-life in some depth of Erebus.
>
> And life indeed was making the sinister splendor of that spectacle——but life infinitesimal, and of ghostliest delicacy,—life illimitable, yet ephemeral, flaming and fading in ceaseless alternation over the whole round of waters even to the sky-line, above which, in the vaster abyss, other countless lights were throbbing with other spectral colors.[63]

This passage leads into a Buddha-like meditation on the all and nothingness of individuality; and though it does not specifically concern Japan, I cite it as showing the atmosphere in which Hearn bathed his tales of the supernatural and the weird. An admirable supplement to Hearn is Percival Lowell's *Occult Japan; or, The Way of the Gods: An Esoteric Study of Japanese Personality and Possession* (1894).[64]

It would be tedious to hunt down all those who made trips up the Nile, or visited Algeria, or went to Constantinople, or loitered in Mexico, or tried to penetrate the secrets of some strange non-American life. Hearn's interest in Buddhism was not unique. Trumbull Stickney in a poem called "Oneiropolis" pictures Buddha looking on ancient Athens:

> A dying town filled of a feeble race,
> Small gossips of their all-expressing tongue,
> Dancers and frolickers, philosophers

> Drunken and sense-tied to the trembling world.
> Hither from fifty climes men come and come,
> Women and children come to see—'tis strange!—
> This city . . .

In two sonnets he advised Americans to live blindly and upon the hour, since

> The Hanging Gardens were a dream
> That over Persian roses flew to kiss
> The curlèd lashes of Semiramis.
> Troy never was, nor green Skamander stream.
>
> .   .   .   .
>
> The world is very old and nothing is.[65]

And in 1908 William Sturgis Bigelow, a convert, delivered at Harvard the Ingersoll lecture on immortality under the title, *Buddhism and Immortality*. If Buddhism denies the senses, it accentuated strangeness, at least from the American point of view.

The Saracen and Mohammedan cultures also made their contribution. Most American travelers to the Near East either broke into solemn raptures, or lamented decay, or contented themselves with the picturesque. A remarkable exception (a book published just before the Civil War) is Bayard Taylor's *The Lands of the Saracen; or, Pictures of Palestine, Asia Minor, Sicily, and Spain,* into which that inveterate voyager managed to inject a considerable degree of sensuous charm, whether ascending "the celebrated Ladder of Tyre" in Lebanon, at the base of which "the sea rushes with a dull, heavy boom, like distant thunder" into the caves it has made, the whole mountain being "a heap of balm; a bundle of sweet spices," or describing the village of Eden, whose "women are beautiful, with sprightly, intelligent faces, quite different from the stupid Mohametan females" and whose girls of ten or twelve "were lovely as angels." The two "set pieces" in the volume are the tenth chapter, "The Vision of Hasheesh," quite as powerful as De Quincey's opium eater and more convincing, and the eleventh chapter containing a long, detailed, and sensuous description of a Turkish bath, admiration for the nude male body, and a final effect of floating in sensuous peace:

> Mind and body are drowned in delicious rest; and we no longer remember what we are. We only know that there is an Existence somewhere in

the air, and that wherever it is, and whatever it may be, it is happy. More and more dim grows the picture. The colors fade and blend into each other, and finally merge into a bed of rosy clouds, flooded with the radiance of some unseen sun. Gentlier than "tired eyelids upon tired eyes," sleep lies upon our senses: a half-conscious sleep, wherein we know that we behold light and inhale fragrance. As gently, the clouds dissipate into air, and we are born again into the world. The Bath is at an end.[66]

His powerful description of an eruption of Mt. Etna (chapter XXXI) belongs rather to the category of the sublime than of the exotic.

But the *Rubáiyát of Omar Khayyám* as translated by Edward Fitz-Gerald was, as it were, the diploma piece of Muslim exoticism. Of this celebrated masterpiece of skepticism, sensuousness, eroticism, and wine, the Library of Congress up to 1957 held about one hundred and twenty editions printed in America (some of them not translated by FitzGerald), and many British printings and versions in other languages. Celebrated issues were illustrated by Elihu Vedder, Willy Pogany, or artists purporting to be Persians, who, however, did not neglect to include in their pictures some rendering of a cypress-slender minister of wine. In 1896 Liza Lehmann brought out her popular cantata, "In a Persian Garden," based on FitzGerald and sung incessantly in music schools, drawing rooms, and concerts. In 1897 John Hay addressed the Omar Khayyám Club of London in a speech often reprinted. He said he could never forget his emotion when the Fitz-Gerald version first swam into his ken, and went on to describe the wide diffusion of the *Rubáiyát* in America:

> In the Eastern States his adepts form an esoteric set; the beautiful volume of drawings by Mr. Vedder is a center of delight and suggestion wherever it exists. In the cities of the West you will find the Quatrains one of the most thoroughly read books in every club library. I heard them quoted once in one of the most lonely and desolate spots of the high Rockies . . . [by] a frontiersman.[67]

The poem was parodied—"The Rubáiyát of a Persian Kitten," "The Rubáiyát of a Red-Headed Office-Girl," and so on. FitzGerald offered a safe exoticism that fitted into the fin-de-siècle mood of the 1890s, a fusion of the remote and the controlled, so appealing that young bicyclists took their best girls out for a spin, rested in some shady nook, and, leaning on an elbow, recited with appropriate emotions:

A Book of Verses underneath the Bough,
A Jug of Wine, a Loaf of Bread—and Thou
Beside me singing in the Wilderness—
Oh, Wilderness were Paradise enow!

Sometimes he brought along a banjo. This was a far cry from Faya-way, but the line of descent was, in a sense, direct. Omar's ladies were not, at any rate, teachers in the Baptist Sunday school.

Exoticism extended downward into the masses.[68] In 1878 people sang "Aloha Oe," said to be by Queen Liliuokalani of Hawaii; in 1888 Pinsuti's "Bedouin Love Song"; in 1902 Rosamond Johnson's "Under the Bamboo Tree"; in 1911 Irving Berlin's "There's a Girl in Havanna"; in 1916 Raymond Hubbell's "Poor Butterfly." Reginald De Koven produced *The Begum* in 1887, *The Mandarin* in 1896. Victor Herbert came along with *The Wizard of the Nile* in 1895, *The Ameer* in 1899, and *The Rose of Algeria* in 1908. Gustav Kerker produced *Kismet* in 1895. Joe Howard did *The Isle of Bong Bong* in 1905 and *His Highness the Bey* that same year. *Mexicana* by Ray-mond Hubbell was staged in 1906; and Gustav Luders wrote *The Sho-gun* in 1904 and *The Great Mogul* in 1907. A kind of geographi-cal fever swept popular song and the musical stage, as if exoticism were a necessary parallel to our adventures in Cuba, Puerto Rico, and the Philippine Islands. And by and by Theda Bara ("Arab Death" respelled) was to be Cleopatra (1918), Anna May Wong starred in *In Old San Francisco* (Chinatown, of course), 1927, Clara Bow was theoretically nude in *Hula* (1927), and Gilda Gray brought us back to Fayaway in *Aloma of the South Seas* (1926). And, ah! Ro-dolpho Alfonzo Raffaelo Pierre Filibert Guglielmi Di Valentina d'Antonguolla, better known as Rudolph Valentino, in the twentieth century was to show a million American women what Arab passion is in that immortal moving picture called *The Sheik*.[69]

Under the influence of the Eastlake school of decoration and furni-ture design, and the rage for colorful "action" pictures depicting a harem, or a Moorish slave, or Turkish cavalry in action, the middle-class American home went *chi-chi* and exotic in the 1880s and 1890s. A solitary statue of Clytie would no longer do. The hallway, the "den," some corner of the drawing room, or a section of the library began to sprout revolving glass globes with knobs of color, blue, green, orange, crimson, hiding the Welsbach burner or what Howells called the electrics, stained glass windowpanes (or a facsimile of

them) overlooking a turn in the stairway, a Turkish corner complete
with ottoman, tabouret, brass coffeepot, and a nargileh, Moorish di-
vans with Persian carpets beside them on the floor, Buddhas seated
among potted palms, a sleek Nubian in a red fez overlooking a fountain, the basin of which contained goldfish, a wall lined with imitation leather on which hung a scimitar, some chains, or an oil painting of veiled Mohammedan beauties or a print of Chinese maidens
stoically confronting this cultural confusion. American Victorianism
was nothing if not energetic, and when it went in for exotic things, it
overrode all considerations of culture and country and cult. "Exotic"
motives, moreover, played their parts in general architecture as well
—Egyptian gateways still lead into the Mount Auburn Cemetery in
Cambridge, a "Persian" temple of the Bahai faith stands just outside
of Evanston, Illinois, and American "mosques" were built to house
the local clubhouse of the Nobles of the Mystic Shrine, not to speak
of Keith and Albee vaudeville and, eventually, "circus" movie houses.
If the reader is confused by this wealth of borrowings, so were the
borrowers.[70]

Nor has the appeal of exoticism faded from the world of the hy-
drogen bomb. It is a major component of what I may call commercialized cosmopolitanism, as the bravura advertising of travel agencies, airlines, and shipping companies amply demonstrates. These
organizations long to assist you in your search for color, romance, excitement, the sensuous, "difference" and, more discreetly, the sensual
—as their posters, travel folders, publicity for plane trips (a perfectly
trained Japanese stewardess in native costume at your elbow), and
the booklets describing pleasure cruises, hotel resorts, and beaches
exist to show. Always the picture is one of idleness and sensuous
charm. Swimmers are as nearly naked as Madison Avenue dares them
to be. The beggars are picturesque, the servants devoted and smiling.
Others may have to work; the American tourist has only the whimsi-
cal duty of sensations. Other lands are per se exotic; if they have social welfare problems, misery, or slums, the tourist need take no responsibility. For him the world has become a picture-book with
exotic scented pages. He has merely to visit distant lands; he is under
no obligation to understand them.

ADDENDUM

My discussion is confined to what seem to me important tendencies in the expression of American responses to cultures other than their own in the half-century. Since all American civilization is largely made up of other-world patterns, transplanted to the New World and adapted to an environment forever changing, the industry of scholars has been devoted to these "foreign" sources of American life and to American responses to other cultures. Any history of theology, science, technology, the social sciences, business, education, the fine arts, or literature in this country must at some time be concerned with the adaptation or refusal of Old World precedents, and consider responses and parallels in theory and practice between this republic and other nations. Anything from representative government to "mod" styles, immigration and architecture, the railway train and the organ grinder, the parasol and social Darwinism, the problem play and interchangeable parts, photography and diamond-cutting, rock-and-roll rhythms and the Washington Monument—these and a thousand other items owe something, sometimes their very origin, to other parts of the world. Even if one knew enough to do so, merely to list the relevant books and articles would be an impossible chore.

Bibliographical guides and special treatises, whether for individual countries or for particular occupations, abound. Perhaps a few examples will be suggestive. Thus for philosophy one can consult Herbert W. Schneider's *A History of American Philosophy*, 2d ed. (New York, 1963) for valuable hints; and in religion the last (bibliographical) volume of James Ward Smith and A. Leland Jamison, eds., *Religion in American Life*, 4 vols. (Princeton, 1961———). For a list of American travelers abroad see the bibliographies attached to the various chapters on travel literature in the *Cambridge History of American Literature*, 3 vols. in 4 (New York, 1917–1921), and for a more selective one the section on "American Writers and Books Abroad" in the bibliographical volume of the *Literary History of the United States*, 3d ed. (New York, 1963); one should consult both the material on pp. 356–70 and that on pp. 66–67 of the "Bibliography Supplement" (1958), rather awkwardly bound in at the back. A section on foreign influences on American writing occupies pp. 353–64 of

Lewis Leary, *Articles on American Literature, 1900–1950* (Durham, 1954), which can be supplemented by the continuing bibliographies in *American Literature* (1929——) and *American Quarterly* (1949——). The relations of German and American culture have been explored by Henry A. Pochmann and Arthur R. Schultz in *Bibliography of German Culture in America to 1940* (Madison, 1954) and Pochmann's *German Culture in America: Philosophical and Literary Influences, 1600–1900* (Madison, 1961). Something on the same scale though not in depth is Stanley T. Williams, *The Spanish Background of American Literature*, 2 vols. (New Haven, 1955)

Perhaps because the field is both obvious and enormous, there is not now, and possibly there never will be, a similar large-scale study for Anglo-American relationships; one can get a glimpse of thorough scholarship in this area by reading a monograph like Louise Greer's *Browning and America* (Chapel Hill, 1952), which tells us something, among other things, about the Browning Clubs. The same difficulty appears in the case of France. A representative study is Albert J. Salvan, *Zola aux États-Unis, Brown University Studies*, Vol. VIII (Providence, 1943). When one there reads that some of Zola's novels appeared under such lurid titles as *A Woman's Heart; or, A Stray Leaf from the Book of Love* (1880) and *A Fatal Conquest; or, Buried in the Ashes of a Ruined Home* (1883) one learns something about what Americans in the 1880s thought of as "French." (Yet even as early as 1839 Samuel Ward defended Balzac: see John Stafford, "Samuel Ward's Defense of Balzac's 'Objective' Fiction," *American Literature*, 24(2):167–76, May 1952.) Italy offers interesting difficulties since, except in sculpture of the Thorvaldsen-Canova sort, there was no "Italian style" as there was a "Nazarene" style for Americans to adopt. Still, tourists, clergymen, sculptors, painters, businessmen, and dilettanti all went there. One can see the pattern of their curiosity in Paul R. Baker, *The Fortunate Pilgrims: Americans in Italy, 1800–1860* (Cambridge, 1964) and various special articles such as Otto Wittman, Jr., "The Italian Experience (American Artists in Italy, 1830–1875)," *American Quarterly*, 4(1):3–15 (Spring 1952). For more general accounts consult Philip Rahv, ed., *Discovery of Europe: The Story of American Experiences in the Old World* (Boston, 1947); David F. Bowers, ed., *Foreign Influences in American Life* (Princeton, 1944); and Cushing Strout's rather mannered *The American Image of the Old World* (New York, 1963). Asia, the Pacific, and Africa still lack this kind of overview, though Daniel Stempel in "Lafcadio Hearn: Interpreter of Japan," *American Literature,* 20(1):1–19 (March 1948) makes out an excellent case for assuming that Hearn had as keen an insight into Japanese life as Bryce displayed for American life in *The American Commonwealth.*

VIII

Landscape and Microscope

—To man the earth seems altogether
No more a mother but a step-dame rather.

—D U B A R T A S

I

IN ALL PHILOSOPHIES man is a part of nature. He may be a part so differentiated from the material world as to think himself an alien in it; he may be thought of as a special creation partaking of many natural characteristics but not wholly one of nature's children; he may seem to be one with the flora and fauna of the world; or he may even think that from the point of view of the forces that surround him he is an inferior physical animal able to cope with externality only by virtue of his mysterious brain. Nature is the source of all energy, whether energy takes shape as thought, as fuel, or as raw material for exploitation. On great occasions titanic bursts of natural energy—a volcano, an earthquake, a tidal wave—overwhelm these puny creatures, men, and kill them off like insects. Thinking backward into time, man finds that immense tides of energy beyond his comprehension have shaped the universe, and looking inward into things modern man discovers the vast destructive powers inherent in the atom. There are of course score upon score of theories about nature, which now appear as majesty, now as comfort, now as friend, and now as destruction; poets, theologians, metaphysicians, and in these latter days scientists have struggled over the centuries to articulate a theory of nature—or of nature, God, and man—that will not only be consistent with itself but also picture nature as something more than a cosmic deathtrap. One fact dominant in many theories, though it is often politely veiled, is that nature not only nourishes man but also offers him opportunities for exploitation; that is, human energy can release and control energies in nature, whether these be wind, tide, wood, coal, ore, food, or atom. When in the course of history men have come, as it were, suddenly upon large tracts of wild nature, their instinct is to seize upon it with possessive fury and to ward others off, claiming ownership for the tribe, the king, or the gods; then to divide it into parcels of earth that can be bought and sold and quarreled over endlessly; and then to compel it by their own efforts to yield better forage, richer crops, deadlier weapons, finer fortifications, or perdurable wealth.

These commonplaces need to be kept continually in mind when one studies the relation of the Americans to the land. That relation dominates their history. It required energy and encouraged the increase of natural energies that were in turn to extend and enrich the energies of a people who held this concept. The savage, if there is such a being, had been content with vague general tribal ownership, wandering from one locality to another as game, or his medicine men, his enemies, or the seasons suggested, taking, save for festal occasions, only such animal life as nature herself might take, or else, if he lived in fixed settlements, living in settlements so simple as scarcely to interrupt the wilderness. The white man looked upon empty land as his individual treasure to be grasped and held and bargained about as an investor hoards and plays with securities. In this context it is illuminating to remember that one of the few original economic thinkers to emerge from American culture is Henry George, whose *Progress and Poverty* (1879), published three years after the centennial celebrations, traced the ills of the republic to the notion that land is wealth and not commonwealth. From the beginning, land in the New World has evoked the most amazing exhibitions of wild human energy. Of this the rush of settlers into Oklahoma in 1889 is a paradigm, twenty thousand people lining an imaginary border and at a starter's gun rushing upon land and seizing it as drowning men clutch at a plank. To European adventurers and planters in the fifteenth and sixteenth centuries the New World presented itself as an empty landscape without ownership or boundary; their first duty was to tear it apart, expropriate it, and wring from it all kinds of wealth.

From the first landing of Columbus to the statement in 1890 of the official closing of the frontier, the land problem and the exploitation of natural resource have been central problems—perhaps *the* central problem, outdating forms of government—in American history. Indeed, if one considers our battles over highways and beautification, slum clearance and rent control, the pollution of nature and the disposal of waste, it continues to be that central problem. A cynic might write the history of the nation in terms of a gigantic real estate speculation, often corrupt, running from the pope's bulls of the fifteenth century that gave to Spain and Portugal New World real estate he did not own, down to the latest "realtor" development and the indignant assertion of landlords that they have a right to do as they please with what they own.

I suggest that responses to New World landscape fall into four great categories: a sense of delight and terror, a belief in limitless natural resources that must per se produce unending wealth, a greed to possess as much land as possible, and a curiosity to find out what makes nature "work." Throughout New World history these motives conflict and interlock, though one or another may at this time or that be more prominent than the others. Thus, the sense of delight and terror is evident in the age of discovery and exploration; and if it seems to have diminished in colonial and revolutionary America, it was revived by romantic poets and painters. But if American readers were asked by Bryant in 1826 to believe that the groves were God's first temples, the American frontiersmen, struggling with cold, heat, hunger, vermin, bogs, forests, Indians, and wild beasts were not greatly impressed by a sense of divinity lurking in the forests primeval. The American farmer has seldom accepted the Wordsworthian dictum that nature never did betray the heart that loved her; and as for the capitalist exploiters of real estate, coal mines, ore, precious metals, forest lands, water power, wild animal hides, and the like, their trail of destruction is large through the whole history of the country.

These great attitudes continue in the period here under survey. Conflict among them can be summarily viewed in a novel by Stewart Edward White that, said Eugene F. Saxton, brought the East, South, and North to understand the West.[1] Himself a lover of adventure and of the quietness in nature, White wrote *The Cabin* (1911), a charming collection of sketches about healthy life in the High Sierra, the mystery of the great pines, the purity of running brook and mountain pool, the ways of birds, and the humors of domestic animals.

But his best-known work, *The Blazed Trail* (1902), is here in question, for it succinctly presents the conflict among three of the primary attitudes toward nature that I have enumerated.

The story is set in Michigan of the 1870s when the forests still stood and Saginaw was a tough lumber town. It concerns Harry Thorpe, son of an embezzler. Our hero goes to the north woods to get away from his shame and his inheritance, quickly learns the crafts of both cutting and selling timber, and the cheating of government and competitors by the unscrupulous lumber kings,. Morrison & Daly. He throws himself into this competition, outwits his powerful and ruthless opponents, and loses his fortune at the climax, when Morrison & Daly, who had secretly created an artificial freshet in a lumbering stream to hurl Thorpe's logs down river, then send one Dyer to file away the boom-chains that hold the logs at the river mouth, so that these will be driven out into Lake Superior and be lost. At the last risky moment Thorpe himself tries to rechain the weakened boom. He is helped by a hulking lumberman, Big Junko, who, however, falls into the lake, cries out that he cannot swim, and so compels Thorpe to choose between saving his investment and saving a human life. He saves the man. Through a contrived ending we learn that his admiring crew spent the summer retrieving logs from the lake shore to present to Thorpe as a wedding gift. Sentimentalism thus triumphs. Nevertheless we are told that the novel was written in a lumber camp from 4 a.m. to 8 a.m. each day in the depth of a Michigan winter, and that the first reader was the foreman of the camp, who began reading it after supper one evening and was still reading at four the next morning.

White is uneasily conscious of the conflict among three elements in looking at the wilderness. We read, for example, of the exploiter that

> the great struggle to wrest from an impassive and aloof nature what she has so long held securely as her own, took on the proportions of a battle. The distant forest was the front. To it went the new bands of fighters. From it came the caissons for food, that ammunition of the frontier; messengers bringing tidings of defeat or victory; sometimes men groaning on their litters from the twisting and crushing and breaking inflicted on them by the calm, ruthless enemy; once a dead man bearing still on his chest the marks of the tree that had killed him. Here at headquarters [the superintendent's office] sat the general, map in hand, issuing his orders, directing his forces.

Though the story is the tale of a successful campaign, its strategy and tactics, this paragraph is followed by a description of the mystery of the wilderness:

> And out of the forest came mystery. Hunters brought deer on sledges. Indians, observant and grave, swung silently across the reaches on their snowshoes, and silently back again carrying their meager purchases. In the daytime ravens wheeled and creaked about the outskirts of the town, bearing the shadow of the woods on their plumes and of the north-wind in the somber quality of their voices; rare eagles wheeled gracefully to and fro; snow squalls coquetted with the landscape. At night the many creatures of the forest ventured out across the plains in search of food,— weasels; the big white hares; deer, planting daintily their little sharp hooves where the frozen turnips were most plentiful; porcupines in quest of anything they could get their keen teeth into;—and often the big timber wolves would send shivering across the waste a long whining howl. And in the morning their tracks would embroider the snow with many stories.

The heroine, moreover, who is first discovered in the middle of a grove of monster pines with "the awe of the forest . . . in her wide, clear eyes," is both a worshipper of natural beauty and a conservationist. When Thorpe is called upon to explain that he cannot save the grove because lumbering is a battle in which "our ammunition is Time; our small shot the minutes, our heavy ordnance the hours," she responds that she has seen the battlefield and it was dreadful:

> I went walking yesterday morning, before you came over, and after a while I found myself in the most awful place. The stumps of trees, the dead branches, the trunks lying all about, and the glaring hot sun over everything! Harry, there was not a single bird in all that waste, a single green thing. You don't know how it affected me so early in the morning. I saw just one lonesome pine tree that had been left for some reason or another, standing there like a sentinel . . . I don't believe I can ever forget that experience any more than I would have forgotten a battlefield, were I to see one.[2]

The sense of wonder and delight, a belief that the business of nature is to offer endless resources (there is some hint that, southern Michigan being exhausted, the turn of northern Michigan has come, but little sense of eventual exhaustion), and the desire to possess and profit are all in the book.

Clearly no one of the aspects of the relation of the Americans to visible nature can be discussed in isolation from the others. Neverthe-less, I shall in this chapter first concentrate upon the interpretation of nature as the physical world outside us, more particularly the earth with its flora and fauna, neglecting of necessity outer space or the cosmos. The romantic concept sometimes ties itself to a doctrine of vitalism, or of visible nature as beauty, awe, or terror, or of nature as order, and less frequently of nature as vengeance, as in Haw-thorne's "The Ambitious Guest." One attribute of the romantic read-ing of earth is a tendency toward the pathetic fallacy in writing both about the larger aspects of the planet and about its flora and fauna, to whom (or which), especially in the case of animals, human motives are frequently imputed—so much so that Theodore Roosevelt was led to denounce nature fakirs. For Roosevelt a nature fakir erred in two major fashions: either he added to actual observations inventions of his own, or he attributed human motive and intelligence to birds and animals. Roosevelt was quite willing to take *The Jungle Book* as fiction, but he could not permit the Reverend William Joseph Long, who sometimes wrote under the name of "Peter Rabbit," to print what seemed to the huntsman president absurd stories about the wild.[3]

Charming books about nature were written after 1915—for exam-ple, Joseph Wood Krutch's *The Twelve Seasons* (1949); and scientific biology was pursued in this country before the Civil War—for exam-ple, Agassiz became professor of natural history in the Lawrence Sci-entific School at Harvard in 1848. But it is roughly true that during the fifty years from 1865 to 1915 high-minded American interest in nature tended to shift from that of naturalist to that of biologist, and in extreme form the micro-biologist, from outdoors to the laboratory, from vitalism to determinism as explanation (at least for many biolo-gists), and from the point of view of Audubon in *Birds of America,* which came out from 1827 to 1838, to that of Jacques Loeb in *The Mechanistic Conception of Life,* published in 1912. Only three-quarters of a century separate these two books, yet the outlook on earth and its creatures in the one differs totally from that in the other. You pass from macrobiology to the cell as central to research; you pass, in Donald Fleming's useful phrase, from the life style of one sort of scientist to the life style of quite another sort.[4] To Agassiz nature is all delight, order, and wonder; to Loeb, though not every scientist agreed with him, "modern biology is fundamentally an experimental and not a descriptive science . . . its results are not rhetorical, but always assume one of two forms: it is either possible to control a life phenomenon . . . or we succeed in finding the numerical relations between the conditions of the experiment and the biological result (for example, Mendel's law of heredity)." [5] The Hudson River school of painters had seen the glory of God in nature and recorded it, or tried to, on canvas; in 1915 Thomas H. Morgan, after breeding endless generations of fruit flies, brought out *Mechanism of Mendelian Heredity,* which on evidence gathered through high-powered microscopes, established the basis for the modern doctrine of chromosomes and genes. [6] The triumph of the microscope did not mean the passing of interest in the out of doors, it meant only that the superior minute analysis possible in the laboratory diminished the need to observe creatures out of doors. More recently a growing interest in ethology has in some degree returned animals to their native habitats and recorded their behavior there. Of course the Audubon societies not only find birdwatching a compelling hobby, they do much for the conservation of wild life.

II

At the opening of our period we find a huge, overwritten, cumbersome and widely influential book, *Man and Nature* (1864) by George Perkins Marsh, a universal genius from Vermont. [7] If it is not the first formal plea for conservation in America, [8] its most recent editor remarks on Marsh's early impact upon forestry. The book, he says, initiated a reversal of traditional attitudes toward forest use and inspired a memorial that led Congress to establish a national forestry commission and to creating governmental forest reserves. Gifford Pinchot declared the book was epoch-making, and the editor of the edition I depend on notes that Marsh was reprinted on the eve of Roosevelt's White House conference on conservation of 1908. Most of the work traces man's destructive effects upon flora and fauna, gives specific examples of the death of forests, the dire results of tinkering with the water supply, and the problems man creates in deserts and sand dunes. Its last chapter is a potpourri on canals, subterranean water, how to build earthquake-proof buildings, the effects of mining, and the sedimentation in flowing streams. The final paragraph remarks that the legal maxim, *de minimis non curat lex,* cannot apply to nature, since "we are never justified in assuming a force to be insignificant because its measure is unknown, or even because no physical effect can now be traced to it as to its origin."

But though the volume is a classic in the literature of conservation, Marsh's basic intent was philosophical. The last paragraph concludes: "Every new fact, illustrative of the action and reaction between humanity and the material world around it, is another step toward the determination of the great question whether man is of nature or above her." Marsh is writing not merely as a philosopher of nature but also within the immediate shadow of the Darwinian controversy. The key-note to nature is "Harmony." Thus the preface begins:

> The object of the present volume is to indicate the character and, approximately, the extent of the changes produced by human action in the physical conditions of the globe we inhabit; to point out the dangers of imprudence and the necessity of caution in all operations which, on a large scale, interfere with the spontaneous arrangements of the organic or the inorganic world; to suggest the possibility and the importance of the restoration of disturbed harmonies and the material improvement of waste and exhausted regions; and, incidentally, to illustrate the doctrine, that man is, in both kind and degree, a power of a higher order than any of the other forms of animated life, which, like him, are nourished at the table of bounteous nature.

The first chapter is more "philosophical" than its successors. It traces the decay of the Roman Empire both to political tyranny and to the destruction of natural resources, and declares that public attention has only recently been half-awakened to the need of restoring the disturbed harmonies of nature, whose well-balanced influences are so propitious to all her organic offspring, and of repaying to our great mother the debt which the prodigality and the thriftlessness of former generations have imposed upon their successors.

Marsh agrees that natural science, as distinguished from natural philosophy, has been "vastly extended," but, "to the natural philosopher, the descriptive poet, the painter, and the sculptor, as well as to the common observer, the power most important to cultivate, and, at the same time, hardest to acquire, is that of seeing what is before him." Marsh's appeal is to humanity. Sight, he observes, is a faculty; seeing, an art, and "this exercise of the eye I desire to promote, and, next to moral and religious doctrine, I know no more important practical lessons in this earthly life of ours,—which, to the wise man, is a school from the cradle to the grave,—than those relating to the employment of the sense of vision in the study of nature." The reader notes that "vision" is here almost a pun. Of course the strictly scientific man must be a specialist and "confine the researches of a whole life within a comparatively narrow circle," all of which may be necessary. But "every traveller, every lover of rural scenery, every agriculturist, who will wisely use the gift of sight, may add valuable contributions to the common stock of knowledge."

In his introductory chapter Marsh goes on to discuss cosmological and geographical influences upon the earth. He then turns to the geographical "influence" of man, sometimes the product of improvidence, wastefulness, and wanton violence, and at others of foresight and wisely guided, persevering diligence. True it is that our meteorological knowledge is uncertain, but the impossibility of exact predictive judgments suggests caution. Nature is on the whole stable until man interferes. Man, notably "civilized" man, is more destructive than the beasts because he is greedy and thoughtless, despite his nobler attributes—he has forgotten that God prepared the earth for his delight. Unfortunately, "purely untutored humanity" is worse than civilized man.

Within nature, yet above it, man must reverse his bad practices:

> He is to become a co-worker with nature in the reconstruction of the damaged fabric which the negligence or the wantonness of former lodgers [on the earth] has rendered untenantable. He must aid her in reclothing the mountain slopes with forests and vegetable mould, thereby restoring the fountains which she provided to water them; in checking the devastating fury of torrents and bringing back the surface drainage to its primitive narrow channels; and in drying deadly morasses by opening the natural sluices which have been choked up, and cutting new canals for drawing off their stagnant waters.

> The fact that, of all organic beings, man alone is to be regarded as essentially a destructive power, and that he wields energies to resist which, nature—that nature whom all material life and all inorganic substance obey—is wholly impotent, tends to prove that, though living in physical nature, he is not of her, that he is of more exalted parentage, and belongs to a higher order of existence than those born of her womb and submissive to her dictates.

The earth is fast becoming an unfit home for its noblest inhabitant, and another era of human crime and human improvidence, and of like duration with that through which traces of that crime and that improvidence extend, would reduce it to such a condition of impoverished productiveness, of shattered surface, of climatic excess, as to threaten the depravation, barbarism, and perhaps even extinction of the species.[9]

Presumably one's first impression of this last passage is its astonishing modernity. The impression is justified. It is more important, however, to see in Marsh's disorderly pages and engaging footnotes that two philosophies confront each other. Terms like "harmony," "spontaneous arrangements of the organic or the inorganic world," "the sense of vision in the study of nature," "exalted parentage," "higher order of existence," and even the implied antithesis in "man as essentially a destructive power"—these phrases remind us that romanticism, dynamism, the Faustian spirit, the religion of humanity, and the sweep of Humboldt's *Cosmos* are not very far away; whereas the recognition of the specialist doing his work in a comparatively narrow circle and the assertion that we are never justified in assuming a force to be insignificant because its measure is unknown, prophesies the professional microbiologist. Marsh built the gateway to an understanding of "nature" after the Civil War.

III

Various incoming roads lead to this gateway, and various avenues diverge from it, some of which, even at the risk of repetition, it is important to explore. One may take for granted that scores of nineteenth-century nature-writers expressed a simple pleasure in the intimate landscape—flower and tree, brook and pond, bird and squirrel, and all shy woodland creatures—and in familiar seasonal phenomena—the fall of the leaf, snow crystals, spring buds, and the meadows warm in June. This sort of thing was reiterated from 1865 to 1915 (and beyond) by writers of whom Frank Bolles is a type. It may be called the Wordsworthian, even the Thoreauvian approach,[10] and whether the writer is a Darwinian is irrelevant for such interpretations. But nature on a larger scale was awesome, terrible, majestic, indifferent, cruel. Along the frontier the indifference or enmity of the earth had been a common experience, as it still was for dwellers scattered over the high plains or along American rivers that flooded in the spring. As the urban population increased, individual exposure to wild nature on a grand scale diminished, and Americans had to learn from books what their ancestors had experienced as matter of course. The shadow of Darwin and Lyell lay over most of these reports; Darwinism could fuse easily with talk of glacial epochs, elemental energy, and the cosmic cold. Even kindly naturalists had therefore their moments of shudder and withdrawal.

Nature in the large attracted adventurous, solitude-loving souls such as Clarence King (1842–1901), John Muir (1838–1914), and John Burroughs (1837–1921), writers representative of a generation. The dominant note in King's *Mountaineering in the Sierra Nevada* (1871) is pleasure in loneliness:

> In long Sierra journeys the mountaineer looks forward eagerly, and gladly, till pass or ridge-crest is gained, and then, turning with a fonder interest, surveys the scene of his march, letting the eye wander over each crag and valley, every blue hollow of pine-land or sunlit gem of alpine meadow; discerning perchance some gentle reminder of himself in yon thin blue curl of smoke, floating dimly upward from the smouldering embers of his last camp-fire. With a lingering look he starts forward, and the closing pass-gate with its granite walls shuts away the retrospect. . . . It is the mountaineer's privilege to carry through life this wealth of unfading treasure ("Preface," p. x).

King revels in the difficult air of the iced mountain tops, in the occasional dangers he must face, and in the opposite feelings of delight in power and awe before the vastness of the mountains and the littleness of urban life, that "crushing Juggernaut-car of modern life and the smothering struggle of civilization" (p. 348). From a dozen passages about the "stern grandeur of granite and ice" and "the tragic nearness of death" (p. 312) I select these two as representative:

> At the moments of such discovery, one cannot help restoring in imagination pictures of the past. When we stand by the river-bank or meadow of that fair valley [the Yosemite], looking up at the torrent falling bright under fulness of light, and lovely in its graceful, wind-swayed airiness, we are apt to feel its enchantment; but how immeasurably grander must it have been when the great, living, moving glacier, with slow, invisible motion, crowded its huge body over the brink, and launched blue ice-blocks down through the foam of the cataract into that gulf of wild rocks and eddying mist! (p. 189.)

Granite and ice and snow, silence broken only by the howling tempest and the crash of falling ice or splintered rock, and a sky deep freighted with cloud and storm,—these were the elements of a period which lasted immeasurably long, and only in comparatively the most recent geological times have given way to the present marvellously changed condition. Nature in her present aspects, as well as in the records of her past . . . constantly offers the most vivid and terrible contrasts. . . . To-day their burnished pathways are legibly traced with the history of the past. Every ice-stream is represented by a feeble river, every great glacier cascade by a torrent of white foam dashing itself down rugged walls, or spouting from the brinks of upright cliffs (pp. 189–90).[11]

Obviously landscapes like these depend upon a scientific reading of the history of nature. Small wonder that beside this remorseless energy, written in hieroglyphs of "a thousand upspringing spires and pinnacles," "jagged forms standing out against the sky like a procession of colossal statues" (p. 58), the human race, or as much of it as King saw at Tuolumne, seemed "people whose faces and dress and life and manners are sadder than any possibilities held up to us by Darwin" (p. 333). I add that the name of God seldom or never appears in this remarkable book.

John Burroughs took a wider literary range, running from biography to a book about Britain and from the habits of birds to literary criticism (he said Emerson was a pine tree and found a great deal of fault with Thoreau). He is remembered, however, as a naturalist, not as a geologist and engineer like King nor as a biologist after the manner of Agassiz or Spencer Fullerton Baird. That Burroughs made any notable scientific discoveries does not appear, but he was intensely aware of the natural sciences, and his vast literary output,[12] in which nature is too often merely the theme song of a genial writer appealing to cultivated readers, is based upon an interpretation Darwinian in its assumption. Burroughs is a more complicated being than his present repute allows; and if he sometimes indulges the pathetic fallacy, he usually knows it is a fallacy—he says, for example, that the poet interprets his own soul, not nature (V, 112). Though he belongs to the line of informal American philosophers that runs from Franklin to E. B. White, he faced some facts of science unflinchingly[13] and was not afraid to discuss the cruelty and indifference of the Darwinian universe. He was impressed by the casual cruelty of nature. He once removed the young of a cowbird from a nest of warblers and dropped it into the water, not without a pang. "Cruel? So is Nature cruel. I take one life to save two. In less than two days this pot-bellied intruder would have caused the death of the two rightful occupants of the nest; so I step in and turn things into their proper channels again" (I, 58).

Birds, he wrote, are the greatest enemies of birds (I, 109). He has a whole essay on "The Tragedies of Nests" in *Signs and Seasons* (1886) (VII, 64–88); and he also asks indignantly:

> What principle of benevolence, or of justice, or of wise foresight has regulated the distribution of the various human races upon the globe, or determined the relative ascendency of the various nationalities? Just the principle that determines which of a hungry pack of dogs shall get and keep the bone you toss them. Think of the wrongs, the cruelties, the waste, the slaughters of history (VIII, 231–32).[14]

Burroughs was struck by the sublime indifference of nature to man:

> How the revelations of science do break in upon the sort of private and domestic view of the universe which mankind have so long held! To many minds it is like being fairly turned out into the cold, and made to face without shield or shelter the eternities and the infinities of geologic time and sidereal space. We are no longer cosily housed in pretty little anthropomorphic views of things. The universe is no longer a theatre constructed expressly for the drama of man's life and salvation. The race of man becomes the mere ephemera of an hour, like the insects of a summer day. . . . We feel the cosmic chill (VIII, 225–26).[15]

The fecundity of life appalled him;[16] he returns again and again to the struggle for survival and insists upon the paramountcy of physical energy in the universe: "The most advanced science of our time does not regard life as a special and separate principle, a real entity which has been added to matter, but as a mode in which certain physical forces manifest themselves just as heat is not a thing of itself, but a mode of motion" (XI, 33).

But though aware of science, Burroughs is not a consistent materialist, and as a philosopher he contradicts himself:

> This vital Nature out of which we came, out of which father and mother came, out of which all men came, and to which again we all in due time return, why should we fear it or distrust it? It makes our hearts beat and our brains think. When it stops the beating and the thinking, will it not

be well also? It looked after us before we were born; it will look after us when we are dead. Every particle of us will be taken care of; the force of every heart-beat is conserved somewhere, somehow. The psychic force or principle of which I am a manifestation will still go on. There is no stoppage and no waste, forever and ever (XI, 188–89).

For him "the universe is no more a temple than it is a brothel or a library" (XI, 190); yet, holding as he did that the sum of physical forces in it is constant, the laws of causation and the conservation of energy everywhere operative, without initiation and without finality, he could nevertheless say: "The heights and the depths that surround us, and the world of vital forces in which our lives are embosomed, and which the darkness of earlier ages did not permit us to see, baffle speech. Magnitude, perspective, order, system, connection, is what the light of science reveals to us" (XI, 133). So the universe, in which man is "suddenly confronted by abysmal geological time—the eternities past and the eternities to come" (VII, 122), proves to be comfortable after all; and Burroughs vigorously denounced egg collectors, egret wearers and people who "clutch and destroy in the germ the life and music of the woodlands" (VII, 211), even though nature is fecund, indifferent, and cruel.

John Muir is principally and rightly remembered as a conservationist.[17] His deeply ethical temperament and religious training probably conditioned him against waste, just as it conditioned his interpretation of the universe and, by a kind of reverse effect, led him to follow not a church but his instincts and see what the upshot might be. He was an unpredictable compound of Robert Louis Stevenson, a Christian evangelist, and a disciple of Walt Whitman. For him the enormous energy of the world was proof of the grandeur and glory of God, creating beauty and giving health to those who fled from grimy industrialism and dared to live in the wilderness. Glaciers, rugged mountain ranges, and the wilderness were sublime and terrifying. He writes in *The Mountains of California* (1894):

The eye, rejoicing in its freedom, roves about the vast expanse, yet returns again and again to the fountain [*sic*] peaks. Perhaps some one of the multitude excites special attention, some gigantic castle with turret and battlement, or some Gothic cathedral more abundantly spired than Milan's. But, generally, when looking for the first time from an all-embracing standpoint like this [a mountain peak] the inexperienced observer is oppressed by the incomprehensible grandeur, variety, and abundance of the mountains rising shoulder to shoulder beyond the reach of vision; and it is only after they have been studied one by one, long and lovingly, that their far-reaching harmonies become manifest. Then, penetrate the wilderness where you may, the main telling features . . . are quickly perceived, and the most complicated clusters of peaks stand revealed harmoniously correlated and fashioned like works of art. . . . Nature's poems, carved on tables of stone. . . . (IV, 78–80).[18]

The operative words here have to do with love and harmony.

Wild nature had no terrors for Muir, who once described a rattlesnake as desperately embarrassed because it had invaded Muir's cabin (VI, 226),[19] rejoiced in a terrific windstorm during which he clung "like a bobolink to a reed" to the swaying branches of a tree (IV, 280), jumped lightly from rock to rock, glorying in the eternal freshness of nature and in the ineffable tenderness with which she nourishes arctic daisies (IV, 109), and found beauty in an avalanche (VI, 284–85). To such a man there was health in wildness; of the Bitter Root Reservation he could write: "Wander here a whole summer, if you can. Thousands of God's wild blessings will search you and soak you as if you were a sponge, and the big days will go by uncounted" (VI, 20). For him nature was God's great epic, forever beautiful, and though Muir admitted an incessant dynamism in nature, sometimes destructive,[20] he thought that God, using this gigantic energy, means well, and in fact validates the Bible:

> To an observer upon this adamantine old monument in the midst of such scenery, getting glimpses of the thoughts of God, the day seems endless, the sun stands still. Much faithless fuss is made over the passage in the Bible telling of the standing still of the sun for Joshua. Here you may learn that the miracle occurs for every devout mountaineer, for everybody doing anything worth doing, seeing anything worth seeing. One day is a thousand years, a thousand years is as one day, and while yet in the flesh you enjoy immortality (VI, 102).

Man and his greed, not Darwinism, nor materialism, nor mechanism, are the source of evil in this vast and beautiful world. Muir called sheep four-footed locusts, "trampling the wild gardens and meadows almost out of existence" (IV, 112), but the sheep were put there by man. The great forests were swept by man-made fires (IV, 222). Of the California goldminers he wrote: "The hills have been cut and scalped, and every gorge and gulch and valley torn to pieces and disemboweled, expressing a fierce and desperate energy hard to understand" (V, 62). Precisely how greed came into a world so beautiful he does not explain, but he denounced "city pot-hunters" who kill robins (VI, 238), and his sternest rebuke was reserved for the ruthless lumber industry. The Indians had done little harm,

> but when the steel axe of the white man rang out on the startled air [the trees'] doom was sealed. Every tree heard the bodeful sound, and pillars of smoke gave the sign in the sky.

> . . . every mill is a center of destruction far more severe from waste and fire than from use. The same thing is true of the mines, which consume indirectly immense quantities of timber with their innumerable fires, accidental or set to make open ways, and often without regard to how far they run.

> Through all the wonderful eventful centuries since Christ's time—and long before that—God had cared for these trees, saved them from drought, disease, avalanches, and a thousand straining, leveling tempests and floods; but he cannot save them from fools . . . (VI, 361,379,393).

Muir could only appeal to Uncle Sam. But God governs even in the tempest. Muir writes of Yellowstone Park:

> In the solemn gloom, the geysers, dimly visible, look like monstrous dancing ghosts, and their wild songs and the earthquake thunder replying to the storms overhead seem doubly terrible, as if divine government were at an end. But the trembling hills keep their places. The sky clears, the rosy dawn is reassuring, and up comes the sun like a god, pouring his faithful beams across the mountains and forest. . . . The ordinary work of the world goes on (VI, 51).

An amusing inconsistency developed among those who plugged for wild nature and also for Walt Whitman, as Burroughs did. Whitman celebrated virility, the outdoors, and health, and they praised him for it without observing that he was wholly uncritical about the reckless exploitation of resources and the destruction of the wilderness they were struggling to preserve. All this, for the poet, came under the rubric of the divinely ordained march of humanity. The general thesis is evident in such a poem as "Starting from Paumanok," full of passages that tacitly assume nature in America is inexhaustible:

> Interlink'd, food-yielding lands!
> Land of coal and iron! land of gold! land of cotton, sugar, rice!

> Land of wheat, beef, pork! land of wool and hemp! land of the apples
>   and the grape!
> Land of the pastoral plains, the grass-fields of the world! land of those
>   sweet-air'd interminable plateaus!

This goes on for a couple of pages, and then one comes to:

> See in arrière [sic], the wigwam, the trail, the hunter's hut, the
> flatboat, the maize-leaf, the claim, the rude fence, and the back-
> woods village,

"pastures and forest," "countless herds of buffalo," island cities, the "many-cylinder'd steam printing-press," the locomotive, ploughmen, "miners digging mines," and much else, with no sense that destruction is wrought by exploitation. "Our Old Feuillage" is another catalogue of American occupations and energies, "the certainty of space, increase, freedom, futurity" smothering any possible compunction about wastage. "The Song of the Broad-Axe" celebrates the necessary and disastrous tool of its title, and like instruments as well, and sings

> Shapes of the using of axes anyhow, and the users and all that
>   neighbors them.

In "The Song of the Redwood Tree," though the poet hears "the mighty tree its death-chant chanting," "the falling trunk and limbs, the muffled shriek, the groan," he blankets this sort of thing with a vision of "the flashing and golden pageant of California." "Pioneers! O Pioneers!" is an equally uncritical paean of the "Western movement." Whitman grows exclamatory:

> Never was the average man, his soul, more energetic, more like a God

than in this "incredible rush and heat" to conquer space ("Years of the Modern"). But the poet himself was equally blind; if in his prose he lamented the greed of the Grant period, he was unable to make the connection between the irresistible rush of America "forward" and the exploitation that necessarily went with this human tide.

IV

We to whom pollution of air, water, and earth has become a major issue are likely to find difficulty in realizing what a dramatic change in the national psychology was represented by the conservation movement, the second major theme in Marsh's *Man and Nature*. It must be kept in mind that during this half-century the enormous energies of a constantly expanding people, at once greedy and idealistic, individualized and half-believers in a proper commonwealth-to-be, were devoted without hindrance or forethought until the last decades of our period to ravaging a continent. The evidence was all around them—worn-out farmlands, gullied hillsides, flooding rivers, acres of tree stumps, abandoned mines, areas blighted by the fumes from smelters, and cities dingy with the smoke of soft-coal fires. But the idea long held sway that these things did not matter, that nature was always indulgent, that there were somewhere toward the setting sun more farms, more mines, more coal, more ores, more timber, and more water to pollute or waste. But two sentences from widely differing sources may shock the modern reader into a sense of an extraordinary *bouleversement* in American opinion. The first is a sardonic observation from a book of 1947: "the oldest criminal tradition in America is timber stealing." The second appears in a standard reference work of 1929. "Of the original stock of big game in the United States not more than two per cent remains." [21] Let us take these in reverse order, postulating, however, that the conservation movement implied in the remark about lumber means not merely the wise use of natural resources but also such ancillary purposes as the preservation of the wilderness, the keeping of reservation areas under national control, and the retention of sites with some picturesque, historical, or, in a broad sense, scientific importance. [22]

To the advancing horde of white settlers trees and marshlands were impediments to be destroyed if farm and settlement were to be stabilized; Indians were to be massacred; and wild birds and animals, obviously superabundant, were to be killed as dangerous or hunted as food by any conceivable device. If the passenger pigeon disappeared, the wild turkey vanished, and the bison herds dwindled, the infinite wisdom of providence would somehow still provide. Settlers from England did not bring with them the game laws, those symbols of caste; and though there were rudimentary attempts at regulating hunting even in Plymouth Colony, though Cooper through the mouth of Natty Bumppo could deplore the wasty ways of the settlements and Thoreau prefer writing about brute neighbors to destroying them, the right of male Americans to bear arms could scarcely be challenged, just as the right of the first occupier to the wilderness could not easily be gainsaid. There were, therefore, no really effective game wardens in the several states until the 1880s; and it is significant that the New York Sporting Association, founded in 1844, did not change its name until it became the New York Association for the Protection of Game and was so incorporated in 1885.

Eastern hunters of the upper class seem to have become more concerned about game laws and the preservation of wild birds and animals earlier than did the rest of the country. It is interesting that a small library of books connected with big-game hunting [23] proved to be one of the earliest modes of propaganda for conserving wild life. The first Audubon Society was founded in New York in 1886 by George Bird Grinnell, but this movement did not spread to Massachusetts and Pennsylvania until 1895, nor was the National Association of Audubon Societies incorporated until 1905.[24] But perhaps the single most influential group in the earlier phases of game preservation was the Boone and Crockett Club, founded by Theodore Roosevelt at a dinner in New York City in December 1887. Its constitution admitted a hundred members (among the earlier batch was Albert Bierstadt the painter), but there were provisions for associate and honorary members. These categories had to be added since, according to Article III of its constitution, no one could be elected an active member unless he had killed with a rifle in fair chase, by still-hunting, or otherwise one adult male individual of each of three of the various species of American large game,[25] and opportunities for this sort of sport steadily dwindled. Not only was the club opposed to slaughter but as the years went by, it found itself more and more involved with two other of the five purposes stipulated in its constitution:

III. To work for the preservation of the large game of this country and, as far as possible, to further legislation for that purpose, and to assist in enforcing the existing laws.

IV. To promote inquiry into, and to record observations on, the habits and natural history of the various wild animals.

Theodore Roosevelt was president of the club from 1888 to 1894, then, after a few years, William Austin Wadsworth from 1897 to 1918, and George Bird Grinnell after 1918.[26] A Game Preservation Committee became virtually a standing committee of the club. This

society had an exhibit at the World's Columbian Exposition of 1893
and that same year began its program of publishing (originally
through the press of *Forest and Stream*), a series of influential books,
of which *American Big-Game Hunting* (1893) was the first. These
not merely opposed slaughter, they also set up sportsmanship as a
code and plugged for conservation. As a historian of the club rightly
observes, its members for a long time were a minority fighting
against a black cloud of the extermination of big game. But though
they were a powerful minority and captained by a future President of
the United States, neither he nor they represented the conscience of
the hundreds of thousands of Americans who annually went hunting.

As the British Empire is said to have grown up in fits of absence of
mind, so it may be said that the Americans stumbled upon the idea
of national parks and monuments, not at first realizing the larger implications of what they were doing.[27] Yosemite was created in 1865.
But difficulties between the State of California (states' rights were a
rampant doctrine in the Far West) and the federal government postponed its becoming a national park until 1905. Yellowstone National
Park was created in 1872,[28] just ahead of a threatened invasion of
homesteaders and exploiters and largely as a result of propaganda in
magazines by various members of the Washburne-Doane expedition
and a geological survey expedition under F. V. Hayden in 1871.
There was at first no appropriation for maintenance. One of the reasons for the easy creation of this park was the negative idea that,
after all, it was generally inaccessible and of no great agricultural,
grazing, or mineral importance. Not until 1894 was legal supervision
possible. Whoever drew the bill creating the Yellowstone National
Park was, however, gifted with prescience, since its provisions were
basic.

The park being created, the customary greed showed itself. A railroad wanted to run tracks through the park, and the vexed question
of hotel accommodations was not wholly solved by the creation of
the Yellowstone National Park Improvement Company (improvement is an ominous word!) supposed to operate under government
supervision. This was in the early 1880s. Nevertheless the example
of good management at Yellowstone proved heartening, and there a
policy for regulating the flow of tourists could be worked out—before
the automobile swamped the national parks.

A series of conferences on the national park system (1911, 1912,

1913) helped establish a unitary philosophy of park administration, so that by 1914 a superintendency for the whole system was created in the Department of the Interior, and by 1916 the National Park Service Act established uniform and, on the whole, sensible rules for managing parks, monuments, and "sites," even if these were not all under the control of one department. I have already hinted that a surplusage of visitors in recent years, anxious to get out into the open, has tended to overwhelm the original notion of such parks as dreamed by the generation of John Muir, Ferdinand Vandeveer Hayden, and Nathaniel P. Langford. Through the formative years and since, the administration of these areas has tended to suffer from niggardly congressional appropriations and has had to struggle with the two perpetual difficulties of dealing with private landowners within a park and with intrusion, often greedy and commercial, from the outside.

But the creation of national parks, national monuments, and federal game and wild fowl preserves was but a minor element in a major problem—that of conservation as a national issue. As I have already indicated, the spoiling of nature went on almost unchecked for a long time in the nation as a whole, one minor (and prophetic) exception being flood-control projects by army engineers. During these five decades, however, the Great West, which thought itself marked out for damaging treatment in matters of conservation, grew more self-conscious in the proportion that Americans in other parts of the republic learned more about it. Embarrassing paradoxes soon developed. On the one hand, the Great West was so big that few Americans thought this vast area could be permanently harmed. On the other hand, the work of experts like John Wesley Powell [29] and his associates demanded a basic reform in the government's land policy and helped inaugurate a movement that eventuated in modernized laws about irrigation, stream control, withholding land from sale, creating forest reserves for their economic potentiality and their importance to irrigation and flood control, and building dams for these purposes as well as for generating electrical energy.

The Western land problem has always had its peculiarities. To begin with, the tradition that the West is misunderstood is virtually as old as the concept of the Great West, and a states'-rights psychology in the trans-Mississippi area developed with the opening of new territories and states. The result was contradiction. The West wanted population, but the only way to get a stable population except in a few scattered cities was by homesteading, a measure that necessarily broke up the open range. The West boasted it was God's country, the land of equality where the handclasp was forever a little stronger; but equality seldom interfered with the capacity of miners, lumbermen, smelters, and sheepherders to scarify the land, waste its resources, and prevent its use by others. The West wanted government to help it with railroads and banks and cheap money, but it angrily protested against almost every conservation measure on the ground that Washington was robbing the several states of real or potential wealth. The West was a country of endless space, inexhaustible trout streams, fertile soil, masculine virtue, courtesy to women, and a code of honor supposed to be superior to any in the East; but the West violated treaty after treaty with the Indians, whom it massacred or saw massacred without protest, and witnessed with grave, dispassionate irony small civil wars between cattlemen and sheepherders, big ranchmen and little ranchers, the forceful protection of illegal fencing, and feuding between farmers from the East and various sorts of Western men. Vote after vote on conservation bills showed that the West wanted to dominate or divert federal legislation; yet it complained of federal neglect at the same time that it repudiated or avoided or tried to cripple many a statute [30] intended to benefit the whole nation. It wanted free lands as donatives, but it objected to free lands as donatives to railroads while it condemned the withdrawal of areas of the public domain from private sale as a cunning device to enrich Eastern capitalists or, if not that, impracticable legislation dreamed up by Easterners who could not rope a cow. In many ways the Western sense of injury after the Civil War repeated the Southern sense of injury before that conflict.

The need of conserving soil, water, and natural resources, underground or above ground, was not of course peculiar to the West. On the contrary the South had its exhausted farmlands, its leached soils, its wasteful mining, its crude exploitation of timber, its floods, its abandoned shacks, and its hopeless people.[31] So did New England. So did other parts of the republic; for example, the Middle West, where, as I have hinted, the stripping of the State of Michigan of its great timber wealth with no policy of replacement was a scandal. In this survey, however, it will suffice to concentrate mainly on the West as representative of a general situation.

All discussions of conservation go back in the end to the long, confused, and maddening history of the land-grant policies of the federal government.[32] These were supposed to have been modernized by the Homestead Act of 1862 and the ancillary statutes known as the Timber and Stone Acts, the Desert Land Act, and the Preëmption Act, but close students find no basic alteration of general policy in 1862, only a continuation of an extraordinary mixture of good intentions, fraud, conflict of claims, speculation, and genuine advance. The Jeffersonian doctrine of the small farm as the bedrock of democracy simply did not work in the Far West. The philosophy of homesteading had to yield before a radical alteration in American psychology as the conservationists won victory after victory, notably during the presidencies of Theodore Roosevelt.

A change came about when it dawned upon enough people, usually members of a younger generation and characteristically persons out of the colleges and universities,[33] that even in America nature was not inexhaustible, that the energies of wild nature could by the energy of man sometimes be put to increasing social use, and that human expertise might restore exhausted natural energies through scientific treatment.[34] The conservation movement rapidly matured under the leadership of publicists, statesmen, experts in engineering, leaders in geology, specialists in the life sciences, and their kind. Marsh, King, Burroughs, Muir, Powell, and other pioneers of the movement had, it has been seen, some degree of scientific education. Though members of the Boone and Crockett Club, the Audubon societies, and similar groups [35] did much to create a climate of favorable opinion, practical leadership originated mainly among the scientists.

Thus at a meeting of 1874 the American Association for the Advancement of Science appointed a committee to memorialize Congress and the state legislatures "upon the importance of promoting the cultivation of timber and the preservation of forests, and to recommend proper legislation for securing these objects." When nothing much seemed to follow upon this action, at the Toronto meeting of 1889 the scientists reaffirmed their position, this time making their recommendations more specific. They wanted: "the establishment of a proper administration of the remaining timber lands in the hands of the general government for the purpose of insuring the perpetuity of the forest cover to the western mountain ranges, preserving thereby the dependent favorable conditions." [36] T. C. Mendenhall was chairman of this committee, which remained in being until 1894. At the 1891 meeting of the association in Indianapolis he presented on behalf of the committee a lengthy report that included a copy of the memorial the committee (amending one by the association) had sent to both the Canadian and the American governments. The committee had met with one from the American Forestry Association (founded in 1876). The two committees had visited the Secretary of the Interior; after that, their memorial had been sent to President Benjamin Harrison, and by him transmitted to Congress, which did nothing immediately. The new memorial pointed out that the first action of the AAAS had, it was true, resulted in creating a Forestry Division in the Department of Agriculture, but that the seventeen years intervening between that time and memorial two had revealed grave weaknesses in the administration of timber lands, largely because those in charge were ignorant of the significance and theory of forest conservation. The new memorial stressed the necessity of protecting watersheds, hedged on the influence of trees on rainfall, and was vigorous about timber thieves and forest fires (most of these of human origin),[37] and urged the appropriation of sufficient funds and the creation of a trained forestry service.[38] In 1891 national legislation gave the President power to set aside public lands for forest preservation; Harrison withdrew thirteen million acres from sale, Cleveland twenty million more. In 1896 Congress voted to pay for a report from the National Academy of Sciences on a national forestry policy, and in 1897 it passed a basic law governing this service. In 1905 the Bureau of Forestry was taken away from the Department of the Interior, transferred to the Department of Agriculture, and renamed the Forest Service. In 1907 the phrase "National Forests" replaced "Forest Reserves." In 1911 legislation authorized the purchase of private forest lands where necessary to protect the watersheds of navigable streams.[39]

Theodore Roosevelt was an audacious President and an enthusiastic conservationist,[40] and Gifford Pinchot was his right-hand man. On March 14, 1907, Roosevelt created an Inland Waterways Commission, which included members of Congress, an engineer, a statistician, a forester, an irrigation chief, and a geologist. The chairman was Theodore E. Burton, an opponent of pork-barrel legislation, and the vice-chairman was Francis G. Newlands, who, though from Nevada,

supported the Reclamation Act of 1902 and river and harbor legislation in 1907. An important suggestion from this commission led Roo
sevelt to summon a conference of all the governors of the states and
territories in May 1908; and as a result of the joint recommendations
of the conference of governors and the Inland Waterways Commission (which had been serving without pay) in June, he issued invita-
tions for a National Commission on the Conservation of Natural Resources, to be composed of forty-nine members, including the
chairman. A third of the other members were chosen from public
life, a third from industry, and a third from science. The work of the
commission was to be divided into four sections: waters, forests,
lands, and minerals, under an executive committee, of which Gifford
Pinchot was made chairman. The letter of invitation said in part:

> The recent Conference of Governors in the White House confirmed and
> strengthened in the minds of our people the conviction that our natural
> resources are being consumed, wasted, and destroyed at a rate which
> threatens them with exhaustion . . . the inevitable result of our present
> course . . . would ultimately be the impoverishment of our people. The
> Governors present adopted unanimously a Declaration reciting the neces-
> sity for a more careful conservation of the foundations of our national
> prosperity, and recommending a more effective co-operation to this end
> among the States and between the States and the Nation.
>
> No effort should be made to limit the wise and proper development and
> application of these resources; every effort should be made to prevent de-
> struction, to reduce waste, and to distribute the enjoyment of our natural
> wealth in such a way as to promote the greatest good of the greatest
> number for the longest time.[41]

Though Congress continued to refuse funds, Roosevelt directed the
heads of appropriate government bureaus and agencies to cooperate
in assembling a report, which was sent to him January 11, 1909, and
published in three volumes that same year.[42] It illustrates the temper
of Congress that a bill was immediately introduced forbidding government bureaus to do any work for the Commission. It should be
remembered that Roosevelt left office March 4, 1909.

In 1910 Charles R. Van Hise, president of the University of Wisconsin after 1903, published an intelligent and appealing survey of
the need for conservation, entitled *The Natural Resources of the
United States*.[43] This was widely read. Public interest was also

aroused by, and created, a spate of newspaper and magazine articles. One writer said of the Second National Conservation Congress held at St. Paul in 1910 that "this was not the ordinary thing. It's a political revolution," and another wrote: "This is a big movement, for the tide is rolling in." If it was a revolution, Western governors did not wish to yield, for they assembled at Salt Lake City and resolved against conservation measures by the national government. There was also some suspicion that Westerners tried to pack the St. Paul congress against Pinchot, whom they intensely disliked.[44] Perhaps the association of conservationists with the progressive wing of the Republican party and later with the Progressive party partially explains some of the opposition, which nowadays seems curiously wrongheaded.[45] But when the vigor of Roosevelt gave way to the prudence or laxity of Taft, and when the famous Pinchot-Ballinger controversy (mainly over conservation policies in Alaska) ended, Pinchot's hold on the government had been broken and with the resignation of Ballinger as Secretary of the Interior (1911), Westerners may have thought they had succeeded in slowing the momentum of a movement they could not defeat. Today, presumably, they would not take their old intransigent position.[46]

For the sake of simplicity I have clung to the problem of forest lands in the main, but it should be understood that similar conflicts and similar demands were simultaneously developed in the problems of mineral resources, oil, irrigation, soil conservation, the building of power dams and the flooding of canyons, and in the creation and management of recreation areas.[47] The relevance of this discussion to the central theme of this chapter is, I think, threefold. In the first place there is the general reversal of the assumption that the natural resources of the country were inexhaustible and that the business of government was to help private citizens to exploit them.[48] In the second place nature, paradoxically, became more comfortable. Not only did wandering in the wilds grow rarer as tours into the wilderness were further safeguarded, but the increasing number of city dwellers, even after the general use of the automobile, had fewer opportunities to see nature on the epic scale that forms the context of books like those by King and Muir. Men were made uneasy by wildness, but then, they had fewer opportunities to be uneasy. In the third place the conviction spread that nature could be used—in a sense a reversion to a complacent eighteenth-century theory—and since its control

and use increasingly lay with science, terror tended to diminish, both
because it was more rarely experienced and because natural catastro-
phes, though occasionally occurring, could, it was thought, be
anticipated, lessened, or prevented by scientific means and governmental aid. The phrase "disaster area" is a twentieth-century term.
Disasters were no longer thought of as inexplicable chastisements by
an angry or indifferent deity. In this sense terror diminished until
scientists created the atom bomb. This horror, though it vividly illustrates the wild energy of the cosmos, is, after all, something induced
by man himself.

V

The conservation movement altered the American attitude toward
nature-in-the-large just as the growth of cities altered man's approach
to the outdoors. What I may term the gross anatomy of the earth
grew to be a greater problem in applied engineering, albeit geological, petrological, and seismatic research not only continued but increased in refinement as better instruments were devised. The irrigation projects and power dams, the planning of highways and the
designing of proper foundations for buildings, and, for that matter,
the care of millions of acres of forest lands made greater demands
upon engineering expertise in general than they did on minute laboratory research. Moreover, except in such isolated cases as the Klon-
dike gold rush, the prospector disappeared into history as great corporations with their staffs of technologists took over mining. If,
despite embarrassing areas of worn-out soils and eroded terrain, the
practice of agriculture steadily improved (it is true that farming
passed from the retail to the wholesale plan), it does not deny the admirable research work of botanists, plant breeders, and experts in
animal husbandry, who developed fatter beef cattle, sturdier wheat,
and hardier alfalfa. A great achievement in agriculture was, however,
an engineering triumph—the invention, by Stephen Moulton Babcock
of the College of Agriculture at the University of Wisconsin in 1890,
of the milk (milk-fat) tester on a centrifuge principle—a machine
that, as somebody sardonically remarked, did more to keep dairymen
honest than did the Bible. Associated with the agricultural sciences
was medical progress in stamping out or reducing yellow fever, ma-
laria, and hookworm. If this raised the energy of the marginal farm

population, unfortunately it could not eliminate endemic agrarian discontent with mere subsistence farming, a discontent that sent thousands of poor whites and Negroes into mill villages and industrial towns. The United States Department of Agriculture, by 1890 perhaps the best in the world, through pamphlet and yearbook, demonstration and agent, strove to make life on the farm more agreeable.

But the farmer does not characteristically write poems to the landscape, and since my present interest is in the general American attitude toward nature, I return for a moment to the urban population. The outdoors became increasingly a means toward health and recreation for increasing multitudes in populous cities pent. City dwellers were not attracted to wild nature, however; they wanted nature as space, but space robbed of ferocity and incivility. The philosophy of public parks, brilliantly established by the labors of Frederick Law Olmsted and his associate, Calvert Vaux, in Central Park in Manhattan, Prospect Park in Brooklyn, the Boston park system, including the Arnold Arboretum, the Capitol grounds in Washington, and elsewhere, carried with it the concept of open-air playgrounds and playing fields. Neither Olmsted nor his colleagues could foresee a time when city parks would turn at nightfall into danger spots. The nationalization of sports, both amateur and professional, even if matches too often became spectator sports, usually implied open-air activity. Creating public bathing beaches became a responsibility of government, although activities like bobsledding and skiing were commonly left in private hands. In the 1890s bicycles, and late in that decade and increasingly thereafter, thousands of automobiles took people out of the cities on "rides" or to outdoor picnics or on long vacation tours. Simultaneously the good-roads movement was encouraged by contests among automobile makers (for example, the Glidden tours) and sustained by the ire of farmers unable to drive their Model T Fords over roads made impassable by mud, ruts, snow, dust, freshets, or bad drainage. Nobody could then foresee a highway culture of billboards, roadside stands, roadhouses, motels, vegetable stands, and filling stations, all hiding the natural landscape. But if this abuse lay hidden in the future, if in New York the Lower East Side still had its balconies crowded with humanity on August nights, if slum dwellers in other cities sweltered in airless rooms, nevertheless the general outdoors movement expressed the activist principle which runs throughout American history and which was never more evident than in the Age of Energy. The Bible of the new physical culture was presumably Theodore Roosevelt's *The Strenuous Life* of 1901.

I return to nature and science. Some of the millionaire masters of energy were inevitably attracted by the fascinating doctrine developed especially in the 1890s by the new astronomy (astrophysics as contrasted with astronometry) [49] that the universe exhibits not merely geometry and motion but also inconceivably great centers of energy endlessly radiating through billions of years into space. New, gigantic research telescopes had to be built. It is probable that if a man of the caliber of George Ellery Hale (1868–1938) [50] had had to wait on the slow process of congressional investigation and appropriation, American astronomy would have lagged lamentably behind, but the imaginative appeal of size and energy led wealthy men used to dealing with size and energy into financing great astronomical projects for the United States. (Of course their vanity was also appealed to by this chance of enduring fame.) The engineering problem associated with such instruments was something the millionaire, himself often in control of vast machines, could intuitively grasp, and this gigantism appealed to an epic race of financiers. Moreover, just as industrial inventions were the work of "practical" men finding an *ad hoc* answer to a specific manufacturing problem, so, the millionaires could see, scientific engines and instruments were needed because an investigator, coming up against a wall which blocked progress, required a tool or a machine that would penetrate or overcome the obstacle. What wealthy donors did not foresee was that, when the total cosmos was thus put under survey, huge telescopes, modern radio telescopes and spectrographs, and photography so refined as to seem to antiquate the human eye would unite to destroy the friendlier skies of the Bible, not to speak of the teleological heavens of Galileo or Newton. Of course some imaginations—for example, that of Mark Twain—reveled in gigantism.

The antithesis of the telescope is the microscope, an easy apposition that led a good many eighteenth- and nineteenth-century divines to pious dissertations on the thesis that God is everywhere.[51] As the telescope carried with it other necessary astronomical instruments, often complex, so research microscopy would have been crippled if ancillary inventions such as Nobert's test-plate, achromatic and apochromatic lenses, immersion lenses, staining processes, special lighting, and at the end of this period ultraviolet microscopes and after it electronic microscopes had not also been developed. It is, however, sufficient for present purposes to note that up to 1830 American men of science were depending upon a few expensive microscopes imported from Europe; that Dr. Oliver Wendell Holmes returned from his medical studies in Paris in 1835, bringing a modern microscope with him, afterward fitting up a special chamber at the Harvard Medical School as a "microscope" room, and eventually devising a simpler microscope that could be passed from hand to hand by his students.

By 1847 the American Charles A. Spencer had made an achromatic microscope for Dr. C. R. Gilman of New York City, and in post-bellum America manufacturers came to rival European experts in producing excellent instruments, a leading name being that of Robert Tolles and a leading firm Bausch and Lomb (originally the American Optical Company) of Rochester, New York.[52] Intricate technical problems of resolving the image, correcting aberrations, lens immersion liquids, and the like need not here concern us; it is enough to know they were solved. By 1941 Simon Henry Gates's *The Microscope,* a treatise on the use of the instrument for research and teaching, had reached its seventeenth edition [53] and had developed rivals. The microscope, said one writer, took the faculty of sight into a totally new world. Societies were founded to expatiate on its uses, and a man as good as Richard Halstead Ward (1837–1917) devoted himself to the instrument, editing from 1871 to 1883 the microscopy section of *The American Naturalist,* one of the first such departments in any scientific periodical.[54] As in Great Britain, so in America: microscopic societies multiplied, for the instrument owed much to the enthusiasm of amateurs. More important was the founding in 1880 of the *American Monthly Microscopic Journal,* edited and published by Romyn Hitchock.[55] For a time the American Association for the Advancement of Science maintained a special section on microscopy, which became the section on histology and microscopy.

It is difficult for a generation to whom the use of the microscope even in high-school science courses is commonplace to realize the basic shift in the attitude toward living organisms that resulted from this tool for research. Taxonomy did not disappear, nor did the collection and identification of new species, either living or from fossils. But zoological curiosity tended to concentrate upon the cell, and less upon nature-in-the-large. A centenary collection of essays celebrating the hundreth volume of the *American Journal of Science*, the oldest scientific magazine in the United States, divided the history of zoology here into four phases: a period ending in 1847, an era of descriptive natural history; the years from 1847 to 1870, an epoch of morphology and embryology; a period from 1870 to 1890 dominated by the search for, and weighing of, evidence for evolution; and a fourth phase of experimental biology running from 1890 to 1918, during which, says the writer, American zoologists caught up with the Europeans in devising experiments and analyzing results.[56] The watershed year was probably 1880. By 1893 Henry Fairfield Osborn could announce that "we know more about the meaning of the nucleus than we did about the entire cell a few years ago," [57] and by 1915, for the American Association for the Advancement of Science, the brilliant E. B. Wilson wrote: "A few years ago the possibility of investigating by direct experiment the internal structure of atoms, or the topographical grouping of heredity units in the germ cells would have seemed a wild dream. Today these questions stand among the substantial realities of scientific enquiry." [58] That same year Thomas Hunt Morgan, at last converted to Mendelianism, published *Mechanism of Mendelian Heredity*, and Jacques Loeb's *The Mechanistic Conception of Life* was already three years old.

This brief discussion is in no sense a history of the life sciences in America for these five decades, an intricate problem for specialists.[59] If it were, I should have to dwell at length upon the extraordinary research work at Johns Hopkins, Harvard, Columbia, Chicago, Wisconsin, California, and other leading universities, and write not only of the men I have mentioned but also of scores of other investigators of great power.[60] In general bacteriology, cytology, embryology, histology, and in other areas under the rubric of microbiology there were great advances. That the protoplasm was the basis of life was accepted as a matter of course, and terms like "chromosome," "gene," and "hormone," unknown to the generation of Louis Agassiz, became the alphabet of zoology. The cell, cell division, the contents of the cell, problems of fertilization, both natural and artificial, questions of mutants, experimental embryology, and an eventual acceptance of the thesis that the genetic material in the chromosome controls the series of events that constitute development became

standard subjects. Vitalism died, much descriptive taxonomy was left
to museums, and investigators more and more set themselves the task
of reducing zoological phenomena (the same was true in botany) to
physico-chemical processes and of discovering, studying, and manipulating the "ultimate building stones" revealed in molecular biology.
As Ernst Mayr puts it, two biologies developed because every organism is the result of two underlying causes: the blueprint of the genetic program and its genotype, and the decoding of this program as
it interacts with the environment in the making and subsequent life
of the phenotype of the individual.[61] But in 1915 much of this lay in
the future, and the titles of the books by Loeb and Morgan, stressing
mechanism, seem to bring the threat of mechanistic biological control (by no means an unintelligent fear) to reinforce the determinism,
materialism, mechanism, or atheism attributed by many nonscien-
tists to the whole theory of evolution.

A curious paradox developed. If the big telescopes taught anything, they taught the insignificance of man as a biological sport
amid the titanic energy loose in interstellar space, but the populace
at large took pride in this bigness. At various observatories (the
smaller ones mainly) astronomers found it made for good public relations to have weekly "open nights" when people could look through
what Milton called the optic tube and see the moon or Saturn with
its rings. Popularizers of astronomy in books like the French *The
Flammarion Book of Astronomy* (1880) and the American Charles
Augustus Young's [62] *The Sun* (1881), somehow took away the horror
from bigness and the cosmic cold, and perhaps the long succession of
fantastic or imaginary voyages into space since the days of Lucian
(H. G. Wells's *The First Men in the Moon,* dating from 1901, is an
excellent modern specimen) seemed to say that mechanical ingenuity
would overcome all difficulties in sending human beings comfortably
to the moon or Mars. Astronomers, moreover, were too few in number to constitute a threat to the survival of the state, so that from the
days when John Quincy Adams waxed eloquent about observatories
as "lighthouses of the skies" [63] to the first lunar landing, astronomy
has had a good press, its popularity latterly increased by the multiplication of that expensive toy, the planetarium.

Microscopy was, however, another matter. It is true that the public
was grateful for pasteurization, vaccines, immunization, antibiotics,

and a thousand other devices modernized or invented or made applicable to man only because of microscopic research, just as it understood in a general way that the protection of plants and animals
against parasites and diseases was possible because patient men in
laboratories had poured over innumerable slides, developed innumerable cultures, and calculated the minutiae of physico-chemical
changes in cellular life among the tissues. But one could not hold
public sessions for the microscope as one held open nights for the telescope, or at least one didn't; and though one could blow up photographs of slides to any dimension, an enlarged view of a blood cell
was somehow frightening as an enlarged photograph of a comet was
not. Astronomers were not dealing with human life. More people
used microscopes than used telescopes, and microscopes were readily
associated with such disturbing things as clinics, hospitals, post-mor-
tems, and inquiries into crime. When it appeared that biolo-
gists were tinkering with the very primal bases of life, when it was ru-
mored that life had been "created" in the laboratory and
"controlled" by such mysterious things as test tubes, slides, the punc-
turing of eggs to let in sea water, and so on, the comfortable world of
nature seemed threatened from below as it was not threatened from
above. No astronomer ever said he could control the motion of a
comet, but might not a mad scientist control human life? In fact, of
course, reverence for life was constant in the laboratories, but still—
what about vivisection? Would "experts" come to manipulate the elements of heredity for what they deemed the betterment of mankind?
Who was to decide what is "better"? What could prevent somebody in
real life from imitating the crackpot vivisectionist in Wells's *The Island of Dr. Moreau* (1896), who in attempting to breed a race of su-
permen, ends by breeding a race of monsters—or masters? The movies, which love horror as a theme, did not help.

The traditional approach to nature as something created and
sustained for the nourishment and happiness of humanity slowly
gave way in many minds to a vague dread of the modern laboratory.
A Muir of the mountains standing sturdily on his two American feet
and looking the Almighty in the face was one thing; a Jacques Loeb
doing nobody-was-quite-sure-what with the mechanical manipulation
of reproduction was something else. In Tennessee or South Carolina,
Texas or Wyoming, hunting was still an acceptable masculine occu-

pation, and even mountain climbing, though eccentric, could be tolerated. But were microscopists studying nature or manipulating mankind? [64]

I have sketched one general response, popular and uninformed, to the progress of scientific research, principally in the life sciences' exploitation of the potentialities of the microscope. There was another, somewhat more philosophic response which illustrates the feeling that the natural sciences and man's healthy-minded response to nature had somehow been given an odd twist by microscopy and all that microscopy implied. I think I can illustrate the polarities of this interpretation by two passages, one from a great British scientist just before our period opens, the other from a noted American nature-lover who lived vigorously on past the close of these fifty years.

In 1857 Michael Faraday, the dean of British physicists, sent to James Clerk Maxwell, brilliant representative of the rising scientific generation, a letter in which he lamented that the age of the verbal presentation of truths about nature seemed to be ending and a new age of mensuration, mathematical formulae, and statistical tables, inhuman and faceless, seemed to be coming in. Faraday wrote:

> When a mathematician engaged in investigating physical actions and results has arrived at his own conclusions, may they not be expressed in common language as fully, clearly, and definitely as in mathematical formulas? If so, would it not be a great boon to such as we to express them so—translating them out of their hieroglyphics so that we might also work upon them by experiment? [65]

But, however much one may lament the inability of modern scientists to produce so charming a piece of exposition as Faraday's *A Course of Six Lectures on the Chemical History of a Candle* (1861), the future lay with Clerk Maxwell and his generation.

The second passage is found in the *Autobiography* of Theodore Roosevelt, who attended Harvard College from 1876 to 1880, a period when the excitement over the microscope as a teaching instrument and an instrument for research was fresh. Roosevelt had at one time intended to become a scientist, but the new biology turned him away. He wrote:

> . . . Harvard, and I suppose our other colleges, utterly ignored the possibilities of the faunal naturalist, the outdoor naturalist and observer of nature. They treated biology as purely a science of the laboratory and

the microscope, a science whose adherents were to spend their time in the study of minute forms of marine life, or else in section-cutting and the study of the tissues of the higher organisms under the microscope. This attitude was, no doubt, in part due to the fact that in most colleges then there was a not always intelligent copying of what was done in the great German universities. The sound revolt against superficiality of study had been carried to an extreme; thoroughness in minutiae as the only end of study had been erected into a fetich. There was a total failure to understand the great variety of work that could be done by naturalists—the kind of work which Hart Merriam and his assistants in the Biological Survey have carried to such a high degree of perfection as regards North American mammals. In the entirely proper desire to be thorough and to avoid slip-shod methods, the tendency was to treat as not serious, as unscientific any kind of work that was not carried on with laborious minuteness in the laboratory. My taste was specialized in a totally different direction, and I had no more desire or ability to be a microscopist and section-cutter than to be a mathematician. Accordingly I abandoned all thought of becoming a scientist.[66]

Teddy was by temperament impatient, and some part of his complaint is the standard undergraduate complaint of being bored by careful instruction; nevertheless, there were others who shared his view, one of the eventual consequences being a renewed interest in environment, ecology, ethology, and population biology.

E. B. Wilson's *The Cell in Development and Inheritance* (1896; revised editions were issued later) is presumably a classic of American biological science, the product of infinite patience and care. So was Charles Darwin's *The Formation of Vegetable Mould through the Action of Worms with Observations on their Habits* (1881). But it would be difficult to find anywhere in the Wilson book a parallel to this passage from the last page of Darwin's monograph:

When we behold a wide, turf-covered expanse, we should remember that its smoothness, on which so much of its beauty depends, is mainly due to all the inequalities having been slowly levelled by worms. It is a marvellous reflection that the whole of the superficial mould over any such expanse has passed, and will again pass, every few years through the bodies of worms. The plough is one of the most ancient and most valuable of man's inventions, but long before he existed the land was in fact regularly ploughed, and still continues to be thus ploughed, by earth-worms. It may be doubted whether there are many other animals which have played so important a part in the history of the world. . . .[67]

Obviously this sort of writing is in the Faraday, not the Clerk Maxwell, tradition. But the difference between the old biology and the new does not lie solely in the superior charm of Darwin's prose, which, whatever defects have been alleged against it, expresses his personality in a way that American scientists, trained in a tradition that makes a fetish of objectivity, cannot achieve; the difference lies in the human meaning of Darwin's study. Not only, like Faraday, does he think that natural science can be presented in expository prose; he also sets the meaning of his discoveries in a human context, one not merely of common observations about a green turf and a beautiful lawn, but also of the long lapse of years. History exists for Darwin as it does not for Jacques Loeb.

A final paradox presents itself. The biological (or for that matter chemical or physical) laboratory is a creation of an urbanized culture. It requires lighting, heating, services of supply, continual sanitation, the aid of technicians, a capacity to acquire and install new instruments quickly, cold rooms, dark rooms, humidifiers, a continual supply of glassware, of specimens, of chemicals, of technical papers, all housed in a modern building which is theoretically possible on a country site but which in fact is seldom or never found very far away from an urban center. Its grounds may be landscaped, but gross nature with her clumsy feet must be kept out of these laboratories that are somewhere between an immaculate factory and an immaculate hospital. Gross nature might spoil a whole experiment. Members of the laboratory staff in such an institution form, it is true, a secular priesthood, but it is impossible to connect their point of view with such phrases from the history of romanticism as the worship of nature, pantheism, or a *Naturphilosophie*. The staff has as little use for Wordsworth as it has for a medieval bestiary. The gap between such an institution and Emerson's "azure-colored little book" of 1836 is great—as great as the gap between Emerson and the symposium of papers published as *Factors Determining Human Behavior* presented at the Harvard Tercentenary of 1936, even though the preface of that volume quotes Robert Boyle on "that noble and improvable faculty whereby an Inquisitive Soul may expatiate itself through the whole Immensity of the Universe." Emerson spent a good deal of time outdoors. There is not a single passage in the whole Harvard symposium, not even in the closing paper on anthropology by Bronislaw Malinowski, to show that the writer had ever been alone in the woods, gone on a canoe trip, or stalked a wild animal.[68] The truth is not as simplistic as modern literary theory holds—that the Americans somehow lost their innocence. They never had innocence in this sense. What has happened is that in this period (and later) nature, methodized more and more, replaced private and personal contact with wildness. Even greenhouses, places for laboratory animals, special gardens, and "controlled" forest plots, though they simulate nature, are not the wilderness of Wilson and Audubon; even ethologists, if they are to study the habits of animals and birds, require more or less fenced-in areas of the great out doors. The energy of nature is better studied and understood nowadays than it was in 1865, and to scientists it has become grander and more absorbing than ever before. But for most Americans by 1915, and more Americans since that date, the energy of nature has become something canalized, beaten, and tamed.

IX

From Harrison to Havana

—The 1890s, in spite of the Aubrey Beardsleys and
the Oscar Wildes, was a period of savage new gods.

—WILLIAM B. WILLCOX

I

ON MARCH 4, 1877, Rutherford Birchard Hayes was inaugurated, without the violence many had feared, as the nineteenth President of the United States. On February 15, 1898, the American battleship *Maine,* lying peacefully at anchor in the harbor of Havana, Cuba, to protect American interests, was destroyed by an explosion that sank the ship and killed some two hundred and sixty officers and men. "Remember the *Maine!*" became a national rallying cry.

Between these two events, virtually a quarter of a century apart, stretches a period probably as tension-ridden as any other quarter of a century in our national history and certainly the most ominous era since the close of the Civil War. Historians of particular phases of it detect some sort of progress as they trace the story of this or that component—industrialization or social welfare, the perfecting of the democratic process, or the enrichment of higher education, the growth of scientific agriculture or development in the arts. There is truth in each of these studies taken individually. Certainly the nation over which Theodore Roosevelt came to preside was radically different from the nation over which Andrew Johnson had ruled uneasily. But in these years the Age of Energy seemed to turn upon and devour itself, to develop more stress than reason, to have produced a writhing bundle of mighty opposites, a congeries of social and emotional conflicts. The ship of state lurched like a vessel in a storm, driven now this way and now that, as one or another of the ruling powers—financial energy, exploitative energy, mechanical energy, populist energy, political energy of the standard sorts, racial energy, religious energy, or the energy of "progress"—momentarily seized the helm and tried to steer leviathan to some port not clearly located on any map. There were years of relative peace (like the Centennial Year of 1876, though that had its dark undercurrents), periods of such desperation as to lead many to prophesy the downfall of the nation, periods of political stagnation when the forces of sectionalism were so evenly balanced that nothing moved, times when the distrust of the whole frame of government was so widespread that it was supposed a wealthy and cynical class ruled an invisible empire, and times when commotions, often riotous, seemed to follow a red banner inscribed: "All Power to the People." Fear of radicalism or of a debased currency or of a tariff for monopoly only, hope in the vague idealism of the Knights of Labor or of settlement workers or of the social gospel, the thrust of democracy toward governmental control of transportation, natural resources, hours of labor, and the "trusts," the countervailing power of Wall Street as a generic term for all capitalistic enterprise on which "development" fed the warfare among these powers turned history into a satire on the dream of the Founding Fathers that they were creating for all time a rational representative republic. John D. Rockefeller, Mary Ellen Lease, Edwin L. Godkin, "Pitchfork" Ben Tillman, Jane Addams, William Jennings Bryan, Samuel D. Gompers, Cardinal Gibbons, Mark Twain, Henry Adams, Charles Eliot Norton, James G. Blaine, Booker T. Washington, William James—which of these was the true secular savior? Who guarded the Shekinah of American belief? How was one to prove that America was not merely promises but promises fulfilled? Or was the great republic doomed to be one with Nineveh and Tyre?

In 1901 William Vaughn Moody, seizing upon the trite metaphor of Longfellow's ship of state, in "Gloucester Moors" vividly expressed the corrosion of doubt:

> God, dear God! Does she know her port,
> Though she goes so far about?
> Or blind astray, does she make her sport
> To brazen and chance it out?
> I watched her when her captains passed:

> She were better captainless.
> Men in the cabin, before the mast,
> But some were reckless and some aghast,
> And some sat gorged at mess.

The climax and ending of this confusion lay in the 1890s. For some queer reason many crucial phases of our cultural development seem to be just about ten years long; hence such terms as the Twenties, the Feminine Fifties, and lately the Sixties. Legends develop, notably about the 1890s, and it is important to examine and evaluate them. One such lies in the vogue of the phrase, the Gay Nineties; and gaiety is supposed to connote a naïve merriment, sentimentality, an innocent raffishness, a naughtiness that was never very naughty, and a sophistication that seldom rose above a parochial level. What are some elements of the legend?

Examples will make these clear. Ethelbert Nevins' *Water Scenes* was published in 1891, and these pianistic tidbits were soon on a thousand upright pianos or in a thousand music cabinets.[1] In the same year Charles Graham published his popular hit, "The Picture That's Turned to the Wall." The year before, Reginald De Koven had produced *Robin Hood,* the most successful romantic American light opera of the century; he interpolated "O Promise Me" into the score, a melody to which hundreds of thousands of American brides were to float to the altar. When De Wolf Hopper sang in the opera, he added to this saccharine song a burlesque that began: "Oh promise me that some day you will die," and between acts he recited Ernest L. Thayer's "Casey at the Bat," the anthem of American baseball: a hundred thousand Americans sighed or laughed. A year after *Water Scenes* Charles K. Harris brought out "After the Ball," that tear-jerker at which people wept and smiled:

> Many a heart is aching,
> If you could read them all;
> Many the hopes that have vanished
> After the ball.

In 1893 Theodore Moses Tobani (if he wrote it) put "Hearts and Flowers" on the market; it is said that the song sold a million copies by 1900, and certainly in the silent movie days, when there was a pianist in the orchestra pit, "Hearts and Flowers" was as inevitable as the request "Ladies, Please Remove Your Hats." The decade, in truth, was rich in popular songs, producing such masterpieces of sheet music as "While Strolling through the Park," "Everybody Works but Father," "On the Banks of the Wabash" (by Paul Dresser), "Ta-Ra-Ra-Boom-Der-E," [2] possibly the first famous torch song, and "There'll Be a Hot Time in the Old Town Tonight," which became the unofficial tune of the Spanish-American War. The cakewalk was still possible, marches and two-steps were "in," and above all ragtime was supposed to mark the quick, nervous American rhythm.[3] Scott Joplin, it is true, did not compose his classic "Maple Leaf Rag" until 1899, but this crowned, it did not create, a genre. Pryor's band prayed "classical music" such as Liszt's "Second Hungarian Rhapsody"; and John Philip Sousa, conductor of the U.S. Marine Band from 1880 to 1892 and then of his own, toured the country, giving gigantic concerts that usually included a trick piece called "The Band Comes Back," played after the intermission, and always one or more of his immortal marches—"Washington Post March" (1889) or "The Stars and Stripes Forever" (1897), which should have become the national anthem and didn't. The nostalgia created by light or tuneful music in the period is represented by a passage in Richard Harding Davis's novel of a Central American republic (Charles Dana Gibson illustrated the work with drawings of manly men and healthy girls). Two red-blooded Americans are in charge of a mine in Olancho, the republic in question, and Langham, long exiled from God's country, tells Clay: "What I'd like to do now would be to sit in the front row at a comic opera, *on the aisle*. The prima donna must be very, very beautiful, and sing most of her songs at me, and there must be three comedians, all good, and a chorus entirely composed of girls. I never could see why they have men in the chorus, anyway. No one ever looks at them." [4]

It was the golden age of vaudeville; [5] the age of the bicycle, sometimes built for two and sometimes for "scorchers"; the age of lawn tennis, of the Sunday-school picnic, of spooning, of football; the age of the pompadour, the basque shirtwaist, the corset, the full skirt, and the chatelaine chain, not to speak of the pin-on lady's watch; the age of the straw hat (slightly tilted), the cutaway coat, the blazer, and the watch chain for men; of short pants on little boys, big ribbons and sashes on little girls, and of baby clothes three times as long as the infant they concealed. It was also the age of Loie Fuller, the *danseuse* of trick lighting fame and the serpentine twist, of Little

Egypt the belly dancer, of Julia Marlowe as Juliet, and E.H.Sothern
in *The Prisoner of Zenda,* of William Gillette in *Secret Service* and
Olga Nethersole in *Sapho* (1900), of *Way Down East* and *The Heart
of Maryland,* of Uncle Tom shows and Dockstader's Minstrels,[6] of
Weber and Fields, and of McIntyre and Heath. Young George M.
Cohan appeared at the age of twelve in a stage version of *Peck's Bad
Boy,* and Lillian Russell, who was getting on, was still playing the
Casino in 1899. Penny arcades, peep shows, and kinetoscope parlors
began to multiply after 1892; in 1896 at Koster and Bial's Music Hall
a motion picture was projected publicly on a screen. By 1900 vaudeville houses, unwittingly admitting a mortal enemy into their midst,
closed each program with moving pictures designed to get the audience in or out of the theater. By 1900 about one hundred and fifty
thousand phonographs and some three million records had been sold.

It is well to glance at the best sellers, a list more varied and intelli-
gent than tradition allows for, but not, for the most part, rep-
resenting high literary art. In the 1890s best sellers included *The
Sign of the Four, A Study in Scarlet,* and *The Adventures of Sherlock
Holmes; Barrack-Room Ballads; The Little Minister,* Charles M.
Sheldon's *In His Steps; Trilby; Dr. Jekyll and Mr. Hyde, The
Red Badge of Courage, Quo Vadis,* and Winston Churchill's *Richard
Carvel; Black Beauty* and *Beautiful Joe.* The better sellers (I adopt
Frank Luther Mott's useful distinction) were such books as *Peter Ib-
betson,* destined to be revived as an opera by Deems Taylor; *The
Jungle Books;* Lew Wallace's *The Prince of India,* S.Weir Mitchell's
Hugh Wynne, Free Quaker, and Richard Harding Davis's *Soldiers of
Fortune;* Marie Corelli's *The Sorrows of Satan; Elizabeth and Her
German Garden;* Booth Tarkington's *The Gentleman from Indiana;*
and in 1900 *The Wonderful Wizard of Oz.* In 1894 *Coin's Financial
School* was a best seller (largely because of the free-silver campaign)
and in 1895 Max Nordau's *Degeneration* was a "better seller"—
that is, it did not reach the sales figure of six hundred and twenty-five
thousand, the minimum set by Mott for a best seller in the 1890s.[7]
To the significance of Nordau I shall come in a moment. It will be
noted that Henry James, William Dean Howells, and Mark Twain
did not make the best-seller list in the 1890s, although *A Connecticut
Yankee in King Arthur's Court* was a best seller in 1889. With one or
two exceptions the best sellers emphasized activity, obvious motivation, and the sterling American virtues.

In the magazine world the great invention of the decade was the ten-cent monthly magazine. By 1899 *McClure's, Munsey's, The Cosmopolitan, The Argosy,* and *The Overland* were selling for ten cents a copy. The newspapers met the bright contemporaneousness of these periodicals by inventing the Sunday supplement, the Sunday magazine, and the Sunday "comics." The British critic, William Archer, remarked: "there is nothing quite like them [that is, the ten-cent magazines] in the literature of the world—no periodicals which combine such width of popular appeal with such seriousness of aim and thoroughness of workmanship." They were all family magazines, and if they became mediums for the muckrakers in the next age, nothing they published could bring a blush to the most modest cheek. They were, so to speak, edited for the "Iron Madonna,"—a memorable phrase more distinguished for novelty than for truth. If you wanted something risqué, you read *The Police Gazette* at the barbershop. It had a circulation of about one hundred and fifty thousand in the period, and was forever fending off libel suits. Anthony Comstock once prosecuted it successfully for lewdness, but the ladies pictured in its pages, though they had shapely legs and decolleté gowns, were never nude, and, as compared with the vocabulary of contemporary underground publications (and some above ground), the style of the *Gazette* had all the chaste elegance of Augusta J. Evans Wilson or the novels of Ouida.

Whether the world of sports falls under the rubric of gaiety during the decade is arguable. Certainly games and exercises offered participation and amusement to increasing numbers of Americans either as participants or as spectators. The period is characterized by the creation of clubs and associations to further athletic events and to lay down rules for both professional and amateur conduct, no less than by the growing power of coaches, professional or otherwise, in the control of team sports, amateur and professional. Football in our sense began in 1871 when Harvard took on McGill University, and for some time nothing was quite certain, either the rules, the scoring, or the number on a team. Such university presidents as Andrew Dickson White at Cornell and Charles W. Eliot in Cambridge, when it was proposed that their collegiate teams travel to alien areas, expressed amazement, shock, and a deep distrust of the morality inculcated by the game. Some time in the 1890s Princeton took over the rebel yell in a game against Rutgers, the idea being to terrify the Rutgers team by organized cheering, and it may be said that cheerleaders, "school spirit," and the college athlete as a type shortly developed. The flying wedge was invented by Pennsylvania in 1894. Football teams were beefy campus heroes, even heroes on the stage (as in *Strongheart*), and the vigorous Theodore Roosevelt, though he recognized the physical risks in football, encouraged his son, Teddy, to play in order to demonstrate he was not a mollycoddle. He wrote to headmasters and university presidents on his views about athletics in schools and college. Crowd attendance increased, and so did sheer animal brutality. By 1905–1906 it was evident that the rules had to be altered, "open" football being the outcome. Whether alumni betting and football scholarships also increased as a result is anybody's guess.

As for baseball, Abner Doubleday, the putative inventor of it, was honored by a public funeral set in the New York City Hall, and the decade rejoiced in the prowess of such mighty men as Connie Mack and Honus Wagner. Gradually during the period national professional baseball leagues took shape. The first professional tennis court is said to have been built at Boston in 1876; tennis throve after the Boston Athletic Association put up its courts in 1888, and courts were built in New York by the Racquet and Tennis Club in 1891 and in Chicago by the Chicago Athletic Club in 1893. But the creation of tennis courts at Tuxedo, New York, in 1900 underlined the importance of the game for the well-to-do, and in the 1890s the concept of national championship awards was well under way. Basketball was invented by James A. Naismith in 1891 at the International YMCA Training School of Springfield, Massachusetts; the original equipment consisted of a nondescript ball and two peach baskets fastened to the balcony at either end of the gymnasium. In 1893 the Chicago Fly-Casting Club instituted the first national tournament in fly-casting. In 1895 the American Bowling Congress was formed. From 1890 to 1907 Mrs. M. C. Howell held a sort of perpetual post as the champion national woman archer of the United States. The Amateur Athletic Union, formed in 1888, was reorganized in 1889–1890 on a federal system.

Whether professional boxing properly comes under the head of innocent merriment is perhaps questionable. One notes, however, that, fighting with gloves on September 7, 1892 (bare knuckles had characterized earlier contests), James J. Corbett defeated John L. Sullivan at New Orleans; he was in turn defeated by Robert Prometheus Fitzsimmons in 1897. Fitzsimmons was knocked out by J. J. Jeffries in 1899. Doubtless amateur boxing was fun for the male. Obviously some of these sports were good, clean amusements, encouraged by proponents of vigor as an essential quality in the American people. Obviously also such sports as pugilism and horse racing (which I have ignored here) existed in a gray world wherein special care had to be taken against corruption and fraud, the social climate was dubious, and contestants were usually professionals, not amateurs. Indeed, the fiction of the period, when it sends the hero (more rarely, the heroine) to a prize fight often intends in so doing to imply his moral decline. But archery, croquet, lawn tennis, track, rowing, yachting, college football, college basketball, college baseball—physical rivalry of this sort was fun and, what is more important, contributed greatly to ethical norms. A football foul or a horse on drugs was worse than plagiarism in a composition class.[8]

II

Legends, I repeat, have some factual foundation, and so does that of the Gay Nineties. Literary historians are too intent on James's later fiction or on Howells or Frank Norris even to acknowledge John Kendrick Bangs's light-hearted *A House-boat on the Styx* (1896), or Richard Harding Davis's *Van Bibber and Others* (1892), or George Ade's *Fables in Slang* (1899). These books had vogue because they expressed the humor of the age. But the notion that the 1890s were unusually gay is no more authentic than are the restaurants or night-clubs got up as period pieces from that epoch, with gas jets, dark panels, steins of beer, waiters in white aprons bursting into barbershop harmony, and on a stage self-consciously fronted by footlights, dancing girls resembling the sextet from *Florodora* ("Tell me, pretty maiden, are there any more at home like you?" was first heard at the Casino Theater in New York November 10, 1900).

Gaiety, however, is, not the only legend of the period. It also developed an emotional counterpoint, the *fin-de-siècle* spirit, which was a compound of many simples—the influence of the Pre-Raphaelites and Ruskin in America,[9] the vogue of the aesthetic, the allure of decadence, and a fashionable philosophy of pessimism. The *fin de siècle* was, one feels, more European than American, a manifestation of the cosmopolitan spirit among those who agreed that life was bad and progress impossible. It went along with a transient revival of "Bohemianism" in America, but Bohemianism really never took root in the United States during our half-century.[10]

An English translation of Max Nordau's *Degeneration* (*Entartung*) briefly had vogue—a New York edition was reprinted four times in 1895—and occasioned a spate of indignant reviews, replies, and condemnations. Nordau claimed to be scientific:

> In the civilized world there obviously prevails a twilight mood which finds expression, amongst other ways in all sorts of odd aesthetic fashions. All these new tendencies, realism or naturalism, "decadentism," neo-mysticism, and their sub-varieties are manifestations of degeneration and hysteria, and identical with the mental stigmata which the observations of clinicists have unquestionably established as belonging to these. But both degeneration and hysteria are the consequences of the excessive organic wear and tear suffered by nations through the immense demands on their activity, and through the rank growth of large towns.

Among those pilloried were the Pre-Raphaelites, Tolstoi, Wagner, Ibsen, Nietzsche, Zola—in fact, almost everybody of note, but as the instances were drawn from Europe, America escaped. American replies either warned potential degenerates to alter their ways, rejoiced that art here was healthy, or denied that science proved any such thing.[11] An anonymous volume, *Regeneration,* republished in New York in 1896, included a preface by Nicholas Murray Butler (who was outraged), contrasted Nietzsche's gloomy "science" with the "noble conception" of Tyndall, quoted Ribot, one of Nordau's "authorities," that "nothing is more common or better known than the momentary appropriation of the personality by some intense and fixed idea," and demonstrated that Nordau was morbid: "He is himself an abnormality and a pathological type. Every large hospital for the insane knows his representative—the one sane man in a world of lunatics. . . . The higher altruism of our time believes that life is not only worth living but worth working for." [12]

A cry for beauty is characteristic of poets—it sounds in English poetry from Marlowe down—and minor poets forever protest against materialism. Minor poets tend to accept the formula: If I had two loaves of bread, I would sell one and buy white hyacinths for my soul. This truth makes it difficult to distinguish aestheticism as art for art's sake from the general expression of distaste for some unpoetic environment. There was much talk in the 1890s about Art with a capital letter, but aestheticism in the sense of the French symbolists and the Oscar Wilde/Arthur Symons/Ernest Dowson generation never became a major American interest.[13] The best study of poetry for the decade fails to establish any dominant literary movement.[14] This does not mean there were no aesthetes—Edgar Saltus, for example writes:

> My soul is full of tulips, my life is filled with song,
> For food I have the visions that about a poet throng,

but this is far from aestheticism as a philosophy, and most of the expressions of the aesthetic were random and are now forgotten.

Little magazines came and went, the better known being *The Lark,* which lasted for two years (1895–1897), but did not die of a rose in aromatic pain; *M'lle New York,* which ran for eleven numbers (1895–1896) under Vance Thompson and James Gibbons Huneker, and fondly imagined it was "French" and *was* anti-Semitic; and *The Chap-Book,* the best of the lot, which lasted four years (1894–1898). But *The Chap-Book* was cosmopolitan rather than decadent, printing work by authors ranging from Hamlin Garland to Paul Verlaine and from Robert Louis Stevenson to Mallarmé. Possibly one should associate with any aesthetic movement the vogue of Tiffany glass and of other expressions of the Art Nouveau,[15] but once again it is almost impossible to sort out Pre-Raphaelite and Ruskinian tendencies from the art for art's sake idea.

The principal exhibit of the decadence in America was presumably the same Edgar Saltus quoted above, a second-rate writer whose fate it is to be intermittently rediscovered and again forgotten.[16] He produced eighteen novels in a self-conscious style that vaguely finds its ancestry in Apuleius or Góngora; a book of verse; fourteen volumes of nonfictional prose; and he did some translating. Among the novels *Mr. Incoul's Misadventure* (1887) retains some mild fame. It is characteristic that *Mary of Magdala* (1891) begins with an imitation of the chariot race in *Ben Hur* and continues by aping Oscar Wilde's *Salome.* Blood, a mild lasciviousness, a precious vocabulary, and bizarrely named characters (Melancthon Stitt, Viola Raritan, Tancred Ennever, Mrs. Bunker Hill are examples) are part of him.

Saltus's nonfictional prose is of more consequence, particularly *The Philosophy of Disenchantment* (1885), *The Anatomy of Negation*

(1886), *Imperial Purple* (1892), *Historia Amoris* (1906), and *The Imperial Orgy* (1920). *Historia Amoris* scarcely fulfills the implied promise of erotic revelations, but *The Imperial Orgy* is an account of life in Russian court circles, and *Imperial Purple* is a mannered study of decadent Roman emperors. What Saltus does not steal and expand from Suetonius and others, he invents. He wants to be both "literary" and shocking, as in this passage on Tiberius:

> In his cups they all passed, confusedly before him; the hermaphrodites whispered to the rose-breathers the secrets of impossible love; the griffons bore to him women with magical eyes; the Albanians danced with elastic feet; he heard the shrill call of the Psyllians, luring the serpents to death; the column of Panchaia unveiled its mysteries; the Hyperboreans the reason of their fear of life, and on the wings of the chimera, he set out again in search of that continent which haunted antiquity and which lay beyond the sea.[17]

Saltus thirsted after shock and exquisite sensations; he achieved brass and vulgarity.

The Philosophy of Disenchantment and *The Anatomy of Negation* are intelligent journalism presenting a philosophy of pessimism taken from Schopenhauer and von Hartmann and a critique of religions which concludes, apparently, with a plea for theosophy. If, as Claire Sprague remarks, Saltus's existentialism is not much better than a student term paper, his treatises probably diffused something like the *fin-de-siècle* mood in the 1890s and may have prepared the way for the vogue of Freud in the 1920s. The names of Leopardi, von Hartmann, and Schopenhauer were bandied about among "thinkers" and the avant-garde, but at this distance in time it is difficult to know how much was talk and how much resulted in genuine intellectual or aesthetic influence. Despite essays by Howells and W.N.Guthrie, among others, only two books of translations of Leopardi's poems were published and but one of his prose works. Howells, as might be expected, was sympathetic to Leopardi's sad sincerity, but held that playing with the idea of death is neither wise nor helpful.[18] The turgid German of von Hartmann offered difficulties; discussion of his philosophy was confined to professional moralists and philosophers in the main,[19] though his name and the title of his book, *The Philosophy of the Unconscious* were talked about among the intelligentsia. The powerful name in pessimism was that of Arthur Schopen-

hauer, who was discovered or rediscovered by the Western world at
the end of the century, and the clarity of whose style was admirably
turned into English when Haldane and Kemp brought out *The
World as Will and Idea* in London in 1883–1886, a masterpiece of
translation soon known in the United States. A selection from the
Parerga and Paralipomena (1891) was assembled by T.B.Saunders as
Studies in Pessimism (he also did a *Counsels and Maxims* in 1890),
attracting those who did not feel up to metaphysics. This little book
was an early title in the Modern Library. The complexity of Schopenhauer's relation to Kant and the German romantic school, like
the complexity of his metaphysical system, need not here concern us,
as, indeed, one suspects they did not concern most American readers.
But three central tenets were clear enough. The first is that suffering
is the immediate object of life. It is absurd, Schopenhauer argues, to
think of the enormous amount of pain everywhere in the world as
the result of mere chance; on the contrary, evil is positive, happiness
the negation or absence of boredom or pain. The second is that pain
and therefore life itself is an expression of an irrational will to live
that replaces vitalism as an absolute. This will can never be satisfied
since if it were satisfied it would cease to be. Hence it forever struggles with, and hurts itself in an irrational and endless writhing. Terms
like God and soul, immortality and any cosmic scheme on a rational
basis have no meaning to our existence. The third, and to many
American readers, the most alluring part of Schopenhauer was his
doctrine that art is the only possible escape from this incessant agony,
since through art we rise above wanting the object of art and look
down upon the will through the contemplative intelligence. There is,
he thinks, a hierarchy among the arts, architecture being at the bottom and music at the top, for

> music shows us just what the will is,—eternally moving, striving, chang-
> ing, flying, struggling, wandering, returning to itself, and then beginning
> afresh,—all with no deeper purpose than just life in all its endlessness,
> motion, onward-flying, conflict, fulness of power. . . . music never rests,
> never is content; repeats its conflicts and wanderings over and over; leads
> them up, indeed, to mighty climaxes, but is great and strong never by
> virtue of abstract ideas, but only by the might of the will it embodies.[20]

The Immanent Will of Thomas Hardy, who was beginning to have
vogue in this country, is a parallel to Schopenhauer.

This reading of life attracted attention from various groups—
music-lovers, for example, who were glad to learn that Wagner had
sent the philosopher a copy of *Der Ring der Niebelungen* because
Schopenhauer understood the music of the future, and Wagner was
of course a modern controversial figure; the small groups of art for
art's sake people, who were strengthened in their belief that art is the
supreme expression of life; those who viewed evolution through a
glass darkly; and those who held that the nineteenth century was a
failure and Western man faced inevitable doom. A study of some
nontechnical accounts of Schopenhauer reveals, however, that most
American writers were unwilling to go all the way with pessimism.
Thus, Gamaliel Bradford in 1892 dismissed both Leopardi and Schopenhauer as shrieking fanatics, said that whatever pessimism there
might be in the United States was inherited from the Calvinists, and
pictured the typical American as one who "bears his lot as he can.
Without murmur or complaint looking on at the vast and varied
banquet of the world, from which he alone goes away unsatisfied;
gazing, an ideal and yet not uninterested spectator, at the curious and
futile show which the vagaries of language and the traditions of our
ancestors have taught us to call life—" in short, a rather decent sort
of chap. In 1894 the more philosophical G. Koerner said that Schopenhauer's system marked "an epoch in the history of philosophy"
but that his book leads the reader to a fear that he is being duped:
"we hear as from the depth of a cave this secret sneer of the grand
magician, who has built it and who laughs at his work and at
himself"—an *argumentum ad hominem,* if ever there was one. In
1897 the critic William Morton Payne declared that Schopenhauer
had a firm grasp and unblinking view of life in its totality, but—
there was usually an American "but"—his pessimism should be accepted in its nobler aspects only. Edgar Saltus, as early as 1889, characteristically paradoxical, called the pessimist the most contented of
men, one who thinks nothing is as bad as it might be; and a writer
in the *Outlook* ten years later not unexpectedly deplored the fashion
of taking a low view of life, a fashion he traced to the depression of
the 1890s in Europe and the United States.[21]

Undoubtedly, European currents in art and thought such as symbolism, the art for art's sake movement, decadence, and poetical or
speculative doctrines of pessimism were noticed in the United States
and had some vogue.[22] But I doubt that the main currents of Ameri-

can thought and art were greatly deflected by these interests. The leg-end that the 1890s, so far as the country as a whole is concerned, were aesthetic or decadent or "arty" is, in my best judgment, like the legend of the Gay Nineties, a half-truth only. History being a one-way process, it is difficult to ascertain what the situation would have been if magazines and advanced thinkers and critics had ignored these European movements or viewed them with the caution characteristic of ante-bellum critical opinion. My guess is that though European theories of this kind contributed in a minor way to the 1890s,[23] an element of gloomy or tragic thought, not necessarily Calvinistic but indigenous in the United States, resurfaces in the period. The problem is to define the movement with more precision.

III

Movements of skepticism, decadence, pessimism, and the like in contemporaneous European thought and art were, I suspect, absorbed into a deeper current in the "American mind." They did not bring this current into existence, they merely gave an additional modern coloring to this darker American mood, however defined. With this went the more cheerless interpretation of evolutionary theory, in one sense beginning before the Civil War, in another, more important sense, gathering force after the publication of *The Descent of Man* in 1871. The controversy is often interpreted as one between science and religion; it is better considered as the question whether human worth and dignity could meaningfully survive if the evolutionary doctrine of the origin of man and of the universe were true. As I have earlier hinted, to save religion either one had to allegorize or adjust traditional Christian concepts into meanings and patterns remote from their original intent, or one had to deny the truth of evolution, or, as in the case of Christian Socialism, one had to translate the church into a sort of divine settlement house. If one follows William James's famous distinction between the tender-minded and the tough-minded, the tough-minded included Brooks and Henry Adams, William Graham Sumner, Thorstein Veblen, George Santayana, Josiah Royce, and even James himself. They were not optimists. They assumed with Royce that life is valuable enough to be tragic. The social and economic troubles of the last two decades of the century, at least until 1898, inevitably created a sort of end-of-the-line feeling which, though it might be re-enforced from Europe, did not depend upon Europe for its origin.

Certain imaginative writers shared this pessimism—the harsher naturalists, cynics, poetical groups like that in the Harvard Yard, whose productions smack less of Oscar Wilde and Arthur Symons than they do of Frazer's *The Golden Bough* (1890), the English Bible, and classical tragedy. *A Connecticut Yankee in King Arthur's Court* (1889), as I earlier remarked, never pretended to be history, but it pictured the end of the machine age as a smash-up and shows how cosmic catastrophe haunted the imagination of Mark Twain. Donnelly's *Caesar's Column* (1891) ends in fascist tyranny, anarchy, a bath of blood—the return of industrial America to barbarism. Stephen Crane's works are mainly variations on the irony of existence; his *The Black Riders* (1895) includes this succinct statement of cosmic despair;

> A man said to the universe:
> "Sir, I exist!"
> "However," replied the universe,
> "The fact has not created in me
> A sense of obligation."

For a writer of the temperament of Ambrose Bierce American life did *not* mean largely and mean well.

I have touched in another connection on the grim picture drawn by Brooks and Henry Adams of a universe running down like a weary timepiece. The death of Henry Adams' sister in 1870, that of his wife in 1884, the concept of a blind, mechanic universe, the financial troubles of the 1890s, and the threat of populist control engendered in him a melancholy, at first rebellious and then resigned, which neither Buddhism nor the South Seas nor John La Farge nor travel nor the Virgin nor the affection of his nieces nor the admiration of his friends could eradicate. *The Education of Henry Adams* retains this desperate picture of the universe.

For the first time, the stage-scenery of the senses collapsed; the human mind felt itself stripped naked, vibrating in a void of shapeless energies, with resistless mass, colliding, crushing, wasting, and destroying what these same energies had created and labored from eternity to perfect. Society became fantastic, a vision of pantomime with a mechanical motion;

and its so-called thought merged in the mere sense of life, and pleasure in the sense. The usual anodynes of social medicine became evident artifice. Stoicism was perhaps the best; religion was the most human; but the idea that any personal deity could find pleasure or profit in torturing a poor woman [the sister], by accident, with a fiendish cruelty known to man only in perverted and insane temperaments, could not be held for a moment. For pure blasphemy, it made pure atheism a comfort. God might be, as the Church said, a Substance, but He could not be a Person.[24]

This anguish was not derived from Europe.

I turn to some of the systematic thinkers. The mercurial quality of the personality and thought of William James makes him difficult to categorize, but inasmuch as the popular image of him is either that of a man who declared that the cash value of an idea is its truth or that of a happy-hearted member of a highbrow Optimists Club, it is well to remember that, like Carlyle's Teufelsdröckh, James knew the Everlasting Nay, the Center of Indifference, and the Everlasting Yea, and that despite his acceptance of diversity as bracing (he once wrote that "pessimism is essentially a religious disease"), he was by no means blind to the tragic aspects of existence. In *The Principles of Psychology* (1890) he announced that the soul was useless for psychological purposes, and toward the end of *The Varieties of Religious Experience* he wrote: "In all sad sincerity I think we must conclude that the attempt to demonstrate by purely intellectual processes the truth of the deliverance of direct religious experience is absolutely hopeless. . . . We must . . . bid a definitive good-by to dogmatic theology," a sweeping away of almost the oldest American tradition. He said, of course, that he was willing to take the universe as dangerous and adventurous, but he said also that in the deepest heart of man there is a corner in which the ultimate mystery of things works sadly. A catena of passages from his books and letters can be put together that parallels Schopenhauer:

> For naturalism, fed on recent cosmological speculations, mankind is in a position similar to that of a set of people living on a frozen lake, surrounded by cliffs over which there is no escape, yet knowing that little by little the ice is melting, and the inevitable day drawing near when the last film of it will disappear. And to be drowned ignominiously will be the human creature's portion. The merrier the skating, the warmer

and more sparkling the sun by day and the ruddier the bonfires at night, the more poignant the sadness with which one must take in the meaning of the total situation.

The scale of evil actually in sight defies all human tolerance. . . . A God who can relish such superfluities of horror is no God for human beings to appeal to. His animal spirits are too high.

If *this* be the whole fruit of victory . . . ; if prophets confessed and martyrs sang in the fire, and all the sacred tears were shed for no other end than that a race of creatures of such unexampled insipidity should succeed, and protract *in saecula saeculorum* their contented and inoffensive lives—why, at such a rate, better lose than win the battle, or at all events, ring down the curtain before the last act of the play.

But James was always a fighter, and other passages indicate his refusal to accept nescience and defeat as the end of man:

There is no *full* consolation. Evil is evil and pain is pain; and in bearing them valiantly I think the only thing we can do is to believe that the good power of the world does not appoint them of its own free will, but works under some dark and inscrutable limitations, and that we, by our patience and good will, can somehow strengthen his hands.

If this fight be not a real fight, in which something is eternally gained for the universe by success, it is no better than a game of private theatricals from which one may withdraw at will. But it *feels* like a real fight— as if there were something really wild in the universe which we, with all our idealities and faithfulnesses, are needed to redeem; and first of all to redeem our own hearts from atheism and fears.

He thought human nature was notably adapted to "such a half-wild, half-saved universe." If James was not a philosophical pessimist, both his ethics and his psychology took full account of the claims of pessimism.[25]

It would be jejune to say that Royce also views the universe gravely, and more important to note that his first major philosophical book was *The Religious Aspect of Philosophy* (1885), and that *The Problem of Christianity* (1913) was virtually his last one. In between are such titles as *The Spirit of Modern Philosophy* (1892), with its account of German romantic philosophy, Hegel, and Schopenhauer, and *Studies of Good and Evil* (1898). Royce's interest in logic and mathematical theory was great, but all commentators agree

that his reading of life was as often ethical as logical.[26] Indeed, had
he been born in an earlier time, he might have become a powerful
preacher of the Word. Ralph Barton Perry notes that religious prob
lems first drove Royce into philosophy and that Royce fused what he
thought to be the great problems of Christianity with his famous concept of the Great Community. In an address at the University of California on "The Conception of God," published in 1897, he
postulates that all knowledge is something experienced, and comments:

> If this be true, then the total limitation, the determination, the fragmen-
> tariness, the ignorance, the error,—yes (as forms or cases of ignorance
> and error), the evil, the pain, the horror, the longing, the travail, the
> faith, the devotion, the endless flight from its own worthlessness,—that
> constitutes the very essence of the world of finite experience, is, as a posi-
> tive reality, somewhere so experienced in its wholeness that this entire
> constitution of the finite world appears as a world beyond which, in its
> own constitution, nothing exists or can exist,

and the point is not the argument for the Absolute, but the stress on
"the storms of . . . agony and . . . restlessness . . . of an incomplete
experience," "our ignorance, our fallibility, our imperfection," "our
experience of longing, of strife, of pain, of error," and "the bitterness
of our finitude" as a reading of actual existence. Royce, to be sure,
argues from fragmentariness to unity, but the point, I repeat, is the
dark terminology in which he conceives of the human condition.

In an essay entitled "The Problem of Job" he asks us to "rejoice in
the endurance of the tragedies of life, because they show us the depth
of life," and the last chapter in *The Spirit of Modern Philosophy,* entitled "Optimism, Pessimism, and the Moral Order," denies the validity of a passive mysticism, a mere resignation, and, like James, declares that God demands we help Him in his struggle against evil.
Royce accepts pessimism as a first step toward moral victory:

> Pessimism, in the true sense, isn't the doctrine of the merely peevish
> man, but of the man who, to borrow a word of Hegel's, "has once feared
> not for this moment or for that in his life, but who has feared with all
> his nature; so that he has trembled through and through, and all that
> was most fixed in him has become shaken." . . . The mood which really
> opposes [optimism] . . . is just the mood that has learned to demand ab-
> solute standards, and that finds none; the mood that refuses to be com-

forted with such good things as can be bought, because it belongs to the priceless goods of the spirit. This . . . true pessimism is in its very nature the mood of the painfully awakened who cry for God's truth, and who so far find it not. It is the despair of those who want a plan in life, and who see how our ordinary and natural life is planless, accidental, a mere creature of fortune. This despair is the first voice, in many hearts, of the truly devout spirit.

In sum, "the justification of the existence of my evil impulse comes just at the instant when I hate and condemn it." [27] As with James, so with Royce; a darkening outlook exists, but awakens the distinctively American solution of heroic activism.

Santayana's "naturalism," in effect a revival of high-minded classical stoicism, is characteristically expressed in his poetry, to which I shall come. The outlook of two other theorists in the period is relevant to pessimism—Thorstein Veblen and William Graham Sumner. The thought of each is based on a bleaker reading of evolution. Veblen's key work, *The Theory of the Leisure Class,* first appeared in 1899 and has been kept in print ever since.[28] He did not believe in progress, he professed to be indifferent to moral issues; albeit his books appeal to a morality higher than custom,[29] and his obvious irony and more obvious sarcasm make him seem the American economic Diogenes. Of the higher learning, which supported him, however reluctantly, he wrote that it is mainly "an exercise of control and coercion over the population from which the [leisure] class draws its sustenance." Modern society for him was but a late form of barbarism, in which "exploit" looks down on industry. The leisure class is wasteful, its expenditure and its consumption are alike showy, and its "wealth," such as it is, though it may have its foundation in somebody's frugality, is now a means for expressing its dislike of toil. Veblen pursues this theme endlessly—into monetary habits, standards of taste and dress, the "conservation of archaic traits" (including English spelling), religion, education, sports, gambling, the function and place of women, academic costumes, dueling, and even William Morris's Kelmscott Press. The trail of the serpent is over them all, and there is little light at the end of the tunnel.[30] Somebody said of *The Theory of the Leisure Class* that it is as grim as a Norse saga. Tone in such a book is more important than theory; and the tone of Veblen's masterpiece is fairly represented in a paragraph from the opening chapter, which lays a foundation of theory for the whole book:

> Under this common-sense barbarian appreciation of worth or honour, the taking of life—the killing of formidable competitors, whether brute or human—is honourable in the highest degree. And this office of slaughter, as an expression of the slayer's prepotence, casts a glamour of worth over every act of slaughter and over all the tools and accessories of the art. Arms are honourable, and the use of them, even in seeking the life of the meanest creatures of the fields, becomes a honorific employment. At the same time, employment in industry becomes correspondingly odious, and, in the common-sense apprehension, the handling of the tools and implements of industry falls beneath the dignity of able-bodied men. Labour becomes irksome.[31]

"The data employed to illustrate or enforce the argument," the little preface tells us, "have by preference been drawn from everyday life, by direct observation or through common notoriety." Let it be remembered that this sardonic description of the warrior's trade appeared just after the Spanish-American War.

Despite an unexpected vision of a radiant future toward the end of an essay on "Earth Hunger or the Philosophy of Land Grabbing," written in 1896 but not published until 1913, William Graham Sumner took a tough-minded, not to say fatalistic view of the future of humanity.[32] For him man is an animal, not a special creation; as an animal he is born into an overcrowded environment and must forever fight for his existence. His needs are to learn self-discipline, the necessary limitations on freedom, and cooperation in the name of self-interest, not sentiment. "We know," he said, "that the human animal is, by nature, more helpless in the face of nature than many other animals." There are but limited supplies of food and land; therefore such concepts as inalienable or natural rights are chimeras that "never can enter into scientific thinking since they admit of no analysis and can be tested by no canons of truth," having in fact "no footing in reality." A yearning for equality is a mere superstition. Neither the savage nor the civilized man, neither the tramp nor the millionaire is free, and the dream of liberty must always issue in disappointment or revolt. Democracy, he held, accomplishes nothing in politics, social welfare, or industry to bless mankind; on the contrary it usually makes matters worse: "All modern economic developments have tended to level classes and ranks, and therefore to create democracy, and to throw political power into the hands of the most numerous class; the courtiers of power, therefore, turn to the masses with the same flattery and servility which they used to pay kings, prelates, and nobles," and all that the nineteenth century can bequeath to its successor is a new version of the struggle to survive, albeit peaceful capitalism is a possible form of evolutionary progress. But Sumner's famous essay on "The Conquest of the United States by Spain" (1899) is a sufficient commentary on peaceful capitalism.

Altruism as the emotion is commonly understood is therefore a will-o'-the-wisp. In the essay on "War" Sumner flatly says:

> The social philosophy of the civilized modern world is saturated with humanitarianism and flabby sentimentalism. The humanitarianism is in the literature; by it the reading public is led to suppose that the world is advancing along some line which they call "progress" towards peace and brotherly love. Nothing can be more mistaken.

Mixing ethics and economics as reformers do is "utterly ignorant and mischievous." "To act from notions, pious hopes, benevolent intentions or idealism is sentimentalism, because the mental states and operations lack basis in truth and reality." What is worse, the burden created by following these illusions falls upon the honest middle-class taxpayer, Sumner's famous "Forgotten Man." How can it be otherwise when bad ethics are bolstered by poetry and the fine arts, which

> affect the imagination and produce new states of thought and emotion. For the greatest part their effect is dissipated and exhausted in these subjective experiences. . . . As motives of action, these impulses of the emotions produced by artistic devices do not stand in good repute in the experience of mankind. Why? Because they contain no knowledge or foresight, and therefore no guarantee of consequences. . . . It is not possible to cross-examine a picture, even if it is a photograph.

Fortunately this fallacy was no longer increased by the clergy, who have ceased to preach theology and are without authority. Such is the world view of this grim economist.

IV

As poets are commonly supposed to be sensitive barometers in any age, it is, I think, significant that the 1890s nourished a group of philosophic bards who tend to a cosmic point of view. They did not, most of them, suggest pessimism so much as comparative mythology, for they tended to allegorize Greek, Jewish, and Christian (notably medieval) legends by turning them into symbols of emotional and fideistic readings of human life. Before one takes up leading figures in this group one must, however, touch upon two earlier writers supposed to have been neglected by the period, whose points of view may be considered relevant to the problem of endurance and despair. These are Emily Dickinson and Herman Melville.

Three books of poems by Emily Dickinson, who died in 1886, were published in 1890, 1891, and 1896 respectively; [33] and though their editors have been accused of blindness to her power, the charge cannot be quite substantiated. The three volumes received a mixed but not unsympathetic reception,[34] and the period of neglect seems to have run from 1900 to the opening of World War I rather than from 1889 to 1900. Did these collections influence thought in the period? Apparently nobody regarded the author as a cosmic poet. Her work was held to be a belated revival of transcendentalism, or brilliant *aperçus* of psychological insight, or a return upon Blake and the seventeenth century metaphysicians, but did not color opinion.

Melville's *John Marr and Other Sailors* was printed in 1888 and *Timoleon* in 1891, and it is held that the decade ignored both. But as each of them appeared in a privately printed edition of twenty-five copies, it is difficult to see how they could have been influential. More to the point is *Clarel*, printed in 1876 though afterward withdrawn from circulation. That lengthy poem, powerful and confused, is more "cosmic" than the two later collections or than Emily Dickinson. It is an epic reading of religion and doubt, church and state, evolution and mysticism, history and contemporary life; and so far as it is consistent, it seems to say that life is dark and an appetite for intelligent experience your only guide. The puzzle is to know when the sentiments expressed are those of the characters and when they are Melville's own. There can be, however, no doubt about the "Epilogue":

> Unmoved by all the claims our times avow,
> The ancient Sphinx still keeps the porch of shade
> And comes Despair, whom not her calm may cow,
> And coldly on that adamantine brow
> Scrawls undeterred his bitter pasquinade.

> But Faith (who from the scrawl indignant turns),
> With blood warm oozing from her wounded trust,
> Inscribes even on her shards of broken urns
> The sign o' the cross—*the spirit above the dust!*
> .   .   .   .
> The running battle of the star and clod
> Shall run for ever—if there be no God.
> .   .   .   .
> Then keep thy heart, though yet but ill resigned—
> Clarel, thy heart, the issues there but mind;
> That . . .
> Emerge thou mayst from the last whelming sea,
> And prove that death but routs life into victory.

The poem anticipates the doubts and fears of the 1890s; the difficulty is that we know too little about its circulation and influence.

I have remarked that poets of that period tended to construct or reconstruct legendary tales into symbols of modern man. Some of these constructs are of course less weighty than others. Thus Richard Hovey, who flitted from aestheticism to athleticism, planned a poem in dramas on the Arthurian story that was apparently meant to fuse a Hegelian view of history with Christian mysticism. The scheme was left incomplete, but even if it had been carried through, it would not have had much weight. Hovey, so far as he is now remembered, is remembered for his Dartmouth poems, including the famous "Stein Song":

> For it's always good weather
> When good fellows get together
> With a stein on the table and a good song ringing clear.[35]

The "Stein Song" has the merit of reminding us that the spirit of Kipling was quite as important an ingredient of the 1890s as the spirit of Schopenhauer. Moreover, Hovey's romantic Arthurianism was eventually overshadowed by the subtle and profound treatment of similar legends in Edwin Arlington Robinson's great trilogy *Merlin* (1917), *Lancelot* (1920), and *Tristram* (1927). In the 1890s, however, Robinson was still feeling his way, practicing sonnets, French forms, octaves, and blank verse, as well as Browningesque dramatic monologues. Though smaller masterpieces like "Luke Havergal" (1896) and "Cliff Klingenhagen" (1897) appeared, his one succinct philosophical statement from the decade is presumably the "Credo" of 1896:

> I cannot find my way; there is no star
> In all the shrouded heavens anywhere;
> And there is not a whisper in the air
> Of any living voice but one so far
> That I can hear it only as a bar
> Of lost, imperial music, played when fair
> And angel fingers wove, and unaware,
> Dead leaves to garlands where no roses are.
>
> No, there is not a glimmer, nor a call,
> For one that welcomes, welcomes when he fears,
> The black and awful chaos of the night;
> For through it all—above, beyond it all—
> I know the far-sent message of the years,
> I feel the coming glory of the Light.

The blackness of despair is here illuminated by the Light of the last three lines, an incorrigible affirmation that anticipates *The Man Against the Sky* of 1916. Robinson's roots are in the 1890s; his flowering comes later.

More pertinent is George Cabot Lodge, who once made considerable noise in the world or at least in New England. He was more of a cosmopolite than he was a Bostonian, so that Paris, Germany, and the Spanish-American War did as much to shape his outlook as any Brahminical inheritance. True, he dedicated *The Song of the Wave and Other Poems* (1898) to the dead Leopardi; true also that, as Henry Adams pointed out, he had a youthful enthusiasm for Schopenhauer. But in literary studies one commonly finds what one is looking for, enthusiasm and Schopenhauer do not precisely mix, and though "vogue" themes like nescience, resignation, Buddhism, and silence appear in his verse, "The Song of the Wave" and poems like it celebrate natural energies for their own sake. For Lodge, human love is a positive and ennobling fact, not a trap set by the irrational will to live. His *The Great Adventure* (1905) restated this delight in energy; and his two poetical dramas, *Cain* (1904) and *Herakles* (1908), exercises in Biblical or Greek mythology, celebrate the uniqueness of personality and the possibility of choice and proclaim a mystical soteriology. Thus, at the end of *Cain* Eve exclaims:

> Till now my tears have blinded me; at last
> I see and know, thou art the Son of Man,
> Thou art the Saviour—and my son, my son!

Herakles, which has sixteen dramatis personae (Sophocles managed to make do with six in *Antigone*) turns the central figure into a savior, a spiritual twin of Prometheus, whom he instructs in the gospel of individuality:

> . . . the soul of man
> Is, in the universe of force and change,
>
> . . . .
>
> The sole self-realized power, the single strength
> Aimed and reflective and perfectible.
> Therefore alone the mind's conception turns
> Chaos to cosmos, ignorance to truth,
> Force to the freedom of articulate law—
>
> . . . .
>
> Yea, of the soul is all our hope!

Whatever else this may mean, it is no declaration of an irrational will nor a gospel of nescience nor, as has been alleged, a reflection of William Sturgis Bigelow's famous Harvard lecture on Buddhism.[36]

Three other poets of the cosmic and mythological sort are George Santayana, Trumbull Stickney, and William Vaughn Moody. Of these Santayana is the most prestigious. He had already begun laying the foundations for his fame as a theorist of aesthetics, a general essayist, and an austere philosopher. Between 1894 and 1901 he printed all the poetry he cared to preserve—*Sonnets and Other Verses* (1894), an enlarged edition of this book in 1896, *Lucifer: A Theological Tragedy* (1899), and *The Hermit of Carmel and Other Poems* (1901). When he was sixty Santayana brought out a selection of his poems, revised,[37] with a preface from which I quote these excerpts:

> Of impassioned tenderness or Dionysiac frenzy I have nothing, not even of that magic and pregnancy of phrase . . . which marks the high lights of poetry.

> Landscape to me is only a background for fable or a symbol for fate, as it was to the ancients; and the human scene itself is but a theme for reflection.

> For as to the subject of these poems, it is simply my philosophy in the making. . . . I see no reason why a philosopher should be puzzled. What

he sees, he sees; of the rest he is ignorant; and his sense of this vast ignorance (which is his natural and inevitable condition) is a chief part of his knowledge and of his emotion. Philosophy is not an optional theme that may occupy him on occasion. It is his only possible life, his daily response to everything. He lives by thinking, and his own perpetual emotion is that this world, with himself in it, should be the strange world it is.

Few poets have defined their powers and their aims more succinctly.

A refined intellectual hedonism informs Santayana's lyric verse, expressing itself through detachment, irony, belief in *humanitas*, and an unembittered stoicism. A phantom of Platonic idealism floats across the background of many poems—

> Love but the formless and eternal Whole
> From whose effulgence one unheeded ray
> Breaks on this prism of dissolving clay
> Into the flickering colours of thy soul,

runs one injunction. An austerity of melancholy, neither tragic like that of Leopardi nor despairing like that of Hardy, is characteristic of Santayana's younger outlook:

> Sweet are the days we wander with no hope
> Along life's labyrinthine trodden way,
> With no impatience at the steep's delay,
> Nor sorrow at the swift-descended slope.
>
> . . . .
>
> Farewell, my burden! No more will I bear
> The foolish load of my fond faith's despair,
> But trip the idle race with careless feet.
> The crown of olive let another wear;
> It is my crown to mock the runner's heat
> With gentle wonder and with laughter sweet.

The second Sapphic ode in the first volume expresses the poet's reading of earth in terms like that of Lucretius's Great Mother:

> My heart rebels against my generation,
> That talks of freedom and is slave to riches,
> And, toiling 'neath each day's ignoble burden,
> Boasts of the morrow.

No space for noonday rest or midnight watches,
No purest joy of breathing under heaven!
Wretched themselves, they heap, to make them happy,
     Many possessions.

For thou, O silent Mother, wise, immortal,
To whom our toil is laughter,—take, divine one,
This vanity away, and to thy lover
     Give what is needful:—

A staunch heart, nobly calm, averse to evil,
The windy sky for breath, the sea, the mountain,
A well-born gentle friend, his spirit's brother,
     Ever beside him.

What would you gain, ye seekers, with your striving,
Or what vast Babel raised you on your shoulders?
You multiply distresses, and your children
     Surely will curse you.
 .   .   .   .
[Nature] hath not made us, like her other children,
Merely for peopling of her spacious kingdoms,
Beasts of the wild, or insects of the summer,
     Breeding and dying,

But also that we might, half knowing, worship
The deathless beauty of her guiding vision,
And learn to love, in all things mortal, only
     What is eternal.

One can murmur the names of Matthew Arnold, Marcus Aurelius, or Walter Savage Landor after reading these serenities. Santayana puts a cool distance between him and the more fashionable pessimists and decadents of the period.

Except as it represents the use of medieval legend to interpret human identity, "The Hermit of Carmel" need not keep one, but *Lucifer: A Theological Tragedy* must detain us longer. The subtitle is apparently descriptive rather than functional, since a five-act drama involving the Christian story, Greek myth, Talmudic legend, and figures from Goethe and Milton is theological only in a Pickwickian sense. The story is alternately simple and confused. If the chief contention in the play seems to lie between Christ and Lucifer,

Santayana has some difficulty in getting Zeus and Hermes, Mephistopheles and a minor follower and companion of Lucifer into the confrontation. In the last act Hermes returns to Olympus, wondering why St. Peter admitted Lucifer into heaven but refused admission to Hermes. Christ then appears before the gods and in a series of rather unconvincing conversational exchanges with Zeus, Hera, Aphrodite, Ares, and Athena, tells these deities that they have sinned unwittingly. He then disappears, whereupon Zeus announces that if he, too, must disappear, he will at least disappear from his throne, says he expects to see the ghost of Christ enter oblivion, and declares

> The last sad summer of the world is come.

(Lament for the passing of the pagan world was standard in nineteenth-century poetry.) In the final scene Lucifer is alone in the universe, superior, he thinks, to Christ, unhappy because he has loved Hermes and lost him, and firm in his intellectual pride, though he, too, longs for oblivion.

> O truth, O truth, eternal bitter truth,
> Be thou my refuge when all else is blind!
> Thou art the essence of my lofty mind;
> At thy pure wells I will renew my youth.
>
> .   .   .   .
>
> Lo! I lift my head
> Into the void, in scorn of all that live
> Through hope and anguish and insensate wars.
> For, knowing grief, I have forgot to grieve,
> And, having suffered, without tears receive
> The visitation of my kindred stars.

Doubtless Howgate, a thoughtful interpreter of Santayana, is right in saying that the play represents the stage of disillusionment when Christianity embraced all that Santayana held dear, whereas naturalism (personified by Lucifer) stood for all that Santayana held true. He is also right in saying that great issues stalk its pages.[38] But the play is grandiose rather than grand (the author in later life called it extravagant), and one finds it hard to reconcile the maturity of Santayana's poetry of reflection with the adolescent rant in many of the speeches in the play. *Lucifer* is, however, historically important because it shows to what amazing lengths even a genius like Santayana could go in the effort to solve the riddle of the world by what I call the method of comparative mythology.

Central to this poetry of comparative mythology is the soteriological figure—Cain and Herakles in Lodge, Lucifer in Santayana (though less clearly), and in the poetry of Moody and Stickney the figure of Prometheus.[39] As were many of his Harvard contemporaries, Moody was something of a Grecophile, but a wide variety of other literary and philosophical influences poured upon him during his formative years at Harvard from 1889 to 1894, part of which he spent abroad, and at the raw young University of Chicago, whither he went in 1895—the Pre-Raphaelites, Milton, Dante, medieval romance, Provençal poetry, Shelley, Browning, Whitman, and of course, his contemporaries. He jettisoned much of his apprentice work; yet such memorable poems as "Gloucester Moors," "An Ode in Time of Hesitation," "On a Soldier Fallen in the Philippines," "The Quarry," and "The Menagerie" date from the late 1890s or the opening of the new century. "The Menagerie," an ironic view of evolution, concludes:

> If you're a sweet thing in a flower-bed hat,
> Or her best fellow with your tie tucked in,
> Don't squander love's bright springtime girding at
> An old chimpanzee with an Irish chin:
> *There may be hidden meaning in his grin.*

The stanza seems at first sight to have nothing to do with the thesis of salvation presented in *The Fire-Bringer* (1904), *The Masque of Judgment* (1900), and the unfinished *The Death of Eve*. Moody fused an interpretation of Prometheus as the savior of mankind with a doctrine of woman as the creative spirit; and the young bride in the zoo must therefore learn what she ought to be as a mature woman. The argument of the trilogy is that Prometheus the sufferer or sacrificial offering, Eve the symbol of the continuity of life, and God the creator and destroyer are so necessary to each other that the weakening or disappearance of any one of the triad injures the cosmic plan. In *The Masque of Judgment,* once mankind has been condemned, heaven weakens as in *Das Rheingold,* the lamps around God's throne dim their splendor, and Raphael, the archangel who is a friend of humanity, mournfully describes the ruin of heaven and speaks of an enigmatic future:

> The moon smoulders; and naked from their seats
> The stars arise with lifted hands, and wait.

Possibly they wait for a new cycle in time. In *The Death of Eve,* after the lapse of endless ages, the aged mother of mankind is to return to the Garden and restore life to the earth, and as in Lodge's *Cain* she calls the first murderer: "My great son!" The point becomes clearer after one reads a parallel lyric of the same title written before the fragment of the drama:

> Far off, rebelliously, yet for thy sake,
> She gathered them, O Thou who lovest to break
> A thousand souls and shake
> Their dust along the wind, but sleeplessly
> Searchest the Bride fulfilled in limb and feature,
> Ready and boon to be fulfilled of Thee,
> Thine ample, tameless creature,—
> Against Thy will and word, behold, Lord, this is She!

A mystical concept of the Virgin here intermingles with the idea of the mother of man.

In *The Fire-Bringer*—which runs parallel to Trumbull Stickney's *Prometheus Pyrphoros*—once Prometheus has brought back light, intelligence, normality, and affirmation, even if pagan, to humanity, Pandora, beloved of him but fatally separated from him, sings of the absolute necessity of the love of God for man and of man for God:

> I stood within the heart of God;
> It seemed a place that I had known;
> (I was blood-sister to the clod,
> Blood-brother to the stone.)
>
> I found my love and labor there,
> My house, my raiment, meat and wine,
> My ancient rage, my old despair,—
> Yea, all things that were mine.
>
> I saw the spring and summer pass,
> The trees grow bare, and winter come;
> All was the same as once it was
> Upon my hills at home.
>
> Then suddenly in my own heart
> I felt God walk and gaze about;

> He spoke; his words seemed held apart
> With gladness and with doubt.
>
> "Here is my meat and wine," He said,
> "My love, my toil, my ancient care;
> Here is my cloak, my book, my bed,
> And here my old despair.
>
> "Here are my seasons: winter, spring,
> Summer the same, and autumn spills
> The fruits I look for; everything
> As on my heavenly hills."

One can at this point mutter owlish references to Plotinus or Emerson, immanence and panpsychism, but the point of this remarkable lyric is affirmation. Moody's trilogy, too much neglected, is, despite passages of merely rhetorical emphasis, one of the few subtle philosphical poems in the national literature. The savior, Prometheus, must mediate and sacrifice; the woman, Pandora-Eve, must create, love, and endure; and God must temper justice with love, being compelled to do so by the actions of Prometheus and the stubborn love of life in Pandora-Eve. The poem is far from the "vogue" pessimism of the decade; it struggles with theology, evolution, a philosophy of the will, and a mystical yea-saying and seems, despite its incomplete form, a more coherent reading of life than either Santayana's *Lucifer* or the two dramatic poems by George Cabot Lodge. If Royce insisted that life is valuable enough to be tragic, Moody declares it is valuable enough for rapture, insight, and love.[40] Regeneration is possible outside science and theology.

Trumbull Stickney was likewise a classicist and of sufficient interest for a selection from his poetical work to appear recently.[41] His *Prometheus Pyrphoros* first printed in the *Harvard Monthly,* came out in a privately printed edition of *Dramatic Verses* issued by C. E. Goodspeed and the Merrymount Press in 1902.[42] A Greek scholar who taught that language at Harvard, Stickney studied in Paris, was something of an Orientalist, an amateur of the arts in the better sense of the word, and a poet in the British and European rather than in the American tradition. Of his generation he, and only he, might qualify as the equivalent to Leopardi, for he has the same melancholy, the same yearning for the ancient world, the same profound sadness that turns love into a peril and landscape into a ghost. In his lyric and meditative verse Stickney writes with exquisite precision, even if he is occasionally a touch too "literary." "Mnemosyne" is an exercise in nostalgic memory:

> It's autumn in the country I remember.
>
> How warm a wind blew here about the ways!
> And shadows on the hillside lay to slumber
> During the long sun-sweetened summer-days.
>
> . . . .
>
> It's dark about the country I remember.
>
> There are the mountains where I lived. The path
> Is slushed with cattle-tracks and fallen timber,
> The stumps are twisted by the tempests' wrath.
>
> But that I knew these places are my own,
> I'd ask how came such wretchedness to cumber
> The earth, and I to people it alone.

"In Ampezzo" is an exercise in a landscape of sorrow:

> . . . high around and near, their heads of iron
> Sunken in sky whose azure overlights
> Ravine and edges, stand the gray and maron
> Desolate dolomites,—
>
> And older than decay from the small summit
> Unfolds a stream of pebbly wreckage down
> Under the suns of midday, like some comet
> Struck into gravel stone.
>
> Faintly across this gold and amethystine
> September, images of summer fade;
> And gentle dreams now freshen on the pristine
> Viols, awhile unplayed,
>
> Of many a place where lovingly we wander,
> More dearly held that quickly we forsake,—
> A pine by sullen coasts, an oleander
> Reddening on the lake.
>
> . . . .
>
> Across this shadowy minute of our living,
> What time our hearts so magically sing,
> To mediate our fever, simply giving
> All in a little thing.

Stickney of course does not have the sense of national ruin that Leopardi expresses, but he lives in a mood of cosmic melancholy, and his *Prometheus Pyrphoros* begins in blackness, continues in a treacherous light fetched by Prometheus from on high for Deukalion and Pyrrha, and concludes in an ominous thundercloud that takes Prometheus away. In a farewell speech Prometheus seems to validate an Oriental concept of life as an endless cycle in which self-affirmation is the only positive form possible to man:

> Many times I have died and yet shall die,
> For Nature rolls on, while across the chasms
> From hill to hill and round from east to west
> Voices pass on the echo to the stars.
> No forms are laid aside, and if I lived
> I was the creating of the tide wherein
> An endless motion was exemplified.

Stickney is the one true melancholy philosopher among these poets.

I have clung to poetry in this analysis of pessimism in the 1890s. It may be argued that the vogue of naturalism in fiction is more to the point. But like the clergyman in Boswell's *Johnson* who lamented he could not be a philosopher because cheerfulness was always breaking in, American naturalists were in the main unable to breathe within the boundaries of determinism. Most of them—Norris, Crane, Garland, Dreiser (who turned mystic), even Howells so far as he was one, and Twain, whose darker moods are obvious but who is haunted by the thought that the damned human race ought to behave better [43] —wanted to reform railroads, or trusts, or politics, or military conduct, or the capitalist system, or American farm life. The poets saw deeper. None of them, it will be observed, attempted an epic, that form which implies that a great central figure has a powerful will and is one—Aeneas, Orlando, and Rinaldo in *Jerusalem Delivered* are examples—from whom royal houses, nations, races, or empires descend. On the contrary their favorite form is the drama, which implies conflict, tension, and release but not necessarily triumph. The impression they leave is that of men perpetually striving for a unity that perpetually eludes them, and the enigmatic or unsatisfactory nature of the soteriological element in their plays is evidence of a profound struggle in their souls. Determinism and free will, evolution and salvation, despair and hope, a protest against tyranny and a thirst for justice—these are their great themes; and they take, not the United States, but all mankind for their subject. Perhaps in a very large sense their inability to arrive at faith of some sort may be thought of as an expression of the irrationality of Schopenhauer's will, and certainly some of them read Schopenhauer. But it is equally probable that they echo the confusion of the 1890s, which were neither gay nor pessimistic but one of the most vexed and stormy decades in the history of the United States since the Civil War.

V

During most of the decade tensions steadily mounted in the United States until they were suddenly defused, transformed, and directed as a unit against a target outside the country, a redirection that gave the republic an emotional unity it had not known for many years. To understand these tensions and why they increased, it is necessary to retrace one's steps.

The half-century that separates the Compromise of 1850, which proved to be futile, from the assassination (1901) of William McKinley, last of the nineteenth-century presidents, divides conveniently at 1876, the year of the most hotly disputed presidential election in American history. Whatever the bargaining that went on behind the scenes, a peace of exhaustion settled on Washington when Rutherford B. Hayes was inaugurated on March 4, 1877, and a few months later withdrew the last Federal garrison troops from the Southern states. This act of pacifism ended the threat of a second civil war.[44] For a brief period all seemed harmony. The North, which had demanded ratification of the Thirteenth, Fourteenth, and Fifteenth Amendments as a pledge of loyalty, felt that the Union was safe; the South, though it lost the war and gave up its doctrine of states' rights, believed that its white civilization had been restored and its regional autonomy recognized. It became the solid South. The West waited to see—after all, Hayes was from Ohio. If Democrats acquiesced in the defeat of Tilden, who had received a majority of legitimate popular votes, liberal Republicans, fearful that their party would split, devoutly prayed that the honesty of Hayes would erase the corruption under Grant. The Centennial Year was, moreover, a year of rejoicing in a united nation. Southern commonwealths constructed state buildings at the Centennial Exposition in Philadelphia, and Federal officials toured the South on missions of good will. The President decorated the graves of both the Union and the Confederate dead.

Why did the harmony so soon break up? It is illuminating to consider the nine presidents between Andrew Johnson, who left office in 1869, and Woodrow Wilson, who assumed it in 1913. Two of them, Chester A. Arthur and Theodore Roosevelt, both from New York, were catapulted into office by assassination, and both of them had known the fierce friction of intrastate party feuds. Roosevelt of course later became president in his own right. The other New Yorker, Grover Cleveland, the only Democrat among the nine, had been shaped by party feuds and like Garfield was in a way a dark horse. The other six were all originally from Ohio, though Grant was associated with Galena, Illinois, and Harrison, educated in Ohio, made his career in Indiana. But Hayes, Garfield, McKinley, and Taft were citizens of the Buckeye State. In these decades the Middle West rather than the East or the South in the long run determined what the country should do; and even a cursory examination of the politics of that region will show why presidents were unable to establish and maintain a firm program until the arrival of Theodore Roosevelt. They had perpetually to compromise with forces beyond their control. The art of politics is the art of compromise, but the kind of bargaining most of them had to learn through their experience of infighting was not the sort of elegant diplomatic give-and-take that eventuates as high policy. I select Ohio for analysis in this respect, not because Ohio was better or worse than its sister states but because the fact that so many presidents came from the heartland of America makes it typical.

The politics of Ohio from 1865 to 1915 were fascinating, unpredictable, usually irrational, sometimes dull, occasionally corrupt, and now and then violent. At one time or another that state nourished persons as diverse as Clement Vallandingham, the leading Copperhead; Senator Joseph B. Foraker, forced to resign from the Senate because of questionable financial deals, who, as governor, when Cleveland tried to return Confederate battleflags to Southern states, cried out: "No rebel flags will be surrendered while I am governor"; Samuel ("Golden Rule") Jones, four times mayor of Toledo, who practiced what many conservatives thought of as rank socialism; John B. McLean, once a Harvard student, who in alliance with a shady crimi-

nal lawyer turned Cincinnati into the worst-governed city in the republic (he was succeeded by the notorious "Boss" Cox, who "ran" the
town until 1910); Jacob S. Coxey of Massillon, who led a march of
the unemployed on Washington; "Tom" L. Johnson of Cleveland,
who thought there might be something in the ideas of Henry George
and became the best-known mayor in America; Marcus Alonzo
Hanna, who calmly assessed big business some millions of dollars to
insure the election of William McKinley; Henry B. Payne, who admired John D. Rockefeller and who was alleged to have been elected
to the United States Senate by Standard Oil money; Nicholas Longworth, who married Alice Roosevelt in 1906, became a congressman
in 1908, and speaker of the House some years later; and Bellamy
Storer, who got into a row with Theodore Roosevelt because he interfered in Vatican politics and failed to answer the letters of his superior. It is difficult to find any common denominator among these
types, but they reflect the cultural and political confusion of the state.
The lower tiers of Ohio counties were "Southern," and across the
Ohio River bummers were brought to cast illegal votes, paid off by illegal liquor and illegal women. The northern parts of the state had
once been colonies of New England; New England names were still
powerful there and so were New England educational and banking
patterns. Mid-Ohio, save for a few industrialized places, was diversi-
fied farming country, losing population, to be sure, but retaining
enough conservative strength to be a force in politics. It is a mark of
the reactionary agrarian attitude that a state agricultural college was
not open until 1873; and an Ohio historian says that a foreman who
went there in 1877 reported the livestock as consisting of five horses,
three of them worn out, five cows, a few calves and steers; that there
was no working capital; and that Norton S. Townsend, an enthusiastic progressive in agricultural affairs, was supposed to teach agriculture, agronomy, animal husbandry, dairying, horticulture, veterinary
medicine, anatomy and surgery, botany and "vegetable physiol-
ogy." [45]

The polyglot population of the ugly industrial cities tended to live
in racial ghettos. The slums in these cities and the dull blocks of
row houses or "flats," which housed thousands of workers and their
families, were in sharp contrast to the New England loveliness of
older Ohio settlements. The workers were quite capable of violence.
The militia was again and again called out, as it was in 1894, to pre-

vent lynchings, curb rioting, control strikes, stop looting, preserve property, or police disaster areas. Southern Ohio for a time sustained the White Caps, a secret order of vigilantes modeled on the Ku Klux Klan. The law-abiding middle class and the commercial, industrial, legal, and transportation overlords could not of course condone or comprehend the tumultuary side effects of immigration, hasty industrialization, and uncontrolled, laissez-faire economy; they were inclined to dismiss discontent as anarchy. John Hay's novel, once anonymous, *The Bread-Winners* (1884), subtitled "A Social Study," pictures Offitt, Bowersox, and other agitators as conspirators against whose murderous intentions it is necessary for employers and bankers to buy stands of arms. At the polls Republicans and Democrats fought each other, the Democrats, when in power, being especially notable for gerrymandering, but party victory was sometimes endangered by splinter groups—Prohibitionists, Populists, or other dissidents. Republican and Democratic bosses played into each other's hands, and a new constitution, completed after interminable sessions of a constitutional convention, was briskly voted down by the electorate in 1874. I repeat that there was nothing peculiar about Ohio; similar conditions could be found in other states, though this crazy quilt of conflicting pressure groups was perhaps more characteristic of industrial commonwealths in the North than it was of states in the South.

American presidents who had been shaped by such turmoil were necessarily educated in its pattern, and when they reached Washington found the country as a whole no easier to manage than was the state of Ohio. Hayes got to the White House by a single electoral vote, a victory made possible by a confidential understanding between Republicans and Southern Democrats. When he withdrew the Federal troops from South Carolina and Louisiana, he found himself for a time a president without a party. When he vetoed a measure for the free coinage of silver, Congress passed the bill over his veto, and at no time did he have the allegiance of those who elected him. Garfield, eight times elected to the Congress, had to struggle against Democratic gerrymandering, was not nominated for the presidency until the thirty-sixth ballot, and, short though his time was, showed no capacity to mediate between the two halves of the Republican party. Arthur, personally honest, was a high-class party hack. Quietest of American presidents, Benjamin Harrison was elected by a popular plurality, not a majority, could not control his party, had to face the enmity of bosses like Quay, Alger, and "Czar" Reed, and in his last two years a House controlled by Democrats. William McKinley was genial, his chief asset; he had fought off Democratic gerrymandering at his every second election to the House of Representatives. Though he was the first president since 1872 to win a popular majority, he was regarded as a puppet manipulated by Hanna, and he put together one of the great mediocre cabinets in American history, which included Russell A. Alger, a supremely incompetent Secretary of War, and John D. Long, an easygoing Secretary of the Navy —all this on the eve of the Cuban War. Taft need not here concern us, even if his amiability let many of the Theodore Roosevelt reforms slide down hill. He was described by Senator Dolliver as a fat man surrounded by people who know exactly what they want.

Clearly there was no governing theory anywhere. Theories were distrusted by practical men both because they were theoretical and because most of them originated in Europe and were brought in by the new immigration as anarchism, socialism, communism, or some other radical philosophy of the state. The older impulse to found radical communities waned, though there were still some scattered colonies like the one in Fairhope, Alabama (1894), or the Ruskin Community (1894–1899) in Muscogee County, Georgia (which published for a time a paper with an influential title, *The Social Gospel*), and others in California, New Jersey, and elsewhere.[46] Utopian thought now took shape as Utopian romance, of which Edward Bellamy's *Looking Backward* (1888) and William Dean Howells' *A Traveller from Altruria* (1894) and *Through the Eye of a Needle* (1907) are characteristic. Some of these launched or fed into national parties, for it now seemed that not village societies but a national revolution was the key to the future—peaceful in the case of Bellamy, dark and bloody in the books of Donnelly and of London. Laurence Gronlund, indeed, opined: "Socialism . . . holds that the impending reconstruction of Society will be brought about by the logic of Events; [and] teaches that *The Coming Revolution is strictly an Evolution.*" [47]

The gray prose of many standard history textbooks fails to give the reader a sense of the restlessness and violence of the last quarter of the nineteenth century. Between the Centennial Exposition and 1901 two Presidents of the United States were assassinated. In the unlovely cities, whatever the success of the park systems in, say, Boston or Chicago, graft was common, crime and prostitution seem to have increased beyond the control of social agencies, and, except for sporadic improvements in Toledo and elsewhere, city police were often helpless or venal, albeit statistics about criminality are notoriously unreliable and for many states then and later do not exist.[48] The tramp became a national type, offering organized capital a recruiting source for strikebreakers.[49] Lynching and attacks upon foreigners became increasingly notorious in the latter part of the nineteenth century. Negroes, Italians, Chinese, and Japanese were among the racial groups assaulted.

Deeper than these manifestations were the sectional and sociological tensions of the age. The South, suspicious of the North, was itself torn three ways: agrarians against the rising industrial class, the poor against the Bourbons who seemed to run the state governments, and the whites against the Negroes. Sometimes, as in the instance of the tariff, Southern industrialists, transportation magnates, and their kind forgot their Confederate roots and voted for high duties, and sometimes they voted for low ones. Sometimes, particularly in periods of agricultural depression (soil exhaustion and obsolete farming methods continued to plague the area), the poor whites and the Negroes, so far as the latter were allowed any political voice, supported clever demagogues who purported to lead them against the "interests," populism finding one of its main supports in that area.[50] Indeed, the South was suspicious of the East, the Middle West, and the West.

The East, proudly recalling that it was in its own opinion the real United States, that the South was backward and the Middle West and West raw or provincial, was prepared to believe that it, and it only, understood finance and capitalism. The Middle West was vaguely conscious of its role as the heartland of the republic but found itself divided in outlook: the industrialists, the transportation barons, the lumber barons, the "Beef Trust," the "Oil Trust," and Midwestern bankers alternately joined Wall Street in voting against "radicalism" and turned suspicious of the haughty Atlantic seaboard and its self-regarding economic and monetary policies, while the urban proletariat joined in strikes against railroads and industry, and the middle class tried to believe that the Benjamin Franklin virtues were the whole of the American way of life. Furthermore, problems of Catholicism and Protestantism, the new immigration and the old American stock troubled state after state in that region, just as they troubled Boston or New York City. The West was suspicious of the East, though not particularly of the South. In general, though not consistently, the West wanted easy money and tariffs that would protect wool and mining but that would simultaneously reduce freight rates and therefore commodity prices. The South opposed any financial or tariff measures that seemed to permit Northern exploitation of Southern resources, and the East was profoundly suspicious of the crude populist notions they attributed to the West, however defined, and regarded the South as a backward colony out of which money could be made but which ought to be left stewing in its own juice. In Congress political combinations for or against this or that measure exhibited all the wild variety of a kaleidoscope, and though in general terms the Middle West got its way, the results were confusing, and partisanship in New York or Pennsylvania or Massachusetts had its role to play in a troubled time.

In a period when the Blaine-Cleveland campaign of 1884 made something of a record in vituperation and in an age which, as I have earlier hinted, was not distinguished for verbal restraint, it is not surprising that hysterical phrases abounded. The demonetizing of silver in 1873 got to be known as the "Crime of '73," a crime committed by criminal members of a mysterious gold conspiracy here and abroad: even Henry Adams was not immune to the idea of a money trust of Jew bankers. Various tariff bills passed or failed to pass or were vetoed and then buried or passed between 1865 and 1915, few or none of which made any consistent sense, and most of which were soon denounced by powerful groups, regional or economic, as wrongs against the welfare of the people. If the Granger movement had been relatively peaceful (Sunday afternoon picnics and rural fairs were supposed to improve the farmers' lot), the Farmers' Alliance and the People's Party were far more bellicose and lived in a dark atmosphere of charges of conspiracy, chicanery, exploitation on the part of wealth and condign vengeance on the part of the poor during the agricultural decline of the 1880s and the 1890s. We must, said James B. Weaver, Populist candidate for the presidency, who had more dignity than some other members of his party,[51] expect to be fronted by a vast and splendidly equipped army of extortionists, usurers, and oppressors. It is difficult to get into consistent focus farm life in the West as pictured by Hamlin Garland in "Under the Lion's Paw" and the opening chapters of *A Son of the Middle Border,* and in Edward N. Wescott's popular story about a New York village banker and horse trader with a shagbark exterior and a heart of gold, the hero of *David Harum.*

The tariff, the currency, the power of state or federal government to control malefactors of great wealth, the regulation of immigration, the capacity of the people to rule directly through the election of senators or the initiative, the referendum, and the recall (all of these measures came into being in the next century), woman suffrage, the desirability of controlling public utilities and transportation systems —such issues and their solutions are chronicled by historians, but their grave pages do not convey the passionate urgency of the age. Even at the risk of some repetition I think it illuminating to quote from a Populist proclamation:

> The conditions which surround us best justify our co-operation; We meet in the midst of a nation brought to the verge of moral, political and material ruin. Corruption dominates the ballot-box, the Legislatures, the Congress, and touches even the ermine of the bench. The people are demoralized; most of the States have been compelled to isolate the voters at the polling places to prevent universal intimidation or bribery. The newspapers are largely subsidized or muzzled, public opinion silenced, business prostrated, homes covered with mortgages, labor impoverished, and the land concentrating in the hands of capitalists. The urban workmen are denied the right to organize for self-protection, imported pauperized labor beats down their wages, a hireling standing army, unrecognized by our laws, is established to shoot them down, and they are rapidly degenerating into European conditions. The fruits of the toil of millions are boldly stolen to build up colossal fortunes for a few, unprecedented in the history of mankind; and the possessors of these, in turn, despise the Republic and endanger liberty. From the same prolific womb of governmental injustice we breed the two great classes—tramps and millionaires. The national power to create money is appropriated to enrich bondholders; a vast public debt payable in legal-tender currency has been funded into gold-bearing bonds, thereby adding millions to the burdens of the people. Silver, which has been accepted as coin since the dawn of history, has been demonetized to add to the purchasing power of gold by decreasing the value of all forms of property as well as human labor, and the supply of currency is purposely abridged to fatten usurers,

bankrupt enterprise, and enslave mankind. A vast conspiracy against mankind has been organized on two continents, and it is rapidly taking possession of the world. If not met and overthrown at once it forebodes terrible social convulsions, the destruction of civilization, or the establishment of an absolute despotism.[52]

Not until the 1960s do we get language thus irrationally charged as proper to popular discussion. The point is neither the economic nor the sociological truth or falsity of this philippic; the point is the note of desperation and smothered violence in language of this kind. What the Populists wanted in the 1890s are the commonplaces of today, but this rhetoric of fury and despair shrouded the moderation of most of their reforms.

The relations of capital and labor in the 1880s and more especially the 1890s dramatize to the point of incredibility the passions of these years. This violence seemed to justify the view of the English traveler, G. W. Steevens, who said that except where property is concerned, every American is at heart an anarchist who hates constraint, hates regulation, and hates law [53]—except when he wants to restrain somebody else. Perhaps for the reason Steevens alleges, by a kind of masochism in the body politic, anarchists were more feared and received more condign punishment than did either socialists or communists, although general opinion did not really distinguish among these radical groups. Between 1888 and 1903 Congress debated legislation excluding anarchists from the country. The concept of America as a political asylum collided with a doctrine of fear, but an exclusion bill was finally passed, partly as a consequence of the assassination of President McKinley, though the indomitable Senator Hoar of Maine opposed the legislation, stoutly affirming there were governments he would gladly overthrow by force and violence. In December 1894 Emma Goldman, born in Lithuania, experienced her first arrest for a speech inciting workingmen to revolt, though no riot followed upon her oration,[54] but neither this, nor other arrests, nor continual police harassment prevented her from getting out an anarchist monthly, *Mother Earth,* or publishing such books as *Anarchism and Other Essays* (1910), and a fascinating autobiography, *Living My Life* (1931). She was deported to Russia in 1919 and died in Canada. The "Haymarket Massacre" of 1886 and the shooting and stabbing of Henry Clay Frick by Alexander Berkman (the assault was said to have been planned by Emma Goldman) in 1892 were of course proofs of the dangers of radicalism.

Seen in long temporal perspective, most periods of alarm look silly, but the historian, if he will translate himself back into the 1890s, finds this fear of anarchy and "radicalism" more than newspaper hysteria. Never had the conflict been more violent. Early organized and possessing war chests of incredible wealth, big business in the 1890s either defied the courts or under the eye of benevolent judges drew the teeth from adverse legislation, notorious instances being a series of interpretations of the due process clause of the first section of the Fourteenth Amendment, and a second example the decision that strikers came under the ban against contracts, combinations and conspiracies in restraint of trade in the Sherman Act.[55] The use of the injunction in cases of labor violence or the threat of violence, like the use of federal troops, became common. Labor did not have equal access to similar weapons of control. A legal historian writes:

> The transformation of the due process clause into a substantive check upon legislative regulation, the elaboration of the labor injunction as an anti-strike weapon, the emasculation of the Sherman Act in the *E. C. Knight* case, and the overthrow of the federal income tax in the *Pollock* case were related aspects of a massive judicial entry into the socio-economic scene. American constitutionalism underwent a revolution in the 1890's, a conservative-oriented revolution which vastly expanded the scope of judicial supremacy, with great consequences for American economic and political history.[56]

If in the 1880s progressives were mildly encouraged, the 1890s saw a series of setbacks.

Taking a general view of the so-called Gilded Age, still another historian paints an even darker picture of the means by which big business evaded the law or avoided testifying before committees or courts.[57] Commissions investigating the meat-packing industry, for example, found in 1889 that witnesses had been intimidated. In other cases subpoenas were ignored, books ordered to be produced were not forthcoming or were doctored, the motives of critics were insidiously impugned, and leading company officials under examination could not remember salient transactions. Despite investigations, denunciations, exposures, and court decisions, the Standard Oil Company persisted in its dubious ways until the administration of Theodore Roosevelt. It went in, legend to the contrary notwithstanding, for apologists and publicity agents, and shrewd lawyers such as Samuel C. T. Dodd. Corporation lawyers did all they could to nullify national regulation in such areas as uniform railway freight rates. Chauncey Depew, defending the New York Central before the Hepburn Committee, accused critics of communism, the destruction of property rights, and so on; and big corporations welcomed with delight the conversion of an economist of the rank of George Gunton from his earlier labor radicalism to the sounder notions he propagated in *Gunton's Magazine* (1896–1904) as well as in a small library of titles advocating conservative economic theory.[58] The doctrine of social Darwinism taught that unrestricted competition was the law of life and that, as Sumner, Andrew Carnegie, James H. Bridge, and others argued, interference by government (except in the interest of profit) in the war for national or world markets only made matters worse. Except for the pallid notion that Christian charity was a Good Thing and except for the obvious truth that starving customers cannot buy many goods, hard-headed financiers, businessmen, and statesmen really believed that governmental regulatory agencies should be kept weak or abolished. The beatitudes, somebody said, did not build business. And what was to keep or make America great except its economic strength? Slums, poverty, sickness, hunger, unemployment were merely the unfortunate but transitory side effects of a great stream of energy which, if allowed to flow freely, would lead the country into a period of unprecedented prosperity from which starvation and over-population would automatically disappear.[59]

Unfortunately, for millions of Americans the businessman's millennium was slow in coming, or rather, progress toward a stable economy seemed to the many—farmers, laborers, housewives, immigrants, country bankers, small-town merchants, and their kind—perpetually to elude the United States. Sweated labor was still commonplace, child labor widespread; epidemics swept through slums where shoddy tenements swarmed with humanity, and sanitation was primitive. Company towns in the coal-mining areas of Pennsylvania or West Virginia and the mill villages strewn over the Piedmont area in the South were about as cheap, unlovely, and primitive as they could be, their heating, lighting, and sanitary facilities either lacking or below civilized standards. Ideas like unemployment insurance, social security, health care, day nurseries, safety devices in mine or mill, sick care, and employers' liability (despite the success of some of these measures in Bismarck's Germany), were poohpoohed as impractical or socialistic. Charity was dominated by "Christian" psychology the schoolbooks did nothing to check, or was of the casual sort afforded by settlement houses, the Salvation Army, socially conscious but condescending church groups, and rescue homes in the big cities (there was little of it in the country). Of civic responsibility in the public interest there was small trace. If on one hand the tragedy of the period was the denial to the state of the right to intercede, it should be noted on the other hand that the unemployed and the impoverished fiercely resented being regarded as objects of scientific social inquiry —of that

> . . . organized charity, scrimped and iced,
> In the name of a cautious, statistical Christ,

satirized by John Boyle O'Reilly. When the cost of living is compared with real wages, skilled workers were worse off in 1870 than they had been in 1850. The panic of 1873 shrank the pay envelopes of those lucky enough to be still employed, and laid off something between two and three million workers of all kinds. Agricultural distress was widespread in the South and West and even in the Northeast in the 1880s, which, however, showed a shaky upward trend in some parts of the economy. But the panic of 1893, marked by the failure of almost seven hundred banks, the bankruptcy of great, overcapitalized railroad systems, the collapse of industry, and a startling increase in unemployment, led to widening bitterness, the flouting of law, and industrial strife that mounted here and there into civil war. On the side of capital the National Association of Manufacturers, created in 1895 to boost the export trade, abandoned its original purpose by fathering the Citizens Industrial Association of America, virtually the same organization under another name, to combat "radicalism": "Whereas, the strained relations between employer and employee are rapidly reducing the business conditions of the country into a state of chaos and anarchy, and the forces of socialism which are assuming control of the situation regard neither law nor the rights and the liberties of the individual," the association solemnly "disapproved" of lockouts and strikes and demanded the equitable adjustment of differences between employers and employees by "an amicable method." Amicability, however, proved to be one thing when interpreted by the National Association of Manufacturers and quite another thing when practiced in a strike by Pinkerton detectives.

Prior to 1867 American labor unions were negligible forces. After 1867 they become increasingly powerful. The Knights of St. Crispin, founded in Milwaukee in 1867, was for five or six years an important national body, which, however, declined by reason of its amateurish organization and the defalcation of some of its officers. It was succeeded by the Noble Order of the Knights of Labor, founded in Philadelphia by Uriah S. Stevens, which by 1886 under the leadership of Terence V. Powderly had a membership of about seven hundred thousand and was a power in the land. It suffered from bad organization and from being a secret society. Eventually it gave way to the American Federation of Labor, born at Terre Haute, Indiana, in 1881, distinguished by its federal organization and by its sagacity in avoiding weaknesses evident in its predecessor.[60] By 1897 the American Federation of Labor had a paid-up membership of over a quarter of a million, by 1914 of two million, and was effectively organized.

There were unions outside the American Federation of Labor. The powerful railway unions remained independent; and in the West the Western Federation of Miners (1893) by and by spawned a dissident group, the Western Labor Union (1898), out of which (and other radical tendencies) was born the Industrial Workers of the World, which accused the A.F. of L. of putting barriers in the way of progress. Between 1881 and 1905 there were almost thirty-nine thousand strikes and lockouts of more than twenty-four hours duration.[61]

Two notable industrial battles of the 1890s will illustrate the bitterness of conflict, a bitterness that amplified the passions of the great railroad strikes of 1877 and 1886. One is in the East. By 1892 the Carnegie Steel Company, one of the parents of United States Steel, had acquired a number of mills in the vicinity of Pittsburgh, including one at Homestead, a drab company town ten miles up the Monongahela River. Henry C. Frick, with the blessing of Andrew Carnegie, who was in Europe, had become the chairman of the board, a man with small enthusiasm for labor unions. The Amalgamated Association of Iron and Steel Workers, a constituent member of the American Federation of Labor, had about a quarter of a million members in 1892, but among the Carnegie plants only the Homestead works were, so to speak, controlled by the union. This organi-

zation seems to have been moderate in its policy and sought to nego-
tiate with rather than to defy management. But Carnegie, despite his
published essays expressing sympathy for labor, apparently advised
Frick that since most of the Carnegie plants were run on a non-union
basis, the Homestead plant should become non-unionized, or at least
accept the non-union wage scale. A new agreement between management and labor was needed in 1892; at the opening of July, however,
the union was getting nowhere with its proposals, and the company
offer would reduce the income of the employees. Frick presented the
union with a wage scale toward the end of May that reduced wages,
and to this he required an answer by June 24. Meanwhile, he assured
himself of help from the much-hated Pinkerton agency. He built a
stout fence about three miles long around his mills with three-inch
holes regularly spaced, he said, for "observation" and at strategic
points he erected platforms bearing searchlights. On June 25 he
broke off further conferences; on June 28 he shut down the armor
plate mill, locking out some eight hundred men. Effigies of Frick and
a subordinate were hanged in Homestead the next morning. Three
thousand workers turned out at a mass meeting, resolved to reply to
the lockout by a total strike, and set up an *ad hoc* Advisory Committee which told the sheriff it would police the mill, and arranged its
battalions in military order in an around-the-clock watch. All the
workers were paid off on July 2 and discharged.

On July 4 Frick requested the sheriff, William H. McCleary, to
protect the company property, Philander C. Knox, the Carnegie attorney, having already inquired whether the sheriff would deputize
Pinkerton detectives. On July 6 at two in the morning three hundred
Pinkerton agents were loaded on barges at Pittsburgh, prepared with
provisions, arms, and ammunition, and a tug towed these barges toward the company wharf at Homestead. Informed of this action, the
strikers prepared to resist. The barges attempted to land at the company wharf, but the embittered employees broke through the company fence and blocked the attempt. Shots were exchanged. The tug
steamed off with wounded Pinkerton detectives, leaving the barges
helpless. A second attempt at landing was made at eight o'clock,
which occasioned more gunfire. Meanwhile more strikers, more arms,
and more ammunition had come from Pittsburgh and other points,
and help was offered from states as far away as Texas. In addition to
rifles the strikers had a twenty-pound brass breech-loading cannon

and a smaller cannon belonging to the G.A.R., neither of which, however, did much harm to the barges. Dynamite hurled at them failed to destroy the Pinkerton force, a burning raft failed of its mission, flaming oil and waste on a railroad car were likewise futile, and burning oil poured into the river proved ineffective. At noon the Pinkerton forces waved a white flag, which was ignored. In the afternoon it was formally agreed at a mass meeting that the Pinkertons would be allowed to land, disarmed, and leave Homestead in safety. At four o'clock a second white flag was displayed, the Pinkerton men landed, were disarmed, and marched through the town, but in spite of guarantees, they were assaulted by strikers, their wives and children, and about half of them were more or less seriously injured. During the fray three detectives were killed, so were ten strikers, thirty detectives were hospitalized, and an unknown number of other Pinkerton men and strikers were injured.

Sheriff McCleary telegraphed the governor, Robert E. Pattison, saying the situation was beyond his control and that he could not find sufficient deputies. After some hesitation the governor mobilized most of the militia, and about eight thousand men under the command of Major General Snowden, who declared that "revolution was proclaimed and entered upon," marched on Homestead. The management repossessed the plant and introduced strikebreakers, who for some weeks lived as prisoners. Sympathetic strikes broke out at other Carnegie plants, one at Beaver Falls lasting four months and one at Duquesne requiring the presence of a regiment of militia. By November it was evident that the union was beaten. More than half its members lost their jobs. The Pinkertons were "the hireling army" denounced in the Populist platform. When in 1901 the United States Steel Corporation absorbed the Carnegie holdings, they inherited executives who, from the shock of this civil war, came to believe that antiunionism was the only defense against socialism, and the unions had learned what one writer calls "industrial absolutism" could do.[62]

There were other bloody affairs in the East, including the Pullman strike (1894), but the tale of physical violence grows monotonous, and I shall content myself with a Western counterpart. There had been gold strikes along the north fork of the Coeur d'Alene River in Idaho and, later, silver and lead had been discovered mainly on the south fork of the same river. This was in the 1880s. Miners drifted in from all sorts of regions, principally from Montana. It is probable that mining camps in the Coeur d'Alene district resembled such camps elsewhere. But in 1884 disputes over wages convulsed the mining town of Bradford on the Wood River. Miners swarmed in, met at a union hall (where arms and ammunitions had been stashed), and several hundred of them prepared to take forcible possession of the Queen of the Hills mine above the little town. The company meanwhile had enlisted about forty defenders and built a fortification for them on a dump at the mouth of the mine. Bloodshed was averted by the skillful intervention of James H. Hawley. But all this was only a prelude. In 1892 further wage disputes arose in other mining camps in the area; a pitched battle took place at the Gem and Frisco mills in July, in which guards were defeated, six men killed, and an unknown number wounded. Mines were shut down, and companies armed their watchmen. Strikers took possession of the Bunker Hill and Sullivan Mining Company stamp mill. State authorities declared martial law, erected a "bull pen," and requested federal aid. In May the company had brought suit in the United States Circuit Court for an injunction against the miners union. Because the miners had seized the mill, warrants now were issued for the arrest of twenty of their leaders, who, after trial in Boise, a great distance away, were sentenced to jail. In September a grand jury brought in indictments against twenty prominent unionists on a charge of conspiracy—note the word. Four of them (including George A. Pettibone) were tried and convicted, and on appeal all were released. Another trial in a state court produced one hundred and forty indictments for the killing of company guards at Gem. Again the miners were freed and the indictments quashed.

Meanwhile, the Western Federation of Miners seemed to have yielded control to "radical" officials. The companies would not recognize the union. In April 1899 all union members in the vicinity of the Bunker Hill and Sullivan Mining Company marched on that company's office, demanding wages of from $3.00 to $3.50 a day and a closed shop. A like demand was made next day on the Empire State Company and the Idaho Mining and Development Company, both of which promptly closed down. Union leaders then decided to make an example of the Bunker Hill and Sullivan people. On April 29, 1899, about a thousand strikers captured a Northern Pacific train, ran it down the canyon to Wallace, Idaho, stopping at a powder house where they loaded one of the cars with dynamite. At Wallace they were joined by other miners. The strikers forced the trainmen to comply with their orders and conducted their operations with military efficiency, throwing out pickets and marching in regular companies. They blew up the mill at Wallace with dynamite, re-formed, and ran the train back to Burke, Idaho, meanwhile cutting the telegraph wires. The crowd was masked. The governor, Frank Steunenberg, appealed to President McKinley for aid, and on May 1, 1899, the 1st United States Infantry regiment was sent. State officials had sworn in about a hundred deputies. In the interim, James Cheyne and two other company officials had been captured by the miners; ordered to run, they were shot at, Cheyne was killed, and one of his companions wounded. On May 3 the governor again proclaimed martial law in the district. About a thousand arrests were made, including the sheriff of Shoshone County and two commissioners, on the ground that they had failed to take action in time to prevent rioting. On May 29 a special grand jury sitting at Wallace brought in a series of indictments charging murder, in consequence of which some of the miners were found guilty. Martial law remained in force about a year and a half. Some time later Steunenberg, then an ex-governor, was assassinated by a bomb, for which Pettibone, Haywood, Moyer, and Simpkins, miners all, were indicted. Haywood and Pettibone were acquitted, the others found guilty.[63] Many felt that the assassination of the President of the United States in 1901 was the direct consequence of all this lawlessness.[64]

The Age of Energy seldom exhibited more distressing traits of irrational disorder than it did in the 1890s, years in which the conflicts sometimes seemed uncontrollable. Section was still arrayed against section—the West and the South taking on populism, which was viewed with dismay by the conservative East, its anxiety increased by the apparent growth of anarchy and the apparent breakdown of orderly legal processes. Racial tensions did not lessen. On the contrary, race was a central issue, as in the cases of the treatment of Negroes, Indians, and the new immigrants, the instances of agitation over Chinese and Japanese laborers, the attempt of the Immigration Restriction movement to check or stop the inflow of Slavs and Levantines, and the problem of American power and our "brown-skinned brothers" in the Pacific, or, less accurately, in the Caribbean. Class, moreover, was arrayed against class—labor against capital, the farmers against the railroads and the banks, the unemployed against what one would nowadays call The Establishment.

Political language was inflammatory, theories of reform, so it seemed to conservative minds, were demagogic, destructive, or harebrained. It is of course difficult to measure the decibels of noise in one age against those in another, and it is true that there were bloody clashes in the 1870s and the 1880s and that the end of Reconstruction brought a kind of peace to the South. But it was an uneasy peace. Higher education improved in the decade; yet these years saw a succession of violations of academic freedom in departments of economics or sociology or history from New England westward and southward.

There were signs of change in 1897; and, postponing to the next chapter the curious unifying power latent in the Spanish-American War, let me record a ceremony held at the State House in Boston to welcome in the twentieth century. This was at midnight on December 31, 1899, and was staged under the auspices of The Twentieth Century Club. Trumpets were blown from a balcony over the listening crowd, a hymn was sung by the multitude, a selection from the Ninetieth Psalm was read by the aged Edward Everett Hale, another hymn was sung, the multitude recited the Lord's Prayer, and as a finale everybody sang "America," after which another flourish of trumpets ushered in the year 1900. Hale was too deaf to hear anything but the brass instruments, but he said that "the whole service was very satisfactory and I am writing under the influence of its solemnity." [65]

X

<hr>

The Roosevelt Era

I wish to preach, not the doctrine of ignoble ease,
but the doctrine of the strenuous life.

—THEODORE ROOSEVELT

I

IF BY NATIONAL UNITY one means unanimity of opinion and emotion in any country, national unity is seldom or never achieved. In our own Civil War there were powerful elements North and South who thought that the inevitable conflict was not inevitable and who wanted to stop the fighting—just as during the Napoleonic wars there was a vocal minority in Great Britain who regarded Bonaparte as a liberator and viewed the nations arrayed against him as agents of political reaction. Yet out of these years Nelson and Wellington emerged as national symbols of pluck and tenacity, as in our own history Lee on the one side and Lincoln on the other have become symbols of the profounder meaning of an epic conflict. In more recent times Winston Churchill became a metaphor of British endurance. In great critical moments, of course, like the Battle of Britain, the struggle to survive unifies a nation, but even in embattled Israel survival does not altogether mute criticism and protest. In American history, when we talk of the Jacksonian period, we do not mean that Andrew Jackson had no opposition and no enemies; we mean only that a set of compulsions of which he was, so to speak, a magnetic center tended to subordinate other, lesser conflicts to the overriding problem whether Jacksonian democracy, whatever one means by the term, was to be the guiding philosophy of republican development. In that sense one can say with perfect propriety that Andrew Jackson focused and summed up an age. In that sense I suggest that a modern analogue in the decades here under survey is the rise to prominence of Theodore Roosevelt.

The dominant figure of the twenty-sixth President of the United States arose out of the tensions of the last two decades of the nineteenth century. He proved to be the greatest activist in the history of the American presidency, and for that reason he may be said to sum up a great phase of American cultural history. The incarnation of personal energy, as varied in his interests as any other of the amazing personalities of the half-century, Roosevelt assisted destiny in propelling the republic into its place among the great powers of the world. After him the United States could never be again what it had been before; in him the Age of Energy reached a symbolic climax. When he retired from the White House there was a slow slide downward under Taft, a descent partially checked and reversed by Woodrow Wilson's New Freedom, that new edition of Roosevelt's New Nationalism, but the New Freedom was in turn checked by the necessity of preparing the country to participate in the Great War of 1914. Since Roosevelt's time, like it or not, we have been a Great Power. I repeat that controversy did not end when Roosevelt became President. On the contrary it was as lively as ever, but the controversies of the age seemed more and more to whirl about the White House as planets revolve around a sun.

Of course an elder generation wanted to keep him down. It proved impossible. Old-guard politicians tried it and continually failed. Roosevelt began his public life as an assemblyman from a silk-stocking district in Manhattan and immediately created a small but powerful insurgent group in the New York legislature. He was then shunted to the national Civil Service Commission under Harrison, hitherto a harmless body. He galvanized that moribund arm of government, and Harrison was moved to comment that Roosevelt "wanted to put an end to all the evil in the world between sunrise and sunset." [1] He continued for a year under Cleveland; then they tried making him a police commissioner in New York City, and he promptly turned into the most vocal police commissioner in the United States. In the first McKinley administration he was Assistant Secretary of the Navy under an unexciting chief, John D. Long. Roosevelt took advantage of the laxity or absence of the Secretary to alert the navy to the probability of a war with Spain, stationing Admiral George Dewey with a small but adequate fleet where he would be closest to Manila. Roosevelt resigned after raising the 1st Volunteer U.S. Cavalry, universally known as the Rough Riders, principally recruited from the Great West, which he loved; then, declaring that his military inexperience did not qualify him for command, he became lieutenant-colonel under his good friend Leonard Wood. But in the general confusion of military policy in Cuba, Wood shortly found himself commanding a brigade, Roosevelt took over the regiment, and the newspapers made him the hero of the charge on San Juan Hill. When, principally as a consequence of a highly irregular protest written by Roosevelt but signed by most of the general officers, the Fifth Army Corps was recalled from Cuba to Montauk Point on Long Island, Thomas C. Platt, still Republican boss of the State of New York, made Roosevelt the candidate for the governorship, a post to which Roosevelt was elected less than three months after he had disembarked. As governor he struggled so valiantly for reform that the regular Republicans next tried to shelve him by making him Vice-President in McKinley's second administration. He presided over the Senate about a week, but within seven months of his inauguration McKinley was shot, and Roosevelt, who had to be brought down from a mountain top in the Adirondacks to get to Buffalo, was sworn in as president—in Oscar Handlin's phrase, the first modern chief executive of the United States.[2]

Elected for a second term, Roosevelt faced a reluctant or a recalcitrant Congress during the last years of his presidency, but he remained the great popular idol. A biographer said that "the peculiarity about him is that he has what is essentially a boy's mind," and the same writer quotes John Morley as having exclaimed: "He is not an American, you know, he *is America*." [3] Having picked out William Howard Taft as his successor, Roosevelt departed on a long hunting trip in Africa, thriftily combining science with pleasure; the pleasure he himself paid for, but the scientific part—securing birds and animals for American museums—was paid for by Andrew Carnegie, whom many persons considered a malefactor of great wealth. Roosevelt emerged from Africa to make a tour of Europe, during which he was hob-and-nob with monarchs and prime ministers, and received the Nobel Peace Prize for having been instrumental in settling the Russo-Japanese War. Hearing ominous reports that the easygoing Taft had betrayed the progressive cause, Roosevelt came home and after a great deal of maneuvering, when he lost the Republican nomination because administration forces controlled the convention, he took over the Progressive party, became its candidate, broke the heart of Senator Robert M. La Follette,[4] and thundered from the platform (once somebody shot at him) that he stood at Armageddon and battled for the Lord. Unfortunately, he had, many years before, declined to join the then progressive movement, the Mugwumps, saying that one should always work within one's party; unfortunately also, before leaving the White House in 1910, he had repeatedly announced he would not seek a third term; and for these inconsistencies and other reasons the Lord apparently abandoned him and elected Woodrow Wilson. Yet in 1912 Roosevelt polled almost a million more popular votes than did his unhappy successor, Taft. In 1914 Roosevelt departed on a rather bootless exploring expedition to discover the "River of Doubt" in Brazil and returned with a tropical infection that permanently affected his health. Domestic sorrows, age, and petulance clouded his closing years. His later activities included denouncing Wilson for delaying war against Germany, and demanding a military command. But the science of slaughter had developed far beyond the simplicities of the Spanish-American War, and Wilson, a shrewd politician himself, refused to allow a military amateur to compete with professionals. Roosevelt died January 6, 1919. His last letter, written January 3, characteristically denounced "hyphenated Americans":

Any man who says he is an American but something else also, isn't an American at all. We have room for but one flag, the American flag, and this excludes the red flag which symbolizes all wars against liberty and civilization. . . . We have room for but one language here and that is the English language, for we intend to see that the crucible turns our people out as Americans, of American nationality, and not as dwellers in a polyglot boardinghouse; and we have room for but one soul loyalty, and that loyalty is to the American people.[5]

This, to be sure, is strident but it is not that sort of patriotism which is the last refuge of a scoundrel. In truth Teddy had strong views on everything—patriotism, football, simplified spelling, conservation, race suicide, the duties of the female sex, politics and business ethics, the Panama Canal, Tolstoi's novels, muckraking, how to raise children, hunting dogs, the untrustworthiness of Russia, historiogra-

phy, the melting pot, the militancy of Kaiser Wilhelm, and the supposed genius of his two stanch friends, Henry Cabot Lodge and
Leonard Wood. All this exuberance gets in the way of understanding
why he is the climax of the Age of Energy.

The difficulty of comprehending Theodore Roosevelt as the symbol of an age arises from a number of causes. One is that a cartoon
image of him still intervenes between the real man and the modern
reader. He was the delight of caricaturists Teddy with the wide
grin and the big teeth, Teddy carrying the big stick, Teddy in his
cavalry uniform, Teddy as a hunter, Teddy as a cowboy, Teddy as a
simple American telling off the crowned heads of Europe. These images are reinforced by the good-natured yet biting humor of Mr.
Dooley's proposal to retitle Roosevelt's *The Rough Riders* "Alone in
Cubia." [6] A second difficulty is the style, more brassy in his public
pronouncements and moral exhortations than in his historical books,
which are at least competently written. But for the great public he
too often wrote at the top of his voice in a manner that is commonplace, starred with repetitive phrases like catchwords in a Dickens
novel, a style without subtlety, without nuance, without grace. But it
is a style, whatever its defects, everywhere characterized by an extraordinary energy. This energy has been wary of the declamatory
fustian of an orator such as Robert C. Ingersoll. In Roosevelt's case,
moreover, the style is not the man himself. One must learn to look
beyond the barrage of such phrases as liars, mollycoddles, manliness,
the big stick, and other terms in this simple and tiring vocabulary, to
discover, when Roosevelt had his best years, a mind as shrewd and
fertile in expedients as the cleverest machine politician or any Old-
World diplomat. Indeed, there are times when this juvenility of utterance seems to be deliberately adopted as a screen to hide, I will
not say duplicity, but at least diplomatic guile.

A third difficulty is the obvious naïveté of some of Roosevelt's leading ideas. We who are troubled by the population explosion cannot
be moved by Roosevelt's condemnation of race suicide, and in an era
of the Women's Liberation Movement his praise of female domesticity falls flat. We are of course, or think we are, all for honesty; but in
the age of Freud and psychoanalysis and "doing your thing," what is
honesty? Everybody is, I suppose, against vice, yet vice is an elusive
term in an age of sexual permissiveness and drug-taking, so that Roosevelt, though he understood bosses and businessmen better than did

most of the muckrakers, strikes us as being altogether too prone to identify his own program with virtue. His preachments of a simplistic morality do not now appeal. We have passed beyond his boyish belief that manly sports would save the nation; we do not care for his simple-minded excursions into literary criticism, the fine arts, racial qualities, and the meaning of history. His activism of the "Damn-the-torpedoes!-Go-ahead" school seems inapplicable, and we are troubled by the discrepancy between his denunciation of corporations and his pragmatic insistence that there were good trusts and bad ones. Finally it should be noted that the earlier biographical studies, once the stage of adoration was over, took on the debunking flavor of the 1920s and the sociological fervor of the 1930s, each as simplistic as Roosevelt is alleged to be.

The passage of time, the publication of Roosevelt's correspondence, and historical research have permitted sounder judgment. By any conceivable standard the line of American presidents from Andrew Johnson through William McKinley is not, to put it mildly, a line of intellectual giants. After Theodore Roosevelt we have had Taft, Woodrow Wilson, Harding, Coolidge, Hoover, Franklin Delano Roosevelt, Truman, Eisenhower, Kennedy, and Lyndon Johnson. The domestic policies of Woodrow Wilson by and large took up where Theodore Roosevelt had left off, but the once-famous Wilson addresses read rather emptily nowadays, and whatever evil was wrought by Henry Cabot Lodge and his little group of willful men in defeating the League of Nations, one suspects that Theodore Roosevelt would have been less messianic, more politic, and more pliable. The only true succeeding genius is F.D.R., an offshoot of the spreading Roosevelt family tree, over whose qualities we are still divided, but nobody pretends, I think, that Harding, Coolidge, Truman, and Eisenhower, whatever their virtues, were men of extraordinary mental caliber. I refrain from characterizing Kennedy and Lyndon Johnson.

It appears, therefore, that, Lincoln aside, we have had no man in the White House since Andrew Jackson's time of Theodore Roosevelt's extraordinary energy, range, and curiosity, and few Presidents (including Lincoln) have touched life on so many sides. Not only is Oscar Handlin justified in calling him the first modern chief executive, but it is also true, I think, that in Roosevelt the Age of Energy focused upon a chief magistrate who embodied its restlessness, its ambition, its curiosity, its extraordinary faith in activism rather than in contemplation, its inconsistencies, and, above all, its ceaseless search of American life for what I may fairly call a pragmatic sanction that would validate the activities of a modern state. Like other prominent personalities I have earlier discussed, Roosevelt was a man curiously reminiscent of the Renaissance, *a uomo universale,* a hunter, a sportsman, a historian, a soldier, an administrator, a social and political reformer, a moralist, a literary critic, an explorer, and above all, a man who carried out the principles of Castiglione's *Il Cortegiano,* for Roosevelt seized upon his puny boyish body and his defective eyesight [7] and by the sheer power of will transformed himself into the tireless human dynamo admired by John Morley. One of his most characteristic performances occurred when, disgusted with "softness" in army officers, he rode ninety-eight miles in one day to show that it could be done.[8] "I cannot praise," wrote Milton, "a fugitive and cloistered virtue, unexercised and unbreathed, that never sallies out." I suggest that Roosevelt exemplified an important component of sixteenth- and seventeenth-century humanism. It is perhaps unnecessary to introduce testimony to the early and continuing popularity of Roosevelt, but William Archer, in his *America To-Day,* wrote in 1899: "There is no more typical and probably no more respected American at the present moment than Governor Roosevelt, of New York. Even those who dissent from his strenuous ideal and his expansionist opinions, admit him to be a model of political integrity and public spirit." [9] The union of activism and integrity continued to attract Americans, or most of them, during most of the Roosevelt era.

II

The proper contemporary attitude toward the Spanish-American War is a curious mixture of amusement, condescension, and contempt. The amusement arises, I suppose, from two sources: the feeling that much of the war was *opéra bouffe,* and the belief that in comparison with such titanic struggles as the two World Wars, this military adventure is a minor skirmish blown up by politicians and the contemporary press. The condescension arises from the feeling that the management of the war on the American side, with some brilliant exceptions, was a rather amateurish affair. The contempt is a function of our present refusal to see "imperialism" as anything but

evil; and since the Cuban conflict was almost our first step toward
empire, and at that a bellicose one, criticism dwells upon the spe-
ciousness of the American case, the hypocrisy of American diplomacy,
and the gross inconsistency between a noble desire to "liberate suffering Cuba" and opportunism (only too evident in our demand for
Guam and the Philippines, where we put down by force, thus curiously paralleling the actions of the Spanish army in Cuba, a movement of independence like that we were supposed to favor at Havana). The same greed, so the argument runs, led to the annexation
of Hawaii through the connivance of a fraudulent government of
American landowners on the islands, the acquisition of Guam and
various other bits of real estate here and there, and eventually to
Roosevelt's hasty recognition of the Republic of Panama in order to
build a canal. In the manner of Frederick the Great, Roosevelt seized
the canal strip first and let the lawyers and the diplomats argue
about it afterward.

There is much truth in these points of view, but some assumptions
seem to require correction. It is held that American opinion was in-
flamed by yellow journalism into declaring war on Spain. Certainly
sensational journalists, in New York and Chicago particularly, played
up atrocities in Cuba weeks before the sinking of the *Maine,* a catastrophe which, whatever its real cause, was almost certainly not the
work of the Spanish government. Harrowing tales were printed of
virtuous women stripped bare by Spanish officers, and much was
made of Spanish tyranny in shutting "innocent" Cubans into concentration camps. The newspapers seldom or never commented on atrocities committed by the virtuous Cubans throughout a great part of
the nineteenth century, nor was it noted that a primary reason for
the lack of food for prisoners in the concentration camps was the insurgent policy of starving out the Spanish garrisons (and therefore
their prisoners) in the towns by setting fire to the crops or murdering
those who tried to harvest them. Spanish government in the island
had varied from mediocrity to tyranny for almost a century, the quality of the governor-general being a function of the government, revolutionary or royalist, in Madrid. Cuban dissatisfaction rose and fell
with the recognition or withdrawal of political or economic liberty
from the island, which on the whole was better off economically in
1880 than it had been in 1820. Newspaper reporters are not required
to be historians; and readers were left ignorant of the truth that—in

view of the famous, or infamous, Ostend Manifesto of 1854, the attempts of Presidents Pierce and Buchanan to acquire Cuba by purchase, diplomacy, or force, the laxity of American governments in checking filibustering expeditions to Cuba from convenient ports in the United States, and the basing of revolutionary juntas on New York or some other American city—the image of virtuous Columbia rescuing tormented Cubans from bullying Spanish tyrants was not necessarily the correct image. Unfortunately, a recent Spanish governor, General Weyler, had acquired a reputation for ferocity that led to his being nicknamed Butcher Weyler. That he was more sanguinary than some of the guerrillas is an arguable point. But shortly before the war he had been withdrawn by a government at Madrid anxious not to lose its Caribbean possessions.

The point would seem to be that most wars have their roots in partisan bitterness and misrepresentation, but that it is also possible for persons more idealistically minded to go along with a movement. It is at least an open question whether the great mass of the American people, most of whom enthusiastically supported the war, were as greatly influenced by a handful of metropolitan dailies as legend makes them out to have been; and it is well to remember that the partisan press, North and South, before, during, and after 1861, was quite as misleading. But does this fact influence one's real estimate of heroism and idealism North and South? Liberal historians make much of American business interests in Cuba, which certainly increased after the war. There is, however, little persuasive evidence to show that in 1898 American business interests wanted a war with Spain, and a good deal of evidence to show that American business interests, on the contrary, were opposed to war and deprecated the bellicose attitude of the expansionists. As the country was just pulling out of the long financial depression that began in 1893, this is understandable. What seems to be true is that of all the events connected with the outbreak of hostilities, the sinking of the *Maine* in the harbor of Havana in February 1898, from unknown causes was the focal point for American emotion. One can of course argue that the vessel should not have been sent there in the first place. But being there, it should not have been destroyed with the loss of hundreds of American sailors.

As for the comic opera aspect of the war, the navy was better prepared than was the army, but although a succession of naval secretaries and activist members of Congress had succeeded in "modernizing" the fleet, we were not in 1898 a first-class naval power. We possessed only four first-rate armored battleships, one second-class battleship, three or four first-class cruisers, and others not so good. We also had various types of vessels obsolescent or obsolete; for example, a dozen and a half "monitors," useless in any kind of rolling water, some gunboats, a peculiar "dynamite destroyer," the *Vesuvius*, fewer than a dozen torpedo boats, and other small craft. Roosevelt's quickness in alerting Dewey to prepare for action, together with the utter inadequacy of the Spanish ships and gunfire, insured us a striking naval victory at Manila. Yet American naval intelligence was so undeveloped that nobody really knew what the rest of the Spanish navy was like, nor, for a long time, where most of it was. Political pressures kept a so-called "flying squadron" to protect the Atlantic seacoast cities against a Spanish bombardment which never occurred, and this squadron was finally ordered to Cuban waters to join the rest of the Atlantic fleet. Nobody had thought his way through the coaling problem, a vexing matter that often confused ship movements.

Admiral Sampson was in general command. He sent most of his fleet on May 19 to blockade Cienfuegos, the chief harbor on the southern coast of Cuba, where it was thought the Spanish fleet under Admiral Cervera was to come. But Cervera slipped into the harbor of Santiago, which Commodore (later Admiral) Schley then blockaded. On the morning of July 3 Sampson steamed off in the *New York* for a conference with General Shafter, liaison between the navy and the army being somewhat less than perfect. On this particular morning Cervera decided to make his desperate effort at escape, and the command of the American vessels immediately present seemed to rest with Schley, though Sampson turned around and managed to be in at the finish. The resulting victory thrilled the nation, but created a bitter controversy concerning the commander rightfully entitled to the credit, a controversy that led to a board of naval inquiry of 1901. The board's decision, itself not clear-cut, pleased the adherents of neither officer, each of whom had been jumped over the heads of officers who had seniority.[10]

Despite this bitterness, the navy was efficient and harmonious in comparison with the American army of 1898. Though individual soldiers and most of the officers of the regular forces were well trained and toughened in many cases by campaigns against the Indians, the

War Department had apparently learned nothing since the Civil War. The Secretary was mediocre. The army numbered (April 1, 1898) fewer than thirty thousand officers and men scattered all over the country and Alaska, and no maneuvers by any large unit such as a brigade or a corps were possible. Enlistments increased this total by August to about sixty-seven thousand, but by then the war was virtually over. The sinking of the *Maine* in February was a clear omen of trouble, but there was on April 20, 1898, when Congress forced the president to declare war, no sufficient provision of anything, not excepting rifles and ammunition. The medical service was woefully inadequate. As for the militia, states'-rights difficulties emerged as of old; one New York regiment refused to go, and in other states the same old quarrel between politically minded governors and legislatures and the federal government broke out again. McKinley called for volunteers (one hundred and twenty-five thousand in April, seventy-five thousand more in May), but the relation among the three kinds of regiments remained uneasy, and most of the army never got to Cuba. Such forces as did land were outnumbered by the Spanish army, which, fortunately for the Americans, made about every defensive military mistake in the vocabulary of war.

Transportation and planning were equally defective. At Tampa, the principal embarkation port for Cuba, a single railway track ran the nine miles from the city to the harbor, and it occurred to nobody that other tracks could quickly be laid. Bills of lading and receipts were not received or not validated (who was to receive them?), cars carrying rifles were left on passing tracks in one place, cars carrying ammunition in another, and those loaded with summer uniforms either did not arrive or were lost in the shuffle. Since the war was a popular war, moreover, tourist trains ran at intervals into the little town or even to the port, and a local factory responsible for the one railway track to the harbor insisted on receiving freight and goods. Transports were leased, but there seems to have been a good deal of fraud or misunderstanding, since vessels theoretically hired to carry twenty-five thousand men could take on only eighteen thousand. Nobody had prepared the ships for this number, nobody had any embarkation plans, and when orders came to embark, parts of regiments were lost, and enterprising commanders seized freight trains and ships to get their men or some of them on board. Then the troops were kept on these crowded vessels for a week under the blazing sun, detained by fear of a Spanish fleet that never showed up. When the convoy put to sea, it kept no order, at night the vessels were ablaze with light, bands played, and every opportunity was offered the Spaniards to destroy the expedition. Fortunately no Spaniards appeared. Descriptions of the landings at Daiquirí or Siboney reveal the same anarchy as at Tampa. Army intelligence was inferior to that of the navy; in consequence nobody knew how formidable the Spanish forces were, where they were, or where the Cubans might be. Men got ashore without much order until the navy took over, albeit two transports carrying about two thousand troops simply disappeared for the day.

The fights at Las Guásimas and San Juan Hill went on in a like disorder for the reason there had been no adequate reconnaissance and the incompetent maps showed "roads" which were in fact trails through a sort of tropical jungle. Individual pluck carried the Americans forward, despite the smokeless powder used by the Spaniards, until they were able to entrench themselves in the hills above Santiago. But food was lacking, there was only one field hospital, clothing was worn to rags under the hot sun, men fell ill (it is estimated that for the less than three hundred Americans killed or mortally wounded in battle many times that number fell ill of disease), and finally a round robin of sorts, written by Theodore Roosevelt, was sent to Washington, and most of the attacking forces were recalled to the United States soon after the Spanish surrender.[11] In *The Rough Riders,* a less egotistical book than legend makes it out to be, Roosevelt writes that war correspondents thought the Americans fought better than the Turks, but that on the whole our system of military administration was rather worse than that of the Greeks (there had been a Greco-Turkish War in 1897 "covered" by Richard Harding Davis, among others), and, Roosevelt adds, it seemed to him curious that "we should have broken down precisely on the business and administrative side." [12] In view of this odd lapse in American expertise, one of Roosevelt's jobs, when he became president, was to insist on increasing and modernizing the navy and on the creation of a general staff corps for the army, together with an improvement in the education and special training in both services. Congress usually balked at his demand for more ships, but in the long run Roosevelt's policy prevailed.

The emotionalism which centered on the Spanish-American War was, one suspects, basically a Protestant Christian emotionalism. Expansionists, to be sure, took advantage of the victory in Cuba and the lack of any coherent American policy beyond "freeing" the oppressed [13] to push forward their design of an American empire, a design going back to the manifest destiny of the ante-bellum United States, when all the New World was to come under one glorious government. Their plans were obvious in the annexation of Hawaii by a joint resolution of Congress, and still earlier evident in the interpretation of the Monroe Doctrine that made the United States the paramount power in the Caribbean. A traditional American attitude led Seward to try to buy the Danish West Indies, Grant to attempt the annexation of Santo Domingo, and Cleveland to warn off Great Britain in its dispute with Venezuela over the boundary between that republic and British Guiana. If the expansionists rode the horses of destiny, their opponents took a high moral tone, evident in so typical a passage as this from *The Bookman* in 1901:

> Will Cuba be less grateful to us if we scrupulously keep our promises to her in a high-minded, generous, gracious way than she will be if we continue an unwelcome occupation, deny to her those rights to gain which for her was the ostensible motive of our war with Spain, and give as a reason our belief that her inhabitants are lawless and incapable? . . . We have everything to gain by honesty and everything to lose by sophistry. The hour has struck when our flag should cease to float over an inch of Cuban territory, and when it should be furled with honour because as a people we are strong and generous and wish to see no taint upon the national escutcheon.[14]

This was published in McKinley's lifetime and validates, as it were, John Hay's remarkable pen portrait of that President. McKinley had, wrote Hay, no original ideas, but "he had the art . . . of throwing a moral gloss over policies which were dubious, if not actually immoral, and this he did with a sort of self-deceiving sincerity. . . . I was more struck than ever with his mask. It is a genuine Italian ecclesiastical face of the fifteenth century." [15]

Around this face of an Italian ecclesiastic of the Renaissance, Protestant sentiment enthusiastically rallied for a variety of reasons. In the first place, the American Protestant missionary movement was at its height, and both in the Caribbean and in the Pacific we were to bring salvation to the heathen and redemption to the lost. In the second place, although the American Protective Association probably reached its peak in 1896 and by 1898 was beginning to decline, it had reminded all right-thinking Christians that the pope was a foreign power, the Scarlet Woman of Babylon, suppressing religious freedom, Cubans, and benighted Filipinos. To sweep back the Spanish Empire was somehow supposed to convert Roman Catholic immigrants to the ideals of the United States. In the third place, ever since the Armada and before, Spain had been the enemy of progress and of man, a nation corrupt, fanatical, and obsolete, virtually the last European power save our cousins, the British, to hold any quantity of territory in the New World. This Spain was supposed to misgovern with the same mixture of medieval and ecclesiastical obscurantism that had prompted the revolt of mainland colonies in South America. In the fourth place, a variety of leading men, all of sound Protestant faith, impeccable morality, American vigor, and progressive, yet scientific views, had argued that the Anglo-Saxons, or in the larger sense the Aryans, and in any circumstances the Americans, were bound to inherit the earth and guide inferior peoples toward the light. In the fifth place, there were the troublesome Chinese, incarnate heathendom, who broke out in the Boxer Rebellion of the spring of 1900. How could we play our part in restoring order and respect for Christian missionaries abroad if (a) we had darkness at our front door in the Gulf of Mexico, or if (b) some European monarchy, presumably hostile, were to occupy strategic positions in the Pacific—for example, Hawaii, or Samoa, or Guam, or the Philippines, or if (c) both of these un-American (and therefore un-Christian) contingencies should occur East and West?

But above all, the Spanish-American War was an example of dedicated American manhood rising in wrath of its own free will to destroy tyranny, free the oppressed, and wave the Stars and Stripes at least for a time over the countries we had liberated, all in the name of a Protestant Christ and a democratic America. Finally, the nation was weary of internal quarrels—quarrels between North and South, East and West, capital and labor, farmer and banker, citizen and corporation, whites and blacks, Indians and settlers, proponents of easy money and proponents of the gold standard; weary, too, of the business depression, the poverty, the unemployment, the vagrancy, the slum problem, and futile party politics—so that when the call went forth to rescue somebody else from trouble the country rose as one man, and American soldiers went off on what proved to be the last war fought in accordance with the canons of romanticism. The war was more humanitarian than selfish; only when the country found itself possessed of power after the war did it experience a desire to use that power in the world.[16]

Whatever truth and error might lie in contemporary interpretations of the Cuban crusade, the war was a vast popular success. It produced three authentic folk heroes—George Dewey, Richmond Pearson Hobson, and Theodore Roosevelt. But Dewey, admirable naval officer that he was, had no adroitness in civil affairs. Presented a home by popular subscription, he deeded it to his second wife; and sounded out on being a presidential candidate, he gravely said: "Since studying this subject I am convinced that the office of president is not such a difficult one to fill." Hobson was heroic and looked the Charles-Dana-Gibson American. He had, moreover, the advantage of being a Southerner. But he was kissed by many girls, his prestige melted away, and he never rose higher than being a congressman from his native state. Roosevelt alone endured, tried and triumphant. Was he not a Bullock of Georgia and a Knickerbocker of New York? Had he not been a graduate of Groton and Harvard College and also a hunter of wild game in the Great West, a cattle rancher in Dakota, a man who brought in horse thieves to the county jail and raised a regiment in San Antonio? He had been shrewder and quicker than the naval bureaucracy, more humane and independent than officers of the regular army, a leader and yet a democratic American, a man who believed in progress, but who sensibly took the pragmatic road when politicians and frontiers blocked the highway of idealism, an American who praised all the virile virtues and all wholesome womanly charms. Now with an honorable record behind him as an assemblyman, a police commissioner, a member of the federal civil service commission, a colonel of a volunteer regiment, a governor of the Empire State who deftly ducked the bosses and yet somehow worked with them, he was President of the United States. An incarnation of the American pragmatic spirit, a combination of a statesman who believed in truthfulness and a politician who believed in truth when it worked, a production of the late nineteenth century who proposed to lead the country and the world into the twentieth century—with him the Age of Energy was justified of its children.

He had, moreover, the right combination of idealism and political savoir faire. Ambitious for power which he thought he could wield, he was nevertheless by no means convinced that idealism would prevail—hence the shrillness of his affirmation of it. To get anything accomplished as governor of New York he had had to deal with machine politicians, just as he was to have to do with the national Congress; he made such pragmatic compromises with them as he could in both cases and "got things done"; when they balked, he appealed over the heads of those who blocked his way to the people at large, and this appeal was couched in such simple terms, public opinion, or most of it, commonly rallied to him—though he was sometimes very wrong, as when during his presidency he discharged some companies of Negro troops who would not testify as to who among them had shot up Brownsville, Texas. But he thought of the governorship, and later of the presidency, as the force to which in the long run the people would turn, and in most instances this combination of guile and straightforwardness seemed to work.

III

When Roosevelt left the White House in 1909 he announced that he and his family had had a bully time. So had the country. His opponents lost a vivid personality whom they could vigorously denounce; his supporters scarcely knew where to turn. Taft was, as one writer says, a man who sought legality whereas Teddy was a man who sought justice. La Follette was too earnest, too reformist, too inflexible, not enough the man of general culture to succeed as an embodiment of American destiny. One is tempted to apply to the ending of Roosevelt's presidency the phrase William Allen White used to describe the effect of Roosevelt's death: it was like the ceasing of the playing of a military band. For almost eight years the White House had been the center of national interest and of the interest of much of the rest of the world. Out of it had flowed an extraordinary stream of commentary, warning, denunciation, exhortation, and moral platitudes. Into it had gone an equally extraordinary stream of visitors—Western sheriffs, Eastern businessmen, diplomats, union leaders, clergymen, historians, sculptors, college boys, authors, naturalists, editors, athletes, explorers, social workers, old classmates, former cowboys, conferences to settle strikes, commissions to study this or that, Booker T. Washington to the indignation of the South,

and J. Pierpont Morgan to the consternation of the liberals. Here was
a President who played at single-stick, boxed, played tennis (and had
a "tennis cabinet"), went on long horseback rides, led friends, army
officers, and strangers on long "scrambles" through Rock Creek, attended college football games, and left the United States (the first
President to do so) to visit the Panama Canal Zone, where "he
tramped everywhere through the mud." His family was also a national possession, sick or ill, active in Washington or away at school;
and Alice Roosevelt's wedding to Nicholas Longworth in February
1906 took on the character of an international event, followed, characteristically, by a meeting of the Harvard Porcellian Club in the
White House. The Executive Mansion had had no such occupants
since Abigail Adams moved into that "unfinished castle of a house"
at the opening of the last century and contemplated with mixed emotions the "trees and stumps in plenty," which in 1800 constituted
most of the capital of the United States.

This endless activity, this ceaseless curiosity, these kaleidoscopic interests, this mixture of public responsibility and private interests, together with the contradictions in the Rooseveltian value system that
enemies liked to dwell on and biographers try to explain, have led
me to call Roosevelt the man and the years of his greatness the climax of the Age of Energy. I think the matter goes deeper than the
obvious similarity between the exuberance of the president and that
of other leading personalities in this half-century. I shall therefore try
to make my meaning clear.

Striking epochs almost inevitably get themselves tagged with the
name of some dominant characteristic or eminent personality; as, the
Elizabethan Age, the romantic period, the Jacksonian period, or the
Age of the Enlightenment. In the chapter on the 1890s ("From Harrison to Havana") I have analyzed both the source and the nature of
the myths supposed to express the special quality in that decade
("The Gay Nineties") and I also dwelt upon the many other activities of the time that contradict the legend. I earlier indicated that the
term "Gilded Age," though legendary, will not quite do as a term for
the period to which it applies. Admitting the difficulty, even the fu-
tility, of an attempt at generalizing for the Age of Energy as a whole,
I think one might do worse than describe these fifty years as a search
for what I have already called a pragmatic sanction for American life
and values.

I borrow the term from history, where it has, of course, a quite different meaning.[17] I reinterpret it by using "pragmatic" in the Jamesian sense that the meaning of a conception is expressed in its practical consequences (this, of course, is a loose reading of James), and I use "sanction" with no profounder meaning than that generally accepted for whatever is proper or permissible. Now the Age of Energy was as filled with contradictions as any other striking cultural era, and I do not hold that all of them can be brought under one roof. Yet some of the contrasts charged against the age and against Roosevelt are explicable by the ability of human beings to believe two or more contradictory propositions at one and the same time and to find each of them a good in itself.

Some of these inconsistencies come readily to mind. The so-called robber barons were capable of pursuing egotistical ends with amazing ferocity, yet most of them were likewise benefactors of the nation and of mankind through their founding of hospitals, museums, libraries, colleges, theological schools, symphony orchestras, and so on. Continental railroads were built by aid of the greatest donative of free land in the history of the world; they were overcapitalized, manipulated, extortionate, careless of the safety of their trainmen and their passengers, unfair in their rates, and eventually had to be brought under state or federal control. Yet the same sovereign people who later complained about the way railroads were run, moved heaven, earth, the legislature, and Congress to get a railroad to tap their town and "build it up," or took joyous advantage of free rides or preferential low fares to locate farms in the West, or beheld with approval their local banks (sometimes major ones) investing depositors' money in corporations notoriously overcapitalized. Many philosophers, social theorists, economists, and clergymen were convinced that evolutionary materialism, however interpreted, was at the heart of things, a doctrine that, if consistently carried through, would, it might seem, deny freedom of choice to man; yet they were also capable of arguing with great passion that evolution means progress, the United States was especially favored by evolution, and the duty of good Americans was therefore to follow light and do the right, for man can half-control his doom, even though there was no deathless angel seated in anybody's vacant tomb.

Literary realists should in theory have been as objective and impersonal as medical students at the dissecting table; in fact, virtually all of them felt that right should prevail, that pity has a human face, and that social ills, once they are analyzed, can somehow be ameliorated. Patriotic statesmen disfranchised whole classes of Americans (Negroes and Indians) for the benefit of the United States; at the same time they really believed in a republican form of government, and neither then nor later was there an attempt to alter the fundamental political structure of the country. Painters, musicians, sculptors, and architects wanted to be "American"; they went to Europe to learn the cosmopolitan touch and returned to apply that touch at home with no inconsistency and without insincerity.

It was argued then and has been argued since that the so-called genteel tradition was only a sentimental evasion of "reality." It was argued then and can be argued now that the idealism of the theory was a necessary corrective to an age lacking refinement and overly given to nauseous ugliness and enormous greed. Laissez faire was a good and proper philosophy. State responsibility for the common welfare was also a good thing. Christianity was excellent. Roman Catholicism was dubious. The American should be distinguished by practicality. The American should be distinguished by idealism. The United States was the refuge of the oppressed of all lands. The United States had a right to refuse a home to any racial or national group it did not fancy. The country was the last, best hope of man. The country must keep its racial superiority under God. One can go on indefinitely. But do not contradictions like these arise from what I have called the pragmatic sanction; that is, the notion that you can affirm any two things as good if they "work" until you find in practice that they cancel each other or that something else or some other pair of opposites "works" better?

The achievements of the Roosevelt administrations were remarkable. The first problem was part of the aftermath of the war. Contentions about who was responsible for victory and who for inefficiency finally subsided. Though the Filipino insurrection under Aguinaldo fed the indignation of anti-imperialists, and the problem in those islands of the "Friars' Lands" (real estate owned by Roman Catholic orders) threatened a nasty quarrel, the rebellion died down, and in 1900 Roosevelt appointed a commission chaired by Taft (succeeding an early, less successful commission) to establish, if it was practicable, a civil government for the Philippines. This was done in July 1901. In 1916 an Organic Act for the Philippines announced a policy of withdrawal and transfer of power to an independent republic, finally completed in 1935. In 1901–1902 the American army left Cuba a theoretically independent republic, though the Platt Amendment permitted the United States to intervene in the case of serious disorders, which it did two or three times. The amendment was abrogated in 1934. Porto Rico, as it was then known, Guam, and some minor possessions offered little difficulty, though there was in Puerto Rico a rebellious mood intermittently expressed. Various enactments gave that island more and more autonomy until in 1917 it became the Territory and in 1952 the Commonwealth of Puerto Rico. Few wars destroying a whole empire have eventuated in so negligible an amount of disturbance. Roosevelt and his appointees should be given the credit for much of this, even if the disharmony between "imperialism" and the doctrine of representative government and self-rule was part of the inconsistency of the pragmatic sanction.

Roosevelt as president "got things done," largely because of his capacity, concealed by his vigor, to work with men who opposed him but who came to realize that in any important contest Roosevelt's pragmatism meant either that he would grant them some concessions in order to get most of what he wanted, or force concessions from them by offering only undesirable alternatives. By such diplomacy (and some threats) he settled the anthracite coal strike, which continued from May until late in October 1902, cost the nation millions, and threatened the prosperity and health of the country. By this method he checked the panic of 1907 when he told J. P. Morgan or his representative that the government would not institute suit under the Sherman Anti-Trust Act if the United States Steel Corporation bought the Tennessee Coal and Iron Company, the impending failure of which threatened the whole business structure. To him the general good in any emergency seemed more important than consistency. Out of this philosophy he appointed a number of White House commissions technically unauthorized by law, from which important legislation came. Furthermore, he surrounded himself with practical-minded men, idealistic without being mere idealists; and he rejoiced in a letter from James Bryce, in which Bryce declared he had never seen a more eager, high-minded, and efficient set of men working in government posts than under Roosevelt.[18]

An extraordinary series of important laws seemed to strengthen popular government and ward off the corruption of big money.

Thus, by the Newlands Act of 1902, money from the sale of public lands in sixteen states was directed to be spent in financing irrigation projects for the general good. In 1903 legislation created a Department of Commerce and Labor, which included a Bureau of Corporations with power to investigate and report on big business. The Elkins Act of 1904 strengthened the Interstate Commerce Commission, and the Hepburn Act of 1906 further broadened the jurisdiction of this body and empowered it to fix just and reasonable railroad rates and to establish uniform systems of accounting.[19] The Pure Food and Drug Act and the Meat Inspection Act protected the national health, and in 1907, the panic year, the Aldrich-Vreeland Act strengthened the currency. At the same time there was created a National Monetary Commission, which, reporting four years later, laid the foundation for our present Federal Reserve system. Of the great service of Roosevelt to conservation I have already spoken. Even La Follette, who had reason to detest him, wrote: "When the historian . . . shall speak of Theodore Roosevelt, he is likely to say that he did many notable things, but that his greatest work was inspiring and actually beginning a world movement for staying territorial waste and saving for the human race the things on which alone a peaceful, progressive, and happy life can be founded." [20]

Roosevelt's foreign policies, apart from the American "empire," are perhaps more important than all his domestic successes except conservation. Of course they aroused controversy, but in general Roosevelt insisted that the country could no longer be ignored in the counsels of the great powers. One is here struck by a remark in the *New Cambridge Modern History* in a chapter by F. H. Hinsley that until Russia overreached herself in a program that led to her defeat in the Russo-Japanese War in 1904, the colonial activities of the powers were subordinate to the necessity of preserving the balance of power in Europe.[21] This truth Roosevelt instinctively grasped, though he would not have put it that way, and he also shared the hope of European liberals that "progressive governments" developing over the world would make for peace. If the United States was to take its proper place among the nations and yet avoid war, it must show itself both strong and flexible—hence the doctrine: Speak softly but carry a big stick. This man of boyish mind and undiplomatic language at home showed himself a superb tactician in international affairs. He was the first President of the United States to win the Nobel

Prize for Peace. Without wounding the pride of either nation he brought Japan and Russia to a peace conference at Portsmouth, New Hampshire. His suavity smoothed the feelings of the Japanese when the San Francisco school board set up ghetto schools for the Japanese and mobs rioted in the streets of that city against the Orientals. Despite the Friars' Lands controversy and others, he never irked the Vatican. He got precisely what he wanted in the Alaska boundary dispute between the United States on the one side and Canada and Great Britain on the other and retained the respect of both nations. He joined other powers in suppressing the Boxer Rebellion and its outrages, but he refused to participate in further partitioning China. His vigor was felt in countries as remote from the American sphere of influence as Morocco, and though he policed the Caribbean and Central America, he declined to think of this country as a universal Galahad rescuing the oppressed all over the globe.

His most controversial acts concerned the recognition of the Republic of Panama, the swift submission to the Senate of a treaty securing rights in the Canal Zone to the United States, and the immediate start of construction of the waterway. Much can be said against this precipitation, but it must be remembered that the Panamanians had been in annual rebellion against Colombia for years. It is also reasonably clear that Roosevelt was at one point deceived by Harran, the Colombian representative.[22] If he sent the fleet around the world, to the terror of the timid and the anger of pacifists, he saw to it that the voyage was expertly managed, countries remained friendly, and the point was made: the United States, too, was a great power.

Like many another who believes in strong administration, Roosevelt was an egoist who sometimes let his egoism get out of hand. We rub our eyes as we read his denunciations of such persons as Godkin of *The Nation,* John Fiske, on occasion Rudyard Kipling, Agnes Repplier the essayist (he hoped she would be chained up in New York City until she got civilized), Hamlin Garland, who had only "half an idea," Henry James, who was too precious, Brooks Adams ("his mind is a little unhinged"), John Jay Chapman and "his little group of representatives of the Extreme Life, or Bedlamite branch, of the ultra-reform movement," Jane Addams ("a confused thinker"), and a wild variety of others.[23] What possible coherence is there among names so various that they stirred Roosevelt to language too outrageous to be even comical? On this point two observations should be made. We must once more reflect on the insufficiency of a vocabulary strictly moral and athletic, unfortunately the only vocabulary Roosevelt on such occasions could command. Then, if one looks beyond the words, one discovers a common ground. These persons—and the muckrakers, the anarchists, capitalists when they are greedy, self-seeking politicians, agitators for women's rights, starry-eyed reformers, sentimentalists who do not live in the world of real struggle that Roosevelt knew—are deviates from his pragmatic idealism and might deviate disastrously. He felt this, in fact, of any man or any group unwilling to accept the plain truth that life is a running battle in which weakness is disaster but fighting should be fair.

This pragmatic idealism was compounded of many elements. He thought of government not so much as having the character of a judge above and remote from conflict as that of an umpire down on the field, prepared to interfere when the playing got too rough, and ready to send offenders to the bench. Government meant a balance among a variety of forces; when any one force threatened to tip this delicate balance, government should step in, arbitrate if possible, and, when necessary, participate and punish. At the same time, as Elting Morison has observed, Roosevelt was well aware that power can corrupt. He therefore held that the excess or long continuance of power should be checked by one or all of three forces: law, custom, and opinion; personal morality; and limiting the time any one could exercise it.[24] That is why Roosevelt went to Africa when Taft succeeded him. Perhaps that is also why he forgot his own principles when he ran for a third term.

His central philosophy in this regard can be illustrated by some passages from his correspondence:

> At times I feel an almost Greek horror of extremes. The same type of mind that wants to make things so easy for the criminal as to encourage crime, shrinks from seeing the nation do the rough work which must be done if nations are to win and deserve greatness.

> The best kind of wageworker, the best kind of laboring man, must stand shoulder to shoulder with the best kind of professional man, with the best kind of businessman, in putting a stop to the undermining of civic decency, and this without any regard to whether it is a labor union or a corporation which is undermining it, without any regard to whether the offender is a rich man or a poor man.

I believe the reformer is absolutely essential, just as the practical politician is absolutely essential. It is because of this belief in both types that I wish unstintedly to condemn the practical politician who becomes a knave and the reformer who becomes a fool.

Now, what we ought all to strive for here is a steady and orderly development along the lines of fair dealing between man and man, and of honesty demanded from all men in business and politics alike. Ours must be neither a movement of the rich or of the poor.

The longer I have been in public life, and the more zealous I have grown in movements of true reform, the greater horror I have come to feel for the exaggeration which so often defeats its own objects.[25]

Roosevelt was genuinely fearful of men, theories, or movements that would so disrupt the traditional structure of American living as to overturn the commonwealth—a fear that seems less visionary now than it did in his own lifetime. The Age of Energy had worked out a practical compromise between exploitation and the state, between force and political control, between activity and expertise, and this he wanted to keep. Yet as did the muckrakers, whom he distrusted, and the insurgent movement which developed under Taft, when Roosevelt talked about the people, he forever failed to define his term. The insurgents professed to speak for the general public weal, though they were essentially the heirs of the Populists and represented the ethos of the Middle West, particularly those states that were still essentially agrarian in outlook. And though he had a vision of a classless society, Roosevelt could not conceive of that society except in terms of the values of the middle class.

It would be superfluous to labor the point that the American middle class believed (then and now) both in ideals and in practicality; in the truth that life is conflict and the truth that you ought to think of the other fellow; in self-interest and in charity; in being strong but not too strong; in brotherhood but within limits; in self-development, provided that culture is the occupation of one's leisure and training for usefulness the principal object of education. Anarchism, populism, socialism, communism could not prevail against the Age of Energy. There was never a threat of revolution. It remained for our time to produce groups that really desire to overthrow the state. Despite millionaires at one extreme and the urban proletariat at the other, the Age of Energy ended by strengthening and enriching the bourgeoisie. Roosevelt was its climax. He fused the activity of Ren aissance man with the values of the middle class. The result was that he became *par excellence* the supreme representative of the prag matic sanction.

IV

What I have called the pragmatic sanction appears to condition much of the literature of the Roosevelt era. Literary historians tend to concentrate upon patterns of writing they find in the 1890s (the polarities are naturalism and the *fin-de-siècle* spirit) and to find in the 1920s an American literary renaissance evident in poetry and postwar fiction. The years from 1898 to 1915, however, they neglect, as a gray and uninteresting area between two epochs of brilliance. Yet significant major characteristics in writing can, I think, be identified. I begin by putting aside certain elements extraneous to the central problem.

The movies from 1898 to 1915 were still mainly in a primitive and nickelodeon stage of development: *The Birth of a Nation* was not released until 1915, the first talking movie was not shown until 1927, and motion pictures had not yet become a major threat to the primacy of fiction as adult entertainment and instruction. The theater in these years, still dominated by the star system and the road company, produced plays such as Augustus Thomas's *The Witching Hour* (1907) and David Belasco's *The Girl of the Golden West* (1905) and aspired to the level of the problem play exemplified in Eugene Walter's *The Easiest Way* (1908). Historians of the American stage do not pay sufficient attention to vaudeville, then in its prime, nor to the amusing line of farce comedies in the period—for example, George Ade's *The College Widow* (1904)—but it should be noted that the dramatization of novels and the novelization of plays were not only common but also emphasized the central position of fiction in that culture. Examples are Francis Marion Crawford's *In the Palace of the King* (1900), originally conceived as a play, and George M. Cohan's theatrical hit, *Seven Keys to Baldpate* (1913) from Earl Derr Biggers' story of that name. Not yet significant was Percy MacKaye's brave theory that masques and pageants really expressed the soul of a people as Broadway did not.[26] The vogue of the one-act play as "art," the idea of the little theater, and an academic drive to rescue the stage from the tyranny of the tired businessman were still unimportant. Writing for children could be good: Baum's *The Wonderful Wizard of Oz* appeared in 1900. Poetry was in the doldrums and was to remain so until the founding by Harriet Monroe in Chicago of *Poetry: A Magazine of Verse* in 1912 and the publication of Frost's *North of Boston* (1915), Edgar Lee Masters' *Spoon River Anthology* (1915), and Carl Sandburg's *Chicago Poems* (1916).[27] Publishing remained a sedate profession, not an industry, the book club had not been invented; there were still serious bookstores; and great houses like Macmillan, Henry Holt, Scribner, and Putnam were nobly carrying on a tradition but mildly threatened through the ten-cent magazine.

Sports aside, reading was therefore still the principal source of art, entertainment, and instruction among the majority. The panic of 1893, it is true, had disturbed the financial tranquillity of Harper and Brothers, but on the whole responsible publishing after 1898 could cultivate the wide range of "readership" that lay between *The Smart Set: A Magazine of Cleverness,* founded in 1900 expressly for its snob appeal, and Wayland's *The Appeal to Reason,* founded in 1895, which, combining socialism and sensation, was launched from Kansas, the home of "Sockless" Jerry Simpson.[28] The space between was a vast area for cultivation. Within it there were of course various classes of readers: a small, elite group who read such books as Henry James's *The Golden Bowl* (1904) and, if they could find a copy, *The Education of Henry Adams;* a much larger public that went in for "good books"; and a still larger but amorphous group that liked simple narrative, simple morality, melodrama, and sentimentality. This group made the fortune of Gene Stratton Porter, whose titles (for example, *A Girl of the Limberlost* in 1909) were invariably best sellers, of Florence Barclay, who published *The Rosary* (1910), of Harold Bell Wright, and of Edgar Rice Burroughs, who brought out *Tarzan of the Apes* in 1914.[29] Books of course cannot always be assigned to any one category of readers. Jack London's novels of animals, Western violence, primitivism, evolution, and the revolution were doubtless read by all sorts of persons, as were Alice Hegan Rice's *Mrs. Wiggs of the Cabbage Patch* (1901) and Upton Sinclair's *The Jungle* (1906), but it is at least difficult to think of buyers of "Pastor" Wagner's *The Simple Life,* which had vogue in 1901, also purchasing

William James's *The Varieties of Religious Experience* in 1902.

Melodrama and sentimentality do not alter greatly from age to age, and our present concern is principally with the "good books" of the Roosevelt years. The novel was the mainstay of publishing. The pattern of the novel has, however, altered so radically since 1920, that it is difficult to be fair nowadays to the achievements of the formalized story. The novel was then thought of as a tale, and not only that but as a story with a plot. It had a beginning, a middle, and a denouement that commonly terminated the love interest by throwing the lovers into each other's arms (never into bed), and in most cases included the exposure of the villain. Dialogue was either informal, lucid, rational and intelligent, or conscientiously in dialect. The stream of consciousness theory of the mind was not yet dominant, and the author himself described what a character was thinking when he thought the reader should be so informed. Motivation was both rational and ethical (or consciously and deliberately immoral) but seldom or never amoral. Nor was it unconscious or primitive except, in a sense, in stories by the Jack London school. In the great majority of these books the cast of characters was as predictable as the dramatis personae in plays produced by stock companies: a hero, a heroine, a villain; the associates of each; and the mothers of one or another, of two types: the eternally maternal "mom" or the worldly social climber or aristocrat. If mothers were "mean," their fall from a proper level of maternity was explicable by their having left the church or ignored it, by having had bad upbringing, or by contamination from the world of men. Fathers were either noble and pathetic characters who couldn't keep up, failure being often the consequence of trusting other men, or capitalists, who in their secret hearts still cherished the memory of some youthful romance, had a soft spot for their spouses, in nine cases out of ten could be managed by their daughters and, if they sometimes quarreled with their sons, usually came around at the end. Characters were divided among two general milieus (country types were no longer necessarily embodiments of rural virtue), the metropolitan characters came either from the slums —in which case they were shrewd, pathetic, comical, and illiterate— or from the upper classes, in which case they were worldly clergymen, domineering bankers, unscrupulous millionaires, and city bosses, who were the agents of upper-class chicanery. Labor, treated gingerly, was either heroic or villainous or suffering. Backgrounds were sketched in as stage sets rather than as environment, but there were notable exceptions like Mrs. Wharton's *Ethan Frome* (1911).

Since contemporary fiction tends to be an outpouring of subjectivism, sometimes narrative, sometimes reflective, but more often than not irrational or emotional, and since the amorphous contemporary novel concerns an anti-hero, modern commentators are suspicious of the well-made novel as written by the generation of Winston Churchill and Ellen Glasgow. They therefore do not look beneath the conventions of the form and are satisfied that Howells said all there was to say when he discussed the duty of American fictionists to register only the smiling aspects of life.[30] Scholarship makes exceptions in the case of Dreiser, Frank Norris, Howells, Henry James, and one or two others, but also seems to assume that conventions governing this literary form were artificial and therefore false to art. Yet conventional ordering of the sonnet into fourteen lines does not falsify poetry, nor does Tolstoi's intermittent intrusion into the vast framework of *War and Peace* reduce that masterpiece to a level below *Madame Bovary*, the author of which follows the convention that he is not writing it. The common attitude nowadays toward fiction of the Roosevelt era, it is clear, simply will not do as commentary.

The novels in question fall into several large categories. First, from about 1895 to about 1905 fiction was fertile in historical romance; second, there were novels about the great open spaces, of which Owen Wister's *The Virginian* (1902) is the great representative; third, there were family novels, like Ellen Glasgow's *The Deliverance* (1904) and Booth Tarkington's *The Turmoil* (1915); and fourth, there were novels about the struggle for power in business or politics or both. Most of these books are activity stories: we had not dreamed of the type of fiction written by James Joyce or Proust or Virginia Woolf. Advanced or "radical" fiction was represented by the heavy-handed naturalism of Theodore Dreiser, though the virtual suppression of *Sister Carrie* in 1900 meant that the public had to wait on *Jennie Gerhardt* in 1911 to learn that sex was primal, marriage was not.[31] Detective stories aside (Mary Roberts Rinehart producted *The Circular Staircase* in 1908), the commonest type of fiction in the period was the novel of political, social, or moral reform. Sometimes all three themes combined in a single book, as they do in Winston Churchill's *The Dwelling Place of Light* (1917).

The novel of reform was nothing new in America; one thinks of Charles Brockden Brown, the determined effort of Cooper to correct the republic in a dozen novels, Hawthorne, *Uncle Tom's Cabin*, books such as Tourgée's *A Fool's Errand*, and Twain and Warner's *The Gilded Age*. Seldom before, however, had so many novelists agreed upon a philosophy and a program. The American ideal was, they felt, sound at heart, and if the republic had gone wrong, if the people had been tricked, the people would on learning the truth turn the rascals out and reform what was wrong. The hero in these stories is usually a representative of the plain people—the Abraham Lincoln type in Booth Tarkington's *The Gentleman from Indiana* (1899) or his Southern equivalent, such as Nicholas Burr in Ellen Glasgow's *The Voice of the People* (1902). Our hero learns of chicanery, discovers how corruption operates, fights these powerful forces, often including the father of the girl he loves (father remains in the background and finances opposition to the hero), opposes a mob, sometimes losing his life in a righteous cause, wins a crucial case in court, or otherwise displays the potency latent in simple morality and an American theory of the state as expressing popular will. At the other pole is the novel, sometimes autobiographical in form, showing an anti-hero commonly born in poverty and determined to rise, who falls in with the machine because his thirst for personal enrichment and power leads him to entrapment by cynical businessmen and venal political leaders. Sometimes this anti-hero marries an innocent girl who believes in him and finds out later that he is crooked. Such books are Robert Herrick's *Memoirs of an American Citizen* and David Graham Phillips's *The Plum Tree*, both published in 1906. The management of the autobiography of a plausible boodler or corrupt lawyer or "statesman" requires considerable literary skill.

Most of these novels include a love story, as standard a part of the tale as is sexual experience today, and in most of them familial relationships are presented affirmatively though the villain may neglect or even exploit his relatives. The heroine is usually a clean-cut, healthy American girl. Even if she is deceived in her husband and has later to suffer, she commonly sticks to him; and sometimes, as in Frank Norris's *The Pit* (1903), the hero is saved by his wife. The heroine, like the hero, may be confronted by a number of moral decisions, and if she consistently makes moral mistakes, as does Lily Bart in Edith Wharton's *The House of Mirth* (1905), the reader watches her gradual descent with pity. The sex-boat, the profligate female, or the alcoholic type appears only in minor roles. The tradition of clean-cut American womanhood runs from the vogue of historical romance to the end of our epoch, the heroines in historical novels being mostly sound American girls in foreign costumes if the novel is set elsewhere than in the United States or the American colonies.

These novels are intelligent and adroit. Their authors write the idiom of their time, not of ours. Their English is clear, not turbid, though it lacks the poetic overtones that create atmosphere in, say, Virginia Woolf's *To the Lighthouse*. Their aim is to present narrative, not introspection. It can be argued that they are too patently optimistic to be faithful to life, but as their primary assumptions are civic and personal morality, one must distinguish between didacticism and ethical postulation. They write in the atmosphere created by the muckrakers and the doctrine of progress rather than by the social Darwinists and the determinists. If life is conflict—and their books assume that it is a battle between Ormuzd and Ahriman—it is not a hopeless conflict. The sympathy that led Lincoln Steffens to try to understand the political boss in *The Shame of the Cities* leads these fiction writers to believe with him and with Ibsen that to let in light and air will produce social justice. They know no such thing as unmitigated evil, they cannot conceive of a Hedda Gabler or an Iago, and they would never dream of producing a book like *In Cold Blood*. But they do not write Sunday-school stories about the virtuous and the idle apprentice; they chronicle resolutions of problems in what they think is the proper American way.

I have hinted that these novelists accept the pragmatic sanction characteristic of the Roosevelt era, and this is evident in their plots when these concern public life, and more notably in their confusion about what they mean when they speak of "the people," who for them rightly possess all power. Like Roosevelt, they thirst after political righteousness, and they assume that the people, if long deceived, can never be defeated, once light is thrown into dark places and the populace rises in its wrath. Without knowing it, they are perhaps still followers of the emotional religion of humanity that swept through the Western world much earlier, producing works like Victor Hugo's *Les Misérables* and the poetry of Whitman. Undoubtedly they profited from the vogue of reform in Toledo and Cincinnati,

Wisconsin and Oregon, and in the federal system, and they welcomed such innovations as the popular election of senators, woman suffrage, the initiative, the referendum, and the recall; I think I may add the commission form of government for cities, which would combine popular control with efficiency. They thought that higher education, notably in state universities as at the University of Wisconsin under La Follette, should be at the service of the people and thereby undercut both corruption and the control of too much of American life by graduates of Ivy League colleges. I do not mean that all these writers were programmatic; yet in many novels the hero or the heroine goes to the university, is exposed to the fraternity-sorority system, revolts against it, and leads the "barbs" to overthrow student government by the wealthy. They were not populists, but they were clearly on the side of the people.

The difficulty is the one that led Theodore Roosevelt to express dislike for the ideas of Thomas Jefferson, whom he regarded as a sentimentalist. Who are the people? The new Americans, systematically voted in gangs by ward bosses? The itinerant workers? The farmers, too frequently "sot" in their ways, despite the Granger movement? The villagers described in Joseph Kirkland's *Zury: The Meanest Man in Spring County* and by Ed Howe in *The Story of a Country Town*? Clearly the basis of democracy was not in the saccharine *Friendship Village* (1908) of Zona Gale. The wants of "the people" in Idaho and the wants of "the people" in Alabama had little in common; was "exposure" to fuse them into a single, high-minded, intelligent electorate? And was not something like this also true of the clash between city and country, county and town? These novelists vaguely knew there were pressure groups, but except by a vague appeal to civic righteousness, their stories do not demonstrate any practicable way by which the clash of such groups was to disappear.

There is a deeper incompatibility. If "the people" were intelligent enough when aroused to defeat villainy at the polls, how could they be so long and so transparently deceived? To quote Lincoln about fooling some of the people all of the time and all of the people some of the time was scarcely a program of practical reform. The novelists dramatized the conflict between good and evil, between machine politicians and the unterrified democracy, but they failed to substantiate the simple postulate of continuing popular virtue and intelligence.

When they narrate the downfall of somebody of good intentions but weak will, they may indeed have demonstrated the truth of Pope's famous lines:

> Vice is a monster of so frightful mien,
> As to be hated needs but to be seen;
> Yet seen too oft, familiar with her face,
> We first endure, then pity, then embrace,

and they asked the reader to sympathize with some political St. George who would slay the monster of corruption and lead its victims to repent. But, like Roosevelt, they were too often better at denunciation and exposure than they were at setting forth a viable philosophy of life in the republic. I do not mean that the novelist has to be a political scientist, but in fact these novels, like novels in other periods, make certain large, simple assumptions, and their narratives, however admirable, left as an impression on the reader only a vague feeling that simple popular virtue was a good thing. Even so forceful a muckraking story as Upton Sinclair's *The Jungle* (1906), which horrified voters—it was the "cause" of passing a Pure Food and Drug Act and a Meat Inspection Act—lives in a simplified universe of black and white, of popular virtue and capitalist brutality. The novelists faced Roosevelt's problem: a specific evil could be analyzed and ameliorated, but practicable working principles were difficult to enunciate and even more difficult to follow generally. The rhetoric of democracy was powerful; like revival meetings, however, it had to be pumped up on each separate occasion. The true weakness of the action novel was not in its conventions, which we find outmoded; it was in its assumptions, which much popular literature has kept today.

V

What many would call a confusion of values, what some have certainly called the hypocrisy of the establishment, and what I have called the pragmatic sanction viable in the Roosevelt era showed itself in fields other than politics and fiction. Education for the people faced a parallel dilemma, to which it could find only a pragmatic solution, if indeed it found any at all, since the dilemma seems more acute today than it was in 1915. Theory and comment on education vibrated, figuratively, between two poles. The first is represented by the theorizing of John Dewey, whose influential *The School and Society* first appeared in 1900, was revised in 1908 and again in 1932, and was followed by *Interest and Effort in Education* (1913), *Schools of Tomorrow* (1915),[32] and *Democracy and Education* (1916). The other pole is represented by the critique of higher education in Thorstein Veblen's *The Higher Learning in America* (1918), published just after the ending of our five decades, a kind of climax to various magazine articles and some books.[33]

The followers of Dewey oversimplified his ideas and ran away with them, so that he felt compelled to repudiate much that passed for "progressive education" in the era, did not in 1919 join the Progressive Education Association (though he later permitted himself to be nominated by acclamation as its honorary president), and again and again warned his followers and well-meaning sentimentalists against the permissiveness too characteristic of what came to be known as the child-centered school. Dewey's real program was not one of mere permissiveness nor aimless creativity, but one of preparation for modern society. Education tends to become merely traditional; Dewey believed that the standard continuing patterns shaping public education at the end of the nineteenth century had become less and less appropriate to the United States in the twentieth century. He believed in democracy, he believed that education is a process of living, and that democracy should begin in the schoolroom, where children will not be overwhelmed by the multiplicity of activities in society outside, and where the school as a form of community life could prepare children gradually for participating in social and economic life and in politics as adults. He wrote:

I believe that education is the fundamental method of social progress and reform.

I believe that education is a regulation of the process of coming to share in the social consciousness; and that the adjustment of individual activity on the basis of this social consciousness is the only sure method of social reconstruction.

I believe that this conception has due regard for both the individualistic and socialistic [34] ideals. It is duly individualistic because it recognizes the formation of a certain character as the only genuine basis of right living. It is socialistic because it recognizes that this right character is not to be formed by merely individual precept, example, or exhortation, but rather by the influence of a certain form of institutional or community life upon the individual, and that the social organism through the school, as its organ, may determine ethical results.

Dewey thought the schoolroom should be dominated by "a spirit of free communication, of interchange of ideas, suggestions, results, both successes and failures of previous experience," that it should be "a social clearing-house, where experiences and ideas are exchanged and subjected to criticisms . . . misconceptions are corrected, and new lines of thought and inquiry are set up," [35] surely a sound basis for popular democracy if it was to be intelligent. No better doctrine of education for a representative republic in the process of adopting technology as a major way of life had been imagined—provided only that the schools could keep the just balance among individualism, societal requirements, and intellectual discipline that Dewey had in mind. Here, could it be carried through, was the foundation, modernized, that would support in the twentieth century Jefferson's great theory of public education. Unfortunately, schools of education were not always capable of educating teachers to grasp and carry out the whole import of Dewey's revolutionary doctrine.

"Radicals" such as Veblen alleged that institutions of higher learning were undemocratic because they were controlled by big business. This control was tantamount to a "sterilization of the universities by business principles." This treason against the people was contrived, according to Veblen, by putting businessmen on boards of trustees and electing presidents and deans agreeable to the prejudices of such boards. Independence of mind was subtly discouraged by various ways of "putting the faculty in its place."

> So well is the academic black-list understood, indeed, and so sensitive and trustworthy is the fearsome loyalty of the common run among academic men, that very few among them will venture openly to say a good word for any one of their colleagues who may have fallen under the displeasure of some incumbent of executive office. This work of intimidation and subornation may fairly be said to have acquired the force of an institution, and to need no current surveillance or effort.

College and university presidents, it appeared, became hypnotized by their own philanthropic (that is, hypocritical) orations:

Particularly do the solemn amenities of social intercourse associated with this promulgation of lay sermons lend themselves felicitously to such a purpose; and this contact with the public and its spokesmen doubtless exercises a powerful control over the policies pursued by these academic executives, in that it affords them the readiest, and at the same time the most habitual indication as to what line of policy and what details of conduct will meet with popular approval and what will not.[36]

As was usual with him, Veblen wrote in general terms. But there had been enough untoward incidents in the academic world to alarm many liberals. The suspicion that Daniel De Leon had been forced to resign from Columbia in 1889 because he had supported Henry George as a candidate for mayor of the city; the charges brought against Professor Richard T. Ely at the University of Wisconsin in 1894 for teaching socialism (the Board of Regents upheld Ely); the obvious politicization of the economics faculty at the Kansas State Agricultural College from 1894 to 1898 and the resultant hiring and firing of economists by Populists and Republicans; the troubled career of the economist and sociologist, Professor E. W. Bemis, at Vanderbilt and Chicago during the 1890s; the dismissal of President E. Benjamin Andrews in 1896 for his financial views from Brown University (he was later brought back); the dismissal of George D. Herron from Grinnell College in Iowa and of Edward A. Ross from Stanford because of their advanced views; the difficulties of Professor J. Allen Smith at Marietta College because he was a free-silver man [37]—these instances and others seemed to prove that colleges and universities were opposing the interests of the plain people by discharging those who spoke for them. Moreover, nothing effective was done by the faculty itself until the organization of the American Association of University Professors in 1915, partly as a climax of mounting resentment against the arbitrary decisions of Nicholas Murray Butler, president of Columbia University. Apparently few university presidents had the courage of Charles W. Eliot of Harvard, who in 1880 in a letter to an English professor laid down the rule that within his own sphere a Harvard professor is absolute, and early outlined a whole philosophy of academic freedom and responsibility.[38]

Freedom of teaching for responsible teachers was of course a goal that had to be reached, but Eliot put his finger on the real dilemma in popular education. As early as 1874, while he was conferring with Daniel Coit Gilman about the nature of The Johns Hopkins University, which was to open in 1876. Eliot said that American institutions of learning "as a class, as a rule, confine themselves too much to producing an average man—a low average quality of attainment . . . we want to work out of that and give more attention to the special capacities and powers of individual men, and carry those individual men to higher levels." [39] Nothing was truer. But how with Dewey could you reshape the grade schools for "democracy" and at the same time reshape higher education so that it would avoid the average man? Clearly colleges, universities, and technical institutions should lie beyond the control of big business, but was the answer to education for all, education for anybody at any level? Could the principle of natural intellectual selection Jefferson believed in be made to work? [40] Or would sentimentality, popularity, and "democracy" take over? The Ivy League colleges and the private preparatory schools that fed them had been more or less committed to education intended to form character, which meant in fact the education of a gentleman, and the career of Roosevelt showed that responsible citizenship could come out of this process—indeed, reformers like George William Curtis and James Russell Lowell had urged the duty of citizenship and political participation on educated men—but now, uneasy at the charge of being snob schools or colleges only for the idle rich, these institutions had begun programs of admission on a more democratic basis. What would come of it? How far was the process to go? The concept of the state university in the service of the people was excellent, but how much of the tax money, how much of the energy of such institutions were to go into extension courses, legislative reference bureaus, adult education, summer schools, and so-called short courses, and how much was to be left to enable the state university to follow its proper calling and rival private institutions not thus encumbered? Moreover, there was an awkward confusion between education that was liberal and education that was vocational, education for expertise and education for the elite. An engineering school could be a fine instrumentality for shaping technologists; was it also a fine instrumentality for shaping an intelligent democracy? As in the instances of politics and fiction, the question of what is meant by "the people" would not be downed; and useful as the pragmatic sanction central to the Roosevelt era proved—it simultaneously sustained the concept of education for all and the concept of education for the able —no real solution for the problem was found. Nor has it been found. As Judge Learned Hand once wisely remarked of many human problems, they are not solved, they are merely postponed.

The problem of proper educational theory for an industrialized and urbanized America produced a flood of books, professional pedagogical journals, and articles in magazines and newspapers. In 1909 another influential writer took up the theme. This was Herbert Croly in his *The Promise of American Life*. He agreed with Dewey on the need of a philosophy for the public schools if the health of the commonwealth were to be preserved, and he agreed with Veblen on the danger to the nation if business values only were to prevail in higher education. By education, Croly said, Americans could be trained for democracy. Like Dewey he repudiated vagueness, sentimentalism, and "progressive education" as commonly undertaken, and like Jefferson he held that some men are born with higher intellectual gifts than others. But he held that in a technological society striving to remain democratic and yet be a powerful nation-state, the great majority of men (his arguments were couched in masculine terms) "gather an edifying understanding of men and things just in so far as they patiently and resolutely stick to the performance of some special and (for the most part) congenial task"; that is, he was all for self-realization. But self-realization was no longer possible in terms of the farm, the village, and the town. He held, perhaps too cheerily, that because of the transformation of American life by invention and industry, great new opportunities were offered to average citizens, and that the demand for expertise required an increase in technical and vocational education. Even farming, he noted, had become a specialist's job. Anything less than practicality was fatal:

> Every American who has the opportunity of doing faithful and fearless work and who proves faithless to it, belongs to the perfect type of the individual anti-democrat. By cheapening his own personality he has cheapened the one constituent of the national life over which he can exercise most effectual control; and thereafter, no matter how superficially patriotic and well-intentioned he may be, his words and his actions are tainted and are in some measure corrupting in their social effects.

In the far background of such utterances one detects the thought of Ruskin, but the rhetoric is that of Roosevelt with a touch of Josiah Royce.

The good work the individual American can be educated to do is, then, "primarily technically competent work." Croly, however, interpreted "technical" generously and added a countervailing value. If the promise of American life was ever to be fulfilled, its citizens must listen to the voice of the critic, by which Croly meant "the voice of the specific intellectual interest, the lover of wisdom, the seeker of the truth," whose essential responsibility was to seek out the truth resident in the lives of his predecessors and his contemporaries, not without looking at both the immediate and the more distant future. In one sense Croly's insistence upon what he calls technical education is that of a Franklin redivivus, but Franklin's morality was general; Croly was trying to get at the heart of a specifically modern American problem. Criticism of the kind he postulates is also a part of expertise, and the program of education he desired was pragmatic and flexible: "There can be nothing final about the creed unless there be something final about the action and purposes of which it is the expression. It must be constantly modified in order to define new experiences and renewed in order to meet unforeseen emergencies." To maintain the political health of a democracy the wisdom of the critic must be embodied in popular doctrinal form. This Roosevelt had seen.

The Promise of American Life was written when its author was forty years old. In writing it he explored the history of the United States, finding as others had done a conflict between Jeffersonianism, which valued individuality and neglected power, and Hamiltonianism, which valued power and underrated individuality, at least for the mass of men. The uncritical simultaneous acceptance of both these points of view seemed to Croly unfortunate, since it had led even intelligent Americans to believe that in the United States progress was automatic. American thinking therefore seemed to imply that the individual had no private responsibility for the nation. The higher American patriotism, he wrote, combines loyalty to historical tradition with an imaginative projection of an ideal national Promise, and this Promise (Santayana's "sort of rainbow in the sky") meant that Americans supposed, as a matter of course, that the future will have something better in store for them individually and collectively than has the past or the present; but a very superficial analysis of this meaning discloses certain ambiguities. What are the particular benefits which this better future will give to Americans either individually or as a nation? And how is this Promise to be fulfilled? Will it fulfill itself, or does it imply certain responsibilities? If so, what responsibilities?

The American political and economic systems had, he admitted, accomplished much to justify a radiant vision of the future, but the difficulty lay in the fallacy of the expectation that the familiar benefits will continue to accumulate automatically.

Automatic progress was no longer a viable idea. Reformers, or most of them, always tend to believe their projects are so excellent that there must be nonpartisan changes to which every patriot will rally. Turn the rascals out and let the people rule. In fact, said Croly, most reforms are not nonpartisan but spring from some interest, sectional desire, vocational demand, or class value. As for the persons who really control life in the United States—and this is the most fascinating part of Croly's analysis—he divided them into four products of a false expertise and analyzed each type. The four were the capitalist in charge of large corporate interests; the representative of the labor union (the old-fashioned "walking delegate"), who could not look beyond the demands of his group to the larger needs of the nation; the political boss; and, most insidious of the quartet, the corporation lawyer, whose interest was confined to advancing the interest of his rich clients, the corporations, for whom laws were a technical game he must master and outwit. These, not large-souled patriots like Roosevelt, were the masters of the American economy. They preached a Jeffersonian individualism (laissez faire) and practiced a Hamiltonian concentration of power.

In Roosevelt's actions and policies Croly thought he saw the proper, not the improper, fusion of Hamiltonian methods and Jeffersonian ends (he seems to have ignored Roosevelt's detestation of Jefferson). In present circumstances, he wrote, "the national advance of the American democracy does demand an increasing amount of centralized action and responsibility." He devoted two chapters to the problems of reconstructing the system, the first of these dealing with the institutional reforms necessary to the state (the government), the second to industrial organization. The regulation of big business, in view of the increase in interstate and international commerce, must lie mainly with the federal government. He thought the distinction between domestic and interstate commerce, so far as it implies a distribution of regulatory power, is a distinction without much importance; then, like the progressives generally, he dwelt upon the undue influence exercised on government by the great corporations (though he admitted that many of these, notably the railroads, had had to defend themselves against foolish or cynical state legislation). On the whole Croly thought the Roosevelt-Taft policy of recognizing the inevitability of larger corporations, but demanding proper regulation of them by government, was wise (the book appeared before the end of Taft's first year as president), but he was chary of praising regulation by commission, preferring the taxation of corporations.

The moral tone characteristic of the Roosevelt era colors Croly's whole discussion, a gallant attempt to retain the best of two traditions, that of Hamiltonian power and that of Jeffersonian individuality intended as excellence. Hamiltonian power meant that industry must support great corporations and a great nation be governed from the center; Jeffersonian individuality meant that life must be enriched for all men. Here are characteristic passages from the concluding pages of Croly's book:

Americans have always associated individual freedom with the unlimited popular enjoyment of all available economic opportunities. Yet it would be far more true to say that the popular enjoyment of practically unrestricted economic opportunities is precisely the condition which makes for individual bondage.

Some men show more enterprise and ingenuity in devising ways of making money than others, or they show more vigor and zeal in taking advantage of the ordinary methods. These men are the kind of individuals which the existing economic system tends to encourage . . .

[But] the truth is that individuality cannot be dissociated from the pursuit of a disinterested object. It is a moral and intellectual quality, and it must be realized by moral and intellectual means.

American public opinion has not as yet begun to understand the relation between the process of national education by means of a patient attempt to realize the national purpose and the corresponding process of individual emancipation and growth. It still believes that democracy is a happy device for evading effective responsibilities. . . . the first necessity of American educational advance is the arousing of the American intellectual conscience.

The American intellectual interest demands, consequently, a different sort of assertion from the American economic or political interest. Economically and politically the need is for constructive regulation, implying the imposition of certain fruitful limitations upon traditional individual freedom. But the national intellectual development demands above all individual emancipation. American intelligence has still to issue its Declaration of Independence.[41] It has still to proclaim that in a democratic system the intelligence has a discipline, an interest, and a will of its own, and that this special discipline and interest call for a new conception both of individual and national development. For the time being the freedom which Americans need is freedom of thought. The energy they need is the energy of thought. The moral unity they need cannot be obtained without intensity and integrity of thought.

Both the rhetoric and the philosophy of *The Promise of American Life* make it a proper code for the Age of Energy. The rhetoric, though free of the intemperate language of even Roosevelt, turns on such words as "energy," "development," "progress," words implying the recognition of power, and "promise" both in the sense of progress and in the sense of an attainable "ideal." Croly sums up the better parts of many elements in an industrialized economy. Yet, despite the excellence of his book, like the muckrakers under Roosevelt and the insurgents under Taft, he was better at exposure than at programming. His ethics were sound, his generalizations were vague. The best he could say was that certain specific reforms seemed to work and, working, were good if they made for "democracy"—a later version of the pragmatic sanction.[42] It is important to note, however, that Croly was writing in a universe of discourse in which rational argument and statement were assumed as a matter of course to be basic in the arts, in education, in industry, and in public discussion. Shortly this was to change.

VI

It is unfair to the Taft administration to dismiss it as casually as I have done, since, despite its wretched tariff bill, the attacks on Cannonism and the "interests" by insurgents and progressives, the unfortunate Ballinger-Pinchot controversy, and the even more unfortunate irruption of an aging Roosevelt into presidental politics in 1912, this presidency saw the enactment of a goodly amount of excellent legislation. Yet the years from 1909 to 1913 seem to represent a slowing down of momentum, a paling of the fires that ever since Appomattox had kept American life at the boiling point. If sectionalism has never entirely disappeared, under Taft it diminished. A pause in the national rhythm occurred; and though the election of Woodrow Wilson in 1912 led to a momentary restoration of reformatory zeal and the election of a chief magistrate even more of a scholar than Theodore Roosevelt, the New Freedom was shortly to be clouded over by war, and the country, willy-nilly, had to drop everything else after the sinking of the *Lusitania* on May 7, 1915, for "preparedness" and eventually for combat. The national life moved on to a total reorganization of its resources, so that when war was declared April 6, 1917, the country was far better off than it had been at the opening of either the Civil War or the Spanish-American War.

There was, however, another, perhaps a deeper, alteration in American culture preparing—that of a basic shift in the concept of discourse itself. After Darwin the next great European revolutionary to alter American thought was not Marx but Sigmund Freud, whose influence, together with that of his school of thought, upon the "American way" has been so profound, that the epoch beginning in 1920 might well be called the Freudian Era. Although Freud attended the notable conference of psychologists at Clark University in Worcester, Massachusetts, in 1909 (William James and G. Stanley Hall were also present), general Freudian influence was not evident until after 1920, when it began to be an important foundation for a postwar psychology of cynicism and sexuality and offered an excuse for intellectuals to turn away from logical solutions to postwar dilemmas by asserting or assuming that rationality was less powerful than the id and the libido.

Freud's early doctrine, as is natural, was received with reserve by professional psychologists in the United States, and moralists were shocked. Whatever news leaked out concerning quarrels between Freud and Jung or Freud and Adler, these were dismissed as evidence of the irritation natural among European savants or as testimony that Freud's theory was not very convincing, after all. National attention was more often fixed on sports, the German debt, the Russian Revolution, and scandals in the Harding administration. That the Freudian gospel, however revised, might utterly change the base of American individualism, family relationships, and the grounds of art, and raise questions about the sincerity of rational discourse did not become evident until much later. My guess is that not until the 1940s did Freudianism and its offshoots, and psychiatry and psychoanalysis as diagnostic or therapeutic methodologies become generally acceptable to physicians, social workers, psychologists, and, let us add gently, the wealthy. But writers were interested before 1915. It is a curious example of American receptivity to new ideas (outside of technology) that the first popular articles Frederick Hoffman, an authority on the topic, could dig out of the magazines were all rather coarse-fibered simplifications of what was thought to be Freud's theory.[43] More professional work is represented by A. A. Brill's founding of the New York Psychoanalytic Society in 1911 and his translations of Freud's *Three Contributions to the Theory of Sex* (1910), *The Interpretation of Dreams* (1913), and *The Psychopathology of Everyday Life* (1914). As Hoffman demonstrates, the non-professional vogue of Freud, and with it a profound influence upon art and literature and communication, began mainly in Greenwich Village during and after World War I. The first great triumph of Freudianism in the novel was possibly Faulkner's *The Sound and the Fury* (1929), though one can make a case for Sherwood Anderson's *Windy McPherson's Son* (1916) and *Winesburg, Ohio* (1919), the "war novels," and Dos Passos' *U.S.A.* Eliot's *The Waste Land* (1922), which has its Freudian moments, is mainly to be referred to anthropology, folklore, and surrealism.

Darwin cannot be made responsible for all the Darwinians, nor Freud for all that passed for Freudianism. An irony in cultural history is that Freud, who thought he was protecting rational culture (one of his idols was Goethe) by making it aware of its subconscious and unconscious contexts, was looked upon as a new messiah, and that he who sought to free men from fear was interpreted as a determinist. But he was thought to release "creativity" from bondage. Some results were unexpected. Universities, once the citadels of rational discourse and creators of a critical habit of mind, came to harbor more and more "artists in residence." In 1915, however, this amazing revolution was not dreamed of, and nobody anticipated a generation that would throw away most of the conventional wisdom and go in for the instant moment and the "relevant" work of art. Nothing can be more remote from either Dewey or Croly, Hamilton or Jefferson, Roosevelt or Woodrow Wilson—or from Freud— than this refusal of civic responsibility for art. And though it goes back to John D. Rockefeller's determination to create popular approval for the Standard Oil Company, the concept of a public relations expert who "builds a favorable image" through the manipulation of subliminal psychology would have been abhorrent to progressives, insurgents, and reformers. The test of public policy slowly shifted from Roosevelt's: "Is it righteous?" and Taft's: "Is it legal?" to the question: "Will it be popular?" in opinion polls.

Energy of personality did not weaken, but its source was now referred not to the soul but to the libido, and judgments of performance were no longer in terms of what is cowardly or heroic, vicious or virtuous, but in terms of frustration, anguish, sexuality, fear, familial relations, and guilt. Mechanical and electrical energy increased, as did that of the atom, but except in such areas as real estate, where buccaneering was still possible, status replaced the injunction to improve. Never had the sciences been more brilliant—consider the list of American Nobel prize winners; never had technology done more, never had expertise been more adroit, but in literature and the arts, as in advertising and "selling," the nonrational became king. The world of Thomas Jefferson was a lost world, indeed.

As late as 1915 most of these drastic alterations lay hidden in the future, but just before the outbreak of the Great War many thousands of Americans were made aware that a new mode of sensibility was upsetting the cosmopolitan tradition of the West. This crucial event was the famous Armory Show in New York in 1913 (parts of it went on tour to cities such as Boston and Chicago). The generation of beaux arts painters, most of them born before the Civil War, were passing from the scene.[44] They were succeeded by a generation that still believed in representational art, but that turned its attention, if not wholly, then characteristically, from the open fields and the wild mountain peaks to urban life—colorful in the instance of Prendergast with his parks and boulevards, elegant in Sargent's portraits, or finding their themes in the picturesque, if unlovely, quarters of a great city, as did the Ashcan school: Bellows with his famous "Stag at Sharkey's," Glackens and his "Roller-Skating Rink," George B. Luks, who painted his charming "The Spielers," Everett Shinn, who liked the garish lights and purple shadows of vaudeville houses, and the prolific and radical John Sloan. Their theorist was that fine teacher, Robert Henri, who was certain that Thomas Eakins was the greatest portrait painter America had produced. Henri's emphasis is forever on craftsmanship, not for smoothness but for energy. If you want to be a historical painter, he advised, let your history be of your own time, of what you can get to know personally. He admired John Sloan's painting of two boys setting pigeons free to fly from a rooftop in lower Manhattan because the canvas would carry into the future the feel and way of life as it happened and was understood.

Not only painting but photography was fascinated by this new urban realism. The dean of photographers was Alfred Stieglitz, whose great "Terminal" and "The Steerage" turned their backs on elegance.[45] But Stieglitz did more than revolutionize photography; at 291 Fifth Avenue in New York in 1905 he opened some small exhibition rooms where, had they cared to go, Americans might have been prepared for the Armory Show by viewing canvases, lithographs, and drawings by such European "radicals" as Renoir, Matisse, Toulouse-Lautrec, Cézanne, Picasso, and their contemporaries. Few, however, cared to go, and conservative critics declaimed against the European wild men. A dissident group of younger painters, following an old custom, seceded from the National Academy to form a "new" Association of American Painters and Sculptors. Out of the matrix of this association the idea of the Armory Show, held at Lexington Avenue and Twenty-fifth Street, was born.[46] When the show was opened, it seemed at times that it might cause a riot.

The radical artists of the Armory Show have become old masters now or have been forgotten, nonrepresentational painting is regularly hung in art museums, some theories of art have gone far beyond the Armory Show, and one is therefore tempted to forget its importance in reshaping American response to the modern world. Photographs of the exhibits there displayed look tame enough nowadays. But at the time this insult to the laws of perspective, these new marriages of ill-assorted colors, these formal distortions, the simultaneity attempted in Duchamp's famous "Nude Descending a Staircase," this sculpture, sometimes creamy, sometimes rude, and often without any obvious "subject," the assumption that a piece of canvas or of paper was a mere two-dimensional flat plane to spread paint on rather than a window into actuality or into an ideal universe beyond mortality

—all this meant that to a powerful group of talents the world had totally changed. Things were no longer things in themselves; they were
not even what they seemed to be to the beholding eye; they were
merely excuses for assembling a private idiom of form, line, and
color. Art was divorced not merely from tradition but from civism itself. The basis of rational dialogue between artist and spectator was
eroded. "Americanism," that long-sought ideal of the arts in the
United States, no longer made any sense, since an international style
inevitably denied nationalism. The arts had always been individual
expression, true; but now art had become the expression of an individualism so remote from the responsibility of either artist or citizen
in the state, that it had nothing to do with the state. Citizens and the
state were called upon to support art, but art here declared itself not
responsible for the support of either the state or citizenship. If individualism might be associated with abstraction, distortion and "les
fauves," this might be democracy; but was something like Seurat's
pointillisme anything more than an unnecessary technical bravado?
The long search for European values for which American sensibility
might profit by associating itself with a great tradition here ended in
a gigantic denial of tradition. Most of the artists represented in the
Armory Show were nothing if not energetic, and in that sense they
sprang from a general age of energy; but if the Armory Show be
granted the historical and symbolic meaning I think it had, the
American Age of Energy ended not with a whimper but with a bang
of denial. Public and rational controls of art were now not possible
except as censorship; and after the Armory Show, after Freud, after
World War I, though energy multiplied, the Age of Energy vanished.
And we were never again to be the nation—heady, adolescent, picturesque, unpredictable, yearning to be loved and fearing to be
outdone—that we had been between 1865 and 1915.

REFERENCE NOTES

INDEX

In these notes the *Dictionary of American Biography* is regularly abbreviated *DAB; the Mississippi Valley Historical Review, MVHR;* and *The New England Quarterly, NEQ.*

Reference Notes

Chapter I: American Panorama

1. This language is the heart of Secretary Olney's famous message to Great Britain in the Venezuelan dispute of 1895.
2. For a more modern view see Blake McKelvey, *The Urbanization of America, 1860–1915* (New Brunswick, 1963).
3. Landmarks in the arbitration of disputes between capital and labor include the agreement in the anthracite coal industry, based on Roosevelt's commission of 1902, and the quasi-judicial machinery established after long travail in the garment trades of New York City.
4. It is of course true that not until the depression of 1929 did the federal government enact legislation for the country as a whole that was upheld by the courts. Nevertheless, the foundations of this philosophy of the relations among employers, workers, and the government were laid in the nineteenth century.
5. Nothing about the Claflin sisters but has its tang. Victoria named a daughter Zulu Maud.
6. Stephen Birmingham, *Our Crowd* (New York, 1967) is here pertinent as a case study in the rise to eminence of a set of non-Anglo-Saxon families.
7. It is curious that the 1890s developed ragtime, the rhythm of which seems characteristically American, and the 1960s go in for popular music influenced strongly by the Beatles of Britain.
8. Fundamentalism is a twentieth-century term, deriving from *The Fundamentals*, 10 (later 12) pamphlets published in Chicago from 1910 to 1915, and financed by two rich men from Los Angeles, Milton and Lyman Stewart. These were sent free of charge, so far as possible, to every pastor, evangelist, missionary, theological student, Sunday-school superintendent, and secretary of a Y.M.C.A. or a Y.W.C.A. throughout the world. The first general editor was Amzi Clarence Dixon; the last, Reuben A. Terry. It is supposed that about three million copies were distributed. See Norman E. Furniss, *The Fundamentalist Controversy, 1918–1931* (New Haven, 1954), "Introduction."
9. If one overlooks the cartoons in this edition, Anthony Comstock, *Traps*

for the Young, originally published in 1883 and edited by Robert Bremmer for The John Harvard Library Series (Cambridge, 1967), is revelatory of real uneasiness. Those who are now troubled by modern pornography will read with interest Chapter VIII, "Death Traps by Mail," and Chapter XIII, "More Liberal Traps."

10. Louis Agassiz, "Contemplations of God in the Kosmos," *The Christian Examiner and Religious Miscellany,* 6th series, 15 (50):1–17 (January 1851).

11. Of various studies, Henry A. Pochmann, *New England Transcendentalism and St. Louis Hegelianism* (Philadelphia, 1948) is succinct.

12. The cosmic theism of John Fiske is set forth in his *Outlines of Cosmic Philosophy,* 2 vols. (1874). It does not seem to differ greatly from the scientific theism of Francis Ellingwood Abbot, which annoyed Josiah Royce and which is presented in Abbot's *Scientific Theism* (Boston, 1885) and *The Way Out of Agnosticism or the Philosophy of Free Religion* (Boston, 1890).

13. An important influence sustaining the "ideal" interpretation of nature and one insufficiently studied is the vogue among the general reading public of Alexander von Humboldt, whose geological journeys in the New World made anything he wrote interesting to Americans. His *Kosmos* is the great *summa* of the romantic interpretation of the universe. An edition in German, presumably abridged (I have not seen it), was printed in Philadelphia in 1855, and according to the Library of Congress catalogue there were three printings of the whole *Kosmos* in translation, one in 1848–1868 and two in 1855–1858. A pastiche entitled *Aspects of Nature* appeared in 1850 and was reprinted as late as 1898 as *Views of Nature; or, Contemplations on the Sublime Phenomena of Creation, with Scientific Illustrations.*

14. A prospectus for the Synthetic Philosophy was printed in 1860. The bibliography is excessively confused since various volumes were from time to time revised. But the scheme is: Vol. I, *First Principles,* 1862; Vols. II and III, *Principles of Biology,* 1863–1867; Vols. IV and V, *Principles of Psychology,* 1870–1872; Vols. VI, VII, and VIII, *Principles of Sociology,* 1877–1897; Vols. IX and X, *Principles of Ethics,* 1892–1893. As the dates reveal, there is overlapping in the sequence. Moreover, the contents of some volumes appeared separately and were then collected into the series. Finally, some of Spencer's most influential writings are not included in the Synthetic Philosophy; for example, *The Proper Sphere of Government,* originally a magazine article, was published as a pamphlet in 1843, and *The Man versus the State* appeared in 1884, two titles of comfort to American businessmen. The *Descriptive Sociology,* 1874–1882, was compiled under Spencer's direction.

15. This seems to be the purport of Laurence Gronlund's *The Co-Operative Commonwealth: An Exposition of Modern Socialism* (Boston, 1884) and of its theory that an enlightened few are to guide an evolving society into cooperation. In Edward Bellamy's *Looking Backward:*

2000–1887 (Boston, 1888) silent change alters the economic, political, and social habits of the nation while the sleeper lies in a long trance.

16. Herbert Spencer, *An Autobiography,* 2 vols., (London, 1904), II, 383–409. Getting home, Spencer wrote: "Thus ended an expedition which I ought never to have undertaken."

17. The essay first appeared in the *Princeton Review,* November 1861, and was collected into *War and Other Essays,* ed. Albert Galloway Keller (New Haven, 1911), from which I quote. It is also available as the first unit in *Social Darwinism: Selected Essays of William Graham Sumner,* with an introduction by Stow Person (Englewood Cliffs, 1963). I find it illuminating that the word "law" or "laws" appears thirty-five times and the terms "science," "sciences," or "scientific" thirty-one times in an essay of twenty-three pages. It is, however, easy to exaggerate Sumner's pessimism. In "Earth Hunger" (1913) he wrote of "a view of the status of the globe as forming a great family of nations, united by a growing body of international law, creating institutions as they are needed to regulate international relations, bound together in community of interest by free commerce, communicating to one another the triumphs won by each in science and art, sharing their thoughts by a common literature in which the barriers of language are made as little effectual as possible, and thus creating one society of the enlightened nations independent of state boundaries," "not in the least," he added, "an ideal or a dream," though the Monroe Doctrine "is a barbaric stumbling-block in the way of enlightened international policy." See Albert Galloway Keller and Maurice R. Davie, eds., *Essays of William Graham Sumner,* 2 vols. (New Haven, 1934), I, 174–207 for the whole essay.

18. The best edition of *Law of Civilization and Decay* is a reprint of the second (1896) edition, with a perceptive introduction by Charles A. Beard, which traces the growth and the reception of the book (New York, 1943). The passage in the text is from Brooks Adams' "Preface," p. 59, in this edition. The bit from Henry Adams is in *The Degradation of the Democratic Dogma, with an Introduction by Brooks Adams* (New York, 1919), p. 260. Of innumerable comments on the thought of the two brothers, I find three succinct, cogent, and useful: Roy F. Nichols, "The Dynamic Interpretation of History," *NEQ,* 8(2): 163–78 (June 1935); Henry Wasser, "The Thought of Henry Adams," in *ibid.,* 24(4): 495–509 (December 1951); and Thornton Anderson, *Brooks Adams: Constructive Conservative* (Ithaca, 1951).

19. A gloomy interpretation of evolution is sometimes found among poets: for example, Edward Rowland Sill, on whom see Newton Arvin, "The Failure of E. R. Sill," *The (American) Bookman,* 72(5): 581–89 (January 1931).

20. *Progressive Orthodoxy: A Contribution to the Christian Interpretation of Christian Doctrine* (Boston, 1885, several times reprinted). The other contributors were William J. Tucker, J. W. Churchill, George Harris, and Edward L. Hincks.

21. *The Andover Case: with an Introductory Historical Statement; a Careful Summary of the Arguments of the Respondent Professors; and the Full Text of the Arguments of the Complainants* . . . (Boston, 1887); *The Andover Defence.* . . . *Arguments of Professor Theodore W. Dwight, Professor Simeon H. Baldwin, Hon. Charles Theodore Russell, and Ex-Governor Gaston* . . . (Boston, 1887); *The Question at Issue in the Andover Case. Arguments of Rev. Drs. Joshua W. Wellman and Orpheus T. Lanphear* . . . (Boston, 1893); Daniel Day Williams, *The Andover Liberals* (New York, 1941) are representative. In a sermon picturesquely entitled *The Andover Bottle's Burst* (Boston, 1882) the Reverend C. A. Bartol ridiculed the attempt of Andover liberals to retain an obsolete creed and talked about "crowding to make the old ecclesiastical omnibus receive the new truth." He poured contempt on the Andover Board. A disciple of Emerson, Bartol had no use for a creed that "yields and budges and sways and warps." He was noted for vigorous figures of speech. The sermon still conveys some of the heat and bitterness engendered by the controversy.

22. This is an oversimplification, since Bushnell altered the doctrine of the atonement and modified other central tenets of the creed.

23. Joseph Le Conte, *Evolution and its Relation to Religious Thought* (New York, 1888), p. 295.

24. John Fiske, *Outlines of Cosmic Philosophy; Based on the Doctrine of Evolution, with Criticisms on the Positive Philosophy,* 4 vols. (Boston, 1902), IV, 259–60. This edition has an introduction by Josiah Royce. *The Destiny of Man Viewed in the Light of his Origins,* 14th ed. (Boston, 1889), pp. 64–65. This was first published in 1884. See also his *The Idea of God as Affected by Modern Knowledge* (Boston, 1886), in which one reads that "the whole tendency of modern science is to impress upon us even more forcibly the truth that the entire knowable universe is an immense unit, animated throughout all its parts by a single principle of life" (p. 145).

25. Examples include a set of lectures given (and repeated) in 1871–1872, *Christianity and Modern Thought* (Boston, 1872), by ten philosophers and clergymen. Among the Americans were Oliver Stearns and Andrew P. Peabody, and among the Europeans James Martineau and Athanase Coquerel *fils,* who, though courteous about Roman Catholicism, thought it was doomed by progress. Another collection, *Freedom and Fellowship in Religion* (Boston, 1876), included essays by Octavius B. Frothingham, David A. Wasson, and Francis Ellingwood Abbot. The Boston Monday lectures were important. In 1880–1881, for example, the printed volume, *Christ and Modern Thought* (Boston, 1881), noted that the masses were unchurched and lamented that "our vague literary rationalism" "drifts from fog bank to fog bank across the seas of discussion, making its protection very often the vapor itself" (Joseph Cook, p. xxix). In *A Critical History of the Evolution of Trinitarianism and its Outcome in the New Christianity* (Boston, 1900) Levi Leonard Paine concludes that theology will be freed from its traditional fetters and

will base itself on the inductive method. George A. Gordon, in *Humanism in New England Theology* (Boston, 1920), which began as an article, "The Collapse of the New England Theology" (1907), argued for updating trinitarianism, as the only answer to the question "How to evolve from an egoistic Deity to an altruistic humanity" (102). An excellent treatment is Frank Hugh Foster, *The Modern Movement in American Theology* (New York, 1939), though John Wright Buckham, *Progressive Religious Thought in America* (Boston, 1919), is by no means outdated.

26. Henry Ward Beecher, *Evolution and Religion* (New York, 1885), p. 52; Lyman Abbott, *The Theology of an Evolutionist* (Boston, 1897), p. 26; Henry Churchill King, *Reconstruction in Theology* (New York, 1901), p. 77.

27. See Sidney Warren, *American Freethought, 1860–1914. Columbia University Studies in History, Economics and Public Law. No. 504* (New York, 1943).

28. George A. Gordon, *Ultimate Conceptions of Faith* (Boston, 1903), *passim*. Shrewd as he was, Gordon does not recognize the real intellectual dilemma. He notes that "the traditional theological system has silently passed out of belief" (p. 74), but he takes refuge in vague sentences such as: Conscience "overflows the channels of mere individuality; it finds itself beyond a multitude of moral centres like itself; it constitutes itself into a world of moral persons, among whom it is one. . . . It must rise into the consciousness of God" (p. 109). This view may owe something to Royce or William Ernest Hocking, but how does such a general assertion validate Christian theology?

29. The phrase "Social Gospel" seems to have spread from a magazine, *The Social Gospel*, edited by Ralph Albertson at the Christian Commonwealth plantation in Georgia, 1898–1901, though it seems to have been printed in Chicago. There is a delicate line to be drawn between the Social Gospel and Christian Socialism. Perhaps the first Social Gospel book was Washington Gladden's *Being a Christian* (Boston, 1876), but the two central titles are the *Encyclopaedia of Social Reform*, edited by W. D. P. Bliss in 1897, and Walter Rauschenbusch, *Christianity and the Social Crisis* (New York, 1907). On the difficulties confronted by the movement see Aaron Ignatius Abell, *The Urban Impact on American Protestantism, 1865–1900* (Cambridge, 1943); Charles Howard Hopkins, *The Rise of the Social Gospel in American Protestantism, 1865–1919* (New Haven, 1940); and Henry F. May, *Protestant Churches and Industrial America* (New York, 1949).

30. I have discussed only the simpler elements in a problem of great complexity. Philosophy and formal ethics in the period passed into the possession of professional academicians, and historians of philosophy have naturally confined their books to tracing professional development. How far these professors of philosophy affected American thought in general until the vogue of pragmatism it is difficult to know. The influence of Hegel on professional thinking was important; the St.

Louis Hegelians seemed at one time to be acquiring popular vogue. They founded the *Journal of Speculative Philosophy* (1867–1893), hospitable to many schools of thought, and in William Torrey Harris colored education. Harris rose to fame as superintendent of schools in St. Louis and served from 1889 to 1906 as the first U.S. Commissioner of Education. But the St. Louis Hegelians were as eccentric as the transcendentalists. The Concord School of Philosophy, a creation of Harris and Bronson Alcott, ran from 1879 to 1887, but it seems to have been a high-level Chautauqua. The great Harvard four—Royce, William James, Santayana, and (as a teacher) Palmer—had enormous repute. Despite the excellence of such moralists as Royce, James, Bordon P. Bowne, George E. Howison, and William Ernest Hocking, it is doubtful whether formal ethics greatly influenced the main current of American thinking. But the reader should consult, among others, Harvey Gates Townsend, *Philosophical Ideas in the United States* (New York, 1934) and Herbert W. Schneider's ampler *A History of American Philosophy* (New York, 1946). A study of Frank Luther Mott's standard history of American magazines reveals a list of philosophical periodicals, including *The Open Court* (1887–1936), but cannot of course answer the question of popular influence.

31. The complex origins of revolutionary theory are traced in the masterly introduction by Bernard Baylin to his *Pamphlets of the American Revolution, 1750–1776*, Vol. I (Cambridge, 1965). Unfortunately, only one out of a projected set of four has yet (1970) been published.

32. The phrases from 1854 and 1858 are to be found in Paul M. Angle, ed., *New Letters and Papers of Lincoln* (Boston, 1930), pp. 134, 176.

33. It is curious, though not necessarily relevant, that "Columbia, the Gem of the Ocean" was originally "Britannia, the Pride of the Ocean."

34. See Chapter 6 of the second part of Asselineau's *L'Évolution de Walt Whitman* (Paris, 1954).

35. These poems are all to be found in Stedman's widely read *An American Anthology, 1797–1900* (Boston, 1900).

36. For the full text of Moody's poems see *The Poems and Plays of William Vaughn Moody*, 2 vols. (Boston, 1912), I, 25–26, 29–30.

37. I quote from the translation by John J. Isler and Alfred E. Mason, 8 vols. (Chicago, 1889–1892), I, 65–66.

38. The records of the celebration were edited by the secretary of the Constitutional Centennial Commission, Hampton L. Carson, in two huge volumes (Philadelphia, 1889). The last item in Vol. I is an admiring account by a French visitor.

39. Straus reworked and published his lectures as *The Origin of Republican Form of Government* (New York, 1887). He did not know it, but he had revived the language of the New England theocracy. The quotation in the text comes from p. 142.

40. Henry St. George Tucker edited his relative's book, 2 vols. (Chicago, 1899); and the quoted passages are to be found in I, 13, 59. The Michigan lecturers included Thomas M. Cooley, Henry Hitchcock of St.

Louis, George W. Biddle of Philadelphia, Charles A. Kent of Detroit, and Daniel E. Chamberlain of New York, once governor of South Carolina, and the collection is called *Constitutional History of the United States as Seen in the Development of American Law* (New York, 1889). I have depended on H. Arnold Bennett, *The Constitution in School and College* (New York, 1935) for my information about civics and addresses to educational institutions. Alfred Bayliss, *Easy Lessons on the Constitution*, an elementary textbook, appeared in Chicago, 1891, but my quotation is from Bennett, p. 97. For John Bascom see *Growth of Nationality in the United States: A Social Study* (New York, 1899). He deplored the "commercial temper" in the United States that separated politics from social life and thought they managed this sort of thing better in Great Britain (pp. 2, 208).

41. Robert G. McCloskey, ed., *Essays in Constitutional Law* (New York, 1957), pp. 4, 18. It is not to be inferred from my text that all treatises and all teaching of constitutional law from 1865 to 1915 partook of the reverential order. Thomas M. Cooley is considered to be the great successor to Story, and both his *A Treatise on the Constitutional Limitations which Rest upon the Legislative Power of the States of the American Union*, which reached a 7th (posthumous) edition in 1903, and his widely influential *The General Principles of Constitutional Law in the United States of America* (1880) are clear legal analyses of the Constitution as a basic document. Moreover, the anonymous *Fate of Republics* (Boston, 1880), dedicated to General Ulysses S. Grant, takes a gloomy view: "the mass of our people will not honor Bible law and practice. Men will remain unrighteous. The invisible forces of the universe, sometimes called God, which countenance nothing but righteousness, will demand a day of reckoning" (p. 250).

42. *Constitutional History of the United States as Seen in the Development of American Law*, p. 13.

43. Thus Gustavus Myers in his *History of the Supreme Court of the United States* (Chicago, 1918) wrote that "the Supreme Court as an institution has throughout its whole existence incarnated into final law the demands of the dominant and interconnected sections of the ruling class," and said that though none of the justice has been venal, their decisions by and large spring from "all-potent class interests" (pp. 7, 8). In *Nine Men: A Political History of the Supreme Court from 1790 to 1955* (New York, 1955), a somewhat splenetic book, Fred Rodell seems to think the court is wrong unless it agrees with Justices Black and Douglas.

44. This statement is credited to Horace Binney (1780–1875), lawyer and constitutional theorist.

45. (Hampton L. Carson, ed.), *The Supreme Court of the United States: Its History and its Centennial Celebration February 4th, 1890* (2 parts) (Philadelphia, 1891), pt. 2: pp. 557–58.

46. Charles Warren, *The Supreme Court in United States History*, rev. ed., 2 vols. (Boston, 1937), I, 753. Warren admires the independence of the

American judiciary and quotes in a final note from a letter of Henry B. Brown, who resigned from the court in 1906, declaring that the court "is a magnificent tribute to that respect for the law inherent in the Anglo-Saxon race, and contains within itself assurance of the stability of our institution" (p. 756, note). Brown had been appointed in 1890. The passage of comment on the lawyers representing Mississippi before the court in 1867 is quoted by Warren from *The Independent,* April 10, 1867 (pp. 456–57). For a characteristic contemporary approach, critical yet sympathetic, consult Alexander Mordecai Bickel, *Politics and the Warren Court* (New York, 1955), and his *The Supreme Court and the Idea of Progress* (New York, 1970).

47. Not all the components of a growing nationalistic mystique continued to thrive. Thus, Memorial Day, instituted by the G.A.R. for May 30, and celebrated on varying dates in the former states of the Confederacy, has virtually lost its religious quality except in time of war, and is now a secular holiday distinguished by baseball games, picnics, and the like. The decline and fall of the Fourth of July as a rededication to patriotism is a parallel instance.

48. Frank Freidel, *The Splendid Little War* (Boston, 1958), pp. 5–6.

49. See the first chapter of Roosevelt's *The Rough Riders* (New York, 1899), and consult the table of enrollments in the appendix.

50. To many medical experts nowadays medical theory and practice in the United States from the Civil War to World War I as well as care for public health seem virtually primitive. Yet the advances were striking. In 1869 the Massachusetts Board of Health was created, the first in the country. More than a hundred medical schools were founded between 1870 and 1890, the practice of anesthesia steadily advanced, appendicitis was correctly diagnosed in 1886, the Mayo Clinic opened in 1889, tuberculosis, yellow fever, typhus, and hookworm were brought under control, the X-ray treatment for cancer began in 1896, the Rockefeller Institute for Medical Research was created in 1901, Abraham Flexner's classical report on medical education (financed by the Carnegie Foundation) appeared in 1910, and Harvey Cushing was appointed professor of surgery at Harvard in 1912. These are but a few among many important discoveries, events, and men.

Chapter II: But Yet a Union

1. The standard history of the conciliatory tendencies is Paul H. Buck, *Road to Reunion* (Boston, 1937). The popularity of such songs as "Tenting Tonight" is illuminating; and for a representative instance of the feeling of a Union private see the letters of William H. Brown and Emma Jane Frazey during the 1860s, as edited by Vivian C. Hopkins, *Bulletin of the New York Public Library* 73(2): 114–36 (February 1969).

2. This is not to assume the existence of monopoly or the lack of competi-

tion among large-scale industries, and means only that technological and business enterprises found what we now call "planning" valuable, first on a regional, then on a national, and in many later cases, on an international scale.

3. Chicago is a classic example of this process, the most American of cities and the most mongrel of our metropolises. See Chapter IV, "The Urban World," in Arthur M. Schlesinger, Sr., *The Rise of the City, 1878–1898* (Vol. X of the *History of American Life* series, New York, 1933).

4. Despite some absurdities (the writer puts the Great Valley of the Hudson in western New York), the chapter by J. W. Watson, "The Natural Scene," in *American Civilization: An Introduction*, eds. A. N. J. den Hollander and Sigmund Skard (London, 1968) is a suggestive survey of the physiography of the United States in relation to national development.

5. Tensions between Old Americans and immigrant groups were, I think, lowered by the influence of such humorous masterpieces as the utterances of Mr. Dooley, the Hans Breitmann ballads of Charles Godfrey Leland, the "Leetle Yawcob Strauss" of Charles Follen Adams, such collections as *A Norse Nightingale,* and poems like "I gotta Carlotta." Nor should one forget tales of sentiment and sympathy; an instance is Myra Kelly's *Little Citizens* (1904), and the vogue of German-Jewish comedians like Weber and Fields. It is regrettable that the stiff propriety of racial groups nowadays neither permits them to laugh at themselves nor lets others laugh with them or at them. Leo Rosten's *The Joys of Yiddish* (New York, 1969) is a delectable exception, but another Uncle Remus seems unlikely.

6. The characteristics of leading Eastern cities are too well known to require comment; yet consider these brief phrases from G. W. Steevens, *The Land of the Dollar* (New York, 1897): "New York is a city of offices and palaces; Boston of parks and villas; Washington of public buildings and houses let for the season. Philadelphia is a city of homes." "Philadelphia is the most English of them all—English, that is, not in the way of outward seeming or slavish mimicry, but in the circumstances of its growth, and the life and character of its people," whereas in New York "the very buildings cry aloud of struggling, almost savage, unregulated strength. No street is laid out as part of a system, no building as an architectural unit. Nothing is given to beauty, everything centres in hard utility. It is the outward expression of the freest, fiercest individualism" (pp. 11–12, 115).

7. Riis wrote among other books *How the Other Half Lives* (1890), which spurred Theodore Roosevelt, then president of the board of police commissioners, into action; *The Children of the Poor* (1892); *Out of Mulberry Street* (1898); the autobiographical *Making of an American* (1901); *The Battle with the Slums* (1902); and *Children of the Tenements* (1903). Most of these are products of what he called "the heroic age of police reporting."

8. Mary Lease is the woman who advised Kansas farmers to raise more

hell and less corn. See Dale Kramer, *The Wild Jackasses: The American Farmer in Revolt* (New York, 1956); John D. Hicks, *The Populist Revolt* (Minneapolis, 1931); Anna Rochester, *The Populist Movement in the United States* (New York, 1944); Norman Pollack, *The Populist Response to Industrial America in Midwestern Populist Thought* (Cambridge, 1962); Robert F. Durden, *The Climax of Populism: The Election of 1896* (Lexington, 1965).

9. Thus Grant's secretary of war, impeached by the House of Representatives, had been colonel of an Iowa regiment. There was some embarrassment in the fact that Grant had been born in Point Pleasant, Iowa, and made his military reputation as a "Western" general, but the embarrassment was lessened by assuming that he had gone east and fallen into the clutches of crooked politicians and shady financiers.

10. The book version of *The Treason of the Senate* (Chicago, 1964), eds. George W. Mowry and Judson A. Grenier, entitles the first chapter "New York's Misrepresentatives," the second, "Aldrich, the Head of it All," and the third, "Left Arm of the Monster" (Arthur P. Gorman of Maryland); but though Phillips went as far west as Wisconsin (Spooner) and as far south as Texas (Bailey), the twenty senators "exposed," twelve of them from Eastern states, are represented as controlled by the Morgan interests or the Standard Oil Company. Vice-President Charles W. Fairbanks of Indiana, who had been a senator for a term and a half, is pictured as having been launched on a legal career by the Morgan interests and as "always quick to rally with the faithful round Aldrich, against the people" (p. 100). This scholarly edition concludes with Theodore Roosevelt's famous "The Man with the Muck-Rake" (1906) and Senator Joseph W. Bailey's explicit attack on Phillips that same year.

11. Thus that excessively healthy American female, the Gibson girl, was created by Charles Dana Gibson, born in Roxbury, Massachusetts, who also drew the Arrow Collar man, modeled on Richard Harding Davis of Pennsylvania, the lineage of both was continued by James Montgomery Flagg of Pelham Manor, New York. The founder of physical education in this country is traditionally Dr. Dio Lewis, once a student at the Harvard Medical School; and whatever the birthplaces of the Ashcan painters, they characteristically moved to the East to paint their vigorous canvases.

12. The best study is John Donald Black, *The Rural Economy of New England* (Cambridge, 1950), which contains some illuminating maps and charts.

13. For an early and ironical discussion of the general problem see "The Decay of New England," *The Nation*, 8: 410–11 (May 27, 1869).

14. Iris Saunders Podea, "Quebec to 'Little Canada': The Coming of the French Canadians to New England in the Nineteenth Century," *NEQ*, 23(3): 365–80 (September 1950). It is thought that about forty thousand French Canadians served in the Union armies. Immigration reached its height in 1898. From 1870 to 1900 the textile mills employed about

sixty thousand. French Canadians often evaded the school laws so that child labor became a problem among them, and they sometimes served as strikebreakers. The writer says that in many Massachusetts cities "Little Canada" was usually described as a hellhole. By 1900 this ethnic group numbered about half a million.

15. Howells' *The Landlord at Lion's Head* (1896–1897) records the change from despair to hope in upper New England as the summer business grew. In "Summer and Winter People," *Yale Review*, 32 n.s.(4): 742–59 (Summer 1943), John A. Kouwenhoven discusses the gains and losses from the summer influxes.

16. Van Wyck Brooks, *New England: Indian Summer, 1865–1915* (New York, 1940), p. 330. Brooks gives a general description of a "Howells story" (pp. 206–207), which to anybody familiar with Howells indicates either gross ignorance on the part of the critic or a determination to think of Howells as a shallow social commentator. Yet between 1882 and 1904 Howells published among other books *A Modern Instance* (1882), *A Woman's Reason* (1883), *The Rise of Silas Lapham* (1885), *The Minister's Charge* (1887), *Annie Kilburn* (1888), *A Hazard of New Fortunes* (1890), *The Quality of Mercy* (1892), *The World of Chance* (1893), *The Landlord at Lion's Head* (1896–1897), and *The Son of Royal Langbrith* (1904), none of which can be dismissed as summer veranda fiction. Moreover, on pp. 222–23 Brooks contradicts the picture he gives of Howells' fiction on p. 330.

17. Alvin F. Harlow, *Steelways of New England* is a fair picture. For a more detailed study see Edward Chase Kirkland's *Men, Cities and Transportation*, 2 vols. (Cambridge, 1948), an economic classic. The financing of the New York, New Haven & Hartford was a scandal through this period, and so was its management.

18. George Sweet Gibb, *The Saco-Lowell Shops: Textile Machinery Building in New England* (Cambridge, 1950) is illuminating.

19. See Robert G. Albion, "New York and its Rivals," *Journal of Economic and Business History*, 3(4): 602–29 (August 1931); and *Boston Looks Seaward* (Boston, 1941), an intelligent survey by a Federal Writers Project group.

20. By 1950 four out of every ten New Englanders worked in factories.

21. On that singular institution, the "fool-proof trust," see Donald Holbrook, *The Boston Trustee* (Boston, 1937). So far as the United States is concerned the investment trust, or mutual fund, is said to have originated in Boston with the creation of the Massachusetts Investors Trust in 1924. The idea seems to have come from the British Isles.

22. William B. Gates, Jr., *Michigan Copper and Boston Dollars* (Cambridge, 1951).

23. On the ups and downs of an interesting intellectual life at a typical college see Thomas Le Duc, *Piety and Intellect at Amherst College, 1865–1912* (New York, 1946).

24. I find it difficult to dismiss Mrs. Eddy, the founder of Christian Science, as a "dusky genius" possible only in "a time of declining vitality" in

an area where "presupposed hysteria" was regarded as "the normal condition." That Mrs. Eddy's "rising fortunes showed how far [spiritualism and Christian Science] answered a deep, insistent need of the population" seems to me to be contradicted by church statistics, including those for the Roman Catholic Church. Or are Roman Catholics, Anglicans, Baptists, Unitarians, and so on not part of the population? (Brooks, *New England Indian Summer*, p. 337).

25. Not so remarkable as a Richardson storage warehouse near it. Both structures have been demolished.

26. Gilbert Chase, *America's Music from the Pilgrims to the Present* (New York, 1955), p. 381. He earlier discusses John Knowles Paine, who wrote, among other things, the incidental music to the notable performance of "Oedipus Tyrannus" at Harvard in 1891, and the careers of Charles Martin Loeffler and Horatio Parker, to which I shall come later. It is interesting to contrast Edward MacDowell's unhappy experience at Columbia University (1896–1904). The MacDowell Colony, which nourishes the creative arts, is, it will be recalled, at Peterboro, New Hampshire.

27. The sonata, one of the most radical piano compositions written in the United States, gives musical impressions of Emerson, Hawthorne, the Alcotts, and Thoreau, but all this is incidental to musical values.

28. In my discussion of the East as a concept I said nothing about the academic brilliance of institutions like Columbia, Cornell, the University of Pennsylvania, The Johns Hopkins University and so on, so that my analysis of New England seems lopsided. The point in stressing the intellectual and creative energy of New England in the period is not to deny this quality to other areas but to correct the common assumption that the New England mind, whatever that means, had atrophied. Another example of New England intellectual energy is the creation of the Peabody Museum from 1877 to 1914, largely at the instigation of O. P. Marsh of Yale and George Peabody Russell of Harvard.

29. For a survey of the influence of Eliot and others on secondary education in the period see "On the Conflict between the 'Liberal Arts' and the 'Schools of Education'" ("Report of the Committee on the Teaching Profession of the American Academy of Arts and Sciences"), *ACLS Newsletter*, 5(1): 17–38 (n.d.).

30. Charles Francis Adams, *Chapters of Erie and other Essays* (Boston, 1871) and *Three Episodes in Massachusetts History*, 2 vols. (Boston, 1892); Henry Adams, *History of the United States during the Administrations of Thomas Jefferson and James Madison*, 9 vols. (1889–1891), *inter alia;* Brooks Adams, *The Emancipation of Massachusetts* (Boston, 1887) and so on. Commentators are frequently so bemused by the ironical depreciation of self and family in Henry Adams' *Education,* they undervalue the revolution in the interpretation of history represented by this Adams library.

31. Quoted in the *DAB*, XIII, 570, from an unpublished letter. Norton by no means confined himself to aesthetics. He translated Dante, edited

Donne, Anne Bradstreet, and George William Curtis, admired Whitman, Niagara Falls, and the World's Columbian Exposition, got out textbooks in literature for the schools, helped to found *The Nation* (1865), and at Ashfield held annual conferences on public issues anticipating the Pugwash Conferences of our time. I touch this side of him later.

32. I have sketched Scudder's activities and other aspects of the renascence of New England in "Massachusetts, There She Is," *Violence and Reason: A Book of Essays* (New York, 1969), pp. 183–202, reprinted from the *Proceedings of the Massachusetts Historical Society* for 1968. This is superseded by Ellen B. Ballou, *The Building of the House: Houghton Mifflin Company—The Formative Years* (Boston, 1970).

33. On this extraordinary pair see Sidney Kramer, *History and Bibliography of Stone and Kimball and Herbert S. Stone* (Chicago, 1940).

34. Transcendentalists saw the struggle as a conflict between two theologies —the justice of God and the optimism of their own faith, according to Robert C. Albrecht, "The Theological Response of the Transcendentalists to the Civil War," *NEQ*, 38(1): 21–34 (March 1965). No doubt. But the general New England opinion was that righteousness had won.

35. In *At Sundown* (Boston, 1890), p. 53.

36. I base this on the perceptive essays on Longfellow in William Charvat, *The Profession of Authorship in America, 1800–1870* (Columbus, 1968).

37. Important as precursors of the Freudian fiction of our day.

38. See *Miscellanies*, Vol. XI of the Riverside Edition of Emerson (Boston, 1883).

39. And was formally censored by the Great and General Court of Massachusetts for doing so.

40. Addressing a shoemakers' union in 1872, Phillips said: "Take a power like the Pennsylvania Central Railroad and the New York Central Railroad and there is no legislative independence that can exist in its sight. As well expect a green vine to flourish in a dark cellar as to expect honesty to exist under the shadow of these upas-trees." A Phi Beta Kappa address of 1881 declared among other things: "When the easy class conspires to steal, what wonder the humbler class draws together to defend itself? True, universal suffrage is a terrible power; and with all the great cities brought into subjection to the dangerous classes by grog, and Congress sitting to register the decrees of capital, both sides may well dread the next move." The speech attacks the sacred cows of the Harvard alumni and defends labor, the Irish Fenians, and the Russian Nihilists. These themes and speeches may be found in any collection of Phillips's addresses.

41. Two admirable studies are Arthur Mann, *Yankee Reformers in the Urban Age* (Cambridge, 1954), which adds to names in my text John Boyle O'Reilly, Solomon Schindler, Frank Parsons, Frank K. Foster, Vida D. Scudder, and others; and Geoffrey Blodgett's more particularized monograph, *The Gentle Reformers: Massachusetts Democrats in the Cleveland Era* (Cambridge, 1966).

42. An interesting commentary on the apathy alleged of New England is found in Albert Bigelow Paine's *Life of Mark Twain* (I used the 4-vol. edition of New York, 1912, part of the *Author's National Edition* of Mark Twain, but the original is in 3 vols.). Twain, he says, always found congenial fellowship in Boston at the Lyceum headquarters on School Street, where Petroleum V. Nasby, Josh Billings, and other stars of the lyceum circuit gathered. Outlying towns were try-out towns, but the final test was the Boston Music Hall (II, 444). Charles Eliot Norton and Francis James Child were early devotees of Twain, and Howells printed *Old Times on the Mississippi* (the first version of *Life on the Mississippi*) in the *Atlantic* serially from January through July 1875. Paine quotes Major Pond, the lecture bureau manager, to the effect that in the winter of 1888–1889 Bill Nye and James Whitcomb Riley were lecturing in Boston. Pond met Twain at the Parker House and persuaded him to introduce them as a surprise. "When they recognized him the demonstration was tremendous. The audience rose in a body, and men and women shouted at the very top of their voices. Handkerchiefs waved, the organist even opened every forte key and pedal in the great organ, and the noise went on unabated for minutes" (III, 876). Scholarship has apparently taken Mrs. Thomas Bailey Aldrich's chilly reception of Twain in the 1860s for the temperature of that city in the 1880s.

43. Consult Lois Kimball Mathews, *The Expansion of New England: The Spread of New England Settlements and Institutions to the Mississippi River, 1620–1865* (Boston, 1909) and Richard Lyle Power, *Planting Corn Belt Culture: The Impress of the Upland Southerner and the Yankee in the Old Northwest* (Indianapolis, 1953) for the older period, and Stewart H. Holbrook, *The Yankee Exodus: An Account of Migration from New England* (New York, 1950) for a general view. There are innumerable special studies. This diaspora was not disinterested. Power quotes the Boston *Daily Advertiser* as saying there must be a Yankee school in every county so that people in the future would march arm in arm with Massachusetts. For the remarkable hold of New England on education see Edward H. Reisner, *Nationalism and Education since 1789: A Social and Political History of Modern Education* (New York, 1922) and Ruth Miller Elson, *Guardians of Tradition: American Schoolbooks of the Nineteenth Century* (Lincoln, 1964). Particular instances are often illuminating. The first public school board in San Francisco was made up of New Englanders, Stanford has streets named for Amherst, Bowdoin, Dartmouth, Harvard, Wellesley, Williams, and Yale, and Whitman College, Walla Walla, Washington, is both in architecture and outlook New England. New England educational influence on the South was necessarily great.

44. The missionary push that Christianized the Hawaiian Islands under the American Board of Commissioners for Foreign Missions, which had its training school in Cornwall, Connecticut, was extraordinary. The white steeples of New England churches and clapboarded New England

houses miraculously sprang up in this once pagan archipelago; and as early as 1835 an American naval officer, having had tea with Mr. and Mrs. Hiram Bingham, both from New England, wrote: "The party was so much like one in America, that had I been placed there by accident, or could I have forgotten the circumstances of my visit, I should have fancied myself in New England." Gerrit P. Judd IV, *Hawaii: An Informal History* (New York, 1961), p. 57.

45. In the 1840s, when the Chicago Irish were about to riot over the loss of a priest who had made the church, its lands, and its appurtenances his personal property in defiance of canon law, the Catholic bishop of St. Louis had to be called in to quiet the disturbance. This I find in Bessie Louise Pierce's invaluable anthology, *As Others See Chicago: Impressions of Visitors, 1723–1933* (Chicago, 1933), p. 90, upon which, together with the third volume of her *History of Chicago: The Rise of a Modern City, 1871–1893* (New York, 1957), I heavily depend.

46. An illustration of the difficulty of defining a region. *The Story of a Country Town* is supposedly set in Fairview, Missouri, and the Gopher Prairie of *Main Street* is of course in Minnesota and not in the Old Northwest.

47. Jacob Burnet, *The Annual Address Delivered before the Cincinnati Astronomical Society June 3, 1844* (Cincinnati, 1844).

48. Charles Fenno Hoffman, *A Winter in the West*, 2 vols. (New York, 1835, but available as No. 75 of the *March of America* facsimile series), I, 49–50.

49. Charles Augustus Murray, *Travels in North America during the Years 1834, 1835, & 1836*, 2 vols. (New York, 1839), II, 75–76.

50. "The Prairies" can be found in any collected edition of William Cullen Bryant and in most anthologies. It repays careful reading.

51. Caroline M. Kirkland, *Forest Life*, 2 vols. (New York, 1842), I, 129–130.

52. Mrs. John H. Kinzie, *Wau-Bun: The "Early Day" in the North-West*. This minor classic is best read in a Chicago edition of 1932, with an introduction by Milo Milton Quaife.

53. Travel accounts are full of picturesque descriptions or anecdotes about these human types. There were continuing complaints of drunkenness, spitting, bad food, coarse familiarity and curiosity, cheating, quarreling, and assassination. In *The Prairie and the Making of Middle America* (Cedar Rapids, 1926) Dorothy Dondore quotes a description of border ruffians—Mississippi boatmen, frontiersmen, and the like, notes election frauds up and down the rivers, and chronicles accounts of the bodies of murdered men left hanging on trees or rotting on the prairie or in some ravine (pp. 198–200). On the Ohio, Timothy Flint had to take his possessions on shore every night against theft (*Recollections of the Last Ten Years*, Boston, 1826, p. 22); and Bryant locked his stateroom every night because Detroit was full of thieves (*Prose Writings*, II, 53, New York, 1884). Flint asserts that no minister of a Protestant denomination ever received a sufficient living for two years in succession (p. 113). The French and Germans settled in groups, as at Gal-

lipolis, Cincinnati, Chicago, or Milwaukee, and gave little trouble, though they were hard to "Americanize," and their Sunday habits shocked the godly; but the Irish, sometimes imported as contract laborers, tended to be riotous, turning Piqua, Ohio, on weekends into the wildest town on the continent (Harlan Hatcher, *The Buckeye Country: A Pageant of Ohio*, New York, 1940, p. 153). In the early 1830s E. S. Abdy found that in southern Indiana freed Negroes owning their own prosperous farms excited increasing hostility from the whites, partly because that state was increasingly burdened "with a class of people . . . sent to it from the other side of the Ohio, in return for its 'comity' in hunting up their run-aways" and with slaves no longer useful, set free with a few dollars for Indiana to bury when they died. (*Journal of a Residence and Tour in the United States of North America from April 1833 to October, 1834*, 3 vols., London, 1835, II, 363–79). A colony of Nantucket whalers settled in a suburb of Cincinnati; and as for the incredible spectacle of Mexicans in Chicago, Bessie Louise Pierce (*As Others See Chicago*, p. 147) quotes this paragraph from Isabella Lucy Bishop, *The Englishwoman in America* (London, 1856): "Mexicans and hunters dash down the crowded streets at full gallop on mettlesome steeds, with bits so powerful as to throw their horses on their haunches when they meet with any obstacle. They ride animals that look too proud to touch the earth, on high-peaked saddles, with pistols in the holsters, short stirrups, and long, cruel-looking Spanish spurs. They wear scarlet caps or palmetto hats, and high jack-boots. Knives are stuck into their belts, and light rifles are slung behind them. These picturesque beings—the bullock-waggons setting out for the Far West—the medley of different nations and costumes in the streets— make the city a spectacle of great interest."

54. There were at least thirty communal settlements in Ohio alone.

55. Land speculation goes back to pre-Revolutionary America and companies like the Ohio Company and the Scioto Company. In 1799 a congressional enactment replaced the concept of larger-tract sales (4000 acres being a minimum) by sales of 640 or 320 acres, after which thousands of farmers moved to the Middle West from the East and South. Nevertheless, land speculation ran riot and was constantly remarked. Timothy Flint (*Recollections*, pp. 170–82) called the Mississippi Valley a "paradise of puffers." In *Main Street on the Middle Border* (Bloomington, 1954) Lewis Atherton notes the boom-and-bust psychology of new Western towns, usually as ugly as those in the Far West were later (see his Chap. I, "Early Days on the Middle Border"). J. M. Peck, in *New Guide for Emigrants to the West*, 2d ed. (Boston, 1837), said that despite the "exhaustless fertility" of the soil of Illinois, "hundreds of men can be found, not yet fifty years of age, who have settled for the fourth, fifth, or sixth time on a new spot" (p. 121).

56. Chester A. Arthur, who succeeded Garfield after Garfield's death by assasination, and Grover Cleveland were from New York.

57. *The Land of the Dollar,* p. 110. In a smoking compartment on a train to Richmond, Steevens discovered that one of his two companions would not speak to the other because he thought this third person a Yankee.

58. One may consult such pronouncements as these: Frank L. and Harriet C. Owsley, "The Economic Basis of Society in the late Ante-Bellum South," *Journal of Southern History,* 6(1): 24–45 (February 1940); Alfred Holt Stone, "Fact and Tradition in Southern History," *Journal of Mississippi History,* 17(1): 1–23 (January 1955); Charles Grier Sellers, Jr., *The Southerner as American* (Chapel Hill, 1960); James McBride Dabbs, *Who Speaks for the South?* (New York, 1964). It is illuminating to compare discussions some twenty years apart: Francis B. Simkins' address at the annual meeting of the Southern Historical Association in 1946, "The Everlasting South," *Journal of Southern History,* 13(3): 307–22 (August 1947), and C. Vann Woodward, "The Search for Southern Identity," *Virginia Quarterly Review,* 34(3): 321–38 (Summer 1958). The standard contemporary treatment is the 10-volume *History of the South,* eds. Wendell Holmes Stephenson and E. Merton Coulter, the first volume of which appeared in 1949 from the Louisiana State University Press, Baton Rouge.

59. See W. J. Cash, *The Mind of the South* (New York, 1941), the opening pages, and John Hope Franklin, *The Militant South, 1800–1861* (Cambridge, 1956). Ellen Glasgow used to say that belligerency was a continuing element in Southern culture.

60. See the informative, if uncritical, study by Theodore Britton Marshall and Gladys Crail Evans, *They Found It in Natchez* (New Orleans, 1939), and compare this with Gerland M. Capers, Jr., *The Biography of a River Town* (Chapel Hill, 1939) and William D. Miller, *Memphis during the Progressive Era, 1900–1917* (Memphis, 1957).

61. Cash, *The Mind of the South,* p. 46.

62. Edited by John K. Bettersworth and James W. Silver (Baton Rouge, 1961). "Retrospect" does not go beyond 1865.

63. The standard study of desertion is Ella Lonn, *Desertion during the Civil War* (New York, 1928). Dr. Lonn's statistics are based as far as possible on official records, and the book contains maps showing the territories out of ordinary civil or military control. The books and articles on Reconstruction are endless. The general drift of the revisionist school of historians is to soften the pictures of corruption, violence, and horror of earlier writers and to indicate that Reconstruction legislation and Reconstruction governors were not all evil but accomplished much for the modernization of the South. However they came into power, the later white supremacy governors controlled by the former Southern gentry might have been less severe on the Negroes than governments like those of "Pitchfork" Ben Tillman and Cole Blease, who, if they sponsored "progressive" legislation, fed the fires of interracial bitterness. For a useful compilation of revisionist statements see Kenneth

M. Stampp and Leon F. Litwack, eds., *Reconstruction* (Baton Rouge, 1969). For the modern view read C. Vann Woodward's study, *The Strange Career of Jim Crowe* (New York, 1955).

64. The best general survey is again by C. Vann Woodward, *Origins of the New South*, Vol. IX of the *History of the South* series (Baton Rouge, 1951). Raymond B. Nixon, *Henry W. Grady, Spokesman of the New South* (New York, 1943), is conscientious. Broadus and George Sinclair Mitchell's *The Industrial Revolution in the South* (Baltimore, 1930), is still useful. John F. Stover, *The Railroads of the South, 1865–1900: A Study of Finance and Control* (Chapel Hill, 1955), is valuable. The rise of the tobacco industry (a typical record) can be traced in such studies as Milton Whitney and Marcus L. Floyd, "Growth of the Tobacco Industry," *Yearbook of the U.S. Department of Agriculture, 1899* (Washington, 1900); Meyer Jacobstein, *The Tobacco Industry in the United States, Studies in History, Economics and Public Law*, XXVI(3), Columbia University (New York, 1907); William Kenneth Boyd, *The Story of Durham, City of the New South* (Durham, 1925); John Wilber Jenkins, *James B. Duke, Master Builder: The Story of Tobacco, Development of Southern and Canadian Water-Power and the Creation of a University* (New York, 1927); and John K. Winkler, *Tobacco Tycoon: The Story of James Buchanan Duke* (New York, 1942). This array of titles neglects the powerful Reynolds interests.

65. The title essay of Page's *The Old South* (New York, 1892) shows how deeply Page felt all this. The Old South "combined elements of the three great civilizations which since the dawn of history have enlightened the world. It partook of the philosophic tone of the Grecian, the dominant spirit of the Roman, and of the guardfulness [*sic*] of individual rights of the Saxon civilization. And over all brooded a softness and beauty, the joint product of Chivalry and Christianity" (p. 5). One there reads that the "sudden supremacy" of the American people "is largely due to the Old South," that "gentle blood and high connection . . . undoubtedly existed in a considerable degree," that after the Revolution Virginian civilization in particular showed "peculiar and strongly marked traits" which made it "distinctive," and that "government was the passion of the Southerner" (pp. 5–46). A like fantasy informs the opening essay in George Cary Eggleston, *A Rebel's Recollections* (New York, 1875).

66. On Southern oratory see Waldo W. Braden, "The Emergence of the Concept of Southern Oratory," *The Southern Speech Journal*, 26(3): 173–83 (Spring 1961). This essay does not touch upon the Southern pulpit nor the grandiloquence of Southern revivalists (not that revivalists were not grandiloquent elsewhere), amusingly parodied in William P. Brannan's "The Harp of a Thousand Springs" in Franklin J. Meine, ed., *Tall Tales of the Southwest* (New York, 1930), pp. 235–37.

67. Mark Twain's jibe that Sir Walter Scott helped destroy a sense of reality in the South seems to have some basis in truth. In "Sir Walter Scott and His Literary Rivals in the Old South," *American Literature*, 2(3):

255–76 (November 1930), Grace Warren Landrum, though she modifies
the notion that the South accepted Scott uncritically, demonstrates the
vogue of such romanticists as Bulwer and Byron. There are other studies.

68. The appeal is wholly emotional with biblical phrases studding the text:
"having eyes, see not, and, having ears, hear not," "peace, peace, and
there is no peace," "why stand ye here idle?" and "betray with a kiss."

69. *Library of Southern Literature*, eds. E. A. Alderman and others, 17 vols.
(Atlanta, 1907–1923), XIII, 6038–39. The speech was delivered September 21, 1860; Lincoln had been nominated in May, the election did not
occur until November 6.

70. I find this attributed to G. Dawson of Georgia in Richard Sterling, ed.,
Sterling's Southern Orator (New York and Greensboro, 1866–1867).
Here are two characteristic later specimens. Benjamin H. Hill, receiving
a flag from Ohio visitors in Atlanta in 1876, declared: "It was not the
Union, my countrymen, that slew your children; it was not the Union
that burned your cities; it was not the Union that laid waste your country, invaded your homes and mocked at your calamities; it was not the
Union that reconstructed your States. . . . No! No! Charge not these
things upon the Union of your fathers . . . the South never made war
upon the Union. . . . We did not leave the Union to make war upon it.
We left the Union because a sectional party seized it and we hoped
thereby to avoid a conflict." (William T. Wynn, ed., *Southern Literature: Selections and Biographies*, New York, 1932, p. 135.) And here is
the chief justice of the supreme court of Mississippi on June 3, 1903,
paying tribute to Southern womanhood: "And so in the midst of the
gloom the woman of the South rose resplendent to the occasion. . . .
Her sublime faith has lived to see the resurrection angel of the South
roll back the stone from the sepulcher, destroy the seal, break the fetters of political disability, shatter the bonds . . . and raise, radiant
from the grave of the old, the figure of the new South, to stand in
transfigured beauty, fronting the deepening glories of the twentieth
century, 'like the winged god breathing from his flight.' She remembered that whatever was sublimest in the annals of Christianity looms
o'er the ocean of time, like the northern lights, more resplendent for
the surrounding shadows." Albert H. Whitefield, "Tribute to the
Women of the South," in Edwin Dubois Shurter, *Oratory of the South
from the Civil War to the Present Time* (New York and Washington,
D.C., 1908). This anthology is filled with quotable quotes.

71. C. Hugh Holman, "Rhetoric in Southern Writing," *The Georgia Review* 12(1): 74–86 (Spring 1958). For a sample of high-toned literary correspondence read the letters printed in James S. Patty, "A Georgia Au-
thoress Writes her Editor," *Georgia Historical Quarterly*, 41(4): 416–31
(December 1957).

72. Mark Twain's account of the conduct of the King and the Duke at the
Wilks funeral in *Huckleberry Finn*, and of the minister and congregation at the false funeral in *Tom Sawyer*, like "The Harp of a Thou-

sand Strings," burlesques this rhetoric. I find Louis Budd's "The Southward Currents under Huck Finn's Raft," *MVHR*, 46(2): 222–37 (September 1959), a refreshing contrast to most contemporary interpretations of this picaresque novel. Somewhere I have read of a Southern justice of the peace who pronounced the following marriage service: "By the authority vested in me as an officer of the State of Georgia, which is sometimes called the Empire State of the South; by the fields of cotton that spread about in snowy whiteness around us; by the howl of the coon dog and the gourd vine whose clinging tendrils will shade the entrance to your dwelling-place; by the red and luscious heart of the watermelon, whose sweetness fills the heart with joy; by the heavens and earth in the presence of these witnesses, I pronounce you man and wife."

73. Esther J. and Ruth W. Crooks, *The Ring Tournament in the United States* (Richmond, 1936). The authors list ring tournaments in thirteen states; the spectators sometimes numbered ten thousand. One such tournament was held at the Centennial Exposition in Philadelphia in 1876.

74. Arthur Burton La Course, *New Orleans Masquerade: Chronicles of Carnival* (New Orleans, 1932), an illustrated history. The author provides a vocabulary for the uninitiated.

75. One would never guess from the novel that Stuart's failure to return to Gettysburg when Lee expected him seriously embarrassed Lee. I find "quicksilver" and "champagne" particularly hard to take, inasmuch as the three-day battle was fought in some of the hottest weather of the year, Longstreet took ten hours to march four miles and prepare for combat, and Ewell's inability to capture Culp and Cemetery hills was owing to the fact that his soldiers were jaded by twelve hours of marching and fighting, and there were no fresh troops at hand. For Cooke's real opinion of war read the extracts from his notebooks published by Jay B. Hubbell, *Journal of Southern History*, 7(4) : 526–40 (November 1941). I think the extracts from *Mohun* are fairly representative of the hyperbolical style of the novel. Philip Pendleton Cooke's romantic ride is chronicled by John D. Allen, *Philip Pendleton Cooke* (Chapel Hill, 1942), p. 30. For the defense of the duello see George Tucker "On Duelling," *Essays on Various Subjects of Taste, Morals and National Policy* (Georgetown, 1822). Francis O. Ticknor's "The Virginians of the Valley" (1862?) may be found in most anthologies of Confederate or Virginia poetry. One should not forget the language of James Ryder Randall in 1861: "For life and death, for woe and weal,/ Thy peerless chivalry reveal,/ And gird thy beauteous limbs with steel,/ Maryland, my Maryland!"

76. A rash of "Southern" magazines, most of them short-lived, should also be noted, *The Southern Metropolitan, Scott's Monthly Magazine, The Southern Family Visitor,* and *The Old Guard Magazine* among them. Of these the most important was possibly *The Southern Review,* edited by the unreconstructed Albert Taylor Bledsoe. These periodicals car-

ried sentimental poetry about the Lost Cause, appeals to "Southrons," vindications of secessionist political theory and Confederate military tactics, and spirited attacks upon the Republican party. The critical quality of *The Southern Review* may be guessed from an unsigned notice of *Valerie Aylmer*, a forgotten novel of 1870, which says it is from the pen of a Southern lady, the personages are Southerners, the action is chiefly in the South, and the tone and coloring represent the "best Southern society." A review of *Autobiographical Sketches of Alumni of the University of Virginia who Fell in the Confederate War* (1871) declares that the two hundred who died had occupied "high social position" and left "luxurious homes to fight." John Hay's harmless *Pike-County Ballads* "effectually popularize Swinburne's uncleanness and blasphemy, while they add a nauseous vulgarity all their own." (Hay was Lincoln's secretary). These gems are in the volume for 1871. One should also note William Gilmore Simms's *The Poetry of the South* (1867), James W. Davidson's *The Living Writers of the South* (1869), "Ida Raymond's" *Southern Writers; Biographical and Critical Sketches of the Living Female Writers of the South. With Extracts from their Writing* (1876), and, a late bloomer, the embattled Mildred Lewis Rutherford's *The South in History and Literature* (1906), which avers among other interesting statements that "General Grant had to free his slaves when the war closed."

77. Albion W. Tourgée, "The South as a Field for Fiction," *The Forum*, 6(4) : 404–13 (December 1888). Tourgée is writing two decades after his original prophecy. C. Alphonso Smith, "The Possibilities of Southern Literature," *The Sewanee Review*, 6(3) : 298–305 (July 1898).

78. The extent of this controversy is amazing. Here are a few representative items: Rebecca Washington Smith, *The Civil War and its Aftermath in American Fiction, 1861–1899* (Chicago, 1937); Richard M. Weaver, *The Confederate South, 1865–1910: A Study in the Survival of a Mind and Culture*, abstracted in Curtis Wiswell Garrison, ed., *The United States 1865–1900*, 2: 424–25; Frank E. Vandiver, "How the Yankees are Losing the War," *Southwest Review*, 40(1): 62–66 (Winter 1955); Robert A. Lively, *Fiction Fights the Civil War: An Unfinished Chapter in the Literary History of the American People* (Chapel Hill, 1957); Richard B. Harwell, "Gone with Miss Ravenel's Courage; or, Bugles Blow so Red. A Note on the Civil War Novel," *NEQ*, 35(2): 253–61 (June 1962); Cecil D. Eby, Jr., "'The Real War' and the Books," *Southwest Review*, 47(3): 259–64 (Summer 1962). And consider *I'll Take My Stand* of 1930 and its controversial offspring.

79. The pueblos and cliff dwellers are sufficiently known to require no comment. On Western ghost towns consult Muriel Sibell Wolle, *The Bonanza Trail: Ghost Towns and Mining Camps of the West* (Bloomington, 1953), and Perry Eberhart, *Guide to the Colorado Ghost Towns and Mining Camps* (Denver, 1959), each profusely illustrated.

80. George Catlin, *Illustrations of the Manners, Customs, and Condition of*

the North American Indians, 2 vols., 7th ed. (London, 1848). II,16–21. The book was first published in 1841; later travelers confirm his description.

81. Albert D. Richardson, *Beyond the Mississippi; From the Great River to the Great Ocean* (Hartford, 1867), pp. 321–22.

82. Samuel Bowles, *Our New West: Records of Travel between the Mississippi River and the Pacific Ocean* (Hartford, 1869), pp. 140–41. See also the thunderstorm described on p. 35. Breckenridge Pass (now Hoosier Pass) is 11,542 feet high. Hamilton has disappeared. It once stood near Miners' Delight and Whiskey Hole, and a young teacher who went to Miners' Delight in the 1860s rode horseback two and one-half miles through snowdrifts to the schoolhouse, carrying two pupils with her on her horse. Her salary was fifty dollars a month. Wolle, *The Bonanza Trail*, pp. 169–70. But there is some confusion between Colorado and Wyoming nomenclature at this point.

83. John C. Van Tramp, *Prairie and Rocky Mountain Adventures, or, Life in the West* (Columbus, 1870), p. 183. This was in southern California and, I infer, in Death Valley.

84. Charles Howard Crawford, *Scenes of Earlier Days in Crossing the Plains to Oregon* (Chicago, 1962), pp. 139–40. This is a reprint of an edition brought out at Petaluma, California, in 1898.

85. Bruce D. Nelson, *Land of the Dacotahs* (Minneapolis, 1946), pp. 149–50; J. A. Munro, "Grasshopper Outbreaks in North Dakota, 1808–1948," *North Dakota History*, 16(3): 145–63 (July 1949).

86. One must also allow for the prelude to war that justifies the term "Bleeding Kansas," and, as I have indicated, for settlements along the west bank of the Mississippi in the 1840s and 1850s.

87. Washington Irving, *Astoria*, Chapters XXIV–XXVIII, *passim*. Rose is introduced (Chapter XXII) as "a dogged, sullen, silent fellow, with a sinister aspect, and more of the savage than the civilized man in his appearance." Irving chronicles other deserters from the Hunt party, the hostility of a rival expedition representing the Missouri Fur Company, led by Manuel Lisa, and the dissensions that virtually wrecked the party on the *Tonquin*, the ship that sailed to the mouth of the Columbia. Though written at second hand, *Astoria* is a tough-minded book of hardship and heroism which should be read by those who identify its author only with *The Sketch Book*. There are more "authentic" Western narratives; the point is how quickly certain conventions developed. On the ballooning of life-size human beings into giants see Kent Ladd Steckmesser, *The Western Hero in History and Legend* (Norman, 1965), and for a particular example Henry Blackman Sell and Victor Weybright, *Buffalo Bill and the Wild West* (New York, 1955). Contrast with all this the life dimension in Anne Ellis, *The Life of an Ordinary Woman* (Boston, 1929). This author was brought up in Central City, Colorado!

88. Harold E. Briggs, *Frontier of the Northwest: A History of the Upper Missouri Valley* (New York, 1940).

89. See the contemporary photographs of Virginia City, Donner Summit, Ophir City, Central City, and other mining hamlets included in Ralph W. Andrews, *Picture Gallery Pioneers, 1850 to 1875* (Seattle, 1964), which contrast sharply with that of the San Xavier Mission and photographs of unspoiled landscape in the same collection.

90. Quoted from one of Draper's lectures by Donald Fleming in *John William Draper and the Religion of Science* (Philadelphia, 1950), p. 99.

91. A modern edition is available in The John Harvard Library Series (Cambridge, 1961).

92. From pp. xiv–xv of Stegner's "Introduction" to an edition of Powell's book in The John Harvard Library Series (Cambridge, 1962).

93. Contrast the romanticized picture of "epical" wheat farming in Frank Norris's *The Octopus* (1901). Lanier's essay, "The New South," a plea for Southern homestead farming, was first printed in *Scribner's Monthly* and is conveniently found, slightly altered, in *Retrospects and Prospects* (New York, 1899) or any reprint of this collection. Lanier anticipates the neo-Confederate theory of *I'll Take My Stand* (New York, 1930).

94. The Dawes Act, the far-off result of agitation and propaganda like that embodied in Helen Hunt Jackson's *A Century of Dishonor* (1881), was meant to civilize the Indians by granting to individuals and families landholdings within the reservations. Inadvertently it opened the door to landgrabbers. The reservation system was, however, also opposed by those who wanted to "build up" the West, for, said Governor E. M. McCook of the Territory of Colorado (at one time the largest owner of real estate in the territory), "God gave to us the earth, and the fulness thereof, in order that we might utilize and enjoy His gifts," a testamentary bequest in which Indians were, apparently, not supposed to participate. See Loring Benston Priest, *Uncle Sam's Stepchildren: The Reformation of United States Indian Policy, 1865–1887* (New Brunswick, 1942), *passim*, and the sketch of Governor McCook in the *DAB*, XI, 602–603.

95. The so-called "Utah War" was between the Federal government under Buchanan and the Mormons. The most objective treatment I have read of the massacre is Mrs. Juanita Brooks, *The Mountain Meadows Massacre* (Stanford, 1950). Mrs. Brooks is a Mormon. She clears Brigham Young of direct responsibility, but validates participation in the slaughter of the immigrant train by Mormons whom she names. A plaque commemorative of this miserable affair says only that the immigrants were attacked by "white men and Indians."

96. In "The New England Origins of Mormonism," *NEQ*, 26(2): 147–68 (June 1953), David Brion Davis traces the links between Mormonism and seventeenth-century Puritanism and ascends to the revelations vouchsafed to the Anabaptist, John of Leyden.

97. See Lynn I. Perrigo, "Law and Order in Early Colorado Mining Camps," *MVHR*, 28(1): 41–62 (June 1941).

98. See Louis Pelzer, "A Cattleman's Commonwealth on the Western Range," *MVHR*, 13(1): 30–49 (June 1926).

99. See that minor classic of the West, Thomas J. Dimsdale, *The Vigilantes of Montana* (Virginia City, 1866).

100. Mark Twain's "Disgraceful Persecution of a Boy," refused publication in a San Francisco paper, is a vivid example of Caucasian brutality. A footnote runs in part: ". . . Brannan Street butchers set their dogs on a Chinaman who was quietly passing with a basket of clothes on his head; and while the dogs mutilated his flesh, a butcher increased the hilarity of the occasion by knocking some of the Chinaman's teeth down his throat with half a brick." See *Sketches Old and New* (1875) or any reprint of it.

101. A fascinating casebook is that compiled by Nyle H. Miller and Joseph W. Snell, *Why the West was Wild: a Contemporary Look at the Antics of some Highly Publicized Kansas Cowtown Personalities* (Topeka, 1963), a selection of "action" newspaper stories from towns like Abilene. Dodge City called itself in 1878 the "beautiful, bibulous, Babylon of the frontier," in Wichita "pistols are as thick as blackberries"(pp. 5–6), and the Junction City *Union* referred to Hays City, its rival town, as "the Sodom of the Plains." But there was always a respectable part to the cow town, which gradually won control.

102. Low rates on persons, household goods, and farm implements were frequently offered westward, but nothing was said about the high rates of shipping back east again.

103. For a sardonic view of land speculation in this area see the chapter, "The Grafters' Share" in Angie Debo, *And Still the Waters Run* (Princeton, 1940). Cf. also the chapter entitled "The Fight between Despoilers and Defenders."

104. Leslie E. Decker, *Railroads, Lands, and Politics: The Taxation of the Railroad Land Grants, 1864–1897* (Providence, 1964), from an examination of sample counties and their records in Kansas and Nebraska concludes that the railroads or their patrons paid a greater proportion of taxes during the earlier years of settlement and a high proportion later.

105. In "Was the West a Safety Valve for Labor?" *MVHR*, 24(3): 299–314 (December 1937) Joseph Schafer argues that it was psychologically such an instrument but that nothing else can be proved.

Chapter III: The Age of Energy

1. Floyd not only transferred an excessive quantity of arms from Northern to Southern arsenals but also allowed Indian trust funds to be "abstracted." Dismissed as a brigadier general from the Confederate army in 1862, he was commissioned a major general by the Virginia Assembly, a striking example of the conflict between state and national jurisdictions in the Confederacy. In *Lincoln and the Tools of War* (Indianapolis, 1956) Robert V. Bruce argues that the North was

right to stick to the muzzle loader because the efficacy of the breech-loader was not demonstrated until the Austro-Prussian War of 1866.

2. Colt's biographer tells this amusing tale: "A Confederate prisoner, while being led through a Union artillery park, was observed to stop and examine the breech of each of the Napoleons [cannon]. When asked why he did this, he remarked: "Ah sweah, yo'all got as many of these 'U.S.' guns as we'uns.'" William B. Edward, *The Story of Colt's Revolver: The Biography of Col. Samuel Colt* (Harrisburg, 1963), p. 372.

3. Because of the destruction of the records of the Confederate medical service in the Richmond fire, we are not as well informed about the matter as we should be. See, however, George W. Adams, "Confederate Medicine," *Journal of Southern History*, 6(2): 151–66 (May 1940); Kate Cumming, *Journal of Hospital Life in the Confederate Army of Tennessee, etc.* (Louisville and New Orleans, 1866); and the appropriate excerpts on the topic in J. L. Underwood, *The Women of the Confederacy* (New York and Washington, D.C., 1906). The literature for the Federal side is vast. See for representative instances Mrs. A. H. Hoge, *The Boys in Blue; or, Heroes of the "Rank and File"* (New York, 1867), especially good on hospital nursing though highly sentimental; Mary A. Livermore, *My Story of the War* (Hartford, 1890), on nursing; Major Albert Gailard Hart, "The Surgeon and the Hospital in the Civil War," rpt. from *Papers of the Military Historical Society of Massachusetts*, vol. 13 (read before the Society April 1, 1902); Julia C. Stimson and Ethel C. Thompson, "Women Nurses with the Union Forces During the Civil War," *Military Surgeon*, 62(1): 1–17; (2): 208–30 (January and February 1928); Marjorie Barstow Greenbie, *Lincoln's Daughters of Mercy* (New York, 1944); Nina Brown Baker, *Cyclone in Calico* (Boston, 1952), the biography of "Mother" Bickerdyke, of whom even General Sherman stood in awe; George Worthington Adams, *Doctors in Blue: The Medical History of the Union Army in the Civil War* (New York, 1952). The initial incompetence on both sides during the first months of the war was appalling and was only slowly overcome. Young medical students were sent to field hospitals to learn their trade, and political appointments of regimental "surgeons" were at first commonplace. The caliber of the medical service, however, steadily improved on the Union side and also in the Confederate army, but the latter was handicapped by lack of supplies and personnel. Perhaps the best comment is that in Whitman's *Specimen Days:* "I must bear my most emphatic testimony to the zeal, manliness, and professional spirit and capacity generally prevailing among the surgeons in the hospitals. There are, however, serious deficiencies, wastes, and want of system in the commissions, contributions, and in all the voluntary and a great part of the government nursing, edibles, medicines, stores, etc. (I do not say surgical attendance, because the surgeons cannot do more than human endurance permits.) . . . Always plenty of stores, no doubt, but never

where they are needed, and never the proper application." *Complete Prose Works* (Boston, 1898), p. 52.

4. On the vexed question how far war helps or hinders industrial and scientific progress the standard work is John U. Nef, *War and Human Progress: An Essay on the Rise of Industrial Civilization* (Cambridge, 1952). On the Civil War see Chapter X in Roger Burlingame, *Backgrounds of Power* (New York, 1940); Thomas C. Cochran, "Did the Civil War Retard Industrialization?" *MVHR*, 48(2): 197–210 (September 1961); and among the replies to Cochran, Pershing Vartanian, "The Cochrane Thesis: A Critique in Statistical Analysis," *Journal of American History*, 51(1): 77–89 (June 1964).

5. The first crude armored ship was possibly that of a Korean admiral in a war against Japan. Under Napoleon III, an artillery enthusiast, the French made remarkable advances in armoring vessels, no wooden ship-of-the-line being laid down after 1855. The first use in battle of armored ships of a sort was apparently the allied naval assault upon the Russian fortress of Kinburn during the Crimean War, where the French employed floating armored batteries (as ships they were unseaworthy). The French also designed armored gunboats for use on the lakes and rivers of Italy. The *Monitor* of Civil War fame was not the desperate improvisation legend makes it out to be. The federal government had authorized the construction of the *Monitor,* the *Galena,* and the *New Ironsides* some months before the battle at Hampton Roads, and later authorized the building of nine more armored vessels. In November 1861 it authorized an additional twenty. The *Merrimac* was in a sense really improvised, and the great achievement of the *Monitor* was not so much that it was armored and low in the water as that it demonstrated the practicability of the revolving gun turret under fire. See H. W. Wilson, *Ironclads in Action: A Sketch of Naval Warfare from 1855 to 1895,* 2 vols. (Boston, 1896); James Phinney Baxter, Jr., *The Introduction of the Ironclad Warship* (Cambridge, 1933); and Philip Cowburn, *The Warship in History* (New York, 1965), more popular in tone. The "locomotive" torpedo (that is, one that travels under water by its own means of propulsion) was not invented until 1866 by Whitehead.

6. The term "sanitary service" is likely to mislead the modern reader. The United States Sanitary Commission, a volunteer civilian organization created by doctors and patriotic women, was officially authorized by the War Department on June 9, 1861. It undertook to prevent the enlistment of the medically unfit, to insist on elementary sanitation in the camps, to correct the diet, to assist doctors and nurses, to provide medical supplies, to supplement the original crude ambulance service, to find books, music, flowers, letter writers, and amusement for the army, and to assist the discharged (especially the disabled) soldier. For excellent accounts see Katharine P. Wormeley, *The United States Sanitary Commission* (Boston, 1863) and Charles J. Stillé, *History of the United States Sanitary Commission* (New York, 1868); and for a modern view,

William Quentin Maxwell, *Lincoln's Fifth Wheel: The Political History of the United States Sanitary Commission* (New York, 1956).

7. In *America To-Day* (New York, 1899) William Archer was to marvel at New York City where "the material world seems as clay on the potter's wheel, visibly taking on the impress of the human spirit" among a "superbly vital people" (p. 24); and in *The Land of the Dollar* G. W. Steevens noted that "in England business is business, and there's an end of it; here business is everything and there is no end or boundary to it. It affords the one career in the country" (p. 264).

8. A prime mover is a machine which moves other machines without the intervention of animal or human power; as a windmill, a steam engine, a dynamo.

9. John H. Girdner, *Newyorkitis* (New York, 1901), pp. 148–49, 150–51, 159. According to the title page, Girdner also wrote on "The Plague of City Noises," and he defines the physical symptoms of the Newyorkitic (his term) as "rapidity and nervousness and lack of deliberation in all muscular movements. . . . This is especially marked in the patient's walk, and in all movements where the feet and legs are involved" (pp. 119–20). On Bayard Taylor see Robert Warnock, "Unpublished Lectures of Bayard Taylor," *American Literature*, 5(2): 123–32 (May 1933).

10. I trust the comparisons are illuminating; they are not original. Henry Adams suggested that the men who looted the Erie Railroad acted as if they had been invented by a French novelist. "One of the earliest acts of the new rulers [of the railroad] was precisely such as Balzac or Dumas might have predicted and delighted in. They established themselves in a palace." See the whole passage in Frederick C. Hicks, ed., *High Finance in the Sixties: Chapters from the Early History of the Erie Railway* (New Haven, 1929), pp. 126–27.

11. See the amusing article, profusely illustrated, by Dorothea D. Reeves, "Come All for the Cure-All: Patent Medicines, Nineteenth Century Bonanza," *Harvard Library Bulletin*, 15(3): 253–72 (July 1967). The standard history of patent medicines in America is James Harvey Young, *The Toadstool Millionaires* (Princeton, 1961).

12. In Confederate prisoner-of-war camps, which sometimes lacked housing or a stockade, a line was drawn on the ground to mark the boundaries of the prison.

13. For variations on this tirade see some of Ingersoll's speeches in *Works*, 12 vols. (New York, 1900), Vol. IX, including one at Bangor, one at New York, and one in Indianapolis, all delivered in 1876.

14. From "Ad Finem" in *Poems of Passion* (Chicago, 1883). Although the trail of Swinburne is over them all, the poems in this collection are worth study by those who think that the genteel lady was the only female ideal of the age.

15. Miss Alcott's potboilers were often melodrama or sentimentalism of the simplest sort, and in *Moods* (1865) and *A Modern Mephistopheles* (1877) she showed herself quite capable of "strong" situations.

16. Richard Bridgman, *The Colloquial Style in America* (New York, 1966) is full of suggestions about the relation of energy to style.

17. *O Strange New World* (New York, 1964), pp. 146–53.

18. This paragraph paraphrases certain passages in my "The Renaissance and American Origins," *Ideas in America* (Cambridge, 1944), pp. 140–51.

19. On the fancy women of Colorado see Forbes Parkhill, *The Wildest of the West,* 4th ed. ([Denver,] 1957); and on San Francisco, Curt Gentry, *The Madams of San Francisco* (New York, 1964).

20. I suppose the best biography is still Robertus Love, *The Rise and Fall of Jesse James* (New York, 1926), but I find it sentimental and melodramatic. Homer Croy, *Jesse James Was My Neighbor* (was he?) (New York, 1949), is fictionalized but quotes testimony from the inquest. Carl W. Breihan, *The Day Jesse James Was Killed* (New York, 1961) at least clings to judgment: "No bandit in history came to a more ignominious end."

21. Custer's *My Life on the Plains* (1874) is nevertheless a classic of its kind. The best edition is that edited by Milo Milton Quaife for the Lakeside Classics (Chicago, 1952).

22. In *The Great Rascal* (Boston, 1952) Jay Monaghan does all he can to sort out fact from fiction in the life of the "ten-cent millionaire." One notes the carefully posed photograph as a frontispiece and reads with a sense of total stupefaction the resolution adopted by the G.A.R. Commandery of Philadelphia: "His spirit was wafted to the side of the great patriots of our land who have gone before and whose deeds and works while in the flesh will be remembered in the brightest pages of our national history" (p. 288). The classic study of the dime novel is in Albert Johannsen, *The House of Beadle and Adams* (Norman, 1950).

23. The turmoil over Mrs. Eddy's career is reflected in the judicious biography in the *DAB,* VI, 7–15.

24. The standard biography is Courtney Ryley Cooper, *Annie Oakley* (New York, 1927), which should be read in the light of Walter Havighurst, *Annie Oakley of the Wild West* (New York, 1954).

25. Joseph G. Rosa, *They Called Him Wild Bill: The Life and Adventures of James Butler Hickock* (Norman, 1964), seems reliable. My material comes from pp. viii, ix–x, 214–15.

26. See the excellent accounts by C. P. Connolly, "The Fight of the Copper Kings" (two parts) and "The Fight for the Minnie Healy" in *McClure's Magazine,* 29 (1–3): 1–16; 214–28; 317–32 (May–July 1907). On one occasion Heinze was fined twenty thousand dollars for illegally taking more than a million dollars' worth of ore out of a mine. Men fought each other in the mines with steam, floods of water, explosives, and gunfire. Heinze in his famous speech to a crowd of hostile miners cut off from work by the shutting down of all the Amalgamated Copper Company's installations in Montana, told the crowd (whom he won over): "I will stake my life on the statement that there are within the sound of my voice a hundred men, now in my employ, who have been

offered bribes all the way from a thousand to ten thousand dollars to commit perjury for the purpose of defeating me in my law-suits." The School of Mines at Butte still has the wonderful glass models used in some of these lawsuits to show where veins "apexed" and where they ran underground.

27. For some reason biographies of Mark Hopkins seem to be scarce, his name not appearing in the *DAB*. On this whole incredible quartet the best book is Oscar Lewis, *The Big Four: The Story of Huntington, Stanford, Hopkins, and Crocker, and of the Building of the Central Pacific* (New York, 1938).

28. His real name was Joshua A. Norton (1819–1880), and San Francisco took a grave, Western delight in his imperial performances. Like Mark Hopkins, he did not make the *DAB*, but see the charming biography by Allen Stanley Lane, *Emperor Norton: The Mad Monarch of America* (Caldwell, 1939).

29. Amid other literature on these tangled lives see Helen Holdredge, *Mammy Pleasant* (New York, 1953), and George D. Lyman, *Ralston's Ring: California Plunders the Comstock Lode* (New York, 1937), neither of which, unfortunately, has an index. The most detailed history of Nevada I know is Sam P. Davis, ed., *The History of Nevada*, 2 vols. (Reno and Los Angeles, 1913), in which fact is fog-bound in loquaciousness, and in which Sharon and his mortal enemy Sutro scarcely appear. But the California-Nevada relation during the days of the Comstock Lode is so obscured by gossip, it is hard to know what the facts truly are. Nevertheless, Mammy Pleasant really existed. A. Russell Buchanan, *David S. Terry of California. Dueling Judge* (San Marino, 1956) is objective.

30. The student has his choice among, *inter alia*, Bernard Falk, *The Naked Lady; or, Storm over Adah* (London, 1934); Allen Lesser, *Enchanting Rebel: The Secret of Adah Isaacs Menken* (New York, 1947); and Paul Lewis, *Queen of the Plaza; A Biography of Adah Isaacs Menken* (New York, 1964). The mystery of her birth has never been satisfactorily solved. At one time or another she claimed six different fathers.

31. One could go on indefinitely. To avoid overloading the page with excessive annotation I add that the materials here excerpted are all in standard biographies which I believe to be reliable. The student who wishes to inquire further should consult the *DAB* and note the references there to relevant titles. I have annotated only matter not to be got at without a little special search. Let me add two random references: the denunciation of the gaudy Fisk funeral in a sermon by the Reverend C. A. Bartol, *Sensations in the Church and on the Exchange. A Sermon Preached in the West Church, Boston, January 11, 1872* (Boston, 1872); and concerning a career that combined ostentation with a genuine "concern" for culture and social service, Ishbel Ross, *Silhouette in Diamonds: The Life of Mrs. Potter Palmer* (New York, 1960).

32. *Atlantic Monthly*, 40(1):95–96 (July 1877).

33. The Blue Blazer, which the original drinker barely survived, was the

invention of "Professor" Jerry Thomas, world traveler and king of the bartenders of his age. See Richard A. Van Orman, *A Room for the Night: Hotels of the Old West* (Bloomington, 1966), pp. 134–35, and the section on bartenders in Russel Crouse, *It Seems Like Yesterday* (Garden City, 1931).

34. On the brothels see Herbert Asbury, *The Barbary Coast* (New York, 1933), on San Francisco; *Gem of the Prairie* (New York, 1940), on Chicago; *The French Quarter* (New York, 1936), on New Orleans; and *The Gangs of New York* (New York, 1928). See also Edward Van Every, *Sins of New York* (New York, 1930), based on files of the *Police Gazette*. On the Smith pantry (the other two faucets ran hot and cold water) see Emmett Dedmon, *Fabulous Chicago* (New York, 1953); and for the water tank full of champagne, Charles Howard Shinn, *The Story of the Mine as Illustrated by the Great Comstock Lode of Nevada* (New York, 1897), p. 160.

35. Allan Nevins, *Hamilton Fish: The Inner History of the Grant Administration* (New York, 1937), pp. 571–73. If the biographer of Diamond Jim Brady is to be believed, George Rector's father took him out of Cornell Law School and sent him to Europe to learn how to make the sauce for sole Marguéry. He worked for two months, fifteen hours a day, before a jury of seven master chefs pronounced him perfect, then cabled his father, was met at the dock by his parent and Brady, and served a dinner at eight o'clock that night demonstrating his new art to Sam Schubert, Dan Reid, Marc Klaw, Abraham Lincoln Erlanger, Marshall Field, Alfred Henry Lewis, Adolphus Busch, Victor Herbert, Brady, and the elder Rector. Brady's praise was: "George, that sole was marvelous. I've had nine helpings—and even right now, if you poured some of the sauce over a Turkish towel, I believe I could eat all of it." Parker Morell, *Diamond Jim: The Life and Times of James Buchanan Brady* (New York, 1934). *Si non vero, e ben trovato.*

36. This is soberly chronicled in Parker Morell, pp. 126–28. For my account of manners I have depended on Ralph Pulitzer, *New York Society on Parade* (New York, 1910); Dixon Wecter, *The Saga of American Society* (New York, 1937); Cleveland Amory, *The Last Resorts* (New York, 1953); Elizabeth Drexel Lehr, *"King Lehr" and the Gilded Age* (Philadelphia, 1935); Albert Stevens Crockett, *Peacocks on Parade* (New York, 1931).

37. George Makepeace Towle, *American Society*, 2 vols. (London, 1870), II, 159–61, 179–80. Though making a living in England, Towle was an American.

38. Oscar Lewis and Carroll D. Hall, *Bonanza Inn: America's First Luxury Hotel*, p. 273.

39. *Ibid.*, pp. 269–70. This singer is not, however, to be measured by the hysteria of this reception. Dictionaries and encyclopedias of music treat her respectfully, she was regarded as the equal of Patti, and her daughter, Mignon Nevada (so named because Ambroise Thomas was a witness at the mother's wedding), has also sung on the operatic stage.

40. I follow with helpless admiration the details set forth in Lewis and Hall, *Bonanza Inn.*

41. Jefferson Williamson, *The American Hotel: An Anecdotal History* (New York, 1930), pp. 94–96. This hotel burned in 1898.

42. James Remington McCarthy, *Peacock Alley* (New York, 1931), *passim.*

43. Rudyard Kipling, *American Notes* (Boston, 1899), p. 92. A cab driver took him to a Chicago saloon where the floor was covered with coins sunk in cement as in the Palmer House. "A Hottentot would not have been guilty of this sort of barbarism" (p. 93). For Kipling's account of spitting in the Palace Hotel, see p. 16.

44. Emmett Dedmon, *Fabulous Chicago*, pp. 147ff; Herbert Asbury, *The French Quarter*, pp. 448–49; Matthew Hale Smith, *Sunshine and Shadow in New York* (Hartford, 1869), pp. 375–76. Smith says there was a great increase in prostitution in New York after the Civil War, when female camp followers were thrown on the town.

45. After the death of Sandy, Mrs. Bowers took to spiritualism.

46. Hildegarde Hawthorne, *Romantic Cities of California* (New York, 1939), p. 281. There is a fine photograph of the Carson house in John Maass, *The Gingerbread Age* (New York, 1957), p. 79. See also the house pictured on p. 18 at Redlands, California.

47. The novels of Edith Wharton on New York and the fictions of Robert Grant and John P. Marquand on Boston and New England are here illuminating.

48. In *The Saga of American Society* Dixon Wecter quotes the New York *Times* for March 27, 1883: "Mrs. Vanderbilt's irreproachable taste was seen to perfection in her costume as a Venetian princess taken from a picture by Cabanel [Cabanel's painting is entitled "Une Vénitienne"— "princess" is an American touch]. The underskirt was of white and yellow brocade, shading from the deepest orange to the lightest canary, only the high lights being white. The figures of flowers and leaves were outlined in gold and lined with Roman red. Almost the entire length of the train was caught up at one side forming a large pull. The waist was of blue satin covered with gold embroidery; the dress was cut square in the neck, and the flowing sleeves were of transparent gold tissue. She wore a Venetian cap, covered with magnificent jewels, the most noticeable of these being a superb peacock in many colored gems" (p. 338). Peacocks, by the by, were very much "in." On the facing page in Wecter's book is a photograph of Mrs. Vanderbilt in costume, surrounded by white doves, but it does not appear that these accompanied her at the reception.

49. Clews' tribute to William H. Vanderbilt is found on p. 356 and his admiring passage on the Vanderbilt ball on p. 366 of his *Fifty Years in Wall Street* (New York, 1908). The address, "Is Great Individual or Corporate Wealth a Menace to the Country and its Republican Institutions?" was printed in pamphlet form at Boston. See p. 6.

50. James Ames Mitchell, *The Silent War* (New York, 1906), *opp.* p. 200.

51. "Trionfo di Bacco ed Arianna." Let everyone open his ears. No one

eats of tomorrow; We are here today, old and young; everyone joyous, women and men. Hide every sad thought, Let us do nothing but be gay. Let him who will be happy, for tomorrow is not certain. . . . O how lovely is youth that forever flies away!

Chapter IV: Energy, Expertise, and Control

1. It is curious that the period had to await the arrival of Theodore Roosevelt in the White House to produce a chief magistrate as forceful as any of the figures I have described. See Chapter X.
2. In "America and the Great Exhibition of 1851," *American Quarterly*, 3 (2): 115–27 (Summer 1951), Marcus Cunliffe demonstrates that British condescension to America there gave way to at least a modicum of admiration for mechanical shrewdness and skill in yacht racing.
3. In S. Edgar Trout, *The Story of the Centennial of 1876* (Lancaster, 1929), *passim*.
4. Although at Philadelphia, Department VI, group 60, of the classification included as class 603, "electro-magnetic motor engines," either few were exhibited or they did not draw significant comment.
5. For a detailed description see *The Illustrated Catalogue of the Centennial Exposition, Philadelphia, 1876*, pp. 97–100.
6. [Bentley], *The Illustrated History of the Centennial Exhibition*, p. 362.
7. Edward C. Bruce, *The Century: Its Fruits and its Festival. Being a History and Description of the Centennial Exhibition, with a Preliminary Outline of Modern Progress* (Philadelphia, 1877), p. 150.
8. The use of electricity for both power and lighting was commented upon again and again, so much so that J. R. Cravath, in his admirable article, "Electricity at the World's Fair," *Review of Reviews*, 8: 35–39 (July 1893), begins: " 'Electricity at the World's Fair' has almost become a tiresome subject to the electrician who has been a faithful reader of the technical papers for the past ten months."
9. The letter to John Hay, written from Washington October 18, 1893, is in Harold Dean Cater, *Henry Adams and his Friends: A Collection of his Unpublished Letters* (Boston, 1947) pp. 291–94. As for provincialism, consider this passage from *The Education of Henry Adams* (Boston, 1918), pp. 340–41: "The first astonishment became greater every day. That the Exposition should be a natural growth and product of the Northwest offered a step in evolution to startle Darwin; but that it should be anything else seemed an idea more startling still; and even . . . admitting it to be a sort of industrial, speculative growth and product of the Beaux Arts artistically induced to pass the summer on the shore of Lake Michigan—could it be made to seem at home there? Was the American made to seem at home in it? Honestly, he had the air of enjoying it as though it were all his own; he felt it was good; he was proud of it; for the most part, he acted as though he had passed his life in landscape gardening and architectural decoration."

10. See Chapter XXV in *The Education of Henry Adams*. A curious collection, *The American Girl As Seen and Portrayed by Howard Chandler Christy* (New York, 1906), not only contains pictures of this regal creature but also proudly announces that "there is in the world none to compare with this gracious queen of our own land," a woman who "has successfully appropriated to herself the best qualities from all the different races to which she owes her origins." "The American Girl is not of a city or a state, but the whole boundless continent is hers" (21, 25, 108). This energetic being apparently abounded from New York to California. On Catholic dissatisfaction with Henry Adams' interpretation of the Virgin see Hugh F. Blunt, "The Mal-Education of Henry Adams," *Catholic World* 145 (865): 46–52 (April 1957).

11. In 1906 Adams could think only of Walt Whitman and "one or two painters" as having insisted on sexual energy as a part of life. He seems to have overlooked or been ignorant of the healthy females in Frank Norris's novels, Garland's *Rose of Dutcher's Coolly*, the alluring Laura Hawkins of *The Gilded Age*, and Dreiser's *Sister Carrie*.

12. Josiah Flynt Willard (his pen name was Josiah Flynt), 1869–1907, was the son of a Methodist minister and his wife. He had a habit of running away from school and became a college drop-out. He stole a horse and buggy twice, was caught the second time and sent to a reform school, then lived as a tramp, served a jail sentence for vagrancy, in his early twenties got to know Arthur Symons and others in England, went to the University of Berlin, worked as a day laborer on the estate of Leo Tolstoi, and, returning to America, became an inspector of railroad police for the Pennsylvania Railroad. Drink proved his undoing, though before his death from pneumonia, he published at least six books and several magazine articles. *The World of Graft* (1901) is said to have promoted "graft" from thieves' slang to the vocabulary of the polite. He left also an incomplete autobiography, *My Life* (1908).

13. My sketch is based on what I used to know of the Middle West, but with due changes it will apply equally to almost any other agricultural region before 1910.

14. I do not mean there were no books recounting the pleasures of a quiet country life. "David Grayson's" (Ray Stannard Baker) *Adventures in Contentment* (1907) is one such.

15. Here I follow Sigfried Giedion, *Space, Time and Architecture* (Cambridge, 1941) and his *Mechanization Takes Command* (New York, 1948). There are later editions.

16. The famous "slaughterhouse cases" of 1872 and 1883 concern, for example, a New Orleans problem.

17. William K. Vanderbilt and others formed a syndicate to build the *America* in 1895 and hold the cup against the British.

18. Seymour Dunbar, *A History of Travel in America*, 4 vols. (Indianapolis, 1915), Vol. III, gives some vivid accounts of early railroad accidents.

19. Robert S. Cotterill, "Early Agitation for a Pacific Railroad, 1845–1850," *MVHR*, 5(4): 396–414 (March 1919).

20. *Reports of Explorations and Surveys . . . made under the Direction of the Secretary of War,* 12 vols. (Washington, D.C., 1855–1860). The 12th volume was issued in 2 parts. Jefferson Davis was then Secretary of War; not unnaturally he recommended the so-called southern route along the thirty-second parallel. The volumes are enriched with superb plates, many in color.

21. A typical contest was that waged between the Santa Fe and the Rio Grande for control of a right of way through Raton Pass and again through the Grand Canyon of the Arkansas. For a pungent account see Chapter XVIII of Stewart H. Holbrooks' *The Story of American Railroads* (New York, 1947), a lively and entertaining book.

22. Robert S. Henry, "The Railroad Land Grant Legend in American History Texts," *MVHR,* 32 (2): 171–94 (September 1945), notes that only 18,389 miles of road or about 8 per cent of the total mileage in the country depended upon federal land grants, that government loans of some $64,500,000 brought back in principal and interest $167,746,490, that by agreement the roads carried government personnel and supplies free or at half the usual rate, and concludes that Washington was not so much munificent as "sharp."

23. It is amusing to note that when locomotives bore names instead of numbers, they were at first called by such titles as Apollo and Mercury, but that the second round of nomenclature used names that emphasize speed and energy, such as Rover, Tornado, Meteor, and Samson. The Arnold Bennett passage is in Chapter V of *Your United States* (New York, 1912).

24. See Paul Wallace Gates, *The Illinois Central Railroad and its Colonization Work* (Cambridge, 1934). Let me add that throughout this discussion of the railroad I have found Emory R. Johnson, *American Railway Transportation,* rev. ed. (New York, 1905), an excellent guide.

25. See Wallace C. Stegner, *Beyond the Hundredth Meridian: John Wesley Powell and the Second Opening of the West* (Boston, 1954). Eighty per cent of the area settled by homesteaders in Montana proved unfit for crop agriculture.

26. Typical is this passage from the opening paragraph of Edward W. Byrd, *The Progress of Invention in the Nineteenth Century* (New York, 1900): Invention "has been a gigantic tidal wave of human ingenuity and resource, so stupendous in its magnitude, so complex in its diversity, so profound in its thought, so fruitful in its wealth, so beneficent in its results, that the mind is strained and embarrassed in its effort to expand to a full appreciation of it. Indeed, the period seems a grand climax of discovery, rather than an increment of growth. It has been a splendid campaign of brains and energy, rising to the highest achievement and the most fertile resources, and conducted by the strongest and best equipment of modern thought and modern strength." To this writer the "practical embodiment" of "labor-saving inventions" partakes "of the sacred quality of creation." For the most part a like attitude is found in later books such as Waldemar B. Kaempffert, ed., *A Popular*

History of American Invention, 2 vols. (New York, 1924); Roger Bur-lingame, *Engines of Democracy: Invention and Society in Mature America* (New York, 1940); James Blaine Walker, *The Epic of American Industry* (New York, 1949); Roger Burlingame, *Backgrounds of Power* (New York, 1949); Courtney Robert Hall, *History of American Industrial Science* (New York, 1954); John W. Oliver, *History of American Technology* (New York, 1956). Only the Burlingame books seem to me to have some notion of the sociological implication of applied science. For the social side consult Samuel P. Hays, *The Response to Industrialism, 1885–1914* (Chicago, 1957), which, however, does not go very deep. Charles H. Cochrane, *Modern Industrial Progress* (Philadelphia, 1904) is virtually a prose lyric about inventions.

27. In "The Anatomy of Prejudice: Origins of the Robber Baron Legend," *Business History Review*, 33(4): 510–23 (Winter 1959), John Tipple points out that few of the muckrakers had suffered at the hands of big business, but that in the years 1865–1914 the promise latent in the re-organization of business into large corporations had not, from the point of view of the average American, been fulfilled. The "people," seeking somebody to blame, pitched on the big businessman as the most con-spicuous directing force.

28. Quoted by Hugo A. Meier in "American Technology and the Nine-teenth-Century World," *American Quarterly*, 10(2): 116–30 (Summer 1958). Meier points out the line of connection between admiration for Yankee skills at the opening of the century and the praises heaped on invention and engineering at its close.

29. Apparently reliable is "Prof." Thomas J. Dimsdale, *The Vigilantes of Montana; or, Popular Justice in the Rocky Mountains,* already cited.

30. Even as late as 1921 Thorstein Veblen in his (nonfictional) *The Engi-neers and the Price System* ironically argued that if not by conspiracy, then at least by "understanding" American entrepreneurs were using "sabotage" to keep prices and profits up.

31. D. C. Cloud (Muscatine), *Monopolies and the People*, 3d ed. (Davenport and Muscatine, 1873), pp. 9–10. One reads toward the end: "The abso-lute power of the brokers of Wall Street over the financies [*sic*] of the country, cannot be more forcibly illustrated than by a careful examina-tion of the case of Jay Cooke & Co." (p. 509). The failure of this com-pany in September 1873 initiated the panic of 1873.

32. For more judicious recent interpretations see Thomas C. Cochran, "The Executive Mind: The Role of Railroad Leaders, 1845–1890," *Bul-letin of the Business History Society*, 25 (4): 230–41 (December 1951), which analyzes about ten thousand letters by business executives and attempts to define their role in the period; Marian V. Sears, "The American Businessman at the Turn of the Century," *The Business His-tory Review*, 30 (4): 382–443 (December 1956), which notes a kind of "trust epidemic" at the end of the century involving both overcapitali-zation and the fact that by 1900 "American business was rapidly out-growing its administrative breeches"; and Cedric B. Cowing, "Market

Speculation in the Muckraker Era: The Popular Reaction," in *ibid.*, 31 (4): 403–13 (Winter 1957), which notes the public ignorance of the economic function of the market, various state and federal acts that tended to identify stock speculation with gambling and tried to put down bucket shops, and the shift in the basis of liberal protest from the agrarian world to the professional classes. Cowing also makes the important point that Americans tended to admire the "bulls" for their boldness and constructive impulse and to dislike the "bears" for opposite reasons.

33. For representative comment within the period see *inter alia* Bruce Wyman, *Cases on Restraint of Trade*, 3 parts (Cambridge, 1902–1904); Albert Walker, *History of the Sherman Law of the United States of America* (New York, 1910); and William H. Taft, *The Anti-Trust Act in the Supreme Court* (New York, 1914). A later study of considerable interest is Carl F. Taeusch, *Policy and Ethics in Business* (New York, 1931). Taeusch says that the Sherman Act "first represented the awakening self-consciousness of the American people to the broader social problems engendered by our business behavior" and notes that its passage coincides with Turner's date for the closing of the frontier (p. 53). But surely this is to ignore the Granger movement, the Populist revolt, and much else.

34. A second conference held the next year in Chicago, since it was explicitly a "National Anti-Trust Conference," came to a hostile conclusion. See *Official Report on the National Anti-Trust Conference held February 12, 13, 14, 1900, in Central Music Hall, Chicago* (Philadelphia, 1900).

35. *Chicago Conference on Trusts . . . Held September 13th, 14th, 15th, 16th, 1899, Civic Federation of Chicago* (Chicago, 1900), p. 626; Jeremiah Whipple Jenks, *The Trust Problem* (New York, 1900), p. 211; James H. Bridge, ed., *The Trust: Its Book* (New York, 1902), p. 167; John Moody, *The Truth about the Trusts: A Description and Analysis of the American Trust Movement* (New York, 1904), p. 494; James Roscoe Day, *The Raid on Prosperity* (New York, 1908), pp. ix, 349. See also John R. Dos Passos, *Commercial Trusts: The Growth and Rights of Aggregated Capital*, rev. ed. (New York, 1901); and John Bates Clark, *The Control of Trusts* (New York, 1901).

36. I paraphrase the admirable article of Alfred D. Chandler, Jr., "The Beginnings of 'Big Business' in American Industry," *Business History Review*, 33 (1): 1–31 (Spring 1959). For a more philosophic statement see Joseph A. Schumpeter, "The Creative Response in Economic History," *Journal of Economic History*, 7(2): 149–59 (November 1947). For a typical case of an increasing demand for expertise (the Pennsylvania Railroad) see Leland H. Jenks, "Early History of A Railway Organization," *Business History Review*, 35(2): 153–79 (summer 1961). This should be contrasted with the history of the Erie Railroad.

37. An issue of the *Bulletin of the Business History Society*, 20(2) (April 1946), was devoted to the topic of "Government Control." N.S.B.

Gras, in a penetrating essay on historical background, has this to say: "By about the 1890's, the new industrial capitalists were getting into financial difficulties; they were over-competing inside the framework of governmental liberalism. Factory was wrecking factory, railroad was outdoing railroad, and one steamship line was bankrupting its nearest rival. All this redounded to the disadvantage of investing capitalists, though often to the temporary advantage of consumers. In the interest of their clients, investment bankers and stockbrokers undertook to change this condition. They introduced control over the distressed industrial capitalists in the interest of dividends on stocks and interest on bonds. The bankers and their friends formed voting trust arrangements, appointed presidents of failing companies, and installed more able directors. There is no thought that the bankers *aimed* at a new business *régime*, though in fact they established one of brief duration—financial capitalism, the money power, or Wall Street dominance . . . the bankers made serious mistakes" (pp. 40–41). Perhaps for this reason the banker, not the businessman, is the villain of folklore. See Kenneth Wiggins Porter, "The Business Man in American Folklore," *Bulletin of the Business History Society*, 18(5): 113–30 (November 1944).

38. Veblen of course held that the corporation exploited the expert, but the modern business historian is not so persuaded.

39. Though the Roman Catholic organization remained one and indivisible, the life of Bishop England shows that it was threatened by what came to be known as the Charleston Schism (1815–1819) and by the possibility of an "Independent Catholick Church of the United States." See Peter Guilday, *The Life and Times of John England, First Bishop of Charleston*, 2 vols. (New York, 1927), Vol. I, Chapters VI–IX.

40. My discussion omits labor unions. Determining whether an association is really national in scope is often a matter of guesswork, since many societies with "American" or "National" in their titles are not therefore countrywide in scope. But I think my figures are roughly accurate.

41. A succinct history of the early decades of the AAAS is to be found in its *Summarized Proceedings* (Washington, D.C., 1940). Note the graph on p. iii showing the steady increase in membership since 1870. In 1914 the membership was 8325.

42. There may be some connection between this indifference to long-run safety and the psychology of miners in the period. See the admirable book by Charles Howard Shinn, *The Story of the Mine as Illustrated by the Great Comstock Lode of Nevada* (New York, 1897), especially Chapter XX. I do not say that foremen were reckless men, but that the mine owner was likely to be impatient of restraints upon production. Writes Shinn: The miner is "a sane, thoughtful, responsible person as far as mining goes, no matter how lawless of social conventions he may choose to be in other directions. He knows himself responsible for the lives of his fellow-workmen; his own life hangs upon the honesty of another's work, and that other's life hangs upon the honesty of his own work" (p. 242). But the foremen and superintendents had to be men of

heroic stature to govern these underground kingdoms. "Men might toil with dull persistency for months in a dark, dripping vault, picking down a wall and wheeling out rock; one twist of the pick might fill the drift with a foaming, resistless river of water. . . . miners become, in the course of years of toil, magnificent examples of the power of such environment to stimulate the emotions and intellects of labourers, and to produce a people with vast capacities for love and hate, for sarcasm and laughter, for terrible wrath and for sublime self-sacrifice" (p. 243). Much of the self-sacrifice would have been unnecessary with modern safety methods. For life in the lumber industry see Anita Shafer Goodstein, "Labor Relations in the Saginaw Valley Lumber Industry, 1865–1885," *Bulletin of the Business History Society*, 38(4): 193–221 (December 1954).

43. *Proceedings*, 4 (1896): 31–50; 242–49; 8 (1900): 11–27; 28–101; 157–80; 213–22; 17 (1909): 79–104; 20, Part I (1912). This last volume is a symposium on the sin of waste.

44. In *More Fables in Slang* (Chicago and New York, 1900), pp. 61–68. For the Dooley items see *Mr. Dooley's Philosophy* (New York, 1900), pp. 24, 32, 49, and *Mr. Dooley's Opinions* (New York, 1900–1901), pp. 199–204. R.T.Crane's book, a curious, embittered attack, was published in Chicago in 1909. The immensely popular *Letters from a Self-Made Merchant to His Son* was serialized in *The Saturday Evening Post*, published in book form in 1902, often reprinted, and sold by tens of thousands of copies.

45. One of the most curious educational pronouncements of the period, showing how the mechanical conception of waste crept into all areas of higher education, is an address by William Rainey Harper, the first president of the University of Chicago, "Waste in Higher Education," delivered before the Regents of the University of New York June 27, 1899. See his *The Trend in Higher Education* (Chicago, 1905), pp. 118–50. With one exception it is the longest address in the book.

46. The best available edition is that edited by David Lowenthal for The John Harvard Library Series (Cambridge, 1965). I shall discuss this book at greater length in Chapter X.

47. *Proceedings*, 6 (1898): 11–36. The speaker was John B. Johnson.

48. *Proceedings*, 16 (1908): 2046.

49. *The Education of Henry Adams* p. 457; "The Tendency of History" in *The Degradation of the Democratic Dogma*, p. 260. The essay was intended as the presidential address before the American Historical Association in 1910.

50. See the biography in the *DAB*, XXI, 489–90. Lee's *Human Nature and the Railroads* (Philadelphia, 1915) and his *Publicity: Some of the Things It Is and Is Not* (New York, 1925) are characteristic collections of articles and addresses. Modern practice in public relations is set forth in a standard treatise by Raymond C. Mayer, *How to Do Publicity*, rev. ed. (New York, 1937), though later textbooks include television. On the rise of the public-relations departments in great corpora-

tions see N.S.B.Gras, "Shifts in Public Relations," *Bulletin of the Business History Society,* 19(4): 97–148 (October 1945).

51. Two brief treatises are Henry Eilbirt, "Twentieth-Century Beginnings in Employee Counselling," *Business History Review,* 31(3): 310–23 (Autumn 1957), and his "Development of Personnel Management in the United States" in *ibid.,* 33(3): 345–64 (Autumn 1959). The Tuck School of Dartmouth College offered the first training program for employment managers in 1915, and World War I gave the movement an enormous impetus.

52. A representative instance is the case of Louis Levine at the State University of Montana. Asked by the chancellor of the state university system to study the taxation of mines in that state, Dr. Levine produced a monograph, *The Taxation of Mines in Montana,* published by B.W.Huebsch in New York (1919). Pressure from the mining interests, particularly the Anaconda Copper Mining Company, on the state university led the chancellor to refuse publication of the monograph by the university as originally agreed, and, indeed, to forbid Dr. Levine to publish it anywhere. Dr. Levine nevertheless proceeded and was suspended from his function as a faculty member on the charge of "insubordination." Professional opinion in the academic world rallied to his support, a "trial" was held before the state board of education, Dr. Levine was vindicated, his salary and rank were restored, and having made his point he resigned from the institution.

53. *Autobiography of Andrew Carnegie* (Boston, 1920), footnote, pp. 157–58. In this connection it is interesting to read William T.Doherty's article, "The Impact of Business on Protestantism, 1900–1920," *Business History Review,* 28(2): 141–53 (June 1954).

Chapter V: Culture and Race

1. This was the year of its formal creation, but Theodore Thomas had been regularly giving symphony concerts in Chicago after 1872. He wrote in that year: "Chicago is the only city on the continent, next to New York, where there is sufficient musical culture to enable me to give a series of fifty successive concerts." Quoted in Bessie Louise Pierce, *A History of Chicago,* III, 493.

2. They printed *The Chap-Book* and publications ranging from Hamlin Garland's *Crumbling Idols* to the fables of George Ade. When Kimball departed, the firm became Herbert S.Stone and Co.

3. The gap between the exiguous programs of the Chicago Literary Club, founded in 1874, and the hopeful sub-culture of the Bohemian group and the literary world could not be greater. See on this organization Frederick William Gookin, *The Chicago Literary Club: A History of its First Fifty Years* (Chicago, 1926). The list of forty-two presidents of the club from 1874 to 1914 does not contain a single name memorable in the history of imaginative or critical writing, with the pale exception

of William Morton Payne, associate editor of *The Dial* from 1892 to 1915, club president in 1911–1912.

4. The efforts of Bronisław Malinowski and Clyde Kluckhohn to clarify the term are instructive. See the article, "Culture," *Encyclopaedia of the Social Sciences,* 15 vols. (New York, 1930–1935), Vol. IV for the first, and the section on culture in Julius Gould and William L. Kolb, eds., *A Dictionary of the Social Sciences* (Glencoe, 1964) for the second. Both articles make much of social conformity, religion, magic, familial traditions, and so on, and speak of the economic basis of the concept, as in the phrase "a pastoral culture." It is needless to remark that the extraordinary development of anthropology in the twentieth century has played havoc with any simple meaning of the term.

5. For the ante-bellum period we have an excellent study, Carl Bode, *The Anatomy of American Popular Culture, 1840–1861* (Berkeley, 1959), but nothing as good for the post-bellum years. The only weakness in Bode is a failure to distinguish between mass culture (his term) and the commercial appeal of certain kinds of art and entertainment to what I shall call the middle middle-class.

6. It is not pretended that "juveniles" were read only by the "folk," but the exploitation of the juvenile market obviously included more than highbrow families. The bibliography headed "Popular Literature" in Vol. III of the revised edition of the *Literary History of the United States* (1963) is suggestive for the decades here studied.

7. In 1940 Louis Adamic brought out *From Many Lands,* subsidized by the Carnegie Corporation as part of his project for a Common Council of American Unity. This book sympathetically surveys the contributions of immigrant groups to American culture. It is amusing to note that Adamic then edited a "Peoples of America Series," one volume of which, by Gerald W. Johnson, *Our English Heritage* (Philadelphia, 1949), was devoted to explicating the traditional Anglo-Saxon heritage. "The English in America," Johnson writes, "have been partially defeated by their own success—that is to say, they were so very important that everyone takes them for granted and proceeds to study other people. This has gone so far that some of us seem to forget that the English had any hand in the job at all." I quote the dust jacket, but see Johnson, Chapter VI of Book II, "The Philosophy."

8. Chapter III of my *America and French Culture* (Chapel Hill, 1927) is an attempt to characterize the American middle class, but it now seems to me oversimplified.

9. It will be recalled that a female figure with uplifted hand, a palm branch in the other, precedes the general. On this an impish Southern sympathizer commented: "Just like the Yankees. The man riding and the woman walking."

10. See Chapter CCXLI of Albert Bigelow Paine, *Main Twain: A Biography.* One suspects that the root of the difficulty was that Gorki was a "red," and the newspapers therefore had a field day.

11. A general historian uses the term "elite" with the same trepidation that

accompanies his use of "culture." For C. Wright Mills the elite are powerful persons who get things done (see his *The Power Elite*, New York, 1956, particularly Chapters 1, 6, 7, 8, 14, 15). M. Kent Jennings, *Community Influentials: The Elites of Atlanta* (New York, 1964) is a laboratory report on decision-making by the elite in an important American city. The tendency to think of the elite in terms of activists appears in Floyd Hunter, *Community Power Structure* (Chapel Hill, 1953), and Robert Presthus, *Men at the Top: A Study in Community Power* (New York, 1964). Activism is generally taken for granted as a necessary characteristic of the elite in American sociology. But an older study, Paul de Rousiers' *L'Élite dans la Société Moderne: Son Rôle* (Paris, 1914), distinguishes between the functions of a political and economic elite and those of an intellectual and moral elite. Hans P. Dreitzel, *Elitebegriff und Sozialstruktur* (Stuttgart, 1962), emphasizes the utopian element in elite thinking but gets involved in fascism and communism. I suppose my own concept is nearer the "strategic elite" of Suzanne Keller, *Beyond the Ruling Class: Strategic Elites in Modern Society* (New York, 1963). That sociological and psychological concern about the concept is relatively novel is easily demonstrated. In the first volume of the *London Bibliography of the Social Sciences* (1931) there is no entry under "Elite," but in Volume Ten, for the years 1950–1955 (London, 1958), an entry under this heading lists seven items and gives four cross references.

12. "Leadership" is as authentically American as "democracy," to which it has a queer, symbiotic relation, but I share the sardonic amusement of Henri Peyre: "In no country have as many volumes on the subject of leadership appeared as in the United States. The reading of most of them is a dismal, when it is not a ludicrous, experience. They dissert [ate] at length on the necessity for candidates for leadership to make friends, to coordinate, to get things done, to lead 'the strenuous life' once dear to Theodore Roosevelt, to learn how to conduct conferences. The last item must be a source of considerable embarrassment to many men of affairs: for they are laboriously advised . . . to devise well planned recesses, during which background music should be played softly; not to hang abstract art on the walls, for it makes uneasy 'those who don't know what the garish splotches mean.'" ("Excellence and Leadership: Has Western Europe Any Lessons for Us?" *Daedalus*, Fall 1961, p. 629). M. Peyre notes that "leaders" in America are found to be of taller stature than ordinary mortals, and after citing some of the absurd statistics, exclaims: "Shades of Napoleon, of John Keats, of Stalin, who never reached the height of even a sub-salesman or of a dean of a very insignificant college!"

13. *The Idle Man*, No. IV (New York, 1832), "Musings," pp. 37–38. My attention was first called to this interesting passage by Dr. Jane Johnson.

14. There was no preface to the original edition of Cooper's first novel, *Precaution*, but in one written for a "new edition" Cooper says: "It can scarcely be said that the work was not commenced with any view to

publication; and when it was finally put into a publisher's hands, with 'all its imperfections on its head,' the last thought of the writer was any expectation that it would be followed by a series of similar tales from the same pen." Cooper later became a professional writer; yet the Effingham family, the history of which begins in *The Pioneers* and reaches a climax of fatuity in *Home As Found,* is composed of persons who do nothing in particular and do it very well. Cooper seems to have regarded them as models for the American upper class. So far as I can remember, no hero of Poe's soils his name or fame by regular occupation.

15. Mary Thacher Higginson, *Thomas Wentworth Higginson: The Story of His Life* (Boston, 1914), pp. 47, 51, 56. When he was a Harvard undergraduate, he went to a phrenologist who told him that he had "splendid talents" but no application (p. 36). In his maturity Higginson of course became an activist.

16. Alexis de Tocqueville, *Democracy in America,* 2 vols., trans. Henry Reeve, Book III, Chapter III. Grund, *Aristocracy in America,* ed. George B. Probst (New York, 1959). The book was first published in London in 1839. Grund keeps up the fiction that his study is written by a German nobleman. His conclusion is that because of the growing power of the West, the "aristocracy of America," which he ends by defining as a considerable portion of all people worth from fifty to a hundred thousand dollars is, if not inoffensive, at least harmless (p. 301).

17. In *Learning How to Behave: A Historical Study of American Etiquette Books* (New York, 1946), Arthur M. Schlesinger, Sr., studied the attempts, usually after some financial or social upheaval, of the parvenu to learn correct behavior. The wellborn of course did not need such manuals, and the opening chapters of Mrs. Wharton's *A Backward Glance* (New York, 1934) show how the discipline of the elite was maintained.

18. One can exaggerate the parochialism of Southern cities. An undated (1895) clipping from the *Atlanta Constitution* describes a "Trilby" evening in Atlanta and discusses Miss Lollie Belle Wylie in terms that at least show some apprehension of general values: "Though cultured New England has long been recognized as the cradle of American letters, the south is rapidly gaining upon the record of that brilliant center of thought and authorship and is hastening to receive the homage of future generations as the favored citadel of American literature. . . . People have had time to muse and meditate. Literature is a product of a nation's leisure, and poets, scholars, authors and historians, though rarely prosperous in the measure of this world's abundance, belong to prosperous and contented areas," of which the South is becoming one.

19. Convenient compendiums are his *Essays from the Easy Chair* (New York, 1892), *Other Essays from the Easy Chair* (New York, 1893), and *From the Easy Chair. Third Series* (New York, 1894).

20. Arlo Bates, *The Philistines* (Boston, 1889), pp. 43–44, 276–77, 280. *The Puritans* contains a satirical portrait of Mrs. Eddy.

21. Margaret Allston, *Her Boston Experiences: A Picture of Modern Boston Society and People* (Boston, 1900), pp. 11, 98. The novel had been serialized in *The Saturday Evening Post*.

22. Sidney McCall, *Truth Dexter* (Boston, 1901). Her husband being asked by his puzzled young wife whether Boston wives had nothing to do, responds with a diatribe against their pursuit of culture. Having finished with hairdressers, masseuses, and so on, "they have soul-ecstasies over Ibsen, fall into trances at the symphony concerts, and flirt with Jean de Reszke. They infest the business part of the town, demanding that men shall sign long scrolls of woman-suffrage petitions, go off to their club-houses, where we are not allowed to follow, and afterward grovel at the feet of Oriental priests, large fat priests with melting eyes, and a transcendental appreciation of American flesh-pots. They rush from clinical lectures to spiritual séances, from sociological meetings to swell afternoon teas, from Olympic games where Harvard darlings get their collar-bones cracked to Zoroaster, from Professor Choice's exposition of the Unknowableness of the *Ding an Sich* to a performance of Shakespeare by females in tights" (pp. 120–21). The novel is laid in the second Cleveland administration.

23. As a setting for fiction New York (like Chicago) drew tales of getting ahead in wealth, often by melodramatic means, whereas the Boston novel more commonly plays up snobbery and social adjustment.

24. For some indication of the liveliness of Hartford in the last half of the nineteenth century, see Kenneth R. Andrews, *Nook Farm: Mark Twain's Hartford Circle* (Cambridge, 1950).

25. Saint-Gaudens, pp. 140–42. He goes on to say how he admired the Metropolitan Museum, Charles A. Platt's "noble design" for the Freer Gallery, and Freer's wisdom in buying Whistler. He liked Anna Held and the historical romances of the period, and found the Columbian Exposition "stunning."

26. An ambitious series of articles on men's clubs organized for the promotion of the arts was begun in *The (American) Bookman* for June 1905, but by January trailed off in sets of photographs. The clubs discussed were The Century, The Authors, The Players, The Grolier, The Franklin Inn (Philadelphia), The Bohemian (San Francisco), The St. Botolph (Boston), The University (Indianapolis), The Literary (Cincinnati), and The Cosmos (Washington).

27. The General Federation of Women's Clubs, organized in 1889, grew out of an earlier organization, the Sorosis. *The Chautauquan* has a good deal of information, but the general history of the women's clubs can be read in J.C. Croly, *The History of the Woman's Club Movement in America* (New York, 1898).

28. See my article, "Arnold, Aristocracy and America," *American Historical Review*, 49(3): 393–409 (April 1944), reprinted in *History and the Contemporary* (Madison, 1964).

29. One is again confronted with the haziness of social classification. Chautauqua reading lists went to the wives of ranchers in the Far West, as-
piring laborers and their families, and other miscellaneous groups. It
seems to have had less appeal in the South.

30. The best discussion of *The Chautauquan* is in Frank Luther Mott, *A
History of American Magazines, 1865–1885*, pp. 544–47, and his *A History of American Magazines, 1885–1905*, pp. 264–65.

31. No other class followed this example in selecting a symbol from the
hardware store. Subsequent classes chose flowers, plants, or nuts. The
unhumorous quality of the enterprise is shown when the class of 1905
("The Cosmopolitans") took as their emblem the cosmos; one has to
think twice to see that a flower, not the universe is meant. The class of
1917 ("The Emersons") for mysterous reasons picked out the cattail.

32. For example: "All persons are concerned in that which shapes the life,
the destiny and the greatness of the nation of which they form a part.
This great movement . . . is a plan by which men and women, boys
and girls, may learn the truths which Christianity has nourished, that
they may enter into sympathy with those things that are pleasing to
God, in order that the best, the grandest, and noblest of all ideas may
have expression in their thoughts, their writings, and in their literature, thus pervading their homes, so that the national life will be rich
in all that constitutes the best in human history." I base my discussion
on John H.Vincent, *The Chautauqua Movement* (Boston, 1885); Jesse
Lyman Hurlbut, *The Story of Chautauqua* (New York, 1921); Rebecca
Longworthy Richmond, *Chautauqua. An American Place* (New York,
1943); and Victoria and R.O.Case, *We Called It Culture: The Story of
Chautauqua* (New York, 1948). And of course the files of *The Chautauquan.*

33. Gay Wilson Allen, *William James: A Biography* (New York, 1967), p.
384. James went there in 1896.

34. The tent chautauqua was the invention of Keith Vawter about 1904.
See Harry P.Harrison, *Culture under Canvas: The Story of Tent Chautauqua* (New York, 1958).

35. Josiah Strong, *Our Country*, ed. Jurgen Herbst (Cambridge, 1963), p.
18, John Harvard Library edition. Strong's opening chapter, "The
Time Factor in the Problem," is illuminating. *Our Country* was first
published in book form in 1886. This edition is a reprint of the revised
version of 1891.

36. James Freeman Clarke, *Self-Culture: Physical, Intellectual, Moral and
Spiritual. A Course of Lectures.* The 21st edition was printed in 1895.
The book first appeared in 1880.

37. See the fine study by Samuel Kliger, *The Goths in England: A Study
in Seventeenth and Eighteenth Century Thought* (Cambridge, 1952);
and on the domestication here of the doctrine, John Higham, *Strangers
in the Land: Patterns of American Nativism* (New Brunswick, 1955).

38. *The Goths in New-England. A Discourse Delivered at the Anniversary
of the Philomathesian Society of Middlebury College, August 15, 1843*

(Middlebury, 1848). Some tincture of the same doctrine appears in his *The American Historical School. A Discourse Delivered before the Literary Societies of Union College* (Troy, 1847), where one learns that the Old Norse chronicles are superior to later historical works (p. 20) and that our social organization has much in common with European forms made better in "our free institutions . . . based upon certain traits of character and certain hereditary principles, the maintenance of which is absolutely essential to the permanence of the valued features of our social and political system" (p. 28). Of course Jefferson cast a backward glance on what he thought was Anglo-Saxon law in justifying the Revolution and was one of the earliest American advocates of the study of Anglo-Saxon.

39. *The American Whig Review* 7(1): 28–46 (January 1848).

40. *North American Review*, 73(152): 34–71 (July 1851). For later examples of the doctrine see J.E.Chamberlain, "A Dream of Anglo-Saxondom," *Galaxy*, 24(6): 788–91 (December 1877); Lyman Abbott, "The Basis of an Anglo-American Understanding," *North American Review*, 166(5): 513–21 (May 1898); F.W.Chapman, "The Changed Significance of 'Anglo-Saxon,'" *Education*, 20(6): 364–69 (February 1900). On the need for replacing Greek and Latin by Anglo-Saxon and the classical literatures by literature in English see J.M.Garnett, "The Study of the Anglo-Saxon Language and Literature," *National Educational Association Journal of Proceedings and Addresses* (1876), pp. 141–56; A.B.Stark, "The Place of English in the Higher Education," in *ibid.*, (1877), pp. 24–32; H.B.Sprague, "The Place of Literature in the College Course," in *ibid.*, (1887), pp. 448–60; C.F.Richardson, "Anglo-Saxon as a College Study," *School and College*, 1(7): 385–97 (September 1892); George Beardsley, "English Literature at the Colleges and Universities," *Educational Review*, 16(2): 185–91 (September 1898). The bibliography is extensive.

41. The thesis is repeated in the final paragraph of Chapter I of *Montcalm and Wolfe:* "It was the strife . . . of the past against the future; of the old against the new; of moral and intellectual torpor against moral and intellectual life; of barren absolutism against a liberty, crude, incoherent, and chaotic, yet full of prolific vitality" (1884). Motley also celebrates the superior virtues of Germanic Protestantism as against Latin Catholicism.

42. See the opening pages of Tyler's *A History of American Literature During the Colonial Time, 1607–1765*, 2 vols. (New York, 1878), and *The Literary History of the American Revolution 1763–1783*, 2 vols. (New York, 1897).

43. *The Beginnings of New England or the Puritan Theocracy in its Relation to Civil and Religious Liberty* (Boston, 1902), pp. 8, 28, 53–54. Edward N.Saveth has written the standard book on this theme, but for a succinct account see his "Race and Nationalism in American Historiography: The Late Nineteenth Century," *Political Science Quarterly*, 54(3): 421–41 (September 1939).

44. Fiske, *A Century of Science and Other Essays* (Boston, 1899), pp. 122–53; *Civil Government in the United States, etc.* (Boston, 1890), especially Chapters II and VII.
45. *The Descent of Man and Selection in Relation to Sex,* new ed. revised and augmented (New York, 1888), p. 142.
46. This was the first pamphlet in the *Johns Hopkins University Studies in History and Political Science* (Baltimore, 1882), pp. 13, 19. See also Freeman's *Some Impressions of the United States* (London, 1883), pp. 137, 139, 153–55.
47. Madison Grant, *The Passing of the Great Race,* 4th rev. ed. "with a Documentary Supplement, with prefaces by Henry Fairfield Osborn, Research Professor of Zoology, Columbia University" (New York, 1921), pp. xii, 22, 16, 49, 228, 230, in that order. The subtitle is "The Racial Basis of European History," and Grant's indebtedness to various European racists is evident. One should note, however, that in *Publications of the American Statistical Association,* n.s., 14(107): 215ff. (September 1914), F. S. Crum presented some alarming figures on the "Decadence of Native American Stock."
48. *Mr. Dooley in Peace and War* (Boston, 1899), p. 56.
49. Elting E. Morison and others, eds., *The Letters of Theodore Roosevelt,* 8 vols. (Cambridge, Mass., 1951–1954), I, 525, 620–21, 724. There are many other passages of like import in the correspondence.
50. The standard study is the admirable *Expansionists of 1898: The Acquisition of Hawaii and the Spanish Islands,* by Julius W. Pratt (New York, 1938), reissued in 1951.
51. For the Moody poems see *Poems and Plays of William Vaughn Moody,* I, 15–30. The Mark Twain material is also in Janet Smith, ed., *Mark Twain on the Damned Human Race* (New York, 1962); and Albert Bigelow Paine in his *Mark Twain: A Biography* prints an unpublished document (as of 1912), "The Stupendous Procession," in which "Christendom" appears as "a majestic matron in flowing robes drenched with blood. On her head a golden crown of thorns; impaled on its spines the bleeding heads of patriots who died for their countries—Boers, Boxers, Filipinos; in one hand a slung-shot [slingshot?], in the other a Bible, open at the text 'Do unto others,' etc. Protruding from pocket bottle labeled 'We bring you the blessings of civilization.' Necklace—handcuffs and a burglar's jimmy." There is more to the description. The best over-all study seems to be Foster Rhea Dulles, *The Imperial Years* (New York, 1956), but one should also consult two analytical articles by Fred H. Harrington, "The Anti-Imperialistic Movement in the United States, 1898–1900," *MVHR,* 22(2): 211–30 (September 1935) and "Literary Aspects of American Anti-Imperialism, 1898–1902," *NEQ,* 10(4): 650–67 (December 1937).

Chapter VI: The Genteel Tradition

1. *The Genteel Tradition at Bay* (New York, 1931). In *NEQ*, 15(3): 427–43 (September 1942), Frederic I. Carpenter published "The Genteel Tradition: A Reinterpretation," one of the better attempts at definition. Santayana tended to equate the tradition with "Puritanism" modified in the direction of amiability and patriotism; after some hesitation Carpenter tended to think of it in terms of American humanism, which becomes reactionary, he thought, when it divorces itself from change and renewal. Others interpret the genteel tradition as a set of middle-class Victorian values, which they condemn.

2. In "The Drift to Liberalism in the American Eighteenth Century," *Harvard Tercentenary Publications: Authority and the Individual* (Cambridge, 1937) I struggled with the varying statements about romanticism in histories of American literature. The admirable *Romanticism in America: Papers Contributed to a Symposium Held at the Baltimore Museum of Art May 13, 14, 15, 1940* (Baltimore, 1940) illustrates the difficulty in distinguishing romanticism from sensibility and sentimentalism.

3. Excellently traced in William Charvat, *The Origins of American Critical Thought, 1810–1935.*

4. "In landscapes the painter should give the suggestion of a fairer creation than we know. The details, the prose of nature he should omit and give us only the spirit and splendor." "As far as the spiritual character of the period overpowers the artist and finds expression in his work, so far it will retain a certain grandeur, and will represent to future beholders the Unknown, the Inevitable, the Divine" ("Art"). "The depth of the notes which we accidentally sound on the strings of nature is out of all proportion to our taught and ascertained faculty, and might teach us what strangers and novices we are, vagabond to this universe of pure power, to which we have only the smallest key" ("Inspiration"). "A wild striving to express a more inward and infinite sense characterizes the works of every art" ("Thoughts on Modern Literature"). "For we do not speak now of men of poetical talents, or of industry and skill in metre, but of the true poet. . . . Our poets are men of talents who sing, and not the children of music" ("The Poet"). These passages are from various essays by Emerson.

5. So did Powers. See his letters to Nicholas Longworth, 1856–1858, in *Quarterly Publications of the Historical and Philosophical Society of Ohio*, 1(2): 33–59 (April–June 1906). Powers complained that having created, as he thought on commission, a "colossal" statue of "America," President Pierce had neglected him, and, moreover, Crawford's equally colossal "Liberty" (which became "America") had been commissioned for the dome of the Capitol. His "Webster," which, he feared, had been lost at sea, was eight feet high and he was thinking about doing a "Washington" and a "Franklin" on the same scale.

6. Elliot S. Vesell, ed., Louis Legrand Noble, *The Life and Works of Thomas Cole* (Cambridge, 1964), p. 129. This is in The John Harvard Library Series. Vesell notes how from 1829 to 1842 philosophical and historical themes overcame Cole's early devotion to landscape. Cole, by the by, thought Turner's later pictures "had an artificial look" (p. 81).

7. Tuckerman, *Artist-Life*, pp. 109, 138. A later volume, *Book of the Artists: American Artist Life* (New York, 1867), is more hard-headed, but twenty years had elapsed between the two volumes.

8. E. McClung Fleming draws a line at 1840. "Early American Decorative Arts as Social Documents," *MVHR*, 45(2): 276–84 (September 1958).

9. On Stedman's debt to the classics see John Paul Pritchard, "Stedman and Horatian Criticism," *American Literature*, 5(2): 166–69 (May 1933). Stedman's judgment was erratic, but I cannot follow G. E. DeMille, "Stedman, Arbiter of the Eighties," *PMLA*, 41(3): 756–66 (September 1926), in accusing him of intellectual dishonesty.

10. In *Americanisms and Briticisms* (New York, 1892).

11. See "An Apology for Technique" in *Inquiries and Opinions* (New York, 1907), a book dedicated to that master of the well-made play, Sir Henry Arthur Jones.

12. Francis Marion Crawford's *The Novel: What It Is* (New York, 1893) is an intelligent defense of fiction as well-managed entertainment.

13. *Studies in American Literary Life* (Philadelphia, 1901). "Now the special laws that govern written words when used for the expression of thought and emotion have been worked out by the rhetoricians and reduced to a system; these laws concern, for example, the value and use of separate words, the combinations of words into sentences and of sentences into paragraphs, and so on and so on." He urges the reader to think about the implications of various literary forms and "to trace out the peculiar ways in which the author . . . has employed the elements of an art-form so as to make them express his individual temperament and his characteristic moods and emotions" (pp. 54–55). The essay is the more interesting because it was a hack job done for the Booklovers Reading Club, Course XXII.

14. The leading titles are *French Traits* (1889), *French Art* (1892), *Victorian Prose Masters* (1901), *American Prose Masters* (1909), *Criticism* (1914), and *Standards* (1917). A new, enlarged edition of *French Art* was issued in 1908; and *American Prose Masters* has been reissued in The John Harvard Library Series (Cambridge, 1963).

15. *French Art*, new and enlarged edition (New York 1908), pp. 3–4, 144.

16. See Chapter VII of *Standards*.

17. See Donald Sheehan, *This Was Publishing: A Chronicle of the Book Trade in the Gilded Age* (Bloomington, 1952). When Walter Hines Page asked Charles Scribner to define publishing, Scribner replied: "Publishing is neither a business nor a profession. It is a career." Some leading publishers were "family houses" with a tradition of culture.

18. See the appreciative article by Mark A. De Wolfe Howe, "Updike of

Merrymount, The Scholai-Printer," *Atlantic Monthly*, 169(5): 588–96 (May 1942).

19. *Book Decorations by Bertram Grosvenor Goodhue* (New York, The Grolier Club, 1931).

20. *Posters in Miniature*. With an Introduction by Edward Penfield (New York, 1897).

21. These critics constituted the Old Guard, who still tended to approach music from a literary point of view, but they were nevertheless influential by reason either of their superior technical knowledge or of their superior knowledge of European music and musical theory, or both. See Edward G. Lueders, "Music Criticism in America," *American Art*, 3: 142–51 (Summer 1951). On Huneker see Arnold T. Schwab, *James Gibbons Huneker: Critic of the Seven Arts* (Stanford, 1963). Among his volumes of musical commentary Huneker published biographies of both Chopin and Liszt. Consult also Huneker's autobiography, *Steeplejack*, 2 vols. (New York, 1918). The Leichtentritt quotation is from his "Music in Boston in the 'Nineties'," *More Books*, 22(1): 11–19 (January 1947).

22. *My Life in Architecture* (Boston, 1936), pp. 36–38.

23. An augmented edition in 2 volumes, edited by William S. Jordy and Ralph T. Coe, appeared in The John Harvard Library Series (Cambridge, 1961).

24. *The Art Work of Louis C. Tiffany* (Garden City, 1914).

25. The famous Report of the Committee of Fifteen (1895) insisted on drawing as a public-school subject. David Howard Dickason, *The Daring Young Men: The Story of the American Pre-Raphaelites* (Bloomington, 1953) is suggestive. On the vogue of Ruskin see Roger B. Stein, *John Ruskin and Aesthetic Thought in America, 1840–1900* (Cambridge, 1967), and for another point of view, Albert Bush-Brown, "Get an Honest Bricklayer: The Scientist's Answer to Ruskin," *The Journal of Aesthetics and Art Criticism*, 16(3): 348–56 (March 1958). The honest bricklayer first appears in Thomas Henry Huxley's address at the inauguration of Daniel Coit Gilman as president of The Johns Hopkins University in 1876.

26. *Learning and Other Essays* (New York, 1910), pp. 5, 11–16, 20, 25, 26–28, 29. "Enthusiasm comes out of the world and goes into the university. Toward this point flow the currents of new talent that bubble up in society; here is the meeting-place of mind. . . . A university brings the spirit in touch with its own language, that language through which it has spoken in former days and through which alone it shall speak again" (35–36).

27. *The Greek Genius and Other Essays* (New York, 1915), p. 124.

28. *Herbert Baxter Adams. Tributes of Friends*, p. 46. Quoted in Charles Franklin Thwing, *The American and the German University: One Hundred Years of History* (New York, 1928), p. 165.

29. Among them the American Philological Association (1869), Archaeological Institute of America (1879), Society of Biblical Literature (1880),

American Historical Association (1884), American Philosophical Association (1901), Bibliographical Society of America (1904), College Art Association (1912). Of the five societies dating from before 1861 only two (American Oriental Society, American Numismatic Society) are in a strict sense organizations of specialists in a single field.

30. Charles Franklin Thwing, *The American College in American Life* (New York, 1897), p. 35; Guy Potter Benton, *The Real College* (Cincinnati and New York, 1909), p. 25; Henry Parks Wright, *From School Through College* (New Haven, 1911), p. 7; Norman Foerster, Frederick A. Manchester, Karl Young, eds., *Essays for College Men* (New York, 1913), pp. 235, 237. Dean Birge's essay, "A Change of Educational Emphasis," first appeared in the *Atlantic Monthly*. He looks back on his undergraduate years that began in 1869 and, rather regretting the pressure of research upon the college faculty, nevertheless argues that the "new college" will teach a "truer justice and a wider magnanimity," and fulfill Milton's ideal of a complete and generous education (p. 262). The best survey in print of higher education in the period is Laurence R. Veysey, *The Emergence of the American University* (Chicago, 1965).

31. Wendell's *Liberty, Union and Democracy* (New York, 1906) was originally a set of lectures delivered at the Sorbonne and repeated at the Lowell Institute in Boston. The chapter on the privileged classes parallels William Graham Sumner's famous essay, "The Forgotten Man," the privileged classes being workingmen the industrious middle class is unfairly called upon to support. The argument is repeated in *The Privileged Classes* (New York, 1908). Wendell wrote Mrs. Jack Gardner in 1902: "More and more, it seems to me that the future of our New England must depend on the standards of culture which we maintain and preserve here. The College, the Institute, the Library, the Orchestra,—and so on,—are the real bases of our strength and our dignity in the years to come." M. A. De Wolfe Howe, *Barrett Wendell and His Letters* (Boston, 1924), p. 145. President Eliot wrote Dean Briggs in 1901 he regretted Wendell's preoccupation with birth or family, finding his "frequent discourse on the subject . . . snobbish in an American." Henry James, *Charles W. Eliot*, 2 vols. (Boston, 1930), II, 134–35.

32. Herbert W. Schneider, *A History of American Philosophy* (New York, 1946), pp. 465–66. But see his whole discussion of "Idealisms."

33. But the nice fusion of scholarship and artistic technique in Sidney Lanier, *The Science of English Verse* (1888), shows the possibility of a combining tendency in scholarship.

34. Although Laura Stedman and George M. Gould's *Life and Letters of Edmund Clarence Stedman*, 2 vols. (New York, 1916), does not say so, I infer that he read the translation of von Hartmann by W. C. Coupland, published simultaneously in London and New York in 1884.

35. This summary view is based on *The Nature and Elements of Poetry* (Boston, 1892), but I find little in Stedman's other critical pronounce-

ments to alter it. I think John Paul Pritchard is wrong in categorizing Stedman as one of Lowells' "Epigoni," but his discussion of Stedman in *Criticism in America* (Norman, 1966), pp. 147–56, is one of the best in print.

36. Rosalind enters the writer's study and "in her I suddenly found the key to the mystery which I had sought in vain to solve by process of thought, for in her I saw the harmony of law with beauty and joy, the rounded circle of right action and a temperament . . . with light and song and the sweetness of nature" (p. 17). Even Shakespeare's Rosalind cannot approach this.

37. "Race" in Mabie generally means the human race, but as is often the case with his generation, this is commonly identified with the Aryans. In Robert Grant's *The Opinions of a Philosopher* (New York, 1894) Josephine discusses with her husband, de Musset, Herbert Spencer, Darwin, Austin Dobson, George Eliot, and Philip Hamerton. Apparently all these wives were as bookish as Poe's Ligeia.

38. See Martha Hale Shackford, "George Edward Woodberry as Critic," *NEQ*, 24(4): 510–27 (December 1951). The best general article I have seen on Woodberry is Richard B. Hovey, "George Edward Woodberry: Genteel Exile" in the same magazine, 23(4): 504–26 (December 1950). This seems to me more hard-headed than Louis V. Ledoux, *George Edward Woodberry: A Study of His Poetry* (Cambridge, 1917).

39. Woodberry wrote Charles Borrows in 1916: "Do you think at all of the *meaning* of the ills that science seems to have brought into the world, like a new apple of Eden?" He was fearful of the "approaching supremacy of the yellow races." He wondered in a letter to George Danton in 1919 whether the Arab genius "will blossom again round the Eastern Mediterranean and the Persian Gulf." *Selected Letters* (New York, 1933), pp. 166, 215.

40. As the following three passages show: "Nobody seems to care, and the years go on remorselessly. No one would ever believe the hours of desolate bitterness and of privation I have myself known in earlier times, and the low dejection of later years" (to T. W. Higginson, 1904). "It is curious how often I feel a disposition to write of the things I see [in America] in a Pickwickian style . . . New York was like a new (and lower) world of vertebrates, whose habits I had well nigh forgotten" (to Lewis Einstein, 1907). "I have come to think of America as a backward nation, in all those things that are in a region above the material and mechanical parts of life and civilization. I think we lack ideas and emotions of the sort that forge greatness in spiritual ways—both as a nation and as individuals" (to John Erskine, 1911). He thought the prettiest sight he saw in the country was the collection of Elizabethan first editions at the Yale Elizabethan Club. *Selected Letters*, pp. 30, 57, 97, 114.

41. He went there to teach in 1880 and wrote that the skies were warm like the Italian ones but that "there is, of course, here and there ugliness, dirt, a general lack of cleanliness and attention to the trifles of life, an

unthrift, as it strikes a Yankee, a waste, neglect and disorder." *Selected Letters*, p. 8. Charles Eliot Norton stoutly adjured him: "What a splendid chance to study primitive institutions!"

42. As in *The North Shore Watch and Other Poems* (Boston, 1890).

43. See *The Torch* (New York, 1903). The subtitle is revealing: "Eight Lectures on Race Power in Literature."

44. The least cloudy of his general volumes is *Studies in Letters and Life* (Boston, 1890).

45. *Essays in Literary Interpretation*, new ed. (New York, 1899), pp. 36–37. See also Woodrow Wilson, *Mere Literature and Other Essays* (Boston, 1896), and Charles Dudley Warner, *Fashions in Literature* (New York, 1902), for variants of the doctrine.

46. William Wetmore Story, *Conversations in a Studio*, 2 vols. (Boston, 1890). See especially I, 3, 73, 148, 166; II, 309, 320, 332, 335, 336, 338, 340. "Nothing is true in art unless it be assimilated by the imagination to the idea which is the soul of the work. . . ." (II, 330).

47. "If this public won't accept my better work, I must wait until a new one grows up. . . . One thing I swear to you. I will go on trying to do intrinsically good things, and will not yield a hair's breadth for the sake of conciliating an ignorant public. If there is any virtue in faith. I'll try to deserve that, if nothing more." Bayard Taylor to Thomas Bailey Aldrich, May 29, 1872, in Marie Hansen-Taylor and Horace E. Scudder, eds., *Life and Letters of Bayard Taylor*, 2 vols. (Boston, 1884), II, 588.

48. Brownell, *French Art*, p. 149; Rosamond Gilder, ed., *Letters of Richard Watson Gilder* (Boston, 1916), p. 186; Lloyd Mifflin, *Collected Sonnets* (London, 1905), p. 56; Story, *Conversations in a Studio*, II, 318, 321. Gilder seems to have been selected as a whipping boy by commentators in the 1920s and later, for all the sins of the Genteel Tradition, but as Robert Berkelman points out in "Mrs. Grundy and Richard Watson Gilder," *American Quarterly*, 4: 66–72 (Spring 1952), accused of barring *The Century Magazine* to Whitman, Garland, and Crane, Gilder could say that all three were printed in this periodical. He carried Whitman's poems in his pocket and liked to read them to his friends.

49. Perhaps the most melancholy passage in Norton's printed correspondence is found in a letter of November 3, 1895, acknowledging the gift of a book of poems by Howells: "Your voice is strangely in harmony with those of the poets who have felt most deeply and suffered most from the riddles and paradoxes of life. One hears in it the tone of the voices of the Greeks, and might match each of its utterances with the sweet verses of the [Greek] Anthology. Here is one which came into my memory as I read your book: 'How can one escape from thee, O life, without dying? thy sorrows are myriad and neither to escape from them nor to endure them is easy. Sweet are thy beautiful things,—the earth, the sea, the stars, the circles of the moon and the sun, but all the rest are fears and pains, and if a good thing befall to one a corresponding Nemesis follows.' " The book was *The Stops of Various Quills*

(1895), and Norton's copy is in the Houghton Library. The volume, unduly ignored by critics of Howells, is strong and somber. The epigram, ascribed to Aesop, is number 123 of Book X ("Hortatory and Admonitory Epigrams") of the *Greek Anthology*.

50. My discussion is based on Sara Norton and M. A. De Wolfe Howe, eds., *Letters of Charles Eliot Norton with Biographical Comment*, 2 vols. (Boston, 1913), Vol. II.

51. "Arnold, Aristocracy, and America," in my *History and the Contemporary*.

52. "It is important . . . to discriminate between listening to Mr. Arnold and reading him. It is well known that some of the ablest Englishmen scandalously neglect the elementary rules of elocution. In the United States almost every person, from the farmer who speaks in a town meeting to the accomplished orator who addresses the Senate of the country, considers that the second part of the sentence should be as audible as the first." E. P. Whipple, "Matthew Arnold," *North American Review*, 138(330): 428–44 (May 1884). Whipple considered Arnold's poetry "weak and melancholy." A writer in *The Literary World*, 14(25): 446 (December 15, 1883), thought Arnold and Arnold's visit to the United States created different impressions. "The impression of the man is pleasant; the impression of the visit unpleasant." H. T. Tuckerman, "English Criticism," *Hours at Home*, 2(1): 5–10 (November 1865); E. S. Nadel, "Matthew Arnold," *The Critic*, 2(36): 135–36 (May 20, 1882); "The influence of Matthew Arnold," *The American Magazine* 8: 37 (October 27, 1883); "Mr. Arnold on America," *ibid.*, 7: 198 (January 5, 1884); Louis J. Swinburne, "Matthew Arnold in America," *Lippincott's Magazine*, 33: 90–96 (January 1884). For general statements occasioned by Arnold's death see *Andover Review*, 9(53): 512–18 (May 1888); *The Dial*, 9(97): 5–7 (May 1888); *The Century Magazine*, 14(2) n.s.: 185–94 (June 1888); and the article by John Burroughs, *The Princeton Review*, 6(3) n.s.: 355–69 (November 1888).

53. The Fuller article is in *The (American) Bookman*, 2(3): 203–205 (November 1895), and is perhaps more pessimistic than I represent it as being. For Theodore Roosevelt see the volume of *Literary Essays* in any edition of his collected works, particularly the essay, "History as Literature" ("History, taught for a directly and immediately useful purpose to pupils and the teachers of pupils, is one of the necessary features of a sound education in a democratic citizenship"). The Stedman essay was reprinted as a preface to *The Writings in Prose and Verse of Eugene Field*, (New York, 1901), Vol. V. When Stedman lectured before the Twentieth Century Club in Chicago, Field gravely pictured a welcoming procession stopping at the packing yards, and the art galleries, composed of the club, the Browning Club in buses, the Homer Club in drays, ten millionaire publishers, ten pork-packers in chariots, and two hundred Chicago poets on foot.

54. *Jeffersonianism and the American Novel* (New York, 1966), Chapter IV.

55. Between 1878 and 1900 thirty-one American publishers brought out at

least one hundred and eighty books by Zola, but most of these were paperbacks sold from twenty cents to a dollar. The advertising emphasizes the supposed lurid or prurient qualities of the fiction, and the titles were vulgarized. Thus *La Conquête de Plassans* came out once as *A Mad Love; or, the Abbé and His Court;* once as *A Fatal Conquest; or, Buried in the Ashes of a Ruined Home;* and once as *The Conquest of Plassans; or, The Priest in the House.* Malcolm B. Jones, "Translations of Zola in the United States Prior to 1900," *Modern Language Notes,* 55(7): 520–24 (November 1940).

56. George Santayana, *Interpretations of Poetry and Religion* (New York, 1900), pp. v, ix. See also his *Three Philosophical Poets* (New York, 1910).

57. The poems are by (1) Frank Dempster Sherman; (2) Lizette Woodworth Reese; (3) Richard Watson Gilder; (4) Lloyd Mifflin. The first two are in the Stedman *Anthology;* Gilder's (entitled "Brothers") is in *Poems* (Boston, 1908), pp. 155–56; and the sonnet is from Lloyd Mifflin's *Collected Sonnets,* rev. ed. (London, 1905), p. 56.

58. *Sonnets and Other Poems* (Cambridge, 1894).

59. Who can forget Mrs. Wharton's description of a performance of *Faust* at the Academy of Music in the early 1870s? "An unalterable and unquestioned law of the musical world required that the German text of French operas sung by Swedish artists [Christine Nilsson was Marguerite] should be translated into Italian for the clearer understanding of English-speaking audiences." *The Age of Innocence* (New York, 1920), p. 3.

60. An equally amusing case is that of the New World tenor, Edward Johnson, unsuccessful under that name, who went abroad, took lessons, sang in Europe, changed his name to Edoardo di Giovanni, and returned to have a *succès fou* with the Chicago Opera Company.

61. John C. Van Dyke, *The Art Tradition in America* (New York, 1919), p. 5, and *American Painting and Its Tradition* (New York, 1919), pp. 5, 61–62, 241; Charles H. Caffin, *American Masters of Painting* (New York, 1913), p. 137; Samuel Isham, *The History of American Painting* (New York, 1905), p. 561.

62. I have found the following biographies of painters useful: Katharine Metcalf Roof, *The Life and Art of William Merritt Chase* (New York, 1917); Lloyd Goodrich, *Thomas Eakins: His Life and Work* (New York, 1933); Ira Glackens, *William Glackens and the Ashcan Group: The Emergence of Realism in American Art* (New York, 1957); Marie de Mare, *G. P. A. Healy: American Artist* (New York, 1954); Helen Appleton Read, *Robert Henri* (New York, 1931); Lloyd Goodrich, *Winslow Homer* (New York, 1944); Henry C. Angell, *Records of William M. Hunt* (Boston, 1881); Royal Cortissoz, *John La Farge: A Memoir and a Study* (Boston, 1911); Van Wyck Brooks, *John Sloan: A Painter's Life* (New York, 1955); Nelson C. White, *Abbott H. Thayer, Painter and Naturalist* (Hartford, 1951); Henry C. White, *The Life and Art of Dwight William Tryon* (Boston, 1930).

63. Robert Henri, *The Art Spirit* (Philadelphia, 1923), *passim*.
64. But in 1967 there appeared in the New York *Times* an advertisement for replicas of Michelangelo's "David," "Fig Leaf Optional."
65. Marie de Mare, *G. P. A. Healy*, p. 235; Katharine Metcalf Roof, *William Merritt Chase*, pp. 21–22; Lloyd Goodrich, *Thomas Eakins*, pp. 77–90; Van Wyck Brooks, *John Sloan*, pp. 13–15.
66. Story thought the sharp, thin air of America has its effects upon the American, since "everything runs to form rather than to color in his mind." Perhaps he was trying to correct the obsession with outline. *Conversations in a Studio*, II, 324.
67. The standard history is Pauline King, *American Mural Painting: A Study of the Important Decorations by Distinguished Artists in the United States* (Boston, 1902). See also the important article by James Watrous, "Mural Painting, Sculpture, and Architecture, 1890–1915," *American Quarterly*, 2(3): 227–33 (Fall 1950). Watrous' conclusion is: "It is true that this whole movement was a transplanted, peripheral part of a European eclecticism, but from the standpoint of our cultural history, we must regard it as more than a casual phenomenon of a latter-day classicism because it was the unique attempt to create for America a 'great' art through an alliance, which some hoped would foster a quality and impressiveness without equal since the Renaissance." I hope my indebtedness to Oliver Larkin throughout this discussion is clear.
68. Caffin, *The Story of American Painting*, pp. 173–74.
69. Originally published under the title "Why We Have No Great Novelists" in *The Forum* in 1887, this was retitled "The American Novelist and His Public" and included in *Literary and Social Silhouettes* (New York, 1894).
70. Saint-Gaudens, *The American Artist and His Times*, pp. 116–17.
71. William A. Coles, ed., *Architecture and Society: Selected Essays by Henry Van Brunt* (Cambridge, 1969), "Architecture of the World's Columbian Exposition," pp. 267–69. This group of essays was originally printed in *The Century Magazine*, May–October 1892. I shall refer hereafter to this collection as Van Brunt.
72. This statement is given in various forms and attributed to various meetings, but there is no doubt of its authenticity.
73. Oddly enough, not admired in their prime. Montgomery Schuyler, who fancied himself as an aesthetician in the matter of bridges, though he considered the Brooklyn Bridge "one of the mechanical wonders of the world," is harsh in judging the towers and anchorages. See "The Brooklyn Bridge as a Monument" (1883) in Jordy and Coe, *American Architecture and Other Writings by Montgomery Schuyler*, II, 331–44. Hart Crane's *The Bridge* expresses of course the modern mystical view.
74. Van Brunt, p. 89.
75. In order to house all the exhibits proposed for the Manufactures Building, George B. Post had to erect an unencumbered hall 1687 feet long and 787 feet wide, or 32 acres. The structure was three times the extent

of St. Peter's in Rome and required seven million board feet of lumber for its floor. Yet, as any set of photographs of the Fair will show, Post not merely solved the extraordinary structural problem but also fitted his building into the over-all scheme of the Court of Honor.

76. Even though there were strikes, the statement is still true. Unskilled laborers worked in the depth of winter and in drenching rains to get the job done.

77. Some fears were expressed that the congress on labor would incite civic disturbances, but it did not. Speakers as various as Henry George, Clarence Darrow, and Bishop Samuel Fallows addressed an audience estimated at about twenty-five thousand.

78. John Fullerton Muirhead published *America the Land of Contrasts,* which reached a third edition in 1898; and William T. Stead published his article in 1894. Both are excerpted in Bessie Louise Pierce's *As Others See Chicago: Impressions of Visitors, 1673–1933.* As good a general summary of the Fair as I have found is Harvey M. Watts, "The White City," *The T Square Club Journal of Philadelphia,* 19(6): 24–27 (May 1931), but both Van Brunt and Montgomery Schuyler give intelligent contemporary reviews of its architecture.

Chapter VII: Cosmopolitanism

1. See *Democracy in America,* Part II, Bk. III, Chapter XVII.

2. Henry James, *Hawthorne* (New York, 1879), pp. 41–43.

3. Thomas Colley Grattan, *Civilized America,* 2 vols., 2nd ed. (London, 1859), I, 81, 114–15; II, 106. See also Chapter III of Vol. II, "Comparison and Contrasts between England and America."

4. Edward Augustus Freeman, *Some Impressions of the United States* (London, 1883), p. 238.

5. See Part IV of Arnold's book.

6. James Bryce, *The American Commonwealth,* 2 vols., 2nd ed. rev. (New York, 1893), II, 819, 827, 828. The extraordinary vogue of Bryce may be inferred from the fact that American editions were brought out in 1888, 1889, 1893–1895, 1899, 1910, 1922–1923, 1924, 1926, 1926–1927, 1928, 1931–1933, and abridged editions in 1896, 1902 (2), and 1908 (the chapter on the Tweed Ring).

7. I confine myself to British observers, though Frenchmen sometimes reiterated the charge of mediocrity. Among other English travel books one might read the young Kipling's brash, if amusing, *American Notes* (1891), George Warrington Steevens, *The Land of the Dollar* (1897), the bias of which is evident from its title, and William Archer's more judicious *America To-Day* (1899). It is curious that if one is to judge by anthologies of excerpts from travel books and by special studies, historians have devoted more time to an analysis of travel books by Europeans to the United States before 1870 than to the period from 1870 to the present.

8. Elisabeth Luther Cary, *The Novels of Henry James: A Study* (New York, 1905), p. 57.

9. For a sketch of this earlier situation see my "The Influence of European Ideas in Nineteenth-Century America," *American Literature*, 7(3): 241–73 (November 1935), the title of which is, however, misleading since the article deals only with the first half of that century. And see also the discussion of the cosmopolitan spirit in my *America and French Culture*, pp. 15–41.

10. Although in *The Old World and the New: or, A Journal of Reflections and Observations made on a Tour in Europe*, 2 vols. (New York, 1836), Dewey is less intransigent than some, he devotes a whole chapter (Chapter XXI in Vol. II) to "the Roman Catholic System," which, whatever its merits, entails "mental slavery" upon the ignorant and, for the enlightened, sets "religion apart from the free action of their own minds" (II, 166). See his final chapter on the irresistible tendency of the republican form of government to prevail. Norton's contempt for Roman society is evident: "Hypocrisy is the rule, not only of the Jesuits, but of those who have been governed by Jesuits" (*Notes of Travel and Study in Italy*, p. 74). His preface announces: "I have not hesitated in the following pages to express myself strongly in regard to some of the corrupt doctrines of the Roman Church and methods of the Papal Government," though "I retain the highest respect for many of its members" (p. vi). The book was reprinted without change in 1887.

11. The Treaty of Washington (1871), which provided for the arbitration of boundary disputes between the United Kingdom and this country, the settlement of the *Alabama* claims, the definition of disputed fishing rights, and other matters, did more than any other political events to lessen tension between the two countries.

12. William Winter, *Gray Days and Gold* (New York, 1892), p. 11; *The Trip to England* (Boston, 1879), pp. 39, 40, 58, 60. He spends a good deal of space on Byron and the Byron collection then exhibiting at the Albert Memorial Hall and speaks of the "strange, dark, sad career of a wonderful man" (p. 104)—a far cry from the moral reprobation of that poet formerly common among Americans. This book, by the by, is virtually the same as his *Shakespeare's England* (1892).

13. Katharine Lee Bates, *From Gretna Green to Land's End: A Literary Journey in England* (New York, 1907), pp. 78–80, 121–24. Chester "is the mediaeval made actual" (p. 124).

14. Originally published in New York (1899), *Among English Hedgerows* went through seven reprintings by 1925.

15. A book by Huish reproduces a great many water colors; and Joseph and Elizabeth Robins Pennell are representative artists who capitalized on the English picturesque in several works, among them: *A Little Book of London* (Boston, 1913) and *Haunts of Old London* (Boston, 1914). Their *A Canterbury Pilgrimage* (London, 1885) is an amusing account of an attempt to follow the route of Chaucer's pilgrims by riding an enormous tricycle. They note a vast number of tramps in the

hop-picking season, but everybody is good-natured and Dickensianly English.

16. Andrew Carnegie, *An American Four-in-Hand in Britain* (New York, 1933), pp. 148, 165, 233, 249–50. Carnegie admired Julius Caesar (p. 138) and Richard Wagner (pp. 152–53), thought the Marquis of Stafford, who owned almost all of Sutherland, praiseworthy because he was a "painstaking director of the London and Northwestern Railway," and yet let the Scotch Duke of Atholl, whose possessions stretched for thirty miles, go unrebuked, albeit "never, till England changes its practice and can boast a peasant proprietary working its own acres in small farms, untrammeled by vicious laws, will she know what miracles can be wrought by those who call each spot their own—their home" (pp. 23, 138, 152–53, 220–21, 290).

17. *English Hours* (Boston, 1905) was compounded out of scattered periodical essays and some papers from *Portraits of Places* (1883) and illustrated by Joseph Pennell.

18. James was driven after dark from Euston Station to Morley's Hotel: "the low black houses were as inanimate as so many rows of coal-scuttles, save where at frequent corners, from a gin shop, there was a flare of light more brutal still than the darkness." His lodgings later struck him "as stuffy and unsocial . . . a sudden horror of the whole place came over me, like a tiger-pounce of homesickness which had been watching its moment." "The absence of style, or rather of the intention of style" was characteristic, and he could not ignore "the uglinesses, the 'rookeries', the brutalities, the night-aspect of many of the streets" nor "the immense misery," yet the crescendo of his observations of the lower classes is a Dickensian, even a Rabelaisian, account of Derby Day (pp. 5, 7–8, 31, 177ff.).

19. Price Collier, *England and the English from an American Point of View* (New York, 1909), pp. 5, 7, 15ff., 27–29, 40, 104, 105, 169, 313, 374ff., 390.

20. James's letters to the New York *Tribune* (by August 10, 1876, Whitelaw Reid complained they were too literary) have been collected and edited by Leon Edel and Ilse Dusoin Lind as *Parisian Sketches* (New York, 1957). *French Poets and Novelists* (1878) is of course a collection of literary essays, and *A Little Tour in France* (New York, 1900) was apparently commissioned as literary sketches to accompany a set of drawings. The drawings were not made, but the book was published in 1900 with the situation reversed; that is, Joseph Pennell illustrated James's literary essays which had originally been written to comment upon somebody else's drawings. All this of course does not concern the picture of French life in *The American* or short stories with French settings.

21. Mrs. Henry M. Field, *Home Sketches in France, and Other Papers* (New York, 1875), pp. 15, 74–75, 83, 97ff., 137, 151ff.; Albert Rhodes, *The French at Home* (New York, 1875), p. 240; Stuart Henry, *Paris Days and Evenings* (Philadelphia, 1896), p. 88, and *passim*; Richard

Harding Davis, *About Paris* (New York, 1895), pp. 218–19; Frank Berkeley Smith, *How Paris Amuses Itself* (New York, 1903). As late as 1882 John W. Allen, Jr., in *Paul Dreifuss: His Holiday Abroad* (Boston 1882) complained of Paris that "the modest traveler's eyes encounter on all sides statues and paintings in the nude" (p. 250). I have deliberately chosen books by less well-known authors as being more representative.

22. William Wetmore Story, *Roba di Roma*, 3d ed. (London, 1864) pp. 4, 25, 56. The bibliographical history of this influential work is a bit confused. The preface is dated November 1, 1862, but I can find no copy of an 1862 edition; the first I have seen is a London edition in two volumes of 1863. By 1887, either in one volume or in two, the work had reached an 8th edition, and in 1877 certain chapters omitted from the 2nd (?) edition were published separately as *Castle St. Angelo and the Evil Eye* (London and Philadelphia). There was a printing of the "standard" text as late as 1894.

23. F. Hopkinson Smith, *Venice of To-Day* (New York, 1896), p. 5; *Gondola Days* (Boston, 1898), preface. The second book has over two hundred illustrations by the author.

24. William Dean Howells, *Roman Holidays and Others* (New York, 1908), p. 35. This volume records a revisiting of places first seen in the 1860s, when he thought he "would like to have the ducal cities of North Italy, such as Mantua, Modena, Parma, and Ferrara, locked up quietly within their walls, and left to crumble and totter and fall, without any harder presence to vex them in their decrepitude than that of some gray custodian. . . ." *Italian Journeys* (Boston and New York, 1872), p. 16.

25. Henry James, *Italian Hours* (Boston, 1919), pp. 5–6, 159–60, 164. The whole book is not only unexpected in its sociological flair but also stylistically one of James's best nonfictional performances.

26. John Hay, *Castilian Days* (Boston, 1899), pp. 248–49. The book was first published in 1871; for the revised edition Hay, in a preface dated 1890, says that though he has corrected "the most obvious and flagrant errors," he lets most of his text stand because, with all its faults, he cannot regret the honest enthusiasm and candor of his original opinions (pp. iii–iv).

27. Kate Field, *Ten Days in Spain* (Boston, 1875), *passim*; James Albert Harrison, *Spain in Profile: A Summer among the Olives and Aloes* (Boston, 1879), pp. 19, 51, 139, 148; William Howe Downes, *Spanish Ways and By-Ways With a Glimpse of the Pyrenees* (Boston, 1883), *passim* (this writer "loved the southern lands . . . perhaps I have a sneaking sympathy for laziness, and immorality, and dirt, and decay"); Charles Augustus Stoddard, *Spanish Cities with Some Glimpses of Gibraltar and Tangier* (New York, 1892), pp. 98–99; Fanny Bullock Workman and William Hunter Workman, *Sketches Awheel in Modern Iberia* (New York, 1897), pp. 159ff. There is no anti-Catholicism in the Workman volume. Perhaps mention should be made of two curious, superficial, and cheerful travel books: Edward Everett Hale, *Seven Spanish Cities and the Way to Them* (Boston, 1883), and Mrs. Susan Hale,

A Family Flight Through Spain (Boston, 1883), a fictionized account of travel by a family with several children.

28. Books about Germany offer dramatic contrasts between the Germany of the "storied Rhine" and the efficient Germany of the Emperor William II. For a specimen of the first see Robert Haven Schauffler, *Romantic Germany* (New York, 1909), and of the second, Ray Stannard Baker, *Seen in Germany* (Chautauqua, 1901). The latter observes that "all government in Germany smacks strongly of the military camp" (p. 15).

29. Sold by subscription, *John L. Stoddard's Lectures* (1897–1898) in 10 volumes (there were supplements) were widely distributed and must have brought romantic notions of the world into many American homes. The *National Geographic Magazine* was published but irregularly between 1888 and 1895 and appeared monthly only after 1895.

30. F. Hopkinson Smith, *A White Umbrella in Mexico* (Boston and New York, 1889), p. 122. For romantic tales about that country see Thomas A. Janvier, *Legends of the City of Mexico* (New York, 1910), and for shrewd social insight into the country of Porfirio Díaz, Charles Macomb Flandrau, *Viva Mexico!* (New York, 1909). Even Flandrau succumbs to romance, as why should he not? "It is at this hour . . . that one should walk through the Alameda, inhale the first freshness of the wet roses and lilies, the gardenias and pansies and heliotrope in the flower market, and, undisturbed among the trees in front of the majestic cathedral, listen to 'the echoed sob of history' " (p. 294).

31. Professor and Mrs. Louis Agassiz, *A Journey in Brazil* (Boston, 1868); Reverend Titus Coan, *Adventures in Patagonia: A Missionary's Exploring Trip* (New York, 1880); Charles Augustus Stoddard, *Cruising among the Caribees: Summer Days in Winter Months* (New York, 1895); Richard Harding Davis, *Three Gringos in Venezuela and Central America* (New York, 1896). The quoted matter in the text is on pp. 84–87. The passage about the beautiful Rio Negro girls is from John Esaias Warren, *Para: Or, Scenes and Adventures on the Banks of the Amazon* (New York, 1851), p. 94.

32. Andrew P. Peabody, *Reminiscences of European Travel* (New York, 1868), pp. 6, 28, 77, 149, 231; Harry Thurston Peck, *The New Baedeker* (New York, 1910), pp. 19–22.

33. On the relation of the piracy of foreign books before 1891 to the paperback book of the 1870s and the 1880s, see Raymond Howard Shove, *Cheap Book Production in the United States, 1870 to 1891* (Urbana, 1937), and Frederick A. Stokes, "A Publisher's Random Notes, 1880–1935: First of the R. R. Bowker Memorial Lectures," *Bulletin of the New York Public Library*, 39(11): 843–61 (November 1935).

34. Art Young in his youth was thrilled by Doré's illustrations to Dante and later on knew the work of Daumier, Rowlandson, Tenniel, Keene, Leech, Cruikshank, Franz Stuck, Phil May, and many more. (Art Young, *On My Way*, New York, 1928, pp. 49–50.) The idea of the humorous weekly seems to have been borrowed from such European successes as *Charivari*, *Punch*, *Fliegende Blätter*, etc. (Allan Nevins and

Frank Weitenkampf, *A Century of Political Cartoons*, New York, 1944, p. 14). *Puck*, transferred out of the German language into English at New York in 1877, long had for its chief cartoonist the Austrian-born Joseph Keppler. On valentines see Ruth Webb Lee, *A History of Valentines* (London, 1953). Both comic valentines and lithographed ones were commercially manufactured in the United States after 1840, but as early as 1823 "Peter Quizumall, Esq." published *The New Quizzical Valentine*, which seems to show influence from Rowlandson and Cruikshank and from the European notion of the grotesque (William Murrell, *A History of American Graphic Humor*, 2 vols. New York, 1933, I: 102).

35. Henry A. Pochmann's, *New England Transcendentalism and St. Louis Hegelianism* goes beyond the Civil War. The indebtedness of American pragmatism to Pareto and F.C.S. Schiller is acknowledged by William James. John Fiske virtually duplicated Herbert Spencer in his *Outline of Cosmic Philosophy*. But the interrelation of American and European thought is a complex subject.

36. *Entartung* was first published in 2 volumes in Berlin in 1892–1893. Omitting fiction, plays, and discussions of Zionism by Nordau, one notes that American translations of his principal "philosophical" works are *Degeneration* (1895), *The Right to Love* (1895), *Paradoxes* (1895), *The Drones Must Die* (1897), *The Malady of the Century* (1898), *The Interpretation of History* (1911), and in 1922 *Morals and the Evolution of Man*. I discuss Nordau later.

37. The *Atlantic Monthly*, 38 (225): 89–90 (July 1876). The successive articles are on pp. 85–91, 233–39, 350–59, 492–501, and 732–40 of this volume. Howells' "A Sennight of the Centennial" is in the same volume, pp. 92–107. He said "the finest of the pavilions" was that of an Oswego starch manufacturer "where an artistic use of the corn and its stalk had been made in the carved ornamentation of the structure." Of the French exhibit he observed that whole rooms "were barred against the public, but enough was visible to emphasize the national taste for the nude." The anonymous *Atlantic Monthly* writer thought the English "immensely in advance of us in all that makes a dwelling comfortable and attractive to the eye" (p. 31), and in view of the dates, it seems possible that the Philadelphia Exposition began and the Columbian Exposition continued the movement to improve American household furnishing evident in the publication of Clarence Cook, *The House Beautiful* (New York, 1877); Harriet Prescott Spofford, *Art Decoration Applied to Furniture* (New York, 1878); Oliver B. Bunce, *My House: An Ideal* (New York, 1884); and Edith Wharton and Ogden Coleman, Jr., *The Decoration of Houses* (New York, 1897). The last-named volume was enthusiastically reviewed in *The Bookman*, 7(2): 161–63 (April 1898), by Walter Berry. One must also allow for the American vogue of Eastlake.

38. *Annual Report of the Board of Regents of the Smithsonian Institution . . . to July 1892* (Washington, D.C., 1893), pp. 513–20.

39. In view of the contemporary tendency to denigrate the Columbian Expostion it is refreshing to find Merle Curti stoutly declaring: "We have yet to realize the impact of the learned congresses at Chicago on the intellectual and cultural life both of the United States and of the world." "America at the World Fairs, 1851–1893," *American Historical Review* 55(4): 833–56 (July 1950).

40. *Congress of Arts and Science, Universal Exhibition, St. Louis,* 1904, ed. Howard J. Rogers, 8 vols. (Boston, 1905–1907). The first volume gives a history of the congress, together with Münsterberg's too metaphysical "scientific plan" for the unity of knowledge; the last contains an index of the set. On the significance for American thought of this gathering see George Haines IV and Frederick H. Jackson, "A Neglected Landmark in the History of Ideas," *MVHR,* 34(2): 201–20 (September 1947), and A.W. Coats, "American Scholarship Comes of Age: The Louisiana Purchase Exposition 1904," *Journal of the History of Ideas,* 22(3): 404–17 (July–September 1961). On St. Louis as an intellectual center, in addition to Pochmann, see Denton J. Snider, *The St. Louis Movement* (St. Louis, 1922), and the appropriate chapters in Daniel S. Rankin, *Kate Chopin and her Creole Stories* (Philadelphia, 1932).

41. Frank Luther Mott, "The Magazine Revolution and Popular Ideas in the Nineties," *Proceedings of the American Antiquarian Society,* 64(1): 195–214 (1954).

42. Miss Wormeley translated not only all of Balzac, but also works by Dumas, Daudet, Paul Bourget, Molière, and sets of French mémoires. See Raymond L. Kilgour, *Messrs. Robert Brothers, Publishers* (Ann Arbor, 1952), pp. 214–15.

43. The play was part of the repertory of the Bobbie Warren Stock Company, which toured Texas in the second decade of this century, producing such sound dramas as *The North Woods, St. Elmo,* and *Lady Audley's Secret.* Even if my memory is wrong and the heroine was not an American girl, the exposure of English snobbery and European villainy thrilled American audiences. Bertha M. Clay, when she was not a writing syndicate, was in actual life Charlotte M. Braeme, an English Catholic.

44. Richard Harding Davis, *Novels and Stories,* (Crossroads edition, New York, 1916), III, 228. *Chantage,* by the by, is hush money.

45. My discussion looks at this problem from the American end. If the reader would like to reverse the telescope, he may care to consult such an article as Edgar F. Harden, "The American Girl in British Fiction, 1860–1880," *Huntington Library Quarterly,* 26(3): 263–85 (May 1963), and so magisterial a study as Simon Jeune, *De F.T. Graindorge à A.O. Barnabooth: Les Types américains dans le Roman et le Théâtre français* (1861–1917) (Paris, 1963), and Cushing Strout, *The American Image of the Old World* (New York, 1963).

46. The judicious are referred to the collected expressions of Mr. Dooley for acute observations in the period on foreigners and their ways; see, for example, that great man on "King Edward's Coronation" in *Obser-*

vations by Mr. Dooley (New York, 1902), pp. 133–38. A generation which knows not the philosopher of Archey Road may need to be reminded that his opinions were reported by Finley Peter Dunne.

47. From Chapter XI. In "Melville's *Mardi*," *American Quarterly*, 2:(1) 71–81 (Spring 1950), Newton Arvin points to a fact of some significance; namely, that the Utopian fantasy of that book is colored by the exoticism of *Typee* and *Omoo*.

48. *Army Life in a Black Regiment* has been several times reprinted. My own edition was brought out by Michigan State University Press in 1960.

49. Lafcadio Hearn, *Two Years in the French West Indies* (New York and London, 1890), pp. 63–64, 88, 90. In "The Utopia of Lafcadio Hearn —Spanish America," *American Quarterly*, 6(1): 76–78 (Spring 1954), Sidonia C. Rosenbaum makes out a good case for believing that at one period in his life Hearn dreamed of Latin America as an exotic Utopia, where he could find "women with skin the color of gold" and "palms shaking their plumes" against the sunrise.

50. Here as elsewhere in this chapter I can hope to be suggestive only. Prior to the half-century under survey there was a considerable publication of missionary books about Oceania, often British but occasionally American: typical is *The Night of Toil; or, A Familiar Account of the Labors of the First Missionaries of The South Sea Islands* by the author of the "Peep of Day," published by the American Tract Society, n.d., apparently an abridgement of a British missionary's account. More "American" is, apparently, *Life in Feejee, or, Thirty Years among the Cannibals* "by a lady" (M.D. Wallis), (Boston, 1851). The subscription book business created Edward Walter Dawson's *The Isles of the Sea* (Hartford, 1886). Political excitement over the Samoan Islands and the Sandwich Islands (Hawaii) produced their spate of books; for example, Charles Martin Newell, *Kaméhaméha The Conquering King . . . A Romance of Hawaii* (New York, 1885); and "adventure" interest was responsible for Rosalind Amelia Young ("a native daughter"), for *Mutiny of the Bounty and Story of Pitcairn Island 1790–1894* (Oakland, 1894), which reached a 3d "edition" in 1895, and for the Reverend James Paton, *The Story of John G. Paton Told for Young Folks; or, Thirty Years among South Sea Cannibals* (New York, 1896). Anthropologists also contributed to this library. In modern times it is amusing to note the reiteration of titles containing words such as "paradise," "pearl," and "Eden." The prize in nomenclature goes to Newton A. Rowe, *Voyage to the Amorous Islands: The Discovery of Tahiti* (London, 1955), which contains an account of a voyage of 1766 that has little to do with amorousness. The contemporary anthropological best seller is presumably Margaret Mead, *Coming of Age in Samoa* (New York, 1928). One ought not forget the vogue of R.L. Stevenson.

51. Charles Warren Stoddard, *South-Sea Idyls* (Boston, 1873), pp. v, 47–48, 328. For other books by him, some of them exotic in character, see the excellent sketch in the *DAB*, XVIII, 52. His *The Lepers of Molokai*

(1885) occasioned Stevenson's famous outburst on the subject of Father
Damien. I find it easy to confuse him with Richard Henry Stoddard,
one of whose fortes was Chinese poetry. See William Purviance Fenn,
"Richard Henry Stoddard's Chinese Poems," *American Literature,*
11(4): 417–38 (January 1940).

52. The historical work is *Memoirs of Arii Taimai E Marama of Eimeo
Teriirere of Tooarai Teriinui of Tahiti Tauraatua I Amo* (Paris, 1901).
I give the full title; it is better known as the *Memoirs of Marau Taa-
roa, Last Queen of Tahiti,* and Robert E. Spiller has republished it
(New York, 1947) under the more manageable name of *Tahiti.* For
Adams' immediate responses to Oceania and for the sentences and
phrases in the text consult *Letters of Henry Adams (1858–1891),* ed.
Worthington Chauncey Ford (Boston, 1930), Chapter XV; Harold Dean
Cater, ed., *Henry Adams and His Friends: A Collection of His Unpublished Letters* (Boston, 1947), pp. 197ff. ("The Samoans are . . . the
most attractive race I ever met"); Henry Adams, *Letters to a Niece*
(Boston, 1920), pp. 31–55; and the sympathetic account in Ernest Samuels, *Henry Adams: The Major Phase* (Cambridge, 1964), Chapter I.
Samuels notes Adams' "elaborate struggles of taste and conscience" in
respect to Mr. and Mrs. Stevenson and records that in the islands "he
fell back on the lowliest tourist resource, novel reading."

53. *Reminiscences of the South Seas,* (London, 1914), pp. 87, 92–93.

54. Louis Becke, the British author of *Pacific Tales,* who had some American vogue, occasioned this comment in *The (American) Bookman,* 6(1):
69–70 (September 1897): "The luxurious color and riotous vegetation of
the tropics form the background of these tales; and as onlookers, the
artist in the author has the power to make us quicken with sympathy
or sicken with disgust, as he unveils the wickedness, the weakness, the
crime existing alongside of the loveliness, the pathos, the strange, wild
beauty of life in the islands afar off in the South Seas. A weird spell
falls upon the reader when he comes under Mr. Becke's sway—a spell
that seems of the land, the atmosphere, the clime." This is a succinct
statement of the exotic appeal.

55. I find little "exotic" in Bayard Taylor's *Poems of the Orient* (1854),
William Alger's *Poetry of the East* (1856), and Charles Godfrey Leland's curiously awkward *Pidgin English Sing-Song* (1876). Stoddard's
Book of the East (1871) contains about fifteen "Chinese" songs, based
on English or French translations. But when one gets down to the days
of Florence Ayscough, Amy Lowell, and Vachel Lindsay ("The Chinese
Nightingale") one can make a case for Chinese exoticism.

56. Joseph Hergesheimer, *Java Head.* With an introduction by James D.
McCallum (New York, 1926) pp. xv, 25–26.

57. I do not mean there are no studies. Exoticism is, as I have said, a
subjective value. But see Arthur Christy, *The Asian Legacy and American Life* (New York, 1945); Earl Miner, *The Japanese Tradition in
British and American Literature* (Princeton, 1958); George H. Danton,

Culture Contacts of the United States and China (New York, 1931); and Clay Lancaster, *The Japanese Influence in America* (New York, 1963). Perhaps I should add two pamphlets edited by Walter C. Young, *Some Oriental Influences on Western Culture* (*Bulletin of the Institute of Pacific Relations*, New York, 1929). In "The Novelist Discovers the Orient," *The Far Eastern Quarterly*, 7(2): 165–75 (February 1948), Charles S. Braden lists novelists, but they seem to me not to be notably exotic.

58. Long's short story appeared in *The Century Magazine* for January 1898, Belasco's play was produced in March 1900, and Puccini's opera, composed in 1904, was given five performances by the Metropolitan Opera Company during its 1906–1907 season in New York.

59. The extraordinary place of the poster, notably in the 1890s, as a revolutionary force in pictorial art, is seldom thought of. But see Brander Matthews, "The Pictorial Poster," *The Century Magazine*, 44(5): 748–56 (September 1892); Arsène Alexandre, et al., *The Modern Poster* (New York, 1895) (contains a chapter on American posters with about thirty illustrations); *Les Maîtres de l'Affiche: Publication Mensuelle contenant la reproduction des plus belles affiches illustrées des grands artistes, français et étrangers*, 5 vols. (Paris, 1896–1900); *Posters in Miniature*, introduction by Edward Penfield, foreword by Percival Pollard (New York, 1896); *A Catalogue of Foreign and American Posters from the Collection of Mr. Ned Arden Flood* (Meadville, 1897); Charles Hiatt, *Picture Posters* (London, 1895); Charles Matlock Price, *Posters: A Critical Study of the Development of Poster Design in Continental Europe, England and America* (New York, 1913); E. McKnight Kauffer, *The Art of the Poster* (New York, 1925), a history of the poster from its European beginnings down to the 1920s, a good deal of emphasis being placed upon the Far East. American illustrators owing much to the poster and to Japanese elements in pictorialism include Jessie Wilcox Smith, Maxfield Parrish, F. X. Leyendecker, and Rockwell Kent. An amusing fusion of the vogue of the poster, Pre-Raphaelitism, and American humor is found in Carolyn Wells's poem, "The Poster Girl," who "leaned out / From a pinky-purple heaven; / One eye was red and one was green; / Her bang was cut uneven; / She had three fingers on her hand, / And the hairs on her head were seven." *Masterpieces of Wit and Humor*, Vol. IV (New York, 1903), pp. 148–49.

60. The first, in 2 volumes, was published in Boston in 1917; the second in Boston in 1885.

61. Fenollosa died in London in 1890. His literary executor was Ezra Pound.

62. The first is in Vera McWilliams, *Lafcadio Hearn* (Boston, 1946), pp. 131–32; the second was printed by Ray M. Lawless, "A Note on Lafcadio Hearn's Brother," *American Literature*, 10(1): 80–83 (March 1938).

63. *Shadowings* (Boston, 1900/1907), pp. 197–98.

64. On the trustworthiness of Hearn as an interpreter see Yone Noguchi,

Lafcadio Hearn in Japan (London and Yokohama, 1910); and Daniel Stempel, "Lafcadio Hearn: Interpreter of Japan," *American Literature*, 20(1): 1–19 (March 1948).

65. *Dramatic Verses* (Boston, 1902).

66. Pp. 38, 175. Note Taylor's delight in a chance-seen Circassian girl: ". . . a slight lurch of the steamer caused her to loose her hold on the garment, which, fastened at the neck, was blown back from her shoulders, leaving her body screened but by a single robe of light, gauzy silk. Through this, the marble whiteness of her skin, the roundness, the glorious symmetry of her form, flashed upon me, as a vision of Aphrodite . . . a momentary glimpse; yet that moment convinced me that forms of Phidian perfection are still nurtured in the vales of Caucasus" (pp. 156–57).

67. *Addresses of John Hay* (New York, 1906), pp. 45–50.

68. And in the American circus (after about 1820). Perhaps it had been there a long time.

69. "Araby," or the Saracens, or Mohammedanism occasioned novels such as Francis Marion Crawford's *Khaled: A Tale of Arabia* (1891), the dreamy verse of Arlo Bates's *Told in the Gates* (1892), and Nathan Haskell Dole's *Omar the Tentmaker* (1898).

70. Consult in this connection Clay Lancaster, *Architectural Follies in America* (Rutland and Tokyo, 1960).

Chapter VIII: Landscape and Microscope

1. This statement is from a pamphlet, *Stewart Edward White* by Eugene F. Saxton, apparently published by Doubleday, Page & Co., n.d.

2. Stewart Edward White, *The Blazed Trail* (New York, 1902), pp. 35–36, 311–12. Note also the first chapter devoted to a description of the pioneer (that is, the lumberer); resourceful, self-reliant, bold, "he presents to the world a picture of complete adequacy," his passions elemental, his pleasures orgiastic. It is characteristic of the Age of Energy that this picture concludes: "This is not the moment to judge him. And yet one cannot help admiring the magnificently picturesque spectacle of such energies running riot. The power is still in evidence, though beyond its proper application." Among the sentimental elements is a crippled boy who dies in the woods playing a love melody on his violin while the hero courts the heroine. But White is better than this concession to "romance," and belongs with Norris, Jack London, Hamlin Garland, and other celebrators of the West. I do not know why he is now neglected.

3. For a characteristic diatribe read Roosevelt's letter to George Bird Grinnell, then editor of *Forest and Stream,* protesting against Long's contribution to the magazine. "He writes about subjects that I know, that is, about large wild creatures; and his tales are simply preposterous. It is an outrage that such books should be admitted as having a proper place outside of libraries of avowed fiction." Letter 2640 in

Morison, *The Letters of Theodore Roosevelt*, III, 467–70. Teddy wrote from Gardiner, Montana, April 24, 1903.

4. The best edition of *The Mechanistic Conception of Life* is edited by Donald Fleming for The John Harvard Library Series (Cambridge, 1964). Fleming enriches the subject by his discussion of the scientific and philosophic origins of Loeb's *Weltanschauung*.

5. Loeb, *ed. cit.*, pp 5–6.

6. I greatly simplify. Though scientists were aware of Morgan's scientific papers before the book appeared, there is the famous case of two of them contradicting each other, but I assume that the book sets forth the considered theory.

7. See the edition edited by David Lowenthal for The John Harvard Library Series. Lowenthal notes various editions and translations, one in 1874 being retitled *The Earth as Modified by Human Action*. The third edition (1885) was reprinted in 1898 and 1907.

8. See the remarkable essay by Gilbert Chinard, "The American Philosophical Society and the Early History of Forestry in America," *The Proceedings of the American Philosophical Society*, 89:444–88 (1945).

9. *Man and Nature, ed. cit.*, "Preface" and Chapter I, *passim;* and pp. 464, 465.

10. It is, however, fatally easy to categorize minor nature-writers and poets as sentimental. Take, for example, Celia Thaxter, who later went in for theosophy and whose *An Island Garden* (1894) was illustrated by Childe Hassam. One of her poems, "A Trust," grim as anything in Crane's *The Black Riders*, tells of an iceberg moving irresistibly to find a ship it is destined to collide with and sink. For some reason this poem comforted Lieutenant (afterward General) A. W. Greely when he was trapped in the Arctic ice in 1881–1883. A student of Celia Thaxter writes: "The meaningless destruction of birds and flowers, shipwreck, drowning, the bereavement of women whose men have been lost at sea, all appear to her as evidence of an unfeeling, a mechanistic Nature. Often she sharpens the feeling by pointing the inexplicable contrast between benignant and malignant moods of nature." Life on the Isle of Shoals was at times as pagan as that in Iceland during the saga period. See Perry D. Westbrook, "Celia Thaxter's Controversy with Nature," *NEQ,* 20(4): 492–515 (December 1947).

11. I quote, however, from a revised and enlarged edition of 1874, though the Widener Library copy (New York, 1902) includes a preface to the *fourth* edition. References are to this edition. King's lively account of the Newtys of Pike in a chapter so titled anticipates twentieth-century accounts of the Okies, and I call attention as well to tributes to a fine horse ("Kaweah's Run"), to Cotter for saving King's life at the expense of his own, and to Western plainsmen and mountain men, who "strike out boldly and arrange the universe to suit themselves" (p. 350).

12. John Burroughs, *Writings*, 23 vols. (Boston, 1904–1922). References in the text are to volumes in this edition. Burroughs began publishing books in 1867, and there were 3 posthumous volumes.

13. It is interesting to quote Burroughs on the interplay of race and climate: "You cannot have a rank, sappy race, like the English or German, without plenty of moisture in the air and in the soil. Good viscera and an abundance of blood are closely related to meteorological conditions, unction of character, and a flow of animal spirits, too; and I suspect that much of the dry and rarefied humor of New England, as well as the thin and sharp physiognomies, are climatic results. We have rain enough, but not equability of temperature or moisture—no steady, abundant supply of humidity in the air." This first appeared in *Locusts and Wild Honey* (1870), and is in *Writings* IV, 77. Shades of Hippolyte Taine!

14. But this passage is followed two pages later by an appeal to humanism: "This alone, and this is enough: To love virtue, to love truth, to cherish a lofty ideal, to keep the soul open and hospitable to whatsoever things are true, to whatsoever things are beautiful, to whatsoever things are of good report." (VIII, 234). This is from *Indoor Studies* (1889).

15. In this same essay ("An Open Door") he waxed ironical about a clergyman who thanked God he was not wrecked on a train that went into the river. But why was the train wrecked at all? The only way God "interferes or takes a hand is through the eternal laws which He has established" (VIII, 231).

16. Burroughs has an essay entitled "Plenitude" in *Fresh Fields* (1884), his book on Great Britain, which includes this passage about herring on the Scottish coast: "The herrings appear in innumerable shoals, and are pursued by tens of thousands of birds in the air, and by the hosts of their enemies of the deep. Salmon and dog-fish prey upon them from beneath; gulls, gannets, cormorants, and solan geese prey upon them from above; while the fishermen from a vast fleet of boats scoop them up by the million. The birds plunge and scream, the men shout and labor, the sea is covered with broken and wounded fish, the shore exhales the odor of the decaying offal, which also attracts the birds and the vermin. . . . Yet the herring supply does not fail" (VI, 188–89). The passages, he says, owes something to *Natural History and Sport in Moray* by Charles St. John.

17. Two biographical studies should be consulted: William F. Badé, *The Life and Letters of John Muir*, 2 vols. (New York, 1923–1924), and Minnie Marsh Wolfe, *Son of the Wilderness: The Life of John Muir* (New York, 1945). Minnie Marsh Wolfe also edited *John of the Mountains: The Unpublished Journals of John Muir* (Boston, 1938). An amazing bundle of skills, Muir was an inventive mechanical genius who, in 1867, injured an eye while working in a wagon factory and decided to abandon the inventions of man to study "the inventions of God." He later became a successful horticulturalist in California. Then he sold his ranch at a profit, provided his family with money enough to live on, and took to a solitary life as a student of the wilderness. Charles S. Sargent, once director of the Arnold Arboretum in Boston,

was attracted to Muir; and in 1889 Robert Underwood Johnson of *The Century Magazine* at Muir's behest went to Yosemite to see the damage done by sheepherding. Propaganda by Muir, Johnson, Sargent, and others eventuated in the creation by Congress of the Yosemite National Park in 1890 on the model of Yellowstone National Park (but Muir was unsuccessful in preventing the damming of the Hetch-Hetchy Valley for a water reservoir). This group got a bill through Congress creating or re-creating (the facts are in dispute) a commission on forestry as well as a bill empowering the president to set aside public land as forest reserves. Cleveland created thirteen of them totaling about twenty-one million acres; efforts to reverse this policy failed. Theodore Roosevelt later added one hundred and forty-eight additional million acres, besides doubling the number of national parks and setting up a number of national monuments. In order to anticipate a bill ending the power of the president to create forest reserves in the West, a measure he felt compelled to sign, Roosevelt created or increased acreage for thirty-two forest reserves on March 2, 1907; four days later he signed the law that forbade him to do so. See Morison, *The Letters of Theodore Roosevelt*, V, 603–604.

18. Edited by William F. Badé, *The Writings of John Muir* (Sierra Edition) were published in 10 volumes in Boston, 1919–1924. My citations are from this. Five of Muir's volumes were posthumous. The relevant titles here are *The Mountains of California* (1894), *Our National Parks* (1901), *My First Summer in the Sierra* (1911), and *The Yosemite* (1912).

19. " 'What are rattlesnakes good for?' As if nothing that does not obviously make for the benefit of man had any right to exist; as if our ways were God's ways!" (VI, 64). This recalls the regret of the Reverend William Paley, who in the midst of a hymn to the felicity of the universe, yet paused to regret that the provision of venom for poisonous snakes had been overdone.

20. "If among the agents that nature has employed in making these mountains there be one that above all others deserves the name of Destroyer, it is the glacier. But we quickly learn that destruction is creation . . . it is just where the glaciers crushed most destructively that the greatest amount of beauty is manifest" (VI, 106). Note also Muir's celebration of rhythmical motion "chasing everything in endless song out of one beautiful form into another" (VI, 107). This reads like an idealist's gloss on Spencer.

21. The first is from an admirable popular history of the lumbering industry and forest conservation, Richard Gordon Lillard, *The Great Forest* (New York, 1947), p. 156. Lillard's chapter, "Baronies in the Making," is especially illuminating on the lumber kings, particularly on the career of Weyerhaeuser, the author noting that he came to see that the conservation of forests was economically sound. The second sentence is from an article on game laws by William Temple Hornaday, former director of the New York Zoological Park, in the 14th edition of the

Encyclopaedia Britannica, X, 4. "Unfortunately," Hornaday then wrote, "the American machinery for the destruction of American game is now so vast, so varied, and so uncontrollable, its momentum is so great, that it is a question whether it will be possible to curb its power, or reverse it before the end of the game supply is reached." Though his prophecy was too gloomy, he notes that in 1926 5,183,353 hunting licenses were issued in the United States, that modern firearms and the automobile had proved more deadly than the loss of forest cover, marshland, or lake, so far as game is concerned, and that hunters were themselves largely to blame for the disappearance, virtual or real, of game between 1909 and 1929.

22. These categories sometimes overlap, but in a general sense Yellowstone Park and the Grand Canyon are principally preserved as landscape, Verendrye Park in North Dakota and Fort McHenry in Baltimore are kept for their historical meaning, and Montezuma Castle in Arizona is, I infer, of primary interest to archaeologists and anthropologists, just as Katmai Park in Alaska ("The Valley of Ten Thousand Smokes"), though obviously picturesque, has continuing interest for geologists and seismologists. Scientific interests wax and wane. I assume for instance, that ethologists continue their interest in Sullys Hill, North Dakota, a wild animal preserve, but that arboriculturists and their kind have by this time found out about all they can from the Muir Woods in California. The original concept of the national park as a wilderness area is now so threatened by good roads, the automobile, the trailer, the speedboat, the ski tow, the snowmobile, and commercialized "sports," that mass recreation threatens to overwhelm it. See a set of articles in the *Atlantic Monthly*, especially that by Devereux Butcher, "Resorts or Wilderness," 207(2): 45–51 (February 1961).

23. I have in mind such books as John Dean Caton, *The Antelope and Deer of America* (New York, 1877); Richard Irving Dodge, *Hunting Grounds of the Great West* (London, 1877); Theodore Strong Van Dyke, *The Still-Hunter* (New York, 1883); various publications by Robert Barnwell Roosevelt, such as *Florida and the Game Water-Birds of the Atlantic Coast and the Lakes of the United States* (New York, 1884); and of course works by the political leader of the conservation movement, Theodore Roosevelt, of which *The Hunting Trips of a Ranchman* (New York, 1885) is representative. A professional magazine like *Forest and Stream*, of which George Bird Grinnell was long editor, was also influential. On hunting mazazines see the appropriate entries in Mott's *History of American Magazines*.

24. Bird protection laws suggested by Audubon societies were adopted by about thirty-nine states between 1895 and 1905, and the national society was influential in promoting the Migratory Bird Treaty Act of 1918. See in this connection Robert Henry Welker, *Birds and Men . . . 1800–1900* (Cambridge, 1955).

25. Fair chase excluded killing a bear or a cougar in a trap, "crusting" moose, elk, or deer in deep snow, or calling, "jacking," or killing them

from a boat while the animal was swimming, or using any other method than "fair stalking and still hunting."

26. The best history of the Boone and Crockett Club is James N. Trefethen, *Crusade for Wildlife: Highlights in Conservation Progress* (New York, 1961). I quote the constitution from the annual yearbook of the club.

27 The earliest such action by the federal government was setting aside one and one-half square miles around the hot springs of Arkansas in order that their healing properties should be a perpetual national possession. This was four years before Arkansas became a state (1836).

28. See W. Turrentine Jackson, "The Creation of Yellowstone National Park," *MVHR*, 29(2): 187–206 (September 1942); and Paul Herman Buck, *The Evolution of the National Park System of the United States*, U.S. Department of Agriculture, National Park Service (Washington, D.C., 1948).

29. The famous document is *Report on the Lands of the Arid Region of the United States with a More Detailed Account of the Lands of Utah*, 1878, 2nd edition 1879. Utah of course was already a well-organized commonwealth. Powell associated with himself in this report Captain C. E. Dutton of the U.S. Army, A. H. Thompson, Grove Earl Gilbert, and Willis Drumond, Jr., experts in geology or related topics. The report was submitted through J. A. Williamson, the U.S. Land Commissioner, to Carl Schurz, perhaps the first Secretary of the Interior to take conservation seriously, and by him sent to Congress, which on April 3, 1878, ordered the document printed.

30. A favorite device was to refuse, or cut down, appropriations needed to put conservation measures into effect on the pretense, not of course confined to Western representatives, of "economy." There were, it must be remembered, a handful of devoted Western senators and congressmen who saw the long-run necessity of conservation, just as there were Easterners who opposed such laws.

31. Because it came into the union after having been an independent republic, Texas offered special problems. The federal government had no public lands in that state.

32. Discussion of the public land policy is voluminous and I do not pretend to have mastered a tithe of the material. But I have found the following illuminating: Benjamin Horace Hibbard, *A History of the Public Land Policies*. This was first published in 1924 but is now available in a new printing by the University of Wisconsin Press (Madison, 1965) with a foreword by Paul W. Gates. Fred A. Shannon, "The Homestead Act and the Labor Surplus" and Paul W. Gates, "The Homestead Act in an Incongruous Land System" are in *American Historical Review*, 41(4): 637–81 (July 1936). See also Harold Hathaway Dunham, *Government Handout: A Study of the Administration of the Public Lands 1875–1891* (New York, 1941), and Roy M. Robbins, *Our Landed Heritage: The Public Domain, 1776 1936* (Ann Arbor, 1942). Aside from the remarkable opportunities for false entry, speculation,

conflict of claims, and inaccurate surveys offered by the several laws, the fundamental difficulty was that rectangular surveys into townships, sections, and quarter-sections, sufficient in the Middle West, proved wildly inapplicable to mountain country, arid lands, and desert regions. The concept of a homesteader simply did not work in many parts of the Great West. The extraordinary opportunities for fraud in the operation of the various laws governing homesteading after 1862 are grimly set forth in the Gates article on our incongruous land systems.

33. A random sampling of some leading names in the conservation movement, not all of them mentioned in the text, shows that Liberty Hyde Bailey was a graduate of Michigan State Agricultural College; F.V. Hayden was a graduate of Oberlin and of Albany Medical College; the impassioned William Temple Hornaday attended Oskaloosa College and Iowa State Agricultural College; John Muir attended the University of Wisconsin; Louis Hermann Pammel, distinguished botanist, was a graduate of Wisconsin and took his doctor's degree at Washington University, St. Louis; Theodore Roosevelt was a Harvard graduate; Charles R. Van Hise took his Ph.D. at Wisconsin; and Henry Wallace was a graduate of Jefferson (now Washington and Jefferson) College in Pennsylvania. There were of course self-educated men like W.J. McGee, but their number diminished. It is interesting also to note how many conservationists were sons of ministers, or thought of entering the ministry (some did), or attended strongly "church affiliated" schools, something that helps explain the high moral fervor of the movement. Carl Schurz, the first Secretary of the Interior to be "concerned," had been a student at the University of Bonn.

34. Although farmers often scorned theorists and instructors from agricultural colleges that came into being after the Morrill Act, in the long run scientific farming, particularly as taught in such patterns of instruction as the "short-course" unit at the University of Wisconsin, had its beneficial effects in the improvement of soil chemistry, proper fertilizers, proper drainage, proper ploughing, the rotation of crops, improved stock breeding, improved plant breeding, better sanitary standards, and the use of machinery in agriculture.

35. I emphasize that the Boone and Crockett Club is merely representative. In 1892 John Muir was instrumental in founding the Sierra Club, on which see Holway R. Jones, *John Muir and the Sierra Club: The Battle for the Yosemite* (San Francisco, 1965). George Oliver Shields, who created *Recreation,* an influential magazine of outdoor life in 1894, helped to found the League of American Sportsmen in 1898. William T. Hornaday, first director of the New York "Zoo," raised one hundred thousand dollars for a Permanent Wild Life Fund. The Isaac Walton League was (and is) another "concerned" association, and the Boy Scouts of America and the Camp Fire Girls are taught the elements of conservation.

36. Note the emphasis on "western" in this wording. Though the area had

not yet become a national park and forest, one can observe as typical the way forests were nibbled at if one reads the report of testimony before the committee of the California Assembly on Yosemite Valley and Mariposa Grove of Big Trees, published as *In the Matter of the Investigation of the Yosemite Valley Commissioners* (Sacramento, 1889). The famous Oregon land frauds, exposed in 1908–1909, simply repeat the pattern on a larger scale.

37. A "Dark Day" in New England (1870), a "Yellow Day" in 1881, and a "Smoky Day" in Ohio (1887) were all manifestations of huge forest fires.

38. I gather this information from appropriate pages in the *Proceedings of the American Association for the Advancement of Science* for 1874, 1875, 1889, 1891, and 1894.

39. A commission report of 1897, the commission being chaired by Charles S. Sargent of the Arnold Arboretum in Boston, found that the United States government was unable to protect the public domain "because the sentiment of the majority of the people in the public land States with regard to the public domain, which they consider the exclusive property of the people of those States and Territories, does not sustain the Government in its efforts to protect its own property, juries, when rare indictments can be obtained, almost invariably failing to convict depredators." It is also noted that civil employees were appointed for political reasons. Congress was continually torn between active pro-conservation sentiment in the East, and an irate West fighting every withdrawal. The Eastern people were better organized. E. Louise Peffer, *The Closing of the Public Domain; Disposal and Reservation Policies, 1900–1950* (Stanford, 1951), pp. 16–18.

40. I earlier noted Roosevelt's dramatic performance in adding millions of acres to the national forest reserves in thirty-three locations on March 2, 1907, under the act of 1891 just four days before he felt compelled to sign an act forbidding the creation by the president of any more forest reserves in Oregon, Washington, Idaho, Montana, Colorado, and Wyoming, and reserving the right to create such reserves to the Congress. His memorandum blithely said that failure on his part to do so would mean "that valuable timber would fall into the hands of the lumber syndicates before Congress has an opportunity to act." The West was furious, or at least Western wealth was furious, at this combination of the wisdom of the serpent and the blandness of the dove. See Morison, *The Letters of Theodore Roosevelt*, V, 603–604. For his invitation to the governors see *ibid.*, pp. 838–39; and for his summoning the Commission on the Conservation of Natural Resources, *ibid.*, VI, 1065–69.

41. Three important side-effects of the first National Conservation Conference were the creation of about forty-one state conservation commissions, besides commissions set up by various national organizations; the notion of regular meetings of state governors; and the calling of a North American Conservation Congress by Roosevelt, which met Feb-

ruary 18, 1909, and included representatives from Canada, Newfoundland, and Mexico. The passage and enforcement of such measures as laws governing migratory wild fowl were made easier by this conference.

42. *Report of the National Conservation Commission,* Senate Document No. 676, 60th Congress, 2nd Session, 3 vols. (Washington, D.C., 1909).

43. Van Hise's book has been called "the most concise and authoritative statement of the situation which the United States has faced in the care and use of its natural resources." In 1917 he was called upon by the United States Food Administration to get out a pamphlet, *Conservation and Regulation in the United States during the World War* (Washington, D.C., 1917). His original volume, which in a sense is the twentieth-century parallel to Marsh's *Man and Nature,* was reworked into unrecognizability under the editorship of Loomis Havemeyer as *Conservation of our Natural Resources: Based on Van Hise's The Conservation of Natural Resources in the United States* (New York, 1930). The various chapters in this are by specialists, and I have depended on them. But this is essentially a new book, not a new edition of Van Hise. Henry Clepper, ed., *Origins of American Conservation* (New York, 1966) is a useful brief anthology.

44. Arthur W. Page, "The Fight for Conservation," *World's Work,* 21:13607–10 (November 1910).

45. See J. Leonard Bates, " 'Fulfilling American Democracy': The Conservation Movement, 1907–1921," *MVHR,* 44(1): 29–57 (June 1957).

46. I say this despite reports by the Sierra Club of encroachments on the public domain. These seem to be more sporadic than the determined opposition before World War I.

47. For a later, more messianic interpretation see Lucy Sprague Mitchell, *et al., My Country 'Tis of Thee: The Use and Abuse of Natural Resources* (New York, 1940).

48. "The public land and the public water, in the form of fuel, power, timber, navigable streams, irrigable plains, and valuable minerals, have been so administered as to beget a confidence in the eternal bounty of nature and a habit of treating public property as a source of private fortune. . . . We are accustomed to think and to speak of America as a land of unlimited resources. Suddenly we are confronted with the appalling fact that these resources are, in fact, very limited and that the limit is in sight." John L. Mathews, "The Conservation of our Natural Resources," *Atlantic Monthly,* 101(5): 694–704 (May 1908).

49. The bases of astrophysics were laid earlier, but by 1890 it had become a major field of astronomy.

50. A distinguished astrophysicist and one of the founders of *The Astrophysical Journal,* Hale was also gifted with extraordinary mechanical talent and with wonderful administrative and diplomatic capacities. He was the first director of the Yerkes Observatory (built in 1892, dedicated in 1897), director of the Mount Wilson Observatory from 1904 to 1923, and the genius who drew up the central plan for the great

200-inch telescope eventually installed on Mount Palomar, though Hale would be the first to insist that he had been helped by others. See Helen Wright, *Explorer of the Universe: A Biography of George Ellery Hale* (New York, 1966).

51. For example, the noted Scotch preacher, the Reverend Thomas Chalmers (1780–1847), used to fill the great Tron Church in Glasgow by a set of sermons later printed as *Astronomical Discourses* or, more frequently, *Discourses on the Christian Revelation Viewed in Connection with Astronomy*, which were widely read in America, editions being available in this country from 1817 through 1871. Despite the title, Chalmers' lectures demonstrated to the satisfaction of readers and hearers that the glories of God could be seen not only through the telescope but also through the microscope.

52. Among various histories of the microscope I find S. Bradbury, *The Evolution of the Microscope* (Oxford, 1967) most satisfactory. But see the papers collected in S. Bradbury and G. L'E. Turner, *Historical Aspects of Microscopy. Papers Read at a One-Day Conference held by the Royal Microscopical Society at Oxford, 18 March, 1966* (Cambridge, England, 1967).

53. Gates was professor of microscopy, histology, and embryology at Cornell University and the New York State Veterinary College at Ithaca. So far as I can make out, this standard manual dates from his *Notes on Microscopical Methods* (Ithaca, 1886–1887). Instrument makers did not lag behind. Edward Bausch published for Bausch and Lomb his *Manipulation of the Microscope* in 1891; and a catalogue of that firm, *Microscopes and Accessories*, issued in 1900, proudly says they have made and sold over thirty thousand compound microscopes and thousands of dissecting microscopes. In this catalogue the simplest "Continental" microscope sold for from fourteen dollars to twenty-seven dollars, and instruments intended for research cost from one hundred and twenty dollars to two hundred and seven dollars.

54. See the sketch of Ward's career in *DAB*, XIX, 435–36. He was one of the first to demonstrate microscopically differences in the cellular structure of blood.

55. The difficulty in getting people to regard the microscope as more than an elegant toy was real, and so for a time was the hope that the microscope would not prove antireligious. In the first number of the *American Microscopic Journal*, pp. 28ff., there is an address to the national microscopic society saying: "We are brought together by an enthusiasm almost unknown in any other branch of science. . . . We are stimulated by the study of these little things which lead a philosopher to call God great in great things, greatest in the smallest."

56. *A Century of Science in America with Special Reference to the American Journal of Science* (New Haven, 1918). The several chapters are by specialists, Chapter XII, "A Century of Zoology in America," being by Wesley R. Coe. In the 50th volume, looking back on the history of the magazine, the elder Silliman had written: "In the retrospect,

we realize a sober but grateful feeling of satisfaction, in having, to the extent of our power, discharged these self-imposed obligations. This feeling is chastened also by a deep sense of gratitude, first to God for life and power continued for so high a purpose; and next, to our noble band of contributors . . ." (p. 37). Modern editors, it is needless to say, do not use this vocabulary. It is relevant in this context to call attention to Marston Bates, *The Nature of Natural History* (New York, 1950), a book that defines the naturalist "as one who studies the phenomena of life as shown by whole organisms." But since it is difficult to find a universal genius who can cope with all the specialisms, while admitting that "the word 'naturalist' has got rather into academic disrepute in recent years" because it has come to mean a mere nature lover, Bates refers "naturalist" to a point of view, which he leaves rather undefined.

57. In a paper, "Present Problems in Evolution and Heredity," *Annual Report of the Smithsonian Institution for 1893* (Washington, D.C., 1894), pp. 313–74.

58. "Some Aspects in Modern Biology," *Annual Report of the Smithsonian Institution for 1915* (Washington, D.C., 1916), p. 395.

59. I have been guided by such surveys as Erik Nordenskiöld, *The History of Biology* (originally published in 1929), new issue, trans. Leonard Bucknall Eyre (New York, 1935); William A. Locy, *Biology and its Makers,* 3d ed. rev. (New York, 1930); Emmanuel Radl, *The History of Biological Theories,* trans. E. J. Hatfield (London, 1930); L. C. Dunn, ed., *Genetics in the 20th. Century: Essays on the Progress of Genetics during its First 50 Years* (New York, 1951); Raymond N. Doetsch, *Microbiology* (New Brunswick, 1960), a symposium; and M. J. Sirks and Conway Zirkle, *The Evolution of Biology,* trans. (New York, 1964).

60. Let the interested reader look up the accounts,. among others, of Hermann M. Briggs, Calvin B. Bridges, Francis Delafield, Edward M. East, William J. Farlow, Reginald H. Fitz, Alpheus Hyatt, Charles S. Minot, Thomas H. Montgomery, Roland Muller, Hideyo Noguchi, Thomas Schickel Painter, Alfred Sturtevant, Roland Thaxter, and Charles S. Whitman, representative instances only, in the *DAB* or elsewhere, if he wishes to learn how microscopy transformed research in many fields.

61. I have derived much illumination from a series of essays and reviews by Ernst Mayr—his contributions to *Boston Studies in the Philosophy of Science,* and to the *Journal of the History of Biology;* "Footnotes on the Philosophy of Biology," *Philosophy of Science,* 36(2): 197–202 (June 1969), and "Introduction to the Role of Systematics in Biology," in *Systematic Biology* (Washington, D.C., 1969). This last is a record of the proceedings of an international conference held by the National Academy of Sciences, and the statement about the two biologies is on p. 125.

62. My statement about Young must not be understood as dismissing him as a "mere" popularizer. On the contrary he had a distinguished career in solar astronomy and astrophysics.

63. Often misquoted as "lighthouses in the skies." The phrase comes from Adams' first annual message to Congress in 1825.

64. But the "bad" image had its offset in Sherlock Holmes and his literary descendants using magnifying glass and microscopic analysis for beneficial ends.

65. This important letter was called to my attention by Professor I. Bernard Cohen of Harvard and appears in Howard Mumford Jones and I. Bernard Cohen, eds., *A Treasury of Scientific Prose. A Nineteenth-Century Anthology* (Boston, 1965), pp. 9–10.

66. In book form the *Autobiography* was apparently first issued in 1913, but the bibliography is complicated, and the first edition is sometimes thought to be that of 1919. I quote from Vol. XX of the National Edition of Roosevelt's *Works* (New York, 1925), pp. 26–27.

67. I quote from an American edition (New York, 1896), p. 313.

68. The preface is unsigned. The book was published in Cambridge, 1937. Malinowski at least remarks: "If anthropology is to become the comparative science of cultures, it is high time it stepped out of its herodotage [the improbable stories in Herodotus] and anecdotage. It must turn to the fundamentals of human culture, in simple and complex, primitive and highly developed forms alike" (p. 155). This is admirable, but self-consciously living with a primitive tribe to take notes on its behavior is not quite what Thoreau had in mind when he wrote in *Walden:* "Every morning was a cheerful invitation to make my life of equal simplicity, and I may say innocence, with Nature herself."

Chapter IX: From Harrison to Havana

1. Nevins' *A Day in Venice,* published in 1898, was bound in purple covers with silver lettering, and the packaging included free doilies for the table. Here as elsewhere I am indebted to Arthur M. Schlesinger, Sr., *The Rise of the City, 1878–1898.*

2. I give the official title of the song, but as sung by Eva Tanguay it came out as "Ta-Ra-Ra-Boom-De-Aye." Sigmund Spaeth, *Read 'Em and Weep* (Garden City, 1926) is a collection of songs of the period—and others. See also appropriate passages in Arthur Loesser, *Men, Women & Pianos* (New York, 1954). There are various phonograph records of songs of the 1890s.

3. The best succinct discussion of ragtime I have seen is that in Chapter XXI of Gilbert Chase's invaluable *America's Music: From the Pilgrims to the Present.*

4. Richard Harding Davis, *Soldiers of Fortune* (New York, 1897), p. 48.

5. Albert F. McLean, Jr., *American Vaudeville as Ritual* (Lexington, 1965) strives to give this lost art both a sociological and a psychological meaning.

6. On the minstrel show see Dailey Paskman and Sigmund Spaeth, *"Gentlemen, Be Seated!" A Parade of the Old-Time Minstrelsy* (Garden City, 1928).

7. The list of best sellers and better sellers I find in Frank Luther Mott, *Golden Multitudes: The Story of Best Sellers in the United States* (New York, 1947), pp. 311–24. My instances are representative only. Needless to remark, what I have to say about magazines is gleaned from Mott's *A History of American Magazines.* The passage from William Archer is in Mott, IV, 7.

8. My history of athletics is based on Frank G. Menke, *The Encyclopedia of Sports,* as revised by Roger Treat, 4th ed. (South Brunswick, 1969). This monumental work should be better known. A brief history is Herbert Manchester, *Four Centuries of Sport in America, 1490–1890* (New York, 1931), which, however, emphasizes hunting and fishing.

9. David H. Dickason's *The Daring Young Men: The Story of the American Pre-Raphaelites* seems to me to show that the connection between the American Pre-Raphaelites and the *fin-de-siècle* movement was tenuous. I draw the same inference from Roger Breed Stein, *John Ruskin and Aesthetic Thought in America, 1840–1900,* an important distinguishing difference being the Ruskinian emphasis on social responsibility and moralism.

10. Two standard treatments are Albert Parry, *Garrets and Pretenders: A History of Bohemianism in America,* 3d ed., rev. (New York, 1963) and Harry Levin's more incisive "The Discovery of Bohemia," Chapter 64 of *The Literary History of the United States.* Parry finds reflections of an American Bohemia in Charles de Kay, *The Bohemian: A Tragedy of Modern Life* (1878), Robert W. Chambers' *In the Quarter* (1894), Howells' *The Coast of Bohemia* (1893), and Henry Blake Fuller, *Under the Skylights* (1901), a collection of tales. I have not been able to see the Chambers novel, but Charles de Kay's novelette is mostly melodrama, Howells stays on the coast of Bohemia but never goes beyond it, and I fail to find much in the Fuller tales. I suspect the common American attitude was that expressed by Wetmore, a character in *The Coast of Bohemia* (pp. 216–17): "We Americans are too innocent in our traditions and experiences; our Bohemia is a non-alcoholic, unfermented condition. When it is diluted down to the apprehension of an American girl it's no better, or no worse, than a kind of Arcadia." Most magazines with "Bohemian" in their titles quickly perished, and The Bohemians of San Francisco has become a highly respectable club for business and professional men.

11. It can of course be said that Nordau is simply re-enforcing the doctrine of "Newyorkitis" I have earlier noticed.

12. *Regeneration* (New York, 1896), pp. iii–xii. The book was really by Alfred Egmont Hake.

13. Lloyd Lewis and Henry Justin Smith's amusing *Oscar Wilde Discovers America* (New York, 1936) fails to reveal that Wilde created many disciples, and the commentaries dredged up by these writers from magazines and newspapers of the 1880s are principally derisory. Satire sometimes indicates that a personality creates a lasting influence, but does not necessarily prove the creation of a cultural or literary movement.

14. Carlin T. Kindilien, *American Poetry in the Eighteen Nineties* (Providence, 1956), a work of amazing patience, tells us that the Harris collection of poetry at Brown University contains more than two thousand four hundred volumes of verse of all kinds printed in the 1890s. Kindilien divides these into (a) the continuing tradition; (b) the new traditionalism; (c) the poet-critics of society and religion; and (d) Whitman and the Vagabondians. Chief among the Vagabondians are Bliss Carman, a Canadian, and Richard Hovey. Hovey worked hard for a while at being picturesque and dressed at one period in the knee breeches and buckled shoes of Oscar Wilde fame. At some distance from Carman and Hovey are Maurice Thompson, Henry R. Remson, and the exiguous Francis Saltus, "standing," says Kindilien warily, "as a pathetic example of what the Poe tradition experienced." As Kindilien also observes that Saltus "never escaped the tone of the boy who expected any moment to be caught smoking behind the barn," I cannot take Francis Saltus seriously as a representative aesthete or decadent. In verse his brother Edgar never got much beyond the literary wickedness of "Beautiful as an uncommitted sin/ You stood before me" (*Poppies and Mandragora*, New York, 1926, p. 18). This volume runs to only fifty-seven pages, and all the poems from p. 33 to the end are by Marie Saltus.
15. Mario Amaya, *Art Nouveau* (London, 1966) is a useful handbook.
16. The best study is by Claire Sprague, *Edgar Saltus* (New York, 1968).
17. *Imperial Purple* (New York, 1892), p. 49.
18. William Dean Howells, "The Laureate of Death," *Atlantic Monthly*, 56(335): 311–22 (September 1885). Long quotations from De Sanctis and a translation of Leopardi by Howells make up much of this undistinguished article, which was collected into *Modern Italian Poets: Essays and Versions* (New York, 1887). W. N. Guthrie, "Leopardi and Evolutional Pessimism," *The Sewanee Review*, 4(2): 129–52 (February 1896) is a catch-all essay, concluding with a long translation. New York editions of the poems in translation appeared in 1887 and 1904, and the *Essays, Dialogues, and Thoughts of Leopardi* in New York and London in 1905. Discussions of Leopardi are surprisingly scanty, though I have not of course exhausted all the magazines.
19. Typical is Walter Caldwell, "Von Hartmann's Moral and Social Philosophy: I. The Positive Ethic. II. The Metaphysics," *The Philosophical Review*, 8(5): 465–83 and 8(6): 588–603 (September–November 1899). Caldwell also wrote an excellent book on Schopenhauer. This essay is clear-headed and unexpectedly sympathetic. Caldwell finds von Hartmann's attitude to be this: "It was an illusion for me to think that I would some day find myself happy . . . an illusion that I allowed myself for some time to think that the development of the world must be *towards something,* and that my working *with* that process would accomplish a result of some sort" (p. 481). He finds von Hartmann's fundamental difficulty to lie in his confusing three meanings of the "Unconscious": (1) the unconscious in nature and history; (2) the unconscious as desire; (3) the unconscious as evil (failure, illusion, suf-

fering, etc., whether positive or negative). But Caldwell praises the German for recognizing the necessity of a metaphysic of ethics, and, like Royce, thinks that God needs our help. Apparently von Hartmann does not think so.

20. This passage is found in the eloquent presentation of Schopenhauer's thought by Josiah Royce in *The Spirit of Modern Philosophy* (Boston, 1892), Lecture VIII.

21. Gamaliel Bradford, Jr., "The American Pessimist," *Atlantic Monthly*, 69(413): 363–67 (March 1892); G. Koerner, "Schopenhauer, the Man and the Philosopher," *Open Court*, 8(339): 3983–89 (February 22, 1894); William Morton Payne, "The Philosophy of Schopenhauer," *The Dial*, 22(255): 115–18 (February 16, 1897); Edgar Saltus, "What Pessimism Is Not," *Lippincott's Magazine*, 43: 594–97 (April 1889); *The Outlook*, 61.1(7): 393–95 (February 18, 1899). W. R. Tuttle in "Does Education Produce Pessimists?", *The Arena*, 21(3): 385–89 (March 1899), traced the appeal of pessimism to the laissez-faire doctrines and rationalist systems taught in the universities, and urged educated men to throw themselves into the midst of social movements, thus anticipating the contemporary demand for "relevance." Various books by or about Schopenhauer received intelligent reviews in magazines like *The Nation*. But I think the instances I have selected fairly represent the spectrum of opinion. Virtually no critic or reviewer but objected to the basic assumption of Schopenhauer that life is pain and only pain.

22. Not only *The Chap-Book* and its kind but more standard periodicals, such as *The Atlantic*, *The (American) Bookman*, *The Cosmopolitan*, *The Critic*, *The Dial*, *Harper's Monthly*, *Poet-Lore*, and *Scribner's*, among others, published essays and reviews on Baudelaire, Mallarmé, Verlaine, Maeterlinck, D'Annunzio, Fogazzaro, Huysmans, Ibsen, Strindberg, and German representatives of aestheticism, decadence, and so forth. Arthur Symons printed his influential "The Decadent Movement in Literature" in *Harper's*, 87(522): 858–67 (November 1893). Nor should one forget books; for example, James Gibbons Huneker, after a self-conscious career as a young *bon vivant*, brought out *Mezzotints in Modern Music* in 1899, the first of a readable and perhaps influential library of gossip and criticism, which, however, even the admiring H. L. Mencken characterized as "florid and baroque." In his first book Huneker let it be understood that he had known Flaubert, Hugo, Brandes, Shaw, Ibsen, Maeterlinck, Strindberg, and others. Surprising things turn up. Thus, in an introduction to Stuart Merrill's translations from the French, *Pastels in Prose* (New York, 1890), William Dean Howells remarks: "What struck me most was that apparently none of them [that is, the French poets translated] had abused his opportunity to saddle his reader with a moral. He had expressed his idea, his emotion, and then left it to take its chance in a way very uncommon in English verse. . . ." Less surprising is the appearance of Richard Hovey as a translator of Maeterlinck: *The Princess Maleine, The Intruder, The Blind,* and *The Seven Princesses* in 1894, and *Alladine and Palom-*

ides, Pelléas and Mélisande, Home, and *The Death of Tintagiles* in 1896. Both collections were published by Stone and Kimball in Chicago. Hovey calls Maeterlinck a poet of the sepulchre, like Poe. On "little magazines" consult Frederick J. Hoffman, Charles Allen, and Carolyn F. Ulrich, *The Little Magazine: A History* (Princeton, 1946). Two amusing articles are Claude Bragdon, "The Purple Cow Period: The 'Dinkey Magazines' that Caught the Spirit of the 'Nineties'," *The (American) Bookman,* 69(5): 475–78 (July 1929), and Carolyn Wells, "What A Lark!" in *The Colophon,* Part Eight (1931). The Wells article reproduces various things from *The Lark,* which was edited by Bruce Porter and Gelett Burgess. The latter wrote for it under a variety of pseudonyms, a fact that suggests caution about the influence of magazines.

23. The distinction is that between the vogue of Schopenhauer and his kind as an intellectual fashion among the avant garde and others, and his influence on the thought of persons as mature as Royce, Santayana, Lester Frank Ward, and William James.

24. *The Education of Henry Adams,* pp. 288–89. Note that Adams retained this intimate confession in all editions of the book.

25. Most of these passages are too familiar to require identification, but these and others can be found in E. P. Aldrich, *As William James Said: A Treasury of His Work* (New York, 1942), or in Ralph Barton Perry, *The Thought and Character of William James,* 2 vols. (Boston, 1935).

26. For example, Peter Fuss, *The Moral Philosophy of Josiah Royce* (Cambridge, 1965).

27. Royce, *et al., The Conception of God* (New York, 1897), pp. 47–48; Royce, *Studies of Good and Evil: A Series of Essays upon Problems of Philosophy and of Life* (New York, 1898), p. 23; *The Spirit of Modern Philosophy,* pp. 463–64. In his life of Royce in the *DAB,* XVI, 205–11. Ralph Barton Perry says that in effect Royce's position came to be: if science postulates simplicity and order, why should not religion postulate goodness at the heart of things? Goodness, however, has to be fought for against great odds.

28. The subtitle originally read: "An Economic Study of the Evolution of Institutions," but this was changed to "An Economic Study of Institutions." The earlier one is preferable in emphasizing the determinism in Veblen's philosophy.

29. One must distinguish between the peculiarities of his private life and his ethical assumptions.

30. The standard study is Joseph Dorfman, *Thorstein Veblen and his America* (New York, 1934), but see also the excellent chapter, "The Amoral Moralist" in Morton White, *Social Thought in America* (New York, 1949). It is fair to note that Veblen's later books are less somber in tone.

31. *The Theory of the Leisure Class* (New York, 1912), p. 18.

32. My summary is based on the great edition, Albert G. Keller and Maurice R. Davie, eds., *Essays of William Graham Sumner,* 2 vols. (New

Haven, 1934), most of them written between 1883 and 1913. I have particularly used "The Forgotten Man" (1883), "Strikes and Industrial Organization" (1887), "Liberty and Responsibility" (1889–1890), "The Absurd Effort to Make the World Over" (1894), "Earth Hunger" (1896), "The Power and Beneficence of Capital" (1899), "Purposes and Consequences" (1900?), "The Bequests of the Nineteenth Century to the Twentieth" (1901), "War" (1903), and "The Mores of the Present and the Future" (1909), but the essays are very much of a piece. *Folkways* (1907) is probably Sumner's most enduring book.

33. Republished in facsimile with editorial comment by George Monteiro as *Poems (1890–1896) by Emily Dickinson* in the Scholars' Facsimiles & Reprints series (Gainesville, 1967). Mr. Monteiro does justice to the fine intelligence of Thomas Wentworth Higginson in introducing the first volume and in writing critical essays on the poet. Higginson was aware of Emily's anfractuosities, but he did yeoman service in readying the reader's mind to take in "poems . . . of extraordinary grasp and insight, uttered with an uneven vigor sometimes exasperating, seemingly wayward, but really unsought and inevitable. After all, when a thought takes one's breath away, a lesson on grammar seems an impertinence." ("Preface," *Poems*, Boston, 1890).

34. Anna Mary Wells, "Early Criticism of Emily Dickinson," *American Literature*, 1(3): 243–59 (November 1929) is rather unsatisfactory.

35. The Dartmouth poems are collected in *Dartmouth Lyrics*, with an introduction by Francis Lane Childs (Hanover, 1938). Hippies would not, I fear, find the *Songs from Vagabondia* "relevant."

36. William Sturgis Bigelow, *Buddhism and Immortality* (Boston, 1908). This was one of the Ingersoll lectures on immortality and, becoming mildly notorious, was reprinted three times in one year. The standard biography of Lodge is Henry Adams, *The Life of George Cabot Lodge* (Boston, 1911). To the posthumous *Poems and Dramas*, 2 vols. (Boston, 1911), Theodore Roosevelt contributed an introduction that speaks of the poet's "abounding vigor . . . his veins thrilling with eager desire, his eyes fronting the future with dauntless and confident hope." This at least corrects the view that Lodge was a soul-mate of Leopardi. It is a commentary on the fading of repute that Lodge's name does not appear in the index of the standard *Literary History of the United States*.

37. *Poems* (New York, 1925).

38. George W. Howgate, *George Santayana* (Philadelphia, 1938), p. 72. Santayana's *Interpretations of Poetry and Religion* (New York, 1900) throws light on his general intention in *Lucifer*.

39. See Thomas Riggs, Jr., "Prometheus, 1900," *American Literature*, 22(4): 399–423 (January 1951). Riggs argues that the Prometheus figure reflects the point of view that came to Henry Adams in the Hall of Dynamo at the Paris Exposition. Perhaps.

40. Although I find Pandora's song central, in a letter to Mrs. Daniel Gregory Mason, who thought *The Masque of Judgment* "destructive," Moody wrote: "For me the kernel of the thing was Raphael's humanis-

tic attitude and Uriel's philosophy, especially his 'confession of faith' in Act III, Scene ii." Daniel Gregory Mason, ed., *Some Letters of William Vaughn Moody* (Boston, 1913). The best current study of Moody is Martin Halpern, *William Vaughn Moody* (New York, 1964).

41. James Reeves and Sean Haldane, eds., *Homage to Trumbull Stickney* (London, 1968). The introduction is informed and sensitive.

42. The one "public" collection of Stickney, aside from the *Homage* of 1968, is *The Poems of Trumbull Stickney*, eds. George Cabot Lodge, William Vaughn Moody, and John Ellerton Lodge (Boston, 1905). Stickney's turgid, though impressive, sonnet, "Be still. The Hanging Gardens were a dream," still lingers in some anthologies.

43. Even in the mechanistic *What Is Man?* by Mark Twain the Old Man, who is presumably instructing the Young Man in his duties as a victim of the Moral Sense, urges him: "Diligently train your ideals *upward* and *still upward* toward a summit where you will find your chiefest pleasure in conduct which, while contenting you, will be sure to confer benefits upon your neighbor and the community." This compound of Adam Smith and the Golden Rule is ludicrous when posited of a machine.

44. One must take this threat seriously. Not only was waving the bloody shirt a favorite rhetorical device North and South, but the success in 1876–1877 of the Red Shirts, a South Carolina paramilitary organization, in intimidating Negro voters and eventually forcing the inauguration of Wade Hampton as governor and white supremacy as a policy, seemed ominous to many, and there were armed forces like the Red Shirts in other Southern states. In *Road to Reunion* Paul Buck describes a cartoon in *Harper's Weekly* (1871) picturing an opossum playing dead, a man poking its ribs, and Jefferson Davis whispering: "Don't you be afraid; that animal ain't dead. Just wait and see." Buck does justice to the distemper of the 1870s. See him, pp. 74ff.

45. Philip D. Jordan, *Ohio Comes of Age: 1873–1900*, (Columbus, 1943), an invaluable study, which is Vol. V of the *History of the State of Ohio*, 6 vols., edited by Carl Wittke for the Ohio State Archaeological and Historical Society. Jordan's fifth and sixth chapters are especially good.

46. Mark Holloway, *Heavens on Earth: Utopian Communities in America, 1680–1880* (London, 1951) is a good survey. For California see Robert V. Hine, *California's Utopian Colonies* (San Marino, 1953). On the Georgia enterprise consult Ralph Albertson, "The Christian Commonwealth in Georgia," *The Georgia Historical Quarterly*, 29(3): 125–42 (September 1945). In "Social Utopias in American Literature," *International Review for Social History* (1938), pp. 287–300, J. F. Normanno concludes that the triumph of capitalism in the United States put an end to communal social experimentation. He lists Utopian fiction, but his list should be supplemented by Allyn B. Forbes, "The Literary Quest for Utopia, 1880–1900," *Journal of Social Forces*, 6(2): 179–89 (December 1927), and Robert L. Shurter, "The Utopian Novel in Amer-

ica, 1888–1900," *South Atlantic Quarterly*, 34(2): 137–44 (April 1935). The Mormons are of course a special case.

47. Though not fiction, Gronlund's *The Cooperative Commonwealth* (Boston, 1894) perhaps belongs here. The quotation from the text is from p. 6 of the first edition.

48. For the National Commission on Law Observance and Enforcement Sam B. Warner prepared a *Survey of Criminal Statistics in the United States* (Washington, D.C., 1951), but even at that late date he said that for many states and parts of states no statistics exist or, if they do, are incompatible with each other. In *A Critique of Federal Criminal Statistics* published in the same way Morris Ploscowe remarked that "for 80 years the Federal Government has been publishing criminal statistics which are inadequate." My statements in the text are therefore impressionistic. Most books about crime published from 1865 to 1915 are anecdotal or lurid or both. An example is Part II, "Satan's Invisible World Displayed," in William T. Stead's notorious *If Christ Came to Chicago* (Chicago, 1894). The curious may care to look into the anonymous *Boston By-Ways to Hell* (Boston, 1867) and Edward Crapsey's *The Nether Side of New York; or, the Vice, Crime and Poverty of the Great Metropolis* (New York, 1872). Riis's classic studies deal principally with poverty. There are of course the annual reports of the National Prison Association, which begin in 1884 (there were previous volumes in 1872, 1874, and 1877), and such *ad hoc* studies as the report of the Vice Commission of the City of Chicago, *The Social Evil in Chicago* (Chicago, 1911). But it takes somebody more expert than I am to make much sense out of the national picture.

49. Josiah Flynt (Willard), *Tramping with Tramps* (New York, 1899), *Notes of an Itinerant Policeman* (Boston, 1900), *The World of Graft* (New York, 1901), and *The Little Brother: A Story of Tramp Life* (New York, 1902); Walter A. Wyckoff, *The Workers: The East* (New York, 1897), and *The Workers: The West* (New York, 1898), illuminate the fear of the hobo and the itinerant worker generally.

50. Of the innumerable studies of agrarian grievances I have found Chapter IX, "The Restless Farmers" in H. Wayne Morgan, *From Hayes to McKinley: National Party Politics, 1877–1896* (Syracuse, 1969) graphic and useful.

51. Populism is here loosely used to include movements like the Farmers' Alliance and the People's Party as well as the fusion of "radical" economic theory, racial and religious distrust, agrarian conservatism, and Bible-belt psychology which, if it had its principal expression in the Populist platforms, strongly influenced the platforms of the two major parties. In "The Populist Heritage and the Intellectual," *The American Scholar*, 29(1): 55–72 (Winter 1959–1960), C. Vann Woodward gives a shrewd appraisal of current interpretations of this movement, pointing out how widespread it was in the South. Concerning that area, amid the rich historical literature on Populism, I have found the following items useful: Charles E. Otken, *The Ills of the South* (New

York, 1894), which calls the credit system ominous and the future dark; Benjamin B. Kendrick, "Agrarian Discontent in the South: 1880–1890," *Annual Report of the American Historical Association for the Year 1920*, pp. 267–72; Daniel M. Robinson, "From Tillman to Long: Some Striking Leaders of the Rural South," *Journal of Southern History*, 3(3): 289–310 (August 1937); Herbert J. Doherty, Jr., "Voices of Protest from the New South, 1875 1910," *MVHR*, 42(1): 45–66 (June 1955). On individual states: John Bunyan Clark, *Populism in Alabama, 1874–1896* (Auburn, 1927); Alex Mathews Arnett, "The Populist Movement in Georgia," *Studies in History, Economics and Public Law*, 104(1), whole number 235, Columbia University (New York, 1922), and C. Vann Woodward, *Tom Watson, Agrarian Rebel* (New York, 1938); Melvin J. White, "Populism in Louisiana during the Nineties," *MVHR*, 5(1): 5–19 (June 1918); Simeon Alexander Delap, "The Populist Party in North Carolina," *Historical Papers published by the Trinity College Historical Society*, Vol. XIV (Durham, 1922); John D. Hicks, "The Farmers' Alliance in North Carolina," *North Carolina Historical Review*, 2(2): 162–87 (April 1925); Clarence Poe, "L. L. Polk: A Great Agrarian Leader in a Fifty-Year Perspective," *South Atlantic Quarterly*, 41(4): 405–15 (October 1942) (Polk was a North Carolinian); Francis Butler Simkins, *Pitchfork Ben Tillman, South Carolinian* (Baton Rouge, 1944); J. H. Easterby, "The Granger Movement in South Carolina," *Proceedings of the South Carolina Historical Association* (1931), pp. 21–32; Gustavus G. Williamson, Jr., "South Carolina Cotton Mills and the Tillman Movement," in *ibid.* (1949), pp. 36–49; Daniel Merritt Robison, *Bob Taylor and the Agrarian Revolt in Tennessee* (Chapel Hill, 1935); Roscoe C. Martin, *The People's Party in Texas: A Study in Third Party Politics*, University of Texas Bulletin 3308 (Austin, February 22, 1933); William Dubose Sheldon, *Populism in the Old Dominion: Virginia Farm Politics, 1885–1900* (Princeton, 1935). The classic study is John D. Hicks, *The Populist Revolt: a History of the Farmers' Alliance and the People's Party*. I am thus detailed about the South because of the supposition, still prevalent, that the movement was mainly Western.

52. From the "Preamble" to the platform adopted at the first national convention of the People's Party at Omaha, July 4, 1892, said to have been written by Ignatius Donnelly. See Walter Rideout, "Introduction" to his edition of *Caesar's Column* (Cambridge, 1960), pp. x–xi.

53. G. W. Steevens, *The Land of the Dollar*, p. 204.

54. Basic studies are Theodore Schroeder, *Free Speech for Radicals* (New York, 1912); Eunice Minette Schuster, *Native American Anarchism*, Smith College Studies in History, Vol. XVII (Northampton, 1932); and James J. Martin, *Men Against the State: The Expositors of Individualist Anarchism in America, 1837–1908* (De Kalb, 1953).

55. An important case was that of U.S. *v* Workingmen's Amalgamated Council of New Orleans *et al.* (1893), in which the decision held that labor organizations came under the phrase "or otherwise" in the Four-

teenth Amendment. The decision read in part: "It is conceded that the labor organizations were at the outset lawful. But when lawful forces are put into unlawful channels—i.e. when lawful associations adopt and further unlawful purposes and do unlawful acts—the associations themselves become unlawful. The evil, as well as the unlawfulness of the act of the defendants, consists in this: that, until certain demands of theirs were complied with, they endeavored to prevent, and did prevent, everybody from moving the commerce of the country. . . . One of the intended results of their combined action was the forced stagnation of all the commerce which flowed through New Orleans." The reader will note the overshadowing influence of the doctrine of conspiracy. See for this and excerpts from other documents of the period, Robert Birley, ed., *Speeches and Documents in American History*, 4 vols. (London, 1942–1943), Vol. III, especially pp. 174–76.

56. Arnold M. Paul, "Legal Progressivism, the Courts, and the Crisis of the 1890's," *Business History Review*, 33(4): 495–509 (Winter 1959). In the Knight case (1895) the Supreme Court held that the Sherman Anti-Trust Act of 1890 did not apply to the American Sugar Refining Company, though this organization controlled ninety per cent of the industry, and in the Pollock case it declared a federal income tax (1894) unconstitutional.

57. Chester McArthur Destler, "The Opposition of American Businessmen to Social Control during the 'Gilded Age'," *MVHR*, 39(4): 641–72 (March 1953).

58. One should read the biography of Gunton in the *DAB*, VIII, 55–56, by Davis R. Dewey to correct bias.

59. Two standard studies are Richard Hofstadter, *Social Darwinism in American Thought*, rev. ed. (New York, 1959) and Robert G. McCloskey, *American Conservatism in the Age of Enterprise* (Cambridge, 1951).

60. "Federation" in this context means a federation of trade groups, not a federation of individuals.

61. My details are gathered from an old but substantial study, George Gorham Groat, *An Introduction to the Study of Organized Labor in America* (New York, 1916), which I have chosen because it is written in the spirit of impersonal inquiry characteristic of social studies in our period.

62. I have depended on the detailed account by Henry David, "Upheaval at Homestead," in Daniel Aaron, ed., *America in Crisis* (New York, 1952).

63. I depend for this account of the Idaho turbulence upon the narrative of a participant, James H. Hawley, *History of Idaho: The Gem of the Mountains,* 4 vols. (Chicago, 1920), Vol. I, *passim.* Other important and bitter strikes include the tying-up of the bituminous coal industry except in West Virginia by the United Mine Workers in 1897, the points at issue being wages, an eight-hour day, a recognition of the union, and

safety devices. There were also violent labor struggles in Colorado in 1894.

64. It is possible to paint too dark a picture, but here is another general estimate: "The year 1892 witnessed the beginning of 'state martial law' in industrial conflicts. Militia had been used against strikers as early as 1828, and both state and federal troops were called out in the eastern half of the country in the Great Riots of 1877. Before about 1892, the military was regarded as an extension of the civil power. They assisted the civil officers and the courts to preserve order and protect life and property. The so-called 'martial law' meant only that the soldiers were called in as police. It did not mean, as it has come to mean since, the imprisonment of men by hundreds, a trial by military commissions, suspension of the writ of habeas corpus and a supplanting of the courts. At this time the soldiers had no more right than a chief of police to exercise such powers." But the extract is careful to indicate all this describes the situation before 1892. Leon Whipple, *The Story of Civil Liberty in the United States* (New York, 1927), p. 227.

65. E.E. Hale, Jr., *Life and Letters of Edward Everett Hale,* 2 vols. (Boston, 1917), II, 372–73.

Chapter X: The Roosevelt Era

1. This amusing remark is quoted by a number of Roosevelt biographers. It can be found in G. Wallace Chessman, *Theodore Roosevelt and the Politics of Power* (Boston, 1969).

2. In a preface contributed to the foregoing book.

3. Joseph Bucklin Bishop, *Theodore Roosevelt and His Time,* 2 vols. (London, 1920), I, 63, 341. With Bishop, Morley spent three or four days at the White House, and after an exhausting but characteristic day he sank into a chair, murmuring: "Look at him! And he has been doing that all day long!" Morley told Bishop that Niagara Falls and the President of the United States were two great wonders of nature (I, 338–39, 341).

4. The concluding chapters of *La Follette's Autobiography: A Personal Narrative of Political Experiences* (Madison, 1913) express the senator's bitterness.

5. To Richard M. Hurd, a representative of the American Defense Society, read to an audience in the Hippodrome, New York City, as "Colonel Roosevelt's last message to the American people." Morison, *Letters of Theodore Roosevelt,* VIII, 1422.

6. "A Book Review," the first essay in Finley Peter Dunne's *Mr. Dooley's Philosophy* (New York, 1906). Mr. Dooley proposed some amusing alternatives: "Th' Biography iv a Hero be Wan who Knows," "Th' Darin' Exploits iv a Brave Man be an Actual Eye Witness," and "Th' Account iv th' Desthruction iv Spanish Power in th' Ant Hills." Roosevelt, who of course read the essay long before it was collected into this

book, was much amused. He cordially invited Dunne to visit him at Albany (Roosevelt was then governor), and wrote Henry Cabot Lodge December 14, 1899: "Yes, I saw Dooley's article and enjoyed it immensely. How he does get at any joint in the harness!" *Letters of Theodore Roosevelt*, II, 1099, 1110, 1134.

7. It took the boy a long time to realize that his eyesight was defective, and when at the age of twelve or thirteen he was fitted with spectacles, a whole new world opened out to him. Roosevelt, *Autobiography*, National edition of the *Works* (New York, 1925–1926), XX, 80.

8. See his letter to Kermit Roosevelt of January 14, 1909, *Letters*, VI, 1475–76. But Roosevelt's concern over "softness" appears again and again in his writings and his correspondence.

9. *America To-Day*, p. 195.

10. In warfare confusion is inevitable, and it should be remembered that the Spanish-American War occurred before the days of radio and airplane, that communication by cable was only partially possible, the cablegrams having to be picked up at Key West by a dispatch boat and delivered to a vessel at sea, which then signaled commands to other ships. The navy had had no experience in shepherding convoys. Transports straggled, refused to obey orders, and were more interested in avoiding the danger of Spanish fire than in getting close enough to shore to facilitate debarkation. Although other modern navies were using smokeless powder, there was none in the American fleet; and Richard Harding Davis tells an amusing anecdote about Lieutenant Mulligan on the *New York* during the bombardment (largely useless) of Matanzas, who cried out "Take your damned smoke out of my way!" because whenever Lieutenant Marble in charge of the turret guns above his head fired a shell, the smoke filled the lower deck and Mulligan could not see a thing. Richard Harding Davis, *The Cuban and Porto Rican Campaigns* (New York, 1898), pp. 31–33. The accounts of Sampson and Schley in the *DAB*, XVI, 321–22, 436–39 are quite impartial. For an able *ex parte* defense of Schley see James Parker, *Rear-Admirals Schley, Sampson, and Cervera* (New York, 1910). The most professional account of the war seems to be French Ensor Chadwick, *The Relations of the United States and Spain: The Spanish-American War*, 2 vols. (New York, 1911). Walter Millis, *The Martial Spirit: A Study of Our War with Spain* (Boston, 1931) is readable and well informed, but to my mind is written in the debunking atmosphere of the period of its publication. Allan Keller, *The Spanish-American War: A Compact History* (New York, 1969) gives an excellent overview of the conflict.

11. Difficulties were increased by the age, avoirdupois, caution, and illness of the commanding officer, General Shafter. When transports brought most of the army home, the sick, wounded and convalescent among the first, he was reproached for the ragged condition of the men and the lack of attendants, medicine, and water on the vessels, to which he very properly replied that since the army left Tampa there had never been enough of anything.

12. *The Rough Riders*, p. 185.
13. That there was no Machiavellian program for conquering the Philippines seems clear from the lack of any thought of an occupying army after Dewey's astonishing victory, the ambiguity of our attitude toward Aguinaldo evident in Dewey's (and others') dealing with him and what he stood for, and McKinley's naïve but sincere anguish of spirit when he took the problem of keeping the Philippines to God and reported that God told him not to abandon the islands.
14. "H.T.P.," "Here and There," *The (American) Bookman*, 13(1): 81 (March 1900). This is followed by a sentence saying that "In the last election, men of all parties stood by President McKinley in the matter of the Philippines, because they honestly believed that the sad condition of affairs in those islands was due to inexorable circumstances whose results no wisdom could possibly have foreseen."
15. William Roscoe Thayer, *The Life and Letters of John Hay*, 2 vols. (Boston, 1915), II, 136–37, 153.
16. The doctrine that the Latins are by nature inefficient, cruel, and corrupt goes back to the epic struggle of England and Holland against Spain and was possibly re-enforced by Parkman's histories of the defeat of bureaucratic and Catholic France in the New World by democratic, Protestant and Anglo-Saxon Britons, and colonials. See on this whole question A. E. Campbell's fine chapter, "The United States and the Old World" in *Material Progress and World-Wide Problems*, Vol. XI of the *New Modern Cambridge History* (Cambridge, England, 1962). As a study in opinion-making see Marcus M. Wilkerson, *Public Opinion and the Spanish-American War: A Study in War Propaganda* (New York, 1932; rpt. 1967).
17. In history the term has had both theological and secular meanings. Thus in 1438 it referred to a French doctrine that a church council is superior to the pope (Gallicanism), and in 1718 it meant a scheme for keeping the Austrian empire intact if the emperor, Charles VI, should die without a male heir.
18. Roosevelt, *Autobiography*, p. 346. Note Roosevelt's preference for an activist conception of the presidency as opposed to the legalism of Taft. Roosevelt again and again expressed his admiration for Lincoln, who had been a "strong" president, and one whom, if he sometimes exceeded the strict powers of the executive, Roosevelt thought preferable to those who did as little as possible in that office.
19. The act also abolished free railroad passes and forbade the roads to transport at their own prices (except for railroad purposes) commodities manufactured and shipped by companies the railroads owned or in which they had a dominant interest.
20. I owe this passage to its citation by Noel F. Busch, Jr., *T.R., The Story of Theodore Roosevelt and His Influence on Our Times* (New York, 1963), p. 195. I do not find it in La Follette.
21. *New Cambridge Modern History*, XI, 42.
22. There is not much to be said for the devious Bunau-Varilla. Contro-

versy arose over the government of the Canal Zone, supervision of the work, and labor policy. Neither Congress nor the public was aware of the technical difficulties involved in one of the most complex engineering jobs ever undertaken. Changes in the design of ships further troubled the engineers. It is, however, characteristic of Roosevelt's pragmatism that, believing as he did in free enterprise, when private companies failed to rise to their opportunity, he turned the job over to the U.S. Corps of Engineers.

23. *Letters*, I, 151, 152–53; II, 1015, 1095, 1101 (on Godkin); I, 175 (on Fiske); I, 286, II, 299 (on Kipling); I, 309 (on Repplier); I, 379, 389–90, 410–11 (on Garland); I, 390 (on Henry James); I, 520, 535, 554, 620 (on Brooks Adams); II, 969 (on John Jay Chapman); VI, 942–43 (on Jane Addams). Similar citations could be indefinitely multiplied, though it is fair to say that Roosevelt often changed his mind about these and others he denounced.

24. See Morison's penetrating analysis in the introduction to Vol. V of the *Letters*.

25. *Letters*, in this order: III, 8 (to John St. Loe Strachey, March 8, 1901); VIII, 1063 (to Rudolph Spreckels, June 8, 1908); III, 18 (to Philip Henry Goepp, March 18, 1901); VI, 954 (to Grafton Dulany Cushing, February 27, 1908); V, 222 (to Owen Wister, April 27, 1906).

26. The first widely publicized masque by MacKaye was *Caliban by the Yellow Sands,* produced in New York for the anniversary of Shakespeare's death in 1916.

27. I may be unfair to Amy Lowell, that vigorous propagandist, but I cannot see that either *A Dome of Many-Coloured Glass* (1912) or *Sword Blades and Poppy Seeds* (1914) made much impression. As it is sometimes argued that American poetry before 1914 suffered from being too "literary," it is amusing to note that reading T. S. Eliot's *The Waste Land* and the poems of Ezra Pound demands an erudition beyond most readers. Poetry in the Roosevelt era may have been buried at the bottom of the magazine pages, but it seems true to say simply that the literary energy of the period from 1898 to 1915 found its characteristic expression in prose. Robinson's first successful book, *The Man Against the Sky,* appeared in 1916.

28. *The Appeal to Reason* began as *The American Freeman,* but is best known as the *Appeal.*

29. I suspect, though I cannot prove, that the success of Elinor Glyn's "daring" and "sexy" *Three Weeks* (1907) was owing to this public, as was, of course, that of Robert W. Service's *The Spell of the Yukon* (1907).

30. The history of this phrase has been unfortunate. In *Criticism and Fiction* it appears in section xxi of Howells' workman-like discussion of the threefold relation of novelist, art, and publisher in the United States. He writes with a mingling of irony and shrewdness: "Whatever their deserts, very few American novelists have been led out to be shot, or finally exiled to the rigors of a winter at Duluth; and in a land where journeymen carpenters and plumbers strike for four dollars a

day [this was in 1891] the sum of hunger and cold is comparatively small, . . . though all this is changing for the worse. Our novelists, therefore, concern themselves with the more smiling aspects of life, which are the more American, and seek the universal in the individual rather than the social interests. . . . We have death too in America, and a great deal of disagreeable and painful disease, which the multiplicity of our patent medicines does not seem to cure, but this . . . tragedy is not peculiarly American, as the large, cheerful average of health and success and happy life is. . . . it is well to be true to the facts, and to see that, apart from these purely mortal troubles, the race here has en joyed conditions in which most of the ills that have darkened its annals might be averted by honest work and unselfish behavior." This is very similar to the assumption of the muckrakers. Like James, Howells goes on to lament the weakness of the American novel when it is an "instinctive response to the vacancy of our social life" and to say that "our grasp of more urbane life is feeble." Howells is explaining why the American novel is as it is, he is not drawing up a program for its future, and I have long been unable to understand why he is, as he would say, "faulted" by critics and scholars who fail to grasp the mingled truth, humor, and irony in this famous passage.

31. One should add David Graham Phillips's later masterpiece, *Susan Lennox: Her Fall and Rise* (1917). I do not discuss sociological awareness in Howells, since it is notorious that his reaction to the Haymarket Riot trials and his reading of Tolstoi were forces that pushed him further to the left in a series of books running from *A Hazard of New Fortunes* (1890) through *Through the Eye of the Needle* (1907) and beyond. He was not strident, and many critics tend to dismiss him as ineffectual. The fable of the sun and the wind betting as to which of them could get a man to shed his coat would seem applicable.

32. His daughter Evelyn helped Dewey to put this volume together.

33. Upton Sinclair's *The Goose Step* (Pasadena, 1923) is a brassy rewrite of Veblen.

34. Dewey's language is famous for offering difficulties in interpretation. I think what he means here by "socialistic" is "social" or "societal," since, though he was a progressive, he found that socialism possessed "too specific political and economic associations to be appropriate." This judgment is somewhere in *Individualism, Old and New*, and is quoted by Joseph Ratner, ed., *Intelligence in the Modern World; John Dewey's Philosophy* (New York, 1939), p. 406. Elsewhere Dewey talks about the "sociality of man."

35. Dewey's educational theory is condensed in Martin S. Dworkin, ed., *Dewey on Education: Selections with an Introduction and Notes*. (Paperback) Classics in Education No. 3, Bureau of Publications, Teachers College, Columbia University (New York, 1959). My citations are from pp. 30, 40, and 66. On Dewey's general theory of democracy see Jerome Nathanson, *John Dewey: The Reconstruction of the Democratic Life* (New York, 1951).

36. Thorstein Veblen, *The Higher Learning in America: A Memorandum on the Conduct of Universities by Business Men* (New York, 1918), pp. 252, 257, 275.

37. On De Leon, see Lewis Hanks, "The First Lecturer on Hispanic American Diplomatic History in the United States," *Hispanic-American Historical Review*, 16(3): 399–402 (August 1936); on the Ely case, Merle E. Curti and Vernon Carstensen, *The University of Wisconsin: A History, 1848–1925*, 2 vols. (Madison, 1949) I, 508–27; on the Kansas case, J. D. Walters, *History of The Kansas State Agricultural College* (Manhattan, 1909) and Julius Terrass Willard, *History of the Kansas State College of Agriculture and Applied Science* (Manhattan, 1940), *passim;* on Bemis, Charles A. Towne, "The New Ostracism," *The Arena*, 18(95): 433–51 (October 1897); on President Andrews, Elizabeth Donnan, "A Nineteenth-Century Cause Célèbre," *NEQ*, 25(1): 23–46 (March 1952); on Herron, *The American Review of Reviews*, 20(49): 713–16 (December 1899); on Ross, his autobiography, *Seventy Years of It* (New York, 1936), *passim* (Mrs. Stanford printed her side of the story in a pamphlet, *Address on the Right of Free Speech, etc.*, n.p., April 25, 1903); on J. Allen Smith, Arthur G. Beach, *A Pioneer College: The Story of Marietta* (Chicago, 1935), pp. 225–27. There was also a quarrel between John R. Commons and Chancellor Day at Syracuse in 1899, but one might go on indefinitely.

38. James, *Charles W. Eliot*, II, 26.

39. *Ibid.*, II, 6.

40. A succinct account of Jefferson's educational doctrine may be found in Gordon C. Lee, ed., *Crusade Against Ignorance: Thomas Jefferson on Education* (New York, 1961), in the same series as Dworkin's anthology of Dewey's work.

41. Croly apparently put no trust in any after-effects of Emerson's "The American Scholar."

42. I have used the edition of *The Promise of American Life* edited for The John Harvard Library Series by Arthur M. Schlesinger, Jr. (Cambridge, 1965). Schlesinger notes that Croly's father, to whom the book is dedicated, was a disciple of Positivism and that his mother, who wrote under the pen name of Jennie June, was both a Comtean and a positivist. He notes shrewdly that just as the insurgents in the Taft regime expressed the dissatisfactions of the Middle West, though they couched these in national terms, so Croly, though he talks nationally, is really writing from the point of view of Eastern, urban, and industrial progressivism.

43. Frederick J. Hoffman, *Freudianism and the Literary Mind* (Baton Rouge, 1945), a well documented study. The magazine articles include two by Max Eastman, "Exploring the Soul and Healing the Body," and "Mr.-er-er—Oh! What's His Name?", both in *Everybody's Magazine* in 1915. They are not in the French sense even good vulgarizations.

44. Thus, Inness died in 1894, Twachtman in 1902, La Farge in 1910, Francis D. Millet in 1912, William M. Chase in 1916, Weir in 1919, and

if others lived into the 1920s, their influence was negligible. The most astonishing case is that of George De F. Brush, who reached eighty-six before he died in 1941.

45. On Stieglitz's transition from realism to aestheticism see Neil Leonard, "Alfred Stieglitz and Realism," *The Art Quarterly*, 29(3–4), 277–86 (1966).

46. In various editions of his invaluable *Art and Life in America* (New York, 1949, but since revised), Oliver W. Larkin lists in his bibliography contemporary accounts of the Armory Show.

Index